MW00851171

ONE THOUSAND VINES

To my families in blood, sap and wine, wherever they may be
And to my secret weapon

PASCALINE LEPELTIER

Best French Sommelier
Meilleur Ouvrier de France

ONE
THOUSAND
VINES

A New Way to Understand Wine

Illustrations: Loan Nguyen Thanh Lan

MITCHELL BEAZLEY

CONTENTS

Foreword by Rajat Parr   6
Foreword by Ava Mees List and René Redzepi   7

One is not born, but rather becomes, a sommelière   9
Reading *One Thousand Vines*   12

READING VINES   15

DOMESTICATION
The origins of grape vines   16
Homo sapiens domesticates *Vitis vinifera*   19
Cépage – a concept   22
The classification of cépages   27
Cépages galore!   31
Hybridization – the past, present and future of grape vines   34

NATURE
The grape vine – from roots to leaves   40
The grape vine – from flowers to berries   45
Is a grafted vine an "artificial plant"?   49
Rootstocks and new viticultural landscapes   55
Grafting – a contemporary issue   57
Which *Vitis* to plant?   64
Thinking differently about vines   70

ECOLOGY
The vine and its underground world   76
The world of vines above ground   85
Envisaging the viticulture of tomorrow   92
Cohabiting with vines   96

READING LANDSCAPES   103

CLIMATE
Meteorological elements and vines   104
The geography of climate   113
Is there an ideal climate for viticulture?   117

GEOLOGY
Why read the geology of vineyards?   124
Understanding igneous rock   130
Understanding sedimentary rock   133
Understanding metamorphic rock   136
Is there an ideal soil for viticulture?   139
Climate, soil and terroir   146

TERROIR

A revolutionary reading of terroir and viticultural landscapes   150
Constructing terroir   158
The architectural heritage of vineyards   164
Wine roads   172
Cities shape vineyards, and vice versa   178
The invention of *appellations d'origine conrôlée*   183
Old Europe versus the New World – a distinction
   to be discarded   192
Preserving viticultural landscapes   198

READING WINES   203

MAKING WINE

What's in a grape?   204
From grapes to wine – a journey of microbial ecology   208
Vinification – art, craft and science   217
The alchemy of ageing   225
The oenologist's century   234
A defect – or a characteristic?   239

TASTING WINE

Wine tasting tells a story of expertise and quality   244
Wine tasting – from the senses to the brain   252
Seeing wine   258
Smelling wine   263
Tasting wine   271
The language of wine   278
Tasting minerality – myth or reality?   284

SERVING WINE

Wine containers   288
Looking for closure – how can wine be sealed?   295
Label mythology   300
Drinking wine   305
The art of serving wine – pairing with food and the role
   of the sommelier   317

CONCLUSION

So, what shall we drink tomorrow?   331

APPENDICES   334

Foreword by Rajat Parr

Sommelier and winemaker, Phelan Farm, California

I remember meeting Pascaline at Rouge Tomate in 2011; I realized immediately that something special was about to happen. At that time, the New York wine world was a classically male-dominated industry – even more so than it is now. Quietly but persistently, over time and through the sheer force of her determination, intelligence, dedication and unrelenting activity, Pascaline became an unprecedented leader in the industry.

At that time, I was a well-established sommelier on the West Coast of the United States, and I thought I knew all I needed to know. But every time I visited New York, I found myself drawn back to Rouge Tomate to be astonished and delighted by Pascaline. What wine would she surprise us with? What essential bit of knowledge would she convey?

Pascaline has trained, mentored and casually advised countless people over her illustrious career, and I too became a student. Even though she has received stupendous recognition for her tireless work, she has never stopped being the humble and caring person I first met. And while so many of us have left the exhausting world of fine dining, she admirably continues to work the floor at her restaurant, Chambers, the place where her genius can reach the most people – at least until this volume became a reality.

Though Pascaline has been involved with the production of several books, this is her first as a solo author. When she told me about it, years ago, I was intrigued. And when I read it, it exceeded my expectations. It breaks all the moulds of a wine book; she has carefully intertwined her background in philosophy with her career in wine. This book is about the truth in wine – and even more so, Pascaline's truth.

Pascaline has dedicated no small part of her life to championing the practice of organic and biodynamic farming. Even in her youth in Angers, she understood the importance of how farming affects the taste of food and wine. This book takes us on a journey from the domestication of grape vines to the nuances of wine tasting, speaking along the way to the essential subjects of climate, geology, terroir, winemaking, and serving wine. I could not agree more with Pascaline when she says, "*One Thousand Vines* is the book I'd like to have got my hands on when I began my life in wine."

This book is destined to become essential reading in the wine world. Reading it once or twice will not be enough; it will be a weekly or daily reference. If you have never met Pascaline, this book reveals her soul. And we who love wine are lucky to have such a brilliant and passionate soul among us.

Foreword by
Ava Mees List and René Redzepi
Head Sommelier, and Owner and Founder of Noma, Copenhagen

Standing on a slope after a drive in an old clunker over a forest road that seems to be used more often by deer, we overlook a wild field. The earth under our feet is so soft that it feels almost unstable. "I don't plough my land," the farmer says, stating the obvious, as we kneel to grab a handful of the thick humus. The soil smells oddly flowery and fragrant. The neighbour's adjoining land looms nearby, with neat rows of plants standing in line like soldiers. We try to do a comparative smell test but can't even dig our nails into the hard ground; we end up having to lie flat on our chest just to breathe in a faint odour of dust.

We are in Kamo, Kyoto. The tea trees are of the Sayamakaori cultivar, and their leaves will one day be dried, fermented, roasted, and served in our restaurant as a cold-infused hojicha blended with cacao and paired with a hand-dived Norwegian scallop. But this kind of crazy, contrasting landscape can be found all over. We may as well have been standing on the Côte de Py, with its organically farmed Gamay vines full of life, next to parcels that look unhappy in their barren enormity. You wonder how it is even possible that this tea farmer – who stopped using pesticides after it made him sick – is ridiculed by his neighbours for having, in their eyes, unkempt tea fields that are farmed along the principles of Masanobu Fukuoka. Or how, four decades after Marcel Lapierre started to resist the mass production of Beaujolais for the Nouveau market, we are still constantly having to defend his principles. When it comes to public perception, there is still much to fight for. Luckily, awareness is expanding, even though we are moving toward a complicated future.

At noma, we have been serving natural wines for more than two decades – because we believe in it, and because it tastes so damn good! But the best part of this movement is the people. It has been such fun to tell the stories and be part of a community that is so tight-knit. Over the course of time, we have forged connections through a shared philosophy and a common thirst with countless people – from right here in Copenhagen, to the smallest mezcaleria in Oaxaca. Because whether it be wine, tea, sake, coffee, beer, or snaps, wherever you travel there is always a friend who knows a friend who will help you find your way to the best restaurants, farms, or coffee shops. Want to know where you can eat well? Start by looking at the wine list. A place that cares for how its grapes are grown will probably also care for where – and how – its fish is caught, who bakes the bread, and exactly when local strawberries are in season. You are what you drink – or pour.

The beauty of wine, as you can read in Pascaline's *One Thousand Vines*, is that it encompasses so many facets of life. It is inherently both natural and cultural, communal and spiritual, intertwined with economies and subcultures. It sparks conversation, enthralls our tastebuds, and accompanies us on some of the best moments of our lives. In your hands you are holding a masterfully written book on just about every aspect of wine you can think of – in case you were wondering is why it's so heavy. Use it as a reference book, an encyclopaedia, whatever you like – but our advice is this: read it from cover to cover.

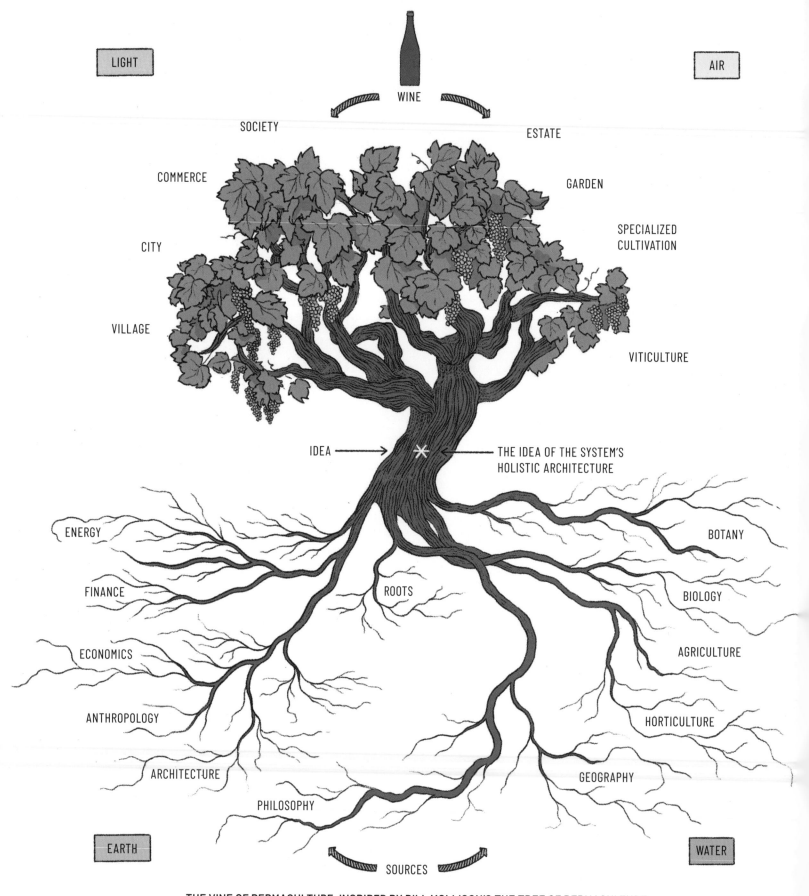

LIGHT

AIR

WINE

SOCIETY

ESTATE

COMMERCE

GARDEN

CITY

SPECIALIZED
CULTIVATION

VILLAGE

VITICULTURE

IDEA →

✳

← THE IDEA OF THE SYSTEM'S
HOLISTIC ARCHITECTURE

ENERGY

BOTANY

FINANCE

ROOTS

BIOLOGY

ECONOMICS

AGRICULTURE

ANTHROPOLOGY

HORTICULTURE

ARCHITECTURE

GEOGRAPHY

PHILOSOPHY

EARTH

WATER

SOURCES

THE VINE OF PERMACULTURE, INSPIRED BY BILL MOLLISON'S THE TREE OF PERMACULTURE

One question remains unanswered for me: what if other living beings had educated mankind – if horses had taught them to run, frogs to swim, and plants to have patience?

André-Georges Haudricourt,
Les Pieds sur terre (1987)

One is not born, but rather becomes, a sommelière

I'm going to level with you: I wrote this book for me more than for anyone else. As a literature professor once informed me some years ago, you write the books you'd like to read, and he wasn't wrong – *One Thousand Vines* is the book I'd like to have got my hands on when I began my life in wine, which is more than 17 years ago now. There was a wealth of publications on viticulture at the time, of course, with works for beginners, encyclopaedias, reference books, first-hand accounts, magazines for the general public and in-depth articles, and my shelves were soon groaning, and continue to, under the weight of fascinating books about wine and viticulture; but the vast majority were either too elementary or too recondite. I seemed to be missing a book – the one that would square the circle between super-specialized knowledge and popular understanding. A book that would also forge a link between the disciplines involved in this oh-so-complex subject, with a view to cross-fertilization of points of view gleaned from areas of expertise that all too rarely meet, from ampelography to botany and even anthropology, from climatology to geology via geography, from microbiology to history, from economics to aesthetics. A work of synthesis, simple enough to guide my first steps, that would invite an attempt at understanding the whys and wherefores rather than inveigling me into just learning by rote. A book that would provide me with a compass to orient myself on a voyage that would become my life. A book that would point me toward the issues raised by all my questions. A book that would ultimately nourish the sense of wonder I had felt at that first sip of wine that turned my world upside down. It took years of study, tastings and time served on the restaurant floor before I felt sufficiently equipped to put my ideas down on paper, years of travel and chance encounters, of bottles opened and vineyards visited, of exhilarating evidence and constant questioning before I felt capable of writing the book you now hold in your hands.

An opportunity to have tried the "right taste" of things

I was not born into wine, and nothing predisposed me to take an interest in it, not even having grown up in Angers, the heart of the magnificent wine-growing region of Anjou in the Loire Valley; I knew practically nothing about this wine area until I turned 23. There would occasionally be a bottle of wine on the family dinner table, often a "little Côtes de Blaye" dug out by my paternal grandfather, the taste of which has left no mark on my memory. We rarely dined out, and my mother, by her own admission, did not appreciate that you have to serve your time at the stove and so cooked as simply as possible, as her mother had before her. This said, we were lucky enough always to have fresh produce on the table: that same grandfather sold fruit and vegetables at the markets in the Orne and Manche regions of Normandy and had shaped the family's taste for natural foods and artisanal produce.

Entirely unwittingly, and from a very early age, I had acquired the "right taste" of things, to quote Jacques Puisais, the famous French oenologist who was crazy about flavour and promoted the education of palate and nose his whole life long. I can still smell the sweet and spicy notes of punnets of Mara des Bois strawberries or Charentais melons at the beginning of summer, the herbaceous scent of fresh peas and podded beans, the slightly sour sapidity of cider apples and the fire of farm Calvados, the ocean spray of prawns and plaice after a fishing trip, or even the smells of the *tripe galettes* and Normandy Camembert that made up my grandfather's lunch once the market stall had been packed away. Those were so strong that I couldn't stand them, and I still can't, despite all the fond memories they evoke. Although I didn't know it at the time, my taste-buds and my nostrils were well prepared to reveal to me the complex flavours and aromas of the world about me; I just needed 20 years to realize it.

From the "right taste" to a taste of philosophy

Until adulthood, I barely looked up to take in my surroundings; instead, I had my nose buried in a book. I had been reading as far back as my parents can remember, starting as soon as I could. Books had aroused an insatiable curiosity within me, and none more than one that will probably mean nothing to readers born into the internet age: *Tout l'univers* (Hachette, from 1961), the large, illustrated French-language encyclopaedia of general knowledge that I discovered on my maternal grandparents' shelves. I read it until the pages were falling apart. Every subject fascinated me in volume after volume, with a presentation of hieroglyphs sandwiched between a detailed exposition of alternating current and a description of the geography of Japan, each with a concise explanation and cartoonish scientific illustrations. I will admit that *Tout l'univers* was an inspiration for this book, the difference being that, with my study of philosophy having taken me in that direction, I have tried to link fields of knowledge rather than simply juxtaposing them.

Just like wine a little later, philosophy turned my life upside down; while curious about everything, I was certain of nothing – still less of what I wanted to do with my life – until my first lessons in philosophy. I know that there are plenty of people who have had bad experiences – or even no experience at all – with this discipline that all too often is considered obscure, useless and divorced from reality, and this saddens me, as I believe that true philosophy is quite the opposite: it is an accessible, essential and enlightening discipline that, like taste, should be taught to all. It is a permanent invitation to be amazed, to question knowledge, sensations and experiences, to learn to think for yourself and to accept the limits of what can be understood.

Here, too, I was fortunate; I had an exceptional teacher in my last year of school who introduced us to philosophy with a text taken from Alain's *Idées* (Paul Hartman, 1932). I had previously never heard the nuances of such a simple and obvious way of thinking that, by shining a light on the whys and wherefores of things, begets a fourth dimension to the world that until then had been invisible to my eyes: that of meaning and its value. Like Eve tasting the forbidden fruit – which according to certain specialists, such as renowned geographer Jean-Robert Pitte, was doubtless a bunch of grapes and not an apple – I had had a taste of the critical wonder that philosophy inspires. When I finished the course, I knew it would never leave me.

From clouds of ideas to the transcendence of wine

When I love something, my passion will often turn into obsession, and this is what happened over the five years that followed; I rapidly developed a taste for metaphysics, the study of language and the philosophers of life who posit existence as a creative and qualitative vital impetus beyond the grasp of logical, quantitative and mechanical concepts and the like, as these are too narrow and rigid to comprehend it. I read the pre-Socratic thinkers, Nietzsche, Bergson and Deleuze in a frenzy that would leave its mark on my later approach to wine. I liked concepts and was pretty adept at juggling them – enough to hope that I could teach.

But the inevitable came to pass: live too long with your head in the clouds of ideas, and you will lose your footing in reality. Petrified at the notion of teaching topics I knew of only in theory and not at all in practice, and exhausted by the frantic pace of my studies, I had to take a forced break – and it was here that wine serendipitously entered my life. A philosophy teacher whom I admired was a great fan of wine; why not try working in a wine shop for a couple of months?

And so it began. I was hooked – internships and side jobs followed one after another, and my prep for my lecturing qualification turned into a master's in hotel and catering. I spent my weekends in vineyards and signed up for every oenology course at the faculty. Wine was taking up more and more space in my life, but I still only saw it as a hobby – until my eureka moment. At the end of my MBA internship at renowned Parisian catering house Potel & Chabot, the *premier maître d'hôtel*, knowing my burgeoning passion, brought a bottle of Château d'Yquem 1937 that had hardly been touched, a leftover from a meal served earlier in the day. This sweet wine from Sauternes is one of the most celebrated in the world, and 1937 is a legendary year. That day was the first time I tasted Yquem. That I had the chance to experience it in such conditions (perfect provenance, in a period, hand-blown bottle, and a superb vintage) was already exceptional, but this tasting was to prove literally transcendent. From the very first sip, I felt totally transported; I had never drunk anything like it. There were so many interweaving aromas and sensations, a multiplicity of memories and thoughts racing through one another as the moment seemed suspended. . . The wine had an incredible, exquisite flavour, but what took my breath away was the impression that it transcended space and time, conjuring worlds that had long since passed – I imagined harvest time, I recognized familiar smells from childhood – projecting one against the other, with seemingly never-ending colours, sounds and textures.

The second sip was just as intense, at once identical and different, and two irrepressible ideas then arose in my mind – I was experiencing wonder, the sensation that Plato had called the original philosophical sentiment. I was in wonder at what I was feeling, but I was also experiencing an idea that I had tried and failed to understand during my studies, the experience of what Bergson calls *durée*, or "duration". Unlike numerical, clock time, *durée* is an immediate index of our experience when "the self allows itself to live" with no attempt to divide, abstract, or count this "succession without distinction", as in a tune when the "notes follow one after another", in an experience of creative vital impetus and pure quality.

Thanks to the wine, I was suddenly living out philosophical experiences that until then had remained abstract to me. Thanks to the grape vine and its anchoring in the senses, its literal rooting in the earth and metaphorical entrenchment in the history of humanity, I realized that I could satisfy my philosophical curiosity through the prism of wine and wine tasting. I enrolled in a sommellerie course at a vocational school that same evening, beginning my apprenticeship and my first shifts on the restaurant floor three weeks later.

From theory to practice – the necessity of wine that is "alive"

It was at that moment that I wished I had found the book that you are now holding in your hands. I knew I wanted to understand wine, but like so many, I had absolutely no idea of where to start; what I *did* know was that I didn't know very much, neither in theory nor even less in practice. I was starting from square one but was lucky enough to know how to learn and, above all, once again to have exceptional teachers and chefs by my side. They quickly taught me that wine is first and foremost found in the vine and in the glass, in the intentions of the men and women who make it, and only then in books; you first had to learn how to taste, to smell, to touch. I realized that however elevated my "higher" education may have been, it had totally neglected these senses that were suddenly providing me with a new way of viewing the world. From these first days of my new life, vines and vineyards imposed themselves upon me as the alpha and omega, the be-all and end-all of life. I met wine-growers of every stripe and understood very quickly that in the absence of a wine-growing culture that respected the living world, there would be no wine of emotion or of terroir, no wine for sharing, no energetically charged wines with such unique and transcendent taste and *durée* – and that what was "alive" was much more than just the vine; it encompassed communities that were tangible and intangible, of the present, the past and the future, and human, plant-based or microbial. And that everything was indeed interconnected in an incredibly diverse and vital dynamic.

The wonder of those first few days therefore became the driving force of a quest better to understand, and in particular better to defend, the work of these men and women in the vineyards who, through their daily dedication to the living world, bring us a taste, in the most immediate fashion, of what is all around us. Wine is one of mankind's most beautiful creations and has undoubtedly contributed – as you will soon read – to the creation of humanity; it is a reflection of our way of living on Earth. While we humans more than ever have become "masters and possessors of nature" at the cost of ecological crises whose consequences we are only beginning to perceive, living wine – rising above an ocean of deracinated, industrial agri-food "plonk" – is becoming a symbol, indicating that another way of living is possible – indeed, even essential. In its myriad incarnations, it invites us to marvel anew at ourselves and all that surrounds us. Behind all the codes and rules, the prejudices and systems created to perform and control, there lurks the imperfect beauty, so diverse and unexplored, of human liberty and the vitality of life that, ultimately, are one and the same. It was to share this taste of the living world with others that I became a sommelière, and it was to provide a key to understanding this wondrous world that I have written *One Thousand Vines*.

Reading *One Thousand Vines*

One Thousand Vines is, I believe, a unique book of its kind, combining my experience as a working sommelière and my critical training as a student of philosophy. As I progressed in my career, I became aware that I didn't understand the way wine was being explained to me; too much of the information was partial and contradictory, with too many oversimplifying explanations that seemed to be either commonplace or prejudices with no grounding in reality – myths maintained for reasons that often remained hidden. The wines I found the most expressive of their terroir were rejected from accreditation tastings for their "atypical nature", while the approaches to viticulture that seemed most obvious to me, being the most respectful of the living world and the results of a sustainable economy, were shouted down with often fallacious arguments. Rather than encouraging people to think critically, wine teaching encouraged, under the pretext of objectivity, the unthinking memorization by rote of numbers of hectares, levels of alcohol or residual sugar, percentages of grape varieties or "traditional styles" and so on – solid information, no doubt, but it totally omitted to explain the whys and wherefores and so failed to acknowledge that wine is above all a creation born of human desires and needs, a self-interested and mutable creation if ever there was one. There was something wrong, and it was becoming more obvious to me with every bottle I tasted and every vineyard I visited. The standardized teaching and tasting of wine was missing one essential point: wine is the embodiment of our ability to play with natural constraints and to transcend them for our own pleasure, an invention constantly re-conceived by the various civilizations that have embraced it. So there is not one wine, but a thousand wines; not one vine, but a thousand vines.

If oenology and sommellerie are the "official" science and practice concerned with this incredible diversity, in fact they exist only at the nexus of all the physical and human sciences, as wine touches on all areas of "nature" and "culture", transcending the fundamental dichotomy on which our Western world-view is based. Even as the tendency in the evolution of knowledge is toward ever-greater specialization and expertise, wine reminds us that all these skills are fundamentally interconnected, forming dynamic systems of thought that must interact if we hope to be able to comprehend its complexity – and therefore our own complexity and that of our world.

This is how this book was conceived: to get disciplines talking to one another and, as in philosophy, to revisit their basic concepts and examine them, to discover their genea-logy and their raison d'être, with a view to uncovering the presuppositions that lie hidden beneath our contemporary notions of wines and vines. In other words, to teach readers to deconstruct prejudices and provide them with a key to unlock for themselves what is at stake with one of humanity's most beautiful and essential creations – and these stakes are high.

Vines, landscapes, wines

I therefore make no claim to have the perspective of a specialist in this book, but rather of a sommelière who has tried to synthesize the knowledge of multiple disciplines relating to wines and vines in order to examine them through the lens of my experience on the ground. This is an interpretation that I wish to be as rigorous as possible, but it is also founded on the limits of my skills, so I shall be offering a position that is committed to defending a certain idea of wines and vines that I shall attempt to justify in the pages to follow. To do so, I have immersed myself in the exceptionally rich field of research into viticulture and winemaking, from which all too few works unfortunately escape their ivory tower to reach the general public, or even professionals in the field. I hope to have grasped to the best of my understanding the thinking of the authors I quote and to have relayed their arguments faithfully.

My research began with what is taught least in sommelière training: the grape vine. There are no wines without vines, however. What do you need to know and understand about the plant to capture the taste of modern wine? You have to learn to read it in the language appropriate to each discipline: ampelography first of all, then botany, physiology and ecology. How did *Homo sapiens* discover *Vitis vinifera*, and why, of all the plant species, did we embark upon such a long period of companionship with it? How has this domestication transformed both people and the plant? Why are there so many cépages, and what do they tell us about vines and about humans? How has the evolution of science and technology shaped their relationship? How much is left of the original plant in the hyper-domesticated incarnation we know today? What vision of nature underlies our understanding of *Vitis*? Can we rethink it differently? Can we cultivate it differently? Reading the vine will lead us to discover the challenges facing contemporary agriculture and the necessity of learning to coexist with the visible and invisible diversity of ecosystems, and to bridge the problematic gap between nature and culture.

I wanted to find out more about these ecosystems, the wine-growing areas themselves. For several years, there has been a cult of climate and geology to explain the quality of wines – there can be no great wine without a great physical terroir. But what does this really mean when you learn more about vines and their impressive plasticity – and the wealth of their microbiota? Are some climates more propitious than others? Can you grow grape vines anywhere on the planet today? How is technology always pushing the envelope of viticulture? What about the soil? Why is it still so miscons-trued and misunderstood even as the adulation of geology has spread from amateurs to professionals? Why is it so difficult to admit that a vineyard, far from being a miraculous gift from the gods or the bounty of Earth, is first and foremost a human contrivance? That what has sculpted the landscape of viticulture is "the desire to drink", and even the "desire to drink well", revealing the potential of a terroir at the price of "civilizational single-mindedness"? That France's AOCs are as much political as viticultural? To read landscapes is to read the history of humanity, to understand terroir as a social fact, not just as climatic and geological facts, as a construction symbolizing the freedom of civilizations.

Which brings us to wine, this artifact for which the human mind has developed miracles of ingenuity. Why is it so complex, so fascinating? Just as a vine is nothing without its microbiota, is wine nothing without its microbial ecology? Do winemakers really *make* wine, or are they not rather reduced to controlling as best they can an infinite number of biochemical phenomena at work in the alchemy of fermen-tation and aging? What are the consequences for the quality of wine of the evolution in winemaking from a practice that was largely intuitive until the 18th century into an oenological science? By trying too hard to standardize it and eliminate its "defects", has this not killed the taste of wine? But if wine is born in the vineyard and in the cellar, is it not also born in the heads of those who taste it? Physiology or education, innate or acquired; what are the mechanisms at work in tasting? Isn't it fundamentally subjective? What are the languages of wine? Are they hurdles or springboards? And finally: why do we drink wine? Why do we like talking about it so much, pairing it, celebrating it? How does it reveal to us the mechanisms of fabricating taste and society? To read wine is ultimately to recognize that it is the symbol of the human condition, that it reflects back to us a mirror image of ourselves, of our culture and its values, of our liberty and the way we live on Earth.

How to read *One Thousand Vines*

In the beginning were the roots of the vine. Much like the "vine of permaculture" – which was inspired by the "tree of permaculture" designed by Bill Mollison, one of the leading theorists of the practice - this book has not one, but several ways in, all interlinked. In fact, rather than as a root system that implies the idea of hierarchy and a subordination of knowledge systems, imagine *One Thousand Vines* as a rhizome where any element can influence any other, whatever its place in the system; think of the internet. So it is possible to start at the beginning, the middle or the end; each section, each chapter and each subdivision can be read independently of the others, but they all also enrich each other. There are thus multiple readings of this book, depending on the reader's needs and desires, which are no less than original connections to be drawn between the disciplines and a symbol of both the reality of our world, which is also being constantly developed at every point, and of the taste of wine, which is reborn with each fresh sip, at once identical and different, in an experience that is eternally returning.

I hope that reading this book will be an opportunity for you to experience wonder.

A NOTE ON CÉPAGE

Cépage, like terroir, is a French term commonly used worldwide in wine conversation due to the importance of ampelographic studies in France. Yet its definition is proble-matic, and even if it is usually translated as "grape variety" or "cultivar" in English, its acceptance is slightly different. Cépage in this book is understood as a collection of clones sufficiently related to one another to fall under the same name (like Pinot), and variety or cultivar are understood as a subgroup of cépages (like Pinot Noir, Pinot Gris and so on).

READING VINES

Our journey begins with the genesis of our grape vine, also known as *Vitis vinifera* subspecies *sativa*, the *Vitis* domesticated specially to make wine. Understanding the complexity of the modern universe of wine-growing and winemaking requires a deep dive into the botanical genealogy of this unique climbing plant. Where does it come from? How was it discovered and chosen by mankind? The aim here is to highlight the stages in this unique domestication that has transformed both people and the vine.

Evolving over millennia, this relationship has shaped *Vitis*, just as it has structured social organization, giving rise to differing visions of nature and the world. The history of Western viticulture demonstrates human will – to understand the vines that were once sacred plants and then became tools of production and came to dominate our environment. The vine is unique in the plant kingdom and has played an agronomic role of major importance. Viticulture is the most extensively studied farming practice, and many of the techniques and solutions adopted by global agriculture have their origins there, from crop selection to genetic modification. While the positive sciences may have permitted analysis of physiological phenomena in ever-greater detail, a reductionist and productivist approach has sometimes encouraged the idea of a stand-alone vine decoupled from its ecosystem. But just like human beings, vines are only part of incredibly complex and dynamic biotopes that are often invisible but always interconnected. By questioning our vision of the world, which is based on a fundamental division between nature and culture, we may be able to invent new relationships with not only vines but also with our ecosystems, helping to find solutions to the ecological crises of today and tomorrow.

DOMESTICATION

The origins of grape vines

Vitis vinifera ssp. *sativa* is the scientific name of the plant that is a symbol par excellence of humanity. Resounding like a magical incantation, the name is an invitation to study its botanical history, because the grape vine did not appear out of thin air; it is the fruit of long domestication. To appreciate its unique place in the plant kingdom and find our way through the labyrinth of its denominations, we have to go back to its genealogy as defined by the sciences that classify the living world. Where does it come from?

A unique place in the plant kingdom

We can understand the origins of the grape vine through its ancestry. Taxonomy, the classification of living things, works like a Russian doll: each individual is a member of a group which in turn is part of a larger clan and so on. Officially, the grape vine is therefore a member of the genus *Vitis*, in the family of the Vitaceae and the order of the Vitales, which is in the subclade of the Rosids that in turn is a member of the eudicots, the angiosperms and the metabionts, which belong to the plant kingdom, part of the domain of the eukaryotes, one of the groups of living things that includes all cellular organisms with cell nuclei (animals, fungi, plants and other protozoans). This one-sentence genealogy attests to the millions of years of speciation of living things that have given rise to the grape vine. But what remarkable characteristics has this also given it?

The grape vine is a green, shrubby, climbing perennial with unique adaptive and agricultural potential. As a eukaryote, it possesses a complex cell system with a long genome that was fully decoded in 2007, revealing it to be rich in genes associated with the production of enzymes and essential oils that play a key role in the organoleptic complexity of wine. As a metabiont (or more precisely chlorobiont, since the grape vine is a green plant), it is an autotrophic organism that generates its own organic matter via photosynthesis. As an angiosperm, or seed plant, its flower is fertilized to give a fruit, a berry, whose embryo or pip is surrounded by a nourishing albumen (the grape flesh) with unique characteristics.

As a dicotyledon, it has a main, burrowing taproot and can grow and form wood thanks to its cambium, or woody tissue, but its most remarkable property has been revealed by recent analysis of its genome: as a climbing plant with such discreet flowers, the grape vine is thought to be a living fossil among flowering plants, one of the species closest to the common ancestor of all inflorescent plants. Unlike one of its relatives, the rose, domesticated for its flowers, the grape vine has favoured its vegetative system and its lianescence, which explains its notably protean nature.

An ancient plant

The Vitaceae family appeared 100 million years ago during the Cretaceous period and dispersed and spread during the Eocene, a period of intense development for flora and fauna. While there is a lack of evidence to date older speciations since these will have decomposed, the species multiplied from the Palaeocene onward. The oldest known fossil of a vine leaf dates from this period 56 million years ago: *Vitis sezannensis*, discovered in the Champagne region.

Since then, the Vitaceae are thought to have differentiated into 17 genera growing in tropical regions in particular,

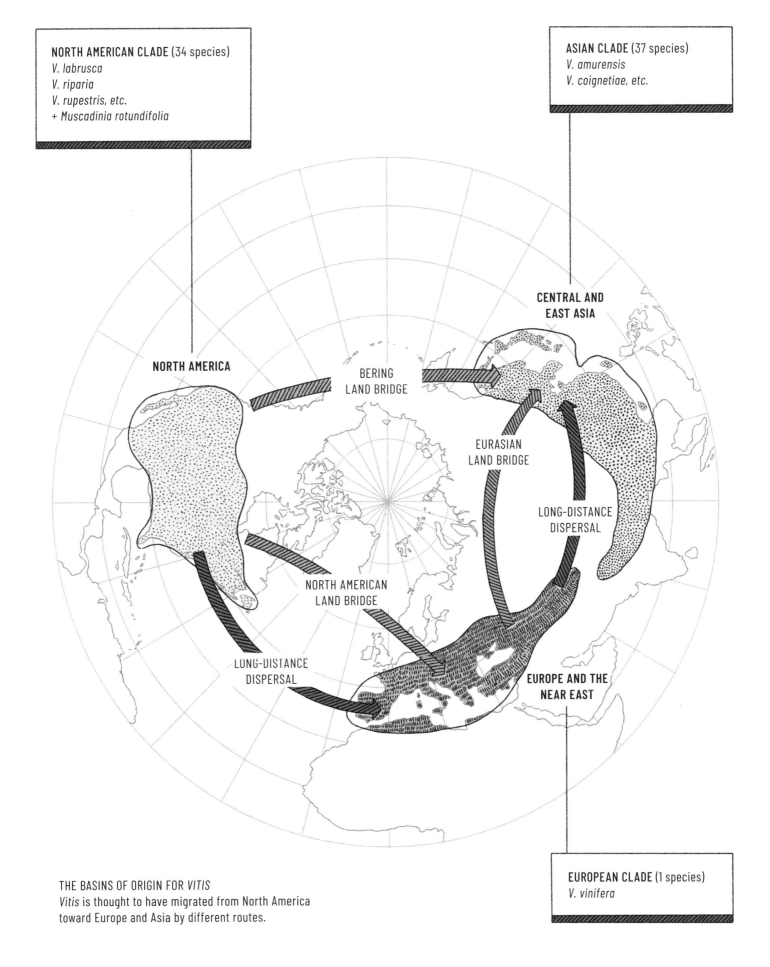

NORTH AMERICAN CLADE (34 species)
V. labrusca
V. riparia
V. rupestris, etc.
+ *Muscadinia rotundifolia*

ASIAN CLADE (37 species)
V. amurensis
V. coignetiae, etc.

**CENTRAL AND
EAST ASIA**

NORTH AMERICA

BERING
LAND BRIDGE

EURASIAN
LAND BRIDGE

LONG-DISTANCE
DISPERSAL

NORTH AMERICAN
LAND BRIDGE

LONG-DISTANCE
DISPERSAL

**EUROPE AND THE
NEAR EAST**

EUROPEAN CLADE (1 species)
V. vinifera

THE BASINS OF ORIGIN FOR *VITIS*
Vitis is thought to have migrated from North America
toward Europe and Asia by different routes.

with the continents of the time not having yet taken their current form. Of these genera, certain strains took to the humid subtropical and temperate zones in the northern hemisphere: *Ampelopsis* and *Parthenocissus*, known to us as Virginia creepers, and *Vitis*, thought to be the most recent addition. Two sub-genera, *Muscadinia* and *Euvitis*, appeared as the vine spread, differentiated by the number of chromosomes – 40 for the former and 38 for the latter. Originating in the southeastern United States, *Muscadinia* has spread only as far as America and comprises just three species, of which only one, *M. rotundifolia*, still attracts scientific interest for its resistance to certain pathogens. *Euvitis*, on the other hand, has produced so many offspring that it has become the dominant sub-genus, taking the name of the genus itself: *Eu-vitis*, the "true vine".

Does the future of global winemaking lie with its origins?

While genetic research suggests the American rather than the Asiatic basin as the origin of *Vitis*, the discipline studies both with a view to finding solutions for the future. In 1907 in Asia, Russian researchers became the first to take an interest in Shan Pu Tao, as it was known in Chinese, or Amurskii Vinograd in Russian, a species of *V. amurensis* growing on the Sino-Russian border, for its resistance to winters of -45°C (-49°F) and soils at -16°C (3°F). Its success has more to do with the ease with which it can be hybridized than the first wines that were produced commercially from it in 1936 by the Jilin Changbai Mountains Wine Company; the acidity was too intense. A relative of Cabernet Severny or Solaris, it has become a part of the world's winemaking future through its descendants, and perhaps for its own part, thanks to the progress made in Chinese viticulture. In the US, *Muscadinia rotundifolia*, the oldest known living vine there (thanks to a Scuppernong plant christened Mother Vine that dates back to 1500 and is still thriving on Roanoke Island in North Carolina), is highly promising; its resistance to certain nematodes is now being studied to develop rootstock resistant to the grape-vine fanleaf virus, the deadliest threat to vines, which is transmitted by these worms.

Conquering the world

Vitis extends across three geographical basins that are now separated but were still linked during the Mesozoic era:

- **The Asian Far East** is the largest of the three basins. The majority of the 37 species found here have berries that are not very tasty and have barely been domesticated; local communities also use other resources to produce alcohol. Nowadays, they are of interest for their tolerance of freezing temperatures, in order to create plants capable of surviving in ever more extreme latitudes.

- **North America**, the second basin, is home to 34 identified species that also remained wild for millennia. The Amerindians took little interest in their berries, preferring beer for their ceremonies, and the colonists then struggled to get along with *V. labrusca*, the most cultivable species. These various forms of *Vitis* nonetheless all spontaneously diversified, evolving in tandem with local bio-aggressors that were to become the principal threats to European vines. Their resistance to these pathogens is the focus of current genetic research.

- **The Near East** and **Europe** form the third and most recent basin. These, the regions with the richest viticultural history of all, paradoxically boast just a single species of *Vitis*: *Vitis vinifera*. Why might this be? It would not have needed to speciate during the geographical upheavals and the most recent glaciation of the Eocene epoch, because it would have found a sufficiently isolated refuge in an adapted environment, the Caucasian basin and the Near East.

Vitis encounters *Homo sapiens*

Vitis vinifera has therefore undergone two parallel evolutions, differentiating two subspecies. The first, *V. vinifera* ssp. *sylvestris* (Latin, "of the forest"), has remained a wild climber, never cultivated, and is also known in France as *lambrusque* (from Latin, *labrusca*, "wild vine"). It is still dioecious (either male or female) and grows in rich, alluvial soils beside watercourses, *V. vinifera*'s natural environment, climbing up any woody support it encounters to seek the light, hence its name *sylvestris*. It covered Europe 10,000 years ago but is now endangered and has been a protected species in France since 1995. The second evolution of *V. vinifera* is "our" grape vine: *V. vinifera* ssp. *sativa*, or the cultivated grape vine, which arose from the boom in viticulture that followed the dawn of agriculture around 9000 BCE. It is now the most diversified species, which it owes to its encounter with *Homo sapiens*.

Homo sapiens domesticates *Vitis vinifera*

Given its nature as a forest ivy that grows by climbing to the tops of trees, producing only tart little berries that are difficult to reach, the grape vine seems far from being a plant of the greatest interest or the easiest to domesticate – and yet it is one of the few ivies (others include vanilla and hops) to have caught mankind's eye sufficiently to be selected, propagated and improved. How and why were we able to cultivate this plant, with its seemingly low nutritional appeal and scant fruit yields?

The Palaeolithic hypothesis

According to American anthropologist Patrick McGovern – head of the Biomolecular Archaeology Laboratory for Cuisine, Fermented Beverages, and Health at the University of Pennsylvania – it was tasting naturally fermented wild grape juice that led early humans to domesticate the vine; this is known as the Palaeolithic hypothesis. Observing birds pecking at the berries, the nomadic hunter-gatherers of the Palaeolithic would indeed have been able to harvest the fruit and taste the liquid that resulted after a few days' travel in hide containers, and they would have been seduced by the euphoric and addictive effect of the few grams of alcohol contained in the beverage. Already possessing the genetic mutation for the enzyme allowing for consumption of fermented fruit – alcohol dehydrogenase – and probably a fan of proto-beer to boot, *Homo sapiens*, or rather *Homo imbibens*, to quote McGovern, would have discovered in this an alcoholic drink that was easily obtained because it did not require the conversion of starch into fermentable sugars as cereals do. The problem was that it quickly deteriorated into vinegar; so how could this phenomenon be reproduced and preserved? The history of viticulture had begun.

An 8,000-year-old wine, but two 11,000-year-old domestication centres

The origins of wine are still shrouded in mystery. With pieces of direct evidence being few and far between, artifacts have long been only indirect clues open to interpretation – but as technological advances have opened up new avenues in molecular archaeobotany and ampelography, the potsherds have begun to talk. Besides revealing possible winemaking practices through their shape and patterning, their porosity and electrical charge have proven an ideal trap for preserving over millennia traces of liquid that can be analysed with spectrography and chromatography. In 2017, a team of scientists that included McGovern discovered what was thought until recently to be the oldest wine production sites to date, bringing to light eight jars with traces of tartaric, malic, citric and succinic acids; their presence in jars suggests that the grapes had been vinified deliberately. This discovery also implies that wine and pottery know-how are intimately linked, suggesting a certain social organization.

McGovern was based at the Gadachrili Gora and Shulaveris Gora sites in Georgia, 50 km (31 miles) south of Tbilisi, the capital. His hypothesis was corroborated by the presence of resin and grape pips, along with confirmation of human habitation between 6000 and 5800 BCE through radiocarbon dating of charcoals and seeds, and palaeoclimatology has confirmed that environmental conditions at the time were close to our own. These eight 300-litre (80-US gallon) jars, one of which has been dated to 5980 BCE, are decorated with dancing men and bunches of grapes and are evidence of the manufacture of unadulterated wine, with no resin or other additives. (None has been found there, unlike a mixture of rice, honey and wild berries discovered in China, dating to between 7000 and 6600 BCE.) It was also the site of significant production that assumes the beginnings of organized winemaking.

However, in 2023, a study led by Yang Dong and 88 other scientists from 23 research centres ("Dual domestications and origin of traits in grapevine evolution") shed new light on the origin of grape vine domestication. This groundbreaking paper revealed that there were probably not one but two separate yet contemporaneous domestication areas 11,000 years ago – one in the Caucasus, as expected, and one in a location at first more surprising, the Near East (the Levant: Lebanon, Jordan, Palestine, Israel). This discovery was based on the genetic analysis and the sequencing of 3,525 varieties, revealing a unique genotype for 2,448 of them, 1,604 *V. vinifera* and 844 *V. sylvestris*. From there, the scientists were able to organize them in groups, six for *V. vinifera* (West Asian table grapes, Caucasian wine grapes, Muscat table and wine grapes, Balkan wine grapes, Iberian wine grapes and Western European wine grapes), and four for the wild sylvestris. And

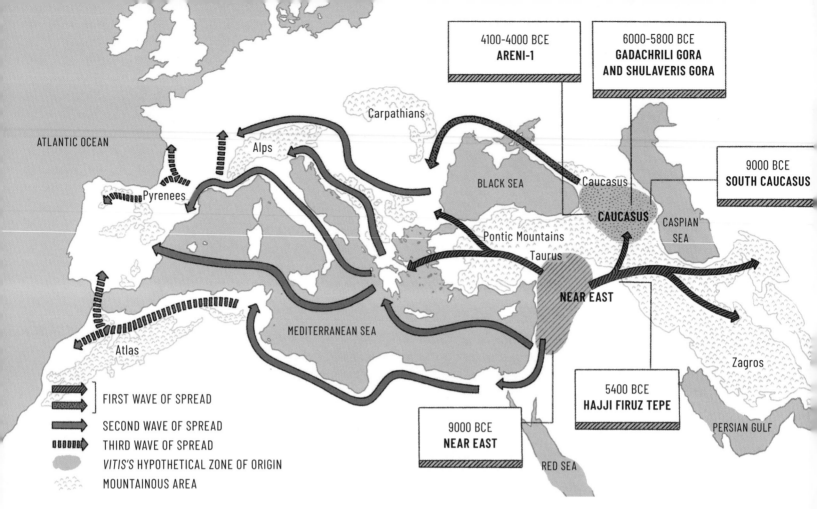

Map legend and labels:

4100-4000 BCE **ARENI-1**

6000-5800 BCE **GADACHRILI GORA AND SHULAVERIS GORA**

9000 BCE **SOUTH CAUCASUS**

ATLANTIC OCEAN

Carpathians

Alps

Pyrenees

BLACK SEA

Caucasus

CAUCASUS

CASPIAN SEA

Pontic Mountains

Taurus

NEAR EAST

Zagros

MEDITERRANEAN SEA

Atlas

5400 BCE **HAJJI FIRUZ TEPE**

9000 BCE **NEAR EAST**

RED SEA

PERSIAN GULF

FIRST WAVE OF SPREAD

SECOND WAVE OF SPREAD

THIRD WAVE OF SPREAD

VITIS'S HYPOTHETICAL ZONE OF ORIGIN

MOUNTAINOUS AREA

THE POSITED FIRST CENTRES OF DOMESTICATION OF *VITIS VINIFERA*

There were two simultaneous centres of *V. vinifera*: the South Caucasus (relatively isolated with weak diffusion) and the Middle East from which *V. vinifera* would have spread to Europe, Africa and Asia in three waves following human migrations.

here lies the most disruptive discovery: "They found that although the South Caucasus domestication is associated with early winemaking, the origin of wine in Western Europe is associated with cross-fertilization (introgression) between Western Europe's wild populations and domesticated grapes originating from the Near East that were initially used as food sources" (Robin G Allaby, chair of genomics, University of Warwick, UK, "Two domestications for grape"). In other words, our grape vines migrated from the Levant while the vine population of the Caucasus, until today, remained more isolated with indigenous grapes quite different from the rest.

A new story of grape-vine domestication

This discovery only confirms an age-old hypothesis: that the first major centres of domestication of wild *V. vinifera* were located in a large region stretching from the Caucasus to the Near East, the historic territories of Mesopotamia and the Fertile Crescent. One of the reasons why South Caucasus was thought to be the original centre was the presence of archaeological findings: the two Georgian sites were part of Shulaveri-Shomutepe culture, which extended into Azer-

baijan and Armenia. Viticulture was therefore thought to have appeared somewhere between Georgia, Armenia (home of the Areni site with its 6,000-year-old stone press) and Iran's Zagros Mountains, where evidence of winemaking dating back to 5400 BCE has been unearthed at Hajji Firuz Tepe. These archaeological findings were backed up by studies of the foundation myths of Asian, Near Eastern and European societies such as the *Epic of Gilgamesh* and Dionysian mythology. There is no such evidence in the Levant, and only scientific progress - like genetic sequencing - could allow such a discovery, corroborating the myths not by archaeological proof, but by botany. The Levant is home to many domesticated plant species (wheat, barley, lentils, flax), with the earliest forms of domesticated cereals appearing about 11,000-11,500 years ago, explains Professor Allaby.

What happened? In the Pleistocene (500,000 years ago), glacial episodes split the wild grape-vine population into two ecosystems, western and eastern, each leading to simultaneous domestication. The genetic analysis showed that the Caucasus one mostly spread to the Carpathian Basin, thus playing a limited role in grape diversification.

On the other hand, the Levant group, originally domesticated for eating not making wine, spread east to Central Asia, India, China; north to Caucasus, and west through Anatolia and the Balkans, then to Western Europe and Iberia: these grapes crossed then with local wild grapes that had thicker skins and less sugar but were more suited to making wine. Even though there is no vestige of the materials required for wine production and storage, these new data, supported by the scientific community, improve our understanding of the mechanism of domestication, shaped by humans and environments alike.

The hermaphrodite hypothesis

Domestication means, above all, controlling reproduction. In the hermaphrodite hypothesis, Swiss molecular ampelographer José Vouillamoz explains how genetic evolution may have facilitated the work of *Homo sapiens*, although it remains a theory, as the physical evidence no longer exists.

In its wild state, *V. sylvestris* is a sexual creeper with both male and female plants, but it also has considerable genetic instability, and rare hermaphrodite mutants arising from male plants have appeared over time. In parallel, the vine also developed another characteristic, vegetative apomixis: it can reproduce from a single twig with a bud planted in the ground. The new plant is a clone of the parent plant. *Homo sapiens* is thought to have identified these particular hermaphroditic, self-pollinating individual plants and understood how to preserve them by taking cuttings, giving rise to *V. vinifera* ssp. *sativa*.

The millennium that followed saw phases of improvement as humans migrated and trading subsequently became more frequent between 3500 and 3000 BCE. Secondary wine-growing centres developed gradually around the Mediterranean. The proto-varieties here were cross-fertilized deliberately or inadvertently by local wild vines, and exceptional individual plants were gradually selected. The berries and clusters became less acidic and tannic, fleshier and balanced in sugar, with variations both in colour and in the size and shape of the pips and leaves.

What Egypt can teach us about these proto-varieties

Funerary frescoes from Egypt's Old Kingdom (2700–2220 BCE) feature the first known representations of the pigmentation of grapes: all the bunches are black. While Egyptologists assume that the pigmentation of the berries must have ranged from green to mauve, they know that there was higher production of wines made from red grapes by direct pressing, and sometimes maceration, from the presence of traces of syringic acid in the majority of the jars; this is not produced in the vinification of white wine. These depictions therefore suggest that they were selecting grapes by skin colour.

Near-perfection of domestication is implied in the writing of Roman agronomists, who describe a vast diversity of varieties, with edible and wine grapes adapted for different regions (Greece, the Orient, Italy), so it is during antiquity that we finally encounter the first true *V. vinifera* or primitive varieties. Are they still with us, or have they evolved as well? In 2012, agronomist Thierry Lacombe, a specialist in grape-vine genetics, was able to identify four historic groups by molecular markers: wild vines, and primitive, ancient and recent varieties. Thanks to vegetative reproduction, in some cases going back several millennia, we can still find ancient varieties such as Savagnin or Pinot, which are several centuries old. That said, researchers are yet to turn up an example of a primitive variety; they have either disappeared or we only know of their distant descendants, or they may still be reproducing and encouraging the emergence of a high level of intravarietal diversity.

Maratheftiko – *a* Vitis vinifera with female flowers that is still cultivated

Cyprus has a long wine history. Commandaria, a sweet wine made with sun-dried Mavro and Xynisteri, was mentioned by Hesiod. But Cyprus's island nature has also preserved endemic cépages, like Maratheftiko, which almost disappeared as it is a non-hermaphroditic *V. vinifera*: its flowers are only female. To be pollinated, this red variety must be planted with varieties flowering at the same time. Complantation was widespread before phylloxera but abandoned with modern viticulture. Fortunately, agronomic pragmatism is now responding to the necessity of preserving this heritage.

Cépage – a concept

Cépage, usually translated as "grape variety" is one of the most common terms in the French vocabulary of wine. Very much like the French concept of terroir, the unique concept it represents is more difficult to pin down than it might at first seem, however. This is as much to do with the way it is used as it is with the reality it describes; in France, it is a winemaker's term that corresponds only imperfectly with the real botanical world. Its limitations become apparent the more it is applied and ever greater numbers of different *V. vinifera* are identified. (There are officially more than 12,250 cépages.) Why is the concept of cépage used only for *V. vinifera* and no other plant? What do we actually mean by cépage? Where did this idea originate, and how is it understood and used today in ampelography, the science of its study? Since French scientists largely participated in the development of this science, it matters to understand the conceptual and practical issues implied by this concept.

Cépages before there were cépages

People (French or not) clearly did not have to wait for the appearance of the word cépage to make use of the concept; the first treatises on viticulture appeared as soon as grape vines spread around the Mediterranean basin. A desire to distinguish between grape vines is apparent first among Greek agronomists, for example Democritus and Theophrastus, and then Latin writers. Among the latter, Pliny the Elder (1st century CE) is known to have listed about 50 different grape vines in his *Natural History*, including Falerno, Nomentura, Alba and Aminea, which he tries to distinguish from each other and organize into a system. Much like his predecessors, however, he concedes that counting all the varieties is an impossible task.

While all these agronomic texts provide many and various tips on cultivation, diseases and sizes, they give no precise description of the grapes themselves; the first major works with descriptions of these varieties, and the word cépage itself, were not to appear until the Middle Ages.

Cépage – initially a colloquial term

Jean-Antoine de Baïf (1532-89), a member of the Pléiade group of poets, is credited with inventing the French term cépage in 1573. It is derived from the word *cep*, a vine, with the suffix *age*, designating an amalgamation; a "cépage" is a collection of "ceps". It then became a winemaker's term from its colloquial use and began to be used more frequently and widely. Different types of cépage were increasingly mentioned: author and satirist François Rabelais (1483 or 1494-1553) has his Gargantua and Pantagruel drink Arbois, Muscadet, Breton and Chenin, while agronomist Olivier de Serres (1539-1619) wrote about Pinot, Beaunois and Corinthian in his *Théâtre d'agriculture et mesnage des champs* (1600).

Synonyms, homonyms and other toponymic names presented a plethora of problems, and a cépage might take the name of a place without necessarily coming from there - such as Auxerrois, which is in fact a Malbec and hails from Southwest France rather than anywhere near Auxerre. Confusion was growing, despite these specifications, although knowledge of cépages improved from the 18th century, initially thanks to Swedish botanist Linnaeus (1707-78), who was the first scientifically to systematize the species of vine known at the time: *V. vinifera*, *V. labrusca*, and *V. lupina* (1753). He was continuing the work of German doctor Philipp Jakob Sachs (1627-72), who was the first to dub this branch of botany "ampelography" (from Greek *ampelos*, "vine", and *graphein*, "to describe") in his eponymous work of 1661. As collections of cépages began to increase during this period, it became clear that it had to be possible to compare specimens in order to identify and differentiate them.

"Cépage" enters scientific language

France owes the entry of "cépage" into scientific vocabulary to Count Alexandre-Pierre Odart (1778-1866) and his 1845 publication *Ampelographie universelle ou Traité des cépages les plus estimés dans tous les vignobles de quelque renom*, in which he studied more than 700 of them. He preferred this term to "species" or "variety", asserting its specific meaning within viticulture. His work is the first comprehensive international enumeration based on the morphology of *Vitis*, its identification and its botanical classification by cépage, in addition to their relationships and cultivational and oenological suitabilities. In France by the end of the 19th century, the term "cépage" was supplanting the *qualité* or *race* of a vine or plant, and had entered botanical nomenclature. The word was then used in every ampelographic treatise until the turn of the 20th century, when a need to rethink this conceptual tool became apparent due to the increasing confusion it was causing: the concept of cépage was not capable of encompassing the protean aspect of vines. Renowned ampelographer Louis Levadoux (1912–85) summed it up as follows in 1961: "This term [cépage] is unlikely to be given any exact botanical definition; it is a systematic wine-grower's unit that fits rather poorly into our modern way of thinking. . . The limitations of cépage, a purely subjective and practical unit, are not recognized by all" (*La vigne et sa vulture*, "Que Sais-Je?").

A real epistemological problem

The particularities of *V. vinifera*'s mode of reproduction and multiplication, not to mention its genetic variabi-lity, present a real epistemological problem in that they make it difficult to invent conceptual tools to pin down its complex reality correctly. Only the Italian language has an equivalent (*vitigno*) of cépage as a botanical category for the grape vine. Other languages use "variety", with English notably using "cultivar", a contraction of cultivated variety. This term is already making an assumption; it presupposes that a cépage needs to be cultivated, implying that the *V. sylvestris* or any *V. vinifera* crossed with wild specimens or other types (such as *Muscadinia*) can be called neither a cultivar nor a cépage. But the word "variety" is not correct either. From a botanical perspective, a cépage is not a variety in the strictest sense because, according to its scientific definition, a variety is reproduced identically with a seed. But the grape vine does not breed true because of its genetic instability. Sowing a grape pip necessarily creates a unique plant, one different from its parents.

It was not until 2009 that the matter was put to bed in France with an official resolution from the Institut national de l'origine et de la qualité (INAO; it used to be called Institut national des appellations d'origine), the public body that regulates French agricultural produce, which ended

The enigma of the origins of Zinfandel

The US long believed Zinfandel to be one of its rare native cépages. This myth was shattered in 1968, however, when a professor at the University of California, Davis (UC Davis), noticed that Primitivo from Apulia resembled it. Samples were sent to California, and the first biochemical and ampelographic analyses confirmed the identity of these two cépages in 1975. Shortly thereafter, Italian researchers backed by Mike Grgich, a Croatian-born winemaker in the Napa Valley, suggested that the Primitivo/Zinfandel grape was none other than the Croatian cépage Plavac Mali.

A Zinfandel defence union was formed in 1991, and Professor Carole Meredith was dispatched to Croatia, returning with 150 samples. From the first DNA analyses made of the vine, she was able to confirm that Primitivo and Zinfandel were clones of the same variety but that Plavac Mali was not their direct ancestor, just a member of the clan.

Croatian research in 2002 resulted in the discovery of a vineyard on the Dalmatian coast planted with hundreds of varieties, including nine rows of Crljenak Kaštelanski. Here, they discovered a DNA semi-match: the red Kaštela grape was the original clone of Primitivo/Zinfandel. José Vouillamoz supplied the last piece of the puzzle with further DNA analysis in 2012, matching Crljenak Kaštelanski with a single century-old vine cultivated in a garden in Split. This was Tribidrag, a cépage that had been known since the 15th century. Apparently imported under the name Black Zinfardel of Hungary (not to be confused with Zierfandler, which is an Austrian white cépage) to the east coast of America from the nurseries of the Austro-Hungarian Empire (which ruled Dalmatia at the time), Zinfandel was brought to California thanks to the Gold Rush. By the end of the 19th century, its success had obscured its origins, to which Jancis Robinson MW, Julia Harding MW and José Vouillamoz pay homage in *Wine Grapes*; here, you will find the description of Zinfandel under the Tribidrag entry.

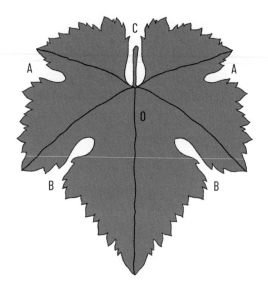

A: LOWER LATERAL SINUSES
B: UPPER LATERAL SINUSES
C: PETIOLAR SINUS
O: PETIOLAR POINT

FIVE-LOBED LEAF

In 1946, Pierre Galet refined ampelometry techniques based on measuring the veins of a leaf along with the number and angles of its lobes.

centuries of confusion by defining cépage, cultivar and clone in line with the work of geneticists and ampelographers Jean-Michel Boursiquot and Patrice This.

Official definitions

Acknowledged as a taxonomic unit applicable to *V. vinifera*, a cépage is a varietal group of varying size. A variety, or cultivar, is a subset of a cépage, which may have several clones, sometimes hundreds. Grenache Noir, Blanc and Gris, along with Lledoner Pelut (Grenache Velu), for example, are cultivars of the Grenache cépage, and Grenache Blanc has three official clones (141, 143, 1213) in addition to many more that have not been accredited by the institutions responsible for grape-vine plants in France. If a variety has several clones, it is polyclonal; if not, it is monoclonal. Here it should be understood that the number of clones per cépage will depend on its genetic instability but also on its age: the older it is, the more clones it is likely to have. Pinot, which has existed for more than 2,000 years, boasts more than 1,000 clonal variations, while Cabernet Sauvignon, which appeared at the end of the 18th century as a cross of Cabernet Franc and Sauvignon Blanc, has 19 official clones and 250 non-certified ones in the national conservatories.

Where the clones have similar quantitative (for example, vigour or yield) and qualitative (for example, minor variations in colour or villosity, or hairiness) characteristics, they will have the same cépage name. When a variation becomes too large and changes the viticultural and winemaking characteristics (this is known as somatic mutation), the clone in question takes on a form different from the initial cépage. Such was the case with Gewürztraminer, an aromatic form of Savagnin Rose, which itself is a mutation of Savagnin Blanc, or Traminer.

The word "cépage" is now normally reserved for wine grapes, "variety" for table grapes and rootstocks. Hybrids are still under debate in the ampelographic community; some would prefer to keep "cépage" for *V. vinifera* alone, although the use of resistant "cépages" is becoming more common when speaking of the varieties that cross *V. vinifera* with other species.

Cépages and their names

In addition to identifying cépages botanically, ampelographers have had to study and map the ampelonyms, the specific names given to a cépage, which have an etymology that may be highly varied – sometimes evocative, or geographical, or morphological. The use of ampelonyms has been spreading since the 14th century. There is no official nomenclature to this day; the international list of grape vines and their synonyms established by the Organisation internationale de la vigne et du vin (OIV; the international body responsible for setting agreed standards in vitivinicultural products) does not promote one synonym over another, while the list kept by FranceAgriMer, France's national institution for agricultural and seafood products, the body that deals with the issue of cépages, makes use of the "principal denomination". This idea, suggested by Robinson, Harding and Vouillamoz, of using a prime name, the description most commonly used in the cépage's region of origin, seems the most sensible. Their work *Wine Grapes* is still the most comprehensive collection of classical and contemporary ampelography available to the general public and includes 1,368 cépages that are found on the market – for a more academic readership, there is also Pierre Galet's *Dictionnaire encyclopédique des cépages* (2000). It is only through use or study that a cépage can survive.

Evolutionary identification criteria

Ampelographic research took on a whole new dimension with the arrival of phylloxera in Europe at the end of the 19th century. The destruction of vineyards and the necessity of finding solutions led to a proliferation of studies to identify resistant species and control the profusion of cross-breeds and hybridizations that de facto were multiplying the number

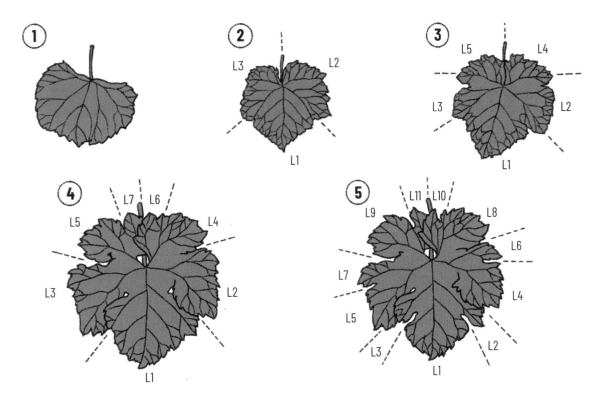

NUMBER OF LEAVES AS AN AMPELOMETRIC CRITERION,
WITH L1 = MEDIAN LOBE; L2 TO L11 = LATERAL LOBES

1. **ONE** (whole leaf). Examples: Melon B, Rupestris du Lot
2. **THREE.** Examples: Chenin, Aramon
3. **FIVE.** Examples: Chasselas, Riesling, Barbera
4. **SEVEN.** Examples: Vermentino, Cabernet Sauvignon, Corvina
5. **MORE THAN SEVEN.** Example: Hebron

THE FIVE TYPES OF LEAF ESTABLISHED BY THE OIV

The OIV has been collating morphological descriptors
to identify cépages since 1983. The leaves are
categorized according to their number of lobes,
among other things.

of varieties. The major researchers of the era included
Victor Pulliat, Gustave Foëx, Louis Ravaz, Victor Vermorel
and Pierre Viala, with the latter two publishing *Ampélographie: Traité général de viticulture* between 1901 and 1910, the
most comprehensive work of ampelography published to
date, describing 5,200 cépages and 24,000 denominations.
Each entry includes elements of historical, geographical,
linguistic (including synonyms), agronomic and (in particular)
morphological relevance, with a description of every part of
the strain according to criteria of size, colour, appearance,
texture and so on. In another advance, 500 of these cépages
are illustrated with a colour plate of a grape cluster. Despite
its wealth of detail, however, this veritable bible is on a collision course with a major problem: it lacks definitive criteria
for identifying known botanical groups and newly created
varieties out in the field.

Since the phylloxera crisis, the issue has become more
than just epistemological; the output of hybridizers and
nursery workers has exploded, the number of plants is
multiplying, and with it merchandise fraud and diseases of
the wood. The consequences are political and economic: to
replant French vineyards with good, healthy plants, you have
to be able to recognize poor quality in the field. The French
institutions have realized that they must therefore monitor
the commercial use of plants, no longer leaving this to the
winemaker or nurseryman as has historically been the case.
But we still have to be able to distinguish between them.

From the revolution in morphological ampelography...

This was to be the work of agronomist Galet, dubbed the "father
of modern ampelography", who in 1944–6 first addressed the
identification of rootstocks. This was an urgent issue; they
appeared as a better qualitative solution to phylloxera than
hybrids (*hybrides producteurs directs*, or HPD, in French), but
they are difficult to identify. A rootstock that is not adapted
to the soil or the graft, or that does not take, will incur the
loss of several years of production. Fraud relating to quality

will only further muddy the waters in times of scarcity. Galet and his colleague Henri Agnel developed a new vocabulary to distinguish rootstocks, codifying the distinctive elements of *Vitis*: villosity, or the hairiness of a vine; the type of budding; the young leaves; the adult leaves that he considered the true "face of the vine"; the tendrils; the shoots; the flowers and the grape clusters, those last being rare for often non-fruiting rootstocks. They listed these according to such criteria in *Les Portes-Greffes, ampélographie pratique* (1946). In 1952, Galet extended his methodology to all the vines in his *Grape Varieties and Rootstock Varieties* (English ed: 1998), insisting on the identification of the morphology of the vine's vegetative organs, its buds, leaves and shoots, which were more distinctive than the fruiting organs, the flowers, clusters and berries.

He also took up the crucial idea of ampelometry as promulgated by Louis Ravaz (1863–1937) at the turn of the 20th century. This was a classification by mathematical ratio based on the measurement of the length of the principal veins of a leaf (seven measurements) and their angles (five measurements). This practical method was to prevail over the decades and was included in part in the OIV's "List of descriptors for the varieties and species of *Vitis*" of 1983. Each entry includes 123 morphological descriptors for eight organs, ampelometry data, an example, a definition and a depiction, since each variety is so complex to identify. While identification is now more straightforward, classical morphological ampelography cannot formally confirm one crucial aspect, however: a vine's lineage.

… to a similar transformation of molecular biology
The arrival of molecular biology in the 1970s was a revolution in our understanding of cépages and their lineage. First of all, biochemistry made it possible to differentiate between varieties by studying the compounds of secondary metabolism (any molecule that is not essential for the growth of the plant – for example, colour pigments such as anthocyanins) and certain enzymes. But it was genetics in particular that was to upset the applecart; using molecular marking and DNA sequencing from a few milligrams of vine cell, research was able to penetrate to the heart of the genome. By locating 20 specific microsatellite markers known as SSRs (simple sequence repeats), which are short repetitive sequences of DNA, genetic ampelographers are able not only to identify cépages but also reveal their parentage through their genotype, which is more reliable than their phenotype (their observable characteristics as modified by their environment). Carole Meredith's teams, working at UC Davis, between 1993 and 2001, managed to establish a similarity between American Zinfandel, Italian Primitivo and Croatian Tribidrag in this manner.

In 1997, the team at UC Davis collaborated with John Bowers to perform the first successful test of parentage and identified the pedigree of Cabernet Sauvignon. Results came thick and fast in the wake of this breakthrough, with Bowers uncovering the kinship of Chardonnay (1999) and Syrah (2000), Vouillamoz showing the descent of Sangiovese (2007), and Boursiquot lifting the lid on Merlot and Malbec (2009), among others. Following rice, thale cress and the poplar, *V. vinifera* became the fourth plant to have its genome decoded, in 2007. The OIV's second edition of the "List of descriptors" (2009) has endorsed this major evolution, adding two biochemical and six genetic characteristics to the 179 criteria for identifying a variety. This list is now the standard global botanical and legal reference text for ampelography.

Identifying to monitor, identifying to preserve
The pursuit of pure botanical knowledge was not the only reason for scientific developments in ampelography. One of Galet's original missions was to combat fraud and exclude cépages considered to be of poor quality, by training technicians who were able to recognize such plants. France was in a full-blown winemaking crisis at the end of World War Two, and a return to the production of fine wines of high quality was a national issue. As expert knowledge increased, monitoring and control of French grape varieties became more rigorous, first in monitoring of plants (uprooting hybrids) and then for diseases of vines and rootstocks. Winemakers' choices of plant stock are now also closely supervised, and they can no longer plant whatever they want.

In France, the varieties authorized for planting, grafting and vinification are listed in a legal catalogue supervised by FranceAgriMer (this is the same for all European Union [EU] countries) and ENTAV-INRA®, which monitors the origins of clones and rootstocks available to nursery workers and is in charge of ratified selections from these cépages. The stated aim is to ensure phytosanitary quality, avoid the spread of disease, and guarantee the genotype of the cépage – but does this approach of restricted and protected biodiversity with a view to sanitary security not fly in the face of the evolution of inter- and intravarietal biodiversity that has been acquired over the course of millennia? By confirming a number of findings from traditional ampelography, molecular ampelography has immeasurably accelerated the identification of cépages and their kinship. In addition to such identification, these two complementary methods are pursuing the fundamental missions of this science: to understand and preserve the incredible diversity of *Vitis* in order to support its adaptation to environmental change and defend it against pathogens – not to limit it.

The classification of cépages

Classifying the abundant diversity found within ampelography is just as difficult as identifying a cépage. Various classifications can be made, depending on the ultimate purpose: a winemaker may be interested in production types, early growth or sugar content; an ampelographer's aim will be to discover the links of lineage and to construct coherent botanical groups; and a lexicographer will rank them in alphabetical order. What are the most common classifications today? How can they help us understand the links between cépages and suggest solutions in an environment in crisis?

Wine and table grape varieties

The classifications that have long proved most useful to wine-makers have been descriptive in nature, grouping cépages according to their technological suitability – that is what they can produce and how. The first of these classifications is the division of *V. vinifera* into two categories according to their domestication: grapes for making wine (grapes) and grapes for consumption or to be dried (table grapes). The former generally have compact clusters of medium-sized berries that are juicy and sweet, with skin that is easy to press but fragile. The latter most often come in loose clusters of large, elongated berries that are more acidic and crunchy, with a thicker skin.

The seeds represent another difference: modern table grape hybrids are often apyrene, or seedless, whereas wine grapes contain pips. These two groups spread around the Mediterranean along cultural lines: the consumers of wine in the Roman world, which became the Christian West,

Unsuspected ancestors

The diversity of cépages in Southwest France has long been a conundrum for ampelographers, with numerous phantom missing parents making it difficult to establish links – for example, for Merlot, which comes from Cabernet Franc and a cépage that remained unknown for a long time. In 1992, an old vine was discovered in Saint-Suliac in Brittany that until 2004 was believed to be a wild vine. Analysis of its DNA, however, revealed it to be an unknown *V. vinifera*. Simultaneously, ampelographic investigations in the Cognac region uncovered four trellises of table grapes known as Magdeleine Noire des Charentes that were identical to the mysterious Breton cépage. In 2009, Boursiquot discovered that this was the absentee parent not only of Merlot but also of Malbec and at least three other cépages.

Magdeleine Noire is not the only "ancestral" cépage that has played a key role as a progenitor and then disappeared from vineyards; Gouais Blanc is the most fertile, with 63 descendants, but there is also Hebén in Spain, Frankenthal in Germany, Bombino Bianco in Italy and Heptaliko in Greece. Some have been highly mobile, such as Gouais, which has long been a missing link in the families of Southwest France and is indirectly linked to Folle Blanche, Colombard, Muscadelle and a host of other cépages, in addition to being related to a number of varieties of Noiriens and Messiles. Magdeleine Noire has not yet given up all its secrets; it seems to be more resistant to flavescence dorée, a fatal vine disease, providing yet further proof of the need to preserve the broadest living varietal diversity.

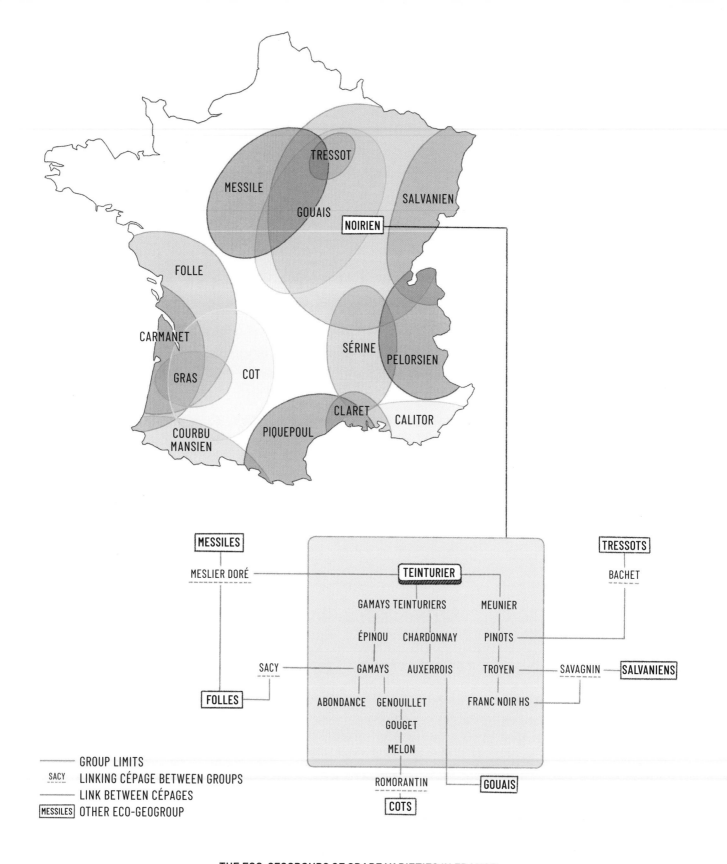

THE ECO-GEOGROUPS OF GRAPE VARIETIES IN FRANCE

Jean Bisson continued the work of Louis Levadoux in establishing eco-geogroups or sorto-types, which were families of varieties having originated and evolved from the same environment. Their members are related, as shown in the detailed illustration of the Noirien eco-geogroup.

took an interest in refining wine grapes, while the Near and Middle East, along with the territories conquered by Islam, where alcohol was forbidden, cultivated table grapes.

Some cépages are both wine and table grapes and stand at the intersection of the two groups. These include Chasselas and Black Muscat, an ancient cépage with a great diversity of clones. Such a distinction is a regulatory categorization based more on use than on any technical reality, however.

Victor Pulliat's classification

In 1879, Beaujolais ampelographer Victor Pulliat (1827–96) developed a classification based on physiological maturity that is still in use to this day. Having observed that cépages do not ripen at the same time, he decided to classify them and took Chasselas Doré, an early cépage, as a point of reference, thereby obtaining five groups:

- **Early cépages** maturing 8-10 days before Chasselas (mainly table grapes and hybrids).
- **First-period cépages** coinciding +/-8 days with Chasselas (Pinot, Melon, Savagnin).
- **Second-period cépages** ripening 12-15 days after (Riesling, Syrah, Chenin, Cabernets).
- **Third-period cépages** ripening 15-24 days after (Grenache, Clairette, Carignan, and cépages used for distillation, such as Folle Blanche or Trebbiano).
- **Fourth-period or late-ripening cépages** ripening 24-36 days after (Mourvèdre, Montepulciano, Trepat).

This classification allows cépage selection according to the climatic conditions enjoyed by the vineyards, and was expanded during the 20th century as geoclimatic know-how was refined. It remains to a certain extent artificial as it does not allow us to understand the relationship between varieties, organizing them only descriptively for their ultimate use.

Natural classifications

It is to French ampelographer Galet that we owe the spread of the concept of "natural" classification, which is based on morphology, cultivational suitability and geographical origin. Since the 18th century, ampelographers had been noting that varieties from the same geographical area shared some resemblances and had common characteristics, seemingly forming families. In 1946, following research undertaken in Russia, Georgia and Central Asia, Russian ampelographer Aleksandr Negrul (1900–71) confirmed these insights, identifying three large ecological/geographical groups, or eco-geogroups, which he called *Proles*. He lists the following:

- **Proles orientalis**, with two sub-*Proles* (*caspica* and *antasiatica*), which includes cépages from Armenia, Iran, Azerbaijan and Afghanistan, with large berries used as table grapes (Dattier de Beyrouth, Sultana, Muscat).
- **Proles pontica** with two sub-*Proles* (*georgica* and *balkanica*), which include cépages from Romania, Hungary, Georgia and Asia Minor, along with Mediterranean cépages; their bunches are average-sized, with round table grape (such as apyrene, or seedless, Corinth grapes), wine grapes, or grapes for both uses (Furmint, Vermentino, Clairette).

> " The task is still a vast one, given the incredible genetic diversity of *V. vinifera*

- **Proles occidentalis** includes cépages from Western Europe deriving from cépages of *Proles orientalis* and *pontica* that were imported during the course of ancient migrations and hybridized with local *V. vinifera*. These are essentially cépages with small clusters of juicy grapes suitable for vinification (Riesling, Cabernet Franc, Aligoté, Aleatico and Verdelho).

This revolutionary classification, incorporating morphological, agronomic, geographical and historical parameters, also confirms the likelihood of the simultaneous domestication of viticulture in the Levant and the Caucasus.

The benefits of Negrul's work

French ampelographer Louis Levadoux translated Negrul's work in 1948 and refined the classification of French cépages within *Proles occidentalis*, using his concept of "sortotypes", or families originating and evolving from the same natural surroundings. It was not until the 1990s that research was published by his pupil Jean Bisson, who continued his work using molecular analysis. It was possible to classify French varieties into 10 sortotypes, named after the most representative variety in the group – for example, Savagnin has given its name to the Salvanien ecogroup, while the Serines group derives its name from Serine, an old synonym for Syrah. Some have very limited distribution zones with little variation – such as the Mansiens, grouped around the Petit Manseng grape in Southwest France, or the Noiriens, around Pinot Noir in Burgundy – while others are less homogeneous and more widespread, such as the Carmenets, around Cabernet Franc. These variations can be explained by the role of humans in spreading varieties.

Crossing and sowing to create diversity

In 1999, French ampelographers Boursiquot and This suggested a new definition of using molecular marking: "A cépage is. . . made up of a collection of clones that are sufficiently related to one another to be conflated under

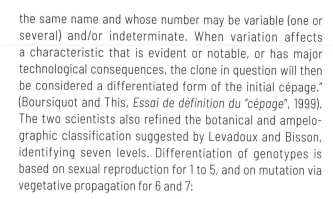

Uncovering the origins of French vines

What are the connections between our contemporary cépages and those cultivated in the Roman era? In 2019, an international consortium made up of teams from the University of Montpellier (including Lacombe), the CNRS sequenced the DNA of 28 seeds discovered on French archaeological sites, some of which dated back to the Iron Age. They revealed their findings in an article published in *Nature Plants* ("Palaeogenomic insights into the origins of French grape vine diversity"), showing that these seeds and the varieties from which they came are closely related to the cépages now used for vinification in Western Europe. A seed dated to around 1100 was genetically associated with Savagnin Blanc, a classic Jura cépage used in the production of France's Vin Jaune; it has been preserved by vegetative propagation for more than 900 years. This work has also shed light on the kinship between Pinot Noir, Syrah and the Roman cépages that the winemakers of the time propagated on imperial territory.

the same name and whose number may be variable (one or several) and/or indeterminate. When variation affects a characteristic that is evident or notable, or has major technological consequences, the clone in question will then be considered a differentiated form of the initial cépage." (Boursiquot and This, *Essai de définition du "cépage"*, 1999). The two scientists also refined the botanical and ampelographic classification suggested by Levadoux and Bisson, identifying seven levels. Differentiation of genotypes is based on sexual reproduction for 1 to 5, and on mutation via vegetative propagation for 6 and 7:

1 – Espèce/Species (*Vitis vinifera*)
2 – Sous espèces/Sub-species (eg. *sativa*)
3 – *Proles*/Divisions/Unités/Units (eg. *occidentalis*)
4 – Familles/Families/Groups/Sortotypes (eg. Noiriens)
5 – Cépages/Sortogroups/Tribus (eg. Pinot)

---

6 – Sous cépages/Varieties/Forms/Cultivars (eg. Pinot Noir N)
7 – Clones/Selections/Types (eg. 115)

Research carried out in molecular ampelography by Thierry Lacombe in 2012 also backed up some of Negrul's insights. From an analysis of the 2,344 cépages in the Vassal-Montpellier ampelographic collection, he refined their ecological and geographical distribution, suggesting secondary centres of domestication around the shores of the Mediterranean. He also noted that there are fewer new varietal generations in the West than in the East. Those that found approval were quickly "fixed", preserved and made into cuttings, while "Eastern" table grape varieties have passed through more numerous generations of descent.

Study of DNA has since made it possible to narrow down and correct the family relationships between cépages. The task is still a vast one, given the incredible genetic diversity of *V. vinifera*, which seems due in part to reproduction from seed until recent times, with this sexual reproduction creating a new cépage each time. Seed-sowing and genetic cross-breeding from seed are therefore the future for adapting vines, which is why the technique has never been used as much as it is today, either in breeding carried out by research bodies or by certain winemakers who employ it to construct resistant varieties of table or wine grapes, or rootstock, and so diversify their vineyards.

The task of identifying the pedigree of cépages is still a vast one, given the incredible genetic diversity of *V. vinifera*.

Cépages galore!

In Book II of his *Georgics*, Virgil asserts that there are as many wines and vines as there are grains of sand in the desert. Ampelography carried out by Viala and Vermorel in 1910 describes 5,200 cépages, while a century later, in 2000, Galet counted 9,600. By 2021, the international database of *Vitis* accounted for more than 21,000 varieties, including 12,250 names for *V. vinifera*, yielding probably 6,000 cépages once the homonyms had been eliminated. What is the explanation for such diversity? And why do only 10 cépages dominate global production despite this glut of complexity, representing a problematic standardization of tastes, markets and wine manufacturing?

Two modes of reproduction

Vitis has two modes of reproduction: sexual, by pollination, and vegetative propagation. These two methods have their advantages and disadvantages, which have been spontaneously exploited, initially by the plant itself and then by humans. All sexual reproduction entails a genetic cocktail, and *Vitis* is no exception. It possesses 19 pairs of chromosomes that combine to create a diploid embryo (the seed within a grape berry) when the flower is fertilized by the pollen from the stamens (the male gamete) inseminating the ovule of the pistil (the female gamete). A key aspect of *V. vinifera* is that its extremely high heterozygosity of between 50 and 95 per cent means that there is a high probability of different alleles, or genetic variations, for the same gene. In other words, this multiplies the probability of the new individual being different from the parents. Add to this a tendency for gametes to exchange characteristics when they are formed, and you have 274 billion different possible descendants per fertilization. If you plant this seed, the variation between the cépage-parents and the progeny is generally so great that you will get a new cépage, with unique morphological qualities and a distinct genome. Molecular ampelography can now identify the markers specific to the mother's DNA and thus determine its kinship.

The first instances of *Vitis* propagation

Vitis was originally disseminated by birds and other animals spreading the plant after eating its sweet berries and transporting the seeds in their plumage or fur. Its sexual, dioecious nature originally made it dependent on the proximity of other plants, wind and sometimes even insects to reproduce, but the appearance of a hermaphrodism gene was a decisive evolutionary step for its propagation and domestication. Hermaphrodism did not entail a cessation of genetic mixing, however, and fertilization between sexual plants and/or hermaphrodites was to continue until the 18th century. This mixing, which is presumed to have been necessary for the original survival and adaptation of *Vitis*, was to become problematic for the first domesticators, however, who wanted to preserve its characteristics of interest: organoleptic (size, flavour, berry yield) and phytosanitary (minimal susceptibility to parasites), along with its capacity for adaptation, and so vegetative reproduction entered the fray.

> " Unlike sexual reproduction, asexual vegetative propagation repeats inherited genetic traits instead of combining them

Vegetative propagation

Unlike sexual reproduction, asexual vegetative propagation repeats inherited genetic traits instead of combining them: planting a cutting, regardless of whether it is still connected to the mother plant, as with layering, or not, will preserve the genome of the individual parent. An individual plant will develop from this cutting, and the technique makes it possible to fix and propagate the genotype. It is known as clonal reproduction, and the clones are identical to the parent except for the occasional minor mutation. This method of reproduction is an extremely practical way of multiplying a variety of interest and is also much faster than sowing, which entails a wait of at least two to three years before seeing the first grapes develop from seed plants, without knowing whether the new variety obtained is viable or not. It is easy

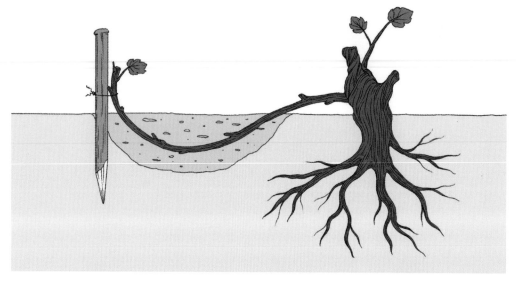

LAYERING

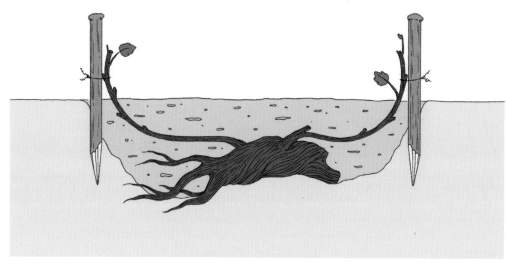

PROVIGNAGE

to understand why vegetative propagation has established itself in wine production.

Thousands of cépages...

In its wild form, *Vitis* was spread naturally by these two methods of reproduction. In domesticating it during the Neolithic period, humans improved and continued to develop the diversity of *V. vinifera*. While sexual reproduction invigorated the genetic pool, adapting individuals and creating the diversity of cépages that we know today, vegetative propagation stabilized characteristics and created clones. Until the 18th century, Europe was almost the only cradle of genetic evolution for *V. vinifera*, which was carried out by crossing individuals within a single species, a process known as intraspecific hybridization. Hybridization between different species was essentially unknown in Asia and America, the other *Vitis* basins, before the Age of Exploration.

As every vineyard was planted with multiple cépages until the end of the 19th century, numerous individual plants continued to appear, the most interesting of which were preserved with layering or with provignage. These planting techniques were predominant until the phylloxera crisis. The former involved burying a branch from the mother vine, along with its buds, which as they grew would develop a root system of their own and create a new vine. When the new plant was sufficiently robust, the winemaker could cut the initial branch, making it independent of the mother. The latter, provignage, followed the same procedure but involved burying an entire vine. Vines were multiplied at low cost using these techniques, and planting density could reach tens of thousands of vines per hectare.

Vitis vinifera has been monitored, crossbred and refined according to its environment and ultimate intended purpose for more than six thousand years. Over the course of history, the formation of nation states has led to the movement of populations, who have taken their best cépages with them, stirring the melting pot of varietal diversity, and because *V. vinifera* boasts high interfertility with no generational problems, thousands of grape cépages have appeared over the centuries. To a certain extent, *V. vinifera* was born to evolve and diversify.

But endangered genetic diversity

Of the 337 varieties authorized as wine varieties in France, 10 accounted for 71.9 per cent of all French vineyards in 2017. In the whole world, the figure was 49.4 per cent in 2015. Why is there so little diversity when there is so much expertise? The reasons lie primarily in agronomic and oeno-logical characteristics of quality and consistency, but this concentration around a few varieties has also arguably been accelerated by the industrialization of production and standardization of tastes as much as by the regulation of standards in viticulture, winemaking and grape varieties.

Can this trajectory be altered? One possible way is to rediscover and appreciate this complexity. On the one hand, there are signs of a growing interest among buyers and producers in indigenous and "modest" cépages, many of which had been neglected since the phylloxera crisis, and in others that survived that crisis but have been neglected during the gradual standardization of AOCs from 1935 onward. Recultivation is under way, such as that practised by the members of France's Rencontres des Cépages Modestes union, which promotes lesser-known varieties. Its efforts to preserve the genetic diversity of varieties have been assisted by the work carried out by conservation and selection bodies such as the 180 French regional conservatories, which alone have protected more than 20,000 different clones. It has been possible for ENTAV-INRA® to approve 47 Pinot Noir clones that are available to French winemakers, and more than 800 other individual vines are under ongoing observation. There is still more work to do on less popular varieties, and it is up to the industry – in the form of selection bodies, nurseries, winemakers and critics – to make them public, and up to the consumer to drink them, in order to preserve their unique genetics.

Indispensable ampelographic collections

Establishing and maintaining ampelographic collections has always played a key role in our understanding of cépages, even if their preservation has not always appeared to be a matter of fundamental importance for political or scientific bodies. We owe the first modern and systematic collection to botanist François Rozier (1734–93), who in 1779 planted out a field near Béziers that was destroyed by the city's bishop in order to build a road that would allow him to see his mistress. Rozier died in penury and without ever finishing the *Traité de viticulture*, his treatise on winemaking.

Before him, Carthusian monks had established a nursery in the Jardin du Luxembourg in Paris, which was enlarged by Jean-Antoine Chaptal (1756–1832) and then Auguste-François Hardy (1824–91), who recorded 1,300 varieties in his *Catalogue de l'Ecole des vignes de la pépinière du Luxembourg* (1848). It was destroyed by Haussmann's urban renewal programme in Paris but inspired the creation of regional collections.

In Saumur, Auguste Courtiller (1795–1875) turned the botanical gardens into an experimentation centre that by 1848 housed 750 cépages, including American hybrids such as Jacquez and Herbemont. In 1876, Gustave Foëx (1844–1906) began a collection in Montpellier that was to become the Vassal-Montpellier Grape Vine Biological Resources Center, which now boasts 2,700 cépages, 350 wild grape vines, 1,100 interspecific hybrids, 400 rootstocks and 60 species of Vitaceae sourced from 54 countries. It is the largest planted database in the world and is complemented by other collections, notably those at UC Davis, or at Cornell University, specializing in cold-resistant varieties. Parallel local, public and private initiatives are now flourishing as winemakers, nursery owners and institutions become aware of the need to preserve this diversity.

Hybridization – the past, present and future of grape vines

Since around 2010 or so, the question of interspecific hybridization of grape vines has emerged from the realms of scientific research and caught the attention of the general public. Often viewed as unnatural, this evolutionary phenomenon, which involves crossing two different species (rather than two individuals of the same species) has always occurred spontaneously and allows for adaptation of the genome through evolution; ferns, strawberries, *Homo sapiens* – all are hybrids. What happens, however, when hybridization is not natural but guided and controlled by humans? How did this technique once save the world's vineyards, and why is it so much discussed today?

A traditional hand-crafted technique

Hybridization is simple: all you need is a clamp, a pair of scissors and a brush. This hand-crafted technique is still in use today, both in research laboratories and vineyards. Just before a hermaphrodite *Vitis* is about to flower, its floral cap must be removed and its stamens cut. Pollen is taken from the chosen male plant with a brush and placed on the stigma of the female plant's trimmed inflorescence, which has been protected to guarantee offspring and avoid any contamination by other pollen. This operation must be repeated several times to increase the chances of success. Once the berry ripens, the seeds are harvested. These will not be numerous on the vine (four per berry at most, and often less), and those with an embryo are germinated. The characteristics that allow for selection (or not) will appear after several years of cultivation. This seemingly simple technique, which has the benefit of renewing the genetic pool, is fiddly, long and dependent on the fundamental randomness of the 274 billion possible combinations. The preservation of specific genes will improve with technological developments, however.

The roots of scientific hybridization

There was no talk of creating cépages in the sense of deliberate hybridization of two identified species until the end of the 18th century. New individual plants were the result of spontaneous cross-pollination between vines. Those that survived (a rare event in nature, in fact) and were of interest were preserved by the winemaker. It could be said that there were as many cépages as there were terroirs.

This was all to change in the 19th century with attempts to simplify grape varieties, specialization by terroir, the global spread of *Vitis* and the advent of modern botany, which took an interest in the phenomenon of introgression. When two individuals of different species are crossbred, simple hybridization occurs, with equal sharing of the genetic pool. If this progeny is then re-crossed with one of the two original species over several generations (repeated backcrossings), the result is an individual that is very close to the latter but with several genes from the other original parent. Introgression bolsters genetic diversity and allows species to acquire new traits more quickly than waiting for a genetic mutation; for grape vines, this might be a change in berry quality, resistance to disease or new climatic conditions, and so on.

The pioneers of directed hybridization

In 1790, British agronomist William Speechly (1723–1819) first described his hybridization method, which had been used on the Duke of Portland's *V. vinifera* in Nottinghamshire, United Kingdom (UK). The first interspecific hybridization was carried out in the United States (US) at the beginning of the 19th century (the *V. vinifera* imported there had all died, unlike the local *Vitis*), the Concord hybridization being one of the best known. In 1843, Ephraim Wales Bull (1806–95) planted 22,000 *V. labrusca* and *V. vinifera* seeds, selecting after six years a plant with remarkable qualities that he named Concord after his village in Massachusetts. Many others, such as Delaware, were long believed to be indigenous *Vitis* until molecular analysis showed them to have *V. vinifera* DNA.

Hybridization remained intraspecific in France during the same period. The pioneers were Louis Bouschet de Bernard (1783–1876) and his son Henri (1815–81) at the La Calmette estate, where they created cépages that would be influential in Languedoc viticulture. In 1824, they created Petit Bouschet (a cross of Aramon Noir and Teinturier du Cher), which was considered one of the first successful targeted varietal creations, before crossing with Grenache Noir to create Alicante Bouschet in 1855.

Phylloxera – an accelerator of hybridization

When phylloxera arrived in France (1863), *V. vinifera* was scarcely able to survive the devastating aphid pests. American *Vitis* resisted but, with very few exceptions, was poorly tolerant of French soils, the pH of which was different from that of American soils. Hybridization also presented itself as a solution to restore viable production levels as quickly as possible, and two approaches were explored: one involving hybridized rootstocks onto which *V. vinifera* was grafted, and another with direct producers (also known as French hybrids or HPDs – *hybrides producteurs directs*, which, as their French name suggests, are planted without a rootstock and produce grapes directly).

The two techniques each had fierce advocates, with some backing the partial preservation of the potential quality of French vines via grafting, while others defended HPDs for their astonishing yield in all kinds of soil, despite a bouquet often marked by methyl anthranilate, an aromatic molecule considered to be "foxy", somewhere between musk, rose and jam, that was specific to American *V. labrusca*. While grafting was ultimately implemented at the behest of the French government in the mid-20th century, there was no let-up in research to create hybrids that produced grapes: the majority of rootstocks are not fruit-bearing.

The four major periods of hybridization

The production of grape-bearing hybrids can be divided into four periods.

• **The original hybrids (1820–70).** These were the crossbreeds of *V. vinifera* and *V. labrusca* occurring in the US before the phylloxera crisis. The best known are Clinton, Herbemont, Isabella, Jacquez, Noah and Othello. Despite the methyl anthranilate that dominated the aromatic profile of some of these, their yield and formidable resistance made them so popular in France during the crisis that their spread threatened the replantation of grafted *V. vinifera*. These six hybrids were banned by a 1935 law that attempted to curb overproduction by making claims of toxicity. The acreage planted with these was not to dwindle into insignificance until the 1970s, persisting only for home producers and consumers.

• **Hybrid direct producers, HPD (1878–1950).** This was the golden age of private hybridizers, and France led the field, thanks to its agricultural colleges. Tens of thousands of experiments were carried out by agronomists, nursery workers and ordinary enthusiasts, and many distinguished themselves by producing plants that are still in use today: Albert Seibel produced 16,000 hybrids, including Chancellor and Rayon d'Or; François Baco created Baco 22A, the only hybrid authorized for a long time in France for an AOC, Armagnac; Eugene Kuhlman was responsible for Maréchal Foch and Léon Millot; the Seyve family created Seyval, Chambourcin and Villard. Couderc, the so-called god-

> **" When phylloxera arrived in France (1863), *V. vinifera* was scarcely able to survive the devastating aphid pests**

father of modern viticulture, was the most prolific, scoring more success with his rootstocks (3306 and 3309 C) than with his direct producers, as did Alexis Millardet (with 41 B and 101-14 Mgt). But this proliferation was uncontrolled, and the planting of hybrids became unmanageable.

• **Modern hybrids (1950–75).** The advent of phytosanitary products, the establishment of the AOC system and the chronically poor quality of red grape hybrids prompted change, with the French state stepping in to regulate, and then ban, planting and vinification of direct producers, whose acreage had risen to 32 per cent of French vineyards (402,000 ha) by the mid-1950s. Institutions took control of hybridization, which declined in France but continued elsewhere, notably in Eastern Europe and the Soviet Bloc. Other interests emerged, with the universities of Geisenheim (Germany), Cornell and Minnesota (US investigating resistances to severe cold and hybridizing such grapes as Rondo and Cayuga White, which have been authorized for vinification by their national legislative bodies.

• **Resistant varieties, PIWI and GMOs (1975–2022).** With the word "hybrid" having negative connotations, the International Organisation of Vine and Wine (OIV) officially adopted the expression "resistant variety" in 1994. In 1995, a group of German winemakers created PIWI International (*pilzwiderstandsfähig*, "resistant to fungal disease") to promote them. Researchers are currently exploring mutagenetics and transgenetics and can now go beyond classic genetic selection to introduce genes from non-Vitaceae and develop GMO vines. Since the late 1990s and with a lot of controversy in France, Institut national de la recherche agronomique (INRA) has experimented on GMO rootstocks and has developed one resistant to the grape-vine fanleaf virus. Several GM vines were made experimentally, but there is for the moment a voluntary global moratorium on GM commercial use in viticulture, though not on research.

Quality hybrid wines recognized in Europe

Hybridization is a powerful tool to address current issues in winemaking (pathogens, climate and so on). Research is focusing on multiple resistance (known as polygenic resistance), which is more difficult to obtain than single (monogenic) resistance. For example, the ideotype targeted in Alain Bouquet's pioneering work of the 1970s had to resist both powdery and downy mildew. Genes resistant to powdery mildew (gene Run1) and downy mildew (gene Rpv1) were taken from *Muscadinia rotundifolia* and introduced into *V. vinifera*, and the plant was restored as closely as possible to its original characteristics with a series of backcrossings. This was the basis of the INRA-ResDur (for *resistance durable*, or "lasting resistance") programme, which developed the first vinifiable polygenic varieties in France. Red wines have been made with Artaban and Vidoc, and whites with Floréal and Voltis, since 2017. Introgressed with less than two per cent of American genes, they are officially considered to be *V. vinifera* and are recorded as "cépages suited for winemaking" in the official catalogue, an essential pre-condition for commercial production. This recognition as cépage is not without

issues for some researchers and scientists who strongly disagree: for them, it is a way to make them acceptable, but it is not scientifically right. However, more than 130 varieties are authorized in Europe and mainly planted in the east and the north, in Germany, Switzerland, Austria, Belgium, Scandinavia and the UK. They include Regent, Rondo, Solaris, Muscaris and Souvignier Gris and are now recognized for their production of quality wine.

Genetically modified vines

There have been spectacular advances in genetics. Genome editing, in particular using the CRISPR technique of DNA sequencing, considerably reduces the development time of new varieties, since it is no longer necessary to sow seeds. Geneticists can also modify a gene while preserving the rest of the genome, unlike the classic technique of crossbreeding, which necessarily creates a new genotype. Using transgenetics, a mutation can be specifically introduced into the targeted gene. Such genes may come from the plant kingdom but also from the realms of animals or bacteria. Leaving aside specific technical uncertainties, GMOs present a number of ethical questions that transcend the world of wine.

Creation, cure and prevention

An increasing number of winemakers have come to believe that contemporary disease is the result of genetic weakening

Seeding: the future of vines?

Randall Grahm has been an iconoclast in American viticulture for 40 years, but Popelouchum, his most recent project, is also the most pioneering. In 2017, he planted 10,000 seeds in Santa Barbara that had come from self-fertilization of Sérine, an old clone of Syrah. A thousand germinated, with some expressing more or less desirable recessive genes. This was what was of interest to him, because his objective was not to find a better-performing clone (which would not be possible, since every seed is a new variety) but to diversify the variety's biotype, the best expression of which he believed to come from a variety of new individuals from the same parents but with differences. He is not alone. Elisabetta Foradori has been doing the same with Teroldego in Trentino, Italy, for 20 years.

Their approaches were indirectly corroborated in 2015 by a study carried out by the Italian biologist Stefano Meneghetti, who had observed self-fertilization in seeds from Gaglioppo and Magliocco, two varieties from Calabria, over more than 14 years, demonstrating an improvement in organoleptic qualities and adaptation to the environment from the new varieties. While the future of vines may be dictated by genetics, is it not also embodied within the seed, especially if that seed has come from different parents that offer it the potential to be of superior quality to themselves? Be it in the vineyards of Grahm and Foradori or in a laboratory, breeding with nature's rules should still be considered.

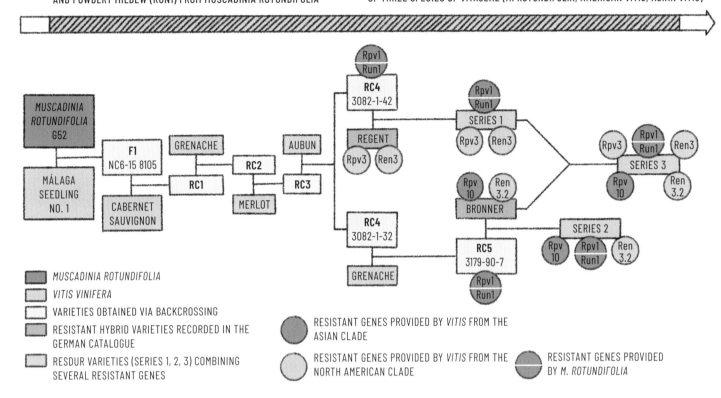

INRA – BOUQUET (1975-95)
INTROGRESSION OF GENES RESISTANT TO DOWNY MILDEW (RPV1)
AND POWDERY MILDEW (RUN1) FROM MUSCADINIA ROTUNDIFOLIA

INRAE – SCHNEIDER (AFTER 2000)
GENE PYRAMIDING OF RESISTANT FACTORS VIA SEQUENCE ALIGNMENT AND MODELLING
OF THREE SPECIES OF VITACEAE (*M. ROTUNDIFOLIA*, AMERICAN *VITIS*, ASIAN *VITIS*)

Legend:
- *MUSCADINIA ROTUNDIFOLIA*
- *VITIS VINIFERA*
- VARIETIES OBTAINED VIA BACKCROSSING
- RESISTANT HYBRID VARIETIES RECORDED IN THE GERMAN CATALOGUE
- RESDUR VARIETIES (SERIES 1, 2, 3) COMBINING SEVERAL RESISTANT GENES
- RESISTANT GENES PROVIDED BY *VITIS* FROM THE ASIAN CLADE
- RESISTANT GENES PROVIDED BY *VITIS* FROM THE NORTH AMERICAN CLADE
- RESISTANT GENES PROVIDED BY *M. ROTUNDIFOLIA*

RESISTANT VARIETIES CREATED BY THE INRA TEAMS SINCE 1975

Bouquet's work resulted in the creation of the first monogenic varieties through introgression of the resistant genes Rpv1 (downy mildew) and Run1 (powdery mildew) sourced from *Muscadinia rotundifolia*. Working from these varieties, Christophe Schneider has used a technique of gene pyramiding of several resistant genes provided by three species of Vitaceae (*M. rotundifolia*, American *Vitis* and Asian *Vitis*) to create ResDur varieties (series 1, 2 and 3).

linked to excessive vegetative propagation (despite the introduction of new parasites that have probably played a greater role) and are suggesting a return to sowing seeds. They also argue that the majority of vineyards planted with hybrids, most of which are rated "tolerant" or "non-resistant" rather than "resistant", make use of phytosanitary products. However, the OSCAR monitoring body (France's national authority overseeing the use of resistant varieties) has recorded an 80 per cent drop in their use on the polygenic varieties resistant to powdery and downy mildew that are planted in the network's vineyards. Others have taken an interest in "historic" hybrids and are replanting them.

Going further, we might join researchers like Elizabeth Van Volkenburgh, a specialist in plant behaviour, in thinking that domestication by selection that is oriented toward anatomy and physiology has upset and caused the decline

of essential functions within plants, including grape vines. A return to wild individuals is an avenue under increasing scrutiny, with a view to introgressing any characteristics that are of interest and restoring to *V. vinifera* adaptive abilities that have fallen by the wayside.

Behind these strategies lie differing visions of the problem and of the world: prevention, or curing with the least harm and cost; the creation of tolerant cloned varieties; and not only rediscovering but also regenerating varieties. But these solutions make sense only when seen in perspective with contemporary cultivation methods like monoculture and industrial viticulture.

Preserving, improving, regenerating, returning to wild vines – these four avenues overlap far more than they run in parallel as long as we think of both vines and viticulture within the totality of the ecosystem of which we too are a part.

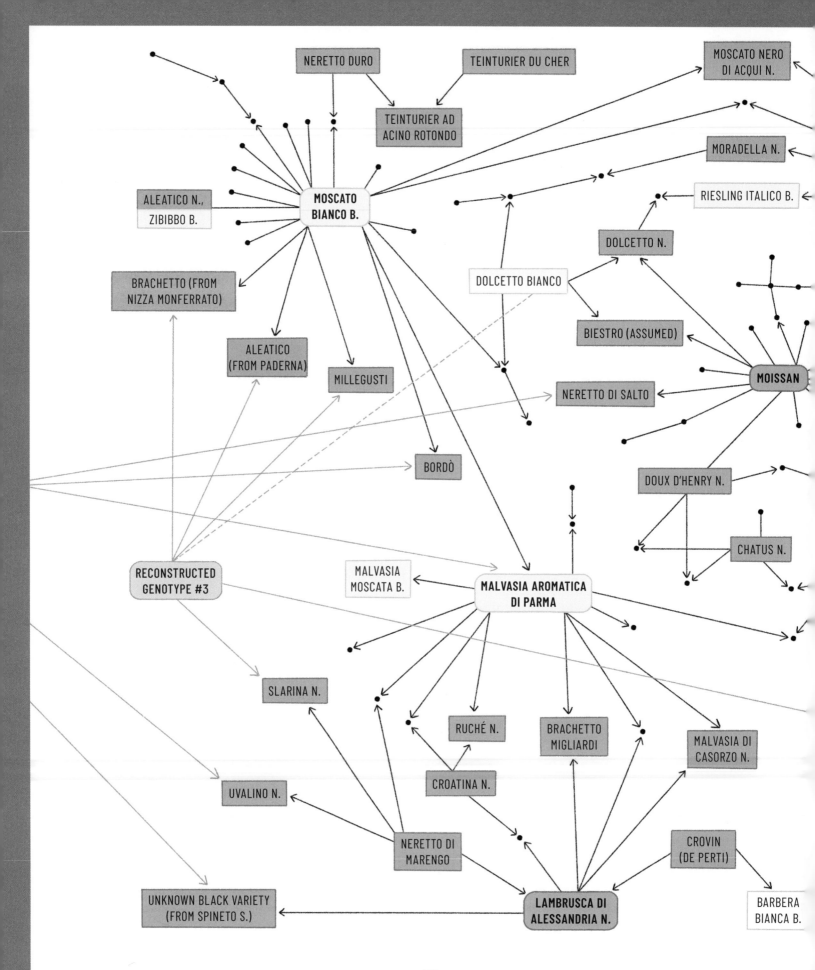

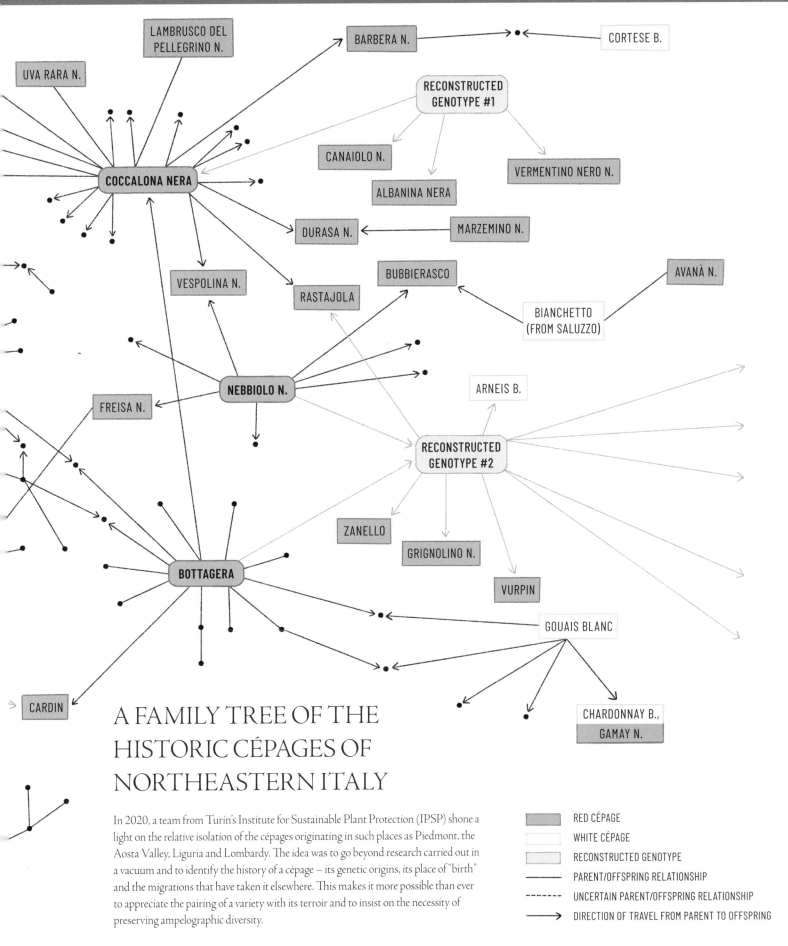

A FAMILY TREE OF THE HISTORIC CÉPAGES OF NORTHEASTERN ITALY

In 2020, a team from Turin's Institute for Sustainable Plant Protection (IPSP) shone a light on the relative isolation of the cépages originating in such places as Piedmont, the Aosta Valley, Liguria and Lombardy. The idea was to go beyond research carried out in a vacuum and to identify the history of a cépage – its genetic origins, its place of "birth" and the migrations that have taken it elsewhere. This makes it more possible than ever to appreciate the pairing of a variety with its terroir and to insist on the necessity of preserving ampelographic diversity.

LAMBRUSCO DEL PELLEGRINO N.

BARBERA N.

CORTESE B.

UVA RARA N.

RECONSTRUCTED GENOTYPE #1

COCCALONA NERA

CANAIOLO N.

VERMENTINO NERO N.

ALBANINA NERA

DURASA N.

MARZEMINO N.

VESPOLINA N.

RASTAJOLA

BUBBIERASCO

AVANÀ N.

BIANCHETTO (FROM SALUZZO)

NEBBIOLO N.

ARNEIS B.

FREISA N.

RECONSTRUCTED GENOTYPE #2

ZANELLO

GRIGNOLINO N.

BOTTAGERA

VURPIN

GOUAIS BLANC

CARDIN

CHARDONNAY B., GAMAY N.

RED CÉPAGE

WHITE CÉPAGE

RECONSTRUCTED GENOTYPE

PARENT/OFFSPRING RELATIONSHIP

UNCERTAIN PARENT/OFFSPRING RELATIONSHIP

DIRECTION OF TRAVEL FROM PARENT TO OFFSPRING

NATURE

The grape vine – from roots to leaves

We know that *V. vinifera* has been domesticated, but what does it actually look like? The aim of plant physiology is to study the morphology, anatomy and metabolism of plants, all of which provide us with a botanical understanding. Because vines are creepers, all the elements involved in vegetative growth – roots, stalk and leaves – are particularly well developed in the grape vine. We rarely take an interest in these structures, however, even though they play an essential role in the plant's functioning and the production of high-quality grapes. How can an understanding of them shine a light on *V. vinifera* in general and on the notion of a terroir wine?

Roots – so essential, but so misunderstood

Roots are the part of a vine that is both hidden and misunderstood. As the direct link between the soil and the specific grape variety, they play an essential role in the expression of a region's viticultural terroir. The technical difficulties involved in studying them in situ, and perhaps even symbolic prejudices against the underworld, might go some way to explain why roots are less frequently studied than other organs of *Vitis*. The use of grafting is another reason; wine production is directly enhanced by the grape variety used as a graft, the part above ground, rather than any part of the vine that is subterranean. However, problems with disease and climate change, not to mention considerations of plant "intelligence" are an invitation to give roots all the attention they deserve.

The growth of roots

The root system of *Vitis* is a complex architectural structure of principal and secondary roots, with the latter also known as lateral roots or rootlets as a whole. These roots are constantly growing longer and larger, with the tip at the end being the node that governs growth via meristematic cells that multiply and grow the roots. This is the underground twin of the top bud (the apex or apical meristem) of the plant, which controls the development of the part of the vine above ground. A root cap that protects it also secretes lubricant substances to allow it to drill into the soil. Beyond this is the actual root elongation zone, followed by a zone covered in root hairs. The latter plays a key role, allowing the absorption of water and minerals and the exudation of molecules that interact with the soil and its micro-organisms. These hairy structures considerably increase the exchange surface area of the root system.

This part of the root is open to its environment. Its bark is protective but permeable to exchanges between the soil and the central root cylinder, which contains two vessels that conduct sap and connect the underground and exposed parts of the plant: the first of these, the xylem, conveys sap that is rich in water and minerals to the branches; the other, the phloem, transports elaborated sap, rich in sugars derived from photosynthesis, to the roots.

The root grows wider and hardens as the vine ages, forming a cambium that separates into a secondary sap-conduction system and phellogen, which produces cork and storage tissue – and herein lies the secret of the resistance of

American *Vitis* species to phylloxera: they generate phellogen far more quickly than *V. vinifera*, isolating the parts attacked by the pest and regenerating them with no necrosis.

Roots influenced by their environment

Clones of rootstock or vines, climate, soil, the rock and viticulture itself all influence the architecture of roots. A vine grown from seed develops a principal plunging taproot and lateral roots; a vine grown from a cutting has more of a tracery of roots that extend laterally. A grape vine, like all living things, operates on the principle of economy and seeks out the most immediately favourable conditions, and the same is true of the root system. With an average length of 2m (6ft 6in), the roots generally find the best conditions for growth at a depth between 15cm (6in) and 50cm (20in) in aerated soil with good access to water and minerals. If necessary, however, they can burrow down tens of metres (30–60ft). In the top 15cm (6in) of soil from the surface, the roots are more exposed to climatic influence (drought, cold) and viticultural intervention (herbicides, intensive working of the soil, irrigation, fertilizer). At greater depths, the roots lack

oxygen (O_2) because the environment is compacted, and they may rot if there is too much water present. They are flattened and hard when the soil is too rocky, and they dry out when it is saline. Disease and parasites will, of course, also have an effect on growth. Each vine is different, with a unique root system, even when grown on the same plot of the same grape variety of the same origin.

The roots carry out essential functions, anchoring the vine in the soil, providing the water and nutrients necessary for its growth and the development of the secondary metabolites that give the grapes their flavour and storing resources. They also play another, long-ignored role, however: they create soil by de-compacting it and modifying it with the substances they exude as they forge associations with micro-organisms such as mycorrhizae, which act upon the vine's metabolism. Roots in symbiosis with living soil are a prerequisite for any consideration of a terroir wine, a wine with a sense of place.

The trunk, from its plasticity…

The trunk is an extension of the root but differs from the latter because of its leaves and buds. Like the root, its principal

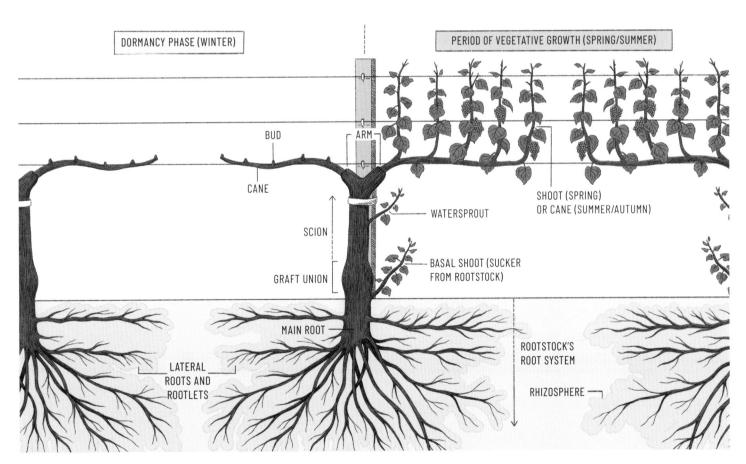

MORPHOLOGY OF A GRAFTED VINE TRUNK

growth is along its length, via the apex and its meristematic cells, while its secondary growth is in width via the production of cambium. The vine survives by forming a protective woody layer that can create scar tissue (from wounds as a result of pruning, for example) and supports the generation of new shoots.

The creeping and climbing nature of grape vines makes them highly plastic, and every variety has its own specific growth habit: Carignan grows upright, Pinot droops, *V. rupestris* is bushy. All seek to clamber up any support to find the sun, which explains why all vines, with very rare exceptions, are pruned to raise *Vitis* from the ground. The training system used depends on a number of different criteria (variety, terroir, logistics, yield), which explains the great diversity in pruning methods; it will always influence the development of the vine trunk, however.

> " Humanity's interest in vines is for their fruit, not for their flowers, their leaves, their wood or their root system

The trunk has three major functions: the lignified section supports the part that is growing, and it acts as a reserve of resources and regulates the nourishment of the vine through the seasons. Last but not least, the sap – rich in sugars, amino acids, vitamins and organic and inorganic acids derived from photosynthesis – circulates through the trunk to the roots. These functions may be affected by poor pruning, which can cut the sap circulation, necrotize the wood and open the door to disease.

... to its architecture

As the trunk grows, it lignifies, developing different kinds of wood – with rough bark on an older growth, or smooth bark on new-season growth. The trunk and the arms consist of the oldest wood; this is the framework of the vine, bearing two-year-old wood, or wood for pruning, which is pruned according to the variety's specific yield. When it is cut short, it is called a spur; when it is left long, a cane. In spring, the buds on the pruning wood produce herbaceous growth known as shoots. As these turn brown over the course of the summer, they are renamed canes. Shoots growing from old wood are called suckers, or in France *gourmands*; these are rapidly removed to preserve the vine's energy.

The shoot and its apex

The shoot consists of a stem with swellings at regular intervals called nodes; the intervals are known as internodes. The node comprises various latent organs: on one side it bears a tendril, a preliminary shoot that attaches the vine to any support; and on the other, leaves that are connected to the shoot via a petiole and the buds. Unlike other fruit-bearing plant species that have specific buds, either for wood or for fruit, *Vitis* buds are all of the same type and produce shoots, leaves or flowers as required, although they differ according to their position on the shoot. The shoot tip, or apical meristem, controls the vegetative growth of the plant by means of hormonal signals. If it is cut back too early, by crop control work such as summer pruning, this influences the distribution of the vine's resources.

The fruit-bearing buds

The other buds are located at the axil of the leaf petioles. These little cones of plant matter contain an embryonic shoot and leaves, as well as a primary bud and secondary buds. The primary bud opens first and produces the largest grape cluster. If it is degraded – for example, by frost – the secondary buds can take over, producing smaller clusters. The fruit-bearing part of the shoot differs with each variety. This variation in fertility, according to the position of the buds and the grape variety, determines the location of the pruning cut on the cane: the basal buds of certain varieties (such as Gamay) are fertile, while those of others (such as Poulsard) are not. In addition to these buds are lateral buds that can produce secondary shoots that are often not fruit-bearing, along with latent buds that remain dormant until the following year and the growth of new shoots. The harvest from a vine is thus always classified as N–1, N and N+1, where N is the current year, N–1 the year before and N+1 the next year.

The vegetal and microbial universe of leaves

While *Vitis* leaves have very different shapes, they all have the same physiological characteristics, developing from buds and dropping when vegetative growth is completed, which can be because of disease or extreme climatic conditions. Once formed, their shape – featuring one or more hairy, serrated lobes – does not change, but their colour develops: when young, they are a pale spring-green; as adults, they turn a deep, dark green; and as summer ends, they become flamboyant, turning anything from yellow to blood red. Each cépage boasts its own colour, subtly influenced by terroir and that year's conditions and viticulture, making leaf coloration a good indication of the plant's environment and condition, whether it is sick, deficient in nutrients, fertilized and so on. The epidermis of the upper side is darker and thicker to protect it from climatic variations and to reduce evapotranspiration, while the underside features microscopic openings known as stomata that permit the exchanges necessary for photosynthesis, respiration and transpiration. Two layers of tissue lie between the upper and lower sides of the leaf. The first

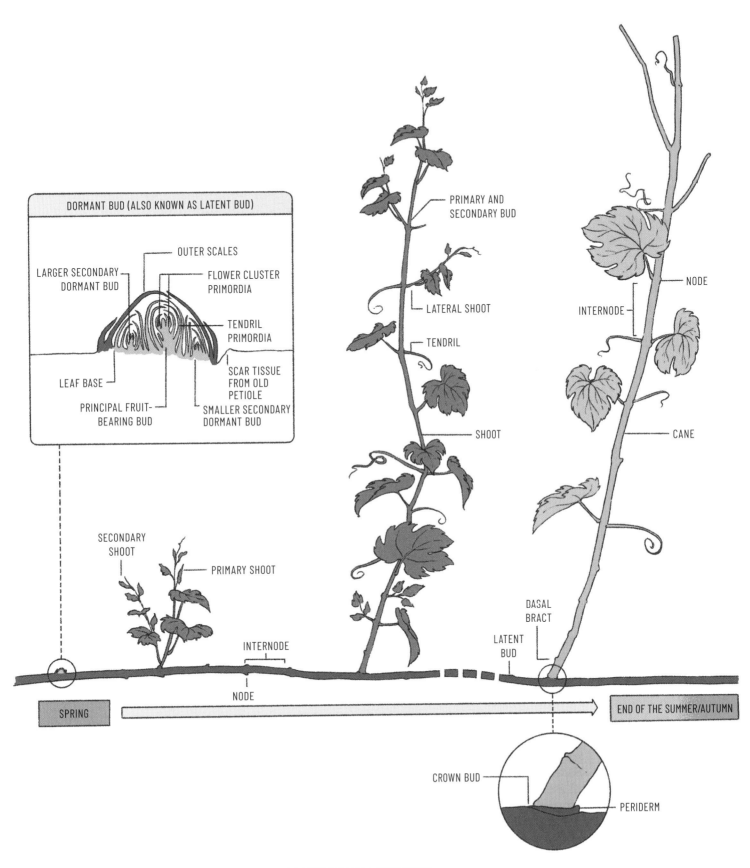

DORMANT BUD (ALSO KNOWN AS LATENT BUD)

OUTER SCALES

LARGER SECONDARY
DORMANT BUD

FLOWER CLUSTER
PRIMORDIA

TENDRIL
PRIMORDIA

LEAF BASE

SCAR TISSUE
FROM OLD
PETIOLE

PRINCIPAL FRUIT-
BEARING BUD

SMALLER SECONDARY
DORMANT BUD

PRIMARY AND
SECONDARY BUD

NODE

INTERNODE

LATERAL SHOOT

TENDRIL

SHOOT

CANE

SECONDARY
SHOOT

PRIMARY SHOOT

DASAL
BRACT

LATENT
BUD

INTERNODE

NODE

SPRING

END OF THE SUMMER/AUTUMN

CROWN BUD

PERIDERM

MORPHOLOGY OF A VINE CANE

The koulouras of Santorini: a jewel in the crown of global viticulture

The Greek island of Santorini, with its magnificent caldera landscape created 3,500 years ago in a gigantic volcanic eruption, boasts a unique viticultural environment. Here, vines are intertwined like Christmas wreaths to form a *kouroula*, or "woven basket", atop the volcanic tuff soil to protect the clusters in the canopy and collect the morning dew, since the island has no springs and receives little rainfall. While a few of the 1,200 ha that have been planted use cordon or Guyot training systems, the EU subsidizes the hundreds of small-scale growers, allowing them to preserve their traditions and heritage: phylloxera cannot survive in these pozzolan (derived from volcanic ash) soils and has been unable to destroy century-old vines and their ungrafted root systems. When the yield becomes too low, the rootstock is cut back and a new trunk is created from a latent site, but the roots remain. This is no doubt one of the reasons why Assyrtiko, the island's leading cépage, achieves such a balance between density of mouthfeel, solar power and saline freshness.

of these is a dense, palisadic layer that is impermeable to water and gases, and contains both the vessels that transport sap and the chlorophyll, while the second contains gaps, leaving space between the photosynthetic cells for both gas exchange and a whole population of microbes whose relationship with their vine host is only just beginning to be understood.

Leaves breathe, transpire and nourish
Vines produce their own substance via chlorophyll photosynthesis which is made possible by chloroplast in the leaves. This endosymbiosis (symbiosis between two organisms, one of which is contained within the other, in this case chlorophyllic cyanobacteria engulfed by a eukaryotic cell) indicates that a leaf is not just vegetal, it also contains a microbial universe: if chloroplast is the descendant of this specific micro-organism, it is in the intercellular space of the leaf that you find most of the bacteria and fungus. Photosynthesis allows the synthesis of substances necessary for the growth and particular development of the vine and its fruit, including glucides, protides and lipids, along with polyphenols such as anthocyanins, aromatic compounds and enzymes. These elements enrich the elaborated sap that is distributed according to the requirements of the various organs - first to vegetative growth structures and then, after veraison (the process in which the grapes change colour), to the grape clusters and storage organs. The intensity of this photosynthesis varies according to the vine (cépage, age of leaves and the structure of the leaf canopy), local viticulture (including plantation density, orientation of the rows and trellising), the environment (sunshine, water supply and temperature) and the respiration and transpiration of the plant. When it "breathes" O_2 and expels Carbon Dioxide (CO_2), sugars are broken down, releasing energy essential for supporting cell life, transpiration and the transportation of sap. It is the young leaves that breathe the most. The vine also loses water, the degree of loss depending on the light, hygrometry and the flow of raw sap from the soil. During its growth period, the more a vine transpires, the more susceptible it is to fungus.

Vitis vinifera, a creeper shaped for its fruit
Humanity's interest in vines is for their fruit, not for their flowers (unlike a rose bush), their leaves (unlike a tea plant), their wood (unlike an ebony tree) or their root system (unlike liquorice). Winemakers are therefore focused on the vine's fruit-bearing organs, while the mission of others working in viticulture is to provide the best possible support for the production of the ripest, healthiest and most numerous clusters. With this aim in mind, we have shaped the morphology and physiology of *Vitis* by constraining its original nature as a climbing plant that more readily puts down roots and forms trunks and leaves rather than fruits. The vine is a vegetative plant par excellence that has been artificially modelled with a view to fruit-bearing, something that we should always keep in mind.

The vine – from flowers to berries

Modern viticulture focuses all its attention on the grape berry, since there would be no wine at all without it – hence the sole aim of the domestication of *Vitis* has been to steer its energy into the formation of its fruit, which, in its wild state, is rare and highly unsuitable for wine production. This is a profound evolution in the physiology of the plant, whose original function can still be seen in the shape of its inflorescences. How do these reproductive organs work? What conditions are needed for a vine to produce fruit suitable for the production of quality wines that reflect their terroir?

Inflorescence

Vine flowers are a rarely seen beauty of nature, with an evanescent scent reminiscent of gardenia; they can be enjoyed only on a few days a year as they appear between the end of May and the end of June, an event that is celebrated in Bordeaux with its famous Fête de la Fleur. The number of inflorescences (the vegetative structures that will form the stalk) that bear flowers often vary from two to five per shoot.

As with leaves, the morphology of the inflorescences varies by cépage: Riesling has a dense inflorescence with few flowers (125 on average), while Tannat features a long stem that is intricately branched with many flowers (more than 440 on average). Ampelographers make use of these to classify clusters by shape (winged, conical and so on) and compaction (loose, average and so on).

These inflorescences are pre-formed in the bud and appear several weeks after bud-burst but do not flower for 8 to 10 weeks. These tiny, ephemeral flowers are visible to those attuned to their dominant green coloration, shot through with white and yellow. With no need for pollinators, they do not have to shimmer obtrusively, and paradoxically, the vine is most striking in the autumn, when its foliage is ablaze with colour.

With *V. vinifera* being almost exclusively hermaphrodite, its flower possesses both male and female organs and is made up of a calyx, a corolla with fused petals that form the cap, an androecium with stamens containing pollen, a gynoecium or ovary comprising a stigma and a pistil, with four ovules, and finally a nectary that secretes nectar. A few rare cépages have sterile male organs and are physiologically female.

The majority of rootstocks are sexual, which complicates their fertilization in a natural setting.

From flower to berry

The key moments in the grape vine's reproductive cycle are flowering, pollination, fertilization and nouaison, or fruit set. Flowers on vines on the same plot of land may bloom for a period of about two weeks, and a shorter flowering period often leads to greater uniformity of cluster quality at harvest.

Good weather is of crucial importance. In order to drop off and trigger flowering, the protective floral cap requires sun, heat and firm pressure from the stamens, otherwise the flowers remain capped and pollination is only partial. Rain, wind and cold during this period may thus also ruin a part of the harvest.

Once it has emerged, the flower may self-pollinate or be pollinated by a near neighbour (allofertilization). The pollen is deposited on the stigma. The pollen produces a growing tube (a pollen grain is a single cell), and this then grows down to fertilize the ovules. One pollen tube fertilizes one ovule.

Once the ovary is fertilized, the four ovules turn into seeds and the rest of the ovary turns into fruit pulp.

If these stages are completed, we are left with a seeded berry with two to four pips. If the stages are only partially completed, several types of berry may result: those with tiny seeds, or apyrene Sultanian berries, typical of the Sultana variety; those with no seeds, or apyrene Corinthians, a notable feature of Black Corinth grapes; or tiny berries with no seeds, in what is known as *millerandage*, hens and chicks or shot berries, arising from the abortion of fertilization. These are often green berries, which are in fact unpollinated ovaries.

So, not all flowers are necessarily fertilized or fruit-bearing. When they fall before pollination, it is known as "shatter" or *coulure*. Some cépages, such as Grenache or Merlot, are more susceptible to this than others, but any variety may be affected during bad weather. Rootstock that is too vigorous may also contribute.

Once fertilization is successful, fruit set - or the phase in which the flower is transformed into fruit - is completed, but it is very rare for the rate of fruit set, or the proportion of flowers pollinated, to exceed 50 per cent. For cépages with a natural dearth of inflorescences, the upshot is few berries, which is one of the reasons why certain varieties are considered to give lower yields.

The berry cycle

Berries develop in three stages. During the first, vegetative growth from fruit set to veraison, they are hard and green, like peas, and behave like chlorophyll organs, with a high content of organic acids such as malic and tartaric. In the second stage, which is maturation - from veraison to full maturity - they grow, soften and change colour, storing up more resources than they consume.

It is at this point that secondary compounds begin to be metabolized, in the case of pigments, or changed, as in the structure of tannins: over the course of 40 days, the berry's sugar content rises from one per cent to 20 per cent; "physiological maturity" is reached during veraison. This does not mean that the clusters are ready for vinification, because their aromas and tannins are not fully ripe, merely

that the pips are ready for germination; the berries are attractive enough to be eaten by birds.

During the final, third stage of post-maturation (with phenolic and aromatic maturity achieved, the clusters can be left to become fully ripe), fruit begins to exhibit the ultimate characteristics of the cépage, and harvesting is usually carried out at this point. While sugar production through photosynthesis has stopped, the chemical composition of the secondary compounds in the berries - sugar and tannins - may still be allowed to evolve if the wine-grower intends to harvest later to make sweet wines. As they lose water, the sugar content of the berries becomes concentrated by sun, cold or the *Botrytis cinerea* fungus that can develop into noble rot in some terroirs, and their secondary compounds continue to change.

The shape and colour of grape berries

Berry shape varies with cépage and is also an important ampelographic marker. Three berry sizes are recognized: small, about 10mm (³⁄₈in) in width, such as Pinot or Sauvignon; medium, 15mm (⁵⁄₈in), such as Gamay or Grenache; and large, greater than 20mm (¹³⁄₁₆in), which is typical of table grapes. The shape, which also varies (flattened, ovoid, spherical and

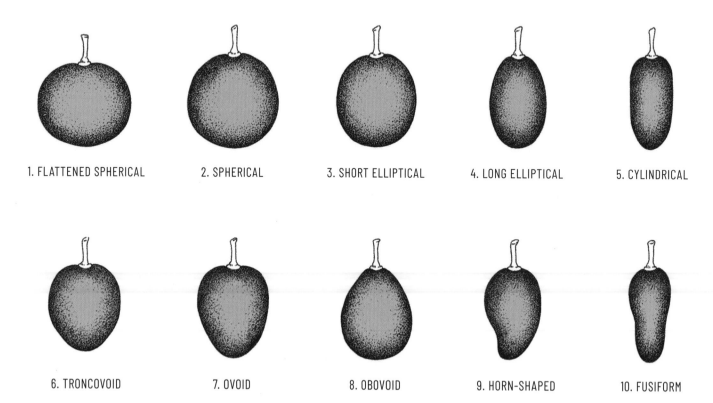

1. FLATTENED SPHERICAL   2. SPHERICAL   3. SHORT ELLIPTICAL   4. LONG ELLIPTICAL   5. CYLINDRICAL

6. TRONCOVOID   7. OVOID   8. OBOVOID   9. HORN-SHAPED   10. FUSIFORM

THE DIFFERENT BERRY SHAPES RECOGNIZED BY THE OIV

so on), has no function in vinification but is important for the fresh grape market.

Berry colour is dictated by MYBA genes, which synthethize anthocyanins, or the red pigments in the skins. Mutations can deactivate one or both genes, however, increasing the possible combinations of active and inactive forms of the chromosomes. Red cépages thus all possess the active form, synthesizing colour for the external and internal skin cells. White cépages have only inactive genes, while *gris*, or pink, cépages generally have internal cells from white skins (inactive gene) and red external skins.

Pinot is an extreme example of evolution: Galet lists Pinot Blanc (Vert or Doré), Rose, Gris, Violet, Noir, Moure and Teinturier. In this last variant, the flesh is red and not translucent as in almost all cépages, owing to the synthesis of specific anthocyanins. These genetic mutations also explain how colour variations can arise on the same cluster or vine.

What the berry brings to wine

A berry is made up of three parts: an external layer, the cuticle or skin of the grape, called the epicarp; a middle layer, the pulp or flesh, called the mesocarp; and an internal layer, the endocarp, a basic enclosure around the seed. This last has little influence on the wine. The skin is a complicated structure, which explains its importance in vinification: the outside of the cuticle is covered with a waxy layer, or bloom, that protects it from water and captures yeasts, bacteria and exogenous aromas that may influence the wine; within the cuticle, the hypodermis, the layer of the skin close to the flesh, contains aromas, aromatic precursors, tannins and even pigment molecules to be extracted.

The mesocarp is the most important layer for the development of the berry; its consistency depends on the breakdown of peptic matter within the cell walls of the pulp. In juicy wine grapes, the skin contains no more flesh cells, only juice. In table grapes, the cells are intact and the berry has a fleshy consistency. Depending on the maturity of the berry, the flesh contains varying levels of water, sugar, organic acids, phenolic compounds and aromatics, minerals and other ingredients essential to wine.

The quantity and quality of the berries depend on multiple factors, including proper functioning of the root system. The majority of fresh berries have a sweet, neutral flavour, with the exception of musky cépages or foxy varieties of *Vitis*, and of Sauvignon Blanc. The enzymes in our saliva can reveal the thiols present in the grape as grapefruit or passion-fruit aromas.

It is vinification that metabolizes the aromatic precursors, and the maceration of the skins that lends colour to the wine. Not all substances are uniformly distributed –

The virtues of uneven fruit set

Known in English almost disparagingly as hens and chicks, grape clusters with uneven fruit set feature healthy, plump grapes interspersed with small, abortively fertilized fruit. These apyrene berries have a thick skin and little juice, and ripen very differently: before maturity, they are very sour but can become extremely sweet very rapidly. It is no secret that they are complicated to vinify, and it would no doubt be better to discard them entirely rather than turn them into wine, but this would risk dismissing their benefits a little too hastily and ignores the history of Burgundy. If the Pinot Noir of 1978 has gone down in the annals, it was mostly due to the uneven fruit set of that year, and the same is true of the vintage of 1995 – legendary Burgundian winemaker Henri Jayer (1922–2006) asserted that this was the reason for its colour and concentration of tannins and aromatics. Uneven fruit set also brings other rewards: better ventilated clusters are less susceptible to disease, a lower yield is of higher quality, with lower levels of potassium leading to more stable acidity. While the parameters are slightly different for Chardonnay, uneven fruit set is deliberately sought for the grape in certain vineyards around the world – for example, in Burgundy for the 1066 clone or Margaret River in Australia, where the Gingin clone, whose berries are genetically prone to uneven fruit set, is considered the most likely to produce wines of high quality.

some are closer to the seeds, others to the skin – so the way the must is pressed influences how these compounds are extracted or not.

The pip

The pip is the seed of the grape, and while it rarely fulfils its propagative potential, its anatomy retains traces of its origins: the embryo is enveloped in the albumen, a nourishing substance rich in lipids that is of interest as an oil but that winemakers avoid extracting because it alters the wine. These are both protected by the seminal tegument, a tough layer that has evolved to resist bad weather and the digestive systems of predators that spread seeds by defecation. This casing contains tannins and nitrogen compounds that are released within the berry at maturity.

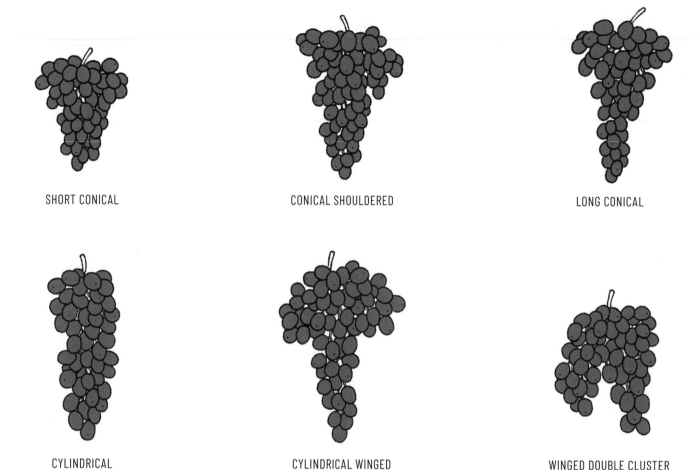

SHORT CONICAL

CONICAL SHOULDERED

LONG CONICAL

CYLINDRICAL

CYLINDRICAL WINGED

WINGED DOUBLE CLUSTER

THE MOST COMMON SHAPES OF GRAPE CLUSTERS

As with the other organs of a grape vine, the shape of the pips varies according to the variety, allowing ampelographers to identify species and assess their age. These seeds are rarely a matter of interest, except when the berries are to be pressed; this is when the winemaker bites on the pips as an indicator of maturity and keeps a wary eye on them during vinification because they are a source of astringency. But this is probably to underestimate their importance – it would seem that no wine of note has ever been produced from seedless grapes, and their complex chemical composition and influence on the development of the plant may be essential for the produciton of wines with truly local characteristics and for laying down.

A cluster of great fragility
Essentially, a grape cluster is a fertilized inflorescence, which can range in size from 5cm (2in) for wild vines to more than 50cm (20in) for White Palestine grapes, and can weigh anything from a few tens of grams in the case of *V. sylvestris* to 100–500g (4–18oz) for the majority of *V. vinifera*, or right up to a kilogram (2.2lb) and more for Muscat of Alexandria and Trebbiano. The berries are linked by a framework of stalks that also provide their nutrition.

The stalk is made up of fibres, tannins and other mineral substances, and it may remain green or lignify upon maturity. Long disregarded and discarded, the stalk is becoming an increasingly important element in vinification.

Pointing skyward when in flower, the grape clusters hang down to earth after fertilization. Once the berries are ripe, they are naturally hidden by the leaves, protecting clusters that are highly susceptible to fungus, insects and bad weather. All vine cultivation is geared toward the production of this fragile crop, unique among the usually hard-skinned fruits of autumn.

Is a grafted vine an "artificial plant"?

There are few vines nowadays that are not grafted. Grafts are ubiquitous, and the practice of grafting would seem to be a technique that has been perfectly mastered and is beyond discussion. The reality is more complex, however. Until the Middle Ages, grafting was viewed as an almost mystical agricultural art capable of miracles, and then it became a major factor in the fight against phylloxera. While it does not produce speciated variation – meaning, for example, a Chardonnay grafted onto a *V. labrusca* does not take on its foxy characteristics, and inversely, *V. riparia's* resistance to certain diseases is unfortunately not transmitted to the scion – it nonetheless has consequences for the physiology of the plant and its interactions with the environment. How does a grafted vine – a combination of two different *Vitis* species that helped to save the world's vineyards – actually work, and why is it ultimately considered to be a chimera or artificial plant?

The ancient practice of vegetal grafting

Wine-growers didn't wait until the phylloxera crisis to graft vines. Vegetal grafting has been practised since antiquity, and a number of the grafts we believe to be modern had in fact been mastered well before the Renaissance; in the 5th century BCE, Chinese writer Pao Tscheou Kon described cleft- and crown-grafting for fruit trees. A century later, the Greeks Aristotle and Theophrastus noted that the success of a graft depends on the botanical proximity of the species grafted. The technique was thus used to preserve the characteristics of varieties, to produce crops more rapidly and adapt them to less suitable soils using a rootstock. The Romans made frequent use of the technique, discovering that the quality of the rootstock was just as critical as that of the scion.

At least five grafting techniques dating back to the 2nd century BCE are still in use today: shield-budding, and cleft-, crown-, approach-, and whip-and-tongue grafting. Although writing in the 1st century CE, in some very modern-sounding texts, Columella and Pliny the Elder left descriptions of various practices from the choice of buds to analysis of the soil and climate as crucial parameters for a good outcome.

Four centuries later, Palladius in *Opus Agriculturae* or *De Re Rustica*, described the ancestor of the bench whip-graft with rooted cuttings, a technique often believed to have been invented in the 19th century.

The other great overlooked experts in grafting were the Arab-Andalusian agronomists of the 11th century. Ibn al-'Awwam wrote *Kitab Al-Filaha* (English ed: *Book of Agriculture*, due 2025), the medieval bible on the subject, in which he collated the knowledge acquired along the Mediterranean coast: it was already known that a perfect graft is only possible if the rootstock and scion are of the same species; that grafting is more successful using healthy and vigorous plants rather than old, tired ones; that the rootstock has multiple influences on the physiology of the scion and so on. With only few exceptions, all the modern techniques of grafting are described by scholars from Al-Andalus (the Iberian territories under Moorish rule from 711 until 1492), but we had to wait until the crises of the 19th century before such prolific research in this field of would be undertaken again.

The grafting scale of affinity

Agronomists of the 12th century were already familiar with the mechanism of grafting, understanding that bringing into contact a sufficiently large surface area of the rootstock's active conductive tissue and the scion welds together their sap ducts, enabling a living relationship between the two individual plants and blending some of their qualities. This takes place at the graft union, the "welding point", a contact zone around which a protective callus forms, encouraging healing and allowing for the exchange of substances. It is here that the union occurs between the xylem vessels carrying the raw sap, rich in water and minerals, and the phloem vessels carrying sap rich in sugar, amino acids and organic compounds from photosynthesis. Not all combinations are compatible, however; tissue may heal poorly or not at all. Perfect harmony is in fact extremely rare, which is why agronomists refer to a scale of affinity between two individual plants. Grafting between different genera has thus proved almost impossible, as demonstrated by the difficulty of grafting *Vitis* and *Muscadinia*. It is more successful with iterations of *Vitis*, but varies according to the species and variety. As professor of viticulture Alain Carbonneau has pointed out, Folle Blanche, a cépage once very widespread in the west of France and recognized as yielding excellent eaux de vie, particularly in Cognac, was progressively abandoned; once grafted it grew larger and more fragile grapes as a result of overfeeding, and rot developed more easily.

> The physiological interactions between the rootstock and scion are unique to a particular pairing and are never entirely predictable

The grafted vine – a new, chimerical vine produced from two varieties

Grafting imposes a shared life on two distinct parts of a vine: the root system of the rootstock and the foliage of the scion, two organs of vegetative growth with their own physiology. It also establishes new dynamics according to the characteristics of the plant chosen for the grafting.

As Jean Branas, one of the 20th century's great professors of viticulture, has pointed out, *V. riparia* and *V. berlandieri*, two species used as rootstocks, do not have the same relationship between the mass of their foliage and their roots; the former has a preponderance of leaves, the latter of roots, and the functioning of the leaf and root systems will be modified according to the nature of the scion selected, which may or may not have its own characteristics. There may be an abundance of leaves and few roots, or vice versa. The foliage and root systems function differently according to the type of graft chosen.

Once a graft has been carried out, the absorption of water and minerals, on the one hand, and photosynthetic activity and the production of elaborated sap, on the other, have to strike a new balance. Added to this is the influence of the graft union, which acts as an obstruction that is both mechanical (the tissues are more or less atrophied, slowing the flow of sap) and physiological (the cell membranes of the two grafted sections have neither the same permeability nor the same selective properties as the compounds circulating in the sap). This is why Branas considers a grafted vine to be an organism formed of populations of cells that are genetically distinct – in other words, a chimera. There are, therefore, always physiological interactions of varying degrees of importance between the rootstock and scion that are unique to that combination and never entirely predictable. This extraordinary interdependence has been noticed, condemned or praised by wine-growers ever since the first grafted vines were planted as a result of the phylloxera crisis.

The discovery of phylloxera

Phylloxera is an insect of North American origin found on vines and oak and pear trees. Its highly complex life cycle delayed its discovery, which occurred five years after the first symptoms appeared in France in 1863. Gaston Bazille, Félix Sahut and Jules-Émile Planchon were the first to notice it on the roots of a vine near Arles. Planchon, a professor of botany, named it *Rhizaphis vastatrix*. Through his brother-in-law, naturalist Jules Lichtenstein, he rapidly realized the link with observations made by American entomologist Charles Riley, whose works on American vines Lichtenstein had translated. In 1871, scientists concluded that phylloxera induced two forms of disease: a gall form on foliage and another on the roots. However, phylloxera's life cycle is in fact more complex, which explains why it has amassed 38 different scientific names, including *Pemphigus vitifolii* (the first name given by American entomologist Asa Fitch in 1855), *Phylloxera vastatrix* (by entomologist Victor Signet) and *Daktulosphaira vitifoliae*, its official name since 1974. Nowadays, the word phylloxera metonymically describes both the disease and the aphid.

Vitis vinifera's killer parasite…

Phylloxera's life cycle consists of 18 stages. It has two forms of reproduction, sexual and parthenogenetic – the female insect can produce an egg without being fertilized. This explains how it can take four different forms: two wingless parthenogenetic females (aptera), almost invisible to the naked eye, that feed and live either on the leaves or the roots, and two airborne sexually reproduced insects, either winged females about 2–3mm (1/16–3/32in) long, or wingless males that live for just a few days to reproduce. Its biological cycle is extremely complicated and alternates parthenogenetic and sexual generations. Males and females mate in summer, and the female lays an egg under the bark of the rootstock in winter. This hatches in spring, producing a wingless female that feeds on young leaves, thereby inducing a gall to form in which the insect can deposit up to 600 eggs via parthenogenesis. Between five and seven generations follow during the summer, migrating to the leaves in American vines and the roots in *V. vinifera*. Here they metamorphose three times in 20 days before becoming adults and, again by parthenogenesis, laying a hundred or so eggs, all of which are female. There are eight or nine generations annually.

Beneath the soil, these thousands of aphids suck the sap, boring into either the lateral roots that produce root nodes or the large roots that form tubers. The latter is fatal for *V. vinifera*; through necrosis and infection, parasites penetrate the root system, which rots and eventually dies away. In summer, the root-based forms turn into winged females that fly away to lay male and female eggs on the leaves. These rapidly hatch, mate and fertilize an egg laid in winter that starts the whole cycle over again.

… that can thrive almost anywhere
Phylloxera spreads very easily under favourable conditions. The insect can reproduce indefinitely by parthenogenesis, its eggs lying dormant in the bark for several months and the wingless females contaminating the vines whose root system or leaves are touching. Meanwhile, the winged females can fly hundreds of kilometres to infest isolated areas. The phylloxera aphids require voids in the soil in order to move about and reach grape-vine root systems, which is why sandy, less compact or saturated soils are less favourable. The deeper the root system, the longer the vine can survive. Most American vines are only susceptible to the gall-inducing form of the aphid - unlike *V. vinifera*, which dies from the root-based instance.

Some areas were spared
Certain parts of the winemaking world have so far escaped the phylloxera invasion, although the net is tightening. Their isolation has allowed them to preserve a legacy of ungrafted vines, some of which are centuries old. These regions include the state of South Australia, where the Barossa Valley and the world's oldest Syrah vines are to be found; large parts of Chile; and extensive wine regions in Argentina and Washington State. The islands of Europe - like Cyprus, the Cyclades and the Canaries - are still relatively protected, as are certain individual regions, such as parts of Germany's Mosel Valley. A few rare vineyards have remained unscathed and are worthy of study to find out why their ungrafted vines have survived. Research is yet to find an alternative chemical or biological solution to hybridization and grafting, and it does not seem to be a scientific priority.

The first grafts in the fight against phylloxera…
When phylloxera struck in 1863, grafting was known in France but took place in only 0.5 per cent of cultivated areas, being used to rejuvenate ageing vines or to combat shatter. It was viewed as expensive and of little appeal, but all this was to change in the struggle against an aphid with no natural predators. The first solutions put forward to address the problem proved impossible to implement on a large scale and too expensive in terms of labour and capital. These included the temporary flooding of vineyards, which required access to vast quantities of water; replanting in sandy soils, which

was unthinkable; or even the injection of carbon disulphide or potassium sulpho-carbonate at the foot of each vine using spikes, which was dangerous and difficult.

While these solutions made it possible to extend the lifespan of several thousands of hectares, they were supplanted by grafting. This was suggested as a solution in 1869 by Léopold Laliman (a Bordeaux landowner and wine-maker who discovered the gall form of the pest in France) and Victor Pulliat. Grafting was to spread through wine-growing areas in tandem with direct hybridization.

… and the first questions raised about grafting and the quality of the wines obtained
Disagreement raged for decades between "Americanists" led by the teaching staff of Montpellier's agricultural college, who championed grafting, and "sulphurists", who supported preserving ungrafted vines using chemical warfare, with the latter including the producers of

> " At issue was the challenge of preserving the character of French vines, once grafted

a number of Bordeaux and Burgundy *crus*. At issue was the challenge of preserving the character of French vines, once grafted; the Americanists argued in favour, their opponents against. Their arguments were analysed by Lucien Daniel (1856-1940), a botanist specializing in grafting, in *La Question phylloxérique, le greffage et la crise viticole*, a report commissioned in 1908 by the French state, which was committed to finding a definitive solution to save the production of high-quality wine and the revenue it generated.

Lucien Daniel's call for careful observation
Daniel asserted that the Americanists' hypothesis that the characteristics of the plants are entirely preserved was mistaken. He thought that American vines had a root system that preferred damper and richer soils and was thus more lateral and less plunging than that of *V. vinifera*, drawing more nourishment from the surface of the soil. The scion would thus receive more water and nitrogen than its physiology might ideally allow, despite the graft union that acted as a throttle. In identical conditions, grafted vines grow more vigorously than ungrafted ones, which might seem an advantage in terms of yield but creates a breeding ground for parasites and fungus such as powdery mildew, a new American disease that exploded in Europe a few years after phylloxera; it spreads more virulently on vigorous plants.

According to Daniel, grafting introduced two major variant factors: a functional imbalance in capacity for absorption and consumption of nutrient elements between the components of the graft; and a graft union that throttled, filtered and retained organic compounds such as starch or nitrogen. These factors were compounded by other problems in re-establishing the vines: the complicated adaptation of the rootstock to European soils and climates that were different from those of North America; variations in resistance to disease; changes brought about by pruning systems; higher yields; and more besides. Grapes from grafted vines could no longer produce the same quality of wine, and Daniel saw proof of this in the fact that the law of 1905 on wine counterfeiting and fraud had the government authorizing the use of additives, like sugars and tartaric acid, to mitigate the weakness of musts. These additives had previously been banned by the Griffe law of 1889, the original legislation on the composition of wine in France. Since he used grafting himself, he was well aware of the technique's advantages and recommended further experimentation and evaluation of the results before making it common practice.

Daniel's conclusions were fiercely rejected by the scientific majority of the time, which was the Montpellier school, and countered by the political desire to deal with and exit the crisis as quickly as possible. His argument also overlooks the fact that a younger vineyard, cultivated using more efficient techniques, is inherently more vigorous and that certain ungrafted cépages of *V. vinifera* develop a more robust root system than many rootstocks. Grafting, which was favoured by the majority, carried the day.

What does contemporary research have to say?
Modern theoreticians and practitioners are in agreement that the vine's rootstock modifies the scion's ability to adapt to the soil, as well as its development. It can be grown on almost all kinds of soil, increasing yields but potentially also opening the door to susceptibility to certain diseases. Pierre Galet has emphasized that grafting affects the levels of starch, water and other organic compounds, and therefore the vigour

Grafted and ungrafted Chenin

A plot of land is divided in two: the larger part is full of strong, slender vines about 10cm (4in) in diameter, and the other with fine, almost delicate plants. The vines are nonetheless the same age and of the same wood, the only difference being that one group has been planted with no graft and the others have been grafted onto Riparia Gloire de Montpellier rootstock.

In 1998, François Chidaine decided to use his plot of land at Les Bournais in Montlouis-sur-Loire, France, to study the difference between grafted and ungrafted Chenin vines. After 22 years, the results were unequivocal: the ungrafted vines exhibit less vigorous vegetative growth than the grafted plants, are less susceptible to disease and require less work as they grow. They also produce fewer clusters with smaller berries. While their vegetative cycle is close to that of grafted plants, phenolic maturity is reached at lower sugar levels and consequently has a potentially lower alcohol content. By the same token, they are more sensitive to climatic variation and the cultivational profile of the soil. The rootstock tends to buffer the influence of a particular vintage and smooth out soil fertility even as it produces greater quantities, permitting higher yields. These can be at least twice the volume of ungrafted vines, which produce only 10–15 hl/ha under the same conditions.

Chidaine understood the need for large areas of France to be given over to the cultivation of vines in order to meet the demand for wine at the time. While the musts tended to ferment in the same manner in the cellar, the results were different: the mouthfeel more opulent and aromatic for the grafted vines, more linear and subtle for the ungrafted vines, with 0.5 to 1% less alcohol. While modern vineyards can obviously not be entirely planted with ungrafted vines, the temptation – and probably the need – to explore this avenue again is entirely understandable, even if isolated results clearly cannot be extrapolated universally. This has become the mission of L'Association des Francs de Pied, a conglomeration of European winemakers working with ungrafted vines; it was founded in the spring of 2021, and its ranks include Germany's Egon Müller, Alexandre Chartogne from Champagne and Loïc Paquet from Bordeaux.

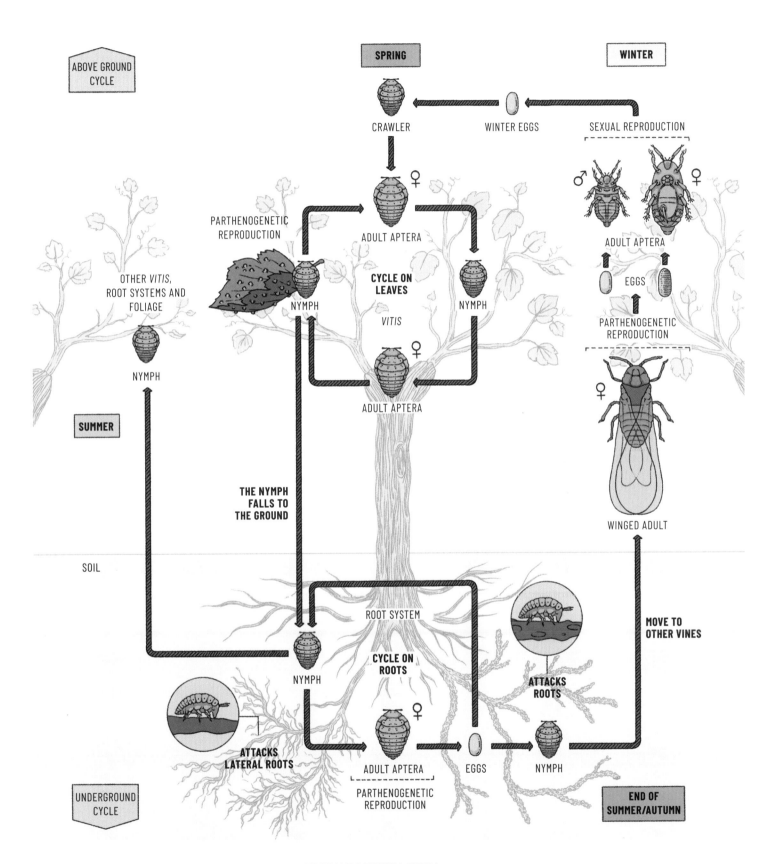

THE LIFE CYCLE OF PHYLLOXERA

of particular parts of the plant. The work of contemporary rootstock specialists such as Nathalie Ollat and Jean-Pascal Tandonnet has confirmed the rootstock's influence on the vegetative vigour of the scion. In a controlled environment, with an identical scion, the volume of wood, foliage and fruit produced may vary by a factor of ten, depending on the rootstock, so influencing the sweetness of the grapes.

The rootstock also plays a role in absorbing water via the architecture of its root system, and it can control the demand for water from the aerial section by influencing its respiration. The same is true for other minerals such as iron, which is absorbed and distributed to a greater or lesser extent depending on the combination of the two components

Australia – guardian of the genetic history of world viticulture

Considered a Johnny-come-lately in the history of global viti-culture, or a country of the New World with sometimes rather disparaging connotations, Australia nonetheless boasts an exceptional ampelographic heritage that is largely lost in Europe; certain Australian regions have indeed escaped phylloxera, and these ungrafted vines, dating back to the 19th century, have since been preserved with great care by wine-growers and federal bodies. The Syrahs of Hill of Grace, Australia's most renowned vines, are said to have been planted in 1868, and the Barossa Valley has created classifications of its Mourvèdre, Grenache and Syrah vines based on their seniority: "old vines" are those over 35 years of age, "survivors" are 60, "centenarians" are 100 and "ancestors" are 125 years old. To protect them, visitors to the valley are asked not to walk among the vines in order not to risk accidental contamination of the soil; the phylloxera aphid can even find its way onto the soles of shoes. Footwear is therefore often disinfected when entering a vineyard after having visited areas where the aphid is present. These old vines, the pride of Australia, are also an invaluable resource for world viticulture and research; the University of Adelaide is at the cutting edge of work on the physiology of these plants and the reasons why they lend such unique balance to wines

of the graft. However, researchers have also shown that the genotype of the scion plays a major role in generating biomass and allocating resources to different parts of the plant, in particular the root system.

A complex and reciprocal influence that is still poorly understood

The scion exerts control over the rootstock and plays a role that is crucial, albeit less well known or understood. The rootstock and scion enjoy a mutual phenotypical influence that is reinforced to a greater or lesser degree by their ecosystem and genotype. Many physiological mechanisms are yet to be fully explained, despite extensive research, with numerous incompatibilities in grafting *Vitis* still unexplained and occasionally producing effects contrary to those expected.

The same is true of our understanding of the coordina-tion (emission, transportation and reception) of chemical and physical signals between different parts of the plant. One of the major difficulties lies in the fact that the beha-viour of the grafted vine is not just the physical sum of the properties of the two individuals but an unpredictable organic combination of these. The potential plasticity of a characteristic varies from one individual to the next in its unique environment, precluding any generalization save that some kind of influence will be observed.

The grafted vine – an "artificial plant"

A grafted plant is ultimately anything but identical to an ungrafted plant, and is, to quote Ollat, an "artificial plant". It is certainly a new entity, with unique behaviour. While the actual physiological mechanisms are still mysterious, we know what is involved physiologically: the dynamics of its ability to absorb, transport, redistribute and store nutrients, and therefore the development, vigour, yield and health of both the root system and the aerial section. The rootstock mitigates environmental conditions, including insects, water and soil pH, and influences the vegetative cycle of the scion, its yield and the quality of the grapes – and so of the wine.

The issue of grafting is of fundamental importance in a viticultural world where it is seen as the best biocontrol solution to combat phylloxera, and as a viable promise of rapid adaptation to climate change, through the develop-ment of drought-resistant rootstocks. It is nonetheless a complex solution that has left an indelible mark on the world's vineyards even as its superior results have discouraged the exploration of other options.

Rootstocks and new viticultural landscapes

In the entire history of agriculture, no plant has benefited in such a short space of time from experimentation on such a broad scale in the search for better rootstocks and affinities between roots and scions than *V. vinifera*, nor enjoyed such rapid and widespread application with so little perspective. Which species were selected on the basis of soils and climates, or for their compatibility and productivity? While we like to talk about root systems and terroir, few pay attention to rootstocks other than winemakers or nursery workers – the people who play a key role in understanding the prevailing viticultural landscape.

The first selection criterion

The first criterion for any rootstock in the fight against phylloxera was obviously resistance to the pest. Pure American *Vitis* were initially chosen, but a major problem rapidly became apparent: French and North American soils were different. Many of France's wine-growing areas are planted in sites with basic pH, containing active limestone, while the younger American soils are principally acidic. The upshot was that American rootstocks had problems absorbing iron, and ferric chlorosis, previously a negligible problem, spread to the scions of grafted vines in Champagne, Burgundy and Cognac; the leaves turned yellow and died, compromising photosynthesis. Consequently rootstocks that were less susceptible to chlorosis had to be found, or American *Vitis* had to be hybridized with other, less sensitive plants or with *V. vinifera*, while taking into account its vulnerability to phylloxera.

The first hybridization of this kind (Aramon [*V. vinifera*] x *V. rupestris*) – AxR1 – was created by Victor Ganzin (1838–1922) in 1879 and is remembered for two reasons: first, as the initial, promising hybridization, although it was rapidly abandoned because it was short-lived and highly vulnerable to the pest; and second, as the rootstock used between the 1960s and 1980s to replant the Napa Valley. It suffered an attack almost immediately, necessitating complete replanting on different, resistant rootstocks less than 15 years later.

Modern rootstocks are century-old creations

The majority of the rootstocks in use today were created over a period of around 30 years between 1869 and 1902. Pure *V. riparia* and *V. rupestris* were the first to be tried, but as the former prefers rich, damp soils and both are sensitive to active limestone, neither could be widely used. They were then hybridized with *V. vinifera*, with limited success. In 1888, agronomist Pierre Viala, reporting from the US, suggested *V. berlandieri*, a species that grows on the Jurassic limestones of Texas and had in fact already been tested in France by agronomists in Montpellier. *Vitis berlandieri* had a major problem, however: it lent itself very poorly to grafting and could not be used directly as a rootstock because it had to be crossed. In 1882, botanists Alexis Millardet (1838–1902) and Charles de Grasset (1830–99) succeeded in hybridizing *V. berlandieri* with Chasselas to create the renowned 41 B; this new rootstock proved the saviour of Cognac and the Champagne region – 80 per cent of these regions were still planted with it 135 years later. *Vitis berlandieri* produced other offspring: 161-49 and SO4, the result of crossing with *V. riparia*, and Fercal from a cross with *V. vinifera*. Hundreds of rootstock hybrids were created in this way – but equally there were the same number of failures.

> Aside from the botanical question, the use of rootstocks has led wine-growers to make changes to both their practices and their environments

Selection criteria and contemporary creations

In 2021, there were no more than 31 rootstocks authorized in France, of which 12 accounted for 84.5 per cent of all production. Production is in fact dominated by six of these: SO4, 110 R, 3309 C, 140 Ruggeri, Gravesac and Fercal. Only the latter two, along with Nemadex Alain Bouquet, were developed after 1922.

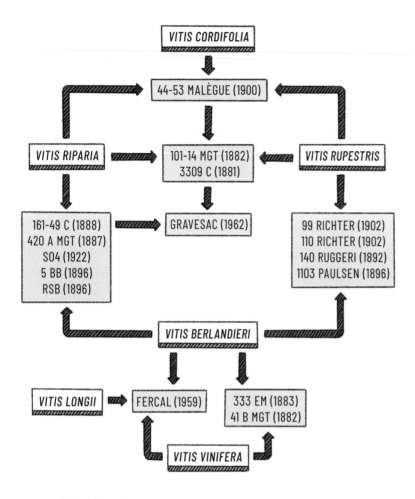

```
                    ┌─────────────────┐
                    │ VITIS CORDIFOLIA │
                    └─────────────────┘
                             │
                             ▼
              ┌──────────────────────────┐
     ┌───────►│   44-53 MALÈGUE (1900)    │◄───────┐
     │        └──────────────────────────┘        │
     │                      │                      │
┌────────────┐             ▼             ┌────────────────┐
│VITIS RIPARIA│───►┌──────────────────┐  │ VITIS RUPESTRIS │
└────────────┘    │ 101-14 MGT (1882) │◄─└────────────────┘
     │            │  3309 C (1881)    │          │
     │            └──────────────────┘           │
     ▼                    │                       ▼
┌──────────────┐         ▼           ┌─────────────────────┐
│161-49 C (1888)│  ┌──────────────┐  │  99 RICHTER (1902)   │
│420 A MGT (1887)│─►│GRAVESAC (1962)│ │ 110 RICHTER (1902)   │
│S04 (1922)     │  └──────────────┘  │ 140 RUGGERI (1892)   │
│5 BB (1896)    │                    │ 1103 PAULSEN (1896)  │
│RSB (1896)     │                    └─────────────────────┘
└──────────────┘                              ▲
       ▲         ┌──────────────────┐         │
       └─────────│ VITIS BERLANDIERI │─────────┘
                 └──────────────────┘
                     │         │
                     ▼         ▼
┌────────────┐ ┌───────────┐ ┌──────────────┐
│VITIS LONGII│►│FERCAL (1959)│ │ 333 EM (1883) │
└────────────┘ └───────────┘ │ 41 B MGT (1882)│
                    │         └──────────────┘
                    └────┐    ┌────┘
                      ┌──────────────┐
                      │ VITIS VINIFERA │
                      └──────────────┘
```

THE MAIN ROOTSTOCKS
The majority of modern rootstocks are century-old creations.

This state of affairs is not peculiar to France – almost all the vineyards in the US are planted with four rootstocks: 101-14, 110 R, Freedom and 1103 P. The work of Andrew Walker, professor of genetics at UC Davis, has highlighted this lack of diversity. Not only have 99 per cent of rootstocks been obtained from a combination of *V. rupestris*, *V. riparia* and *V. berlandieri*, but they are all thought to derive from single and unique clones: Rupestris St George, Riparia Gloire and Berlandieri Rességuier S2 respectively.

This poorly diversified genetic pool represents a real problem: all the individual elements are potentially vulnerable to the same parasites, so diversification is a matter of urgency. Numerous laboratories have taken up the challenge, studying previously unexplored wild cultivars, decoding the genetics of resistant genes, integrating strains by crossing, and more besides. They are working on these vines in response to current problems of nematodes, drought and salinity, but one of the ongoing major obstacles is that rootstocks, buried away and influenced by factors that may be both environmental (soils, climate and so on) and physiological (their relationship with the scion), are bound to function in a way that is immensely difficult to grasp.

The consequences for wine-growing landscapes

Aside from the botanical question, the use of rootstocks has led wine-growers to make changes to both their practices and their environments. Our understanding of the geology of wine-growing areas, once highly empirical, has deepened and become central to the notion of wines of quality. The roots of a rootstock may compensate for the weaknesses of a cépage: Pinot Noir, with its otherwise shallow root system, can take better root when grafted.

Grafting also made it possible to plant on a wider variety of soils, which had the immediate consequence of bringing vineyards down from the hills to colonize the plains. While a bonus for mechanization, this was an evolution that also meant many historic, steep vineyards disappeared.

Grafting disrupted yields too: the productivity of certain plants was favoured over varietal diversity, and these were stimulated by vigorous rootstocks to produce a surplus of wood and grape clusters. It became necessary to control yields – and planting density, pruning and treatments all had to be reconsidered. Some maintain that grafting leads to a levelling-out of the specific peculiarities of wine-growing localities. Rootstocks and grafting were both the saviours and the great transformers of French and European vineyards.

Grafting – a contemporary issue

Almost every French and European vineyard was re-established with grafting as a result of the phylloxera crisis. According to experts and the state, it was the only solution to produce wines of quality, but this "miracle cure" may in fact have been, to quote an expression coined by grafting exponent Marc Birebent, the "original sin of contemporary viticulture". The choice of rootstock and grafting technique is decisive for the sustainability of the plant, the quality of the wine it produces and the profitability of the estate. If grafting is inevitable, what is the best way to graft to ensure the remedy is not vulnerable to wood disease, the great post-phylloxera scourge?

Grafting issues

Planting is a major financial and logistical investment for winemakers. Even if the estate is in a hurry to begin production, at least two or three years – and sometimes much more – are required from preparation of the soil to the selection of varieties for planting and for the whole enterprise to succeed. Downtime of the land, an absence of harvesting and the price of purchasing plants and grafts, and planting, are significant investments that can be lost if the plantation is poorly executed – either immediately, if the young vines fail to take, or a few years later, if the vines die. Success depends on a series of agronomic and economic decisions taken by a whole chain of those involved: researchers, legislators, nursery workers, wine-growers. A good graft depends on the quality of the plants, the accuracy of the grafting cut made (its length, shape and angle) and taking into account the direction of the plant fibres to allow for good healing with minimal necrosis. The location where the graft is to be made determines the technique used. These two parameters are crucial to both the success rate and the potential aging of the vines.

Grafting, over-grafting, regrafting

The type of grafting varies according to the age of the vine. Grafting describes the initial union of the trunk (the rootstock) and the scion when the aim is to propagate a new plant. Over-grafting, an age-old practice used to change variety without having to uproot and replant the vine, consists of grafting a new individual plant onto the part of the vine that is above ground. Regrafting involves creating a new graft beneath the graft union – starting again on the rootstock rather than the scion – and is used to combat the withering of vines or to mitigate climatic or mechanical accidents. It is used if the scion has weakened; the rootstock has a strong chance of being vigorous enough to be regrafted. The latter two techniques are principally used where the climate will be favourable during the procedure, so in the Mediterranean basin, California and so on.

Field grafting (grafting in the vineyard) or bench grafting

Grafting is carried out either as a field graft or a bench graft. The first method consists of grafting onto a rootstock that has already been rooted in the soil for several years, and its advantages include better control of the plants, more certain recovery, immediate adaptation to the environment, and speedier fruiting. It is more demanding as far as soil preparation and monitoring are concerned, however, and is difficult to mechanize, requiring time and a trained labour force. It is also challenging to carry out in cool and damp areas. Field grafting was the most widespread technique at the end of the 19th century and has aroused renewed interest among winemakers who have been disappointed by bench grafts.

Bench grafting, in which the trunk and scion are cut and located mechanically to produce rooted grafts that can be planted directly, was invented in 1878 to mitigate recovery problems in northern regions and as a response to phenomenal demand. The advantages are obvious: industrialized production, less dependence on the climate and use of non-specialist labour. The procedure was improved in 1975 with the invention of omega grafting by the German nursery firm Wagner, making it possible to process up to 13,000 plants per day. This cheaper and more efficient technique supplanted bench whip grafting and became widespread at the end of the 1980s.

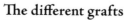

Pruning and curettage to combat esca

Despite its great age, there is no miracle cure for the wood disease esca. The chemical solutions that have been used against it include sodium arsenite, which was banned in 2001 because of its toxicity. Others are being tried, including injections of fungicides, hydrogen peroxide and the use of biological agents or natural molecules, but none has yet proved to be efficient and non-toxic.

Pruning and curettage are also preferred methods for reducing the risks of contamination. A graft that produces no necrosis and pruning that respects sap flow are essential, in addition to the elimination of dead, contaminated wood. At the turn of the 20th century, a certain Mr Poussard working in the wine industry in Charente, France, developed a pruning technique that respected sap flow and protected plant tissue. It has recently been rediscovered and renamed Guyot-Poussard.

As with grafting and over-grafting, the date of pruning, cutting precision and the monitoring of the pruning wounds play crucial roles. Curettage is the most effective approach when a vineyard is infected with esca, and the technique was already being used by Columella in the 1st century CE; contaminated areas are removed using saws or blades, leaving only healthy wood. It is a painstaking, expensive and unpredictable strategy, but it extends the lifespan of the vines. All these once-forgotten techniques have been publicized by pruning and grafting experts including François Dal with the Institute of Vine and Wine Sciences (ISVV) in France and Simonit & Sirch in Italy, but the problem, which affects ungrafted and grafted vines alike, shows the complexity of the question of wood disease.

The different grafts

There is a wide variety of techniques, all of which require careful attention to match the buds and, in particular, the wood; the scion and the graft must be of identical diameter or very close in size to permit a good join and not break when tested for solidity. Of all these techniques, there are essentially four used in viticulture. Semi-mechanical grafting dominates the market yet more and more viticulturists are turning back to the more time-consuming field grafting for its agronomic quality.

- **Cleft grafting** sees the scion cut to a wedge and inserted into the rootstock, which is split across its diameter. This is relatively easy to do but requires wood of identical diameter, or very close to it. It is carried out as a field graft or a bench graft and can be semi-mechanized.
- **Semi-mechanical grafting**, a variation of cleft grafting, is also known as a *trait de Jupiter*, or an English graft. This technique requires wood of the same diameter and a clean cut, otherwise a bulbous graft union will result.
- **Omega grafting**, the most common technique since the early 1980s, accounts for 95 per cent of the plants grafted in France. The rootstock has an inverted omega-shaped (Ω) slit, while the scion is cut to be inserted into this and should be on the same plane as the trunk to ensure it takes well. The semi-industrial automation (with its larger volume of production) that brought the technique its success has attracted criticism nowadays, however. The transverse cut of the sap vessels does not follow the direction of the plant fibres, and the diameters are often imperfectly matched because of overproduction, which can result in tissue necrosis and an increased fragility in the plants.
- **T-bud graft (shield-bud graft) and chip-bud graft**, field grafts that require some dexterity. Writing in the 3rd century BCE, Theophrastus called this *emplastratio*, these are now being rediscovered through over-grafting. A cutting with a dormant bud is taken from the scion, and either a simple cut (chip-bud) or a shallow T-shaped cut (T-bud) is made in the bark of the trunk when the sap is rising. This causes little necrosis in the vine, preserves it well and promises a good recovery, but it is less common because it is more expensive to carry out than mechanized grafts.

Oddly, very few new grafting systems have been developed since the 1970s, the only ones being mortise grafting, by Rauscedo in Italy, and F2 by Hebinger in Alsace, both of which are barely used.

Esca

The primary cause of vine mortality in France is fungal wood disease, with esca being the most common. The disease is not new; the 1st-century-CE Roman agronomist Columella

SEMI-MECHANICAL GRAFTING: ENGLISH GRAFT

SEMI-MECHANICAL GRAFTING: OMEGA GRAFT

SEMI-MECHANICAL GRAFTING: F2 GRAFT

FIELD GRAFTING: CHIP-BUD GRAFT

FIELD GRAFTING: T-BUD GRAFT (SHIELD-BUD GRAFT)

THE PRINCIPAL CONTEMPORARY GRAFTS

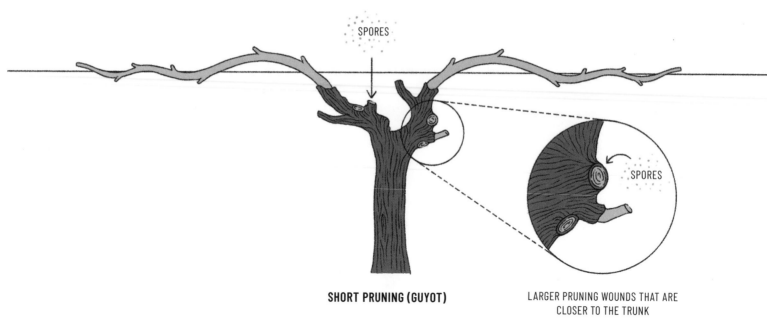

SPORES

SHORT PRUNING (GUYOT)

SPORES

LARGER PRUNING WOUNDS THAT ARE
CLOSER TO THE TRUNK

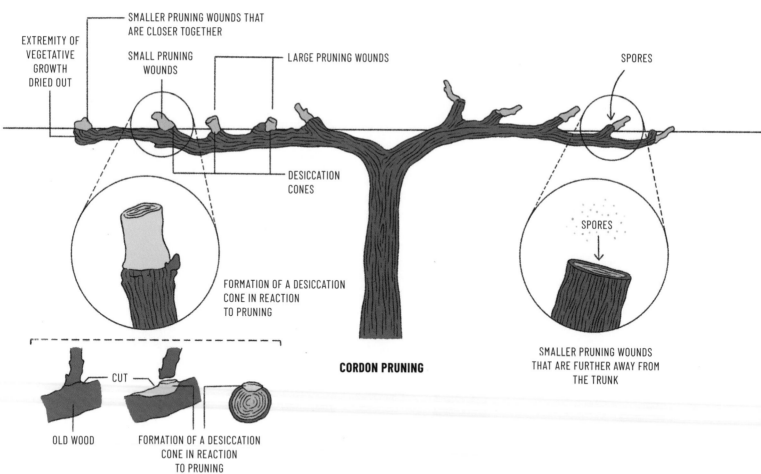

EXTREMITY OF
VEGETATIVE
GROWTH
DRIED OUT

SMALLER PRUNING WOUNDS THAT
ARE CLOSER TOGETHER

SMALL PRUNING
WOUNDS

LARGE PRUNING WOUNDS

SPORES

DESICCATION
CONES

FORMATION OF A DESICCATION
CONE IN REACTION
TO PRUNING

SPORES

CORDON PRUNING

CUT

OLD WOOD

FORMATION OF A DESICCATION
CONE IN REACTION
TO PRUNING

SMALLER PRUNING WOUNDS
THAT ARE FURTHER AWAY FROM
THE TRUNK

PRUNING WOUNDS

Learning how to prune properly has become a priority for the survival of vineyards,
because pruning wounds are the origins of numerous necrotizing wood diseases such as esca.

mentions *sideratio* of the vine, with symptoms that match those of esca, and it was already a problem by the beginning of the 20th century. Esca has spread exponentially over the past 20 years or so, however, not least because of the 2001 ban on sodium arsenite, the only known effective remedy, because of its toxicity.

There are two forms of esca: apoplectic (the vine withers and dies abruptly in the hot season) and chronic (the leaves necrotize, and the vine dies over a number of years). Examination of the trunk reveals the same problem in both cases: a white fungus, known in France as *amadou* ("white rot"), invades the interior of the vine. This is a saprophytic fungus that feeds on dead tissue.

Paradoxically, this fungus plays a fundamental role in the natural world, breaking down dead wood and recycling it into mineral elements, and is ubiquitous, being equally widespread in cultivated nurseries and on vineyard plots. In the particular case of esca, its action is parasitic rather than symbiotic; it simply needs to find the right conditions in order to fulfil its role – it cannot grow if there is no necrotic tissue present.

We therefore need to understand the origins of this necrosis, which often spreads down from the scion toward the rootstock. An increasing number of experts attribute the cause to the imperfect healing of vascular tissue around wounds to the vine sustained during pruning or mechanized work, micro-injuries during the period of vegetative growth and so on. Others, including Marc Birebent, have also cited a poor graft union as an entry point for the disease; the omega-graft in particular may create an almost impassable barrier around the necrotic woody tissue while also reducing the flow of sap, and insects such as termites and ants, which were previously able to find access, can no longer enter and clear away this dead wood and white rot and so play their part in reducing the risk of the vine dying.

Graft types and susceptibility to disease

A 2017 study carried out by Birebent in association with Bordeaux's ISVV has highlighted the influence of the type of graft on plant dieback (progressive death of plant tissue). Working with Cabernet Sauvignon and Mourvèdre, two cépages considered to be vulnerable, and three grafting techniques, they found lower rates of esca in manual cleft grafts carried out in the vineyard than for English and omega industrial grafts. There are thought to be several reasons for this: improved healing through better supply of resources to the callus and a better contact zone with the cambium for grafting carried out in the vineyard versus contamination of the graft union in the nursery.

While the choice of graft type is far from being academic, the problem of esca predates the invention of omega

Grafting and the rise of Merlot

The process of grafting creates a graft-union callus whose size and healing vary with the genetics, age, vigour and so on of the scion and the grafting technique used. In the majority of cases, however, the grafting point acts as a bottleneck, modifying the physiology of the new vine. Professor Alain Carbonneau has developed a little-known model to explain it. The phloem sap, rich in sugars, is normally dispersed to all the plant's organs according to their needs. Because of this partial obstruction, however, the roots receive less sap, while more remains in the aerial parts of the plant. This has benefited Merlot, which was not widespread before phylloxera since it did not fertilize well and had a root system that may not have been best adapted to conditions in Gironde. With the processs of grafting, fertilization and fruiting improved greatly thanks to this sugar bonus. The cépage then spread rapidly throughout the Bordeaux area, to the detriment of Malbec, a once-ubiquitous grape that was susceptible to the grape-vine fanleaf virus and had problems with shatter because of its excessive vigour. The latter thus disappeared almost entirely from the region's vineyards.

grafting and so presents a much larger and more complex agronomic problem for the question of vegetative health. Grafting is therefore just one critical element among several. Traditionally the preserve of the winemaker, these skills have been delegated to vineyard nursery workers who, since phylloxera, have become hands-on specialists under the supervision of the institutions tasked with selecting and certifying plants. The industrialization of both the profession and the sector in general, along with questions of immediate economic profitability at the expense of quality and long-term considerations, are undoubtedly part of the problem.

THE GROWTH STAGES OF A VINE

The vine is a perennial plant with an annual growth cycle consisting of three phases: a vegetative cycle, during which it forms shoots and leaves to allow the roots and trunk to develop; *aoûtement* or cold-hardening of the vegetative organs, during which the plant stores up reserves in the roots and wood for the start of vegetative growth in the following year; and a reproductive cycle, from the formation of inflorescences to fruiting. These three physiological functions are intimately interdependent during the year and from one year to the next.

The 16 growth stages of a vine's life cycle, as described by Galet

The phenological rhythm of a vine varies according to climatic conditions. In a temperate climate, it is discontinuous, with a period of active growth and another of winter rest. In the northern hemisphere, this annual cycle begins around February, with "weeping", when the sap runs out of the pruning cuts, and finishes toward the end of November with leaf drop. Several descriptive models detailing the phenological stages of *Vitis* have been suggested, but a system called the BBCH scale was developed in Germany in order to define with precision the growth stages for most plant species. It features a decimal code from 00 to 100 and was adopted in the 1990s. In 1993, it was synchronized with the Baillod-Baggiolini system, which is specific to vines.

Sprouting/bud development

A – Winter bud: resting phase (dormancy). The bud (eye) is almost totally covered in brown scales. The buds, which are pointed or rounded depending on the cépage, begin to swell as the sap rises; this becomes apparent when the vine is pruned and starts to weep. The buds then elongate within the scales.

B – Cotton bud: the bud continues to swell, and the scales move apart. A woolly protective layer, known as the "cotton bud", is clearly visible and marks the beginning of bud-burst.

C – Green tip: this is the actual moment of bud-burst. The bud elongates sufficiently to show the first signs of a green tip as the young shoot becomes visible.

Leaf development

D – Leaf break: a rosette of rudimentary leaves appears. The base is still protected by the cotton bud, which is progressively expelled from the scales.

E – Leaf spread: a first leaf extends and spreads away from the shoot, followed by three or four others, which are already showing their varietal characteristics. The new-growth cane becomes visible.

Inflorescences emerge

F – Clusters (inflorescences) are visible: inflorescences are rudimentary grape clusters that appear at the tip of the shoot. There are now four to six spreading leaves.

G – Clusters (inflorescences) separate: the clusters grow, although the flower buds are still clumped together.

H – Flower buds separate: the inflorescence appears in its typical form, with separated flower buds.

Flowering

I – Flowering: the stamens push off the cap (corolla). When this falls, the ovary is exposed and the stamens spring up around it. The flowers open progressively. Once in full flower, 50 per cent are open, meaning the cap has fallen and the stamens have spread out. Most of the caps will have fallen off by the end of flowering.

Fruit development

J – Fruit set: after fertilization, the ovaries enlarge and the stamens wither, although the latter often remain attached.

K – Peas: the berries grow from the size of lead shot to that of a pea, to reach around 50 per cent of what will be their final size. The cluster tilts downward into a vertical position and assumes the shape typical for its cépage.

L – Cluster closure: the berries reach 70 per cent of their final size and begin to touch each other. The speed at which cluster closure takes place varies according to the cépage and in some cases may never be complete.

Berry maturation

M – Veraison: the berries begin to change colour or become translucent, depending on the variety. The cluster becomes more compact.

N – Maturity: the berries reach maximum development. Once ripe, they have acquired some colour, or are transparent for white cépages, and soft to the touch. The rise in sugar levels and reduction in acidity indicates readiness for picking.

Senescence

O – Cold hardening, or *aoûtement*: the main canes turn brown and lignify, indicating wood maturity, a phenomenon that begins with veraison and ends after picking.

P – Leaf fall: the leaves change colour, turning yellow, red or brown, and then gradually drop off. This heralds the start of vegetative rest, or dormancy.

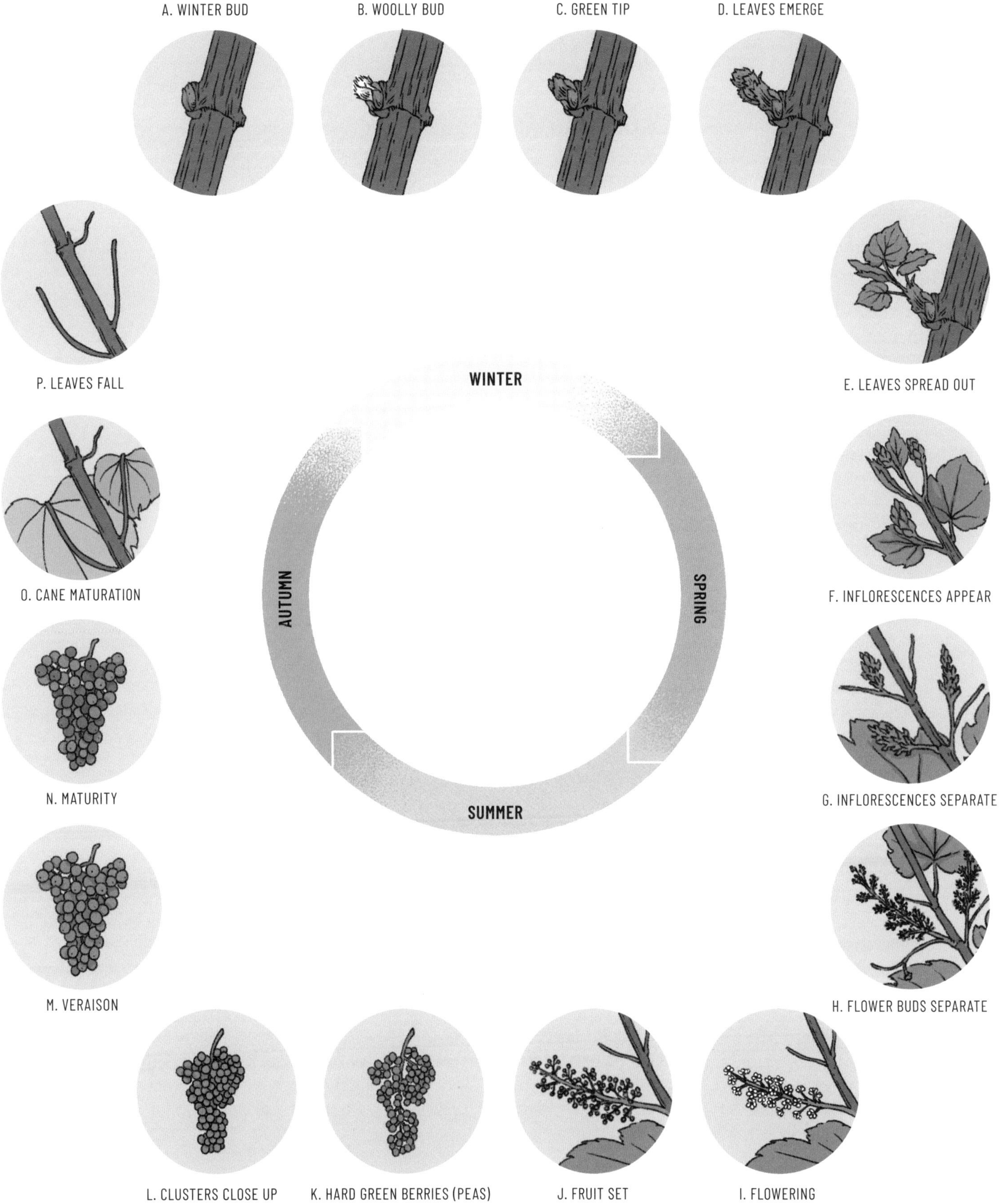

A. WINTER BUD

B. WOOLLY BUD

C. GREEN TIP

D. LEAVES EMERGE

P. LEAVES FALL

E. LEAVES SPREAD OUT

O. CANE MATURATION

F. INFLORESCENCES APPEAR

N. MATURITY

G. INFLORESCENCES SEPARATE

M. VERAISON

H. FLOWER BUDS SEPARATE

L. CLUSTERS CLOSE UP

K. HARD GREEN BERRIES (PEAS)

J. FRUIT SET

I. FLOWERING

WINTER

AUTUMN

SPRING

SUMMER

Which *Vitis* to plant?

What to plant? The problem is complicated by the question of "plant material", a curious expression (with productivist and industrial associations) that has been in use to refer to vines since the first half of the 20th century. A number of choices are made in order to produce wines of quality. The methods of production, sale and use are strictly controlled to reduce the spread of many kinds of vine disease; wine-growers cannot just plant whatever they like however they like. What are the ramifications of these constraints for viticulture and its diversity? Is there a difference between massal and clonal selections?

The birth of the grafting industry

Until the mid-1960s, some wine-growers made grafts out in the field using the wood from particular vines selected for their exceptional qualities. This technique was less expensive and adapted to the biotope, but these advantages were compromised by the state's fight against vine disease, the industrialization of viticulture and the expansion of a professional institution that had first appeared in the 1880s, the vine nursery.

This last was born of the extraordinary demand for plants that occurred after the phylloxera crisis. The vine nursery business grew rapidly and exponentially, with Provence and Carpentras becoming major production and sales markets at the end of the 19th century. Businesses specializing in grafting then mushroomed in the south of France, from Charente to the Alps in particular, as well as in Spain and Italy.

The number of diseased plants grew, and at the request of the French state in 1944, Jean Branas founded the Section de Sélection et de Contrôle des Bois et Plants de Vigne (Section for the Selection and Control of Vine Material), an official unit with a remit to select and monitor vines, to authenticate plant material and eradicate the grape-vine fanleaf virus. National bodies and research institutes have controlled vine production in France ever since.

Healthy plant selection

A distinction is usually drawn between clonal and massal selection in terms of classifying the origins of planted vines. In both cases, however, a vine is selected, propagated and grafted – in other words, cloned. The imprecision of the notion of "massal selection", often understood to be a grower selecting wood cuttings from an existing vineyard, each individual vine bringing genetic diversity to the new plantation, blurs the difference between these two methods of production,

based on an appraisal of a plant's health and its agronomic and oenological value.

Comprehensive clonal selection began in France in 1962 and is now supervised by the French Wine and Vine Institute (Institut Français de la Vigne et du Vin, IFV). Officially authorizing a new clone or a new variety takes 15 years. The first step is for certified selection bodies to research vine stock among vineyards and conservatories or plant collections to identify a strain that combines cultural, technical and organoleptic qualities that are stable and interesting. The strain is then tested for the principal diseases via indexing (grafting onto a plant that will accelerate symptoms of any diseases that may be present) or by serological testing (an ELISA test). If it is impossible to find a healthy stock, an apex micro-grafting method is used; the tip of a virus-free growth shoot is grafted onto a part of the stem of a pip that has just started to emerge. The new vine should not show any symptoms.

The clone head

The healthy strain is then subjected to precise viticultural and oenological monitoring for a number of years, checking the number of buds, weight of wood, distribution and number of shoots, chronology of phenological stages, yield, constituents of the grape, health, susceptibility to disease and more besides. The grapes are vinified in a number of batches over at least three vintages. Vinification is standardized to normalize fermentation. The wines are then analysed for alcohol, sugars, acids, pH, colour intensity, tannins, anthocyanins and so on. Finally, their organoleptic quality is judged against a checklist of criteria, and if all are met, the plant is selected, becoming a "clone head", or "initial material". It will then be submitted for inclusion in the official catalogue, and a maintenance body is tasked with preserving it.

From selection to commercialization

And so the vines begin their journey. Certified/approved establishments propagate the cuttings – the basic material of the mother vine that is sold to nurseries. The nurseries graft the cuttings and offer them to wine-growers as certified products with a phytosanitary passport (ECPP). As of 2022, there were 1,350 clones of 380 varieties registered and available for sale in France, a number of which were selected in the 1970s and 1980s. Certain cépages offer wider choice than others: there are 47 clones of Pinot Noir, 31 of Chardonnay, eight of Riesling, but only one of Gringet. Not all are regularly propagated: three clones of Chardonnay (76, 95 and 96) account for 50 per cent of production. Another 11 are significant, and the rest are propagated in small numbers and are often difficult to find in a nursery. In addition to eliminating viral disease and providing traceability, the aim of clonal selection is to research yield regularity, maturity and cultivation, to showcase the diversity to be exploited agronomically and to meet the industry's various production targets. Selection of this kind has other economic benefits: France now leads the world in sales of certified virus-free plants in a market worth several hundred million euros. The research and selection institutes have trademarked and licensed the plants they have developed, such as the selections registered with ENTAV-INRA®.

What about massal selection?

Historically, winemakers have made massal selections for reasons of practicality and cost, but such choices are now aimed at preserving the genetic heritage of (often old) vines that seem particularly well adapted to their biotope and the production levels sought. The wine-grower identifies the vines

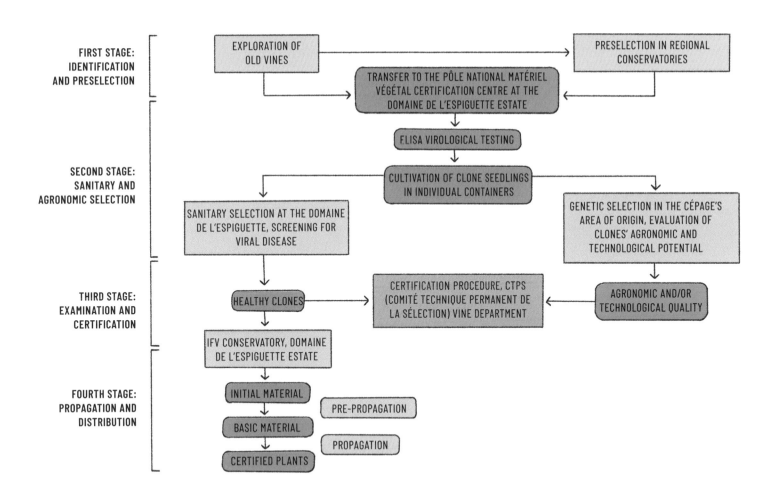

THE CERTIFICATION PATH FOR A CLONE AT THE IFV
The certification path for a clone by the plant-material division of the IFV takes about
15 years from identification to release.

and sends cuttings to a certified nursery, or may propagate them in private nurseries, which are strictly supervised. In either case, to limit the spread of disease, only the wine-grower has planting rights. Legally, a massal plant can only come from the wine-grower's own vineyard. Such a selection differs from clonal selection as it is usually understood, in its desire to preserve the genetic heritage of old vines that might disappear, in its health protocol and in its selection demarcation – here, the wine-grower's vineyard. In either case, however, the genetic diversity of a cépage ultimately depends on the real-world diversity of the number of individual plants: if certain varieties are very widespread or if variability is poor, there will be little genetic diversity.

> "We plant for our grandchildren" – but this old wine-grower's adage no longer holds true, since uprooting vines after less than 30 years is becoming more common

The question of the influence on the vine of its locality may also arise; how can the adaptation of an individual plant to its terroir be evaluated? This raises the question of the importance of the ecosystem from the moment the future vine is selected, propagated and then cultivated, and its effects on the vine's metabolism. Each plant is influenced by its surroundings in a unique way. While epigenetics (the science exploring this influence on the expression of genes and uncoded modifications of DNA sequence) is beginning to provide some answers, it shows that there is no reproduction of epigenetic mechanisms from the mother plants to the young cuttings, since growth and propagation are facilitated by meristems, non-specialized cells. Once the plant has been selected and planted, however, the influence of its environment is once again in play. The issues involved can be better understood by following the production of a grafted plant in a nursery.

Cultivating mother vines

To produce these plants, nursery owners must first have their plots of land approved. The soil in nurseries is often sandy or too rich for viticulture. Two types of vine can be cultivated: the mother vines of rootstocks (a total of about 2,400 ha in France, with 10 varieties covering 90 per cent of the land planted) and scions (about 1,600 ha, with 22 cultivars accounting for 80 per cent); this represents 0.53 per cent of the 750,000 ha of vineyard land in France. Every variety must be registered in the official catalogue of vine varieties overseen by FranceAgriMer, the country's supervisory body. If a nursery wishes to plant a non-approved variety (a forgotten

cépage, for example), it must request authorization to experiment. The massal selection of rootstocks has been banned since 1960 unless sourced from private vineyards where only the owner has planting rights.

Mother vines are cultivated in the open air or forced in a greenhouse. When grown in plots, almost all are planted in soil and are weeded, fertilized and chemically treated. The aim is for the plant to produce as much wood as possible, and the volume varies by rootstock cultivar. Isolated nurseries adopt an organic or biodynamic approach, but there are no organically accredited plants because it is obligatory to use a synthetic insecticide against flavescence dorée, a deadly phytoplasma disease.

The cuttings with their latent buds are taken as scions during the vine's dormant period to produce plants the following year. They should be taken as close to the date of grafting as possible, although this is not always achievable due to the time of year or the stage of the vine's growth. The rootstock's latent buds are cut back to prevent regrowth, while the scion's latent buds are kept intact. Both the rootstock and the scion should have the same diameter to guarantee the best graft.

Some nurseries are generalists, while others specialize in scions or rootstocks. Given the law of supply and demand, the most sought-after clones are the most widely produced, although certain official clones or rare varieties are sometimes hard to source for planting on a large scale. These can be purchased commercially from other nurseries that are often located abroad; nurseries may subcontract to other nurseries without always revealing this. Grafting is a complex market that exerts a major influence on the winemaking industry.

The cost of grafting

Grafting is a process involving high labour costs in a highly competitive sector where the purchase price generally drives sales. There is thus pressure to cut costs. Field grafts are more expensive than bench grafts, the price of which varies with the technique; bench grafts are used for 99 per cent of planting in France. Once the graft has been made, the graft union is waxed to prevent it from drying out or rotting during the forcing process. The aim is to create a solid graft callus; it takes about 12 days in a moist atmosphere at 25–30°C (77–86°F) for this to take place and for the shoots to reach 4–5cm (1½–2in). Hormones can be used to accelerate the process.

The plants, at this stage called *barbus* ("bearded"), are sorted, rewaxed and then stored in a cold room as they wait to be planted out in the field, usually in May. By autumn, they have developed roots and growth above ground, and the wood has lignified. During this period, they are treated and fertilized like adult vines. Before winter, when they are ready, they are dug up and sorted; the graft union is checked by thumb pressure and 40–50 per cent generally break, so there are average losses of 50 per cent. One of the most common criticisms is that poorly sorted plants make it through this process to market. The plants are finally stored to await being sent out for plantation. The whole cycle takes more than a year, with precise logistics and a considerable investment on the part of both the nursery and the wine-grower. It is understandable that quality assurance problems appear in an industry where the main players tend to drive prices down.

The problem of the quality:productivity:price ratio

Industrial grafting is attracting increasing criticism, with some wine-growers and nurseries calling into question the influence of the growing conditions in the nurseries on the viability of the plants, whether this be the treatments the plants receive or the fact that the plants are being produced in terroirs that are very different from those in which they will be planted. Do the apparent initial savings from this practice pay off when the cost:benefit ratio is considered over the short, medium and long term? A basic graft costs €1.30 at the time of writing, as opposed to €2.30 or more for one of better quality. In 2021, the average cost for planting a hectare was somewhere between €25,000 and €30,000, including preparation of the land, planting, maintenance, stakes, trellising and so on, and when a plant dies, a replacement costs at least €10. When we consider that a root system will not find a point of balance for optimum production for 20 to 25 years, which is the average lifespan of today's vines, we realize that the upshot is the impossibility of producing terroir wines. So how can we ensure that the vine ages well?

Are vines getting sick through being understood as "plant material"?

"We plant for our grandchildren" – but this old wine-grower's adage no longer holds true, since uprooting vines after less than 30 years is becoming more common. Replantation and complantation seem to be increasing in parallel with an escalation of ever-worsening climatic events, notably drought and heatwaves. Esca, thyllosis, *folletage* ("sunstroke") and other ailments are proliferating among young vines that seem weak from the outset. It is no wonder that questions are being raised about the cultivation and health of these plants. Might intensive agricultural techniques, like harvesting from year two, immediately seeking a high yield, systematic fertilization and so on, not be major accelerators of dieback? Is it not the case that

Challenging the vine nurseries

A number of the approaches employed by vine nurseries are being questioned by wine-growers, agronomists and even nursery workers. One of the best known is Lilian Bérillon, who knows the industry like the back of his hand. He has criticized the industry's practice of trading plants that are low-cost and of dubious origin – a practice that he himself followed at the beginning of his career – and is promoting radical change. Varietal diversity of rootstocks is one of his passions, and he is now propagating 20 of the 31 authorized rootstocks in his nursery at Jonquières in Vaucluse, France, trellising and cultivating them like vines. He is campaigning for the authorization of their massal selection with a view to reinvigorating the genetic pool.

Faced with the ravages suffered by Sauvignon Blanc (a cépage that is highly susceptible to wood diseases) in Sancerre, SICAVAC, the technical support body for Centre-Loire wine-growers, has been working with four nurseries since 2010 to develop a set of specifications and controls to guarantee the quality of Sauvignon Blanc vines under the Ceps Sicavac brand. It provides the scion plant material (four clones, ENTAV-INRA® 376, 159, 906, 108, and two massals), and the nursery undertakes to cultivate and trellis the mother vines of the rootstocks, while the grafts – which have been produced without herbicides and watered using drip irrigation – must spend one season outside and be harvested after leaf fall to encourage good lignification.

Much like the wine industry, which has had to face the consequences of excessive industrialization, nurseries are being obliged to draw up new protocols to better guarantee the health of their plants.

the demand for productivity and low costs is fundamentally incompatible with the vegetative rhythm of the vine and of plants in general, despite all the advances in agro-technology? Might not vines – not to mention the soil and the whole environment – be getting sick through being thought of as "'material" for production?

THE PRINCIPAL VINE DISEASES IN 1920

In 1920, Larousse's illustrated monthly magazine published a series of scientific diagrams that helped to identify vine parasites, among other pests. The main diseases of this period were principally fungal; having arrived from America in the 19th century, they turned viticulture on its head because *V. vinifera* had no natural defences. To this day, they remain the major diseases that most phytosanitary products seek to combat.

POWDERY MILDEW, *UNCINULA NECATOR*

DOWNY MILDEW, *PLASMOPARA VITICOLA*

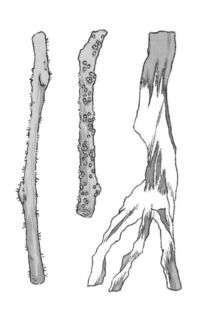

ROOT ROT, *ARMILLARIA MELLEA*

EFFECTS OF APOPLEXY AND SUNBURN

EFFECTS OF CHLOROSIS

BLACK ROT, *GUIGNARDIA BIDWELLI*

WHITE ROT, *CONIELLA DIPLODIELLA*

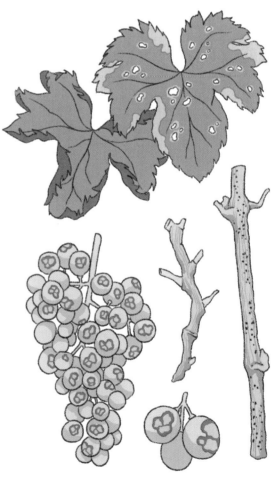

ANTHRACNOSE, *ELSINOË AMPELINA*

Thinking differently about vines

The vine as "plant material"? What notion of nature underpins this idea of the vine as a tool of production? The question is of interest to both wine-growers and scientific researchers in their vision of *V. vinifera* as a plant domesticated to produce grapes. Put another way, the contemporary viticultural world's understanding of vines is based on a specific approach that might be termed "ethnobotanical". All nations and peoples have a specific relationship with their plant environment, a dynamic and historic relationship in the way they identify, describe, understand, use and represent it, even when they wish to be as objective as possible. What are the presuppositions that determine our relationship with vines, with plants, with the plant world? By changing our perspective, new ways of understanding will emerge.

The vine – that great unknown

In Greek mythology, the vine is born from the death of Ampelos (meaning "Vine"), a young satyr with whom Dionysus was in love. The Greeks saw the reincarnation of the young Ampelos and the god in every vine, every bunch of grapes and in the wine itself. This anthropomorphic perspective might seem naive to us now: vines and human beings inhabit two different realms, with one generally being considered superior – but when we talk about vines, they often sound like people: they don't like to get their feet wet, they are working hard, they breathe. We even speak of a vine's growth "hormones" and think of a vine as a unique individual with a limited lifespan. We could continue to give any number of other examples that betray our difficulty in thinking of vines without resorting to concepts and knowledge systems that take the world of humans and animals as a reference point. Thinking about vines from a botanical perspective requires a re-examination of our approach to knowledge: do we truly understand what a vine is? A plant? This question has been occupying those in scientific circles since the 1980s and started to percolate through to a larger public around 30 years later.

Rethinking plants

Francis Hallé, leading botanist and world-renowned biologist specializing in the ecology of tropical rainforests and the co-founder of the Radeau des Cimes scientific expedition to explore tropical rainforest canopies, has developed a new way of approaching and critiquing his discipline. His ideas are not directly addressed to vines but are applicable, and allow us to take a fresh look at vines. His *In Praise of Plants* (2002) seeks to answer the question of what a plant is in a new

way, demonstrating that innocent and unintentional epistemological zoocentrism has blinded botanical science ever since Aristotle by making use of the conceptual approaches of animal biology to understand the plant world. Presumed to be immobile and without speech, and so devoid of soul or intelligence, plants have been relegated to an inferior rank as a result and pressed into the service of superior animals who need them to live. A utilitarian approach has therefore guided how we think about plants. So how should we approach thinking about them and their specific nature? Through an original, interdisciplinary and analytical comparison with animals, demonstrating that each and every one has its own way of being in the world, and thus properties that are fundamentally differentiated.

A plant is neither an animal…

The ontological distinctiveness of plants lies in the way they obtain energy to survive. Plants tend to grow upward to capture solar energy while fighting off competition from other plants and facing down danger from predators. They thus develop a vast surface area of sensors both above ground, for light, and below ground, for water, depending on the availability of resources. They do not need animals to survive, though they sometimes make use of them to be pollinated and to spread their seeds; if animals were to disappear, however, plants would be able to develop other strategies. They are autotrophic, generating their own nourishment, and so have achieved food independence. Fixed in place, they enjoy considerable morphological plasticity, enabling them to adapt their shape, but also possess behavioural and genomic fluidity. Animals, by comparison, have poor plasticity and

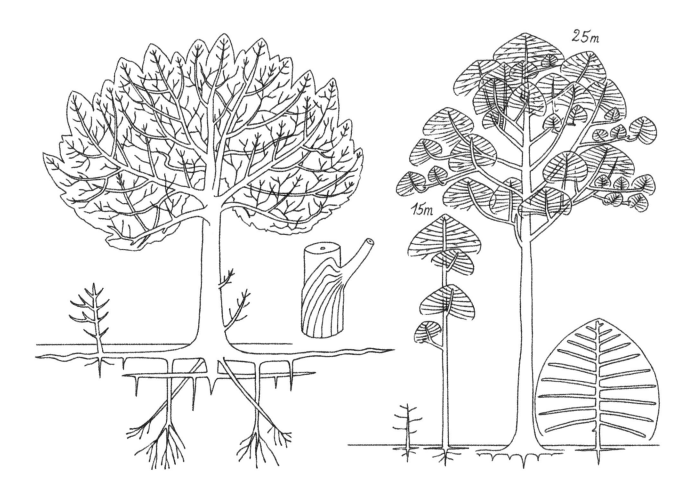

COLONY TREES BY FRANCIS HALLÉ

Leading botanist Hallé has disseminated his work through his writing but also through an original approach to scientific drawing. Influenced by the traditional, schematic architectural model, Hallé brings life and poetry to illustrations without losing any scientific rigour and allows us to perceive plants differently.

settle for a single genome because they are able to flee from danger. The choice facing plants is metamorphosis or death, which is why there can be multiple genomes for the same plant; this has fundamental consequences for the way we understand the idea of the individuality of plants.

… nor an individual…

Cut an animal in half and it dies, but if you divide a plant in two, both halves will live. Taking this a step further, every cell in a plant is capable of reproducing the plant in its entirety; this is known as totipotency and is not possible with animals. Quoting from French poet Francis Ponge's *Le Parti pris des choses* (1942), Hallé suggests that "plants have no vital organs". They have no centralized operating system of

heart, brain, lungs and the like, and in place of a hundred or so distinct organs, they have no more than three - root, trunk, leaf – but these organs fulfil the same functions as in animals, of feeding, breathing and so on. From this, Hallé draws a conclusion that is a major paradigm shift and anything but easy to grasp: etymologically, immunologically and genomically, a plant is not an individual.

… but a colony

Plants have highly attenuated immune systems that do not destroy intruders. They are therefore more accepting of "otherness" than animals, as can be seen from the practice of horticultural grafting. This obliges us to reconsider the boundaries of plants and what we think of as diseases or

71

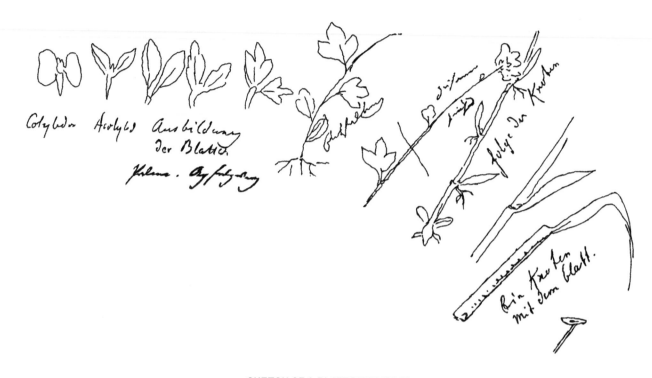

SKETCH OF A *BLATT* BY GOETHE

Goethe illustrated his musings on botany with evocative sketches, such as this of the *Blatt*, the basic unit that constantly metamorphoses during a plant's three periods of growth – from seed to leaf, from bract to flower, and from pistil and stamens to fruit.

pathogens and to examine the relationships that these might establish with plants – not to mention with death, which can coexist with life in the same plant: a vine blighted with dead wood due to esca can still produce fruit.

How can this be? In the 19th century, Charles Darwin (1809–82) and entomologist Jean-Henri Fabre (1823–1915) explained it intuitively by discussing plants in terms of a colony, a collective entity made up of parts that are equally divisible and reproducible from root to bud. A plant in fact reproduces by reiteration, a concept developed by Dutch forest botanist Roelof Oldeman in 1972, increasing its volume by indefinitely reproducing its original architecture from seed. As a colony, it is de facto virtually immortal, and if conditions are right, its life can potentially be infinitely prolonged. A plant never stops growing, in fact – it is only when it is prevented from getting bigger that it dies. Although rooted in the ground, it is neither immobile nor passive (as our anthropocentric prejudices would suggest); it has a fundamental double mobility and its own temporality that does not coincide with ours; this prevents us from properly perceiving and understanding it – and almost certainly from respecting it.

A different mobility

Plants possess another kind of mobility: they move as a species. By taking advantage of the mobility of the animals they attract with their odours, colours, flowers and fruits, plants are able to migrate and colonize new territory. Plants produce these secondary compounds to compensate for their fixed position but also to function as a deterrent against predators by emitting gases or acids and so on. Instead of "fight or flight", they therefore transform and modify their environment through symbioses with other living organisms. This takes place externally – for example, with mycorrhizal fungi or other plants – and internally with bacteria, leading Hallé to assert that foliage is, more than anything, a "bacterial bloom". Chloroplasts, the organelles of chlorophyll, are thus bacteria that have become part of the plant cell but continue to behave like bacteria.

Understanding a plant therefore entails observing it in its own particular environment, which is in turn intrinsically linked to the relationships it has developed with its entire ecosystem. In arriving at these conclusions, Hallé has followed English botanist Edred Corner (1906–96) in developing the study of plant "architecture", the morphology of its aerial structures, and positing its epistemological legitimacy. Before these, the German poet and philosopher Goethe, whose literary success has eclipsed his work as a natural scientist, had made this observation the basis of his biological studies at the end of the 18th century.

The metamorphosis of plants

Goethe outlined a new scientific method in his essay *The Metamorphosis of Plants* (English ed: 2009) that some consider a revolution of Copernican proportions, transcending the fixist or transformationalist theories of the era's nascent science of biology. Before him, plants were classified into positivist categories according to a description of the fully formed plant organism, as practised by Linnaeus, the 18th-century naturalist. Goethe found this approach inadequate: living things were to be understood only in their totality and not by reducing them to their composite parts, and this should be achieved through synthesis rather than analysis. After years of observation, Goethe noted that the cotyledons (the first leaf part of the seed), the leaves and the flowers were just phases of the same dynamic and not differentiated organs.

His great idea was born: every plant is in and of itself nothing but a metamorphosis. Its parts are variations of an original organ with a fundamental and unique form that merely repeats itself in a living process punctuated by expansions and contractions. He called this the *Blatt*. Made up of an internode and a bud, this was the base unit that would change constantly during the three phases of a plant's growth – from seed to leaf, from bract to flower, and from pistil and stamens to fruit. By undergoing metamorphosis through expansion and contraction, it was fulfilling various different functions. Goethe named this concept the *Urpflanze*, the "archetypal plant". The *Urpflanze* does not exist, either as an idea or in reality, and it cannot be perceived or felt; it is the guiding principle of every plant, and only in the material observation of the metamorphosis of each individual can one identify this point that is common to all. Metamorphosis is the very essence of a plant.

The Goethean method

Goethe proposed a new epistemological method to understand this. Our senses, devalued by theories of knowledge since Plato, are in fact excellent tools for understanding the world; conscious perception of odours, textures and colours has real-world epistemological validity. The method comprises three phases: the first is analytical, involving a sensory description of the plant, with no a priori considerations, from its germination to its decay; the second is synthetic and entails recreating, in the imagination, the dynamics of its metamorphoses (in other words, understanding its life and times, its *gesta*); the third is an intuitive perception – the scientific, sensory and intellectual intuiting of the law inherent within the phenomenon (*Urphänomen*) that renders the nature of the plant wholly perceptible to the imagination and the rational mind alike.

Goethe's method has been described as a "systematized imaginative phenomenology" (Nicolas Class, *Goethe et la méthode de la science*, 2005), an experimental approach suggesting the qualitative study of forms as a way of understanding the dynamic force specific to living things that, in its totality, is constantly metamorphosing the living world.

> " Goethe outlined a new scientific method in his essay *Metamorphosis of Plants* that some consider a revolution of Copernican proportions

It may be that only Goethean morphology is able to study this phenomenon in its entirety by complementing the quantitative and mechanistic natural sciences, since the latter's analytical reductionism cannot describe the continuing metamorphosis of the living world. Imagination also permits the creation of ways of thinking specific to each object studied: a plant is neither a rock nor an animal, nor yet a mathematical idea, and each of those should have its proper method of study.

Goethe's theory met with a mixed reception in the 19th and 20th centuries, but contemporary curiosity about nature, research into phenotypes and evolutionary biology have generated renewed interest in these visionary works of modern botanical morphology. In the field of viticulture, this phenomenology of nature profoundly influenced Rudolf Steiner, the founder of the biodynamic movement.

The *gesta* of the vine and biodynamics

Steiner was well acquainted with Goethe's epistemology and was responsible for producing an edition of Goethe's scientific writings in the 1880s. Working from these, he devised objective idealism, his own theory of knowledge that equipped him to establish a theory to describe the practice of biodynamic agriculture. He presented this in 1924 in a series of eight lectures that were compiled in his *Agriculture Course*. These difficult texts are based on the concepts of anthroposophy, a doctrine developed by Steiner of which certain aspects remain controversial. Nonetheless, he suggests in this course a reading of plants that, to this day, influences the practice of biodynamic viticulture, notably as taught by Jean-Michel Florin, the coordinator of the Biodynamic Agriculture Movement (MABD) and co-director of the agricultural department of the Goetheanum.

According to Steiner, a plant is a living being undergoing slow but constant transformation; it is radically different from animals, and zoocentric concepts cannot be applied, although Goethean phenomenology describes this perfectly. The "original plant" exhibits two growth tendencies, vertical and peripheral or spiral, and its aerial parts undergo three metamorphoses. The first of these involves metamorphosis of the leaves: the organs, the leaves, appear successively via a vegetative process in exchange with the plant's environment that forms living matter through photosynthesis. This is followed by floral metamorphosis: the floral organs are formed simultaneously and side-by-side in a process that gives the plant its defining shapes, odours and colours. This transformation attracts insects and animals. The last is fruit metamorphosis, and the organs (pulp and seeds) are a synthesis of the vegetative and floral processes. Each metamorphosis of the organs should be understood not as a function, as with machines, but as a process of integration and differentiation that increases as the plant develops. So how does this happen in detail?

> " Goethe's phenomenology of nature profoundly inspired Rudolf Steiner, the founder of the biodynamic movement

In the beginning was the seed

The seed carries within it all the plant's regenerative potential. The sexual reproduction that produced the seed enables a rebalancing of pathologies, something that vegetative propagation – which has been the basis of vine propagation for centuries – is unable to do. This would explain the vine's current susceptibility to disease. When the seed germinates, its urge to grow vertically is expressed by a root that burrows down into the soil; this is "positive geotropism", which follows gravity. There is a main, privoting taproot – this is found in all plants – while the secondary root system that develops afterward is specific to the species. Cuttings do not have this primary root.

A stem grows up toward the sky; this is "negative geotropism", which fights against gravity. If the seed is viewed as a point, we can see the plant as a dynamic axis between earth and sky. The cotyledons appear, the organs above ground, growing in a spiral around the trunk, up toward the light in order to capture it more effectively. These leaves react to the environment and are "open", as opposed to the trunk, which by contrast is more "closed; this is the "peripheral" impulse of the plant. It is at this point that the three stages of metamorphosis are triggered.

The three stages of metamorphosis

The first stage of metamorphosis involves the leaf, revealing the two growth tendencies that are constantly at work within the plant: a centrifugal force of expansion that expresses its "juvenile" force in vegetative growth, the production of matter through photosynthesis; and a centripetal force of contraction that differentiates this matter, representing the floral process. These growth tendencies are expressed during every stage of the various metamorphoses and in every species. A vine, like any creeping or climbing plant, therefore has a preponderantly centrifugal tendency. The leaf essentially embodies vegetative growth, with a discrete differentiation of its shape that tends toward the production of a flower bud.

The second metamorphosis is that of the flower, furthering the speciation of the plant in a motion of expansion and contraction; it is the former of these two that dominates in flowering. Green leaves make way for flowers that cannot photosynthesize but remain sensitive to the rhythm of the sun. Secondary compounds – like nectar, pigment and aromatic compounds – appear; these are not necessary for the plant itself but, rather, aid its propagation. Opening up to space and heat, the flower grows away from the earth, and is to be appreciated more for its qualities – colour and odour – than quantitatively by weight.

The final metamorphosis involves the fruit in a motion of expansion and contraction like the flower. Cells grow to produce green fruit, to be followed by a process of maturation. The number of cells no longer increases, although they do grow, and substances (sugars, acids, pigments and so on) are transformed. Fruit can therefore be understood as a synthesis of vegetative growth and the floral process, of which the seed is the final result.

By using this method, the observer should be able to understand the dynamics and profound nature specific to each plant in order better to appreciate and cultivate it, if necessary, while respecting its specific tendencies, which exist only in a dynamic relationship with its organic and mineral environment understood as a whole. This method also makes it possible to understand and utilize the powers and synergies of plants in medicines or for biodynamic compounds. When applied to vines, it therefore offers new insights. This is how biodynamists hope to develop a new approach to viticulture and to agriculture in general.

The gesta of vines

How does the vine embody the principle of Goethe's *Urpflanze*, the archetypal plant? In Florin's *Viticulture biodynamic. Nouvelles voies pour régénérer la culture de la vigne* (2018), the author lays a foundation for a Goethean reading of *V. vinifera* and sketches out behavioural nature specific to the vine:

"A vine is, in its origins, a plant that binds deeply with the earth and raises up that earth by forming wood every year. It can live a long time, up to a hundred years and more.

"Highly vegetative, it is wide open and sensitive to the environment to which it is exposed, as can be seen from the formation of tendrils. The weak flowering process, which is still heavily influenced by vegetative forces, is very much set aside, and the vine channels its vigorous vegetative growth directly into its fruit. Winemakers usually use every means at their disposal to guide and control this indomitable vegetative force (pruning, cropping, pollarding and so on). The shoots and even the tendrils (as transformed stalks) are subject to two forces, the instinct to grow upward and gravity pulling the shoots downward. Vines always seem compelled to grow higher without ever really succeeding. They need the support of trees (or stakes) on which they can climb – creating an image of a permanent aspiration to rise up toward the light.

"In comparison with many other plants, vines do not undergo a process of 'devitalization' through a contraction of their successive foliage. Instead, the opposite occurs: the vegetative process is so powerful that, rather than remaining in vegetative dormancy, the secondary lateral buds in the axil of the current shoot develop by forming secondary shoots. Sometimes, even tertiary shoots appear. By the end of spring, we have the distinct impression that we are dealing with a plant that wishes to grow in every direction at any cost, and to fill all the space available without ever stopping. Vines are dominated by a vegetative process that continues right through to the berries, which reveal evidence of this in their watery and earthy character when very young, and which they retain until the start of maturation. Rudolf Steiner described this process in the following manner: 'What other plants save exclusively for the young seedling, all the growth power that is otherwise reserved for the young seedling and does not flow into the rest of the plant, all this flows into the vine and, in a certain way, into the flesh of the fruit as well.'"

The plant and the vine – a unique way of being in the world

Scientific research since the late 20th century, suggests that plants can no longer be thought of as "vegetative" organisms, with all the negative connotations that this term entails – passive, immobile and inferior to humans and animals. The plant kingdom is endowed with abilities and its own way of being in the world, from which we can learn. Epistemological anthropocentrism is a trap, but it has a certain educational value when critiqued and controlled. In fact, critical engagement with it may enable us to reforge links between disciplines in the same way as they existed until the Enlightenment, when thinkers such as Goethe synthesized (in some respects in the Hegelian sense) multiple fields of study, including aesthetics, in their works. This kind of approach is increasingly being promoted today, at universities in particular. A biodynamic reading is a further example of a more holistic approach and, while controversial, has the merit of replacing mere observation of the specificity of the living world in all its dynamics by siting its environment at the heart of any consideration, while suggesting that we think differently about plants – with greater respect and humility.

ECOLOGY

The vine and its underground world

To quote agronomist and mycologist Marc-André Selosse, who has been campaigning for a new understanding of soil since the 1990s, it is "too small, too dirty, too opaque" (*Jamais seul*, 2017); until the 1970s, soil was practically invisible to us. It was, as it were, a simple physical substrate for life above ground or a geological reservoir of raw materials. If acknowledged at all, it is often represented equivocally, and many wine professionals bandy the terms "bedrock", "ground" and "soil" about with indifference. Soil is far from being simple, fixed, dead matter, however. On the contrary, it is a highly complex and fragile agglutination of living ecosystems, providing life support and resources for the entire biosphere. How do vines interact with it? Why is this relationship so crucial for the health of both parties? Living soil is much more than a food reserve – it is an essential prerequisite for long-lived vines and terroir wines.

Soil – a environment that is so little known and yet so complex

Soil is an unknown that is taken for granted, even by those who deal with it on a daily basis. That we have taken such a superficial interest for such a long time has now resulted in the serious problems of soil pollution, degradation and loss, threatening many ecosystems, including vineyards.

Soil represents only 6.5 per cent of Earth's surface; the seas and oceans take up 71 per cent, and non-arable areas account for 22.5 per cent. It was initially simply defined by its position between air (the atmosphere) and rock (the lithosphere). Then, as measuring devices were developed and perfected, it was characterized by its constituent parts, including solid and fluid mineral elements, which until recently hogged all the limelight, and an organic part, both living and dead, the study of which did not really begin until the end of the 1970s.

Historically viewed as a mineral, soil was seen as no more than a habitat for flora and fauna that were visible to whatever degree and often dismissed as of neither use nor harm. Research since the early 1990s has discovered that these organisms, about which we still know so little, do much more than simply inhabit the soil; they are essential to its formation, function and fertility – and probably even to the possibility of life on Earth.

This organic fraction of the soil includes the living biodiversity and the organic matter that appear on its surface. The latter detritus is principally made up of the remains of plants and animals that mineralize after a process of progressive decomposition. Distinctions are made between the coarse, living organic matter moving freely about the surface; the fresh, free and fine organic matter in the lower level; and the transformed, stable organic matter bound together with the mineral portion known as humus. Each has different properties, but it is this last, the clay-humus complex, that is the key to soils and terroirs.

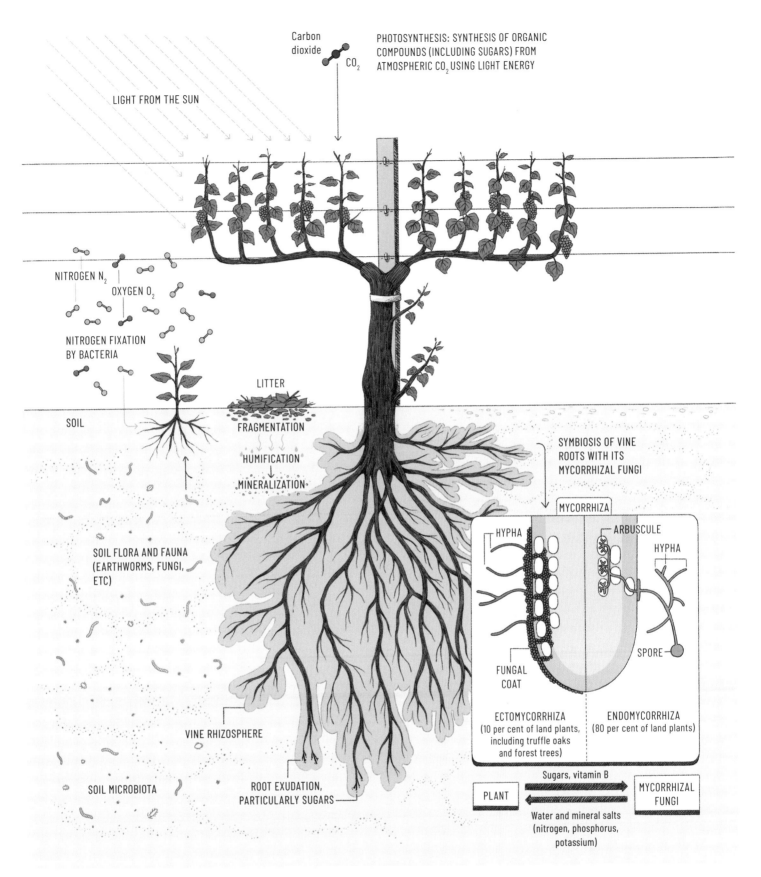

PHOTOSYNTHESIS: SYNTHESIS OF ORGANIC COMPOUNDS (INCLUDING SUGARS) FROM ATMOSPHERIC CO_2 USING LIGHT ENERGY

Carbon dioxide

CO_2

LIGHT FROM THE SUN

NITROGEN N_2

OXYGEN O_2

NITROGEN FIXATION BY BACTERIA

SOIL

LITTER

FRAGMENTATION

HUMIFICATION

MINERALIZATION

SYMBIOSIS OF VINE ROOTS WITH ITS MYCORRHIZAL FUNGI

MYCORRHIZA

HYPHA

ARBUSCULE

HYPHA

SPORE

FUNGAL COAT

SOIL FLORA AND FAUNA (EARTHWORMS, FUNGI, ETC)

ECTOMYCORRHIZA (10 per cent of land plants, including truffle oaks and forest trees)

ENDOMYCORRHIZA (80 per cent of land plants)

VINE RHIZOSPHERE

Sugars, vitamin B

PLANT

MYCORRHIZAL FUNGI

SOIL MICROBIOTA

ROOT EXUDATION, PARTICULARLY SUGARS

Water and mineral salts (nitrogen, phosphorus, potassium)

THE COMPLEX ROLES OF MICROBIOTA IN SOIL

The microbes making up a vine's soil are involved in the humification and mineralization of organic litter, capturing atmospheric nitrogen and, in symbiosis with the vine, creating its rhizosphere through mycorrhization.

Soil, clays and humus

To pick up on the work in particular of agronomists Claude and Lydia Bourguignon (*Le Sol, la Terre et les Champs*, 2015), to understand the health of a vine as its potential for expressing its terroir when being tasted, we need to understand the importance of clays, humus and the clay-humus complex.

Soil is created by the synergy between the mineral and the organic – it is an organo-mineral complex. Deep underground, the bedrock is broken down into primary minerals by the action of microbes, plant roots and water, which recombine to form secondary minerals that include clays. It took some time to find an explanation for this phenomenon, which takes place with all types of bedrock, whether sedimentary, igneous or metamorphic. Clays are in fact an indirect by-product of plant nutrition. The roots and their microbes draw the nutrients they need from the soil, but some are only required in minute amounts, such as silica, iron and aluminium, which are trace elements in plants. The amount present in the soil gradually increases until they crystallize into silicates of iron and aluminium - in other words, into clays.

> Without the clay-humus complex, there could be no talk of appellation wines, let alone the complex idea of "minerality" in wines

The organic matter on the surface is also broken down and mineralized under the action of flora and scavenging fauna like insects and mites that lead to its to decay, causing coarse matter such as leaves, branches and bark, rich in lignin and cellulose, to disintegrate. This is then transformed by fungi and bacteria. The speed at which this cycle of mineralization, the transformation of organic into mineral matter, takes place depends on the environment, the microbial population that is present, and what material is available for decomposition.

Primary mineralization rapidly produces biomass, water, CO_2, mineral salts and sulphur that are immediately available to the vine but easily leached away since they are not solidly fixed. The humification process is much slower and, while also a kind of microbial decomposition and mineralization, produces organic matter that is far more stable, thanks to its electrical charge: humus, made up of humin, and humic fulvic acids. This acts as the vine's foodstore, providing nitrogen and phosphorus.

Secondary mineralization can then further transform raw humus into mineral elements that can be assimilated by the roots. The presence of clays and humus is required for the creation of soil, because these, under the right conditions, form the clay-humus complex.

The clay-humus complex – a key component of soils and the expression of terroir

Without the clay-humus complex, there could be no talk of appellation wines, let alone the complex idea of "minerality" in wines. Why is it so important? It is the key to the biological and chemical fertility of soils, and its electrical interactions are its secret weapon. Clays and humus are colloids, negatively charged particles that naturally repel one another and can very easily be washed away by water. To aggregate, they must therefore find another binding agent – a biological adhesive or mineral bridge. The former is produced by fungi and earthworm digestive processes: on their journey from the depths of the soil to the surface, worms produce them in their digestive tract, which secretes glomalin, a very recently discovered glycoprotein capable of binding clays and humus. This has transformed the way we think about the role of earthworms; the casts, or vermicasts (worm "excrement"), that we see on the surface are clays and humus that have been ingested and aggregated thanks to glomalin. They are essential for soil formation.

Mycorrhizal fungi also produce glomalin that is less visible but just as important: cations – positively charged compounds such as calcium (Ca^{2+}), magnesium (Mg^{2+}) and hydroxydes of iron - are released into the soil through physico-chemical and biological degradation of the bedrock and organic litter, and settle between the humus and the sheets of clay to form cationic bridges, forging a solid connection between them; this is how the clay-humus complex is formed.

The richness and depletion of viticultural soils

The clay-humus complex is the food reserve for plants and the secret to the fertile stability of soils - it is therefore, indirectly, the reservoir of life above and below ground. Its quality depends on its ability to stabilize the cations released by the processing of mineral and organic matter (potassium K^+, ammonium NH^{4+} and so on), large amounts of which are required to nourish a vine. This is known as its cation exchange capacity (CEC). The higher this quotient, the more it prevents these minerals from being leached away by water, and the more it can make available to the plant in one way or another. The clay-humus complex also gives soil a lumpy, pellet-like texture. The better the circulation of air and water, the higher its fertility and plant and microbial biodiversity – and so the more efficient its creation of soil in a virtuous circle.

Here it should be understood that these formation processes are complex and delicate and can be upset by any number of viticultural practices where these are carried out too intensively, including the use of pesticides that kill earthworms, fungi and bacteria; mineral fertilizers that disrupt the soil's chemical composition; ploughing, extrac-

Microbial life; or: Microbes are life!

Microbes "build plants, animals and civilizations", as Selosse pointed out in *Jamais seul*. Because we are part of the very small minority of creatures larger than 1mm, our size, and therefore our immediate field of knowledge, meant that we were unaware of almost all terrestrial species invisible to our eyes until the invention of the microscope in the 17th century. Once such species had been discovered, however, the legacy of Pasteur meant that we were determined to view them solely as pathogens, pushing back knowledge of the role they play in making life possible.

We now know that 90 per cent of the Earth's biomass consists of microbes, comprising something like a trillion species of which we know scarcely 0.001 per cent of their diversity and functions. We do know that they make up our atmosphere and soil, however, and guarantee the cycles of matter (nitrogen, carbon, phosphorus). They allow us to digest our food and detoxify it. They can make us sick, but they can also heal us. They have penetrated to the very heart of cells to create endosymbioses, giving rise to new properties and abilities. Humans, animals and plants are not isolated individuals but veritable zoos, microbial ecosystems. We depend on them, and they depend on us as hosts and shelters in a permanent but delicately balanced dynamic co-evolution. And let us not forget that without microbes there is no fermentation – and thus no wine.

tion and the de-structuring of soils and so on. It is known that French vineyard soils have become poorer, with average levels of barely two per cent of clay-humus complex compared with double that for vineyard soils in Italy's Trentino area, which has pioneered grass cover and the preservation of organic matter in soils.

Billions of living beings, from the surface to the depths

It took a long time to work out the mechanisms of the clay-humus complex, but understanding the living matter in soil has been another story altogether. We now know that just one single gram of living soil – from a forest, for example – contains at the very least more than a billion individual creatures belonging to more than a million species.

Who is lurking within this teeming crowd? The first to be identified are the macro-organisms that are visible to the naked eye: in the case of plants, these are roots and their hairs; and in animals, rodent and insectivorous mammals such as moles, or invertebrates. The latter are members of an extremely diverse range of families of which the best known are insects, arachnids (spiders), crustaceans, myria-pods (centipedes), worms and molluscs. These are classified by size, function or the depth of the soil in which they live: epigeic fauna, on the surface; endogeic, further down; or anecic – from the Greek, *anesis*, "elasticity" – to indicate that they move up and down between these layers.

The last group, not the smallest but the least well known and most mysterious, is that of micro-organisms, microbes that are between 1 and 10 billionths of a metre (10^{-9} metre) in size. They make up almost all of the millions of species we find beneath our feet. A distinction is made between micro-fauna, which essentially comprise amoebae, and microflora, whose astonishing diversity of species and biomass are as nothing compared to the incredible diversity of functions they perform. These include the algae, fungi and bacteria that, metaphorically, are the heart and lungs of the soil.

The microfauna that interact with roots

Vine roots are far from being alone underground; they rub shoulders with a whole subterranean crowd with whom they maintain extremely complex ecological interactions, these being classed as beneficial, neutral or harmful by their frequency, duration and nature. When they benefit all parties, it is known as mutualism or symbiosis; when beneficial for just one party and harmful for another, it is known as parasitism; and when harmful for all, it is termed competition. Certain interactions undergone by root systems are direct, but most are indirect and are mediated by the creation of the clay-humus complex and the supply of nutrients essential to *Vitis*.

The activity of this flora and fauna is now seen as a reliable indication of the life and biological quality of agricultural and viticultural soils. The INRAE Bourgogne-Franche-Comté research centre has even collated an inventory of bacterial

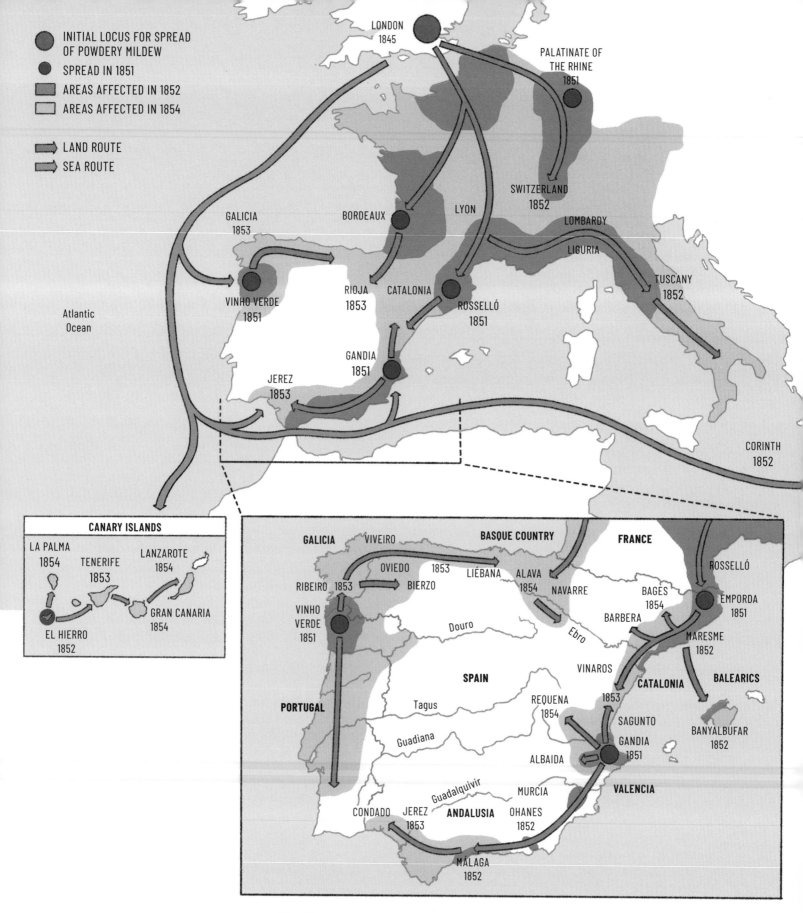

LEGEND

- INITIAL LOCUS FOR SPREAD OF POWDERY MILDEW
- SPREAD IN 1851
- AREAS AFFECTED IN 1852
- AREAS AFFECTED IN 1854
- LAND ROUTE
- SEA ROUTE

LONDON 1845

PALATINATE OF THE RHINE 1851

SWITZERLAND 1852

LOMBARDY

LIGURIA

TUSCANY 1852

GALICIA 1853

BORDEAUX

LYON

Atlantic Ocean

VINHO VERDE 1851

RIOJA 1853

CATALONIA

ROSSELLÓ 1851

GANDIA 1851

JEREZ 1853

CORINTH 1852

CANARY ISLANDS

LA PALMA 1854

TENERIFE 1853

LANZAROTE 1854

GRAN CANARIA 1854

EL HIERRO 1852

GALICIA — VIVEIRO — BASQUE COUNTRY — FRANCE

OVIEDO 1853 — LIÉBANA — ALAVA 1854 — NAVARRE

RIBEIRO 1853 — BIERZO

ROSSELLÓ

BAGES 1854

EMPORDA 1851

VINHO VERDE 1851

Douro

Ebro

BARBERA

MARESME 1852

PORTUGAL

SPAIN

Tagus

VINAROS

CATALONIA

BALEARICS

Guadiana

REQUENA 1854

1853

SAGUNTO

GANDIA 1851

BANYALBUFAR 1852

ALBAIDA

Guadalquivir

MURCIA

VALENCIA

CONDADO

JEREZ 1853

ANDALUSIA

OHANES 1852

MÁLAGA 1852

THE SPREAD OF POWDERY MILDEW IN EUROPE (1845-54)

communities, the *Atlas français des bactéries du sol* (2018). Population-status stress, attacks and stimulation are all linked; vine health and disease depend on the balance of the ecosystem as a whole. Plants can cultivate their pathogens, because the diseases of one may be the friends of another; there is no such thing as a parasite in itself, but only ever in relation to other organisms. It is all a question of the regulatory effect and the balance of competition, although it is generally parasitic relationships that benefit from research because there are so many problems to resolve.

Among the microfauna affecting vines, particular attention has been paid to nematodes, as vectors of the grapevine fanleaf virus, a degenerative disease that is one of the major causes of global vine mortality. Not all nematodes are pathogenic, however; the majority of them, predators and decomposers living principally on the surface of the soil, are necessary for the regulation of bacterial and fungi populations and therefore for the breaking-down of organic matter.

Mycorrhiza – a symbiotic relationship that anchors a vine in its terroir

The microflora population that has been attracting more and more interest for some years is mycorrhizal fungi, first discovered by German botanist Albert Frank in 1885 and unveiled to a wider public in Peter Wohlleben's best-selling *The Hidden Life of Trees* (2017). Their existence is obviously far more ancient: mycorrhizal fungi have been cohabiting with plant roots for more than 450 million years. But viticulture has only recently begun to take an interest in this fundamental and universal phenomenon of the plant world.

Mycorrhiza is a symbiosis, a relationship of mutual benefit that springs up spontaneously between the roots and fungi. There are several different kinds depending on the type of interaction. In the case of vines, as with 80 per cent of all plants on Earth, it is known as endomycorrhizae (from the Greek *éndon*, "within"), because the mycelium penetrates the interior of the cells to form arbuscules (filamentous structures resembling a tree), which is where exchanges take place between the fungi and *Vitis*. At the start of this cohabiting relationship, the vine may react to the fungus as a parasite coming to steal its resources, but it soon understands the benefits of this symbiosis, which fulfils four fundamental roles.

Mycorrhizal symbiosis – invisible but essential to vines

This symbiosis is based on an exchange of nutrients; the vine produces sugars via photosynthesis that the fungus is incapable of making, and in return, its mycelium network explores a volume of soil that is up to a thousand times greater than that reached by the vine's roots, giving it much improved access to essential resources such as water, nitrogen and phosphorus, which it can assimilate only through the fungi. Research is increasingly highlighting fungi's involvement in raising the production of molecules of key importance in wine flavour, such as amino acids linked to aroma or flavonoids such as quercetin.

Fungi also provide protection against pathogens. Since vines are both their hosts and their homes, it is entirely in fungi's interests to safeguard the vine's good health. They trigger a variety of protective mechanisms through spatial competition, the production of antibiotics and the activation of the vine's natural defences. They also mitigate environmental stress, including water stress and certain kinds of chemical pollution, and are able to store heavy metals in their vacuoles. Last but not least, they help in aggregating the clay-humus complex and stabilizing the soil by melding its different elements.

> " Population-status stress, attacks and stimulation are all linked; vine health and disease depend on the balance of the ecosystem as a whole

Energy-saving – a universal principle

Vines are a special case in that they are plants that do not require lots of nutrients. The attraction of using mycorrhizae rather than a vine's own roots lies more than anything in an energy-saving calculation; what uses more energy: feeding fungi or growing roots? And the answer is, it depends.

A vine will indeed adapt to its surroundings and how easy it is to access essential resources. When it is fertilized, especially with mineral fertilizers, so that its main nutrients (nitrogen, phosphates and potash) are provided directly by the wine-grower, there is no need to feed the fungi, which dwindle. In so doing, however, the vine deprives itself (or is deprived, since it is subject to the decisions made by the wine-grower) of all the other functions of mycorrhizae; not only does the vine become dependent on fertilizers for its nutrition, it also becomes more susceptible to pathogens and abiotic stress in the form of heat, drought and so on. Of no use to the plant, the fungi alters its prophylactic and phytostimulatory functions. This is known as mycorrhiza-induced resistance (MIR), the study of which in vines is only now beginning.

An absence of fungi also affects the clay-humus complex and thus the presence of water and minerals that the plant can assimilate. If the fertilization "tap" is cut off, therefore, the vines struggle to protect and nourish themselves in less favourable soil, and are weaker and consequently more susceptible to disease.

THE *VITE MARITATA ALL'ALBERO*, OR ARBORESCENT VINES

Before vineyards were reconstructed post-phylloxera, a training system was in use in certain French and Italian regions that combined vines and trees. Subsistence polyculture was common at the time, and such plots were known in France as *joualles*, with vines, fruit trees, vegetables, cereals and so on being planted side by side. By the 20th century, agricultural consolidation and the rise of monoculture had replaced this type of intercropping almost entirely.

SAVOIE AND COMTÉ DE FOIX

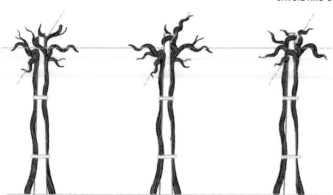

COMTÉ DE BIGORRE AND BÉARN

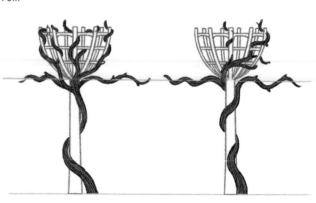

NÉBOUZAN (GASCONY)

TIVOLI (LAZIO)

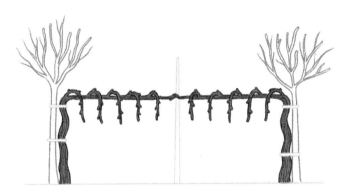

ORIGINAL SYSTEM USED BY THE BELLUSSI BROTHERS (VENETO)

SECOND ORIGINAL SYSTEM USED BY THE
BELLUSSI BROTHERS (VENETO)

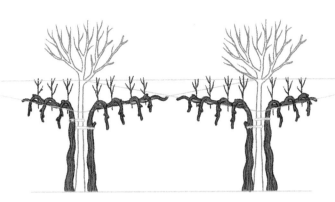

THIRD VARIATION OF THE BELLUSSI
BROTHERS' SYSTEM (VENETO)

SINGLE-FESTOON SYSTEM (LAZIO)

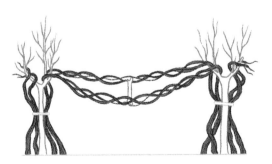

DOUBLE-FESTOON SYSTEM

HIGH TRAINED AND PRUNED VINE (LAZIO, ABRUZZO, TUSCANY)

HIGH TRAINED AND PRUNED VINE WITH MIXED SUPPORTS (CAMPANIA)

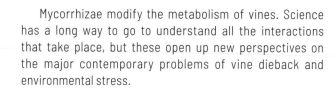

Mycorrhized vine plants

Truffles are the best-known mycorrhizal fungi. A truffle is an ectomycorrhiza that remains outside the root cells of the oak trees with which it lives in symbiosis. While truffles occur spontaneously in nature, their growth can be controlled by planting oak trees that have already been mycorrhized with the desired truffle: Perigord black truffle (*Tuber melanosporum*), *T. uncinatum* from Burgundy, summer truffle (*T. aestivum*) or white *T. magnatum*. Viticultural nurseries have also been selling grafted mycorrhized plants since the early 2010s – not for the fungus itself but for the vigour and capacity for bio-control and recovery that it provides. Spontaneous mycorrhization can also set in after a time, but the question of the difference between fungi imported from an outside environment and indigenous fungi is being explored, as are the development factors, even if it is assumed that a diversity of plant species in vineyards, each with its own mycorrhizae, is a contributing factor.

Mycorrhizae modify the metabolism of vines. Science has a long way to go to understand all the interactions that take place, but these open up new perspectives on the major contemporary problems of vine dieback and environmental stress.

The vine's rhizosphere – its own unique soil

It is clear that, far from being just a passive and inorganic substrate or an inert sponge, the soil is an aggregate of biological and physico-chemical processes in never-ending evolution. It is not pure, lifeless rock, like a sandy desert; it is formed and evolves according to its primary substrate and its environment in a process known as pedogenesis, and there is thus an age, a life, and a diversity of soils. It is the synergy of their elements that allows a certain type of vegetation to grow or be cultivated in soil, and *Vitis* thrives on a number of these elements in a remarkable fashion. Far from being deleterious and pathogenic, microbes are, for their part, at the heart of vital interactions, some of which may be harmful although equally also neutral or positive, but always striving for balance in an ecosystem.

In the heart of their root systems, vines play host to mycorrhizal symbiosis that is the source of many reciprocal benefits whose metabolisms are yet to be explained. This vast network of mycelia and roots is known as the rhizosphere and is the vine's own soil, in which other micro-organisms known as microbiota evolve, differentiating it from the surrounding earth. In the absence of these bacteria, fungi and other single-celled organisms, a vine would have access only to its immediate surroundings and would rapidly exhaust these solubilized resources. Thanks to all these other agents, vines have a field of exploration a hundred times greater. While some micro-organisms may be pathogens, the benefits derived from this cohabitation outweigh the downside: they nourish, protect, detoxify, metabolize nitrogen from the air into proteins, and regulate the growth and respiration of the aerial parts of the vine, which in exchange provide them with air and sugar. You might imagine them to be invincible, but the balances they strike are extremely fragile.

The time-frame of soil is not that of contemporary agriculture, and once destroyed, a soil cannot be recreated either artificially or overnight. The underground part of the vine is far more than just an organism; it is a complex ecosystem whose "community" is compromised by a number of the practices of conventional viticulture.

The world of vines above ground

Looking out over an array of vineyards with serried ranks of trellises, it is difficult to imagine vines in a landscape other than that of monocultural viticulture. Today, grape vines are grown in conditions of isolation created by the wine-grower in the interests of productivity far removed from their original nature as companion vines to other species. While domestication has altered the relationship of the vine to its soil, it has equally disrupted its interactions with animals and plants above ground, with the effect of making these less natural, even to the point of negating them under the pretext of protecting *V. Vinifera*. Who are these companions to the vine, and why are they so important to the viticulture of today and tomorrow?

There's no photosynthesis without bacteria

Microbes are everywhere underground, creating soil and nourishing and protecting the roots of vine plants, but they are also at the heart of the life of *Vitis* above ground. As with mycorrhiza, photosynthesis is a microbial symbiosis that is essential to the plant, whose foliage is not just green plant tissue but a "bacterial bloom" (Hallé). This concept was first put forward at the end of the 19th century by German botanist Andreas Schimper (1856–1901), but it was really the work done in endosymbiotic theory during the 1970s by American microbiologist Lynn Margulis (1938–2011) that established it on the intellectual map: photosynthetic cells contain chloroplasts, originally an endosymbiosis, the engulfment of photosynthetic cyanobacteria by an early eukaryotic cell. Chloroplasts with their high concentration of chlorophyll are responsible for photosynthesis. Unlike human cells, which are in direct contact with one another, there are gaps around plant cells that permit the circulation of O_2 and CO_2 and also provide a habitat for microbes.

As evolution progressed, bacteria colonized the gaps and then penetrated into the cells themselves. As a strategy of self-preservation, cyanobacteria found refuge in the ancestors of our green plants and remained there, becoming phagocytized – eaten, as it were – in order to survive under the protection of their host cells; in return, they endowed their hosts with new physiological abilities. Both entities continued to co-evolve while retaining their own DNA, resulting in a chloroplast that possesses bacterial genetics and carries out photosynthesis inside the cells of the leaf, which has its own genome.

The same is true for us, in fact, but with respiration; microbes are on our skin and in our bellies, but also at the core of our cells: these breathe thanks to our mitochondria, the product of endosymbiosis with bacteria.

A hundred million bacteria per gram of leaf

There are said to be one hundred million bacteria for every gram of leaf. Discoveries such as these have led scientists to realize the limitations of certain concepts, such as that of "organism", in understanding such phenomena. No organism – animal, plant or vine – is an entity in itself, existing alone; everything is intrinsically connected to micro-organisms. A new concept was required – the holobiont, defined as "an ensemble made up of an organism and the micro-organisms that it shelters" (Selosse, *Jamais seul*).

Vines are holobionts, or supraorganisms; they don't exist alone or in isolation. A proper understanding of this involves identifying the other agents with which they are constantly interacting, their function and their ecology. Like mycorrhizal fungi, the microbial populations that occupy the aerial parts of the vine are fragile and delicately balanced. Are they pathogenic or beneficial? Do we know what they are? We are aware of the problems that may be posed by the use of fungicides with active ingredients that are not so discerning in respect of the "enemy" to be eradicated; these can wipe out vine pathogens, but they can also weaken the plant or even affect the fermentation of wine.

Vines are the victims of parasitic relationships…

As a result of the Pasteurian approach that viticulture inherited, the microbiota of the vineyard were first viewed as a pathogen. Although *V. vinifera* is a relatively resistant plant, its domestication exposed it to a growing number of micro-organisms that put viticultural production as a whole in danger, with downy mildew and powdery mildew, which are present in every vineyard, being two of the most harmful fungi. Having arrived from America, they began to contaminate European vineyards in the mid-19th century, in particular in 1845 and 1879. By attacking all the vine's green organs, they can cause a total loss of the harvest. Combating these two diseases accounts for almost all of the fungicidal treatments used in French vineyards – synthetic molecules, of sulphur for powdery mildew and copper for downy mildew in organic and biodynamic agriculture – with knock-on effects on other micro-organisms.

> " The training system known as arbustive or hautain has been described poetically as a *vite maritata all'albero*, a "vine married to a tree"

A number of other vine diseases have microbial origins: bacteria (including Pierce's disease), phytoplasms (flavescence dorée) and fungi (black rot, botrytis, esca, root rot and others). Biochemical control solutions have been developed against the majority of these, but it is now acknowledged in every case that controlling them will require prevention and a better understanding of the ecological interactions within the biotope of the vineyard as a whole, and not in isolated treatments.

... but are in part cared for by microbes

Research is now beginning to focus on biocontrol solutions using microbes with a view to reducing the use of phytosanitary products, although the initial results are still anything but conclusive. *Trichoderma* fungi have thus been studied in the fight against wood diseases esca, black dead arm and eutypiosis. Yeasts (*Metschnikowia fructicola*), bacteria (*Bacillus pumilus*) and amoebae (*Willaertia magna C2c Maky*), not to mention insects and mites, may also feature in the remedies designed to help tackle historic vine diseases. Some producers are even using a mixture of yeasts and phototrophic or lactic bacteria to protect and stimulate the plant; the name for these is Effective Microorganisms, or EM®.

All these avenues of enquiry into vine health have been enhanced by discoveries relating to other microbial populations that have been the focus of significant interest since the turn of the millennium, because the yeasts and bacteria living in vineyards play a role in fermentation. Does the use of fungicides hinder vinification by killing infestations? Are these micro-organisms part of the terroir and a link to the wine's origins? These are hot-button topics in the scientific world, and a minority of specialists in microbial ecology have joined certain winemakers who practise spontaneous fermentation in thinking that this is indeed the case. Research based on genetic sequencing has revealed "microbial terroirs" that are in no way random, with specific taxa of yeasts and bacteria, but these results have been contradicted by many other studies.

Trees and shrubs are essential companions for *Vitis*

In addition to the invisible microbial world, vines live alongside other flora and fauna that are more familiar to us in that we can at least see them. Phytosociology is the science of the interactions between a plant and its environment in the wild. This form of study is biased, however, in the case of *V. vinifera*, because the vine is domesticated and vineyards are anthropogenic environments. It takes a wild vine to make us realize that trees and shrubs are essential companions of the vine, protecting it from flooding and allowing it to take root and climb with little need for lignification, since the solidity of a tree's trunk provides ample climbing support. *Vitis* is the commensal companion of a tree above ground, and there may even be mutual benefit below the surface. So why don't we see trees in vineyards?

The relationship between vines and trees has had a chequered past that is now being rediscovered with the reappearance of viti-agroforestry, a new term that describes an old form of viticulture: trees disappeared from vineyards only recently, as has been pointed out by Léa and Yves Darricau in *La Vigne et ses plantes compagnes* (2019). To produce healthy fruit, vines must climb up toward the light and escape the dampness of the grass. The first wine-growers soon developed pruning and trellising techniques in order to allow this. If the environment is hot and dry, with scattered woodland, vines have less competition and vines are trained in a goblet shape with no trellis. (This method is known as head-pruning and is a Graeco-Oriental legacy to be found along the Mediterranean coast.) If the climate is cool and damp, however, with dominant forestation, support must be used – either dead, in the form of stakes, or living, in the form of trees. This training system is called *arbustive* or *hautain* and is a legacy of the Etruscans, a central Italian people who preceded the Romans. It has been described poetically as a *vite maritata all'albero*, a "vine married to a tree".

From the *joualle* system to re-parcelling of land

The *vite maritata* training system, which is suitable for wooded wine-growing regions such as Tuscany, spread throughout Europe, driven more by the economics of vineyards than by their environment, since the selection of methods to support the vines was dependent on financial means: wealthy proprietors could afford to pay for vast numbers of stakes and labour. It was the less wealthy who resorted to trees and complantation, combining growing

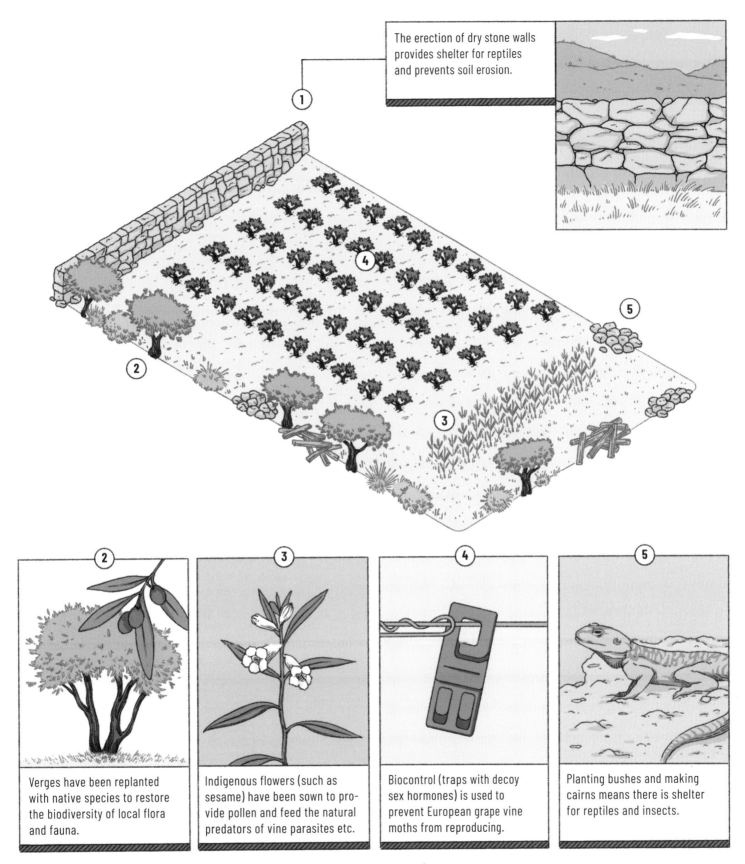

1 The erection of dry stone walls provides shelter for reptiles and prevents soil erosion.

2 Verges have been replanted with native species to restore the biodiversity of local flora and fauna.

3 Indigenous flowers (such as sesame) have been sown to provide pollen and feed the natural predators of vine parasites etc.

4 Biocontrol (traps with decoy sex hormones) is used to prevent European grape vine moths from reproducing.

5 Planting bushes and making cairns means there is shelter for reptiles and insects.

THE AGROLIFE PROJECT IN THE VILLAGE OF LÁNIA, CYPRUS

This has involved the adoption of sustainable viticultural techniques – the replantation of native trees, the creation of shelter for local fauna and so on – to preserve the biodiversity of the island's traditional vineyards.

The aromas arising from the vine's companion plants

Martha's Vineyard Cabernet Sauvignon is a cinch to identify, even blindfolded; the wine from Heitz Cellar, a legendary estate in the Napa Valley, has a bouquet of camphor that many find easy to recognize. What causes it? The giant eucalyptus trees that surround the vineyards were long thought to be the culprit, until more research by Dimitra Capone at the Australian Wine Research Institute showed that this is not the full story. There is a connection, but the relationship is indirect rather than direct – previous experiments had been carried out only in a laboratory, not under real-life conditions, making the results limited and not adapted. This aroma (1.8-cineole, or eucalyptol) is a volatile terpene secreted by the trees and emitted as a chemical gas. The vine is unaffected by this, but the chemical nonetheless settles on the arms of the plant and is absorbed more by the stems than by the berries. Capone's research further suggests that the notes of menthol discernible in the finished wines may also come from leaves that were not sorted during harvest and that have been vinified with the grapes.

In Italy, Diego Tomasi has demonstrated the influence of blackberry plants on the aromatics of Pinot Noir (*Influence of Blackberry Plants on the Aroma Profile of* Vitis vinifera *L. cv. Pinot Noir*, 2017). Here too, however, the study was conducted in a laboratory rather than on the ground, in vineyards. Should such research be halted? While the aromas of a wine are attributed to its cépage, vintage and vinification, perhaps the companion plants of a vine should also be considered as part of the influence of terroir? Research here has only scratched the surface, although in 2021 Canadian François Chartier, in collaboration with his Chartier World LAB and the University of Barcelona, inaugurated the professorship of Gastronomía y Aromas to address this fascinating subject, among others.

vines with vegetables and cereals in a self-sustaining agricultural system known as *joala* or *joualle* in which each plant has to benefit the others.

In the subsistence economy that existed up until the world wars, the trees were clearly not chosen at random. Taking inspiration from the forest species naturally favoured by *Vitis*, the trees selected were hardy and able to withstand hard and frequent pruning (which was necessary to let in sufficient light for the vine) and were of course multifunctional. They could also provide food for the family or livestock, as well as viticultural tools in the form of stakes, barrels, ties, presses and sacks, or domestic materials like firewood or timber, while also being sources of potential additional income. This method of vine cultivation was widespread across the entire continent until phylloxera arrived. From the Roman era onward, however, these practices had attracted criticism from agronomists for limiting harvest quantities. The vines had to compete for water, light, and nutrition. Criticism gathered pace in the 19th and 20th centuries, and monoculture imposed itself gradually as land was consolidated.

Trees – and the benefits they provide – have been driven out by monoculture

As trees became less of a resource to the wine-grower and more of a nuisance, the study of their potentially beneficial relationships with vines was sidelined. Their importance in viticulture was not reconsidered until the 1980s, with the pioneering pilot estate at Restinclières, in the Hérault region of France, being a groundbreaking example. So what do we know today? We now recognize that trees are home to a whole host of natural predators of creatures that ravage vines but they bring even more benefits, helping to create and maintain soils via their root systems, acting as firebreaks and wind protection, and mitigating extreme weather events by providing shade. So in addition to their aesthetic value, they are of genuine ecological interest to vineyards.

What about potential symbioses with vines, however? We know almost nothing about these because it has attracted very little interest as an area of research to date, leaving wine-growers having to act on promising hunches involving pairings that may be alimentary, prophylactic, aromatic or otherwise. This all looks forward to wines and landscapes that are more complex and more beautiful.

Is grass an enemy of the vine?

After having been removed on a regular basis for centuries by mechanical means or with chemical herbicides, grass is also beginning to reappear in vineyards, even becoming a compulsory specification for certain AOCs. We are gradually beginning to recognize its virtues, but why was it historically shunned?

Plant cover competes for water, nitrogen and the nutrients present in the top layer of the soil where its short roots grow, while its moisture content also increases the risk of frost and rot. That is why pruning, tilling, ploughing and de-turfing among other techniques are all used by wine-growers to get rid of these "enemy" plants. However, the condition of modern soils and the intensity with which they are now worked, both in frequency of tilling and to what depth, have little to do with pre-industrial cultivation methods; the alarming deconstruction of soils since the "green revolution" paradoxically calls for grass and plant cover to come to the rescue in an attempt to revitalize them.

From "weeds" to "adventitious plants"

Not only grass but a remarkable diversity of other plants is now being subjected to very serious scrutiny in an effort to get disrupted cycles back on an even keel while maintaining the volume and quality of harvests required to keep wine estates afloat. Plants that grow spontaneously the moment we stop pulling them up are described as "weeds", but behind this term, with all its negative connotations, there lie what scientists now prefer to call "adventitious bio-indicators" – plants that are harmful only in the specific context of production and that, more often than not, prove to be neutral or even beneficial. They reveal the otherwise invisible condition of the soil, its excesses and deficiencies, and naturally strive to restore the ecosystem in which they find themselves to a balanced state known as homeostasis.

This can take years and affect yields, and there can be considerable differences within the same parcel of land, depending on the pedology (evolution of the soil) and the type of viticulture. By turning over the soil superficially, for example, ploughing may select for "steppe" species, adapted to dry and bright conditions, and "heritage" species (so-called because they are dependent on agricultural practices) which grow in the depths below tilled soil: these may be bulbs, such as tulips and anemones, or alliums such as wild garlic or *Allium polyanthum*, a wild onion known as *baragane* and a delicacy in Bordeaux. Knowing how to read these plants in order to control them is a precious skill, as explored in the works of botanist Gérard Ducerf, whose *Encyclopédie des plantes bio-indicatrices* (2005) addresses this.

Bio-indicator and healing plants

What do these plants bring to the table? They often detoxify; their roots restructure the soil by promoting the presence of subterranean flora and fauna that loosen and improve it; and they increase the content of organic matter, creating humus. They may even reduce the vine's vulnerability to certain diseases. To accelerate this process of symbiotic revitaliza-tion, more and more wine-growers are choosing to sow "green fertilizers". These may be plants with roots that de-compact and aerate the soil, such as brassicas (cruciferous vegetables) or poaceae or gramineae (grasses); nitrogen-fixers, such as legumes; melliferous flowers to attract pollinators; or others besides. We have long been familiar with their general benefits, although more recently, other plants have been attracting the attention of agronomists with their ability to combat the threats specific to vines – metallophyte plants can grow on soils contaminated with metals such as copper, for example, and decontaminate them in a process known as phytoremediation.

> " A farm run on "vitipastoralism" harnesses the natural synergies of diversified ecosystems and of companionships both visible and invisible

Other studies have concentrated on the insecticide or insectophile properties of certain species: legumes and fabaceae (alfalfa and hairy vetch) and poaceae (oats) planted in soils on fallow land contaminated by the grape-vine fanleaf virus seem to reduce the population of the nematodes that infest it. When combined with other techniques – like resting parcels of land after uprooting vines, the choice of rootstocks and so on – this seems a promising avenue of opportunity for reducing the use of synthetic chemical additives while promoting biodiversity and revitalization of the soil.

Exploration of the direct relationships between vines and their plant companions – and thus of the influence of certain plants that diffuse aromatic molecules to modify the organoleptic characteristics of grapes, and hence wines – has therefore only just begun. How can we work with these ground-cover plants that are among the sine qua nons of the viticulture of tomorrow?

Vine fauna – pests and helpers

Animals are the last of the vine companions on the list. Their presence and diversity depend on the region in which the vineyard is located and the degree to which the environment has been anthropized. When grown as a monoculture, vines are a highly delicate and extremely simplifed artificial agro-system under constant cultivation; a vineyard is home to a narrower variety of species because it can provide them with neither food nor shelter. What is worse, if a species establishes itself and thrives, it becomes invasive because there is no competition. As with microbes, which we categorize as pathogens, the fauna in vineyards is seen first and foremost as parasitic, as pests to be eliminated.

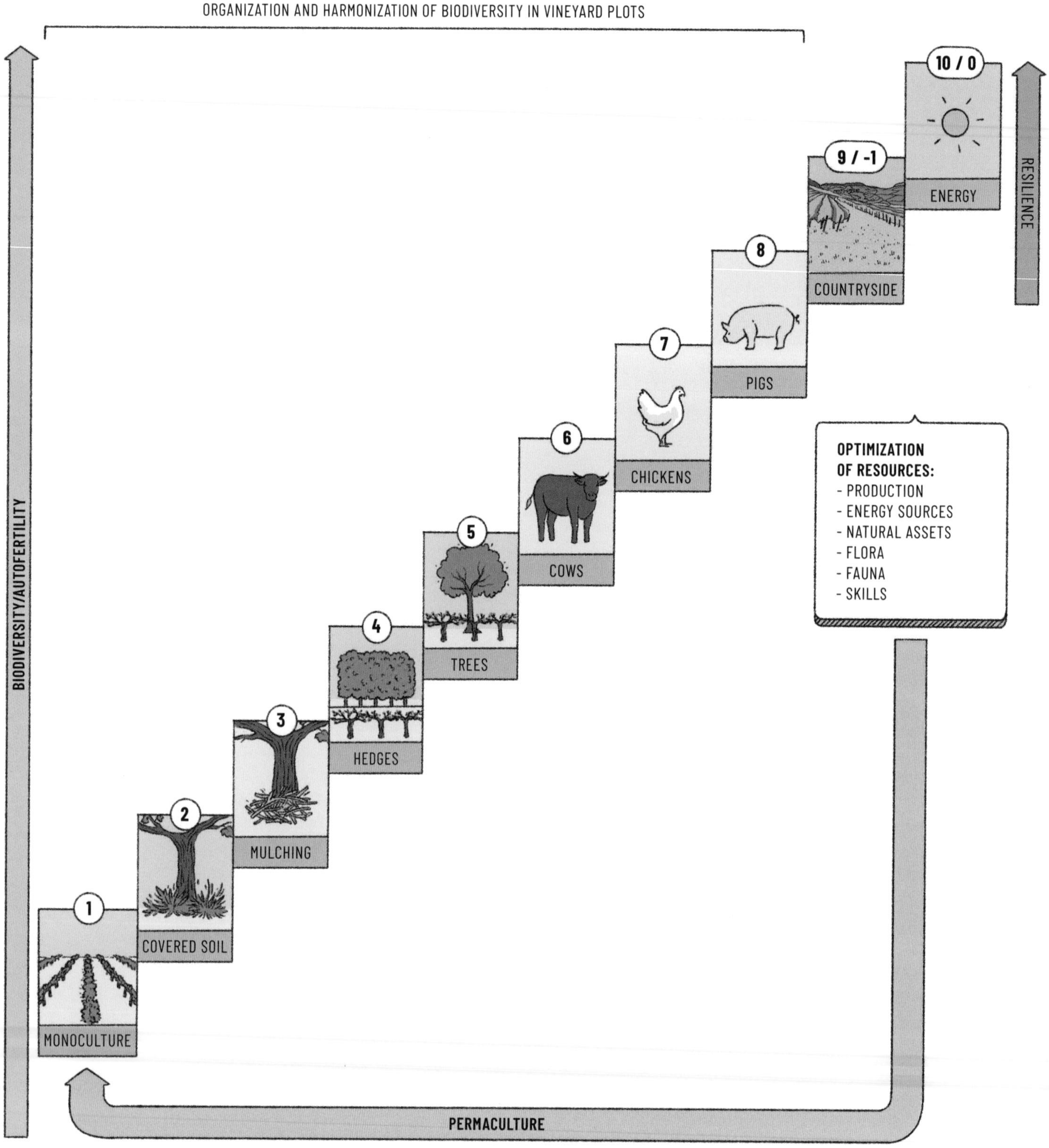

ORGANIZATION AND HARMONIZATION OF BIODIVERSITY IN VINEYARD PLOTS
BIODIVERSITY/AUTOFERTILITY
1
MONOCULTURE
2
COVERED SOIL
3
MULCHING
4
HEDGES
5
TREES
6
COWS
7
CHICKENS
8
PIGS
9 / -1
COUNTRYSIDE
10 / 0
ENERGY
RESILIENCE
OPTIMIZATION OF RESOURCES:
- PRODUCTION
- ENERGY SOURCES
- NATURAL ASSETS
- FLORA
- FAUNA
- SKILLS
PERMACULTURE

PERMACULTURE, ACCORDING TO ALAIN MALARD

Viticultural designer and permaculture specialist Alain Malard, the creator of this evaluation scale for the gradient of biodiversity, autofertility and resilience is a proponent of agroecology and the importance of a permacultural approach to the organization of vineyard plots.

Ecological interactions here are also more complex and rich, however, with mites, spiders, insects, birds and other mammals such as bats – the biocenosis of a vineyard is a veritable bestiary. Phytophagic mites and insects pose the principal threat to vines: grape moths (*Eudemis*, *Cochylis*, *Eulia* and the vine leafroller *Tortrix*), scale insects and leafhoppers. When their populations reach a critical mass, each of these insect species poses a threat to the vine at different stages of its life cycle: egg, larva or adult. To regulate the populations of these pests, we have to understand the reasons for their presence - the condition of the vines, an absence of predators, microclimatic conditions and so on - and identify *their* predators in order to help the vine. This latter group of predators belongs to a variety of species that may be generalists or specialists, occasional visitors or ever-present. However, in each case it is a question of balance; the population of even these predators must also be regulated by other species and so on.

Vines and domestic animals

In addition to wild species, domestic animals are also involved, giving rise to a modern form of viticultural pastoralism. Wine-growers may choose to introduce certain species, but unless suitable habitats are established for them, with a diversity of plants with which they can live, this can have only a very short-term effect. The success of organic pest control relies heavily on the re-creation of a diversified natural environment with a variety of species, through the reintroduction of grassed and uncultivated areas with hedges and trees. Sheep, pigs and chickens in particular have been reintroduced to vineyards to keep grass short, provide fertilizer or loosen the surface of the soil. The use of horse-drawn ploughs and animal traction is becoming popular once again, involving biodiversity, less compaction of the soil and lower use of fossil fuels.

The polycultural farm, a central element of biodynamic agriculture in which animals, plants and humans interact in a self-sufficient system, are becoming a model or an inspiration even for estates that do not subscribe to Steiner's approach, in a form of "vitipastoralism" that aims to harness the natural synergies of diversified ecosystems and of companionships, both visible and invisible. It is thus an invitation to cast our net a little wider, as Erasmus – the humanist philosopher and author of the injunction *non solus*, "never alone" – had already summed up in the 16th century: "Like the vine, which, though the most distinguished of all trees, yet needs the supports of canes or stakes or other trees that bear no fruit, the powerful and the learned need the help of men of lesser station." (Translation courtesy of Elsevier.)

Restinclières – a pioneer of viticultural agroforestry

To the north of Montpellier is an agroforestry research centre that is unique in the world. The Restinclières estate is a 53-ha, open-air laboratory where more than 80 types of tree rub shoulders with vines and field crops. Since 1990, INRA (from 2000, Institut national de recherche pour l'agriculture, l'alimentation et l'environnement, INRAE) has been conducting research on the interactions that take place here. A plot of land planted with Syrah and Grenache along with seven specific tree species (service trees, pines, alders, cypresses and pear trees) in 1996 has made it possible to observe a number of trends: greater production of biomass, a "climatic buffer" effect from the trees, very limited competition, and a capacity for biocontrol and detoxification. The scientists have been cautious about their conclusions, given the multiplicity of parameters and the unique characteristics of every terroir, but the results obtained seem to demonstrate that this biodiversity has had a positive influence, complemented by the aesthetic and marketing value of re-creating landscapes of complex beauty (albeit highly contrived, on occasion) to develop wine tourism.

Envisaging the viticulture of tomorrow

Is the very act of cultivating vines making them sick? While our understanding of *Vitis* has never been so sophisticated and so widely disseminated, its ills come not as single spies but in battalions: vine dieback, climate emergencies, environmental questions linked to the abuse of synthetic chemistry – vines are in a bad way. But exactly which vines are we talking about? Every community has its own image of nature, an ethnobotany that is specific only to that group. Anthropologists and philosophers may study this, but the wine world is less aware of it. We can no longer think of the vine as a passive and isolated plant, however – they never grow alone and in fact can exist only within an ecosystem. Nor are they the sole tenants of vineyards; the land is shared with a multitude of species whose existence and roles are often revealed only through the excessive attempts of human control. How did we reach this point? How can we understand these species properly and integrate them into the way we work – and maybe even find some solutions?

Viticultural modernity and the hopes of the agricultural revolution

It is precisely the excesses of modern viticultural and agricultural practices that have exposed the limitations of our way of understanding and using vines - and natural resources in general. Post-1945, viticulture and agriculture were carried out within a context of major food shortages and economic challenges, and the wine industry was in a parlous state. Faced with a labour shortage that had already made itself felt before the war but had then been exacerbated by a decrease of population and an exodus from the country to the cities, priority was given to a search for efficient, inexpensive techniques that would boost productivity and assure the reliable quality and quantity of harvests. Bold initiatives addressing "quality" with a view to mapping, selecting, uprooting and replanting resulted in a total restructuring of the wine industry within just 60 years. Consolidation of land, the transition from poly-culture to monoculture and a mechanized management system for plots of land all radically transformed the viticultural landscape. From the 1950s to the turn of the 1990s, viticulture felt the benefits as the agricultural revolution intensified and the mechanization of vineyard work, often painstaking and time-consuming, was optimized.

The chemical industry's invention of synthetic phytosanitary products - herbicides, pesticides, fungicides and mineral fertilizers - accelerated, and their use was systematized in preventative and curative treatments with a view to obtaining healthy grapes and facilitating a transition toward high-quality wines with a designated origin in response to changes in consumer demand. This marked the advent of conventional viticulture, and until the 1990s, there followed decades of profitable production, acclaim and the certainty of the sustainability of viticultural terroirs.

From industrial viticulture to the necessity for "thoughtful" viticulture

Worrying signs began to appear from the 1970s onward, however, as public and politicians alike were first alerted to the consequences of chemical pollution by books such as *Silent Spring* (1962) by American writer Rachel Carson (1907–64). While the industry faced a major overproduction crisis at the end of the 1990s, other problems gradually came to take centre stage: the appearance of new parasites, the growing resistance to certain chemical treatments and thus their increasing ineffectiveness; an awareness of the destruction of ecosystems, the pollution of waterways, the erosion of soils; the risks to health for wine-growers and consumers; and more besides.

According to the most recent official French figures available (2002, published 2005; to date, there has been no official update), viticulture in France accounts for 15.6 per cent of the pesticides market and 3.2 per cent of workable arable land. The techniques and results of this productivist viticulture, employing industrial processes in both vineyard and cellar – use, indeed, abuse, of poorly planned synthetic products and increased mechanization whatever the ecological cost, with a view to guaranteeing a certain volume at harvest – became suspect within a context where the economic viability of an estate was beset by ever more complications. For reasons of image as much as of economic interest, ecological concern or social pressure, the age of viticulture that might be called *raisonnée* or "thoughtful", to be followed by "integrated" and then "sustainable" iterations, had dawned.

Changing practices, changing mentality

This thoughtful, reasoned approach aimed to apply phyto-sanitary treatments in an informed and controlled way with a view to limiting their negative repercussions for the environment, while guaranteeing production quality and economic viability. With support from the French authorities since 2000, a sustainable dimension has been added, entailing the controlled and quantified environmental and social management of resource preservation. Champions of organic and biodynamic viticulture have pointed out the limits of this, in particular the ongoing use of synthetic phytosanitary products.

This sustainable viticulture is making progress in vineyards through the introduction of standards such as ISO 14001 and the like, and labels such as HEV (High Environmental Value), but even today it is not yet in the majority.

Why might that be? In *La Viticulture durable, une démarche en faveur de la pérennisation des territoires viticoles français?* (2008), geographer Sylvaine Boulanger-Fassier explains it as follows: "That sustainable agriculture is not booming more is not due to technology. It's more a question of mentalities that are evolving slowly and a fear of change… Wine-growers will thus have to come to terms with taking more time to observe their vines; even so, certain growers still consider this observation time to be time wasted".

Short-term benefits, medium-term problems

The systematic use of phytosanitary products since the second half of the 20th century has eradicated famine in developed countries by quantitatively levelling out agricultural production and has also made it possible to cultivate crops on otherwise unsuitable soils. To return to Selosse's point, however, the benefits accruing through efficiency over the short term have disrupted the natural order and also created a double helix of dependence; force-fed with mineral fertilizer, vine roots have no need of the nutritional symbiosis they would normally maintain with mycorrhizal fungi. By no longer nourishing the fungi, the roots lose part of their immune protection, creating a need for more pesticides that will affect helpful and harmful organisms alike, reducing still further the beneficial action of mutual assistance, and so the cycle continues.

So the question is not a matter of knowing why we started using these products and applying this logic – without them, the world would not be where it is today – but rather of asking why we systematically continue to resort to them when their harmful consequences are known? There is absolutely no doubt that it is to ensure a certain production volume at lower cost.

The limits of the concept of vines as tools of production

In reality, the vast majority of approaches to viticulture (conventional, *raisonnée*, sustainable; even organic and biodynamic when they adopt an industrial model) share a similar idea of vines and their relationships with their environment. They take a naturalist view of *Vitis* in which this inanimate plant follows set natural laws that allow it to be controlled, making it possible to anticipate the consequences of viticultural intervention, just as with any tool. Unlike us, vines are not free to behave and grow as they wish, and they have neither intelligence nor free will, with no choice but to be governed by brute necessity alone. Hence they may be seen simply as a tool of production, and by the same token, it is our duty to ourselves as conscious beings to preserve them.

This world-view seems to have become a truth universally acknowledged since it has been shared by prevailing Western philosophies for centuries, and yet it has been challenged by numerous thinkers and scientists since the 1980s. How can we think differently about nature, and thus about vines? Can this paradigm shift bear fruit and suggest other forms of relationships with vines, and also other approaches to viticulture?

The naturalist "Great Divide"

Our understanding of the world is structured by a dichotomy between culture and nature, separating what relates to free human societies – customs and morals – from what is to do with physico-chemical mechanisms, universal laws that are predictable and knowable. Anthropologist Philippe Descola, who calls this "naturalism", has highlighted the implicit distinction that this idea entails: the existence of "humans" on one side and "non-humans" on the other; in other words, everything that is external to the former, that which people in the Western world still call "nature" and understand as resources belonging to them.

Here he joins philosopher Bruno Latour, who spoke of the "Great Divide" (*We Have Never Been Modern*, 1993) and identified the existence of not one division but two: the first, between "humans" and "non-humans" (society and nature, in

The intelligence of vines

In December 2021, Master of Wine Isabelle Legeron organized Raw Wine Alive!, the first international online conference at which agronomists, physiologists and geologists in particular were invited to present their work on living and natural wines. All appealed for a rethinking of our relationship with nature and the living world, and none more so than Professor Paco Calvo, head of the Minimal Intelligence Lab at the University of Murcia, Spain. Using chronophotography to study the growth of plants, he has laid the foundations for identifying intelligence in plants that adapt and retain behaviours. Aware of the criticism that this has attracted, he has suggested that the point of interest here is to realize that there are other forms of *sapientia*, of knowledge, and that we must extract ourselves as best we can from our anthropocentric vision to learn from these ways of being in the world and reconsider the hierarchies of living things. The vine would then become an ally, and no longer be just a simple resource.

other words), gives rise to a second that manifests itself in the notion of the superiority of "modern" humans, who have mastered the positive sciences, over the "non-modern", whose representations of, and interactions with, nature are nothing but naive and superstitious beliefs. We modern Westerners would thus be the only ones to have "privileged access to nature", to quote Descola, who exposes the limitations of this attitude in his *Beyond Nature and Culture* (2005) and identifies other ways of being in the world and other ontologies specific to other communities, including totemism, animism and analogism. The other conceptions of the world, which have a different understanding of the relationship with the Self and the Other, including our "nature", may prove to be sources of inspiration to get us out of our ecological impasses. Like Latour, Descola invites us to rethink the universality of the fundamental dichotomy of naturalism and its consequences, ethics and practices to suggest new policies that are fundamentally ecological.

Gaia, or the right use of nature

To counter this opposition, Latour makes use of climatologist James Lovelock's concept of Gaia: the Earth as a biosphere made up of all the beings that inhabit it and their environment. Gaia's creatures cannot live without her. She is a superorganism that inclines toward self-regulation, developing and maintaining life in a dynamic and permanent co-evolution. It is no longer a question of nature on the one hand, following its immutable rules, and humans on the other, exercising their free will. Everything done by any terrestrial being, any human or non-human inhabitant of Gaia, affects the Earth. The problem is no longer humans per se or technology per se but certain practices that entail unwelcome consequences; Amazonian tribes therefore have fewer responsibilities in the ecological crisis than industrial societies.

It is this question of how we use nature that philosopher Catherine Larrère and agronomist Raphaël Larrère address in *Du bon usage de la nature* (1998). This use can be good if it is ecocentric and sees humans as part of nature, fundamentally co-evolving with all the species to which they are related – interdependent and not individuated. Philosopher Baptiste Morizot in *Nouvelles alliances avec la terre. Une cohabitation diplomatique avec le vivant* (2017) has gone further still, positing a "diplomatic cohabitation with the living world".

Cohabiting with vines – learning how to live together

Morizot has identified a "crisis of sensitivity" in modern Western Man, whose capacity to observe and understand other living species has been considerably attenuated by the nature/culture dualism. He maintains that we must relearn a "new culture of the living world" in which other organisms are thought of as other ways of "being alive", with their own logic of existence (temporality, extension and so on) in territories that are shared. We live together intimately: we are different, there is an "Otherness", but we are not radically separated; we are interconnected. Fighting against our fellow inhabitants inevitably results in harmful consequences for all that may be direct or indirect, immediate or in the furthest distant future, as demonstrated by the current environmental crisis.

Morizot posits diplomacy as a kind of relationship. Where the modern mind sees only indifference, harm or utility, this win/win diplomacy attempts to understand intertwined interests, common causes and possible vital alliances. So vines are not just *our* tools of production, terroir is not just *our* environment; each of these is a cohabitation, home to a whole host of life, with ways of being in the world that must be respected if we wish to continue to benefit from the fruits of *Vitis* through this diplomatic approach to viticulture.

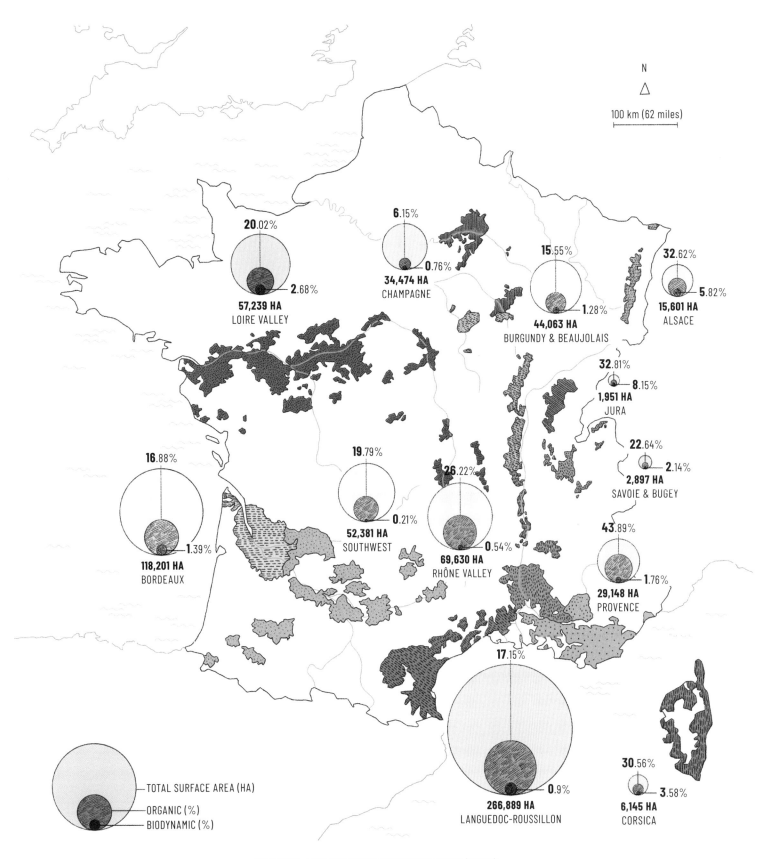

6.15%

0.76%

34,474 HA
CHAMPAGNE

20.02%

2.68%

57,239 HA
LOIRE VALLEY

15.55%

1.28%

44,063 HA
BURGUNDY & BEAUJOLAIS

32.62%

5.82%

15,601 HA
ALSACE

32.81%

8.15%

1,951 HA
JURA

16.88%

1.39%

118,201 HA
BORDEAUX

19.79%

0.21%

52,381 HA
SOUTHWEST

26.22%

0.54%

69,630 HA
RHÔNE VALLEY

22.64%

2.14%

2,897 HA
SAVOIE & BUGEY

43.89%

1.76%

29,148 HA
PROVENCE

17.15%

0.9%

266,889 HA
LANGUEDOC-ROUSSILLON

30.56%

3.58%

6,145 HA
CORSICA

TOTAL SURFACE AREA (HA)
ORGANIC (%)
BIODYNAMIC (%)

ORGANIC AND BIODYNAMIC VITICULTURE (2020)

This diagram shows areas of vineyards cultivated by organic and biodynamic agriculture, both certified and undergoing conversion, in France's main wine-growing regions in 2020.

Cohabiting with vines

If we are to renew our approach to wines and vines, we must imagine other forms of viticulture and envisage a form in which sustainable development is not merely a marketing slogan. To achieve this, we would have to establish "natural contracts" – diplomatic relations, as it were – with vine ecosystems. What practices might become common causes between us and these other living beings, these "holobionts", so that we can "work with" and no longer just "fight against"? What avenues could we open for the viticulture of tomorrow if we view it as cohabitation?

The paradox of the "natural wine" movement

Natural wine has become something of a phenomenon in the 21st century, attracting a reputation as a production movement that is both a source of enjoyment and a bone of contention. But is there not an inconsistency inherent in this term, as its detractors routinely point out? Necessarily cultivated and created by Man, who has domesticated *Vitis* and learned how to control fermentation, is "natural wine" not a contradiction in terms? Just like the "anthropology of nature", however (the title that Descola adopted for his professorial chair at the Collège de France), "natural wine" as a concept is illogical only within the context of a particular, dichotomous idea of nature that is specific to the naturalist vision of the world – and which is but one among many. The natural-wine movement reappeared in France in the 1980s and chose this name in an effort to "change mentalities".

In her book *La Corne de vache et le microscope. Le vin "nature", entre sciences, croyances and radicalité* (2019), anthropologist Christelle Pineau takes what seems to be a nebulous assortment of practices and skills and extracts guidelines based on a new idea of nature and our possible relationships with it.

The cow's horn and the microscope

According to Pineau, there are, in the first instance, dynamic and more or less fluid networks between wine-growers that nonetheless base "their common identity on respect for the soil and the environment, favouring preventative action with a view to moving toward autonomy for both vine and wine". In response to accusations of a lack of rationality, she answers that some of these wine-growers are in fact striving to link disciplines and methodological approaches to find alternatives to conventional viticultural practices. These "researcher/wine-growers" make use of both biodynamic and legacy rural practices, of microbiology, and of approaches considered esoteric in parallel with others incorporating cutting-edge scientific and analytical thought. This interdisciplinary approach has but one goal: to "reawaken sensitive awareness" within us, in order to understand the living phenomena involved in the production of wine when the naturalist approach begins to show its limitations. Nature is thus being reimagined, becoming both a source of inspiration and the objective of this activity "through which and with which wines with a 'primitive' feel are assembled". This involves acknowledging a "wild" dimension beyond the control of any kind of domestication and learning to perceive within this possible channels of communication.

Aligning with the work of plant specialists such as Calvo, Van Volkenburgh and others, some even feel that this will involve "de-domesticating" – a return to wild vines – to allow the plant to rediscover the abilities it has shed during its time of servitude.

Rereading vines and their ecosystems, observing their signals, sharpening our perceptions, accessing an intuitive understanding that is contrary neither to science nor to ethics but is based as much on instinct as it is on reason – these are the practices that will create the conditions for the possibility of a symbiotic relationship rather than just a parasitism in which the sole aim of viticulture is the production of grapes at any cost. This new "natural contract" is clearly not the exclusive prerogative of "natural" winemakers; it is the premise embodied to varying degrees in agroecological, regenerative, vitipastoral and biodynamic viticulture, and even in permaculture, under a variety of guises. Research is flourishing throughout the world, mutually enhancing and joining forces to pool ideas and resources, as in the Regenerative Viticulture Foundation.

The history of "natural wine"

Natural wine has no legal or undisputed definition; instead, there is a variety of meanings based on a common principle – an opposition to wines containing additives. Merchant and oenologist André Jullien (1766–1832) had defined it as early as 1816 in his *Topographie de tous les vignobles connus*: "A natural wine is one into which no substance alien to it has been introduced". He insisted on chemical purity, as did a group of German producers who, to promote their "natural" wines (in other words, with no added sugar), in 1910 founded the Verband Deutscher Naturweinversteigerer (Association of German Auctioneers of Natural Wines), which was to become today's VDP (Verband Deutscher Prädikats- und Qualitätsweingüter or Association of German Prädikat and Quality Wine Estates). Several years earlier, an ill-fated revolt by wine-growers in Languedoc-Roussillon in France had focused on a return to natural wines ("Wine must be the fermentation of the pure juice of the vine!") as opposed to "sugared wines" and modified wines.

The expression reappeared at the beginning of the 1980s, this time to differentiate such wines from "technological" wines that were no longer using only sugar but also added other oenological substances to stabilize and standardize the final product. This time around the approach also included viticulture. Observing the fermentation difficulties experienced with Beaujolais musts, chemist and wine merchant Jules Chauvet (1907–89) identified a link between the excesses of industrial wine production, grape quality, the ostensible necessity of additives and the taste of wines. After decades of work, he formalized the conditions required in both the vineyard and the cellar to bring about natural vinification with no other additives, so using only indigenous yeasts and no sulphur. This inspired the pioneers of the movement, such as Marcel Lapierre and Pierre Overnoy, who followed Jacques Néauport, a disciple of Chauvet; Chauvet never used the term "natural wine" in his publications, however.

Definitions nowadays revolve around one common tenet: natural wine must at the very least come from viticulture, such as organic and biodynamic farming, that makes no use of synthetic products and must be made without chemical additives or recourse to traumatic physical techniques like reverse osmosis, centrifuging and flash pasteurization. Only a minimal dose of sulphur dioxide (SO_2) is permitted. Charter marks have appeared on the back of the commercial success of such production, including France's AVN (Association for Natural Wines), the first of its kind, and Vins SAINS (Sans Aucun Intrant Ni Sulphite, "with no additives or sulphites"). Vin Méthode Nature, the most recently established, is currently the only one in France authorized to add the designation "natural method" on its labels, which is reserved for producers who agree to apply such an approach and to be monitored by an external body.

Observing and accompanying

What these viticultures all have in common is an understanding of vineyards as a complex aggregation of ecosystems whose diversity and dynamic capacities must be preserved in order to produce a harvest of quality, ensure the sustainability of the vines and renew the vineyard's resources. They question the use of synthetic chemistry: the principle of "a molecule for each problem" – a fungicide for this fungus, an insecticide for that mite, a herbicide to combat all the "weeds" – flies in the face of the idea that every problem is multifactorial and requires prevention as much as cure. It is a symptom of an imbalance, often with extremely complex causes, that must be understood, although it remains incomprehensible to some. Practical considerations require a modicum of humility in the face of the functionalities of ecosystems; it is not a matter of planting a vine and then disengaging entirely, leaving it to its own devices, nor of coddling it with extreme interference, but rather of "accompanying" it in its growth within a unique and specific environment.

The One-Straw Revolution

It is to ethnobotanist André-Georges Haudricourt (1911–96) that we owe a distinction made in 1962 (*L'Homme et les plantes cultivées*, 1943) between two types of legacy approaches to agriculture: a *direct, positive* one that is typical of the West, in which the cultivator is permanently making interventions with the domesticated plant, even if this means "overdomestication", and an *indirect, negative* approach in which there is little or no direct contact. Instead, the farmer creates a developmental space for the crop he is cultivating that is almost a "return to nature".

> " There is no one formula, but rather a host of viticultural practices with one common constant: a striving not to destroy ecosystems

It was undoubtedly no coincidence that it was Asia, Haudricourt's preferred research location, that saw the development of "natural agriculture" in the laissez-faire techniques of Japan's Masanobu Fukuoka (1913–2008), a microbiologist specializing in plant diseases. Growing disillusioned with chemical agriculture in the 1960s, he decided to experiment with a form of polyculture that dispensed with machinery, pesticides, fertilizers, ploughing and compost on his farm in Shikoku, limiting his interventions to sowing, mulching, mowing and harvesting, and he tells this story in his book *The One-Straw Revolution* (English ed: 1978). His method of "inaction", which he understands as human intervention carried out in full conformity with the laws of nature, calls into question both the traditional model of ploughing and the modern approach of chemical monoculture, which are viewed as a "desire to do better than nature" that in fact result in the destruction of natural resources and the loss of a sense of purpose in agriculture endeavour. For Fukuoka, agriculture is fundamentally a spiritual practice. Nature is a perfect, albeit entirely incomprehensible, model and offers everything necessary for human agricultural production to those who know how to observe and steer its symbioses. Not only are natural resources not depleted, they are enriched, producing a harvest comparable to that of conventional agriculture, according to Fukuoka's experience with rice, barley and citrus fruits.

Natural agriculture, permaculture and regenerative viticulture

Agriculturalists and other interested parties soon came from all over the globe to study this "natural agriculture". In their book *Permaculture One* (1978), Australians Bill Mollison and David Holmgren described "this sustainable agriculture for self-sufficiency and farming on every scale", emphasizing with such a term the will to produce enough for all.

How does this relate to viticulture, which in its essence is a highly interventionist monoculture? Practically no commercial vineyards are run entirely according to this method, but ever more estates are integrating certain aspects into their practices without losing sight of financial and human considerations. This is certainly the case with those claiming to practise regenerative viticulture.

"Regenerative organic agriculture", a term coined by Robert Rodale (1930–90) at the turn of the 1980s, aims to go further than organic agriculture: the goal is to actively regenerate soils in order to better activate the resilience of ecosystems, capture CO_2 and optimize the water cycle. This approach is ecological, but also social and economic, developing forms of agriculture that minimize their effects on climate change, producing sufficient quantity and quality, and guaranteeing social justice and equitable health for agricultural workers.

Whether in the US, Australia or Europe, the concept of regenerative viticulture has been spreading rapidly in the wine world for several years, with the primary notion being not to cultivate vines but to regenerate the soil and its entire underground ecology. There is no one formula, but rather a host of viticultural practices with one common constant: a striving not to destroy ecosystems, especially by ploughing.

Ploughing and no-tilling

More and more wine-growers are beginning to question the use of ploughing, that "inspired" solution that gets rid of the vine's competitors while at the same time enriching it naturally: the action of ploughing brings mineral salts to the surface while burying the organic matter that will decompose. Ploughing is in fact bioturbation carried out by humans, the mixing of soil horizons by hand on a scale and intensity far greater than when carried out by plants or soil organisms. The pace and depth of ploughing have accelerated since the boom in mechanization at the beginning of the 20th century, and the consequences that hitherto have been less visible are now becoming more and more apparent: depletion of the soil, drought and a loss of capacity to capture CO_2.

The Original Block at Eyrie Vineyards in Oregon, USA, the plot where David Lett planted the first Pinot Noir and Pinot Gris vines in the Willamette Valley in 1965, has not been turned over in 50 years; his son Jason has extended no-till to the whole 24-ha estate. He has noted greater plant diversity on plots that have not been ploughed for longer periods and has learned from studies carried out with the University of Oregon that this diversity is also reflected in the mycorrhizal populations. These vary according to their position beneath or between the rows of vines, suggesting links of mutual assistance that he feels would not exist with ploughing.

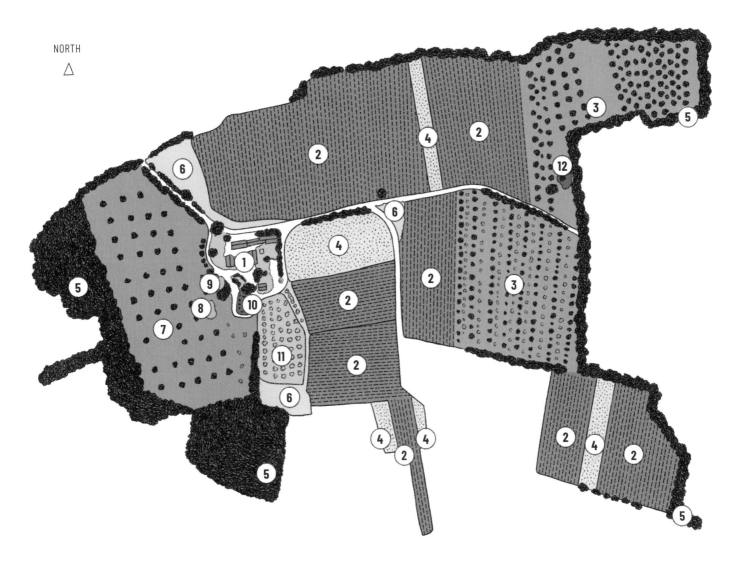

NORTH
△

1 CHÂTEAU DE FOSSE-SÈCHE BUILDINGS

2 VINES

3 AGROFORESTRY GRASSLAND

4 FALLOW LAND WITH WILDFLOWERS

5 FORESTED AR, OF WHICH 5.5 HA ARE OWNED
   (THE FOREST EXTENDS FURTHER BUT IS NOT
   ON THE ESTATE'S LAND)

6 PERMANENT GRASSLAND

7 AGROFORESTRY GRASSLAND PASTURE FOR
   JERSEY COWS

8 WETLAND AREA

9 POND

10 SMALL PERMACULTURE FAMILY ORCHARD AND
   KITCHEN GARDEN

11 NURSERY (CONSERVATORY) ORCHARD
   OF LEGACY FRUIT VARIETIES

12 BRAMBLES FOR HARES AND DEER

A UNIQUE AGROFORESTRY PROJECT: CHÂTEAU DE FOSSE-SÈCHE

Château de Fosse-Sèche, a thousand-year-old estate in Saumur, France, is a shining example of biodiversity preservation: of its 45 contiguous hectares, 15 are planted with vines and 30 are dedicated to protecting and developing a balanced ecosystem. The number of trees planted is far greater than might appear from the diagram (between 4,500 and 5,000).

Forestry engineer Mimi Casteel, Lett's neighbour, also practises "no tilling" and regenerative viticulture on her Hope Well project. She is convinced of the role viticulture and agriculture have to play in combating greenhouse-gas emissions and advocates no-till as a solution to capturing CO_2, while also insisting that this is just one element in the restoration of the fundamentally problematic ecosystems of monoculture. While no-till cannot be practised in every vineyard, because it requires specific environmental conditions, the question of the least disturbance of soils is becoming a central consideration in viticultural thinking.

From traditional vitiforestry...

Vitiforestry combines woodland plantation with viticulture. It has been practised since antiquity but disappeared with the restructuring of vineyards in the latter part of the 20th century, with the exception of a few traces here and there – a few hectares of Asprinio di Aversa DOC in Campania, Italy, are cultivated as "curtains" of vine shoots hanging down from the tops of poplars more than 10m (33ft) in the air.

This practice was widespread in central Italy until the 1960s but is now more folklore, having been replaced by pergola training. Other, less spectacular but more authentic forms of vitiforestry can still be seen in the Meskheti region of the Republic of Georgia or in the Cinti Valley in Bolivia – areas with little or no experience of the restructuring of modern viticulture.

Vitiforestry, which has been a growing force since the 1990s, aims to be more than just an anecdote: it looks to provide viable alternatives, taking various guises depending on the final purpose of production. The most advanced systems combine a diversity of tree species, heights and ages along with plant cover. The trees and vines can be mixed on the plot or planted alongside one another at the edges. A number of different agronomic benefits have been identified; soils are better structured, store more water and nutrients, and are better protected against erosion. Biomass

Vignenvie in Beaujolais: frugal viticulture

Three hectares of land in the Beaujolais village of Charnay have been managed in accordance with the natural agriculture methods of the Vignenvie association since 2007. Its aim is to safeguard these vines in the heart of the village by adhering to the practice of extreme frugality, limiting the time spent on viticulture, money and materials to a minimum. This involves 20 or so people spending just four weekends and a few days a year maintaining the vineyard. Éric Texier, the only professional wine-grower in the group, and his son Martin, are among the leaders of the project, whose progress has been documented in a blog (blog.vignenvie.org). A former nuclear engineer and an avid reader of Fukuoka and Mollison, Éric takes an active role in a project that is far from complete non-interventionism but rather a guided laissez-faire.

The plot was replanted in 2009 after three years of lying fallow; it is low density, with a diversity of clones and rootstocks, mixed natural plant cover, both wild and sown, that is laid down or mown when it gets too high, and a total ban on ploughing. Pruning, de-budding and trellising are reduced to a minimum. And they only use copper – 600g (1.5lb) per year, which is just 15 per cent of the upper limit for organic viticulture – sulphur and biodynamic preparations.

And what are the results after 10 years of applying these principles with no official scientific procedure? Low vine mortality, very low susceptibility to disease, an absence of water stress, a stable yield of 15 hl/ha (a little less than a ton per acre), between 11.5 and 13.5 degrees of potential alcohol and no problems with vinification. Four thousand bottles have been produced and sold for €5 after tax to keep them affordable for everyone. The next phase will involve pergola planting of one hectare with a new generation of hybrids including Artaban and Souvignier Gris to reduce the treatments required even further and allow year-round grazing for sheep.

is boosted thanks to better exploitation of light, water and minerals, with the root system returning nutrients to the soil, and organic matter increasing through the decomposition of leaves and foliage. The microclimate is modified – the presence of a hedge or a stand of trees mitigates climatic extremes, sheltering the plot from wind and sun; acts on the radiation of heat, with a slight increase in night temperatures; reduces the risk of frost; reduces evapotranspiration; and improves photosynthesis. Lignin is broken down more easily, feeding the carbon cycle and thus the microbial population. A broad range of insect species guarantees the longest possible period of flowering, providing room and board for a wider diversity of species throughout the year.

It is also important to use grass paths to link the trees, however dispersed they may be, to connect the different habitats. Château de Fosse-Sèche in Saumur, one of these pioneering estates, has implemented these practices throughout its 45 ha, which consist of 15 ha of vines and 18 ha of managed agroforest. It is one of the large-scale experimental projects that form part of Nature 2050, a collaborative public/private programme with firm goals to be achieved by 2050 in restoring biodiversity and promoting adaptation to climate change.

… to vitipastoralism

Taking this another step further, some wine-growers are integrating livestock, again in many different ways, with sheep, goats, cows, chickens and ducks, and more besides, either permanently in residence or just passing through. They may be led by a herder, be in an enclosure or running free: the idea is to bring in organic matter while keeping the vegetation down. The Léon Barral estate in Faugères in the Hérault, France, has pioneered such an integration of animals, and the approach has been followed by a number of biodynamic estates where the presence of animals is key.

In New Zealand, 59 per cent of the 37,000 ha of vineyards become home to thousands of sheep (the country has 27 million) during the winter months, and the results of this cohabitation have been collated in a study by doctor of ecology Meredith Niles. Focusing on the country's largest wine-growing area, which is famous for its Sauvignon Blanc, the work documented a unanimous response from the wine-growers studied. They included Brancott, the largest producer in New Zealand. The advantages outweighed the inconvenience. As they graze, sheep keep the grass short and also keep down herbicide-resistant plants; this lowers the risk of frost, since short grass is less damp, and reduces the use of herbicides and nitrogen, as well as the need for fuel. Some growers also make use of sheep to remove leaves. Last but not least, there are significant cost savings. The down-

side is that sheep may damage canes and especially trellising wire and irrigation pipes. The study is ongoing, looking at questions of biodiversity and ways of working the soil.

Viticultural agroecology

All these approaches can be grouped under the umbrella term of agroecology. While the word was coined by American agronomist Basil Bensin (1881–1973) in 1928, the science was only really to take off in the 1970s, thanks to the link established by scientists between our agrosystem and ecosystem, and then with the publication of the book *Agroecology: The Scientific Basis of Alternative Agriculture* (1983) by Chilean-American agronomist Miguel Altieri.

> Far from being a reactionary position, viticultural agroecology is an eminently progressive proposition that offers a real future

Agroecology may take different forms, depending on the areas where it is implemented, with powerful social questions raised in the countries of Latin America, where it is understood as a real alternative to agrobusiness and the problems inherent in the green revolution. This is why a social dimension is never far away in Altieri's definition of the term, in particular food sovereignty and security, and goes hand-in-hand with a critique of the use of agroecology for utilitarian, productivist ends, which would alienate it from its very essence. To be relevant and offer solutions for the future, agroecology must be more than just a "greenwashing" of industrial agriculture in its provision of ecosystem services, which in fact would be no more than a continuation of nature/culture dualism. Viticultural agroecology that is able to overcome such dualism has the potential to become a model for the viticulture of the future, with all its environmental, economic and social benefits, in a new ethnobotany of cohabitation. Far from being a reactionary position promoting wildness and "doing nothing" as a default option, it is an eminently progressive proposition that offers a real future for our modern viticulture. On the condition that we rethink the prevailing productivist model that is at the very heart of the problem, these are approaches to viticulture that may lay claim to offering sustainability for vines and production of wines that truly express the complexity of their terroir.

READING LANDSCAPES

Viticultural landscapes are without doubt among the most captivating in the world, as if man and vine had each found their ideal collaborator in revealing such unexpected beauty. Their layout and colours have a powerful ability to stir the senses, proof positive of both the extraordinary inventiveness of humans and the infinite plasticity of both nature and *Vitis*. They embody in their essence the notion of terroir, a powerful concept that has had many different definitions in various cultures through the ages. But how did it come about?

Vines are not found everywhere on Earth but grow in certain favourable locations that have been studied over the centuries. Are some climates more suitable than others? No doubt, but each new technological breakthrough crosses geographical frontiers of where vines can be made to grow that were once thought impassable. Is there a particular geology that suits them, with select minerals that transcend the influence of *Vitis* and provide us with access to "the true taste of the earth", as Colette puts it in *Prisons et Paradis*? The subject is far more complex and fascinating than it might at first seem. Ultimately, we still know very little about soil, its life, its inhabitants and the way it interacts with vines, because there is not just one soil but a thousand soils, and those in vineyards are far more anthropomorphized than we might care to admit. What if we were to follow geographer and historian Roger Dion in viewing vineyards as an embodiment of human genius and liberty, as social achievements rather than merely as physical terrains? In the same way that humanity has moulded and shaped vines, we have moulded and shaped the terroir to suit our needs and dreams – on occasion, without counting the cost.

CLIMATE

Meteorological elements and vines

Intuitively, we often describe wines by referring to the climate: we characterize wine as fresh and crisp, or mild and comforting, corresponding to ways in which the Anglo-Saxon world might describe cool or warm weather. These qualifiers are in fact indicators of climatic conditions that influence the acidity, alcohol, sweetness and tannins of a wine – and its aromas. This shows us that, over the long term, climate defines regional styles and grape-variety choices: these essentially depend on sunshine, temperature, humidity or winds. Vintage, an essential concept that has been valued since antiquity, is the ultimate expression of this over the short term. Climate thus determines vinification as much as it does high-quality viticulture; it is defined in the first instance by its meteorological parameters. What are these in the case of *Vitis*, and how do they shape viticulture?

A plant sensitive to agroclimatic conditions

Agronomists have made their position clear; as professors Alain Carbonneau and Laurent Torregrosa note in their book *Traité de la vigne* (2020), "The climate must be taken into account as a first priority in studies of the environments of vines, given the weight and multiplicity of its effects". While every cultivated plant is dependent on the conditions in its immediate surroundings, vines are one of the most sensitive. American climatologist Gregory Jones considers it "the canary in the coal-mine" – in other words, a bellwether of climate change in its environment. The way that harvesting dates have come forward since the 1960s and 1970s – by two weeks in Burgundy, and a whole month in Châteauneuf-du-Pape – is one of many alarming symptoms of climate change. In response to the climatic extremes the country is experiencing, Australia has equipped itself with a climate atlas known as *Australia's Wine Future* that is freely available at wineaustralia.com. This is a multidisciplinary research project aimed at helping producers to anticipate change in their vineyards by modelling extremes of temperature and precipitation. Observation of the current geography of vineyards shows us that there are zones that vines prefer but that these are also diverse; there is no one ideal climate, but rather many possible climates that first and foremost depend on meteorological elements, including light, temperature, humidity and wind.

Sunshine and light energy

Vitis is a heliophile – a sun-hungry creeping vine that needs precise exposure to solar radiation to ripen its grapes. Sunshine is especially necessary during the period when the berries are developing, between flowering and harvesting, because it triggers physiological reactions that influence the chemical composition of the grape and its yield. Good light exposure is also essential to the seamless completion of flowering and fruit set, affecting the coloration of the berries after veraison, as well as the production of sugar.

The duration of exposure and the intensity and quality of the light depend on several parameters that play a role in the choice of vineyard location and vine training. The angle of solar radiation varies with latitude, season and time of day; the more light vine leaves receive at a perpendicular angle, the more light they absorb. Above the 45th parallel in the northern hemisphere, pruning and row orientation are all largely arranged to capture the maximum amount of sunlight and ripen the grapes.

Cloud cover and the composition of the atmosphere also play an important role. Ultraviolet rays are a part of light, and they interact with vines in ways that are coming under ever closer scientific scrutiny. While they do not bring heat, their intensity and type, filtered by the thickness and quality of the atmosphere, affect photosynthesis and polyphenols. Their radiation is less obstructed at high elevations and increases by three to four per cent with every 300m (985ft) of height. Wines subject to such levels of exposure (those grown in mountainous environments, for example) thus tend to have more phenolic compounds and colours. It seems that the level of UV rays varies across the globe, however; certain regions, such as New Zealand, are exposed to 30–40 per cent more radiation than areas in the northern hemisphere at the same latitude. Higher levels of radiation increase the levels of flavonoids, including anthocyanins and tannins, in the grapes.

Light nourishes but also destroys; sunburn can cause leaves to dry out, and it scorches berries during extreme periods of heat or drought. Some estates in regions exposed to this kind of phenomenon, such as California or Australia's Hunter Valley, apply "sunblock" made of white kaolinite clay to their plants to protect them. In others, the shadows cast by trees, low walls or certain pruning systems such as head-pruning play a role.

Frost without sun

The energy deficit particularly associated with an absence of sunshine during the day, and then during the night, accentuates drops in temperature and so increases the risk of freezing. Frost is first and foremost a drop in temperature to below 0°C (32°F) resulting in a change of state in water to ice. It may occur under the following conditions:
• In autumn, after harvest (early frost);
• In winter, during dormancy (classic winter frost);
• In spring (late frost) – the time that it does the most damage, because it occurs when the primary fruit-bearing buds have already broken.

Frost can also take one of three forms.
• **Advection frost** is caused in northern Europe by the arrival of large volumes of cold air from Scandinavia or Eastern Europe, carried by moderate to strong winds. Generally affecting large areas, these conditions create a black frost that burns and dries out the buds through the combined action of dry air, wind and sunshine. In spring, this causes the blackening of tissue in buds that have broken. This type of frost is widespread.
• **Radiation frost** occurs in calm atmospheric conditions with very weak winds and clear skies. This kind of nocturnal chill is caused by the soil losing more heat than it receives. The absence of solar radiation after sundown combined with a clear sky brings about a drop in temperature until daybreak. This may lead to a strong temperature inversion when cold air remains trapped at ground level, especially in valleys. It may also result in the appearance of hoarfrost, with damp atmospheric water vapour turning into feathery ice crystals. This type of frost is potentially quite localized.
• **Evaporation frost** arises when damp soil releases energy through evaporation to achieve thermal equilibrium with the ambient air at 0°C (32°F). This is a rarer type of frost.

These different frosts often result in disaster, as occurred in France in 2019, 2021 and 2024; in each case, the absence or presence of sunshine played a role.

> " Observation of the current geography of vineyards shows us that there are zones that vines prefer but that these are also diverse

Heat

Temperature is a corollary of light. Soils and vines receive heat in pretty much the same way, although the type of soil clearly influences how it is received. The vegetative cycle of vines reacts to specific temperatures.
• **Below 10°C (50°F)**, there is no vegetative growth. The plant is dormant in winter or, if it has leaves, the temperature limits its photosynthetic activity to less than 25 per cent of its potential.
• **At 10°C (50°F)**, bud-burst may be triggered. This marks the end of dormancy and the beginning of what Galet calls the "annual favourable period", from March to November in the northern hemisphere and November to March in the southern hemisphere.
• **Between 24 and 28°C (75–82°F)** is the optimum temperature for photosynthetic activity, which begins to flag after 30°C (86°F).

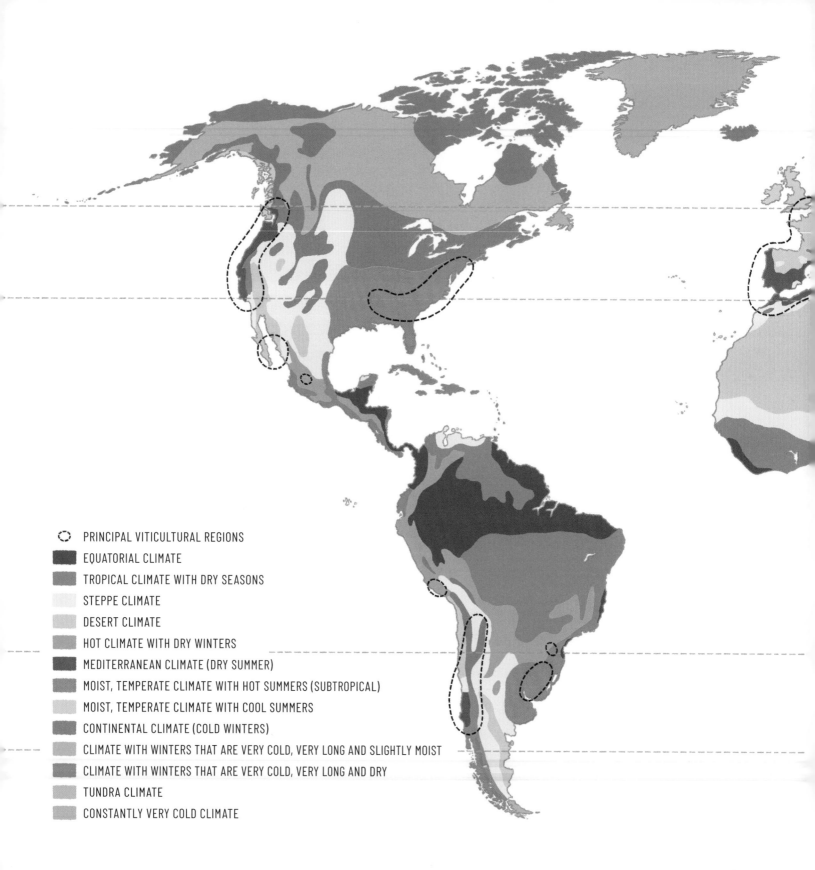

MAP OF THE WORLD SHOWING THE MAIN WINE-PRODUCING AREAS AND TYPES OF CLIMATE,
AS DESCRIBED BY ALAIN CARBONNEAU AND JEAN-LOUIS ESCUDIER

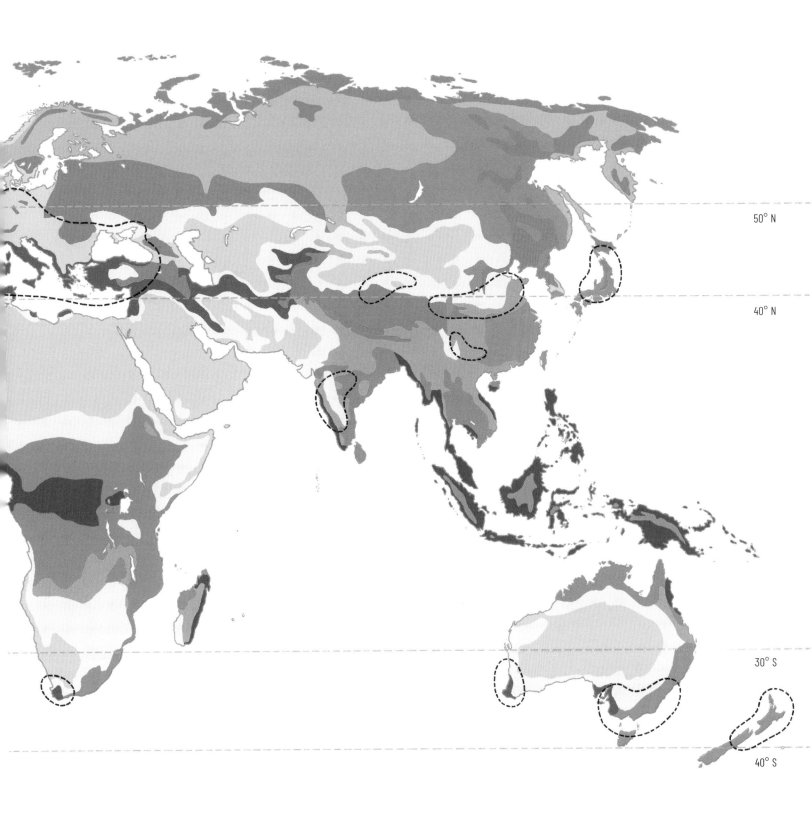

• **At 40°C (104°F)**, photosynthetic activity ceases through a surplus of energy and heat. The cumulative effect of these disrupts enzyme activity, the leaf pores close and tissues dry out.

It can therefore be seen that almost all the world's vineyards are located between the annual 10-22°C (50-72°F) isotherms. Not all regions situated between these two average temperatures are necessarily suitable for vine cultivation, however. Specific monthly averages during the vegetative cycle are required, especially in summer, with areas needing an average temperature greater than 18°C (64°F) and a certain number of days at higher than 30°C (86°F) to trigger physical maturity of sugars and acids and physiological maturity of polyphenols. In the maritime zones of northern Europe, grapes can only mature during exceptionally hot and dry years, unlike inland regions with hot summers at the same latitude. In other words, Normandy is not Champagne - it is too cool in the summer. Variations during dormancy are not so crucial, unless temperatures fall below -15°C or -20°C (5°F or -4°F) in winter: strains of *V. vinifera* can suffer fatal

> "Almost all high-quality vineyards also seem to have one other point in common: cool nights after veraison

damage, while American and Asian *Vitis* can survive down to -30°C (-22°F).

Almost all high-quality vineyards also seem to have one other point in common: cool nights after veraison. When nocturnal temperatures reach about 15°C (59°F), vines respire less and can use their sugars to mature their secondary compounds - their polyphenols, colour and aromatic palette - while retaining their acidity. Determining temperature norms and indices of maturity for different cépages is thus a highly complex business.

From temperature indices to ecoclimatic indices

Americans Albert J Winkler (1894-1989) and Maynard A Amerine (1911-99), who both taught viticulture at UC Davis, began to develop the Winkler Index in the 1940s. Assuming that temperature is the deciding factor in the quality of California wines, they calculated the degree days, in other words, the aggregate number of hours (rather than days, oddly) when the temperature was higher than 10°C (50°F) during the vine's growth period, from 1 April to 30 October. In this way, they identified five standard viticultural zones in California, which were then used primarily to categorize wine regions in numerous non-European countries. Their method rapidly revealed its limitations, however, because it does not take into account the length of the day

Ultraviolet and infrared light come to the aid of vines

While research on the role played by UVA and UVB light in the physiological development of vines is ongoing, it has already resulted in methods to combat certain fungal diseases and to shore up the plants' immune system. In both instances, techniques using robots were devised to expose vines to radiation of this kind. At AgriTech, Cornell University's experimental station on the Finger Lakes in New York State, phytopathologist David Gadoury has shown that ultraviolet light can kill downy mildew and powdery mildew fungi at night, when their defences against UV are inactive. Wine estates have been experimenting with this technique since 2019. With a view to boosting the vine's immune system, ecophysiologist Laurent Urban and physiopathologist Jawad Aarrouf, both lecturers at Avignon University, France, hit on the idea of stimulating the plant's natural defences during its vegetative phase: sustained exposure to UV light triggers the production of salicylic acid, a natural plant hormone that plays a key role in the vine's immune system. Vineyards in Bordeaux, Champagne and the Loire have been experimenting with this technique since 2019. Research suggests there is benefit in long exposure to infrared light to mitigate the risk of frost by inducing hyperthermia in the vines via electromagnetic waves, to warm the tissues of the plant. In all cases, use of the properties of light is part of the search for solutions that have a lower impact on the environment.

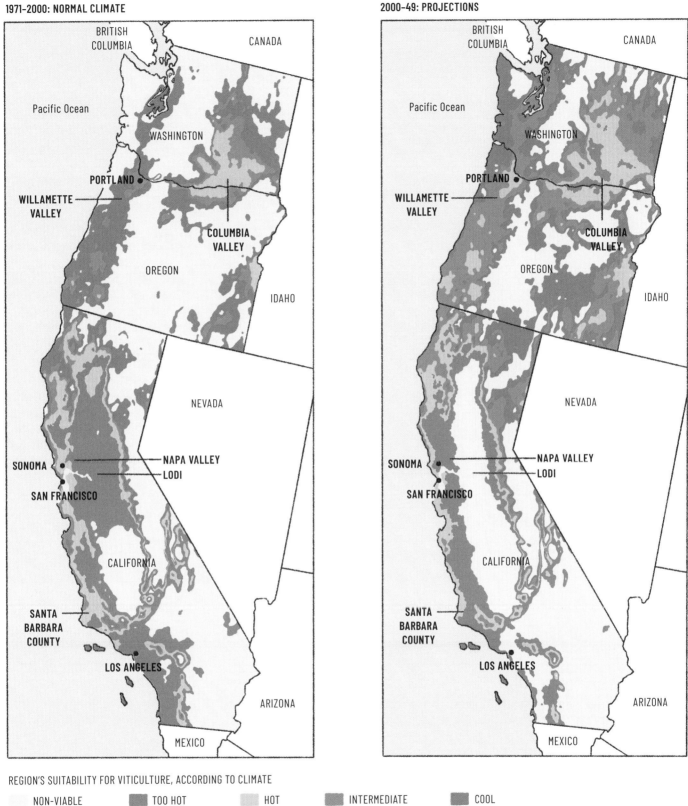

REGION'S SUITABILITY FOR VITICULTURE, ACCORDING TO CLIMATE

NON-VIABLE   TOO HOT   HOT   INTERMEDIATE   COOL

THE WEST COAST VINEYARDS THREATENED BY CLIMATE CRISiS?

In 2000, climatologist Gregory V Jones suggested that the location and cépage choices
of the historic vineyards on the West Coast would evolve under the influence of climate change.

The Winkler Index, soon to be updated

Warren Winiarski is one of the heroes of US winemaking: in 1976, his Stag's Leap Wine Cellars Cabernet Sauvignon, produced in 1973 on the eastern slopes of the Napa Valley, won the blind tasting known as The Judgment of Paris, beating the most famous Bordeaux wines of the time. In Winiarski's view, he owes his success to his reading of the works of professors Amerine and Winkler of UC Davis, on California vineyards in the years 1930–40, and indeed he used their writing on the Amerine-Winkler Index, or simply the Winkler Index, and potential suitability of more than a hundred cépages to plant his vineyard in the 1960s.

Alarmed by the climate crisis that was becoming all the more obvious in California, Winiarski decided in 2021 to get involved in financing an update of the famous Winkler Index. What was he hoping to achieve? To create a new grape-suitability index that would integrate every relevant climatic and environmental factor. Steered by the laboratory in the Department of Viticulture and Oenology at UC Davis, run by Beth Forrestel, a biologist specializing in plants, the project aims to renew the analytical model by re-evaluating the criteria for measuring berry ripeness. To achieve this, the researchers turned their attention to the vines' water status, their soils and the chemistry of the berries throughout the growth cycle, comparing these data with winemaking procedures and meteorological phenomena from more than 74 plots in the Napa Valley. Test vineyards were also planted in Davis and Lodi, making it possible to study the reactions of more than 60 cépages to heatwave. These new data have been compared and contrasted with the observations of Amerine and Winkler. The project, which has been supported by a number of local producers who see it as a practical tool in response to climate issues, will be extended to vineyards on the coast and in California's Central Valley over the next few years.

(included in the Huglin heliothermic index/HI, which is more commonly used in Europe), cloud cover (the insolation index, representing clearness of the atmosphere), the average lowest temperatures at night (the cool night index, or CNI) or even hygrometry (the dryness index, or TVMDI).

After writing his PhD thesis (1999), Brazilian agronomist Jorge Tonietto joined his doctoral supervisor Alain Carbonneau in presenting and publishing a new classification, the Geoviticulture Multicriteria Climatic Classification System, which incorporates the HI, CNI and TVMDI to refine the classification of winemaking macroclimates. Their analyses, which cover more than 29 countries and a hundred or so wine regions, are available online at embrapa.br/en/uva-e-vinho/ccm-geoviticola. These bioclimatic indices are nonetheless still too large-scale to provide a precise answer to the question of how vines react to temperature in all their varietal diversity. While a revision of the Winkler Index is under way with a view to incorporating this perspective, other types of "ecoclimatic" index that include plant phenology have been developed.

Since 2005, American atmospheric scientist and wine climatologist Gregory Jones has been developing a climate scale based on the qualitative potential ripeness of cépages and their different stylistic expressions. Refining the relationship between climate, cépage and high-quality wine has also been the concept behind the work of New Zealand agronomist Amber Parker since 2011. Working with international teams, she has developed two indices: the Grapevine Flowering and Veraison index (GFV), which takes into account flowering and veraison, and the Grapevine Sugar Ripeness index (GSR) which looks at the berries' sugar content at maturity. These indices were determined through analysis of 95 cépages and the climatic conditions observed when they ripened, and have since proved their relevance for application in correlating cultivars and wine areas as a function of climate change. More than just temperature analysis models, these are dynamic predictive tools demonstrating that vine phenology is an important indicator of climate disruption.

Water and vines

Vines consist of more than 85 per cent water, and their ongoing health and the eventual grape harvest are dependent on it. Vines transpire and evaporate 95 per cent of the water that is consumed during photosynthesis, with the remaining 5 per cent being used for all other physiological functions. This may be only a small amount, but it is essential. *Vitis vinifera* can survive and produce grapes while receiving just 250–350mm (10–14in) of water during its growth period, and even less in desert vineyards, but the majority of high-quality vineyards receive 400mm (16in) during this same period: an annual average of 600–900mm (24–36in). Any lower, and irrigation is required. It has been established that producing high-quality grapes requires a certain level of water stress, triggering the plant to produce abscisic acid, a plant hormone that redirects the vine's use of sugars toward ripening its fruit. While there doesn't seem to be an upper limit for precipitation to halt growth, too much water results in excessive vegetative vigour and both retarded development and asphyxia of roots, meaning a poorer harvest with lower yield and a risk of rot. In this case, drainage needs to be appropriately adapted.

The water balance – a complex dynamic

Vineyards take in and lose water in different ways through a dynamic complex of exchanges.

• **Rainfall**. The impact of rain varies according to its intensity, frequency and seasonality. Rain is crucial in spring because it determines the growth of the vines, but it can also affect flowering and allow diseases to develop and parasites to move in. In summer, rainfall mitigates the risk of water stress and can cause the grapes to swell just before harvest, but it can also increase the risk of disease. It can be decisive during the harvest period in autumn, causing more juice to be produced or accelerating the spread of *Botrytis cinerea*, which causes grey mould, and other fungi. Rain in late autumn and in winter has less of an immediate effect but replenishes water reserves and prepares for the following year.

The vine's capacity to absorb and react to water depends on a host of factors.

• **The soil's ability to retain water.** The more intense the rain, the greater the role played by the topography and the soil's capacity to retain water and so attenuate run-off – or in the event of drought, to capture and release water.

• **Ambient atmospheric humidity**. This is a potential aggravating factor for fungal disease, but it can also have beneficial

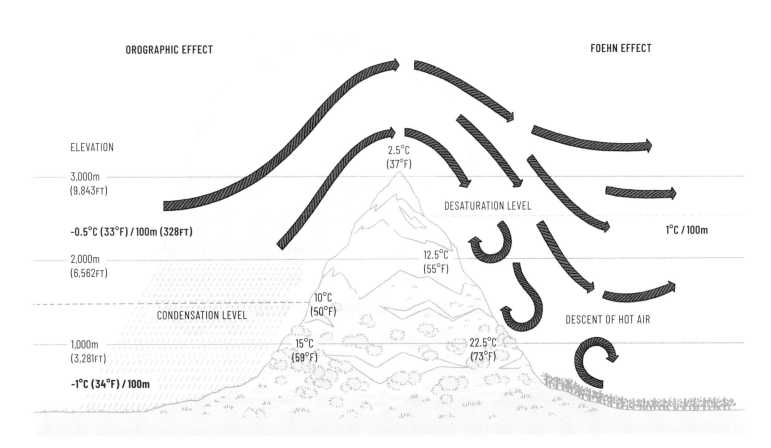

THE PRINCIPLE OF THE FOEHN EFFECT

The Foehn is a cold, damp wind that becomes hot and dry as it passes over high ground.

effects: in vineyards with no water source or water table, such as those on the island of Santorini, dew plays a key role because it alleviates the vines' water stress.

- **The plant's rate of evapotranspiration**. Air temperature and humidity affect the volume of evapotranspiration; vines transpire at variable rates throughout the day and at different times in their growth cycle.
- Finally, **certain extreme events** such as hail, which is historically rare in winemaking regions, are becoming more common, causing significant damage to the vintage but also to the robustness of the vines by damaging the wood.

Making generalizations about the water balance of a vine in any given region is complicated by the extent to which local parameters may vary, despite the large number of indices available (PET/ETa – potential/actual evapotranspiration; aridity index; hydrothermal index). However, we understand just how crucial the balance between water supply and vines is for obtaining a quality harvest, as well as for the best possible vitality for the plant.

Wind

Wind is often forgotten as a primary factor in quality viticulture, even though it is ubiquitous. It has direct consequences for vines and indirect effects on meteorological and geographical phenomena within climate.

Country lore tells us that a change in the wind signals a change in the weather. Wind can affect plants in a variety of ways: physically, by breaking shoots or weakening flower-buds; physiologically, by affecting evapotranspiration and slowing photosynthesis; thermally, by compounding water stress and drying out the plant; chemically, when the air is loaded with suffocating sand, or sea salts that can scorch the leaves; or of course pathologically, by limiting the sporulation of fungi, or indeed promoting the dispersal of their spores in the same way as it does with vine pollen. It therefore has an effect on the health of the vine and its yield, with varying consequences depending on the season.

Wind can indirectly moderate or enhance the effects of temperature – a slight wind reduces the risk of night frosts – and topography: it can play a part in soil erosion. Depending on its strength and frequency, wind can shape the profile of entire vineyards or simply influence the variations in a vintage. In western France, for example, gentle, damp West Atlantic winds of variable strength are the most important, directly defining the character of the wines and viticulture of Bordeaux and Muscadet. The influence of these winds diminishes the further inland you go.

Many winds have been given names, and some are associated with major wine areas or remarkable phenomena – for example, the Mistral and the Foehn. The effects of some winds are so significant that they define whole viticultural areas, such as the Petaluma Gap AVA (American Viticultural Area) in California, or the Van Duzer Corridor AVA in Oregon: in both cases, a gap in the coastal mountain ranges allows cool, westerly winds to pass through, amplifying the influence exerted by the Pacific, slowing down grape-ripening, preserving acidities and thickening the skins of the berries. In South Africa, the Cape Doctor (a "purifying" wind, hence its name) blows from False Bay toward the Western Cape, with the same impact as the winds from the North Pacific.

"Foehn" is the general name for winds of a particular kind, including the Foehn of Jurançon and Alsace. As climatologist Hervé Quénol explains, when a mass of air encounters a mountain range, it undergoes orographic lift. As it rises, the mass of air cools, and as the capacity of an air molecule to contain moisture decreases with temperature, precipitation is triggered. When the air is already heavily laden with moisture, having passed over the sea or over a large body of water, this rainfall will be intense. Once the air has passed over the high ground, it will have lost a large proportion of its moisture. It will then undergo a process known as subsidence (movement toward the ground) on the far side of the high ground, causing a wind that is powerful and very dry – the Foehn. This is a major phenomenon not only in France's Alsace and Jurançon, but also Oregon and Washington State (the Chinook) in the US, on the South Island of New Zealand (the nor'wester), and in Alpine wine-growing areas. It has a cleansing effect on the climate and extends the vine's ripening period. When the terrain is very high, as in the Andes, these winds can be extremely powerful and dry, such as the Zonda and the Viento Blanco. They are sometimes so strong that they can burn or break the buds, while the cold front of air that generally follows can increase the risk of frost in the Argentine regions of La Rioja, San Juan and Northern Mendoza.

Sunshine, rain and wind define the meteorological dimensions of the climate. While often associated with the notion of vintage, they are in fact essential natural conditions to be considered, first for the mere possibility of cultivating *V. vinifera*, and then in the development of high-quality viticulture, first if *V. vinifera* is to be cultivated at all, and secondly, if quality viticulture is the ultimate aim. Their interactions and variability are extremely complex, however, in terms of both season and locality. Providing key data in the definition of climatic zones, wind, rain and sun should be considered in context with the geographical dimension of climate.

The geography of climate

Climate and its meteorological parameters may be reduced or indeed amplified by the geography of a terrain – in other words by latitude, elevation, topography (relief and exposure), continental positioning, the presence of bodies of water and so on. All of these create specific climatic conditions on different scales (macro-, topo-, meso-, micro-), but how might these parameters affect the viability of a viticultural area and the production of high-quality wine?

Is there an ideal latitude?

The 45th parallel has been described as the "ideal latitude for the world's great wines" by Olivier Bernard, director of Domaine de Chevalier in Bordeaux, and journalist Thierry Dussard, co-authors of *The Magic of the 45th Parallel* (English ed: 2014). This latitude, equidistant between the pole and the equator, is, according to the authors, nothing short of "magical", and it does indeed run through many of the northern hemisphere's famous wine-producing areas. It crosses Libournais in Bordeaux and passes between Hermitage and Châteauneuf-du-Pape before moving on to Piedmont and northern Italy and eventually into Georgia, one of the legendary cradles of wine. Then it goes to Xinjiang, China's largest viticultural area; to Oregon, to northern Ontario and to southern Quebec, where viticulture is just beginning. This fascinating "ridge line" will have to be extended to other temperate latitudes to include every area where *V. vinifera* has been planted historically or with great success, such as the Mediterranean coastline. In reality, there is one band enclosed between the 30th and 50th parallels north and another between the 25th and 45th parallels south. The latitude is more restricted in the Antipodes because of the presence of large areas of ocean. This area is sunnier than its northern counterpart, however, allowing grapes to ripen well.

Latitude affects two important parameters in viticulture.
- **Sunshine**. This decreases on average the nearer you get to the poles. However, when considered in relation to the vine's vegetative period, the levels of solar energy are compensated at higher latitudes by the length of the day and a greater angle of incidence.
- **Temperature**. We know that vines do not survive or cannot produce high-quality grapes at latitudes too close to the poles. In effect, 0.6°C (c. 1°F) is lost for every additional degree of latitude between the 36th and 60th parallels North. Commercial vineyards at these northern limits do exist, however, even if growing wine at such a latitude is

uncertain and expensive. Thanks to technological innovations, and perhaps even climate change, vineyards are producing wines in Norway (with hybrid whites and reds planted on the 59th parallel), Sweden and Siberia. Getting closer to the equator, vines have adapted to the heat, humidity and absence of winter and grow continually. Pruning during vegetative growth makes it possible to obtain several harvests per year, as in Thailand, Indonesia and Kenya.

Elevation

For vineyards, elevation means lower temperatures, more intense light and UV radiation, and a decrease in atmospheric pressure, hence a decrease in the driving pressure for gas exchange of O_2 and CO_2. It is physically harder for the plant to breathe at higher elevations. The temperature of the air also reduces with elevation, losing 0.6°C (c. 1°F) for every 100m (330ft), up to a height of 500m (1,640ft), and then 1°C (c. 2°F) for every 170m (560ft) above that. Galet maintains that vegetative growth is slowed by a day for every 30m (100ft) of elevation up to 1,000m (3,280ft), and a further day for every 20m (66ft) above that. We also know that acidity is better preserved when the day/night temperature range varies widely.

> With elevation sometimes compensating for latitude, certain vineyards in low latitudes are planted at great heights

Elevation can sometimes also compensate for latitude, which is why many vineyards in low latitudes are planted at great heights, above 2,000m (6,560ft), such as at Ao Yun in Yunnan, China – the name of the estate means "flying above the clouds" – or those in the Quebrada region of Humahuaca, in northwest Argentina. In addition, there may be enhanced photosynthetic activity and transpiration thanks to greater light intensity, increased shortwave solar radiation and scantier cloud cover, but this is also reduced by the absorption of CO_2, which is more limited as elevation increases. The composition and quantity of certain secondary compounds like aromas are affected, but the grapes obtained generally have more colour and contain more tannins.

Elevation obviously has its limits: the risk of frost increases, and wind, hail and rain are often more intense. Achieving phenolic and physiological maturity and thus a suitable yield can also be problematic, and there are divergent data on the length of (or shortfall in) the vegetative cycle, depending on the exposure and location of the land.

Some wine regions have therefore made elevation a line of demarcation in appellation status. In Sicily, there is an upper limit for Etna DOC (*denominazione di origine controllata*, the Italian equivalent to France's AOC), which varies with exposure: 1,000m (3,280ft) on the southern and eastern slopes, and 800m (2,625ft) on the north face. Above these limits, the wines may lack maturity, with alcohol levels that are too low and acidity that is too high to qualify for the appellation. They are therefore downgraded to IGT (*indicazione geografica tipica*, the equivalent of France's IGP). Galet has established that sugar reduces by 0.8–1 per cent per 100m (330ft) of

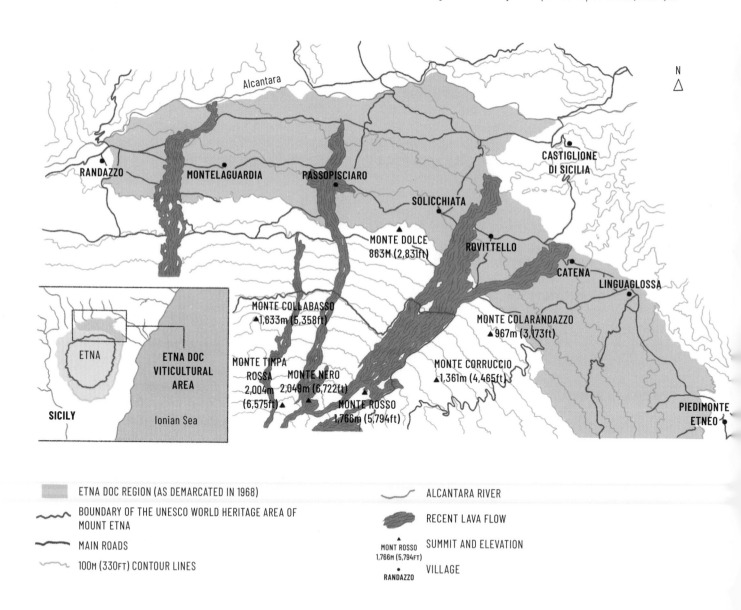

THE VITICULTURAL AREA NORTH-NORTHEAST OF ETNA IN SICILY
Elevation defines the upper borders of the Etna AOC to ensure the grapes ripen sufficiently.

elevation, while acidity increases by 1 per cent; wines produced at between 300m (985ft) and 400m (1,310ft) on the slopes of the volcano generally have an alcohol level of 14–15 per cent; 13–14 per cent between 400m (1,310ft) and 800m (2,620ft); and less than 13 per cent above that.

The Barolo and Beaujolais appellations also have upper elevation limits, tempered by the orientation and gradient of the land.

Relief – the primacy of hillsides

Vines can be found on all kinds of topography, but those grown on hillsides have had a reputation for quality since ancient times. Virgil in the 1st century BCE wrote, "Bacchus loves open hills" in his *Georgics*, while Pliny the Elder's *Natural History* (1st century BCE) set out an enduring hierarchy of Falernian wines based on the vines' position on the slopes: Caucinum, a light wine, in the uppermost reaches; Faustianum, a sweet wine that was the most popular, in the middle; and Falernum, harsh and generic, at the foot of the slopes. The recognition achieved by wine regions such as Burgundy's Côte d'Or, Champagne's Côte des Blancs and the Loire's Coteaux du Layon has only increased the perception of hillsides as the terrain of choice, and rightly so.

Hillsides are sought for their shallow and poorly fertile soils that inhibit the natural vigour of the vines, their sunshine and their exposure to air-flow, but also for their natural drainage, which depends on their gradient and the composition of their soil. The steeper the slope and the greater the exposure, the more perpendicular the sun's rays and the more heat accumulated by the vine and the soil; the soil will also release greater or lower amounts of heat according to its colour and composition. This explains why many historic northern wine areas such as the Mosel and the Ahr in Germany are located on slopes at an angle greater than 35 degrees – these have the best sunshine and drainage.

The other main viticultural terrains are plains and plateaux. Both are flat but differ in their elevation and its effects along with their depth of soil, with plains being generally more alluvial and fertile, although with notable exceptions, such as the sandy vineyards of Contra Costa in California or the smooth pebbles of parts of Châteauneuf-du-Pape.

Relief and exposure

Choice of exposure is of primary importance for every type of relief, since its effects may be significant. In the northern hemisphere:

- **South-southwestern exposure** was preferable until recently. Sunlight is received from daybreak onward, warming the ground and limiting the risk of frost. This orientation also offers better protection against cold north-northwest winds.

- **West-southwestern exposure** provides sunlight until the end of the day, but the soil lies in shade in the morning and is therefore potentially more susceptible to frost. The same is true of easterly exposure, where the sun disappears very early.

- **Northern exposure** was more difficult and was chosen only when another factor, such as wind, needed to be mitigated. Galet cites the northerly *grands crus* from the uplands of Reims in Champagne, which are protected from westerly and southwesterly winds, as illustrated by the Cru de Verzenay with its trademark windmill. (The windmill, incidentally, functioned because of the less frequent but still sufficiently strong winds from the east and southeast. These winds were less damaging to the vines.)

The characteristics of such exposures may be either reversed or tempered, depending on latitude. And now, of course, climate change has a major impact. In southern vineyards, northern and eastern exposure is increasingly sought to mitigate water stress. One last point in respect of terrain and exposure: these both play a major role in the dynamics of soil erosion and are obviously factors in vineyard running costs.

" Choice of exposure is of primary importance for every type of relief, since its effects may be significant

The role of large expanses of water

The heat capacity of soil is much less than water, so soil changes its temperature more quickly than water for the same amount of incoming energy – it heats up and cools down more quickly. Large expanses of water such as oceans thus play their part in determining the temperature range in the viticultural regions that they influence. They affect the "continental" nature of terrain; this is its distance from coastlines, which often entails large annual temperature variations. Oceans tend to temper the cold of winter and moderate the heat of summer, but their effects are also influenced by their own temperature: the Mediterranean is warm; the Pacific, through which the Humboldt Current runs, is cold on the west coast of America; the Red Sea is hot; and the Atlantic varies in temperature.

Where these water masses are cool, they tend to prolong the vegetative period and preserve acidity, as with Pinot Noir, Syrah and Chardonnay from the West Sonoma Coast and Santa Barbara on the coast of California. The Pacific also causes thick fog in California that engulfs San Pablo Bay and penetrates into the Napa Valley, partially covering it during summer afternoons and moderating the temperatures in the vineyards. When oceans and seas are warmer, they mitigate the effects of latitude and allow grapes to ripen, as with the Gulf Stream on the French Atlantic coast, or in Canada's Nova Scotia, or Crimea.

Heroic viticulture

It has been called "heroic" or "extreme" wine-growing. Far removed from the easily cultivated, expansive fertile plains, these vineyards have arisen in environments that defy all practical reason. In 1987, organizations representing iconic regions growing wine in extreme conditions came together to defend and develop their approaches to cultivation, which had sometimes looked in danger of being abandoned because they were so difficult to run and costs were so high. The Centre for Research, Environmental Sustainability and Advancement of Mountain Viticulture (CERVIM) was founded under the auspices of the OIV. To qualify for inclusion, vineyards must be planted on terraces on slopes with a gradient greater than 30 per cent, at elevations in excess of 500m (1,640ft). Wine-growing on small islands, where the challenges arise from isolation and the difficulty of sourcing water, may also qualify for inclusion. CERVIM counts among its members representatives from Italy's Aosta Valley, Cinque Terre and island of Pantelleria; from Spain's Canary Islands, Priorat and Galicia; Banyuls, Collioure and Auvergne in France; the Douro in Portugal; the Mosel in Germany; Styria in Austria; and Valais in Switzerland.

According to CERVIM, what links these regions and individual estates is the size of what are often family-run concerns cultivating niche indigenous cépages on scattered plots of land, on hilly terrain where mechanization is nigh on impossible. Their winemaking activity is also generally supplemented with other sources of income. Ultimately, the aspect of the landscape is of fundamental importance. Plenty of other winemakers practise heroic viticulture without belonging to CERVIM: the northern Rhône Valley or Alsace in France, Lavaux in Switzerland, or the Azores. It comes as no surprise that the vast majority of these unlikely plots of land are located in Europe, with some saying that they account for up to seven per cent of European vineyards, wherever human stubbornness and history have at some point in the course of civilization justified the economic and social viability of such cultivation. Think of the labour and time required to construct the terraces of the Douro, the Mosel or northern Rhône's Côte-Rôtie – the pragmatism constraining contemporary viticultural operations would never have countenanced such efforts.

Marine currents and ocean temperature are crucial in regulating climate on every scale: this can be seen in the effects of El Niño and La Niña on the west coast of the Americas. Oceans also influence rainfall and cloud cover; rain is less seasonal on coasts exposed to moist wind, but sea breezes can also push clouds inland. The level of exposure on the coast is also a factor to be considered. In Europe, western coastal areas are wetter than those in the east, as are those on the Italian peninsula, but the opposite is the case in the Americas, where it is always drier in California and Chile than in New York or Uruguay. Lakes and rivers also have a modifying effect on temperature in proportion to their size, flow and depth. They do not directly bring rain, but they influence air flow in the form of breezes from the sea, lake or ocean, as in Stellenbosch in South Africa, where these breezes help limit extreme summer temperatures, or in the vicinity of the North American Great Lakes, where they have a similar softening effect. Water's influence is also magnified by its power to reflect light (it reflects about seven per cent on average); lakes act like mirrors and may increase the temperature of lakeside vineyards by reflecting the sun's light, sometimes by more than 1°C (2°F). The same is true for the surface of the sea, especially at dawn and sunset. This contributes to the other influences of water masses to create a warmer and milder mesoclimate that is a crucial element for vineyards positioned at the very edges of winemaking territory, as in Switzerland with lakes Geneva and Neuchâtel, Hungary with Lake Balaton, Italy with lakes Como, Garda and Maggiore, and North America with the Finger Lakes and lakes Erie, Michigan and Ontario. It is worth noting that the effects of a lake extend beyond its shores. Vines may not be planted directly on the shore of a lake but can still be within its zone of influence.

Meteorology and geography are intimately interconnected: their interactions are the origins of extreme climatic diversity, and they shape the environments suitable for viticulture. Depending on the latitude, the number of differentiating factors and their relative influence will vary considerably, so selecting a vineyard's site is crucial to its agronomic and commercial viability, with choices made first on a regional then local level, right down to the specific plot of land. Certain topographies have been historically preferred, partly for their specific characteristics. While climate change – with all its complex consequences that may be beneficial or harmful, depending on the situation – can make the siting of vineyards more of a guessing game, the effects of geographical factors on viticulture have remained more predictable. This is why winemakers have always sought to reproduce or to modify topography to compensate for climatic uncertainty.

Is there an ideal climate for viticulture?

The climates under which vines are cultivated should be understood in terms of their meteorological and geographical parameters: how suitable are they for growing vines, how do they vary and where are they headed? The possibility that a vine can be cultivated at all does not mean it can be cultivated in a particular way – each cépage has its own particular requirements but will often reveal its full nuances and complexity only at the very extremes of its zone of viability. Which are the main vine-growing climates, and what are their characteristics? How have they changed over time, and have they been affected by what some people are no longer calling climate change but "climate chaos"?

The main vine-growing climates

It is possible to determine which climates are suitable for viticulture by superimposing a map of wine-producing areas over one showing the principal climate zones. Carbonneau and former INRAE researcher Jean-Louis Escudier have done precisely this in their book *De l'oenologie à la viticulture* (2017), proposing the following classification in decreasing order of size of area planted and identified using the Köppen climate classification scheme for temperature and precipitation.

- **The Mediterranean-style climate** with hot, dry summers and mild, damp autumns and winters is the most common. All the regions around the Mediterranean experience this type of climate, as do areas with comparable topography, such as the coastal areas of Portugal, California, Chile, South Africa (Western Cape), and Australia (Perth, South Australia). These wine-growing areas account for the greater part of global production. The regions where vines originated, such as Georgia, have similar climates but with more tropical aspects in summer and more continental aspects in winter. These are the areas where viticulture is easiest.

- **Semi-arid, steppe or semi-desert climates** are the second most common. These regions have less than 400mm (16in) of rainfall annually, with evaporation often exceeding precipitation and significant variations in temperature between day and night. Growing vines in such locations is more or less impossible without irrigation. Some of these are historic wine-growing areas, such as the Near and Middle East, South America and western China, whose recent commercial development is, however, the result of improved techniques for using the water available. While irrigation is traditional in the Andes (the system was originally created by the Huarpes, the indigenous people of the Mendoza region) and in China (the Turpan *karez* system used by the people of Xinjiang), contemporary techniques – such as sprinklers, drip irrigation, micro-irrigation, regulated deficit irrigation and so on – are far more targeted and have contributed to the emergence of large new production areas, such as in Australia (Riverland, Murray Darling, Riverina), California (Central Coast), Mexico and South Africa. Certain kinds of contemporary irrigation are, however, freighted with agronomic and environmental problems, such as soil salinization.

> Although they require more attention in cultivation and greater precision in vinification, wines from temperate climates are often considered to be those that best express the characteristics of a cépage

- **Temperate climates** with maritime or continental inluence are third in line. A distinction is made for regions with a maritime or oceanic influence, such as the greater part of western France, New Zealand, the coast of Victoria in Australia, and the Willamette Valley; the rest of Oregon's wine areas have a Mediterranean climate. They experience considerable rainfall and moderate variations in temperature. The mean temperature is above -3°C (26.6°F) but below 18°C (64.4°F) in the coldest month, when there is persistant frost.

  The remainder are regions with a continental influence. They have more severe temperatures, with the mean temperatures of the coldest month usually below -3°C (26.6°F), and are found only in Eurasia and North America, with highly contrasting hot summers and cold winters, and potentially heavier summer rainfall: Germany, Central Europe, Ontario and New York's Finger Lakes all fall into this category. Temperate climates are far less common in the southern hemisphere.

The vines, which flourish in such climates despite the increased risk of disease, are often grown at the very edge of their maturation zone under conditions that scarcely allow the cépage in question to ripen. Requiring not only greater attention in cultivation – choosing the most promising varieties, the right terroirs, pruning and so on – but also greater precision in vinification, the wines from these regions are often considered to express most fully the characteristics of the cépage. So the most nuanced, terroir-driven Chardonnays are said to be made in Chablis, the most complex Syrahs in Côte-Rôtie and so on.

Other climates where vines are commercially cultivated account for a smaller percentage of global production. In descending order of vineyard area planted, these are:

• **Subtropical climates** that differ according to their rainfall. In terms of viticulture, a difference is made between vineyards with hot, damp summers such as the south-eastern coast of America as far as Long Island, to the east of New York); the coast of Australia's New South Wales; southern Japan and southwestern China; and those with hot, dry summers, such as southern Brazil or Uruguay. Humidity and heat trigger vegetative growth and increase the danger of fungal disease. However, many of the *Vitis* cépages grown here are adapted to these conditions.

• **Equatorial and tropical climates** both feature annual average temperatures above 18°C (64°F), an absence of winter, and heavy rain spread throughout the year. Vines never stop growing in such conditions, and they bear leaves, shoots and clusters of grapes all at the same time. Besides the high risk of disease, pruning must be very precisely controlled to regulate the plants' vigour, which sometimes permits two harvests a year. While their production yields are slim, there has been increasing media attention on vineyards in India, Thailand and Indonesia, as well as on the islands of Hawaii, Tahiti and Réunion where *V. vinifera* is grown along with hybrids such as Isabella, which have better resistance to fungal disease.

The Anthropocene question

In 2003, American climatologist William Ruddiman shook the scientific community to the core by asserting that humanity brought about the start of climate change not with the Industrial Revolution but, rather, with the Neolithic Revolution and the birth of agriculture. Known as the early anthropogenic hypothesis (EAH), this theory develops the Anthropocene hypothesis, a concept that in turn suggests we have left the Holocene era – the geological epoch that began 12,000 years ago that most scientists consider still to be in progress – and entered a new geological period determined by human activity.

The EAH is based on an understanding of the mechanisms of glaciation cycles and interglacial periods posited by Serbian geophysicist and astronomer Milutin Milanković (1879–1958) and suggests that the increase in the main greenhouse gases – CO_2 over the past 8,000 years, and methane over the past 5,000 years – is not only natural but also due to the establishment of settlements by humans. In the first instance, this was through slash-and-burn deforestation for crops and grazing land, which directly emits CO_2 and indirectly triggers ice melt, thus intensifying gas exchanges between oceans and the atmosphere. This was followed by irrigation for rice-growing, livestock husbandry and the burning of biomass, which produces methane. Although occurring in quantities that would seem negligible to us nowadays, this accumulation of gas would, over the centuries, have resulted in a warming in excess of 1°C (2°F), allowing the world's populations to grow by guaranteeing them a certain volume of agricultural production.

The theory notes in contrast that periods in which temperatures dropped over the past 2,500 years may be linked to the incidence of epidemics, when human activity was lower due to high death rates and reforestation. Ruddiman's hypothesis is innovative but has attracted criticism. Despite the controversy, the theory nonetheless highlights the role of plants, soils and people in the issue of climate change.

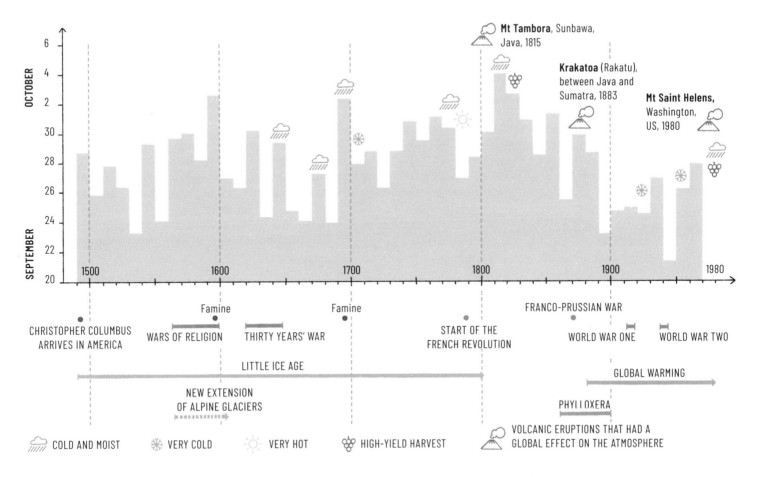

CLIMATE EVENTS AND START DATES FOR HARVESTS SINCE 1500, ACCORDING TO EMMANUEL LE ROY LADURIE

Each vertical bar represents the average start date for grape harvests for each decade; the taller the bar, the later the harvest. The greatest difference established by Le Roy Ladurie was 14 days.

• **Polar climates** are also being increasingly explored, particularly in Scandinavia and at the southern tip of Chile and Argentina. While vines can grow beyond the 50th parallel in the northern hemisphere and the 40th parallel in the southern hemisphere, conditions of extreme cold, modest summer heat and poor light complicate the viability of viticulture in such latitudes.

Harvest dates and climate

Although climates are well defined, they clearly have zones of influence that are not fixed but have been evolving continuously since the earliest days of the Earth. Such changes have indirectly affected viticulture by shaping geology, through the transformation of soils over the last 500 million years, for example. But these changes have also had direct effects; the global warming that followed the last Ice Age, which ended about 10,000 years ago, facilitated the progressive domestication of *V. vinifera* and may well have been caused by the expansion of agriculture.

For modern agroclimatologists, the vine is a bellwether of the symptoms of climate change, while for several decades climate historians have been using vines to identify Europe's climatic cycles over the past 1,000 years. In his *L'Histoire du climat depuis l'an mil* (1967), French historian Emmanuel Le Roy Ladurie has demonstrated that the dates of the grape harvest are one of the most reliable indicators of climatic evolution, along with the those of wheat harvests and the evolution of glaciers. Since vines are in the unique social and economic position of being the most closely monitored plant under cultivation, their history has been documented very precisely over the years, and these preserved records have given rise to the science of historical vendemiology, first practised by Le Roy Ladurie.

Having established that the quality and date of a harvest depend on the climate of that particular year – an early harvest would suggest a hot spring and summer, while conversely, a late harvest would indicate these had been cold or rainy – Le Roy Ladurie analysed the official start dates of harvests recorded in Burgundy and in the rest of France since 1370. He also highlighted the possible interference of social and anthropic causality – socio-economic or political contexts such as war, oenological changes upon ripening, the decisions taken by estate owners and so on – with a determinism that was purely climatic.

> For modern agro-climatologists, the vine is a bellwether of the symptoms of climate change

Taking an interdisciplinary approach, historians, geophysicists, climatologists, ecophysiologists and pattern-modellers have furthered his research, creating a database of phenological observations (called ANR-OPHÉLIE) with a view to refining our understanding of temperatures since the end of the 19th century and to put current climatic trends into perspective. Valérie Daux, a geophysicist specializing in climate studies, has summed up the progress and limitations of their work in her article "La reconstruction climatique à partir des dates de vendanges".

Optima and viticultural glaciation
This research suggests that the climate seems to have been relatively stable for the past 10,000 years, compared to preceding periods, but that it has nonetheless alternated during this time between mild periods, known as climatic optima, and cool periods, or little ice ages. Despite the average disparity in temperature between these being only small, between 0.3°C (0.5°F) and 0.7°C (1.25°F) over multi-decade averages, such variations have had major consequences for the biotope, human societies and viticulture.

Europe experienced a small climatic optimum during the Bronze Age (c.1500–1000 BCE) and a cool period during the Iron Age (c.1000–400 BCE), followed by a rise in temperatures during the Roman era (c.250 BCE–400 CE) that could be compared to that of the present day and is thought to have helped V. vinifera's expansion northward. The Little Ice Age that followed (536–660) played a part in the fall of the Roman Empire and hastened the abandonment of certain northern vineyards.

Medieval Europe experienced a further climatic optimum between 900 and 1300 CE, which seems to correlate with a significant period of conquest and land clearance; England and Belgium had their own vineyards even as the Vikings

conquered Greenland, which was covered in vines. The period from the 14th century to around 1850 saw Europe undergo a minor ice age, with the northernmost vineyards being abandoned once again, principally because of glacial peaks in 1300–80, 1620–70 and 1820–60. Very harsh winters (such as that of 1709, which wiped out numerous vineyards), famine, disease and deadly epidemics of dysentery, plague and so on greatly reduced the populations of towns and villages and also disrupted viticulture and political stability in equal measure. This period was, however, punctuated by the "beautiful 16th century", as it is called in France, and the 1550s beat all records for early harvests in Europe, with grape-picking beginning in Beaune on 16 August in 1556 and on the 21st in 1559. In 2003, the year in which much of Europe baked in a heatwave, the harvest in France began on 19 August.

After 1860, Europe experienced a period of warming during which vineyards achieved their maximum expansion worldwide. Climatic conditions were once again favourable between the 1910s and the 1950s, allowing for rapid redevelopment of the wine industry after phylloxera but also resulting in some problems with overproduction.

Temperatures have been constantly increasing since the 1970s, and the first two decades of the 21st century have been some of the hottest on record. The current global trend is toward accelerated warming. Early harvests have been on the increase since the mid-1990s. The year 2020 was 1.2°C (2°F) hotter than the dawn of large-scale industrialization in 1850–1900. The 1980s were all about achieving greater ripeness in musts, but the aim today is to preserve acidity and control alcohol levels while protecting vines from the various stresses caused by changes in their environment. The world's higher latitudes are the most affected (+2°C/3.6°F on average), with lower latitudes becoming drier. Rainfall patterns have changed; precipitation is less regular and seasonal, with successive episodes of drought; climatic extremes are more severe and so it continues, with repercussions for the entire biotope. For wine regions, the complete phenology of vines has been affected.

Vines and "climate chaos"
What effects has climate change had on vines and the grapes they produce? The consequences have been highly complex, multifactorial, interdependent and dynamic, making them somewhat difficult to analyse. First of all, there has been a change in the vine's phenological cycle. On a global scale, the dates for bud-burst, flowering, fruit set and veraison have advanced by an average of one week as a result of mild winters and springs, with an associated risk of frost. These earlier dates have shifted the seasonality of the vegetative cycle, and thus the intensity of sunshine to which the vines

are subjected: as they receive more light and heat, they will, in theory, photosynthesize more and metabolize polyphenols differently, boosting some and reducing others. By the same token, they may be exposed to greater water stress, evapotranspiration and *grillure* (scorched bunches). Physiological ripening of sugar and acidity is increasingly divorced from phenolic maturity of tannins. With a shortened vegetative cycle, warmer nights, and harvests taking place at the height of summer, there are challenges to the grape-variety choices made by historic viticultural regions in order to pick in the autumn under cool conditions that allow for ripeness and organoleptic maturity and complexity. This is compounded by more extreme climatic episodes of drought, hail and frost that may weaken the plant, which would go some way to explain certain wood diseases.

The biosphere has also been affected, disrupting the environments of micro-organisms, fungi, insects and other animals to varying degrees. In some cases, entire populations have disappeared; in others, they have migrated or multiplied in the absence of predators. The northern regions of Europe, for example, have witnessed the arrival of the leafhopper *Scaphoideus titanus*, which carries a phytoplasm that causes flavescence dorée, a deadly, degenerative, bacterial disease of vines, as well as *Drosophila suzukii*, which attacks red- and pink-skinned cépages, as in the vineyards of Alsace, Burgundy, Jura and elsewhere in northern and central France in 2014. Others have seen changes to their life cycles, like the scale insect, whose number of generations per year has tended to increase. Controlling powdery mildew and downy mildew in the mild winters and hot summers that are favourable to these diseases is becoming more challenging, not least in contexts where a reduction in the use of phytosanitary products is the goal.

Other effects that are less apparent to the general public are also being studied. Researchers from the University of Geisenheim in Germany have looked at rises in the CO_2 content of the atmosphere, which is thought to be a partial cause of the acceleration of climate change by greenhouse gases, and have shown that it intensifies photosynthetic activity in vines. This in turn produces more biomass (acids in particular) but may also leave vines more susceptible to certain pathogens.

A further consequence of warming is soil salinization; in environments that are too hot, water in the soil can, under certain ground conditions, rise by capillary action. It evaporates, leaving mineral ions such as sodium or chlorine at the surface. The phytotoxicity of salt has been clearly established – vines die in salt solutions at concentrations in excess of 1.28g/l (0.2oz/gallon). Irrigation, which might seem to be a solution, paradoxically seems to aggravate the problem, as

has been the case in certain regions of Australia where rivers and water tables have become increasingly loaded with salt in a vicious circle. Rather than climate change, it is easy to understand why scientists like plant biology PhD and wine journalist Jamie Goode from the UK speak of "climate chaos" for viticulture.

New winemaking geographies

New geographies and viticultures are taking shape as the pace of climate change accelerates. The traditional parameters for managing vineyards have practically been reversed: in places where winemakers had long sought heat, they now look to protect vines from it; where damp was once avoided, they now look for water; and where cépages with high levels of alcohol were once in favour, well-ripened varieties with moderate alcohol potential are now preferred. Australia has led the field in the systematic study of these issues, incorporating them into the development of winemaking areas. *Australia's Wine Future: A Climate Atlas* is a project between industry body Wine Australia and the University of Tasmania that maps climate change at a scale of 5 km (3 miles) across the principal regions of the country to help producers adapt their approaches accordingly. It has now become one of the most comprehensive scientific programmes on a national scale,

> " New geographies and viticultures are taking shape as the pace of climate change accelerates

but examples of adaptation and modification of vineyard dynamics are to be found everywhere.

Cooler areas are being sought, as in South Africa, where new vineyards are categorized by cold units, on the model of apple-orchard plantations, and often by proximity to the coast. New latitudes and elevations are being (re-)explored: Britain had more than 3,928 ha planted for wine production in 2023, as opposed to 150 ha in 1975, and Argentinian vineyards have been creeping ever higher up the slopes of the Andes with vines at Tupungato, Uco and San Carlos in Mendoza at elevations in excess of 1,100m (3,600ft). At Bodega Colomé à Salta, there are vines at more than 3,100m (10,170ft) above sea level.

The search for water is turning economies upside down, with the value of vineyard land in Mendoza now indexed to the availability or otherwise of water. The majority of universities specializing in viticulture are looking at new rootstocks that can adapt to drought, while cépages once spurned for their low alcohol levels have been fished out of plant collections and brought back into fashion, including Terret, an old cépage

The VitAdapt programme

VitAdapt Envichange was developed at INRAE's experimental estate in Bordeaux from 2009 until 2022 under the aegis of Professor Kees van Leeuwen. The programme studied the interactions between 52 cépages that are of significance for contemporary viticulture, including five interspecies hybrids that are resistant to fungal disease, and climatic conditions that are increasingly hot and dry. The aim was to map the predisposition for early ripening, resistance and typicity of the cépages with a view to recommending the best-adapted varieties. The research has confirmed that phenologies and ripening dynamics vary greatly depending on the variety. This has made it possible to identify six groups of cépages based on early ripening to mid-veraison, speed of ripening, and the final concentration of sugars. As a parallel undertaking, the project looked into the physiological mechanisms of drought resistance, which vary greatly from one variety to the next and are still poorly understood. In addition to this, monitoring the vinification of some 20 of these cépages was intended to help evaluate typicity and organoleptic potential.

Ultimately, the project highlights the necessity of plant diversity in adapting to climate change. The changes in grape selection for AOC Bordeaux/Bordeaux Supérieur made in 2019 were a direct result of this work – seven new cépages have been authorized for up to five per cent of the land and 10 per cent of the final blend: Touriga Nacional, Castets (an old Bordeaux variety), Marselan (Grenache x Cabernet Sauvignon), Arinarnoa (Tannat x Cabernet Sauvignon) for reds; Albariño, Petit Manseng and Liliorila (Baroque x Chardonnay) for whites. 2023 saw the addition of inter-specific hybrids, including Floréal, Sauvignac, Sauvignier Gris and Vidoc. This was a full-scale, scientifically controlled experiment that is helping to shape varietal development.

from the Languedoc that is being replanted in its region of origin, in Châteauneuf-du-Pape and even in California.

The appearance of vineyards is similarly changing as pruning methods evolve in an attempt to limit water stress and leaf scorch. No-till has been advocated by some to promote better carbon capture. These developments, which are more or less visibly reshaping the world's viticultural landscapes, are summarized in *Quel vin pour demain?* (2021), a reference work by journalist Michelle Bouffard, Master of Wine Jérémy Cukierman and geographer and climatologist Hervé Quénol that addresses this very question.

Climates and high-quality wine regions – nothing is set in stone

Vine-growing is very much climate-dependent. *Vitis* can indeed grow in a good number of different conditions, but its optimum expression depends on the precise match between a cépage and a local microclimate, whose parameters the winemaker has chosen and often modified. While many regions have a macroclimate suitable for grape cultivation, the wines grown are generally classified as local wines; they lack the distinctive assets required to produce high quality and do not have the typicity of fine wines.

The climatic zones that permit optimum expression of a grape variety's complexity are generally located at the edges of cultivation zones, where ripening is not excessive, and were once thought to be fixed and immovable. The French system of appellation by origin has even in some respects fixed them in stone. Because it has failed to take into account the increasing pace of climate change since the 1970s, its historical nature has been highlighted. Indeed, ever since we have been putting the histories of winemaking and of the climate into context, it has become clear that both are also heirs to practices that have adapted, minimized, augmented and anticipated climatic dynamics and their consequences for the agronomic and economic viability of viticulture.

Vineyards have been shaped by vignerons and have evolved according to the quality and quantity of their harvests, their capacity to adapt to changes in demand, and the agronomic, human and logistical costs of production. In this way, climate has always played a part in fashioning these landscapes that were thought unchanging. Viticulture is invariably at the leading edge of agricultural research and is certainly a bellwether for the symptoms of climate change; it may also even be at the cutting edge of solutions in fighting climate chaos, a struggle that also involves understanding the other aspects shaping terroir: the soil and human will.

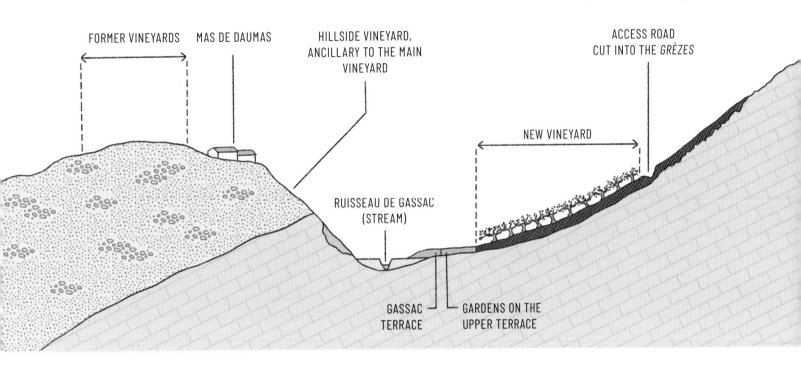

WEST

EAST

FORMER VINEYARDS

MAS DE DAUMAS

HILLSIDE VINEYARD,
ANCILLARY TO THE MAIN
VINEYARD

ACCESS ROAD
CUT INTO THE *GRÈZES*

NEW VINEYARD

RUISSEAU DE GASSAC
(STREAM)

GASSAC
TERRACE

GARDENS ON THE
UPPER TERRACE

SILTS, SANDS, PEBBLES AND
OLIGOCENE LIMESTONES

LIMESTONES

PEBBLES

FORMER VALLEY IN THE LIMESTONE, BACKFILLED
WITH SAND AND SILT

LIMESTONE SOURCE IN THE VALLEY BED

LUTETIAN LIMESTONES

WHEN A GEOGRAPHER CREATES TERROIR: HENRI ENJALBERT AND THE MAS DE DAUMAS GASSAC ESTATE

Renowned geographer Henri Enjalbert (1910–83) advised Aimé Guibert on planting an exceptional terroir with a combination of climatic and soil analysis, as shown in this west-to-east cross-section of the Mas de Daumas Gassac estate. As geographer Raphaël Schirmer commented, you might even say that it was Enjalbert who actually created this top-quality terroir.

GEOLOGY

Why read the geology of vineyards?

Geology shapes landscape, and an educated eye may begin to perceive a world of influences that were previously invisible. Whether limestone, schist, basalt, Carboniferous rock or Portland stone, the underlying bedrock and its geological layers are revealed through the proliferation of wines that claim them on their labels. While climatologist Gregory V Jones has reminded us that geology and pedology play a mediating role between vines and climates by influencing the availability of water and micronutrients, American geologist James E Wilson has gone a step further, suggesting that any proper understanding of viticultural terroirs is incomplete without an understanding of local geology, beyond any climatic parameters. Why is this science so important, and what aspects must be addressed from a wine-growing perspective?

Geology – from invisible to essential

Nowadays, geology is proudly displayed on bottle labels for marketing purposes and touted as an indication of quality by vignerons and sommeliers alike; the unprecedented visibility it enjoys in the way wines and vines are represented may come almost as a surprise but is undoubtedly a revelation. There is nothing new here, however: the local bedrock is already in evidence in an estate's buildings, its low walls, terraces and vineyard outbuildings, and in its *chais* and cellars, which historically were built from locally available stone. Wild plants have, in their own way, also been constant indicators of what is going on beneath our feet.

For some years, however, we have been learning to see viticultural landscapes and terroirs differently. One of the driving forces behind this change of perspective has undoubtedly been the interest shown in wine regions that have made the subsoil an essential part of their identity. There is no better example of this than Burgundy, and the Côte d'Or in particular, where vineyards are organized according to the nature of the subsoil and its topography. Plots of land, known locally as *climats*, have been graded for centuries according to their soil's potential for producing quality wines. The best are designated *grands crus* (33 in total), followed by *premiers crus*, *crus communaux* or village-level *wines*, and then sub-regional and regional wines, in order of anticipated quality. Different *crus* may often be planted no more than a stone's throw apart, but the geology of their terroir might vary so greatly that the wines produced are fundamentally different.

Geology and wine quality – the birth of oenogeology

The French appellation system developed at the beginning of the 20th century was in part inspired by Burgundy's classification, which makes the link to its geological origins one of the essential criteria for defining a wine, its quality and identity. As a result, INAO has increasingly been turning to geologists for advice. Expert counsel is now being sought both by state bodies and by private estates to decipher the rock beneath their feet and attempt an explanation of the link with the final wine. By digging trenches and conducting soil analyses, geologists around the world – like Françoise Vannier in Burgundy, Georges Truc in the Rhône, Michel Campy in the Jura, Brenna Quigley in the US and Pedro Parra everywhere – have been exploring vineyards and drawing up maps establishing the role played by geological variations in the quality of wines.

Laboratories are specializing in the same way, like Adama in Burgundy under Vannier; or Sigales, led by pedologist and agronomist Isabelle Letessier and geologist/cartographer Josselin Marion, which has mapped the geology of Beaujolais and several areas around the Rhône, among others. These maps are created in 2D or 3D, as in the videos made by Pierre Le Hong on the geology of the terroirs of Bordeaux and Tuscany, while in Italy Alessandro Masnaghetti has carried out studies of Barolo, Barbaresco and Chianti.

A new approach is emerging with the specialist work of geologists focusing on the relationships between the soil, the subsoil, the vines and the wine. Truc, one of its pioneers, has named this science oenogeology. Thanks to work that began in the 1990s but has picked up pace since the mid-2010s, a geological reading of terroirs has spread to the point of becoming the focal point of tastings. But what is it, exactly? Can we really say that this or that wine is better and more complex because it comes from vineyards planted on this or that bedrock?

Even the ancients knew that the soil makes the wine

This is anything but a new idea; writers in ancient times had already claimed that it was possible to taste the influence of the land on a wine, and that a wine's flavour was linked to the soil's various properties. Around 29 BCE, Virgil suggests an

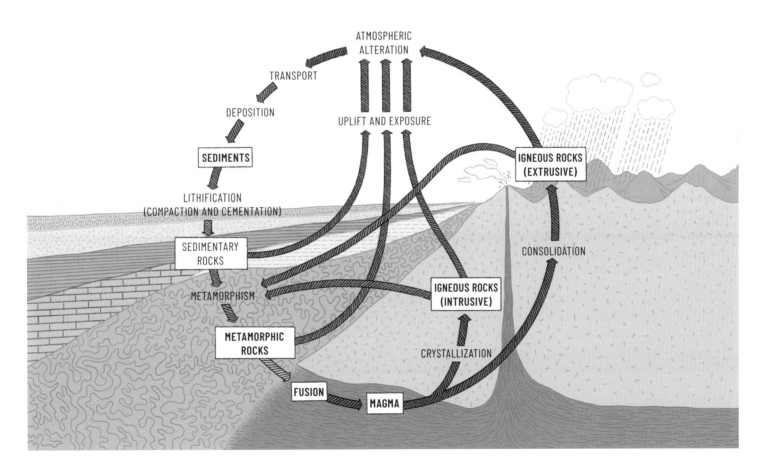

THE ROCK CYCLE

experimental tasting process in his *Georgics*: "Bitter or salty ground, where no seed flourishes, / No ploughing will change the fluid that withers them. / To better test their unpleasantness and nature, / soak the earth thereof with pure water, / placed in a wicker basket, or in a funnel, / if you suspect grapes that are useless for the press. / Thicker and more opaque water will run through, / revealing the flavour of this treacherous land."

> Vines will grow in a wide diversity of soils, subsoils and landscapes

Writing around the same time, Vitruvius confirmed in his *De architectura* that the difference between wines was due to their soil: "Therefore, all these differences in flavour are due to no other thing than the differing qualities of the soil, as can be seen with fruit as well: for if the roots of trees or vines and other plants did not produce their fruit from the moisture that they drew from the nature of the ground, the same fruit would have the same flavour everywhere. We know, however, that the wine known as Protropum [first-pressing wine] is made on the island of Lesbos; the wine known as Catacecaumeniten [burned wine] is made in Maeonia; Tmolites [a blend of wines from Mount Tmolus] in Lydia; Mamertinum on Sicily; Falernian in Campania; Caecubum in Terracina and Fundis; and in a great number of different places, many kinds of wines of different quality; and this could only be the case because the moisture of the earth communicates its properties to the roots, saturating the wood, which then conveys it up to the tips of the branches, and the fruit deepens the particular flavour of its land and type."

The writers of antiquity were thus suggesting that diversity in wines was due to geological variations and the specific properties of soils that had come about over millions of years.

The origins of the geological history of wine terroirs

While the world's vineyards are located within a number of specific climate zones, vines can grow in a wide variety of soils, subsoils and landscapes. Wherever they are grown – on plains or the slopes of volcanoes, on gravel terraces or at the foot of marble quarries, in soils as sandy as a beach, or on white chalk hills, on soils that may be more than 500 million years old or created a mere 20,000 years ago – wines recognized and appreciated for their quality are born of a multitude of substrates. To understand this heterogeneity, we must explore the very long geological history of an Earth that is more than 4.5 billion years old.

The geological substrate that makes up the Earth's crust was formed under the effects of a slow drop in temperature during the Archaean Eon: chemical elements combined into minerals that in turn aggregated into rocks.

This crust then floated on the Earth's mantle and was subject to convection currents. Its pieces broke up and began to drift, moving apart and leaving oceans between them, or crashing together triggering orogeny, the birth of mountain ranges. This is known as plate tectonics, a theory that emerged in 1915 with explorer Alfred Wegener's idea of "continental drift", although it was confirmed only in the 1960s. It is in this movement that the diversity of the world's landscapes has its origins.

Over the course of 3.8 billion years, landslips and collisions, submersions and erosion, compounded by climatic events, have created the world's rocks, soils and topographies. Geology is therefore ironically not set in stone; it is by its very nature in evolution, with the geological timescale being classically based on palaeontology.

Geological eras

The geological time scale was founded on a palaeontological basis, but there are other dating techniques that can be used to construct other systems of chronological classification. The current system was established in 1913 and has been constantly evolving ever since as techniques have improved, with geochronological dating being the most common approach. As Truc has explained, this may be "relative" or "absolute": relative means that the parameters studied relate to stratigraphic and/or palaeomagnetic methods; and absolute, that radio-isotopes of certain substances are used.

Each geological division is identified by its "floor" and "ceiling", its lower and upper boundary. With stratigraphy, these are limits defined by dramatic changes in the fossil record that arose mostly from catastrophic extinction events, as Kevin Pogue, professor of geology at Whitman College, Walla Walla, explains, and whose evolution and presence can be measured; palaeontological "zones" thus make it possible to identify possible disjunctions and "units" between consistent strata that can be examined across larger or smaller areas and are a feature of rocks formed in both marine and continental environments. This technique is always relative.

Isotopic techniques measuring the different isotopes of chemical elements present in rocks and minerals have recently made it possible to refine the resolution scale of geological time entirely, to complement the palaeontological scales. In order of magnitude, these units are aeon, era, period, epoch (a subdivision of a period that can be further divided into early, middle and late; the Early, Middle and Late Jurassic, for example), age and sub-age.

Many of the names in regular use in discussing wine regions derive from Latin and ancient Greek and are linked to their age and their manner of birth: the Palaeozoic Era (once known as the First Era, spanning the period 541 million to 252.2 million years ago) comes from *palaiós* ("old") and *zóé* ("life"). Periods may also take the name of the place, people or geology where the rock was discovered or is most common – the Jura for the Jurassic, the Celtic tribe of the Silures for the Silurian, and carbon for the Carboniferous are good examples.

A spotlight on viticultural geology

Why has viticultural geology become such a talking point in recent years? Soil and subsoil were used to determine the extent of appellations and had come to be seen as fixed, marking the parameters of terroir that could not be reproduced anywhere else. With the accelerating globalization of viticulture over the past 50 years, however, cépages and skills have been on the move and have spread further afield. Since the 1970s, the supremacy of, for example, France has no longer been a foregone conclusion. What is left to justify that superiority? Here we must turn to what might be termed the geopedological aspects of vines, the land and the soil, which cannot be exported. These have become fundamental criteria in justifying the quality and uniqueness of a wine, backed up by an approach to tasting that seeks to identify the "minerality" of a bottle. Whether this is merely a marketing argument or a scientifically demonstrable reality, it is easy to understand why the subject has caused so many heated debates. It is also why we need to try to understand the role of the soil in the idea of terroir and its relevance.

Minerals, rocks, chemical elements – what are we talking about?

The terms "minerals", "rocks" and "chemical elements" are often bandied about when talking about wine, especially its "minerality", but they often result in misunderstandings. What follows is an attempt to clarify.

· **A mineral** is a natural, inorganic, solid substance that occurs in the form of crystals made up of chemical elements. It has a structure and a composition that define its properties (for example, hardness, colour, cleavage, density). Quartz, feldspar, diamond, gold, gypsum, mica, clay (in the mineralogical sense) and graphite are just some of the 4,000 known minerals.

· **A chemical element** is an atom identified by a defined number of protons in its nucleus. In Mendeleev's periodic table of elements, these are represented by a symbol and an atomic number – for example, ^6C is carbon and its six protons. An atom contains neutrons, the number of which determines its isotopes, the "varieties" of the chemical element: carbon has four – ^{11}C, ^{12}C, ^{13}C and ^{14}C, the last being the famous carbon-14 used for carbon-dating. Electrons also orbit the nucleus and, much like protons, have an electric charge. If an atom has an equal number of electrons and protons, it is neutral. If there is an imbalance, it is electrically charged and is no longer an atom but an ion. A sodium ion Na^+ has one surplus proton (a cation), while a chlorine ion Cl^- has one extra electron (an anion). Chemical elements can combine – oxygen O with itself (dioxygen, or O_2) or with others (for example, with hydrogen, to form water, H_2O). Chemical elements may be released during the transformation of minerals and rocks.

· **A rock** is a natural, solid material formed entirely or partly from an aggregate of minerals of one or several kinds. It is defined by its mineral constituents, its chemical composition and the way it was formed. Limestones are thus a family of sedimentary rocks predominantly composed of calcium carbonate ($CaCO_3$).

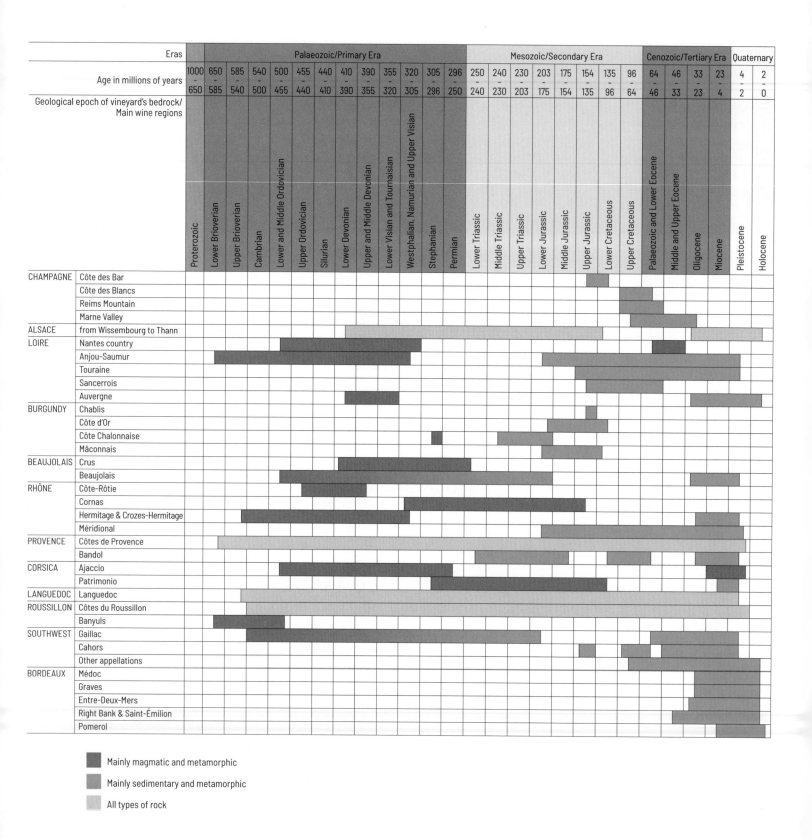

SIMPLIFIED CHRONOLOGY OF THE GEOLOGY OF THE WINE REGIONS OF FRANCE, BY BENOÎT FRANCE

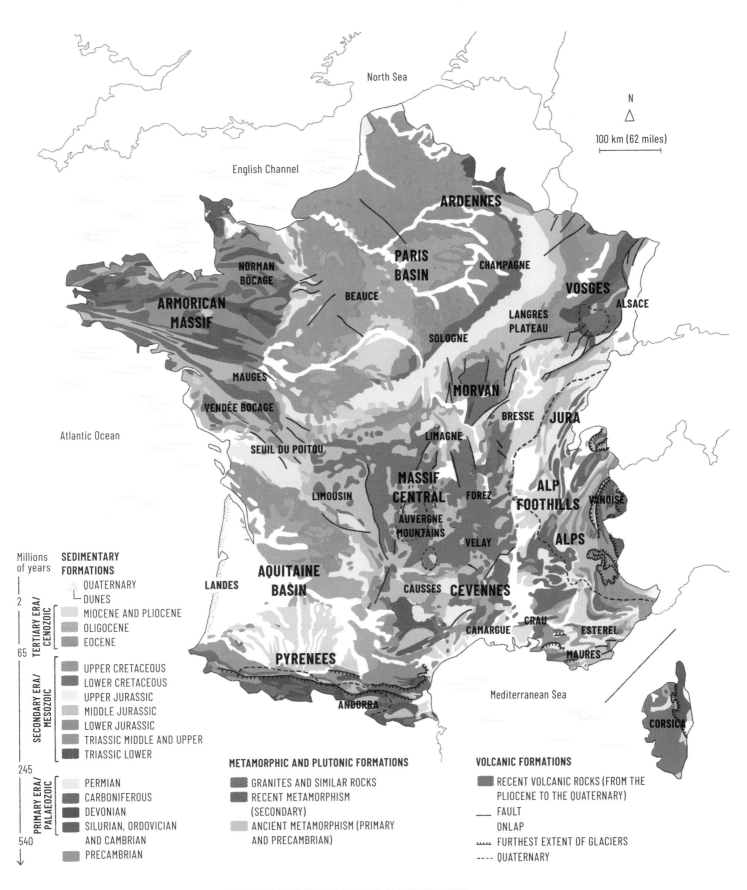

North Sea

English Channel

N

100 km (62 miles)

ARDENNES

PARIS
BASIN

CHAMPAGNE

VOSGES

NORMAN
BOCAGE

BEAUCE

ALSACE

ARMORICAN
MASSIF

LANGRES
PLATEAU

SOLOGNE

MAUGES

MORVAN

VENDÉE BOCAGE

BRESSE

JURA

Atlantic Ocean

LIMAGNE

SEUIL DU POITOU

MASSIF
CENTRAL

ALP
FOOTHILLS

VANOISE

LIMOUSIN

FOREZ

AUVERGNE
MOUNTAINS

ALPS

VELAY

AQUITAINE
BASIN

LANDES

CAUSSES

CEVENNES

CRAU

CAMARGUE

ESTEREL

PYRENEES

MAURES

Mediterranean Sea

ANDORRA

CORSICA

Millions of years	SEDIMENTARY FORMATIONS		
	QUATERNARY		
	DUNES		

TERTIARY ERA/ CENOZOIC
- 2
- 65

MIOCENE AND PLIOCENE
OLIGOCENE
EOCENE

SECONDARY ERA/ MESOZOIC
- 245

UPPER CRETACEOUS
LOWER CRETACEOUS
UPPER JURASSIC
MIDDLE JURASSIC
LOWER JURASSIC
TRIASSIC MIDDLE AND UPPER
TRIASSIC LOWER

PRIMARY ERA/ PALAEOZOIC
- 540

PERMIAN
CARBONIFEROUS
DEVONIAN
SILURIAN, ORDOVICIAN AND CAMBRIAN
PRECAMBRIAN

METAMORPHIC AND PLUTONIC FORMATIONS

GRANITES AND SIMILAR ROCKS
RECENT METAMORPHISM (SECONDARY)
ANCIENT METAMORPHISM (PRIMARY AND PRECAMBRIAN)

VOLCANIC FORMATIONS

RECENT VOLCANIC ROCKS (FROM THE PLIOCENE TO THE QUATERNARY)
FAULT
ONLAP
FURTHEST EXTENT OF GLACIERS
QUATERNARY

GEOLOGICAL MAP OF FRANCE, BY JACQUES FANET

Understanding igneous rock

In recent years, we have seen more and more wine lists being organized according to underlying rock type. There has also been a proliferation of specialist tomes addressing the links between vineyards and geology, including *Vineyards, Rocks, & Soils* (2018) by British geologist Alex Maltman or the work of Kevin Pogue. What is being discussed? How can we understand these rocks, their formation and their differences?

Three great rock families

There are three great families of rocks that are distinguished by the way they were formed: igneous and metamorphic rocks, which are endogenous (formed in the depths beneath the Earth's crust), and sedimentary rocks, which are exogenous and produced on the surface of the Earth.

We shall begin with the rocks that come from the Earth's mantle or crust, igneous rocks – from Latin *ignis*, or "fire". As their name suggests, they are created through the crystallization of the Earth's magma, a molten rock made up of silicates and gases, or from the partial or total melting of crustal rocks. They are found in regions of tectonic activity (the subduction zones and rift zones that form plate boundaries) and "hot spots" (regions within plates above rising plumes of hot mantle, as in Hawaii or the Canary Islands). They can be found at the roots of ancient mountainous areas that have been eroded over time to reveal the plutonic rocks in their depths. But active volcanoes also display this dynamic in real time, as well as the diversity of igneous rock that is possible.

> " All plutonic rock has a volcanic equivalent of the same composition as the type of magma from which it was created

Formation and composition of igneous rock

The slow, deep solidification of magma produces these plutonic or intrusive rocks, while rapid surface cooling creates volcanic or extrusive rocks, the best known of which is lava. Every plutonic rock has a volcanic equivalent of the same composition as the type of magma from which it was created. The way they were formed determines their texture: the crystals that make up the granular texture of plutonic rock can be clearly seen, but most volcanic rock has an "aphanitic" texture: the crystals that compose the rock are not visible to the naked eye because they cooled more quickly. Their degree of hardness and potential for erosion also vary greatly, while their hue comes from the the minerals they contain. All these rocks can thus be classified according to their mineralogical composition (quartz, feldspar and secondary mineral content). Chemically, they are primarily distinguished by their percentage by weight of silica, into ultramafic (less than 45 per cent), mafic (45-55 per cent), intermediate (55-65 per cent) and felsic (more than 65 per cent).

The presence or absence of minerals has been explained by geologist Norman Bowen in a theory, called the Bowen's reaction series. This is a theory of fragmented crystallization of magma in a series of reactions: if the rock is rich in potassium and sodium, it is felsic; if it is rich in magnesium and iron, it is mafic. The terms acidic and basic were once common, but this terminology is confusing and is now no longer used for rock.

Vineyards on plutonic rock

Granites are the largest and best-known group within this family. They underlie several famous wine regions, including parts of the northern Rhône and Beaujolais in France, Dão in Portugal and the Strathbogie Ranges in Australia, as well as the slopes of California's Sierra Nevada, the Simonsberg in South Africa and the Itata Valley in Chile. They differ widely and are classified according to their composition and susceptibility to erosion. Unfortunately, the lingua franca of wine does not often take these differences into account. Granites are often light grey because of their quartz crystals and owe any other nuances in their coloration and hardness to other minerals: the pink in the granite at Fleurie in Beaujolais comes from the potassium in feldspar, and the black speckles in the rocks in Ajaccio from biotite.

Its strength and density makes granite the construction material of choice for *lagares*, the traditional maceration vats used for Port, and for vine stakes in Galicia, but equally these properties make it difficult to dig out cellars in granite regions. Wine stores tend to be above ground in such places.

There are other plutonic rocks that are found more rarely in vineyards and are less well known. Contrary to its

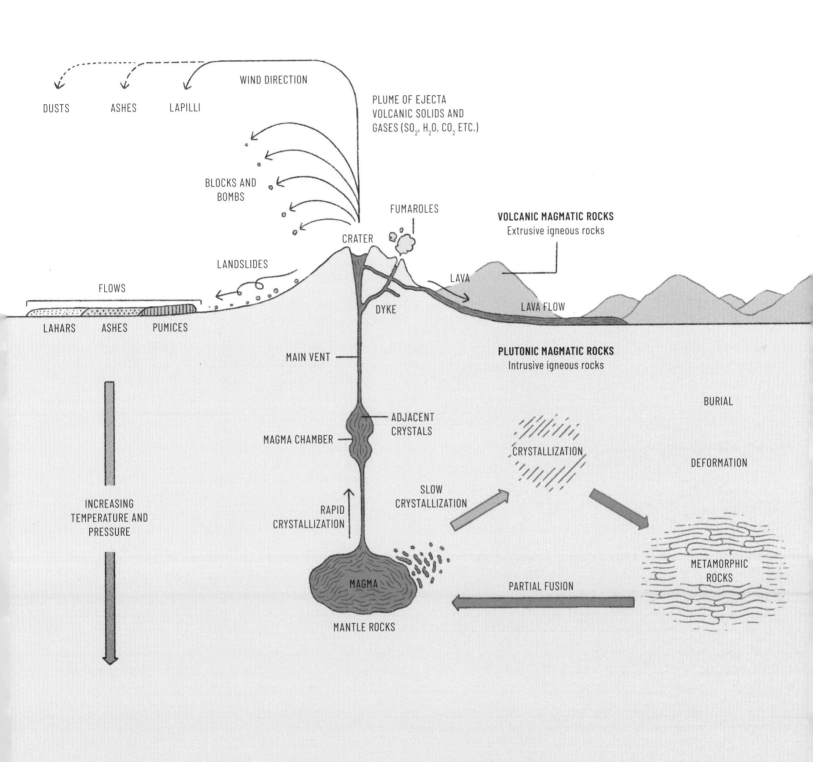

WIND DIRECTION

DUSTS   ASHES   LAPILLI

PLUME OF EJECTA
VOLCANIC SOLIDS AND
GASES (SO_2, H_2O, CO_2 ETC.)

BLOCKS AND
BOMBS

FUMAROLES

CRATER

LANDSLIDES

VOLCANIC MAGMATIC ROCKS
Extrusive igneous rocks

FLOWS

LAVA

LAHARS   ASHES   PUMICES

DYKE

LAVA FLOW

MAIN VENT

PLUTONIC MAGMATIC ROCKS
Intrusive igneous rocks

BURIAL

ADJACENT
CRYSTALS

MAGMA CHAMBER

CRYSTALLIZATION

DEFORMATION

INCREASING
TEMPERATURE AND
PRESSURE

RAPID
CRYSTALLIZATION

SLOW
CRYSTALLIZATION

METAMORPHIC
ROCKS

MAGMA

PARTIAL FUSION

MANTLE ROCKS

THE FORMATION OF IGNEOUS ROCKS

In search of the identity of volcanic wines

Volcanic wines have always been a source of fascination – from the time of Pliny the Elder and the eruption of Vesuvius in the year 79 CE, to the present-day craze. Whether on islands (Madeira, the Canaries, the Azores, Sicily) or mainlands (Italy's Vulture and Vesuvius, Rangen de Thann in Alsace or Kaiserstuhl in Germany), and whether active (Chile), extinct (Soave, Alto Piemonte in Italy, Hungary, northeastern America) or dormant (Santorini, Auvergne), do volcanoes impart a particular characteristic to wines despite the diversity of cépages, climates and cultivation methods? Canadians John Szabo MS (master sommelier) and Benoît Marsan (professor of chemistry at Université du Québec and of wine chemistry at Institut de Tourisme et d'Hôtellerie du Québec) have set about studying just this question. Often very well drained and relatively poor in organic matter, although rich in certain mineral elements, do these terroirs have a distinctive organoleptic signature? Might their concentrations of potassium, sodium and iron affect the taste of the wine? Are there any correlations between the microbiota of these soils and the behaviour of the vines? The results of the study are eagerly awaited.

image, Beaujolais is not just granitic - the *crus* at Juliénas and Côte de Brouilly are principally based on diorite, a rock with no quartz but composed of hornblende, a dark, iron-rich amphibole that is known locally as bluestone because of its colour. Gabbro, a rock containing pyroxene and feldspars but no quartz, is attracting attention with the rise of the new *crus communaux* in the Muscadet region, such as Gorges. Gabbro is also to be found in the Sierra Foothills of California.

Vineyards on volcanic rocks

Basalt, the volcanic equivalent of gabbro, is the best-known and most widespread extrusive rock, and it is the principal component of the oceanic crust of the Earth. It varies from very dark green to black, depending on its pyroxene content, and it originates from slow lava flows that are typical of flattened volcanoes known as shield volcanoes. Weathered basalt releases a large variety of nutritive elements (cations) such as iron, magnesium and calcium carbonate. Many of the original minerals in basalt weather to form clay minerals that give these soils beneficial cation exchange capability – in other words, they are extremely fertile.

Wine regions defined by this type of rock include the Columbia Valley AVA, between the US states of Washington and Oregon; the butte in Somló, Hungary; some of the vineyards in Auvergne; Forst in Germany's Pfalz - and of course, the slopes of Mount Etna. Andesite, which takes its name from the Andes, occurs on the west coast of the Americas and in Santorini. Its best-known form is porphyry, a decorative rock, often green or red, that has undergone two crystallization processes. It is found in the Nahe region in Germany, and in Italy, especially in Gattinara (Alto Piemonte) and north of the lakes around Bolzano (Alto Adige/South Tyrol). Last but not least, there is rhyolite, the volcanic equivalent of granite. This is found in deposits in Savennières and Coteaux du Layon in Anjou, in the Loire, and in the vineyards of the Stags Leap AVA in the Napa Valley, a region where it is often used as a construction material.

Pyroclastic volcanic rocks

The last group to consider is that of pyroclastic rocks. These, unlike lava flows, originate from explosive volcanic activity caused by the pressure of underground gases on magma that is more fluid because it is richer in silica. These rocks are also known as "tephras" and include rock fragments of different sizes that have more or less agglomerated. The best known in wine regions are:

- **Volcanic ash and tuff** (not to be confused with tufa or tuffeau), as in Campania, where tuff has given its name to a cépage, Greco di Tufo;
- **Pumice**, solidified lava foam found on the island of Lipari, north of Sicily, and in Tokaj;
- **Lapilli**, or pozzolans, from the Italian for "little stone", found, among other places, on Lanzarote in the Canaries.

Understanding sedimentary rock

Pebbles, limestone, chert (also known as silex) – sedimentary rocks shape all our landscapes and are part of everyday life. Covering more than 70 per cent of the Earth's crust, from continents to the depths of rivers, lakes and oceans, these accretions of particles that have become rock can be treasure troves of information, often capturing the history of the environment in which they were created – think of fossils trapped in chalk. This familiar nature conceals an exceptional geological, mineralogical and chemical diversity arising from their varied origins. What are the main ways of classifying these rocks, some of which are considered the very acme of great wine terroirs?

From sediments to sedimentary rocks

Unlike igneous rocks, sedimentary rocks are formed on the surface of the Earth through the solidification of sediments. According to Pogue, their classification is based on either grain size (detrital) or dominant mineral (chemical). The most common minerals are quartz (chert, diatomite), calcite (limestone, tufa) and dolomite (dolostone). Mineralogy and textural terms modify these basic subdivisions – for example, calcareous mudstone.

Several key kinds of material give rise to sedimentary rocks, but the most common are detrital particles from the mechanical erosion of pre-existing rocks through the action of frost or water, and the products of chemical or biochemical alteration by bacteria or lichen, for example. These processes cause minerals to be dissolved or transformed, in the way that feldspars turn into clay. These alteration processes can also combine: roots alter the surface both mechanically and biochemically.

In each case, these mechanisms produce particles of varying dimensions that are classified by their grain size:

- **Granulometric clays** (more than 2μm) - not to be confused with mineralogical clays - are invisible to the naked eye;
- **Colloids or silts, sands, fine gravels and coarse gravels** (more than 4mm/⅛in), are visible to the naked eye.

The formation of these sediments is only the first stage in the genesis of a sedimentary rock, however. They must still:

- Be transported by water or ice (these sediments are called **moraines**), wind (**aeolian sediments**) or gravity. The distance they travel depends on the mass of the particle and the energy of the means of transport; think of the different sizes of alluvial deposits on a riverbank. The energy of this movement erodes them to a greater or lesser degree, depending on the hardness of their minerals;

- Arrive at a particular place in sedimentary basins, either in the form of particles or chemical elements in solution (like the calcium ion Ca^{2+}) before being deposited in strata. This is known as **sedimentation**;
- Undergo a transformation, or diagenesis – a succession of varied chemical and mechanical processes, of which the most important are compaction and cementation. The pressure increases as other sediments are deposited, reducing porosity, expelling water and forming a cement between the particles in which bonds are formed between certain ions. The growth of minerals during diagenesis creates variations in the texture of sedimentary rocks.

> 66 To believe that there is any ultimate correlation between a cépage and a terroir of superior quality would be to see things too simplistically

Classification of sedimentary rocks

The classification of such rocks is based on a number of different parameters, including the size of the particles or the mineralogical nature of their constituents. A distinction is typically made between:

- **Detrital rocks**, which may be loose or consolidated. They are loose when the particles, of whatever size, remain free: beach sand can remain in the same state after burial and diagenesis; it is still called "sand" but is considered a rock. The size of the particles makes it possible to distinguish clays (less than 2μm) from silts (2-63μm), fine sands (63μm-2mm/¹⁄₁₆in), coarse sands and fine gravels (more than 2mm/¹⁄₁₆in). They are said to be consolidated when their original porosity, due to diagenesis, is filled with a cement of some kind (for example, carbonate, silica or

Diatomite – a magical sedimentary rock

Almost as light as a feather, diatomite is an extremely porous, friable and abrasive rock formed from the skeletons of diatoms, which are marine and lake algae. Diatomite is often white and can be confused with chalk but is very different from the latter: there is no limestone involved in diatomite, just pure or almost pure silica, which is responsible for diatomite's remarkable properties. Many use it unwittingly every day, perhaps in an exfoliating facial mask, or in the litter tray set out for the cat, when striking a match or brushing one's teeth, or even cleaning silver. It is also widely used in wine processing: kieselguhr is diatomaceous earth, used to filter wines. Some vignerons have been marketing its presence for a couple of decades: the Sta Rita Hills AVA in Santa Barbara, California, has striking diatomite cliffs, which can be seen in the film *Sideways*.

ferruginous). Clays are then designated as argilites or pelites, silts as siltites, sands as sandstone and the largest particles as conglomerates.

- **Rocks of "chemical" origin**: these are formed through the precipitation of ions dissolved in water, such as certain limestones (travertines), silex, or better still evaporites (gypsum and salt). We know, however, that in most cases micro-organisms play a role in the crystallogenesis of minerals of this kind.
- **Rocks of biochemical and biological origin**: their creation essentially depends on the presence of living organisms with shells or skeletons, animal or plant plankton, or macroplants. They are of crucial importance to winemaking, and most limestones are of this type. Chalk and coal are the best-known examples of this kind of rock.
- **Sedimentary rocks that are the products of alteration, or alterites**: these are often the result of alteration processes that create mineral concentrations such as bauxite, aluminium ore, ochres, certain iron ores, or manganese ores.

What about vineyards?

Sedimentary rocks account for the vast majority of wine terroirs, and all types may be home to vineyards.

- **Detrital rocks**. The best-known conglomerates are puddingstones (Jurançon, Dry Creek AVA), sandstone (Alsace), safres (sandy marl found in Châteauneuf-du-Pape) and greywackes (New Zealand). Shales make up more than 46 per cent of all sedimentary rocks and are often confused with schists because of their laminated structure, but they are less well represented, except in the Finger Lakes AVA.
- **Rocks resulting from chemical precipitation** are rarer. Examples are Sancerre's renowned silex, gypsum in Franconia and Alsace, travertine in Pouilly-Fumé and Lazio formed in hot water – for example, in thermal springs – and its cold-water equivalent, the tufa of Rioja and Ribera del Duero. Note that the latter, a chemical precipitate of calcium carbonate, should not be confused with tuff, which is a pyroclastic, volcanic rock, or tuffeau, which is a biochemical, low-density Loire Valley marine limestone composed primarily of the skeletons of foraminifera.
- **Biochemical rocks** are without doubt the best known of all sedimentary rocks, with one in particular – limestone – being especially revered. Limestone deposits form the bedrock of the Paris Basin, encompassing the Cognac region and the central and eastern areas of the Loire, Champagne and Burgundy. Limestone consists of at least 50 per cent calcium carbonate ($CaCo_3$) but is rarely pure, containing other elements that subtly influence its colour but not its solubility or susceptibility to erosion, its good water retention and high pH.

  There is a wide range of limestones, depending on the period and the seas in which they were formed. Some are very rich in fossils, and these include oolithic (Côte d'Or) and entroques limestones (Pouilly-Fuissé). Those containing high levels of magnesium are known as dolomites after the eponymous Italian region where they are common. Chalk is a very pure limestone formed from coccoliths (minuscule plates made up of the exoskeletons of algae that accumulated in the oceanic depths after their death) and is found in parts of Champagne and England. The term is frequently overused, however; school chalk often contains gypsum, and tailor's chalk is actually talc (magnesium silicate).

  Marls are a mixture of limestone and clay in equal proportions; if one were to take precedence over the other, the result might be called clay, calcareous marl, argillaceous limestone or limestone. There is a remarkable diversity in the colour of the marls in the Jura, arising from the mineral composition. There are also some biochemical rocks whose origins are to be found in organisms that are not calcareous but siliceous: diatomites.

Finally, some terroirs are identified by sediment and grain size, with no direct consideration of either diagenesis or chemical composition. In fact, the key compound here is what lies beneath: the clay. Vines are rarely grown on pure clays, but these may be found under silts, especially on loess, an aeolian sediment, as in Austria's Kremstal and Kamptal regions; or under sands, such as in Contra Costa, California. Clays are also of course to be found under a large number of terroirs in Bordeaux, and under cobbles, as in Châteauneuf-du-Pape or Washington State, where they lend their name to The Rocks District of Milton-Freewater AVA. While cobbles offer excellent drainage, they are chemically inert in soils, and the interest comes from the underlying clays.

Whether by sheer chance or natural predetermination, some of the world's most iconic wine regions – Burgundy, Champagne and Bordeaux – are located on sedimentary rocks, especially limestones. It therefore comes as no surprise that ambitious producers have set off around the globe in search of similar geologies, in the hope of producing wines of equivalent quality. After working at the Romanée-Conti and Dujac estates in Côte d'Or, France, Josh Jensen spent several years prospecting for limestones in the US before founding Calera in 1974, planting Pinot Noir on the slopes of Mount Harlan in California. However, to believe that there is any ultimate correlation between a cépage and a terroir of superior quality would be to see things too simplistically and to deprive ourselves of a multitude of hitherto unexplored possibilities.

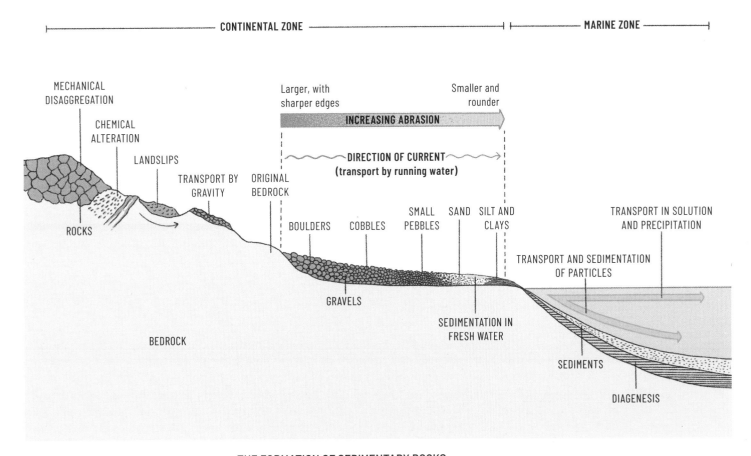

THE FORMATION OF SEDIMENTARY ROCKS

Understanding metamorphic rock

It was the Roman poet Ovid who gave us the concept of metamorphosis, the notion of a change of form and matter into an entirely different reality, when he made it the leitmotif of his poem *Metamorphoses*, a retelling of Greek and Roman myths. In much the same way, metamorphic rocks are created through a transformation of pre-existing rocks into completely new geologies. How are they formed? Which are the iconic metamorphic wine regions? What should we make of this cycle of rock transformation?

The formation process of metamorphic rocks

Metamorphism is a process that takes place unseen beneath the Earth's crust over thousands, indeed millions, of years. Most metamorphic rocks are related to the subduction of igneous, sedimentary and/or metamorphic rocks when one tectonic plate is forced beneath another, but others are created by "baking" rocks through contact with large bodies of magma as explained by Pogue. Rocks metamorphosed by subduction are said to have undergone "regional" metamorphism; rocks baked by contact with plutons, "contact" metamorphism.

As it sinks down, the original rock, the protolith, is subjected to increased external pressure, equal on all sides. On occasion, tectonic stress, the pressure caused by plate movements, can alter the external shape and texture of the original rock, which creates folds, fractures and layering. This pressure is compounded by a temperature rise of 25°C for each additional kilometre (45°F per mile).

> Far from being immutable and eternal, all the rocks on Earth are in fact undergoing perpetual transformation via different geological processes

The majority of metamorphic rocks are not formed at great depths, however, but between 12 km and 24 km (7.5-15 miles) beneath the Earth's surface, where the pressure is up to 12 times greater and temperatures are anything from 300°C to 600°C (570°F to 1,110°F). The original rock does not melt under such conditions, but remains solid; as it sinks and leaves its "domain of stability", its mineral composition becomes unstable. In seeking equilibrium, the minerals making up the rock, such as the clays in shale or mudstone, which themselves are more or less stable, gradually recrystallize into new minerals, such as micas that are stable in the new higher-temperature, higher-pressure environment.

The composition of metamorphic rocks is generally layered, a result of the pressures exerted during their formation. This is known as foliation, a laminated structuring that has different grades: at first a slate, the lowest grade metamorphic rock, then a phyllite, which is a shiny slate, with barely any visible mica grains; this is also low-grade. Then comes schistosity, or the alignment of coarse visible micas; this is intermediate-grade metamorphic rock. The last stage is gneissosity, the highest grade, represented by gneiss.

The geological history of a rock can thus be reconstructed from its crystallization, analysis of which reveals the degree of metamorphism it has undergone: contact metamorphism (with low pressure, along a magma chamber, for example), regional metamorphism (where temperature and pressure rise progressively), cataclastic metamorphism (with high pressure from the crushing and shearing of rock during tectonic movement), or the very rare impact metamorphism (due to a impact from meteorites, so a different process from the other sorts of metamorphism). These are all a matter of gradation rather than strict divisions between the rocks that are formed. Even though there are many parameters in combination – including the original rock, the type of metamorphism, and mineral compositions – it is nonetheless possible to classify rocks by petrographic facies (their foliation and the nature of their minerals) or by metamorphic sequence (the order of their transformations): basalt is transformed into green schists, then amphibolite and finally eclogite; clay transforms into slate, phyllite, mica-schist, paragneiss and ultimately migmatites.

But the usual classification is based on index minerals, which are minerals associated with specific temperatures and pressure regimens – for example, chlorite is a green mica associated with low-grade metamorphism. Ultimately, with enough heat and pressure, any protolith can be become a migmatite – a hybrid metamorphic-igneous rock that has undergone partial melting.

The metamorphic rocks of the world's vineyards

Metamorphic rocks are brought to the surface by erosion, often at the roots of mountain ranges that have been worn away over time. An example is Muscadet, on the edge of the Armorican massif, which itself is part of the Hercynian Chain that, 360 million years ago, had an elevation in excess of 6,000m (c. 20,000ft), as opposed to the 60m (200ft) of today. Outcrops of metamorphic rocks may take various forms.

- The best known is **slate** that has come from shale or mudstone (a fine, detrital rock) and has been gently transformed by weak metamorphism. It is unfortunately often confused with schist. Slate is lower-grade metamorphosed rock that has no visible mineral grains; schist is composed of coarse-grained micas visible to the naked eye. Slate can be split easily; its fissility makes it useful for roofing; schist doesn't break as cleanly.

- **Schists** are the result of additional metamorphism and occur with mica crystals - white crystals mean muscovite schist, and black mean biotite schist, for example. These extremely durable rocks can be used for vineyard buildings that clearly betray the local geology. Various regions owe their identities to schists, including parts of Anjou, Faugères, parts of Roussillon, the Côte Brune in Côte-Rôtie, Cap Corse in Corsica, Germany's Mosel and Rheingau, Priorat and Galicia in Spain, the Portuguese Douro, Cederberg in South Africa and Central Otago in New Zealand. However, these

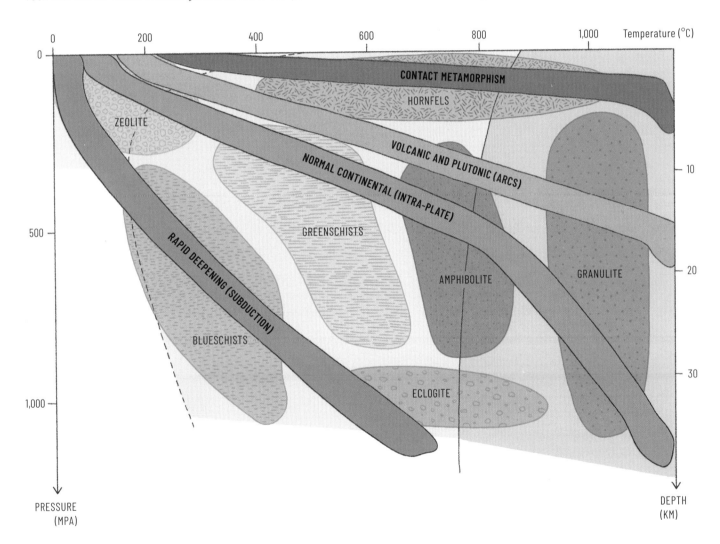

THE DIFFERENT FACIES OF METAMORPHIC ROCKS

This diagram shows the spectrum of different metamorphic facies in terms of temperature, pressure and depth conditions. Metamorphic facies are one of the subdivisions used by scientists to classify metamorphic rocks.

regions are far from being identical, and their mineral composition is varied and difficult to typify. What they have in common is their schistosity. Schists associated with sandstone break down into clay-schisto-sandstone soils with a low pH that retain water well.

- **Gneiss** is the next stage of metamorphism. A hard and dense rock made up of micas, quartz and feldspars, it is known as paragneiss when of sedimentary origin, and orthogneiss when made up of igneous rock. *Crus* from Le Pallet in Muscadet, Caramany in Roussillon and Austria's Wachau are rich in this type of rock.
- The final stage before the protolith melts to form magma is **migmatite**, which is typical of Tupin-et-Semons in Côte-Rôtie, Côtes du Forez in the Loire and Okanagan in Canada.

With the exception of slate and schist, metamorphosed sedimentary rocks are less common in wine regions: few vines grow on real marble, and the famous "marble of Comblanchien" is in fact a very pure limestone from the Middle Jurassic. Dark green amphibolite has become an iconic symbol of Muscadet, used in many wine names there, as well as to define some of the *crus*, and as it alters, it gives rise to clays from the montmorillonite family. The extremely hard hornfels,

which is found in Andlau in Alsace, is known as "Steige schist". Serpentinite is even a vine repellent – the distribution of vineyard land in the Troodos Mountains on Cyprus is a clue. Its high levels of magnesium and other minerals hamper the plant's assimilation of potassium and calcium.

The Earth's infinite rock cycle

Far from being immutable and eternal, all the rocks on Earth are in fact undergoing perpetual transformation via different geological processes; in particular circumstances, any of them can be plunged underground to merge and form new magma. Once on the surface, they all undergo change in great cycles of emergence, transformation and destruction. Some of these cycles are long – the journey from magma to magma takes between 10 million and 100 million years – while others, such as from rock to rock, are shorter, from 100,000 to 1 million years. This would explain how the rocks that we know are relatively young by comparison with the age of the Earth: the oldest rocks are just over 500 million years in age, while our planet has been around for 4.6 billion years. The formation of subsoil rocks takes place within this dynamic of recycling, the "potting compost" of the landscapes in which our vines grow.

The multicoloured slate schists of the Mosel River in Germany

The amphitheatre of vineyards facing the little hamlet of Pünderich, tucked into a great loop of the Mosel River, is breathtaking, with Riesling trained on stakes defying gravity on stone terraces that fall away dramatically to the river. Clemens Busch produces around 20 cuvées from the 19 ha he farms biodynamically on this small hillside near Marienburg. Identified by the age of the vines, the positioning of the different plots within the *cru*, the style of vinification and the underlying bedrock, three wines come from three different types of slate schist: *Vom Roten* (red), *Vom Blauen* (blue) and *Vom Grauen* (grey). Tasting them in order is an astonishing experience. They seem so different even though they come from vines planted in the same way just a stone's throw apart, and from grapes that are vinified in exactly the same way. Is it due to the rock?

For geologist Alex Maltman, this relationship is dubious in the case of coloured schists. He maintains that the mineral elements that differentiate them are absorbed by the vines either in tiny quantities or not at all; they are either of no use (the carbon that the grey schist has to offer is already obtained from photosynthesis), too small in quantity, potentially too toxic (titanium, vanadium and chrome) or they may still be impossible to assimilate (ferric iron, Fe^+, must be dissolved to form Fe^{2+}, a process promoted by mycorrhizae via particular molecules known as siderophores). However, Maltman goes on to add that we should perhaps be looking not so much for a direct relationship between plant and geology as for an indirect and more complex link: these mineral differences might be influencing the albedo, through variations in solar energy wavelength, and more generally the mesoclimate and the microbiological life in the soil. An increasing roster of agronomists takes another view, however, maintaining that these trace elements are the metallic co-factors of enzymes that may be involved in the genesis of aromatic molecules. The minerality of wines is a question of vast proportions.

Is there an ideal soil for viticulture?

Discussion of the geology of wine areas has become standard practice these days. The granites of Beaujolais, the basalt of Mount Etna, the Terra Rossa of Coonawarra in Australia, the slate schists of the Mosel river in Germany – the bedrocks of these areas are emblazoned on brochures and labels, both by the regions and the producers. While vines might seem to spring straight from the rock, however, it is a fact that they grow in soil, however thin and easily overlooked it might be. Located between sky and Earth, this relatively thin layer of mineral elements and organic matter is a structure undergoing a perpetual transformation that makes viticulture possible. Far from being a static list of ingredients, soil is dynamic; it is formed, it changes and it can disappear, just like rocks. This transformation is known as pedogenesis, the study of which (pedology, or soil science) was invented in 1883 by Russian scientist Vasily Dokuchaev. What processes does it entail? Are some soils more suitable for viticulture than others? How do soils determine the growth of vines and so influence the quality of the wine?

The formation of soil

The camera does in fact lie; the vines at Châteauneuf-du-Pape do not grow directly on cobbles.

Plant a vine in a pile of slate or pebbles, and it will wither and die, unable to survive for the thousands of years required for these rocks to degrade into soil. It needs a complex organo-mineral substrate, developed over time, from the breakdown of organic matter and the alteration of bedrock.

This creation of soil involves two major series of transformations, the bio-physico-chemical alteration of rocks and the formation of new minerals; in some respects, soil begins with the "rotting" of rock. Everything on the Earth's surface is inexorably being worn down and degraded. The rate at which this takes place depends on the type of bedrock, the topography and the climate, which also determine the intensity of the meteorological, biological and other processes involved: basalt alters 10 times more quickly than granite; high temperatures promote degradation, and heavy rainfall accelerates migration within the soil. Pedogenesis does not have the same dynamic in temperate climates as in tropical climates, or on hills as on plains; different organisms colonize basic or acidic soils. These factors explain the almost infinite variety of soils on Earth.

The birth of soils

There are three ways in which rocks may be broken down.

• **Biological degradation**, initially not visible, occurs when a microbial biofilm including algae and bacteria develops on exposed rocks, attacking them mechanically and chemically.

• **Physical degradation** is more apparent, with wind, heat, water, freezing and thawing abrading and fragmenting rocks and promoting chemical change.

• **Chemical degradation** may take multiple forms, including solution and oxide reduction. Water plays a key role here: rainfall, which contains carbonic acid from dissolved CO_2 and therefore has an acid pH, is corrosive. It transfers and precipitates minerals, causing new concentrations. It rapidly attacks and leaches out limestone, leaving behind the more solid elements of the original material, like quartz. It alters silicate rocks (basalt, granite) and facilitates the creation of clays - for example, through the hydrolysis of feldspars and micas. Air is also an agent of change - O_2 plays a role in the oxide reduction of elements such as iron on the surface and in the pores of rocks. CO_2 promotes the creation of $CaCO_3$ - better known as calcium carbonate.

A lithosol, a skeletal covering of soil, is eventually established, along with pioneer plants, followed by colonies of ever-more-complex living communities, depending on the type of bedrock and the environment. As they die, they create litter, which decomposes to form humus. Next to appear is the clay-humus complex, and the soil turns brown. Organic and mineral elements migrate, and strata are formed. This entails the forming of "horizons", homogeneous layers of varying depths that distinguish the soil from its bedrock and

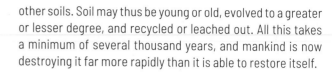

Why is soil pH so important for wine?

Study of the soil always involves the terms "acid" and "basic", but what exactly do they mean? The pH (potential of hydrogen), is a measure of the acidity or basicity of an aqueous solution; the pH scale represents the concentration of hydrogen ions (H^+) and hydroxide ions (HO^-) in a solution, which in turn determine its degree of acidity. If a solution contains an equal amount of both, it is neutral – so water has a pH of 7. If the level of H^+ is higher, the solution is acidic (pH between 0 and 7); if it has more HO^-, it is basic (pH between 7 and 14). The scale is logarithmic – a solution with a pH of 4 is 10 times as acidic as one with a pH of 5.

Assessing the pH of a soil from its bedrock is not straightforward. To begin with, it is not the soil itself but the water in the soil that has a pH value, and there are several external factors that come into play, including climate, agricultural techniques and microbiota. As a general rule, rocks that do not contain carbonates (like granites, sandstone and schists) give acidic soils, while those that are rich in them, such as limestone, give basic soils; the schist soils of the Mosel river have a pH lower than 6, but the chalky soils of Champagne have a pH between 7.9 and 8.5. In addition, pH varies with soil depth.

But why is it so important for vines? Rootstocks have affinities that vary with the pH, and the pH level influences the way minerals and trace elements are assimilated by vines. The cation exchange capacity (CEC), which determines the fertility of the soil, varies with pH, with acidic soils having a lower CEC than basic soils. In addition, microbial and biological activity is more intense in soils with a pH between 5.5 and 7. The pH value is thus crucial and is a factor often corrected by wine-growers. One last point: might there even be a link between soil pH and the pH of the wine? The question is far from being a simple one.

other soils. Soil may thus be young or old, evolved to a greater or lesser degree, and recycled or leached out. All this takes a minimum of several thousand years, and mankind is now destroying it far more rapidly than it is able to restore itself.

Types of soil

Soils are classified into taxonomies, just like living species, and here the determining features are their characteristics and morpho-pedology, or structure; their granulometry, or texture; their composition; their horizons; and the dynamics of the transfer of elements within them, whether by gravity or the action of living organisms such as earthworms or humans (bioturbation).

Types of soil are identified by digging pedo-geological trenches, revealing horizons that are interdependent and often only gradually demarcated. These divisions are the soil's "fingerprint". The different strata are classified by letter code into the following main subdivisions.

- **Horizon 0 or humus** is the organic layer at the surface, made up of litter and humus.
- **Horizon A or topsoil** is the arable, organo-mineral layer where the clay-humus complex is metabolized. This rich but fragile layer enables crops to be grown.
- **Horizon B or subsoil** is the mineral layer, poorer in organic matter and humus but richer in clay, minerals and rock fragments.
- **Horizon C or parent material** is the bedrock's zone of change in which mineralogical breakdown starts with the loss of soluble ions.
- **Horizon R or bedrock** consists of the pure, unaltered, underlying rock.

As pedogenesis is highly dependent on climate and the environments that climates create, the different types of soil with their specific horizons follow the major climatic zones – a polar soil, for example, would not be found at the equator. The World Reference Base for Soil Resources (WRB) is a global database that recognizes 32 major soil groups and many national soil classifications based on the particularities of each country; in France, the *Référentiel pédologique* identifies 34 soil types known as *grands ensembles de références* (GER).

As the vine grows, its roots will thus penetrate a series of horizons. The interactions involved are incredibly complex, depending on many different factors: the type of soil, the age of the plant and its rootstock, agricultural practices and more. Roots reaching depths of 1.0–1.5m (3–5ft) are common in most viticultural soils, as opposed to 50cm (20in) in top-soils and depths in excess of 10m (33ft) in very deep but accessible soils, as in some of the gravel slopes of the Médoc. If the soil allows, vines may develop a double-root system, with the roots in the upper layers extracting water and nutrients, and

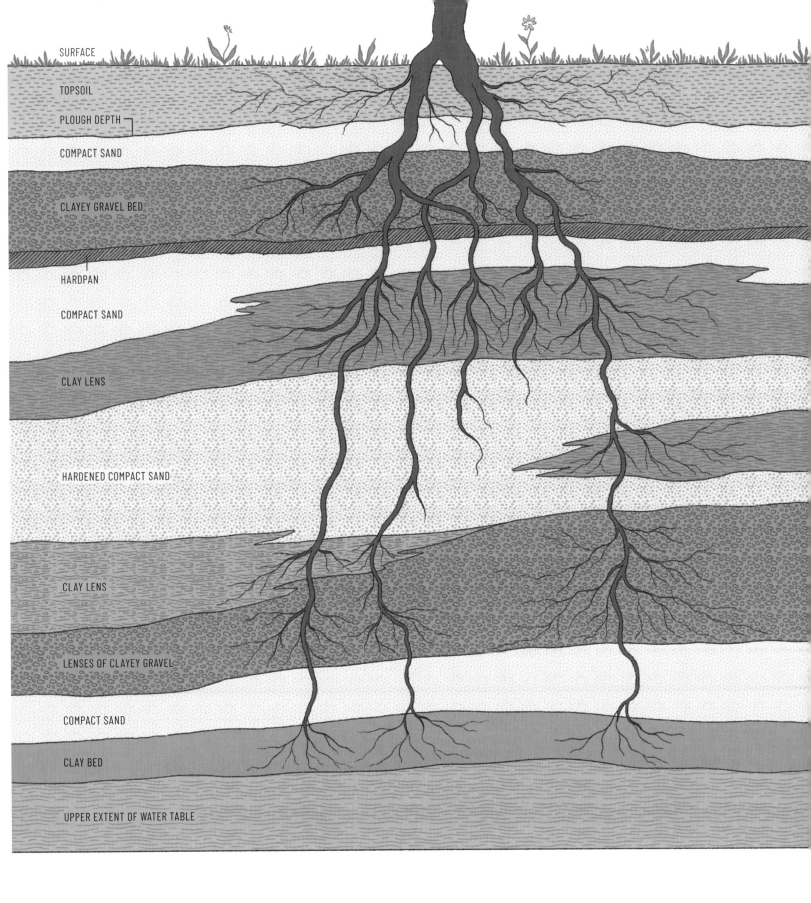

SURFACE

TOPSOIL

PLOUGH DEPTH

COMPACT SAND

CLAYEY GRAVEL BED

HARDPAN

COMPACT SAND

CLAY LENS

HARDENED COMPACT SAND

CLAY LENS

LENSES OF CLAYEY GRAVEL

COMPACT SAND

CLAY BED

UPPER EXTENT OF WATER TABLE

CROSS-SECTION OF A VINE IN GRAVES SOIL IN THE MÉDOC, AS DRAWN BY GÉRARD SEGUIN AND JAMES E WILSON

deeper roots able to source water in the event of excessive drought. There is not just one type of soil but a thousand soils, with vines needing to adapt to each on a case-by-case basis, according to their requirements and potential.

Residual vs transported soils

A point needs to be made here, according to specialists including Pogue: the difference between residual soils or transported soils is crucial to understanding the potential of terroir based on its geology. To quote his comments, "Many vineyards are planted on transported (alluvial, glacial, aeolian) soils that are quite thick so that the vine roots are not at all influenced by the underlying bedrock. A good example is the Columbia Valley AVA, where 90+ per cent of the vines are planted in thick wind-deposited loess and glacio-fluvial flood deposits. Chemically and texturally, the soils developed in these transported soils have no relationship to the underlying basalt bedrock, so it is incorrect to think of the Columbia Valley as a 'volcanic terroir' since vine roots do not encounter the bedrock. Many soils in France and in California are on thick alluvial deposits that insulate the vines from the bedrock. These vines are thus growing in soils derived from the prolonged weathering of the complex mixture of all the bedrock outcrops that lie upstream." This perspective finds a resonance with the work of geologist-agronomist Pedro Parra as exposed in his book *Terroir Footprints* (2020).

What a vine needs, or the functions of viticultural soil

World expert in viticulture Professor Kees van Leeuwen and his team at the National School of Agricultural Engineering, Bordeaux, have contributed to a body of research suggesting that vineyards that create great wines are enormously diverse geo-pedologically and that any hierarchical classification of these would be a mistake. Proof is provided by the 51 *grands crus* of Alsace, which are planted in a veritable mosaic of bedrocks from limestone to granite, including marl, sandstone, schist and more besides, in every possible combination. Fine or coarse-textured, acidic or basic pH, rich or poor in organic matter, young or old and so on – there is certainly more than one ideal type of soil for growing wine. Studies covering 400 ha of seven of the most renowned areas of Bordeaux have identified nine GERs, some of which have a greater correlation with the finest wines produced here than others.

> " Vineyards that create great wines are enormously diverse geo-pedologically, and any hierarchical classification of these would be a mistake

What is more, the soil often varies a great deal across a small area; extensive homogeneous tracts of land are very rare nowadays, because the vineyards have been consolidated.

The mechanisms explaining the links between soil and wine quality remain a mystery, however. Research has established only that some viticultural soils respond better than others to the needs of the vine in general, but each in its own way. So what functions should the soil ideally fulfil to satisfy the needs of *Vitis*? The first is to provide a sufficiently stable substrate for the plant, so it can take proper root and ward off any physical and chemical disturbance or biological attack that might alter its physiological capabilities. The second is to provide the vine with the mineral nutrition necessary for growth.

The minerals of viticultural soils and the "minerality" of wine

This is where considerable confusion arises around the link between the elements, or nutritive cations, that vines require, the minerals in the soil, and the notion of "minerality" in wines. Vines are extremely frugal creepers that by nature need very little, and less still when they are cultivated for the controlled production of grapes rather than indefinite production of biomass. This is why poor soils that are unusable for any other crop suit vines very well. All they need is a "Goldilocks zone" with no deficiencies or excesses – no overly high levels of active limestone or aluminium, for example. In addition, vines only ever take from the soil what they strictly need, in quantities that vary throughout the vegetative cycle. Six elements are essential: nitrogen, phosphorus, potassium, magnesium, calcium and sulphur, along with a number of trace elements.

Another common misconception that should be put into perspective is the origins of the nutrients that the rootstock requires: do they come from the bedrock or from organic matter?

Since they are neither solubilized nor in usable ionic form, minerals in the bedrock are not immediately available to the vine's roots. Microbiota, soil pH and the clay-humus complex therefore play a key role in the bioavailability of these elements, with the latter acting as a kind of repository, storing and redistributing the minerals. It operates principally via complexolysis, a chemical reaction in which mineral is taken from rocks exposed to weathering. Georges Truc explains that newly formed clays in the soil constitute a kind of cationic "bank", supplying solutions formed through contact with water and transmitting them to the rising sap via the hyphae of the mycorrhizae in the cells of the lateral roots. The mineral nutrition of a vine depends almost entirely on the mineral constituents of the subsoil that have been extracted from the bedrock. Nitrogen can only come from organic matter and would be rapidly exhausted after a number of vegetative cycles if there were no external input, hence the need for the wine-grower to add nitrogen, either directly, with organic or synthetic fertilizers, or indirectly, by sowing legumes between the rows of vines. A healthy vine grown on good soil with an active mycorrhizal system can source everything else itself.

What should be done if there is also a lack of mycorrhizae? The immediate solution would be to alter the soil, but if the mycorrhizae come to rely on this, there is a risk of creating a vicious circle of dependency without solving the underlying problem, which is the weakness of the microbiota. The most telling example here is potassium, which is widely present in French soils; a lack of aerobic bacteria gives the impression that vines are failing to assimilate it, and so the unsuspecting wine-grower uses fertilizer with salts of potassium, saturating the soil and creating an ever greater imbalance.

Bedrock, if it is within reach of the root system, can play a complex role in the mineral nutrition of plants and in the flavour of wines; the substance left when a wine is evaporated – the ashes – comes from the mineral load provided by the subsoil, but its influence on aromas is almost certainly indirect. It is also influential in other ways, such as in managing the vine's water supply, the soil's third function.

The vine's water regime

In 1986, professor of viticultural pedology Gérard Seguin, a pioneering researcher of the influence of soil and climate on the quality of Bordeaux wines, published a groundbreaking study on the famous vineyards of the Médoc (*"Terroirs" and Pedology of Wine Growing*) stating that the quality of the wines produced in these soils could not be correlated with the soils' mineral fertility. Paradoxically, his analysis even identified a deficiency of nitrogen and magnesium in the most renowned of the Médoc soils. He therefore posited that the principal factor for quality was the soils' capacity to regulate water supply at key junctures in the vine's vegetative cycle, in particular with a slight deficit after veraison to reduce the vigour of the vine while concentrating sugars and polyphenols in the grapes. Too much or too little water, and the vine and the grapes will not achieve optimum development.

The available water capacity of a soil depends on several factors.
• **Structure**, or its texture and porosity, which depends on the size of its constituent particles. Clays are thus identified by particle size (less than 2μm); they retain water and nutrients well but may be compact, making it difficult for vines to develop roots. Alluvial soils are lighter, aerated, and generally fertile. Sandy soils are light and well drained, but retain little water or mineral elements. Loam is considered the best soil for agriculture; it is an equal blend of

Albedo

In terms of soil, albedo refers to its capacity to reflect sunlight, measured on a scale of 0 to 1, according to the colour and nature of the soil surface.
· The darker the soil, the lower the albedo value, with basalt achieving an average of 10 per cent, while limestone scores an average of 35 per cent.
· The more the soil is covered with stones or grass, or broken up by ploughing, the lower the albedo value. An absolutely flat surface like a calm lake will thus reflect a great deal more energy, which is one of the reasons vines can be grown on slopes around the Great Lakes of the northern US. Even so, the main reason is the lakes' thermal mass, tied to the water's heat capacity: the warmth of the water moderates the climate near the lakes.

Reflected light boosts certain metabolic activities in vines, such as the production of polyphenols, and partially compensates for climate; the sun's rays not only provide light, they are also a source of heat. The soil's reflective capacity for light is inversely proportional to the thermal energy that it stores, so these two complementary functions should not be confused. A soil's ability to radiate and conduct heat depends on its type and texture, so dark soils like schists and basalts heat up more quickly and to higher temperatures than lighter-coloured material, and such soils radiate heat to the vine, primarily in the afternoon; not at night as mistakenly thought, because they also cool quickly.

Poor drainage and moisture, however, hamper this process. Clay soils take longer to warm up but can store more heat than sands, which has an impact on the vine's growth cycle. The nature of both bedrock and soil once again exerts a key influence on the vine's microclimate and conditions for growth.

sand and silt, with a smaller proportion of clay that assures good porosity and oxygenation of the roots while retaining sufficient quantities of water and nutrients.
• **Permeability and drainage**, or how water infiltrates and percolates through the soil. Excluding the role of human activity, it is the geological history of the bedrock that is of essential importance here. Rock type is of first importance; sedimentary rocks tend to be more permeable, while some clays and the majority of igneous and metamorphic rocks

are less so. The level of fracturing is another consideration; rock may develop fissures over time, which, even if only microscopic, still allow water to penetrate. Many viticultural soils in damp northern regions, including limestone soils, owe their interest to viticulture to these cracks, and the same is true for granitic substrates.

- **Gradient**, where the angle of orientation of the rock plane in respect of the slope and the degree to which it may or may not hinder the flow of water.
- **Topography**, where water run-off differs according to whether a plot of land lies on a plateau, a hill or a plain.
- **Stoniness**, where the amount of stones and gravel, along with their type and size, affects the water regime in several ways. Their quantity is one: they tend to limit the soil's capacity to retain rainwater and irrigation water even though they improve aeration, and they may also block water rising by capillary action. Horizons made up of impermeable clays can have the same effect but may also have an asphyxiating influence. In addition, a stony surface alters the amount of

solar energy received by the soil, affecting evapotranspiration, thermal inertia and compaction, and thus indirectly modifying its water regime.

Clays – the key to soils

Clays (in the mineralogical sense) are a further parameter of a soil's water regime and quality. These mineral compounds of sheets of aluminium and magnesium silicate form fascinating rocks that are of vital importance to agriculture, since their structure gives them a very large surface area for the volume they occupy. This allows them to retain water and ions with great efficiency, and thus makes them potentially very fertile. There are, however, differences in the layering of clays that affect to what degree water is extractable and accessible; kaolinite and illite are clays that swell and contract very little, while smectites, which include montmorillonites, expand greatly when moist and crack as they dry out.

In 2002, agronomists Claude and Lydia Bourguignon, the founders of the *Laboratoire d'Analyses Microbiologiques*

The soils of Châteauneuf-du-Pape, according to oenogeologist Georges Truc

A sea of orange pebbles, head-pruned vines, a clear blue sky and a ruined castle: the image of Épinal in Châteauneuf-du-Pape conceals far greater geological complexity than first meets the eye. Oenogeologist Georges Truc is an expert in the geology of the Rhône and has closely examined these sedimentary soils dating from the Mesozoic to the Quaternary Period.

- **To the west** lie the Lampourdier massif and Urgonian limestones from the Cretaceous period. Clayey sands have infiltrated beneath these small, hard, fissured slabs, creating a water reservoir in what is an otherwise stressful environment for vines. The wines here are more restrained but crisper, especially the whites.
- **To the east** lie pockets of red sandstone and a sandy marl made up of large shells that have been cemented by limestones. This rock is also widely used in local architecture but crumbles easily. Roots plunge down into red clays altered from marls. The wines have complex aromas, with interesting, tightly knit tannins.
- **At the eastern extremities** are the safres. Unexpectedly, vines do not suffer stress here because the roots find the underlying clays. This soil produces delicate and open wines with fine tannins.
- **At the heart of the AOC**, there are terraces of round pebbles, the famous *galets roulés*. These are the last remnants of rocks transported by the Rhône during the Quaternary period that have all been dissolved away to leave only quartz, the most resistant material, in the form of quartzite pebbles. They provide neither water nor nutrients, but hidden beneath them lies a further product from the dissolution of the rocks: clays of high quality. The wines are opulent, rich and tannic.

The different sectors of the appellation are explained by geology and expressed by Grenache, a cépage that invariably betrays its terroir, making it possible to taste the typicity of different sectors.

des Sols (LAMS), analysed the individual total surface areas of the clays of 53 *cru* vineyards in Burgundy, and the colour of the *cépage* planted. Their conclusion was that there was a correlation in 86 per cent of cases between the family of the clays and the planting of Chardonnay and Pinot Noir, and that these empirical decisions had been prompted by geological, pedological and topographical considerations.

In *Terroir and the Côte de Nuits* (2011), a study of the *grands crus* of Burgundy, the British importer and Master of Wine John Atkinson has noted that those devoted to reds contain more smectites than those set aside for whites, which were richer in kaolinite; a water balance had thus been struck between the *cépages* and the underlying types of limestones and clays.

In a complementary study (*Great Burgundy Wines: A Principal Components Analysis of "La Côte" Vineyards*, 2004) covering 2,816 vineyards in the Côte d'Or that sought to identify a unique factor that would make it possible to account for the difference between *grands crus* and *premiers crus*,

researcher Frank Wittendal concluded that it was neither elevation nor gradient nor bedrock and still less morphology that was the deciding factor, but rather the structure of the soil: *grands crus* contained less active limestone and a larger proportion of gravel scree from erosion of the hillsides. From this he concluded, as Seguin had already demonstrated in Bordeaux, that the most important factor in the production of Côte d'Or red wines of high quality is the soil structure, which needs to place the vines in a situation of slight water deficit around veraison.

On a more global scale, scientists have understood that the availability of water partially determines the style of wine that may be produced – and obviously the quality of that wine. The great viticultural soils thus offer a certain consistency of quality and quantity that marks them out over the long term. Soils are created within their environment and alter over time, and it is these complex dynamics that scientific models of terroir seek to replicate.

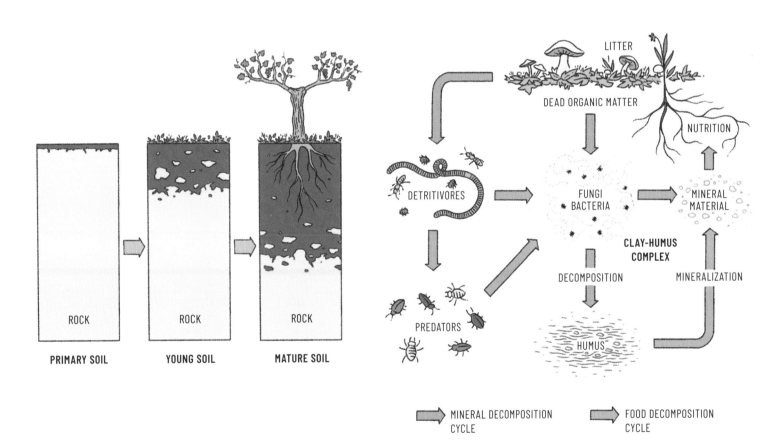

THE FORMATION OF SOIL, AS DESCRIBED BY ALAIN MALARD

Soils are born, and soils die. Their formation depends on numerous factors in their unique environment, and these may be biotic (flora and fauna) or abiotic (air, temperature, water and wind).

Climate, soil and terroir

There would be no vines without soil, and there would be no fine wines without particular types of soil. Similarly, there would be no prospect of any profitable, quality viticulture without a certain type of climate; climate and soil are the warp and weft of the production of fine wines. How do they interact? Is it possible to classify the plethora of different combinations in which they appear? Can we define terroir wines using climate and soil alone? What definition of terroir might such an approach imply – and is it enough?

The scientific approach and classification of terroir

The growing interest that the scientific study of viticultural soils has attracted since the 1960s is revealed particularly in the desire to find a rational basis for a complex and vague concept that has no status in law – that of terroir. One approach to classifying terroir would involve understanding and differentiating the natural potential of viticultural areas and then using stated parameters to establish hierarchies that could be considered objective; so soils could be considered to have potential for a given level of production. Or this method could even legitimize the idea that a wine's quality is necessarily linked to its origin, as is the case with the French AOC system.

> The wider the definition of terroir, the more interdisciplinary the modelling of its systems

This would explain why the geo-pedological analysis of wine areas and terroir that had taken its first steps in France at the instigation of INAO at the end of the 1930s began to pick up pace from the 1970s onward. Such studies have been regional, with Bordeaux, Burgundy, the Loire, Alsace, the Rhône and so on having differing approaches, and are mostly based on a narrow definition of terroir: the soil in which the vine is planted, including its geology and lithology, and the climate and its interactions with soil conditions. In other words, the soil is understood as an ecological locus, including its texture, pH and content of mineral and organic material. Since the first international conference on the scientific study of wine terroirs in 1996, however, some approaches have emerged as more relevant and effective, both in accounting for the diversity of combinations of soil and climate, and in zoning vineyards on the smallest scale possible ($\frac{1}{10,000}$ in the Côte d'Or, for example), ideally on a plot-by-plot basis. The idea in each instance is to identify consistent "units of terroir".

Tools to identify wine terroirs scientifically

In the 1970s, problems with chlorosis and the water regime of Cabernet Franc planted on the limestones of Saumur and Chinon prompted a team from INRAE d'Angers led by agronomists René Morlat, Jean Salette and Christian Asselin to study the geo-pedological aspects of the vineyards of the Loire, examining their climate and its influence on the local vines. Their work took an eco/geo/pedological approach, and the upshot was the development of the concept of a "basic terroir unit" (BTU); each unit is defined by its mesoclimate, its geological substrate and its state of degradation (rock/alteration/alterite – the extent to which it has turned into a clay). Thousands of geological trenches were dug, and weather stations were installed, first in Anjou and then in other regions of the Loire Valley. This information was then collated using algorithms and juxtaposed with wine-growers' knowledge and experience in the field, and supervised tastings.

The results led the team to conclude that there is a relationship between a wine and its terroir of origin that is to a greater or lesser degree identifiable and features three principal influences: precocity, or early ripening; potential vigour; and potential water supply, all of which are essentially determined by the lithology of the substrate (in other words, whether it has been altered or not). A BTU can be defined from these starting points.

With an end goal that is both theoretical and practical, this research has led to the production of an atlas that can be used by wine-growers on a plot-by-plot basis to fine-tune their vineyard management. For example, it has suggestions for the selection of rootstocks and cépages. With the inclusion of more than 400 BTUs from the Fiefs Vendéens to Touraine, it has now become the world's most comprehensive geo-pedological wine terroir-mapping project and can be accessed free of charge at eterroir-techniloire.com.

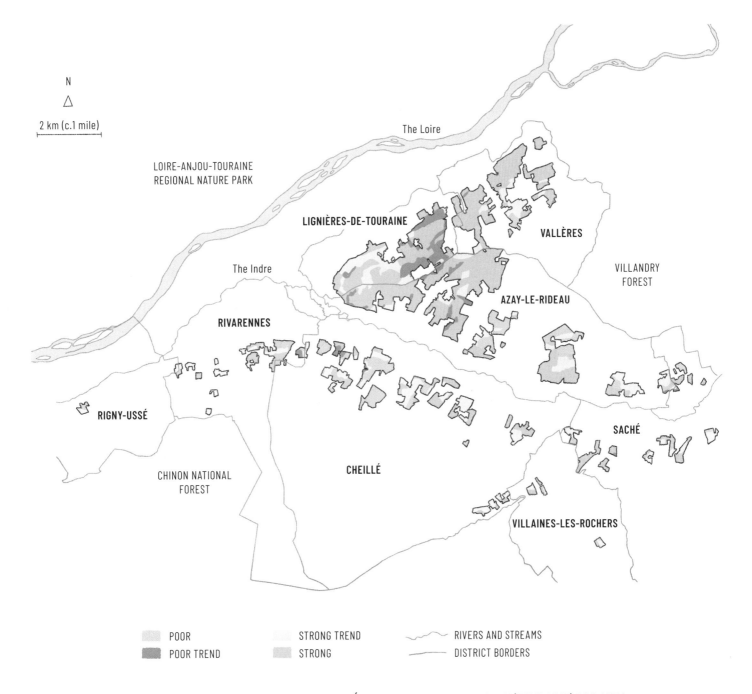

N

2 km (c.1 mile)

The Loire

LOIRE-ANJOU-TOURAINE
REGIONAL NATURE PARK

LIGNIÈRES-DE-TOURAINE

VALLÈRES

The Indre

VILLANDRY
FOREST

RIVARENNES

AZAY-LE-RIDEAU

RIGNY-USSÉ

SACHÉ

CHINON NATIONAL
FOREST

CHEILLÉ

VILLAINES-LES-ROCHERS

| | POOR | | STRONG TREND | | RIVERS AND STREAMS |
| | POOR TREND | | STRONG | | DISTRICT BORDERS |

ADVISORY MAP OF THE ADAPTATION OF THE CHENIN CÉPAGE IN THE AZAY-LE-RIDEAU (TOURAINE) AOC AREA

It is possible to use BTU (basic terroir unit, a concept developed by René Morlat's teams at INRAE in Angers) mapping to identify the suitability of a cépage and its rootstock for a terroir in relation to the styles of wine desired.

The BTU has been extrapolated from the Loire as an operational tool; Carbonneau and Alain Deloire, professor of vine physiology at Montpellier SupAgro, have used it in their *Traité de la vigne* to identify the major groups of global terroirs according to four dominant factors:
• Terroirs where **topography** is the dominant feature;
• Terroirs where **mesoclimate** is the dominant feature;
• Terroirs where **soil** is the dominant feature;

• Dry terroirs in regions where **irrigation** is necessary and therefore becomes a determining factor in the typicity and quality of the wines.

Carbonneau takes this a step further in suggesting the concept of a wine terroir unit (WTU), of which the BTU is but one component, interacting with the cépage and the cultivation system. The WTU can thus encompass a series of BTUs if a strong identity can be discerned in the wine produced,

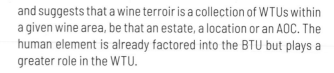

Argentina discovers its terroirs

The wines of Argentina have long been sold on their cépage rather than their origins. For both commercial and historic reasons in new viticultural countries, such blended terroir wines offer more flexibility for production. A revolution has been in progress since 2012, however. At the request of high-profile producers, the geology department of the faculty of agricultural sciences at Cuyo University has mapped the Mendoza region by terroir; previously, only administrative demarcations had been considered. The first geographical indications (GIs) were the administrative provinces; two DOCs were also based on political boundaries created in 1989 (Luján de Cuyo) and in 2007 (San Rafael). Since then, the criteria have been narrowed down, resulting in 2017 in the recognition of the Paraje Altamira GI, which is defined as the alluvial fan of the Tunuyán river, whose tiny pebbles are cemented together with calcium carbonate. Applications and approvals for GI status then followed thick and fast. Wishing to deepen his understanding of his terroir in Altamira, wine-grower Sebastián Zuccardi called on Pedro Parra, who had written a PhD thesis on wine terroirs that developed his own approach to soil classification. It was based on a combination of the following.

- Morlat's "rock/alteration/alterite": degradation, argillation and fissure profile.
- Soil derivation: sedimentary soils that have been moved, or soils coming directly from the bedrock without being transported.
- Soil scientist Michel-Claude Girard's unit of soil landscape with satellite imaging work. This is a unit of virtual and cartographic representations of the "landscape" formed by the mosaic of soils. This particular "landscape" is invisible to the eyes because it lies beneath the plant cover, but it plays a fundamental explanatory role for potential vegetation and certain failures of viticultural practices.
- The electromagnetic conductivity of soils complemented by direct analysis of trenches.

Parra's research identified units of macro-terroir (UMT), which he refined by studying the history of the plot and tasting the wine. He considers the wine-grower to be the interpreter of the land, and thus as much a factor in modifying the environment as the person responsible for the final product. He describes his work in *Terroir Footprints*.

and suggests that a wine terroir is a collection of WTUs within a given wine area, be that an estate, a location or an AOC. The human element is already factored into the BTU but plays a greater role in the WTU.

What is the view beyond France?

France is at the cutting edge of this endeavour, no doubt because it is the cornerstone of the AOC system. Any justification for the quality of a wine largely depends on its terroir, with all the attendant financial ramifications, particularly in respect of real estate. In 2020, a hectare of the Côte des Blancs in the Champagne region was worth an average of €1,658,000, against less than €13,150 for a similarly sized parcel of open meadowland outside the appellation. Scientific validation of the quality of terroir only reinforces the commercial argument for typicity and the link to the wine's origins. Unlike cépage or skills, terroir cannot be exported. Countries that have adopted a more or less similar system of vineyard hierarchy – in particular, the countries of the EU after 2011 – are beginning to make use of it to affirm the demarcations of their appellations.

Switzerland's original approach should be noted. With its vineyards few and far between and often scattered across complex natural and agricultural landscapes, it has focused its attention on spontaneous plant associations, and this "symphytosociological" method (meaning "that which grows together") has been used to identify large units of natural terroir to classify vineyards into bio-geographical zones. In the countries of the so-called New World, where the notion of terroir is still considered by some to be no more than a marketing trick employed by "Old Europe" to counter rising competition from new wine regions, research has principally been centred on climate. The Winkler-based approach of zoning by bioclimate, in the US, or homoclimate in Australia ("homoclimate" meaning areas with almost the same climate) thus implies that soil is less important than climate. This makes it possible to justify recourse to "fertigation" – irrigation plus fertilization – with the claim that this alters neither the quality nor the identity of the wine.

Agronomists and geologists in these countries are beginning to develop a terroir-based approach, however, often using private funding on individual estates, as has been seen in Oregon and South America, in particular with Parra's work. In any event, such work is predicated on collaboration between research institutions, interest from the wine world, and funding, which goes some way toward explaining why certain regions – for example, Languedoc, Loire, Bordeaux, Burgundy, Australia and California – have gone further down this road than others. Readers should be aware of the correlation between the subjects studied by researchers and the financial interests behind them: important subjects may not be funded because there is no commercial interest, even though they should be studied – for example, alternatives to grafting for phylloxera.

A definition to be broadened

A scientific approach to terroir via earth and life sciences is essential if producers wish to improve vineyard cultivation, but it remains limited in and of itself. It must also consider the direct and indirect effects of viticulture and other human interventions, because humankind has had a major impact on the physical environment and on vineyards in particular. Certain viticultural soils could be considered "anthroposoils" under France's pedological classification system since they have been modified by more than 50 per cent through human activity. Climate is more difficult to influence, although attempts have been made in the past by building walls and installing irrigation systems; heating cables and wind turbines are now used to combat frost, and there is no longer any doubt about humankind's hand in the current acceleration of climate change. The definition of terroir must thus be broadened to recognize that humans has been constructing wine terroirs for millennia.

The OIV definition of terroir

In 2010, the OIV enacted an official definition of terroir. It implies that terroir is the combination of physical, biological and cultural components, and that the agricultural product grown from it has some unique characteristics, like flavours and aromas, that can be identified and linked directly to these components.

"Vitivinicultural terroir is a concept which refers to an area in which collective knowledge of the interactions between the identifiable physical and biological environment and applied vitivinicultural practices develops, providing distinctive characteristics for the products originating from this area. Terroir includes specific soil, topography, climate, landscape characteristics and biodiversity feature." (Resolution OIV/Viti333/20210 OIV.) It also means the cultural component is more suited to appear where a community of producers have been adopting similar techniques in their environment, potentially leading to official regulation of these practices by some institutions, like INAO in France.

Humans at the heart of the idea of terroir

In her *Terroirs viticoles. Définitions, caractérisation et protection* (2003), agronomist Emmanuelle Vaudour examines terroir as a concept with four aspects.

- **Agrocultural**, or terroir as material. This is in the naturalist sense, as outlined above. Vaudour defines it as "the natural potential of a given environment to produce a specific product", the matrix that supports the plant within a stratified arrangement of the soil, subsoil and climate. This view of terroir is prevalent in wine estates in particular and is a part of (in Vaudour's words) "the agronomic response of the plant through its specific vertical organization rather than its lateral extent, the space it occupies and its geographical relationships with other elements in the local environment".

- **Spatial**, or terroir as territorial terroir, addressing the need to identify and develop a terroir within human economic and social systems. Vineyards are zones of production that have been carved out of the land over time: structured viticultural areas have been in existence in Europe since the Gallo-Roman period. This avenue of research was pioneered by Roger Dion in his *Histoire de la vigne et du vin en France; des origines au XIXe siècle* (1959), which examines the hegemony of the naturalist meaning.

- **Recognition**, or the terroir of identity/recognition. This includes its cultural and ethnological aspects, memory of place and heritage, deriving from the two aspects above: "terroir-conscience".

- The **slogan terroir**, or brand terroir, incorporating the consumer desire to identify with a place of origin. This is thus a quest for roots and for meaning, underpinned by rural and ecological values: "terroir-slogan".

The wider the definition of terroir, the more interdisciplinary the modelling of its systems; agronomy, geology and agroclimatology have been joined by oenology, economics, sociology, anthropology, geography, history and more besides, with their many and various scientific definitions relating to differing fields of expertise and specific issues. Studies synthesizing these approaches are unfortunately thin on the ground because there is not necessarily any immediate interest; applied research is to an extent determined by the urgency of the problems to be solved, as we saw with the phylloxera crisis and as is now apparent with climate change. This does not mean that other research topics cannot be relevant or that perspectives cannot evolve to move away from pragmatic approaches and short-term solutions; which is why we need to put people back at the heart of the notion of terroir. Humans are both subject and object, agents of transformation of the natural environment, by improving and disrupting it alike, and creators of ways of understanding and ascribing economic, moral and aesthetic value to this environment and its produce. Terroir is man-made – literally and symbolically. Human considerations, and those relating to the commercial viability of a vineyard, in particular, are as much a part of the creation and sustainability of wine terroirs as the soil and the climate that encompass them.

TERROIR

A revolutionary reading of terroir and viticultural landscapes

In his *Le Bon Vin. Entre terroir, savoir-faire et savoir-boire* (2010), geographer Jean-Robert Pitte pays homage to Dion, who revolutionized the geography of wine in the 1950s. For Dion, terroir is "a social fact, not a geological one", a historical construct more than anything else. The essential factors of soil and climate are not enough on their own to make a good wine; access to the market is just as crucial. Since the customer is a vital element of any commercial network, they become "sculptors of terroir". Dion's ideas, which are still so little known, were developed in 1952 in the article "Querelle des anciens and des modernes sur les facteurs de la qualité du vin", offering a new take on viticultural landscapes. What does his work have to say? What new keys to reading a landscape does his historical viticultural geography provide for our times?

Dion's method and historical geography

Geography is an ancient discipline, the practice of which is attributed to the Greek Herodotus (5th century BCE) and the name of which was coined by Eratosthenes (3rd century BCE). It studies the environment of the Earth, the distribution of populations and their relationships with the areas in which they live. As terrain cultivated by humans, vineyards are by their very nature geographical phenomena, but until Dion, no one had studied them systematically as such. Having graduated from a select higher-education institution in France, the École Normale Supérieure, Dion was no ordinary geographer, however; as a classical humanist, his command of Latin and Greek afforded him access to sources that geographers had previously disregarded. Given their economic and symbolic status, vineyards and wines are extremely well documented, appearing in parish records, chronicles, decrees,

accounts, poems, survey maps and harvest notices, as well as travellers' tales. In his dissertation *Le Val de Loire* (1933), Dion had already developed a method for interpreting landscapes that drew on the gamut of human sciences, teaching physical geography from a linguistic, philological, ethnological and historical perspective.

What was Dion's credo? Studying the past makes it possible to understand the invisible social, political and commercial trends that have de facto defined the visible occupation of land. He concluded that rural landscapes are the result of human will and have a technical, cultural and economic history. Dion rejected absolute natural or social determinism in order to highlight the practical transformations of natural matrices by humans. Our relationships with our environment are seen as often complex and mutable, varying over the course of centuries according to our needs, and it is the same with vineyards;

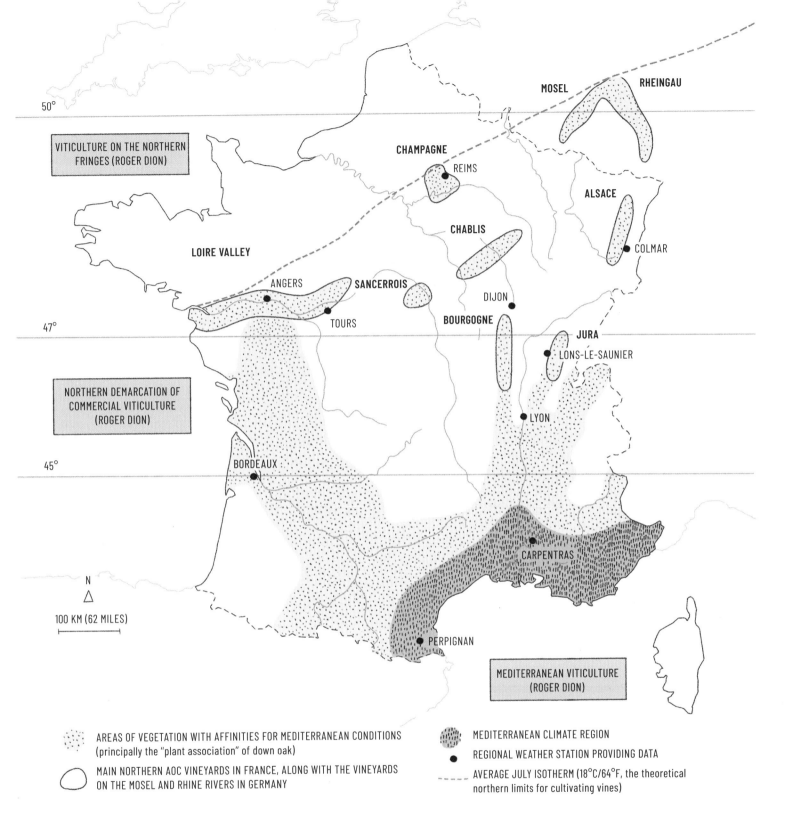

50°

VITICULTURE ON THE NORTHERN
FRINGES (ROGER DION)

MOSEL
RHEINGAU

CHAMPAGNE
REIMS

ALSACE

COLMAR

CHABLIS

LOIRE VALLEY

ANGERS
SANCERROIS

DIJON

TOURS
BOURGOGNE

JURA

47°
LONS-LE-SAUNIER

NORTHERN DEMARCATION OF
COMMERCIAL VITICULTURE
(ROGER DION)

LYON

45°
BORDEAUX

N

CARPENTRAS

100 KM (62 MILES)

PERPIGNAN

MEDITERRANEAN VITICULTURE
(ROGER DION)

AREAS OF VEGETATION WITH AFFINITIES FOR MEDITERRANEAN CONDITIONS
(principally the "plant association" of down oak)

MEDITERRANEAN CLIMATE REGION

REGIONAL WEATHER STATION PROVIDING DATA

MAIN NORTHERN AOC VINEYARDS IN FRANCE, ALONG WITH THE VINEYARDS
ON THE MOSEL AND RHINE RIVERS IN GERMANY

AVERAGE JULY ISOTHERM (18°C/64°F, the theoretical
northern limits for cultivating vines)

VITICULTURAL ZONES AS IDENTIFIED BY ROGER DION (1959) JUXTAPOSED WITH A DISTRIBUTION MAP OF PLANTS WITH
AFFINITIES FOR MEDITERRANEAN CONDITIONS, BY GEOGRAPHER AND CLIMATOLOGIST JEAN-PIERRE CHABIN (2004)

Dion identified three broad viticultural zones defined in part by climatic conditions: viticulture on the northern
fringes, which was rare and poorly documented; Mediterranean viticulture under almost perfect conditions;
and between the two, viticulture in which human ingenuity mitigated difficult conditions to produce the
most remarkable and highly valued wines on the market.

the market for drinking well has just as much to say as the physical potential of terroirs in explaining the advent of fine wine and the distribution of the great historical wine regions. This was the central thesis of his masterpiece, *Histoire de la vigne et du vin*.

Olivier de Serres – without a market, there can be no good wine

How is it that there are high-quality vineyards can be found in northern regions, in cold, damp latitudes far removed from the Mediterranean climatic conditions that are ideal for vines? Why are the wines and terroirs of Vertus in Champagne spoken of in hushed tones, but not those of Sézanne? Why are there vineyards in Sancerre but not in Bourges? Why have vines been planted in locations where the conditions for viticulture seem at best only mediocre - such as at Sables de l'Océan in Capbreton? In seeking to resolve the paradoxes revealed by the geography of French viticulture, Dion revived the question posed by Olivier de Serres in his *Théâtre d'agriculture* (1600): "If you are not in a place where you can sell your wine, what would you be doing with a good vineyard?" Dion took this dictum, borrowed from a connoisseur and author of ancient treatises who is also considered the father of modern agronomy, as a kind of guiding light for his geographical analysis.

Dion's starting point was the observation that modern theories of soil and climate as the sole factors determining quality fail to explain the location, success and sustainability of the great vineyards of the north of France: the Loire, Champagne and Alsace. The naturalist explication is thus misleading and owes its authority only to the long-lived success of French viticulture, which would probably tempt anyone to believe that there is an obvious and natural affinity between a location and a cépage. He maintained that this belief arises only from the fact that we are not witnessing the creation of new vineyards; in fact, we have even forgotten what that costs in terms of investment and ingenuity. To quote Pitte, who is in agreement with Dion, the geography of wine relies far more on the will to produce, drink and sell it than it does on the environment. How else can we explain remarkable wines from mediocre terroirs, or exceptional terroirs that produce nothing special or are left to lie fallow? The introduction to *Histoire de la vigne et du vin* teaches us that it is a desire to drink fine wine and to secure supplies at almost any price that is the source of this motivation to produce the goods by the sweat of one's brow - the hidden premise underlying Serres's ideas.

Three forms of viticulture in France since the Romans

Dion stated from the outset that wine is not essential to the survival of the human race: "In fact, man loves wine like a friend that he has chosen; as a matter of preference, not out of obligation. The history of wine, even in its geographical expression, is also more strongly marked by arbitrary choices than that of wheat or rice."

He explained how the Gallo-Roman taste for wine, which made it worth growing on a commercial basis, and the necessity for *sacra vitis*, the "sacred vine" in Christian worship, developed viticulture beyond its natural home toward northern Europe. However, he also pointed out that the further north this expansion was driven, the less certain and more costly viticulture became, and the more skill was required to produce good wine year upon year. He then went on to define three broad forms of viticulture, each with its own dynamic.

- **Mediterranean viticulture** was primitive, basic viticulture in perfect harmony with its environment, able to produce large quantities well and at low cost. There was little disease (downy mildew and powdery mildew were then unknown); minimal investment in vines was required, with no need for stakes or wires - head-pruning was sufficient; and there was a wide choice of cépages and soils producing wines with alcohol levels that made them easy to keep. Frugal viticulture of this kind had evolved little in terms of equipment or labour since ancient times. It was easy - perhaps even too easy, since it did not demand innovation. Ubiquitous in practice, it produced more ordinary wines for day-to-day consumption than quality wines, with few exceptions. These exceptions included Cypriot wine, which was considered the best in Christendom, or Malvasia from Greece, which was grown commercially by the Venetians. A significant anecdote here is that the popes of Avignon (1305–62) were said to have drunk not Châteauneuf-du-Pape, the local tipple, but wine from Beaune. It was only in the 20th century that the quality dynamic became widespread throughout the Mediterranean coast when competition from other vineyards began to make itself felt.

- **Winemaking on the northern fringes**, near the English Channel and the North Sea, was the precise opposite. Scattered vineyards were found along this pioneering wine outpost, where they depended on "atmospheric, economic, social or psychological phenomena": over the years, these included the Roman or medieval climate optimum for Europe, the Little Ice Age, the need for communion wine to celebrate Mass, or for the prestige and the satisfaction of harvesting your own wine. However, due to the extreme irregularity of harvests, because of rot, poor grape-ripening or unsuitable cépages, along with variations in taste and production costs, there were no commercial exports. The wine produced was consumed only by the limited local market, and only a small minority made a living from it. As soon as imported wine became cheaper, the vineyards were abandoned, with some prestige exceptions, and the workforce and land were transferred to other, more profitable products. Although these regions, including England and Flanders, preferred beer and cider for day-to-day consumption, they became consumers of wine as a luxury when commercial routes opened up – wealthy and discerning drinkers who had been educated to expect the best played a key role in spurring a viticulture of emulation, eschewing local vineyards and demanding imported wines, whose characteristics they were to dictate to Porto, Bordeaux, the Loire and the other regions that produced them.

• Between these two zones, there lay what Dion dubbed the "**northern limit of commercial viticulture**", the area to the north of the Mediterranean vineyards but south of the northern fringes; it included Germany. It was this region that was of most interest to Dion because, paradoxically, it had become the most renowned and successful viticultural area even though its physical characteristics were far from ideal.

In the north, making good wine is essential if you want it to sell

The "northern limit of commercial viticulture" is determined in part by the physical possibility of cultivating vines. One might be tempted to believe that it is only climate that plays a role here, but in fact vines bear fruit too irregularly north of the 18°C (64°F) isotherm in July. This area, where the isotherm value is constant but the temperature is modulated by the influence of the Atlantic or the relief, corresponds more or less to the dividing zone between the northern fringes and the northern limit of the commercial production zone. However, Dion observed that certain wine regions, like the northern Loire, Champagne and the historic viticultural area around Orléans, were not in the most favourable zones. In fact, quite the contrary – other factors influencing development must therefore have come into play. The planting of vineyards also varied with the profitability of other agricultural activities, and indeed even of industry at any given moment.

By the same token, Dion shows that geology does not promote the creation of a vineyard "by providing it with this or that substance necessary for the growth or fruiting of vines, but rather by not favouring the cultivation of wheat, which is in competition with vines". Such is the case in the Côte des Bar in Champagne, where the slopes carved out of the Kimmeridgian marls were not suitable for large-scale cereal cultivation and had thus been left for vine cultivation more or less by default. The hills also had the advantage of proximity to rivers, enabling produce to be transported. It is all a question of agricultural profitability. Dion noted the same for the southern limit of this area, abutting the northern part of the Mediterranean zone: vines and olive trees will often begin to

appear as soon as such crops yield more than wheat or beets, not just because the land is too poor or too rich for them.

A geographer would conclude from this that any decision to site a vineyard is as much a question of making judgments about subsistence and economic profitability because it is about the physical potential of the terroir. Paradoxically, it is precisely this need to cultivate the best possible crop to sell at the highest possible price that makes excellence and originality a prerequisite for such viticulture. The difficult production conditions and agricultural competition require ingenuity, soil management, observation, patience and constant adaptation to produce a wine whose inimitable qualities (which are also commercial arguments) cannot be attributed solely to the physical terroir. None of this can happen in the absence of producers ready to invest in their vineyard and a market rich and powerful enough to buy such produce; and such a market must also be both discerning enough to taste the difference from ordinary wines and enterprising enough to demand progress, as Britain did with Bordeaux and Champagne in its modern, sparkling iteration. Reliable transport is also essential.

There is therefore a financial and logistical price to pay for producing good wine in this intermediate zone: vineyards that are ideally situated for access to local or more distant markets must be purchased; competent farmers must be sourced; the right plants must be selected and maintained; and changes made must not be to excess. Space for vinification and storage must be available, along with the necessary equipment; many vineyards are located close to forests because of the access to wood. There is also the need for a workforce, and the cost of labour, throughout the year to prune, harvest, propagate and generally look after the vines.

Cities – the cradles of high-quality vineyards

Vines are "people plants", said Dion, with vineyards located in centres of population whose growth they will foster – but if any other industry is in competition with them, their development may stop dead, whatever their potential. Besides providing the right conditions for cultivation, vineyards must thus also, he said, "be easily accessible to those who provide the resources and the means required for any such cultivation, as well as those who reward the endeavour with the price offered for its products. The creators and managers of these high-quality vineyards have more often than not been city-dwellers, however."

Quality wine has been produced in urban areas since ancient times, and the network of cities with ecclesiastical connections is a perfect illustration of this. These links explain the creation and influence of the vineyards of Paris, of which only traces remain today, Reims (Champagne), Auxerre/Dijon

(Burgundy) and Trier (Mosel), which expanded greatly during the medieval period. This allowed wealthy urban-dwelling owners speedy access to their vines, which were a symbol of prestige, as well as a source of both pleasure and profit. Cities also provided local markets and trade routes that had been developed for other products, such as salt.

If a vineyard was too far from the city, the incentive to seek out quality became less pressing, which explains the difference between Vertus and Sézanne in Champagne: both towns are equally suitable for viticulture, but the distance from the former to Châlons-sur-Marne is half that of the latter from Troyes, the respective cities that regulated their trade. In addition, Sézanne was too far south to export competitively to northern markets; Vertus has been elevated to the status of a *premier cru*, while the Sézanne region continues to struggle for recognition as a high-quality producer, despite its remarkable wines. Access is thus more important than soil or geography in an environment suitable for the cultivation of vines.

Competitive popular viticulture

There was, of course, another kind of viticulture that was more grassroots and intended for personal consumption; this was driven by volume and the aim was to produce as much as possible, on the smallest possible plot of land with the least possible investment. This usually involved planting high-yield cépages on flat and fertile land, and the result was mediocre wines. These vineyards posed problems, not only for public authorities, since the vines generated lower export taxes and took up space that would otherwise be used for wheat during frequent food shortages, but also for wealthy owners who may have viewed it as a dilution of the potential reputation of their own wines, a competitor for the supply of barrels and an incentive for their agricultural workers to become independent. Decrees issued to uproot such vineyards, while retaining those of high quality, were legion until the beginning of the 19th century. Philip the Bold's famous ordinance of 1395 is well known, forbidding the use of manure and banning from the Duchy of Burgundy "a most evil and highly disloyal plant named Gaamez [Gamay], from which bad seed a great abundance of wines is derived". His aim was to ensure that "our country recovers its good reputation for good wines"; promoting viticultural quality was of great importance to the political and economic strategy of a state that sought to compete with the kingdom of France in the 15th century.

"Let the vine see the river" (Médoc saying)

Whether destined for aristocrats, churchmen or the bourgeoisie, quality wine rapidly became a commercial product from the Middle Ages onward. Since local elites who both produced and consumed the wine were limited in number,

exports were essential, not least because the merchants had access to many rich clients and a market, and so they were willing to invest in their vineyards. Transport of goods was essential, however – until the advent of railway travel, the places where wine was sold for the highest prices were all located near river and sea ports and along several major overland routes. The logistical constraints that prevailed until the beginning of the 17th century make it easy to understand why transport by water was the most efficient method. It was also safer and easier to tax. Jerez, Porto and Málaga were thus all ports before high-quality vineyards began to appear on their outskirts for their northern clients, and the same is true of Cognac and La Rochelle.

Almost all the major vineyards in France are located beside rivers – not just for their effect on local heat conditions or the topography of their hillsides, but because they are navigable: the story is the same for the Loire, the Rhône, the Saône, the Garonne, the Dordogne, the Rhine and the Seine, the Lot, the Cher, the Meuse and the Marne. Overland routes were taken only for easy, safe and short journeys; Orléans became a major commercial vineyard in the 16th century not because of its less-than-perfect alluvial soils or its poor climate, which is affected by northwest winds, but because it had good connections to the Loire and the Parisian market across the Beauce plain. The very success of this vineyard was to spell its doom in the 18th century, however – quantity took over as the watchword, and the wine became so bad that it was distilled or turned into vinegar. By 1787, Orléans boasted 200 vinegar-makers.

Dion's *Histoire de la vigne et du vin* is thus a substantiation of the ideas on the relative nature of natural determinism that Serres had posited more than three centuries previously. Serre in just 10 lines shed more light on the issue than even the most learned geological or climatological treatises. He identified three kinds of favourable locations for major vineyards:

- **Close to large cities and the navigable rivers** that serve them, "such as the Loire, Allier, Seine and Yonne; taking the wines from Auvergne, Burgundy, the area around Auxerre and elsewhere, and carrying them to Paris and other places."
- **Near the sea**, "even the coast of Bordeaux and La Rochelle, where large quantities of wine set sail for England, Scotland, Flanders, Brittany, Normandy and other countries."
- **"Near cold mountains"**. It is only in regions where wine can easily be sold, and thus properly repay the investment required to extend or improve a vineyard, that winemaking is able to offer employment to large numbers of workers and so also influence the distribution of towns and villages and shape the countryside in general – affecting both landscape and society, in other words.

Sake territories seen through the lens of Dion

Nicolas Baumert specializes in the geography of Japan and has used Dion's work to study the areas in which sake is produced. Sake and wine have a number of similarities: cultural importance, a comparable historicity, and a guarantee of commercial quality that resides in specific natural characteristics. For sake, these are the quality of the water and the variety of rice used in the brewing process. As with wine, however, Baumert notes the relative influence of certain prime factors; while water and rice do not have as strong a link with terroir as grapes and are ubiquitous on the Japanese archipelago, sake's highly complex production process requires skills that are hard to source. Quality is, in fact, determined by political power, which manifests as the economic power of those able to pay craftsmen and control trade. Even today, the key regions for sake production are still Kansai and Kyoto, the historic centres of power; the latter, the city in which the drink was perfected for the aristocracy, was the imperial capital in the 7th century. Sake's spread to the rest of the country was sluggish because of the feudal system and the highly technical nature of its manufacture. when Tokyo became the capital during the Edo period and wished to produce its own sake, there were not enough brewers with the necessary skills. The scheme failed, and Kansai retained its dominance.

As water transport became a criterion of quality for a discerning elite in these areas, much as it did with wine, breweries moved closer to ports to make logistics easier, and they are still plentiful in such locations. As was also the case with wine, the historic regions initially maintained their dominance when the innovations of the modern world, such as railways, bottles and an export trade, widened the areas of distribution; they had the financial means, the skill-set and the commercial networks to adapt. A further similarity with wine arose as quality began to suffer with the concentration and industrialization of large-scale producers who were no longer serving "informed enthusiasts". New regions dedicated to the best possible production began to emerge as physical conditions once again began to play a role in differentiating tastes. The history of sake entirely supports Dion's hypotheses for the construction of quality terroirs.

The modern relevance of Dion's approach

To sum up, what has Dion taught us? That the vineyards that have been progressively designated *appellations d'origine contrôlée* are as much based on socio-economic interests as on local conditions or resources, and that all of these are of importance. Physical characteristics demarcate the vast, general zones where vines can be grown, and a geography that is economic, political and historical determines production areas within this territory. Finally, differences in quality between the terroirs in these areas emerge through the specific physical and geographical characteristics that human investment reveals and improves, and it is this that marks out a superior *cru* – privileged terroir and an owner prepared to invest in their vineyard.

Put another way, Dion does not challenge the role of climate and soil on a local scale, which has prompted subdivisions of land that may be extremely ancient – those in Sancerre have existed since the 15th century, for example. But he suggests that, on a regional scale, it is commercial geography that holds the whip hand. Having modelled this hypothesis in their article "Roger Dion, toujours vivant!", geographers Étienne Delay and Marius Chevallier have concluded that his approach is still relevant and that this "quasi-determinism in the definition of production zones of high-quality wine is indeed in part a social construct. If a region has historically always produced quality wines, to assert that it is thanks to particularly propitious soil and climate conditions, would be like drawing a target only after the archer has loosed his arrow."

Justifying the quality of wines by terroir alone is tantamount to an intellectual position of self-justification that is in part erroneous and in any case lacking in integrity. The issues are clear, particularly the financial considerations, but is it not just as important – especially for the future of a viticulture that is staring down the twin barrels of climatic and biological emergencies – to highlight the primacy of human liberty, will and power over fatalism, determinism and absolute relativism? A wine of quality is above all a creative dynamic, rather than a profile set in stone.

THE US: THE IMPOSITION OF PROHIBITION AND ITS CONSEQUENCES (1845–2021)

Prohibition was ratified throughout the US by the 18th Amendment between 1920 and 1933, when all production, importation, sale and consumption of alcohol was banned, but it had also already been implemented piecemeal in previous decades. After it was repealed in 1933, each US state legislated on the management of the alcoholic drinks industry, and there are as many laws as there are states even today. By 2021, 17 states (in pink), plus jurisdictions in Alaska (not illustrated), Maryland, Minnesota and South Dakota, had adopted forms of "control", regulating wholesale purchasing of spirits and, in certain cases, wine and beer, via government bodies. Thirteen of these jurisdictions also control retail sales for consumption outside bars and restaurants via government-run outlets or designated agents.

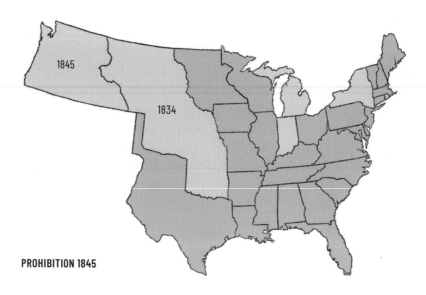

PROHIBITION 1845

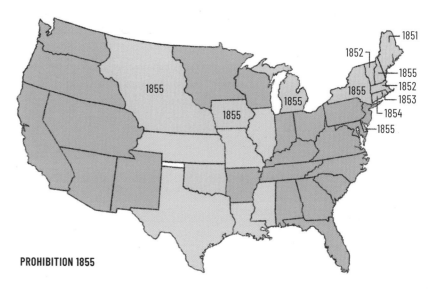

PROHIBITION 1855

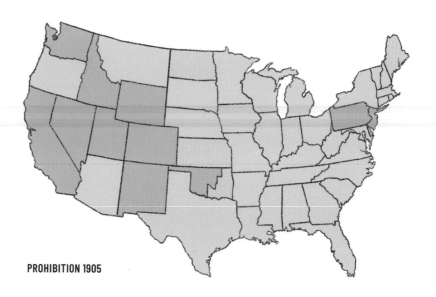

PROHIBITION 1905

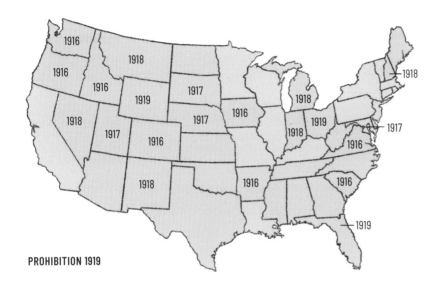

PROHIBITION 1919

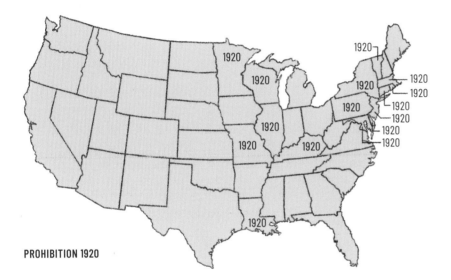

PROHIBITION 1920

ALASKA

HAWAII

2021

	ALCOHOL PROHIBITED
	LOCAL BAN
	ALCOHOL AUTHORIZED
	ALCOHOL CONTROLLED

Dates indicate the implementation of prohibitionist legislation across the entire state.

The states marked 1920 are those designated as dry by the 18th Amendment.

Constructing terroir

The term terroir is often bandied about in the world of wine as an almost transcendental explanation of wine quality, with ideas of absolute and objective excellence strongly associated with the natural, inherent characteristics of a terroir. The great historic vineyards have been idealized as privileged viticultural territories but nonetheless owe their genesis as much to economic considerations as physical conditions; they are, in part, social constructs. More importantly still, few terroirs remain that have not been totally transformed by man. While the process of "anthropization" – the conversion of land into terroirs by human intervention – is now highly controlled (in particular, by the appellation system), this has not always been the case. How have producers constructed their terroirs over the centuries? Does this "artificialization" exclude the possibility and the legitimacy of a link between the taste of a wine and the soil in which it is grown?

Human ingenuity – controlling and improving wine terroirs

Writing in 1952, Dion noted, "The sight of a vineyard of quality being created on new ground has long since become such a rarity that the modern world can no longer conceive of the labour and ingenuity required by such an enterprise to force nature to give us what she would never have offered of her own accord."

The establishment of the AOC system in France has progressively endorsed the idea that there exists a "naturalness" in the original link between wine and its terroir. Recent years have seen INAO declassify plots of vines where soil from outside the vineyard had been shipped in, as occurred in Alsace in 2011. Curiously, however, there is no legislation in France prohibiting the transformation of vineyard land, as Jean-Pierre Garcia, a geoarchaeologist at the University of Burgundy, pointed out in a 2011 study of the viticultural soils of Burgundy (*Le goût du lieu: la mise en place du discours sur la nature des sols comme référence au goût des vins en Bourgogne*). There are only mechanisms designed to prevent abuse of the system; these are provided by defence and management bodies (ODGs in France; Organismes de Défense et de Gestion) that are guarantors of the integrity of their particular appellation. There may also be a clause in the most recent set of specifications for some AOCs, but not all. This clause sets out the conditions for the "reworking of plots" that is likely to "modify the morphology, subsoil or topsoil (including any soil brought in from elsewhere) or elements that make it possible to guarantee the ongoing integrity of the soils in a plot of land intended for production of the AOC, excluding conventional ripping work".

Completely prohibiting the alteration of plots would actually be denying historical reality; for as long as their viticultural efforts have been recorded in treatises on viticulture, wine-growers have worked on soils to control physical conditions as much as possible and to improve the volume and/or quality of the harvest year-on-year. Once the location of the vineyard has been selected, it is time for human ingenuity to get to work, and it is this inventiveness that has created and "artificialized" our viticultural landscapes.

A viticultural soil always has a history

Land occupied by vineyards always has some form of history, whether as uncultivated ground or as pasture, cereal crops or orchards; it might even be a former vineyard. The first stage in the artificialization process - converting land into a vineyard by human hand – is therefore to clear it. All the old vegetation, including any vines, is uprooted, sometimes by deep ploughing or by using modern chemical weedkillers. There are numerous accounts of the almost inextricably entangled network of vine roots produced by *provignage* in vineyards that had to be replanted after phylloxera, such as that written by Gaston Roupnel (1871–1946), a renowned Burgundian historian and regional writer, who highlighted the human effort involved in creating the Côte d'Or vineyard: "When the old, pre-phylloxera vines were uprooted in Chambertin, long chains of rotting stumps were dug out from the soil in which they had been buried and entwined over centuries. This earth, this bed in which they had grown, the cradle in which they had been born, had however become the tomb in which they now lay as unseen, shapeless debris, the vegetal foundations of a hundred successive vines. . . all they had provided, all the chains linking them to the past, had been wiped out like human generations" (*La Bourgogne. Types et coutumes*, 1936). Ideally, although rarely, for economic reasons the ground would be left to rest for seven years, whether it was sown or not, to allow for the natural elimination of carriers of deadly diseases such as the fanleaf virus or root rot.

Clearing, uprooting, and controlling soil structure and depth

Stones must be cleared from plots that are too rocky, while large boulders are broken up and removed using dynamite or a bulldozer. It took 6,000 truckloads and a year of work to remove the limestone boulders from the 45 ha of the Finca Altos Los Hormigas vineyard in Luján de Cuyo (Mendoza, Argentina). Smaller stones can be crushed and reburied to avoid sacrificing soil thickness and to retain a particular granularity, or removed and used in local building work, such as in the drystone walls (*murgers*) and stone huts (*cabottes*) of Burgundy or the cramped outhouses of the Rhône. They are either built at once when the plot is ripped – ripping being

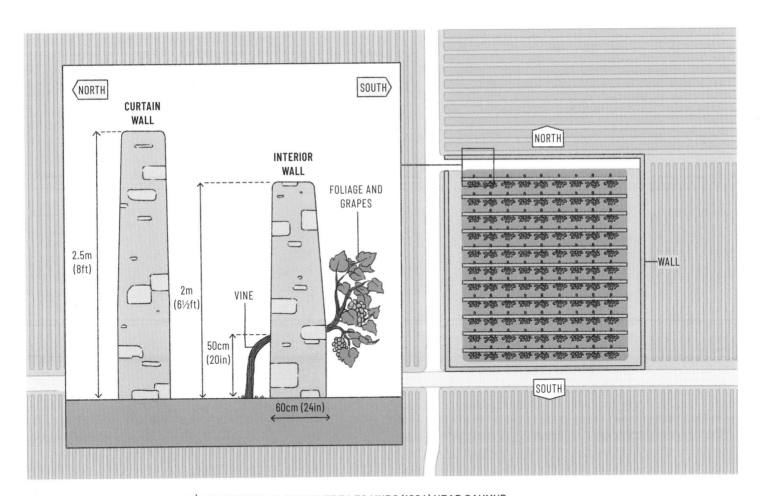

PÈRE CRISTAL'S CLOS D'ENTRE LES MURS (1894) NEAR SAUMUR

Père Cristal was a legendary figure who had walls constructed in two of his *clos des murs* (enclosed vineyards). Running from east to west, they were pierced with holes through which Cabernet Franc vines were threaded in order to keep, as he said, "their feet cool while their heads were in the sun" and thus ripen perfectly. Vines have also been trained against walls with no holes in Thomery since the 18th century to ripen Chasselas. The Clos d'Entre les Murs enclosure at Château de Parnay is today planted with Chenin and is listed as a historical monument.

deep ploughing – or over the years, as stones are collected after rising to the surface; some have stood for centuries, silent witnesses to the historical management of the texture of the soil. They sometimes even lend their names to the location, as with the Saint-Aubin Murgers des Dents de Chien *premier cru*, which is separated from Chevalier-Montrachet by a stretch of bare land known as Mont Rachez or Mont Chauve, and whose name (meaning "houndstooth drystone walls") recalls the pointed shape of the stones that make up the many Jurassic limestone walls. Just as the removal of stones affects the local soil balance, building walls alters the microclimate, protecting from frost, wind, rain and erosion, and promoting particular kinds of biotope while preventing others, like livestock grazing. The ground is often ploughed superficially to create soil depth; this loosens and buries the plant cover and ultimately makes for better rooting. If the soil is too compact, ripping is carried out; this is a delicate task because it can disrupt the structure of soil and subsoil, breaking up layers and bringing to the surface elements that are of less use to vines – layers of clays, active limestone, salt and so on – while disturbing the most fertile layer on the surface. Subsoiling is a less intrusive technique than decompacting and involves tilling the soil without turning it over. By modifying the soil horizons, all this management of the land clearly anthropizes the physical terroir.

> Land occupied by vineyards always has some form of history, whether as uncultivated ground or as pasture, cereal crops or orchards; it might even be a former vineyard

Controlling moisture

For some wine-growers, ensuring vines have a good supply of water, the pre-condition for quality wine, is the primary function of the soil. This is why the majority of soil management systems aim to improve water availability, taking into account the gradient, the soil type, subsoil and fractures, the climate (of course) and the type of grapes and wines to be produced. They address:

- **Excess water** in saturated areas, clays in particular, that block the percolation of water and choke the roots; this is what happens when water takes the place of O_2 in the soil. Such areas are also vectors of disease and make it more difficult to use machinery because tractors get bogged down. Many vineyards, especially on plains, are often drained before the vines are planted, since the work involved is so extensive. Pits of varying depths are dug to accommodate ceramic or plastic drains that collect and channel the water that seeps in, which is usually then removed via ditches and drainage channels.

Some historic vineyards rely on sophisticated drainage systems such as that used at the Gironde estuary, which includes the Médoc. These terroirs were created at royal command between the reigns of Henri IV (1589) and Louis XIV (1715), engaging the expertise of engineers in the Dutch Republic in a titanic endeavour that took more than a century. Using the same methods employed for the polders in their homeland, the Dutch surveyors drained the marshes using thousands of kilometres of channels, sluices and canals known locally as *jalles*, crisscrossing the villages of Saint-Éstèphe, Pauillac, Saint-Julien and Margaux. By lowering the water level, they also exposed mounds – known locally as *mottes*, *cos* or *fittes* – of Günz glacial formations (Quaternary) that were far more suitable for cultivating vines thanks to their gradient and water table, as well as their geological make-up of gravels, clays, silts and sands. In Sauternes, further upstream along the Garonne, you will find Château d'Yquem, a *premier cru supérieur* in the 1855 rankings and undoubtedly the most famous sweet wine in the world. It is planted over 113 ha of land with more than 100 km (62 miles) of drains; such management is essential, since the abundance of water sources and excessively clayey soils were preventing the development of quality noble rot on this unique terroir.

- **The absence of water** is equally a problem. Before the advent of precision drip irrigation, micro-sprinklers and the like, controlled flooding was one of the techniques used to mitigate the lack of water. These irrigation channels now have a heritage value, as well as viticultural use. Examples include the 2,170 km (1,350 miles) of *levadas* on Madeira and the *agouilles en pied de géline*, the local name for the channels that irrigate the vines on the sunny, sloping schist hillsides in Banyuls. In "Grape Valley", the nickname for the historic region of Turpan in Xinjiang, China's largest wine region, in the far northwestern corner of the country, there are more than 1,000 wells and 1,600 km (994 miles) of extraordinary channels; these form the *karez* that have been listed as a UNESCO World Heritage Site. The valley is in a unique geographical position; at 154m (505ft) below sea level, wedged in between the Taklamakan Desert and the mountains of Tian Shan, which rise to over 7,000m (c. 23,000ft). These channels were the solution chosen by the Uyghurs to capture water from melted snow, and they have made Turpan a major grape-growing centre for centuries. The system is also known as *qanat* and may originally have been developed by the Persians around the 1st century BCE. They are also found in the Maghreb (*foggaras*), in the Near and Middle East and in Central Asia.

Less spectacular but equally crucial to the development of Argentinian vineyards in the Andes, the channels dug out of the earth by the Huarpe Indians and copied by their Spanish colonizers are still in use for old Bonarda or Criolla vines. Digging out, opening up, and closing off these channels is the work of the *tomero*, the steward of these centuries-old skills, although oral transmission of this knowledge is gradually dying away. All these techniques for flooding the vineyards are highly complex and require large volumes of water; as a result they are slowly being abandoned. Here too, however, all the irrigation and drainage channels, the ditches dug between or beneath the rows of vines, and even modern drip irrigation systems are part of this artificialization of the terroir, either directly, by modifying the water supply, or indirectly, by influencing the development of the vines' rhizosphere.

Controlling gradient and erosion

Sloping terroirs require considerable management. Depending on the degree of slope, this may involve reducing the gradient to a greater or lesser degree, improving access, making it easier to work the soil and limiting run-off. Imagine the effort, willpower and time it took to construct the endless banks of terraces along the Douro, the northern Rhône and the Mosel, or even in Lavaux in Switzerland, the Wachau, the Aosta Valley and Valtellina. Even on gentler slopes, the gradient must be controlled to limit erosion due to gravity and rainfall.

As upland soils erode, a colluvium of eroded matter accumulates to varying depths on the sides and at the base of hills. If this is not too clayey, it may yield good viticultural soils that are aerated and permeable, as in the foothill vineyards of Alsace, the Côte d'Or and Champagne. This comes at the cost of a loss of upland soil, however. Breaks must be made in the slope, using techniques such as limiting the length of the rows of vines planted across the incline, planting hedges, and leaving plant cover to lend structure to the soil where this is possible and the rainfall is not too excessive. Fine rainfall of 1–2mm (up to ⅟₁₆in) will penetrate the ground, but heavy rain of 100mm (4in) falling in storm conditions will run off and carry away material. The useful layer on the surface is washed away, triggering catastrophic landslides. Levelling or even terracing the land is thus sometimes necessary, especially if the gradient is greater than 10 per cent or 5.7 degrees. Conversely, the vigneron may also have to create slight slopes if the terrain is too flat.

The impact of terracing

Reconfiguring slopes with terraces is an ancient practice. The profile of the terraces – their length, width, depth, whether they are gently sloping or flat – will depend equally on both the topography of the land and the vineyard equipment

Controlling the climate: the problem with anti-hail nets and AOCs

Hail has long been a threat to vineyards and has become a major problem for a number of appellations. Its effects can be devastating, with a wide range of damage possible depending on the growth of the vines and the intensity of the hailstorm. Some solutions have been found, including hail cannons that ignite acetylene, an explosive gas, to create a shockwave to disrupt the formation of hailstones; generators that diffuse crystals of silver iodide to promote the formation of smaller and thus potentially less dangerous hailstones; and balloons loaded with hygroscopic salts, which similarly force the crystallization of smaller hailstones. The use of these three techniques does not present a problem in AOCs, despite the possibly harmful nature of the second, but this has not been the case for anti-hail nets, which were banned for AOCs/IGPs until 2018. The reason for this was that INAO considered their presence might affect the climate – and thus the terroir. It was only after three years of experimentation in Burgundy, monitoring temperature, precipitation, sunshine, ripening and indeed yield, that the institute was ready to concede that these "vertical, single-row nets exert no more than a very limited influence on the vine's mesoclimate. . . and are compatible with protecting an AOC". They have been permitted ever since but are used only infrequently because of the cost of installation and the amount of additional work involved. Another question arises, however: if these nets pose so many problems and threaten the wine's connection to its origins, not to mention their altering of the landscape, why have modifications to the soil like compaction, ripping, soil death through chemical toxicity and so on not been challenged in the same vein?

and specialist infrastructure, like funicular railways, and the labour available. In all cases, however, terracing deepens the soil at the outer edge, often creating a heterogeneity between the front and back of the terrace that can influence vine growth. Water circulation may also be unbalanced, depending on natural drainage, and the water supply is almost always managed. The walls of the terraces create different micro-climates depending on the terrace's construction. Protection from the wind and the amount of reflected light and heat will vary according to the size of the terrace and the materials of which it is made – and here too the effect is to disrupt the layers of soil both physically and in their chemical composition. Pierre Galet suggests that terraces dry out more easily than sloping vineyards where the temperature of the soil is lower and it is not compacted in the same way; grape growth and sugar content are higher in the former case. Wine-growers can also add more soil or alter the existing soil.

> Vineyards are thus invested with the mind of man

Given the enormous financial and human cost, one might wonder if such vineyards would be planted today, and how many terroirs of exceptional potential have gone undiscovered. It also explains the high price of a bottle from vineyards using such heroic methods, even if these often barely cover the cost of production. These terraced terroirs are constructions of human genius.

Nourishing the soil was as important back then...

In Europe, an acceptable level for soil erosion has been estimated at around 1 tonne/ha/year. In 2018, the average loss of European soils was 12 tonnes/ha/year, and in certain appellations in the Val de Loire area it was more than 20 tons/ha/year. Viticulture has historically been one of the crops most susceptible to intense erosion. "In Volnay, in 1468-9, we had to bring earth [to lay down] above the enclosure, which had been eroded down to the bed rock... In Chenôve, in 1383, earth was taken from Chaume de Marsannay and carried into the vineyard enclosure, which took 691 man-days of work," relates Garcia, indicating the considerable rates of erosion in the viticultural soils of Burgundy during the Late Middle Ages. Importing soil is an age-old practice but one that is highly dependent on local resources. Garcia continues, "In Beaune, in 1468, we even see a plot formerly leased to Jehan Dubois being taken over by some gentlemen... to take the earth, as resources are so rare. All these measures taken within the ducal vineyard ultimately resulted in the fertilization of the ground to compensate for the natural erosion of the soil, and we know of similar imports throughout the ages, from the 14th to the 18th century, and

until the turn of the 20th century, where there are still to be found in the minutes of some town councils auctions of dirt and earth from the local area for wine-growers to spread on their vineyards."

It is now easier to understand INAO's position on these questions if we start from the principle of "local, steadfast and ongoing usage" as set out in the AOC; wine-growers have been constructing terroir for centuries.

Viticultural soil has always been enriched, because it is unable to support the annual harvesting of perennial plants without a reduction in quality. While polyculture – as with the *joualles* of the Middle Ages, a cultivation system combining several plant species on the same plot – proved to be a solution for subsistence farming for centuries, many references to the use and abuse of direct imports of organic and mineral matter for commercial agriculture can be found in texts dating back to ancient times. The quality of this manure and the manner of composting are crucial and will determine the fertility of the land over the long term. Nearby cities and the agricultural practices used on the land surrounding a vineyard play a critical role here; municipalities would negotiate with farmers and wine-growers to spread urban waste, including from latrines.

In Sauternes and Champagne, for example, there was an unfortunate lack of organized soil improvement; and in Bordeaux, since few cereal crops were grown, livestock and straw were not as widespread as vines. This has been highlighted by historian Stéphanie Lachaud in a study on the development of terroir in Sauternes in the 17th and 18th centuries (*Le Sauternais moderne. Histoire de la vigne, du vin et des vignerons des années 1650 à la fin du XVIIIe siècle*, 2012). Plants that grew nearby, such as heather, offered some alternative, but it was often the city that met such needs. This would explain Champagne's historic use of waste from Paris – the infamous *gadoues* – although this source became problematic as the habits of Parisian consumers changed with the introduction of plastics, heavy metals, batteries and the like into the general waste mix; the practice was banned in 1997. Being only minimally or not at all biodegradable, this kind of waste will unfortunately leave its mark on vineyards for far too long.

... as it is today

Vineyards are obviously still being modified and altered today, although this is now carried out in a more scientific way to prevent excessive vigour in growth. Before vines are planted, core samples are taken of the ground, allowing soil analysis to establish the pH, the ratio of active limestone to total limestone, the content of organic matter, biological activity levels and even the cation exchange capacity. If the

Madeira – a legendary wine

The archipelago of Madeira, a series of volcanic peaks 647 km (402 miles) off the Moroccan coast, produces a legendary wine. The 740 km² (286 square miles) of the eponymous main island house is all that remains of the viticultural area, some 440 ha of vineyards spread across vertiginous hillsides. Grape vines arrived in Madeira with the Portuguese in 1418 and were immediately cultivated to produce the wine required for maritime exploration. Thousands of kilometres of terraces and irrigation channels (known as *levadas*) were installed across its fertile hills, whose subtropical climate allowed vines to be grown on pergolas. At the peak of production, there were 2,500 ha of vineyards. These initially produced unfortified clairet wines, and it was not until a surplus arose at the end of the 17th century, when the island was no longer a necessary stop on the voyage to the Americas, that the excess was distilled and added to the fresh must.

This fortified wine was then shipped around the world, and it was subsequently discovered that the wine that had travelled (the *vinhos do roda*) tasted far better, the heat to which it had been exposed on the journey having slowly cooked it so that it was almost indestructible. Madeira was thus born of the vagaries of the market and technical innovation. The sea change undergone by the wine was reproduced with the *canteiro* technique (barrels left exposed to the air at ambient temperatures for several years, with no topping-up) and then *estufagem* (vats heated to 45°C/113°F for four months). Professional wine-growers have been working hard since the 1980s to bring up to date a wine that had toasted America's Declaration of Independence in 1776 and survived phylloxera, the Russian Revolution and Prohibition, but traditional Madeira-making is still barely breaking even, if not losing money, and now faces a new threat: the production of unfortified wine from local, international and hybrid varieties. Unless the market shifts, the Madeira once enjoyed by George Washington may become a heritage relic that can be saved from oblivion only by wine tourism.

soil is too acidic (pH less than 6.2), the limestone levels are altered – historically, with lime – to prevent deficiencies like low magnesium and aluminium, which can potentially lead to diseases. "Basal dressing" was introduced to build up reserves of fertilizer material and to improve the soil structure, with the amount added based on annual losses of humus from the soil, which varies with the levels of clay and limestone added: this is between 300 and 1,000 kg/ha/year. Even though levels of organic matter can be very low in viticultural soils, it is nonetheless essential to provide vines with proper mineral nutrition. The trick is thus to ensure good levels of humus that do not mineralize or leach out too quickly. If humic restoration from vine to vine – using pruned vine wood, dead leaves, plant cover and grape marc – is insufficient, wine-growers may add organic matter from external sources, and the choices made, whether they use plant and/or animal compost and the type and level of composting, will depend on the desired rate of humification/mineralization. Specific quantities of phosphorus, potassium or even magnesium may also be added.

Terroir and human inspiration

Instead of taking an overly naturalist approach and refusing to accept the key role played by humans in creating wine terroirs, we should acknowledge the anthropization of terroirs and the human ingenuity involved in cultivating the world's historic vineyards; such an approach may allow us to envisage the potential of tomorrow's viticulture more clearly and with greater perspective. It will also cause us to re-examine the status of the new vineyards created *ex nihilo* since the end of World War Two, not so much in respect of the primacy given to physical geography in deciding their location, but rather in the mere consideration that they exist at all and have been created just as our historic vineyards were created, using the tools available at the time. This demonstrates how the geography of viticulture is first and foremost relative and dependent on the resources available: tools, social organization, ease of exchange of goods and services, the economic capacity to take risks, and the socio-cultural values prevailing within a geographical area that is fixed but varies over time. Vineyards are thus invested with the mind of man.

The architectural heritage of vineyards

Nothing tells us more about the role of man in constructing vineyards than their traditional built heritage; rural architecture is a function of both physical environment and social organization. If we assume that architecture can be read as a discourse with the world or, more exactly, the ecosystem within which it developed at a given time, then learning to recognize the materials used, deciphering the structures and interpreting the aesthetic choices will help us to understand the construction of wine terroirs. What stories can wood, stone and iron tell us? What is this viticultural heritage embedded in the vineyard? What lessons can we learn from the evolution of cellars and barrel stores that are now erected by "starchitects"?

Viticultural landscapes – a history of materials

Stakes and trellises, a half-derelict wall, boundary markers, paths and small huts blend into the vineyard landscape to the extent that we often don't even notice them, all the more so if our attention is focused on the vines and the soil. But they are nonetheless important witnesses to the construction of wine terroirs in historic regions. These structures give the vineyard a voice, often even making it possible to read the vine's geological substrate and environment. Until the turn of the 20th century, wine-growers could not spend all their time with their vines and wines; they were, by necessity, also carpenters, masons and jacks-of-all-trades, following in the peasant farmer's footsteps by using local materials and managing their land with whatever came to hand at the least expense. Other than technical innovations that proved useful or made economic sense, materials from further afield were used only if absolutely necessary. On the face of it, vineyards require only small quantities of simple materials like wood, stone and iron. However, as Jean-Claude Martin, an economist specializing in winemaking issues, has pointed out (in *La création de paysages viticoles: une histoire de matériaux*, 2006), their use provides evidence of physical constraints, technical and social dynamics, and a lack of recognition of the amount of labour required.

Stone

Stone is almost always a clue to the bedrock that lies beneath, and its presence in buildings is often as much to do with how easy it is to work as its capacity to resist time. Until construction costs fell, thanks especially to cheaper transport and alternative materials such as concrete, decisions were guided by pragmatism, and tended toward the most efficient solution achievable with local skills and the labour available.

It is thus no coincidence that the châteaux of the Loire are concentrated in the areas where tuffeau limestone is quarried. Excavated quarries have yielded cellars that are perfect for aging wine, not to mention an abundance of raw materials to build the walls of the vineyard enclosures that can still be seen from Touraine to Saumur. The viticultural landscape changes in the Anjou Noir region, where slate schists are found in multilayered walls, trellising supports and roof coverings – but no subterranean cellars, because excavation is too laborious and costly outside the slate industry. In the Pays Nantais, where the influence of the subsoil is clearly visible in its buildings, all the plaster rendering is made with sand from the Loire, and exposed rubblestones are typical subsoil features in communities that all have their own quarries for sandstone, granite or gneiss.

Granite has long been a feature of the built landscape of Minho, the northernmost region of Portugal, home to Vinho Verde. Skills that migrated with the Celts and from Central Europe have created the enclosures, terrace drains and supports of these tiny, self-sufficient vineyards, and the subsoil is revealed in the basalt, silex, pebbles and serpentine of the local walls.

Wood

The situation is different for wood, which is less resistant to time and fashion than stone. Whether as a living tree or cut timber, it is the primary material chosen for vine trellises, although the type of wood used will depend equally on the local climate and the species' durability in local conditions. Living trees used as trellises are also a sign that wine has been grown somewhere for centuries, in small-scale, peasant farming with little capital, primarily aimed at meeting the needs of a family. Since they are difficult to industrialize and to treat for powdery mildew and downy mildew, such trellising systems are disappearing, except in isolated regions or when used in heritage techniques, such as the *hautains* that marry together trees and vines. The use of stakes is a sign that a wine-grower has the financial power to invest, as in the Médoc, where low vines have historically been trellised 50cm (20in) above the soil and supported by a horizontal frame of stakes made of chestnut (which lasts five years), or resin pine (15–20 years) to which cross-members (the "arms") are attached.

Everything changed in the 1850s with the advent of iron wire, which was more durable and practical. This became widely used after 1875 and facilitated mechanization and a radical transformation in viticulture after phylloxera. Despite the gradual disappearance of wood from vineyards, it is always interesting to note its presence or absence in a wine region.

Rural heritage on a local scale

Regional architecture is both infinite in variety and universal in function, as is immediately apparent from the layouts of estate buildings and the rural heritage of an area where the local climate, materials, skills, social structure and cultural influence have conspired to create distinctive vernacular features that all have the same purpose – to demarcate, protect, manage, transport, vinify and conserve. Geographer Raphaël Schirmer, a vineyard specialist, has studied this phenomenon in his *Civilisations du vin. Comment les vignobles ont façonné le monde et les hommes* (2018).

Enclosed vineyards are primarily a sign of the power and investment ability of their owner, usually a city-dweller or an influential local figure, perhaps a politician or clergyman; the bounds of peasant vineyards tend to be natural, taking the form of hedges and ditches. The maintenance of walls is included in lease contracts, highlighting their importance for high-quality viticulture: they create a protective micro-climate, and they prevent predation and theft; they make the singularity of their wine all the more desirable. The addition of a gate bearing the name of the estate and the owner is the ultimate symbol of prestige, so it comes as no surprise to learn that these are found especially in Champagne, Burgundy and Bordeaux.

While not every region has a wealth of *clos*, vineyard huts are almost ubiquitous. These are a sort of discrete annexe of the wine-grower's residence and would have been constructed during the off-season by the wine-grower himself. They are principally used as a shelter during the working day, and occasionally as a toolshed or stable. In France, there is a whole host of local names for such a structure: *cabotte* in the Côte d'Or, *caborde* in Besançon, where they are the last vestiges of a viticulture that has disappeared, *capitelle* in Languedoc, *casot* in Roussillon, *mazet* in the Cévennes, *loge* in Champagne, *folie* in Touraine. In Rioja, such a building is a *casita*; they are not just a French phenomenon. Some have particular architectural styles, with their roofs often identical to those of local houses, and are comfortably appointed, such as the *lubites* around Tours. In mountainous regions, they may be actual temporary refuges, with one part reserved for local farming and another as a living space, such as in the *grangeons* of the Bugey or the *sartos* of Savoie: in instances where the vineyard is situated far from the village, wine-growers would spend several days here working on the vines, as ethnologist Claude Royer relates in his *Les Vignerons. Usages et mentalités des pays de vignobles* (1980).

> " Regional architecture is both infinite in variety and universal in function

Other heritage relics are equally revealing: milestones, dovecotes (bird droppings were popular as a fertilizer), wayside crosses for Catholic vineyards, and even vineyard paths, some of which are very ancient indeed. Schirmer suggests that whether these are straight or winding is symbolic of the owners' particular vision of nature and the world; when geometry triumphs, it suggests that man considers nature as a possession he can master and control, with himself as the centre of the universe, while winding paths might suggest respect for nature's superiority. This is the overriding aesthetic of the great estates of the Médoc, which can be found at every level of production, from the management of the vineyard to the architecture of the châteaux, and from the final blending of the wine to the structure of the market, with its brokers and merchants.

"It's the cellar that makes the wine"

All vineyards have buildings dedicated to two universal functions: making wine and storing it in situ, whether it is aged for a few weeks, months or years. In France, their names are legion (*cuverie*, *cuvier*, *pressoir*, *vendangeoir* and many more besides), but the architecture of the winemaking floor, with its presses and vats, hardly changes across the regions. The size of the building may vary with the size of the estate, but it is always easy to access, often on the ground floor and with minimal insulation. The same cannot be said for the storage space, which has an even greater influence on the architecture of the building. Since wine has to be kept in the best possible temperature and humidity so it does not spoil, particular attention must be paid to the barrel store, and until very recently, the solutions found were manifested in specific architectural features that were more or less distinctive depending on the region.

In his *La Maison vigneronne en France*, written in 1955, Charles Parain followed Dion in analysing responses to this storage problem (when alcohol levels were lower than now). Wine from central and eastern France was more delicate because it was lower in alcohol and had to be kept in smaller containers at a temperature around 10–12°C (50–54°F), so an underground cellar was ideal. The wine from Mediterranean wine areas was higher in alcohol and more robust; the containers were also larger and the variations in temperature smaller, and in such a case, storage at ground level would do the trick, not least since the wine was often sold and consumed more quickly. The same went for regions exporting wine for distillation, such as southwestern France.

> **Wineries are remarkable windows on the incredible diversity of the dynamic between wine-growers and their physical and cultural ecosystems**

Parain has identified three broad types of traditional estate buildings: those with underground cellars, those with vaulted cellars and others with above-ground cellars. The first are found in northeastern France, Champagne and Burgundy, and have spread as far as Saumur, with its troglodyte dwellings, and Auvergne, as well as the Douro and Tokaj. The ancient Egyptians may have dug storage cellars for their wine, but this practice did not spread along the Mediterranean coast, where buildings with vaulted cellars were the norm. This latter was a Roman technique that spread along the routes of imperial culture to find its way, in certain incarnations, into the estate buildings of Alsace and Germany. It is unknown further west in France, however, where unvaulted, above-ground barrel stores appeared as outhouses to the main building. These are found from Muscadet to Ariège, but the château-*chai* (château/winery) of the Médoc is the most accomplished form, with the symbolic elegance of the estate-owner's "house", the construction, nowadays, of the estate building commissioned from a famous name, and the vat room and barrel store; hidden away and practically invisible, this is supervised by a manager and far removed from a winemaking function that had long been seen as of peasant origin. The burgeoning international influence of Bordeaux was to spread this model throughout the world and bring about a radical evolution in viticultural architecture in the second half of the 20th century – the winery as a marketing tool.

"Starchitecture" – a new way to market wine

Until 1966, the end goal of vineyard architecture was not the wine itself. As Schirmer has demonstrated, the Palladian villas of the Romans and the châteaux of Bordeaux symbolized the refinement of an elite of which drinking wine was merely one aspect. The designs of Gustave Eiffel (1832–1923), including the Byrrh cellars in Thuir, the González Byass bodega in Jerez, and the CVNE cellar in Rioja, are first and foremost hymns to modernity, a triumph of steel over stone and a victory for international business and commerce. The dream-like structure of the Bodegas Güell in Sitges, Catalonia, which bears the name of the famous patron of Antoni Gaudí (1852–1926), is intended to blend into its environment. As with the work produced by the architect's pupils (28 cooperative cellars across Catalonia), it is above all a reflection of faith in progress and social Catholicism.

Everything changed when Robert Mondavi (1913–2008) opened his winery at Oakville in the heart of the Napa Valley, suddenly casting a spotlight on the work involved with winemaking that until then had been hidden away by traditional wine-estate architecture. The buildings, designed to welcome visitors, had to give a sense of their links with European expertise and drinking sophistication, while also highlighting the American spirit of innovation. The public would visit, taste and buy, and thus began the estate/winery as a communication hub and total cultural experience, with restaurants, exhibitions, concerts and more besides. The role of architecture was now to amplify a particular discourse about wine, pushing a narrative developed by a brand strategy. The greatest names were called upon: first of all, Ricardo Bofill for the Château Lafite-Rothschild barrel store (1988), then Herzog & de Meuron (Dominus in 1997, Petrus in 2001), followed by Frank Gehry at Marqués de Riscal in Rioja (2006), Jean-Michel Wilmotte (Château Cos d'Estournel, La Cavale), Christian de Portzamparc (Château Cheval Blanc), Norman Foster (Château Margaux), Jean Nouvel (Château La Dominique, Château La Coste), Philippe Starck (Château Les Carmes Haut-Brion), and even Zaha Hadid (Bodegas López de Heredia). This internationalization, which is mainly found in Bordeaux and the countries it has influenced, such as Spain, Austria, Italy, the US, Chile, Argentina and Australia, as well as in Provence, has not always preserved a link with the local area.

The winery, telling the story of wine

The design of the building, which has to combine practicality with aesthetics, has become a way of making a statement. Schirmer has identified three major recurring themes around the world. The first is metonymy, whereby the architecture picks up on an element linked to wine and reproduces it

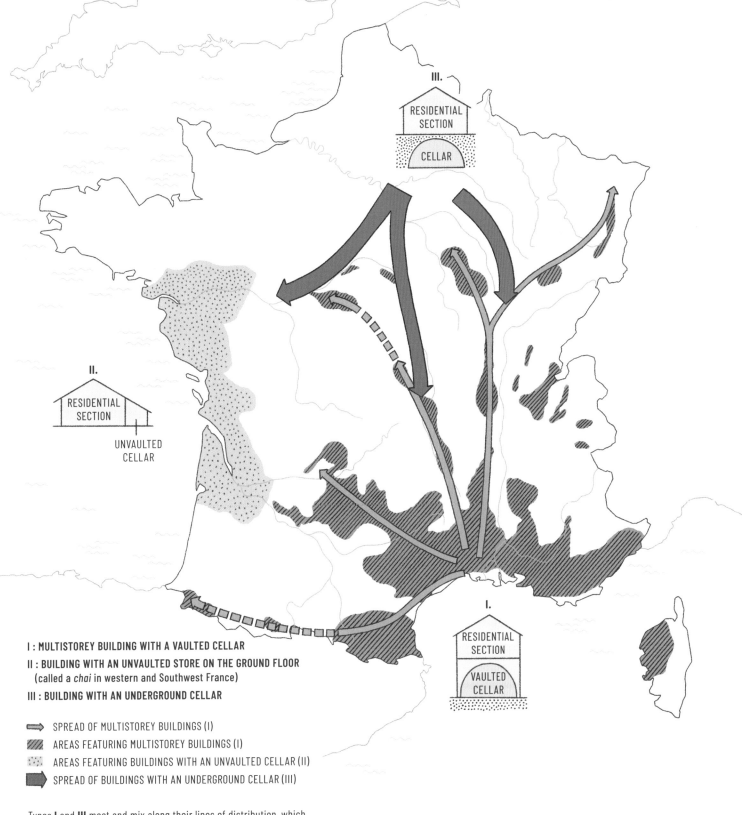

III.

RESIDENTIAL SECTION

CELLAR

II.

RESIDENTIAL SECTION

UNVAULTED CELLAR

I.

RESIDENTIAL SECTION

VAULTED CELLAR

I : MULTISTOREY BUILDING WITH A VAULTED CELLAR

II : BUILDING WITH AN UNVAULTED STORE ON THE GROUND FLOOR
(called a *chai* in western and Southwest France)

III : BUILDING WITH AN UNDERGROUND CELLAR

➡ SPREAD OF MULTISTOREY BUILDINGS (I)

▨ AREAS FEATURING MULTISTOREY BUILDINGS (I)

░ AREAS FEATURING BUILDINGS WITH AN UNVAULTED CELLAR (II)

➡ SPREAD OF BUILDINGS WITH AN UNDERGROUND CELLAR (III)

Types **I** and **III** meet and mix along their lines of distribution, which
largely correlate with waterways.

THE MAIN TYPES OF WINE-ESTATE BUILDINGS IN FRANCE, AS DESCRIBED BY CHARLES PARAIN

The architecture and distribution of wine-estate buildings were determined by climatic and commercial constraints.
Claude Royer has illustrated the three most common types in France, as identified by Charles Parain.

"The Douro is an excess of nature" *Miguel Torga*

The Douro Valley is spectacular – and hostile, with an old proverb promising "nine months of winter and three months of hell" on its vertiginous schist hillsides and poor soils. The region has been cultivated since antiquity, however, and the herculean effort to stamp the authority of man on the terroir is apparent in the thousands of kilometres of drystone terraces, both the narrow *socalcos* and the wide *patamares*, that mark out the Baixo Corgo, the Cima Corgo and the Douro Superior, the subregions of the valley. Despite the economic success enjoyed by Porto's fortified wine since 1678, the region remained fairly isolated until recent years, with Porto and Vila Nova de Gaia, the twin coastal cities that house the lodges (barrel stores) where the Port is aged and exported, connected to the valley only by the river, a railway and around 100 km (some 60 miles) of winding road. Portugal's accession to the European Community changed everything, however, and better roads have been built amid a welter of EU subsidies and private investment. To compensate for the sag in the market for fortified wines, a portion of the economy is moving from west to east; all the estates are exploring unfortified still wines (under the Douro appellation); and wine tourism is taking off.

This trend received a fillip in 2001 with the recognition of the Alto Douro as a UNESCO World Heritage Site, and this has left its mark on the development of the quintas, or estates. The quinta houses built by the great Port shippers were historically the symbol of the city in the valley, even though any temptation toward ostentation was constrained in favour of practicality; all they did here was make wine, and little money was spent on the aesthetics. This was to change after 1986, with the quintas being restored, redesigned or rebuilt to square the circle of ensuring production and marketing while also conserving history. The number of buildings designed by architects, often Portuguese, then multiplied wildly, with each new building being more remarkable than the last, making the Douro one of the most symbolic regions in the history of wine architecture.

metaphorically; this might be a vine, a barrel, a glass or something else entirely. For Schirmer, this produces the most obvious and disappointing results because it reduces the civilizational aspects of wine to a caricature.

The second theme is natural mimicry, or the "synecdoche of landscape", as Eva Bigando calls it in *La synecdoque paysagère, une notion pour comprendre les représentations des paysages viticoles bourguignon et bordelais* (2006), when the building aims to emulate an element of the countryside and blend into its surroundings. This may be through the design itself (the wave of the Bodega Ysios in Rioja, for example) or the materials used (local again, as in the stones at Dominus in the Napa Valley). The implicit message is that the wine is natural and that human intervention has been kept to a minimum.

The third theme is a continuation of the second, and involves introducing as much transparency as possible; the barrel store disappears metaphorically, thanks to see-through walls, or literally, beneath plant cover, or underground. The wine flows directly from nature, indeed from the cosmos, with the role of man almost obviated by a discourse of absolute naturalism that paradoxically turns its back on its cultural dimension. It is interesting to note the great questions of our age reflected in wine-estate architecture: man at the centre of the world, man to be respected as part of nature and so on.

It should come as no surprise that the major trends in the understanding of terroir – naturalism, then as a socio-historical construct – bleed into the architectural evolution of barrel stores and the fundamental ideas of which they are an incarnation, since architecture is in part a reflection of a discourse with the world. There is nothing random about the layout of a winery: whether out of economic or practical necessity, or through the prioritization of investments or marketing concerns, the buildings used to vinify and store wine are remarkable windows on the incredible diversity of the dynamic between wine-growers and their physical and cultural ecosystems. They also reveal an evolution in the links between cities and wine terroirs. The latter were for a long time under urban influence but are now finding emancipation as globalization takes over the wine market. An estate no longer needs to be within a local commercial orbit to be recognized and to grow. Dion's theories have once again been confirmed by the new trading circuits that double the number of the traditional routes and allow new terroirs to emerge. Knowing and understanding these routes is therefore of crucial importance.

PRUNING

Pruning probably began when grape-pickers noticed that vines that had been nibbled by their livestock produced less fruit in subsequent years, but the grapes that were produced were sweeter and the harvests more regular. Ever since Mago I of Carthage's *Agricultural Encyclopedia* appeared in the 3rd or 2nd century BCE, guidelines for training vines have provided a constant stream of suggestions for the best ways of pruning for shape, new growth and grape yield.

The principal pruning methods used in commercial viticulture

Pruning methods once varied widely from region to region but were standardized in the mid-19th century, not least thanks to physician and agronomist Jules Guyot, to whom we owe the method that bears his name. This was followed by the adoption of wire-trellising and machinery, as well as a flood of expert advice as greater and more profitable yields of higher quality were sought after the phylloxera crisis. Pruning methods are generally known as "short" (one to two buds retained per cane), "long" (four to ten buds on average) or "mixed" (somewhere between the two). The most common are as follows.

- **Cordon de Royat**: single cordon trained or spur pruning on a permanent extension of the trunk. This short pruning method features a permanent horizontal arm with two to five spurs bearing buds, aligned to follow the trellising – each will generally have two buds. Variant: Double cordon de Royat.
- **Single Guyot**: a mixed pruning method on a short trunk, or cane pruning. The structure consists of a trunk from which extend one single fruit cane (usually bearing six to ten buds) and one renewal spur with two buds, which will become next year's fruit cane. Variants: Double Guyot; Guyot Poussard (a single Guyot with two arms, one of which has a shoot and the other a cane and a renewal spur).
- **Head-pruning**: short pruning on a free-standing trunk made up of two to five arms, with maybe one or two shoots, each having one to three buds. Head-pruning is generally low to the ground and not trained. This is called *albarello* in Italy, and *en vaso* in Spain.
- **Pergola**: an aerial training system above head height. A long trunk may support one or two arms, forming a horizontal canopy. This is called *latada* in Portugal, and it is related to the *tendone* system in Italy.
- **Stake**: a long prune on a generally short trunk, with the plant creeping along a stake.
- **Lyre**: a pruning method for large vines with low plantation density that involves training arms along two axes of trellising from a long trunk, creating two curtains of canes pointing upward that look like a lyre.
- **Geneva double curtain**: a short prune on a long trunk supported by cordons on both sides.
- **Scott Henry**: a mixed system on a long trunk in which the canopy is divided vertically, with the canes forming two curtains, one rising and one falling.
- **Precision mechanical trimming (PMT)**: a mechanized pruning system based on a single cordon at a height, intended to produce high yields.

Physiology, history, productivity

What should we make of this standardization? There may actually be more to it than meets the eye. In 2007, Carbonneau identified 50 major framing methods and 250 training systems, which he classified according to whether the pruning was selective or not (minimal or no pruning, for example), uniform (cordon), alternating (Guyot), or mixed. While around 10 or so pruning systems predominate today, the others are used only rarely, and it is not difficult to see how standardization is bringing about a loss of intangible heritage; there has been a slow erosion of a local history shaped by wine-growers' choices that are "dictated often by constraints imposed by the environment, occasionally by their own creativity in technical innovation, and nearly always by historic roots and habits handed down from generation to generation", as Carbonneau reminds us in his 2013 article, "Diversité des architectures de vigne dans le monde. Contraintes environnementales et facteurs historiques". While these historical and regional pruning systems may not heed the rules of modern productivism, don't they have something to teach us about the way a particular cépage has adapted and been shaped during its singular history, as well as about the relationship that wine-growers have developed with their ecosystem over the centuries – especially in these times of climate chaos and of wood diseases, for which we know that poor pruning is partially responsible?

Comparison of regional (1867) and international (21st-century) pruning systems

Pruning has become standardized over the course of less than 150 years, and there are now no more than 10 or so international training systems that have supplanted hundreds of regional pruning methods. The illustrations on the following pages show this trend toward standardization, comparing the pruning methods employed in Muscadet (on the left) around 1867 with the main 21st-century international pruning systems (on the right).

TRAINING SYSTEMS (1867–21ST CENTURY)

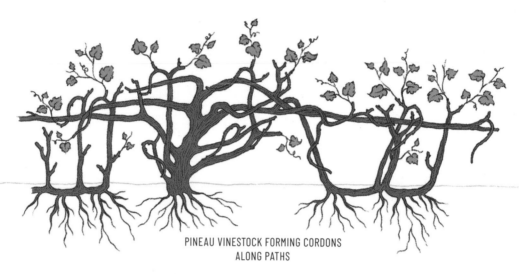

PINEAU VINESTOCK FORMING CORDONS
ALONG PATHS

PYRAMID OF CHASSELAS

ISOLATED VINE
(1ST YEAR)

PINEAU VINESTOCK WRAPPED AROUND A TREE TRUNK
(200 BUNCHES IN 1866 – 67kg/148lb)

FULLY GROWN OLD PINEAU
VINESTOCK

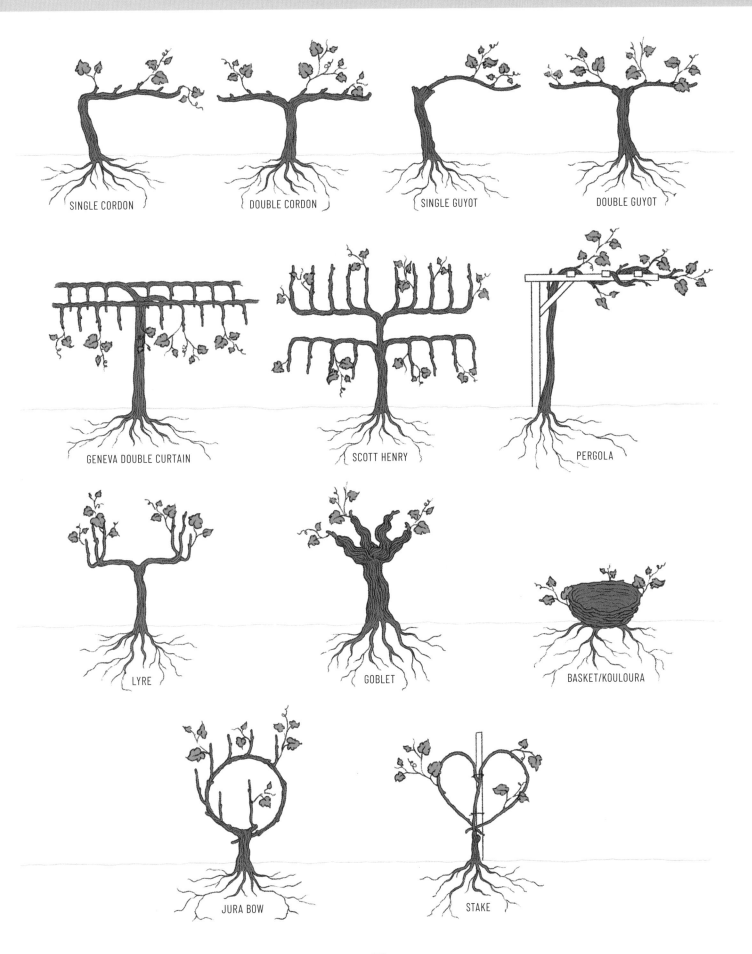

SINGLE CORDON

DOUBLE CORDON

SINGLE GUYOT

DOUBLE GUYOT

GENEVA DOUBLE CURTAIN

SCOTT HENRY

PERGOLA

LYRE

GOBLET

BASKET/KOULOURA

JURA BOW

STAKE

Wine roads

Before the advent of modern transportation, the geography of wine was primarily a geography of distribution. Wine oiled the wheels of society and was a symbol of power, playing a part in worship, diet, and colonization – it got around. Waterways were long the transport routes of choice, and improvements in commercial shipping had a direct influence on the spread of winemaking: barrels and bottles were exported by water, while innovations and influences arrived along the same path. In the absence of waterways, major land routes were the only other option, and these played a similar, if more limited, role. Pilgrimages, crusades and the discovery of the New World in the Middle Ages all promoted cooperation and the exchange of ideas in terms of producing and drinking wine. So how did this geography of distribution shape the historic vineyards?

Water routes

Most trade was conducted via water until the 19th century. Given the volumes to be transported, the economic and human cost, relative speed and other factors, river and sea routes were freighted with less risk than land convoys. From the Gallo-Roman period onward, the first vineyards established in France were on rivers: Bordeaux on the Garonne, Metz and Trier on the Mosel, Vienne on the Rhône and so on. Schirmer expands on this in his *Vignes et vins. Paysages et civilisations millenaires* (2018), and explains, "Wine geography in the Old World more or less maps onto a network of waterways. The major vineyards are located on major rivers. . . By the same token, places that are more difficult to reach, such as central Spain, have had to develop extensive land routes for cities such as Salamanca. For a long time, however, vineyards of this kind scarcely achieved any kind of reputation abroad comparable with that of their counterparts near the coasts and shores." The management of riverbanks, ports and canals played a major role in the establishment of vineyards that were dependent on the smooth running of commercial shipping.

First, let's take a look at the river itself; the presence of obstacles might delay the planting of a vineyard, and Cahors and Gaillac insisted upon "good upkeep" of their river (Dion, *Histoire de la vigne et du vin*, 1959) in the 13th century. In the 18th century, the demolition of the rocky gorge at Cachão da Valeira, the site of many shipwrecks on the Douro, accelerated expansion of the wine area upstream. The rapids at Grand Thoret and La Gratusse on the Dordogne were not addressed until it was too late, and vineyards never made it further than Bergerac, further downstream; the high country remained isolated from busy Gironde traffic and thus missed out on the market for quality produce, despite the construction of the Lalinde Canal in 1843.

Digging canals – a major challenge

Until the mid-19th century, the construction of canals and locks helped to accelerate the expansion of certain vineyards. This could involve canalizing a river prone to flooding, like the Rhine, a political frontier and trade artery whose complex course was channelled to be navigable only late in the day, with consequences for the greater or lesser development of the wine regions through which it passes. Or it could mean connecting up watercourses, such as the completion of France's Canal du Midi in 1680, which opened up a more rapid route to Bordeaux, the Atlantic and Paris for the vineyards of Languedoc by linking the Garonne to the Seuil de Naurouze watershed.

This became the capital's supply route after a devastating frost in 1709 put a large proportion of the vineyards in the north out of action for several years. Vineyards in the south had previously found exporting to the north difficult because of the distances involved. The vast majority of these were simple wines to be drunk on the spot, with the exception of sweet Muscat, Grenache and Malvasia wines. From the 19th century onward, these had been produced to compete with the sweet raisin wines, made with sun-dried grapes in Cyprus or the Peloponnese, that were extremely popular at the courts of the time and were sold by Venice, a major trading hub in the Middle Ages. These were easier to transport because they were vinified in small barrels and were sometimes also counted as medical remedies and so exempted from duty, but their market was nonetheless greatly limited by their rarity and their high price; they were very seldom available in Paris.

Everything was to change for Languedoc after the disaster of 1709, however, as merchants were obliged to seek other sources of supply. Realizing the nature of the emergency, the authorities lowered the duty, prompting the first expansion of modern vineyards in the area. The terroirs planted at this point were still on less fertile land, rather than on the plains – unlike the second expansion, which was triggered by rail transport. This was the beginning, however late in the day, of the prosperity of Languedoc, which was to reshape the local landscape (according to Dion) and last until the overproduction crises that arose in the 1920s.

The same was true of the vineyards of the Rhône, which had long been driven by demand from the Italian market. This market for Rhône wines developed because shipping wine upstream on the river was very difficult: the strong Mistral and the current required many men and beasts to pull the boat along the towpaths. Going downstream was much easier. The strong Italian market justified the continuing production of wine in the Rhône, and Paris became a second market. The preferred route to Paris and the northern markets was via the Loire, not least because of prohibitive taxation, in Lyon in particular. This was despite the length of the route. Construction of the Briare (1642) and Loing (1723) canals, the dredging of the Loire riverbed to make it navigable from Saint-Rambert to Roanne, and lower taxation made it possible to increase the availability in the capital of wines from Beaujolais and the Mâconnais region, along with others from south of Lyon.

The frost of 1709 provided a similar impetus, and the Canal du Midi opened the floodgates to the English market: the capital cities of the north fell in love with Chusclan, Tavel, Côtes du Rhône, Côte-Rôtie, Condrieu and Hermitage, all at prices that justified the cost of production on the area's rolling hills. The high-quality production processes described by Pliny the Elder in his *Natural History* on the terraces of the Pays de Vienne during the High Roman Empire were back in full swing thanks to improvements in river transport, the importance of which had been fully understood by the authorities. They also grasped the role played by legislation; the edict of 1776 that abolished privileges hampering the free distribution of wine in France was decisive, as Dion points out.

Ports – the creators of vineyards for winemaking...

For obvious reasons of accessibility and cost, vineyards have been established in the vicinity of ports for centuries. The importance and commercial influence of these transport hubs even went so far as to forge an identity for viticultural areas and their style of production, as shown by the vineyards of the Atlantic coast, Nantes, Bordeaux, Porto and La Rochelle. The vineyards of La Rochelle are now no more, but their accessibility in the Middle Ages ensured they surpassed even those of

Bordeaux in terms of prestige and trade. The Gironde estuary protects Bordeaux from the bluster of the Atlantic, but it is also the area's Achilles heel, because its narrows are difficult to navigate; docking at La Rochelle is far simpler because it is directly adjacent to the ocean but still protected. No sooner had the straits of the Pertuis Breton and Pertuis d'Antioche been dammed than vineyards were planted to satisfy demand from Dutch merchants who were already port customers for its salt, and the city experienced tremendous growth matched only by Flemish cities like Bruges.

La Rochelle had everything going for it: political stability; a burgeoning population; favourable climatic conditions for regular, high-quality production of white cépages; the considerable added value of wine and salt, the production of which was less precarious than cereal crops; and the possibility of docking large-tonnage boats. The size of boats was measured at the time by the number of barrels shipped, and by 1460 some vessels could accommodate more than a thousand, although these required sufficient under-keel clearance. The wines of Poitou and Saintonge, the regions around La Rochelle, were the most widely consumed in 12th-century England, the crisp whites they produced finding greater favour than clairet from Bordeaux until the 16th century. At this point, the local vineyards gradually entered a slow decline – the New World was offering new trading opportunities, the "burned wine" that would become Cognac was conquering northern Europe and competition from other ports was becoming ever stiffer.

... and for distilling

The spread of distilling was also linked to water transport and the benefits port vineyards had to offer. As Éric Rouvellac, a specialist in wine geography, pointed out in *Vins, vignobles et viticultures atlantiques* (2020), distilling provided alcohol for sailors and a preserving agent for food, and the vineyards of Cognac and Armagnac, which were defined through the export of spirits to the north, had been planted in response. The Pays Nantais is a textbook example here: Muscadet wine style was until recently directly linked to the production of wines for distillation, and high-yield whites that were neutral and crisp had long been in demand from the Dutch.

Historical geography still weighs heavily on recognition of the quality of a region that would in any case deserve it on physical criteria alone. Henri Enjalbert (in *Histoire de la vigne et du vin. L'avènement de la qualité*, 1975) maintains that Cognac carved out a niche for itself at the beginning of the 18th century through the quality of the distilled wines that came from the Grande and Petit Champagne areas, which saved the vines from being uprooted when there was overproduction of white wine. Cognac companies soon saw the advantages in aging its distillates: estates with the

Marsala – the sad fate of a Port vineyard

Marsala, Porto, Jerez – so many ports have given rise to quality vineyards, and so many destinies have been decided by trade with Britain. Such was the case with the rise and fall of Marsala, a viticultural area in Sicily that was one of the great commercial success stories of the 18th and 19th centuries. Legend has it that in 1773, John Woodhouse, an English merchant in search of soda, which was produced in great amounts in Sicily, was obliged to put in at Marsala, where he came across a fortified wine produced *in perpetuum* (a method similar to the solera/perpetual reserve system) that was akin to the Sherry and Port that was so popular at the time. He decided on the spot to market it in England.

Its success, boosted by a personal order from Horatio Nelson, was such that Woodhouse took up residence on the island to begin mass production. In 1806, he was joined by Benjamin Ingham, who set up a company and developed the European and American markets, rapidly becoming the wealthiest man in Sicily. In 1832, the Sicilian Florio family became the third great dynasty of the golden age of Marsala, generating great fortunes and commissioning extraordinary architecture.

Everything abruptly ground to a halt at the beginning of the 20th century, however, when the English market suddenly lost interest; post-phylloxera reconstruction was extremely sluggish and dedicated to the industrial production of wine and *coupage* for vermouths. The small volumes remaining were used to make cooking Marsala. A hundred years later, the landscape still bears the scars of the crisis, with the wine area eaten away by urbanization and polyculture. A mere handful of producers are attempting to keep historic Marsala alive, including Marco De Bartoli, who is determined to preserve the traditional, pre-fortification style using the *perpetuo* method with his Vecchio Samperi. He has nonetheless also had to develop a range of unfortified still wines to meet the expectations of a market that consumes few of these great and historic *rancios*.

resources to store stock were founded from 1643, and the port of Rochefort on the Charente began to boom. By 1875, the region covered 282,000 ha; by 2019, it was only 78,000 ha), exporting 14 hl (370 US gallons) of wine but 400,000 hl (10.5 million US gallons) of spirits.

Mutage, the addition of alcohol to grape must to halt fermentation and stabilize wine, was a practice that had been in use since the 13th century, and it presented the areas around ports with a commercial opportunity that resulted in the expansion and restructuring of vineyards first in Jerez, then Porto, Madeira and Marsala, all of which enjoyed this unparalleled competitive advantage over vineyards further inland. A similar story unfolded with the vineyards founded at ports of call on major maritime trading routes, such as the passages to the Indies and the Americas. These vineyards exported their produce but also imported the commercial and technical skill of the merchants that sold it, as Schirmer clearly identifies (in *Civilisations du vin*) in the establishment of the great merchant families (often from the Hanseatic League, the Rhine or England), who created international networks by introducing regional markets to others from further afield.

Land routes – supporting the expansion of vineyards

Some vineyards clearly also arose from the great overland trails blazed by exploration and commerce where waterways were not available. The network of roads developed by the Romans complemented the river routes and helped the planting of vineyards to spread, initially during the High Roman Empire (1st–3rd centuries CE), extending to the northern marches of the province of Narbonne with the propagation of Gaillac along the Via Domitia and Via Aquitania – the vineyards of Côte-Rôtie and Hermitage were to appear at the same time on the Rhône. Once the adaptation of Mediterranean cépages to northern climes had been achieved through crossing and selection, this triumphal march of conquest was to continue along the Via Agrippa, starting from Lyon and heading toward northern and western Europe; Burgundian vineyards in particular were to benefit directly from this development. Later on, the salt road would also accelerate the expansion of some vineyards, as was the case with Arbois, which took advantage of this trading network to export Jura wine.

The Silk Road – a dead end for wine

By contrast, Jean-Robert Pitte characterized the Silk Road as a "dead end for wine" in his *Le Désir du vin. À la conquête du monde* (2009). Although there is real potential for viticulture in the regions it crosses – from Antioch in modern-day Turkey, to the former capital of China, Chang'an (now Xi'an) – Pitte

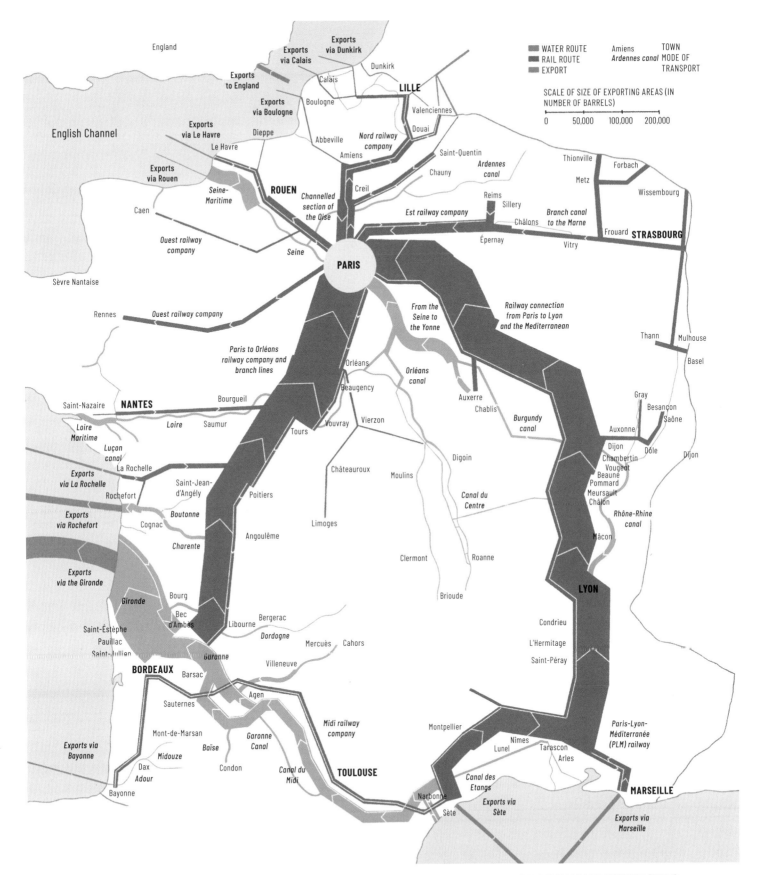

TRANSPORTATION MAP OF WINES AND SPIRITS IN MAINLAND FRANCE DURING THE SECOND EMPIRE, BY CHARLES MINARD (1857)

Charles Minard was Inspector General of Bridges and Highways, and he notably created some extremely modern maps of the commercial transportation of wines and spirits in France during the mid-19th century. (As mapped by Minard.)

considers this a "neat problem of cultural geography": there are still isolated strings of vineyards stretching all the way to China, but they have experienced no growth – why might this be?

The long history of Turkish winemaking slowed dramatically with Ottoman colonization, which resulted in the spread of Islam across the country and the loss of the Russian and European markets, while the Persian market collapsed with the Iranian Revolution of 1979. There was some evidence of wine consumption and winemaking in India, especially under British rule, until phylloxera hit, but the monsoon season seems to have slowed the spread of *V. vinifera*, as did the various religious prohibitions. Since the early 1980s, however, the country has seen a dynamic revival of the industry supported by viticultural improvements and a growing market. There are still traces of a few small vineyards in the high valleys of Muslim Afghanistan, albeit not for wine production; Pakistan, again mostly for grapes but with some very rare, forbidden

home brewing; Tajikistan, mostly for grapes and a little wine; and Tibet, for both grapes and wine. The cultivation of all these vineyards may have begun under Persian influence. It is the Persians we have to thank for the arrival of viticulture in China via the Fergana Valley between Uzbekistan and Kyrgyzstan, and the oasis at Turpan in Xinjiang still bears witness to this, even if the real development of wine production in China was the work of the Soviets after World War Two.

Despite the established presence of vineyards, including in Vietnam and Japan, and the undeniable consumption of alcohol, why has wine not enjoyed the same success here as in the West? Pitte thinks it is because "vines and wines arrived in these regions stripped of a large part of their cultural trappings and resonance". While Islam was not unaware of wine, Buddhism had only faint praise for it – enough to lend a slight religious sheen, although not to the same degree as in Christianity. This is also true of the other animist religions (Taoism, Shintoism and shamanism), where the sacred plant is rice,

The Loire: taming the royal river

In his doctoral thesis *Le Val de Loire* (1933), Dion pointed out the role played by waterways in the geography of wine – and the spread of vineyards across the Loire basin pretty much maps onto the stretches of waterway navigable by river traffic before the advent of the railways.

The Loire is France's longest river, and was it also its number one trade route until trains made an appearance. Paradoxically, however, it is also the most difficult river to navigate, with significant flooding and drought, shifting sandbanks, ice-jams and unpredictable winds along its dangerous and irregular course. The Loire came to rule the waterways and serve so many vineyards only through massive investment by a string of authorities, provided solely because alternative modes of transport were worse and even more expensive. Development of the river fostered expansion of the vineyards; the watercourse was dammed in the 12th century, levees were built and dozens of ports sprang up between Forez and Muscadet, with vines being planted nearby. Customs borders influenced the quality of production, since only the best wines could justify the duty imposed.

The Loire is blessed with a drainage basin of 120,000 km² (46,300 square miles), or about one-fifth of the area of the entire country. It rises in the Ardèche and flows north toward the Paris Basin, linking Lyon, Paris and Nantes before reaching the sea in the Pays Nantais. No effort was spared in improving the connections between these three crucial centres of the national economy, including the challenge of digging the Briare (1642), Orléans (1692) and Loing (1723) canals. Loire wine became ubiquitous on tables throughout France and in northern Europe, and the vineyards began to specialize in fine wines for export overseas and simple wines for everyday use. It was a key route and brought external influences into the valley, with pilgrims who followed the Camino de Santiago sharing cépages and skills, and the markets of the north deciding the style of the wines. The Val de Loire region's centuries-old alliance of nature and culture was recognized by UNESCO as a World Heritage Site in 2000.

not the vine. Wine production thus remained minimal until the 20th century and the advent of Westernization; only now are we discovering that Asia has wine terroirs of great quality.

The Camino de Santiago de Compostela

By contrast, the various routes of the Camino de Santiago de Compostela (the Way of St James), were to give rise to a number of vineyards, on occasion in regions that seemed little suited to high-quality viticulture, as examined by Pierre Casamayor and Éric Limousin in their *Les Vignobles des chemins de Compostelle* (2003). Pilgrims needed wine. Pilgrimage to Galicia was to experience an extraordinary boom in the 11th and 12th centuries thanks to the Gregorian Reforms and support from the papacy; within two centuries, a network of more than 1,200 monasteries associated with the Benedictine abbey at Cluny (founded 909 CE) had been established in the region. The monks allowed pilgrims to stop overnight in their hostels, and they all needed wine, as decreed by the monastic rule of hospitality to travellers. Vineyards were founded, although only traces of some are visible today: pilgrim numbers, which had declined after the 16th-century Reformation fell away more or less completely after the separation of Church and State in 1905 in France. Such was the case with the vineyards scattered along the Via Podiensis, the leg of the Camino that passes through Puy-en-Velay in Auvergne on the southwestern edges of the Massif Central. These included Estaing and Entraygues-le-Fel, on the steep hillsides along the Lot, and on the Truyère in Marcillac, which supplied the abbey church at Conques, or the vineyards in Figeac and Moissac around the crags of the Causses du Quercy and Cahors.

As pilgrimage along the Camino picked up again in the 1950s, wine tourism and the crisis in winemaking that encouraged the renewal of historic vineyards have meant that some are now being restored to their former glory. This is true of the magnificent vineyard of Irouléguy, where the Via Turonensis, Via Lemovensis and Via Podiensis meet to begin the crossing of the Pyrenees at Saint-Jean-Pied-de-Port. A similar role was played by pilgrimage paths on the Iberian peninsula, such as the Camino Francés, which stimulated the growth of vineyards in northern Spain.

The Spanish vineyards of the Camino Francés

There are several pilgrimage routes through Spain to Santiago de Compostela, but the best known and most popular is the Camino Francés, which passes through wine regions that in part owe their survival to the human, religious and commercial traffic that has been following this route for centuries. Starting from Saint-Jean-Pied-de-Port and the vineyard at Irouléguy in the French Basque Country, it crosses the Navarre region, passing on the way the monas-

tery at Irache that has been supplying pilgrims with wine since the 12th century. Since 2009, this has been the home of Prado de Irache, a *vino de pago* (an appellation particular to Spain, designating an exceptional estate). The Camino then passes through Logroño and La Rioja, which is well known for reds and whites good enough to lay down, before reaching the high plateaux of Castile and León. It is here, south of Burgos, that the wines of Ribera del Duero, some of the finest Tempranillo-based Spanish reds, are produced.

The Camino then turns north past León to reach Ponferrada in the Bierzo DO (*denominación de origen*, Spain's equivalent to AOC), heralding "Green Spain", the Cantabrian coast and the Atlantic. Mencía (red) and Godello (white) grapes yield crisp and spicy wines here.

The majestic landscapes of Galicia soon heave into view, and here, on steep schist hillsides carved out by the rivers Miño and Sil, you will find Roman-era terraced vineyards that can still produce uncommon wines. Having been largely abandoned in the wake of the phylloxera crisis and the rural exodus to the cities in the 20th century, they are now coming back to life, in particular under the appellation Ribeira Sacra. The wines made with local cépages (Albariño, Loureiro, Treixadura, Mencía, Brancellao, Sousão, Caíño Tinto and others) are crisp and dense, with bags of personality.

Pilgrims who finally reach Santiago de Compostela can slake their thirst with one of the most refreshing beverages in the country, Rías Baixas – and the subregion of Ribeira do Ulla produces glorious examples of this fine Albariño wine. This terroir of oceans and mountains that has been shaped in part by pilgrimage routes is particularly suitable for making white wine, which has also been historically preferred as a wine for celebrating Mass.

Far more importantly, however, the Camino de Santiago was also to bring cépages to a wider audience. Pilgrims were not slow to help themselves to cuttings of varieties they had enjoyed, and winemaking skills and drinking customs were swapped and shared – the whole of Europe's wine industry was to benefit from the progress brought about by the exchanges of ideas fostered by pilgrimage routes.

"It is impossible to fully understand [the viticultural geography of France] without juxtaposing it with the geography of transport and traffic as it existed in France before the age of rail," asserts Dion in *Histoire de la vigne et du vin*. These dynamics would change profoundly with the Industrial Revolution and the transformation of transport, as is evident not only in the construction of vineyards in the countries of what came to be called the New World, but also in the rebirth of certain European vineyards and the emergence of the wine economy we know today. Cities were also to play an unmistakably decisive role in shaping vineyards.

Cities shape vineyards, and vice versa

Far from being idealized enclaves in rural settings, historic wine areas producing quality wine owe their growth to the many different relationships they have forged with towns and cities; large towns have been planting vineyards and breathing life into them since ancient times. As described by the UNESCO professorial chair in the culture and traditions of wine at the University of Burgundy, the city is both "a place where wine is cultivated and produced and a place of commerce and consumption, where norms, tastes and hierarchies are refined… and a diversity of culture is expressed." Urban areas have had a major influence on the typicity and quality of the wines their citizens wished to drink, and consequently on winemaking as a whole. It is no coincidence that many towns in France have given their name first to wine styles and then to specific AOCs – but what can urban vineyards teach us about the intertwined histories of cities and vines? How does the vineyard shape the city, and the city shape the vineyard?

Vineyards in the city – the role of urban viticulture

Cities play a key role in wine trading routes: wine passes through them on its way elsewhere, but it is also drunk in them – in vast quantities. While vines are now being replanted in cities mostly as a result of wine tourism schemes, urban vineyards initially provided sustenance for city-dwellers until political or economic circumstances forced them beyond the city walls. There are still traces of this in Vienna, where more than 700 ha of vineyard lie within the city limits. There are many *Heurige*, local taverns, often owned by the winemakers, that still serve wine produced directly from the local land. These are generally Gemischter Satz, a wine made by field blends of different varieties that has had official recognition as a DAC (the Austrian equivalent of AOC) since 2013.

Many of Venice's islands housed vineyards during the city-state's commercial glory days between the 11th and 17th centuries; some of these, such as Mazzorbo, have now been restored to life.

Some prestigious vineyards were planted outside cities but soon became swallowed up by the suburbs, which only increased their influence. The most famous examples are Château Haut-Brion (Pessac) and its immediate neighbour La Mission Haut-Brion (Talence), Pape Clément (Pessac) and Les Carmes Haut-Brion (whose postal address is in Bordeaux, although the estate building is in Mérignac and the vines are in Pessac). The 18th-century Clos Lanson in Reims was long forgotten but is now being revived and dubbed the "Haut-Brion de Champagne" under Lanson cellarmaster Hervé Dantan. The current renaissance of vineyards within the city walls of Paris only reinforces the winemaking pedigree of France's capital and emphasizes the links between cities and viticulture.

Vineyards shape cities by making, maturing, selling and drinking wine

To the educated eye, the cobbled streets of old La Rochelle tell a rich story of the city's viticultural past, with Armorican granites, pebbles from England, assorted Dutch stones and more besides, all of which had been used as ballast for the ships that descended on wine ports. Vineyards have helped shape many European cities to a greater or lesser degree, whether in terms of materials, architecture or urban planning. Schirmer (in *Civilisations du vin*) explains it thus: "Vines and wines have a remarkable ability to create spaces entirely dedicated to wine production, maturation and storage… It is undoubtedly the only agricultural produce that has such creative power." In other words, wine has the sway to shape whole districts. Quays and ports are notable examples of this and include the Quai des Chartrons and the Port de la Lune in Bordeaux, Vila Nova de Gaia in Porto, the Barrio de la Estación in Haro (the winemaking capital of Rioja), or even the area around the Halle aux Vins on the Quai Saint-Bernard in Paris.

Railway stations also began to appear, such as at La Rapée in Paris, where Languedoc wines destined for the barrel stores in Bercy would arrive in vat wagons on the PLM

(Paris–Lyon–Marseille) line. Workplaces were constructed too: storehouses and facilities for the production, ageing, distilling and subsequent bottling of wine. To facilitate ease of movement, these were single-storey, high-ceilinged buildings with windowless walls and entrances on streets at right angles to the quays, all carefully orientated to protect from the heat. The urban planning of Haro in Rioja and Sanlúcar de Barrameda at the mouth of the Guadalquivir is still profoundly influenced by such considerations. Infrastructure soon followed, with places of business, such as trading floors, brokerage markets and wine merchants, joining premises for lawmakers, travellers and excise-collectors.

Louis XVI was prompted in part to build the Wall of the Farmers-General around Paris – the last vestiges of which, such as the Gate of Hell on Place Denfert-Rochereau, are still visible – to control more effectively the imposition of excise duty on wine entering the capital. Obviously, there were also places where wine was sold and where people lived, and the influence on the cityscape itself should not be forgotten. Buildings were constructed to celebrate wine and as a symbolic representation of the power that it confers: sculptures, fountains, façades carved with bunches of grapes, vines and similar decorations. The city was putting its commercial and political power on display and wanted everyone to recognize it.

Lastly, there was also a cultural element, expressed in festivals, fairs and exhibitions, and these celebrations of wine are now being revived in wine tourism and the heritage industry. Bordeaux, which has achieved UNESCO World Heritage status, is a shining example: it was the first city to hold a Vinexpo and has opened the Cité du Vin museum space, whose metaphorical architecture aspires to be "an evocation of the soul of wine, between the river and the city", according to its architects Anouk Legendre and Nicolas Desmazières.

Cities shape vineyards

Vines and wines are an integral part of towns and cities in just the same way that towns and cities shape vineyards and determine wine production. While city walls – with both a defensive and administrative function – have long separated urban and agricultural spaces, they have not been entirely able to prevent direct contact between the two. As Schirmer has pointed out (in *Civilisations du vin*), such links were necessarily over short distances in the case of vineyards, because owners had to be able to access their estates in the days before modern transport. As has been shown by J H von Thünen in his 1826 modelling of the organization of agricultural space (*L'État isolé*), this influence is exerted in what is in effect a series of concentric circles and is dependent on production costs, distance to markets and land rent. The

The urban vineyard of Château Haut-Brion

The heart of Bordeaux boasts wine estates of legendary reputation, and none more so than Château Haut-Brion. Located on the border of Pessac and Talence, the 51-ha property stares across at its equally renowned twin sister, Château La Mission Haut-Brion. While the excellence of their wines owes much to their terroir – which consists of gravelly ridges about 30m (100ft) across, protected by the Garonne, with a beneficial climate of hot summers, mild autumns and winters free of frost – the research of Raphaël Schirmer and Hélène Velasco-Graciet in *Atlas mondial des vins* (2010) also acknowledges the role of the wine-grower in developing this quality over the centuries. Since the construction of the château in 1549, the various owners of Haut-Brion have always been at pains to make use of their local and international networks to promote the estate's wines and its international reputation. In 1666, the heirs of Jean de Pontac, the founder of the estate, opened a tavern in London to serve the "new French claret" under the Pontac brand. Keeping track of developments in winemaking (adding sulphites, extending vatting and maturation, topping-up and racking), they produced a colourful and powerful wine that rapidly made a name for itself, and whose fame only accelerated when it began to be sold in bottles at the end of the 18th century.

Thomas Jefferson, future US president, considered it to be one of the greatest Bordeaux. The words "château" and "terroir" both feature on the labels. In 1855, Haut-Brion was rated a Gironde *premier grand cru classé* and then, in 1953, a Graves *cru classé*. American banker Clarence Dillon, who bought it in 1935, continued to make innovations: electricity was installed, and the wooden vats were replaced with stainless steel in 1961. A clonal selection programme was started with INRA in 1972, and a wine laboratory was set up in 1990. Château Haut-Brion is an urban vineyard par excellence, a manifestation of human ingenuity and an embodiment of the role played by cities in discovering and ensuring the survival of quality wines.

TALENCE

CHÂTEAU LA MISSION
HAUT-BRION

CHÂTEAU HAUT-BRION

PESSAC

BUILDING

COMMUNE BORDER

**AMOUNT OF COARSE MATERIAL
AT THE SURFACE**

MORE THAN 50 PER CENT

LESS THAN 25 PER CENT

BETWEEN 25 AND 50 PER

TYPES OF SOIL (as defined by Schirmer and Velasco-Graciet):

CALCISOL: soil with a substantial accumulation of lime.

BRUNISOL: soil found in temperate regions, mainly brown in colour due to the alteration of primary minerals by a weakly acidic environment.

LUVISOL: rich and deep "leached" soil with good agricultural fertility. Water collecting here in winter may cause plant asphyxia.

RED OXISOL: a type of hydromorphic soil in which redox reactions predominate.

PLANOSOL: a type of soil with greatly varying characteristics but a particular water profile whereby the upper, permeable layers retain excessive amounts of water during some seasons.

PEYROSOL: soil featuring large amounts of gravel and pebbles that affect its soil chemistry.

SANDY SOIL

VARIOUS

CF: CABERNET FRANC
CS/CF/M: CABERNET SAUVIGNON, CABERNET FRANC AND MERLOT
CS: CABERNET SAUVIGNON
M: MERLOT
S: SAUVIGNON
S/S: SAUVIGNON AND SEMILLON
SE: SEMILLON
R: REPLANTATION IN PROGRESS (2010)

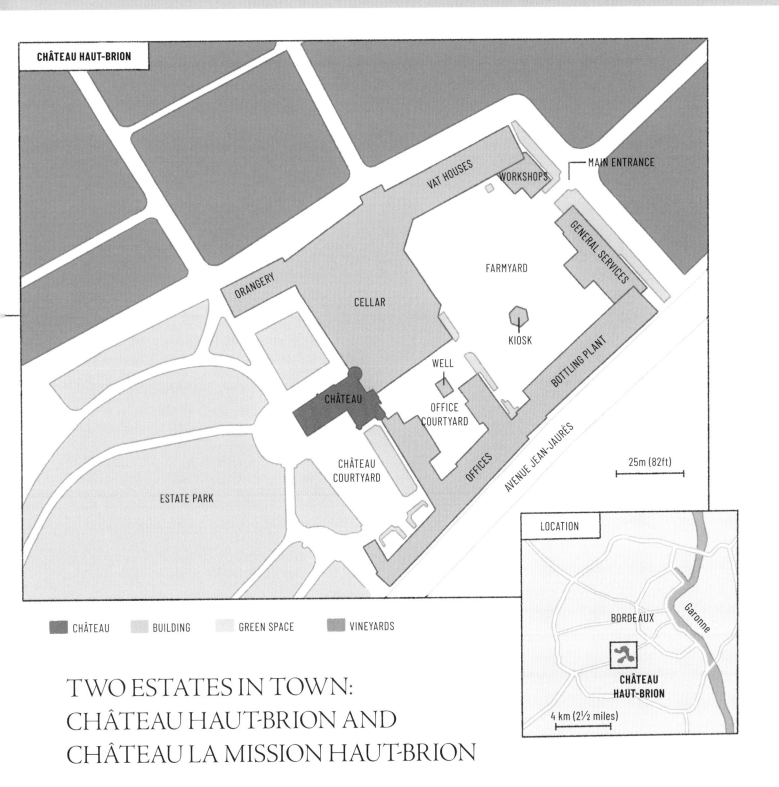

VAT HOUSES

WORKSHOPS

MAIN ENTRANCE

ORANGERY

CELLAR

FARMYARD

GENERAL SERVICES

KIOSK

WELL

BOTTLING PLANT

CHÂTEAU

OFFICE COURTYARD

CHÂTEAU COURTYARD

OFFICES

AVENUE JEAN-JAURÈS

ESTATE PARK

25m (82ft)

LOCATION

BORDEAUX

Garonne

CHÂTEAU HAUT-BRION

4 km (2½ miles)

CHÂTEAU   BUILDING   GREEN SPACE   VINEYARDS

TWO ESTATES IN TOWN: CHÂTEAU HAUT-BRION AND CHÂTEAU LA MISSION HAUT-BRION

In their study of the soils and choices of cépage at Haut-Brion and La Mission Haut-Brion, Schirmer and Velasco-Graciet have shown how the vineyards on Clarence Dillon's estates are perfect examples of the links between cities, vineyards and wine, as well as of the reciprocal influences they exert in shaping one another.

The Chartrons district

As the title of a collective study led by Schirmer suggests (*Bordeaux et ses vignobles. Un modèle de civilisation*, 2021), Bordeaux is justly considered one of the world's wine capitals, and the district of Chartrons is one of its symbolic highlights.

Created by and for the wine trade, thanks to British, Flemish and Irish merchants – collectively known as the *aristocratie du bouchon*, or the cork aristocracy – this area, about 2 km (1 mile) long, saw a large proportion of French produce destined for export pass through its halls between the 14th and 19th centuries. The neighbourhood's layout and architecture are entirely given over to trade, with constantly recurring features: grids of merchants' townhouses, all with ostentatious façades, and a plain barrel-store of two or three storeys at most to the rear, set between streets running at right angles to the Garonne river.

The post-phylloxera period saw activity gradually move away to the outer suburbs or return to the vineyards as estate bottling and ideas of locality and specific origins took precedence over umbrella brands. While only a few buildings remain from this all-but-disappeared era, the crucial role played by the Chartrons area in the viticultural economy and identity of Bordeaux was honoured with the inauguration of the Cité du Vin museum on its northern borders in 2016.

greatest urban investments were made in the innermost ring, which also encompasses (and this is no coincidence) the areas considered the best terroirs, as demonstrated by the geography of these *crus*.

These investments may be highly visible – compare the architectural continuity between châteaux in Médoc and Bordeaux, which were built by the same architects – or invisible, such as in the maintenance and improvement of vineyards, estate enclosures and so on, as recorded in lease contracts, which were often very restrictive for farmers. The end goal of these investments – to improve and publicize the quality of the wines – was as much about social prestige as it was about economic profit. The success achieved in 17th-century London by the wines of "Ho Bryan" (Haut-Brion) came about through a convergence of the political and economic power of the Pontac family of parliamentarians'

investment in the vineyard, the wine's presence on the English market and public awareness of its taste. With the creation of Haut-Brion, a new understanding of single-estate wines was born of the interaction between two cities, Bordeaux and London, as Schirmer noted. This was to be a crucial turning point in the evolution of Bordeaux wines.

The city – the cradle of branded wines

Taste-making cities soon became brands in themselves. Before the advent of wines from specific estates and plots, wines were defined by the urban centre with which they were associated, with the city lending a sense of sophistication and quality.

Wines from Beaune, Bordeaux, Champagne and Cognac were often blends or produced by merchants guaranteeing "local" taste, in a trend that accelerated in the Middle Ages. Jean-Pierre Garcia and historian Olivier Jacquet sum it up as follows in *Le terroir du vin: trajectoire historique d'un objet multiforme en Bourgogne* (2020): "Cities. . . impose upon their resident wine producers and trade corporations their standards, their measures and gauges, their legal and fiscal control, and their privileges. . . It is above all the geographical area where human transformational expertise is applied that allows something to be designated '[produce] of [such and such a city or village]'."

It is precisely this approach that can be found not only in the definition of France's *appellations d'origine*, which must demonstrate "local, trusted and consistent techniques", but also in the concept posited by French agronomist Georges Kuhnholtz-Lordat (1888–1965) in *La Genèse des appellations d'origine des vins* (1963) of an "elite nucleus", whereby the quality of the wine and the integrity of the appellation are inversely proportionate to the distance from the focal point of the town or village.

In other words, terroir is determined at any given moment in its history by the socio-economic interests of a city. Ideas of terroir, *climat* (*cru*) and appellation, and all that they represent, may change over time; just like their physical dimensions, their normative identity is evolving in lockstep with unceasing human efforts of construction and redefinition. A wine terroir is not eternal but profoundly dynamic – a symbolic mirror of our society.

The invention of *appellations d'origine contrôlée*

The ancient world recorded the names of the most sought-after wines on amphorae, and France has a historic tradition of classifying many agricultural products, including wine, according to their region of origin. For centuries, however, there was nothing to guarantee this provenance, and as individual wines became increasingly popular, they were often blended, modified or even completely faked. Any actual connection with a wine's "birthplace" was fading away even as, paradoxically, such origins were being ever-more closely defined during the phylloxera crisis. This link to origins that was formalized in the *appellation d'origine contrôlée* (AOC) system seems a given to us, even as it is now being challenged for its inflexibility, but it is, in fact, a relatively late arrival whose advent was anything but easy. How did the AOC designation come about? What were the criteria and methodology? And why is this system now in crisis?

A fantasy

The creation of the AOC system was anything but straight-forward, and its long and complex genesis came about under great political and social tension. Burgundy, often held up as a paragon of this classificatory system, might be the best example to explore this; the region's well-documented history is based on the precise origin of its wines, which are designated according to their *climats*, a Burgundian term that refers to a plot of land with specific geological and climatic conditions. These sites, which produce wines embodying the typicity of the terroir in all its natural and human complexity, have been compared and ranked over the course of centuries.

The discovery of Burgundy as the land of terroirs dates back to medieval times and the foundation of the abbeys at Cluny (909 CE) and Cîteaux (1098). As they returned to the original principles of the Benedictine monastic rule (self-sufficiency, self-denial, prayer, work and hospitality), the Cistercian monks would have devoted their time to identifying a host of micro-terroirs, tasting and testing the flavours of the hillsides to find out where to plant their vines.

From that time until the French Revolution, the monks seem to have recognized, demarcated and ranked the intrinsic qualities of the individual plots of land whose specific characteristics directly influenced the taste of the wines. This narrative of monks who are at once geologists, agronomists and wine-growers began to spread at the beginning of the 20th century. Since the 1980s, it has been almost syste-

matically co-opted by the majority of professional bodies and marketing communications, lecturing the general public and winemakers alike on the validity of the venerable and sempiternal nature of terroirs that have been "blessed by the gods", which the *climats* of Burgundy and then the AOC could only endorse. A number of studies – including publications by Jean-Pierre Garcia, Guillaume Grillon, Thomas Labbé of the University of Burgundy's UMR ArTeHiS (Archaeology, Land, History and Society) faculty and Olivier Jacquet – show the situation to be very different, however. They suggest that this re-reading of a history that is far more complex is in fact a commercial tool used for *a posteriori* justification of the grand narrative of the creation of the AOCs.

There is no specific mention of the tastes either of the land or the *cépages* in the monastic archives that have survived to our times. Any mention of winemaking suggests instead that the monks were most exercised about selling the largest possible quantities, with no distinction of place of production. In the 15th century, the Cluniac monks of Saint-Vivant de Vergy made no more than one *vin des clos*, a wine from their enclosed land that brought together all their vineyards in Vosne-Romanée, including the modern *grand crus* of La Romanée, La Romanée-Conti and La Romanée Saint-Vivant.

The monastic orders certainly played a fundamentally important role in spreading vineyards throughout Europe and in refining and passing on winemaking expertise, but their invention of the hierarchy of terroirs is a fantasy. The people identifying, developing and promoting *climats* were never the monks; rather they were the legislators, councillors and bourgeoisie of towns such as Beaune and Dijon, 500 years later.

Recognizing *climats*

The *climats* of Burgundy were recognized by UNESCO as a World Heritage Site in 2015, but their construction began in the 16th century and became progressively routine in the 18th

> In a bid to save its viticulture, the French state instituted a system at the beginning of the 20th century that guaranteed the origins of wine

century. The term made its first appearance in wine parlance in 1584 to describe the Clos de Bèze estate in Gevrey-Chambertin as *le climat de Champt Berthin*, and it became more common over the next two centuries, eventually applying only to vineyard plots and their wines.

Over the same period, a large amount of land was being sold by the Church to a newly arrived urban elite, and it was these who would play an active role in identifying particular wines and classifying them for commercial profit. They surrounded themselves with entrepreneurial brokers, the forerunners of wine merchants, whose job was to taste the wine, identify a wine's *climat* of origin and provide a guarantee of this for its sale. They invested in the hillsides that were nearest the town, and these became automatically more prestigious: those around Dijon were first, although they have been swallowed up by urbanization, followed by the Côte de Nuits and the Côte de Beaune. It is no coincidence that Gevrey-Chambertin is the commune with the greatest number of *grands crus* (nine). *Climats* became both the norm for designating the relationship of a wine to its place of origin and an indicator of its quality. They are nonetheless based on land ownership, which does not necessarily take into account the physical homogeneity, the soil, topography or other factors of the land itself.

This demarcation of land was further entrenched during the 19th century with the publication of numerous classifications by elite urban experts that established a hierarchy of *climats* and wines by sorting them according to criteria that were more cultural than geographical. These included classifications by André Jullien (1816) and Denis Blaise Morelot (1831), followed by Jules Lavalle (1855) and the Agricultural and Viticultural Committee of the Village of Beaune (1860).

"Equivalent quality" and "geographical brands"

Such classifications reflect only imperfectly the elite's consumption of wine in France at the time. Almost all the wine

was being sold by merchants who developed a sales system based on "equivalences", both in Burgundy and in France as a whole. The wine-growers were nothing more than suppliers of grapes or must, and in a period when estate-bottling was more or less non-existent, it was the blending and ageing skills of the wine houses in Dijon, Beaune and Bercy that were paramount. Playing on the reputation of certain towns or names (Montrachet, Pommard and so on), they would concoct a specific taste for each blend, which they attributed to each particular wine and adapted to their market as they saw fit, since there was no regulation at all. Consumers would rely on the name and the merchant's reputation. The grapes were generally acquired from local sources and might in some cases come from areas far distant from the geographical brand being sold; Hermitage was often cited as a supplier. The wine merely had to be of "merchantable" quality at the brokers' tasting with a tastevin, meaning clear and without too much volatile acidity.

Two standards of production quality emerged in the 17th and 18th centuries: some very rare fine wines from the owners of individual estates, such as those from certain châteaux in Bordeaux, for example, on the one hand; and branded wines or wines of "substantial quality" conforming to merchants' taste on the other. These latter were greatly in the majority.

Fraud exploded with the arrival of phylloxera. Some merchants continued to use geographical brands but extended their supply base to Italy or Algeria, using wines produced on the cheap, or even completely artificial potions that used no grapes at all. Consumers no longer had any idea what they were drinking. Wine-growers who had painstakingly rebuilt their vineyards found themselves in a crisis of overproduction, with competition from wines from the South, and looking to break free from the merchant system. Under pressure from wine-growers and some merchants, the powers-that-be were forced to institute a legal system that guaranteed the origins of wine in a bid to save French winemaking and avoid civil war within an industry at loggerheads with itself.

"Local, trusted and consistent techniques"

Appellations were born of crisis, but their institution was made possible by very specific political circumstances. France's Third Republic (1870–1940) was seeking to establish itself by reducing the influence of the landed aristocracy in the provinces, and it fostered a middle class of distinguished citizens and Republican property-owners who got involved with setting up *syndicats viticoles* – bodies representing wine producers – and were part of a network of university experts and legislators who were key actors in advancing their own position which was for single-estate wines. In addition to the necessity of combating fraud in respect of the composition of wine and abuse of denominations, there were considerable political and financial considerations. It is therefore easy to understand that decades and multiple revisions were required to arrive at a method balancing the weight of physical factors and historic know-how.

It was the latter that initially prevailed. The first law, passed in 1905, was intended to protect consumers against fraud and counterfeit wine by forbidding deception in respect of a wine's origins – but without specifying how these origins were to be determined. This was corrected in 1908, with areas of provenance demarcated according to "local, trusted and consistent techniques", terms that had been included since the law of 1905. The presupposition was that the age of a terroir's institution would underwrite quality, when in itself, of course, it is neither good nor bad.

Several areas (Clairette de Die, Armagnac, Cognac, Banyuls, Bordeaux and Champagne) embraced the law and defined their official borders. The exclusion of Aube from the last-mentioned of these, even though the department had historically supplied the wine houses of the Marne, resulted in serious rioting in 1911 and 16 years of legal wrangling. The government was obliged to review its statute, and in 1919 a law on *appellations d'origine* was passed, setting out the rights to use a place name and a collective brand. The exact provenance of a wine would appear on the label, and the courts would decide on whether it had the right to do so based on "local, trusted and consistent techniques".

Producers were now required to argue their case by presenting the most credible proof of techniques used, ideally as old as possible, such as orders, awards, scientific assessments and classifications, including any from the 19th century. Evidence that was too recent was very often dismissed without the terroir itself even being examined. Rather than building bridges, this law reinforced the division between merchants and estate-owners, and, among the latter, between owners of single-estate wines who were in favour of the law and owners of vineyards producing wines for immediate drinking who stood to lose the financial bonus inherent in the opportunity to use a name that was more hallowed; having the appellation meant being sure of land rent. The struggle to define the borders of Corton is a good example of this, and it was up to the party with the best network of contacts, not the best terroir, to substantiate its arguments.

A law of 1927 introduced a need for "objective facts", imposing a choice of cépage and introducing the idea of "land suitable for producing the appellation". Geology was invoked, as in Chablis, or for the Kaefferkopf *grand cru* in Alsace, to endorse the superiority of origins over brand through science

in addition to technique. The matter is a complicated one, however; the demarcation of Chablis and Margaux have resulted in five and eight court judgments respectively.

The creation of INAO and the AOCs

France's current system of *appellations d'origine contrôlée* (AOC) is based on a 1935 decree/law proposed by senator Joseph Capus and his friend Baron Le Roy de Boiseaumarié, the owner of Chateau Fortia in Châteauneuf-du-Pape (an appellation that had previously been a victim of multiple frauds). The state then approved of the proposals submitted by the Institut National des Appellations d'Origine (known as the "Committee" until 1947), a private body created for this occasion but reporting to the Ministry of Agriculture. It worked with the *syndicats viticoles* to ratify this new regulatory system that incorporated previous judgments and recognized new appellations, detailing production areas and methods of viticulture and vinification in a set of specifications particular to each AOC.

> " The creation of the AOCs was anything but a foregone conclusion, and their long and complex genesis took place amid great political and social tension

It also instituted monitoring, such as chemical analysis of levels of volatile acidity, for example), verification of cépage selection, checks on yield, and more besides. For the very first time, terroir was defined and protected. Top-quality vineyards complied immediately, and Arbois, Châteauneuf-du-Pape, Tavel, Cassis, Monbazillac and Cognac were the first AOCs to be gazetted, on 15 May 1936, followed by more than 60 others in the same year. This did not, however, result in the commercial success anticipated.

For a start, many of the demarcations were subject to multiple revisions, reductions and extensions, some of which took a very long time to be resolved; it should be remembered that many appellations do not have a homogeneous terroir, despite their recognized techniques and classifications, and vice versa. The institution of the *premiers crus* in 1943 and the debate about *grands crus* such as Clos de la Roche, Bonnes-Mares and Clos des Lambrays (to stick with Burgundy for the moment) was complicated and fraught. The relationship between cépage and soil, as analysed by geologists and agronomists, had already been of great interest in the 1930s but became a criterion in the 1950s and 1960s. The naturalist understanding of terroir became established in the regulations, with the role of the winemaker gradually being eclipsed in the appellation definitions – the principal experts consulted were agronomists, soil scientists and geologists.

THE CLIMATS OF VOSNE-ROMANÉE AND FLAGEY-ECHÉZEAUX IN 1860

In 1860, Beaune's agricultural and viticultural committee, which had been instituted to promote Burgundy at the International Exhibition to be held in London in 1862, created a statistical map classifying the vineyards of Marsannay-la Côte in Santenay into first (1er), second (2e) and third (3e) classes. This map was to be used in the process of demarcating AOCs.

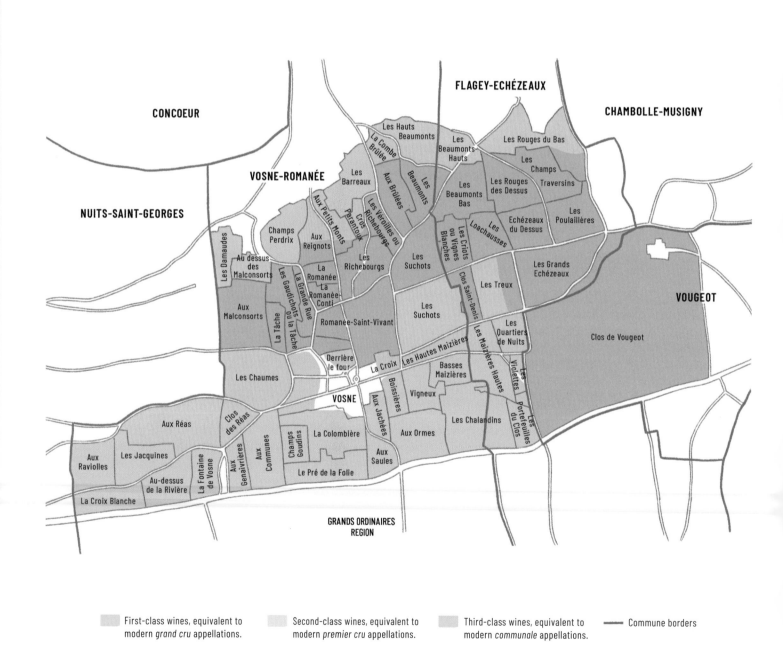

FLAGEY-ECHÉZEAUX

CONCOEUR

CHAMBOLLE-MUSIGNY

VOSNE-ROMANÉE

NUITS-SAINT-GEORGES

Les Hauts Beaumonts
La Combe Brûlée
Les Beaumonts-Hauts
Les Rouges du Bas
Les Barreaux
Aux Brûlées
Les Champs
Les Beaumonts
Traversins
Les Beaumonts Bas
Les Rouges des Dessus
Les Véroilles ou Richebourgs
Cros Parantoux
Aux Petits Monts
Echézeaux du Dessus
Les Poulaillères
Champs Perdrix
Aux Reignots
Les Criots ou Vignes Blanches
Les Loachausses
Les Richebourgs
Les Suchots
Les Damaudes
Au dessus des Malconsorts
La Romanée La Romanée-Conti
Les Grands Echézeaux
Les Treux
VOUGEOT
Aux Malconsorts
Les Gaudichots ou la Tâche
La Grande Rue
Les Suchots
Clos Saint-Denis
La Tâche
Romanée-Saint-Vivant
Les Quartiers de Nuits
Clos de Vougeot
Derrière le four
Les Hautes Maizières
Les Maizières Hautes
Les Chaumes
La Croix
Basses Maizières
Les Violettes
Les Portefeuilles du Clos
Boissières
Vigneux
VOSNE
Aux Jachées
Les Chalandins
Aux Réas
Clos des Réas
Aux Ormes
Les Jacquines
Aux Genaivrières
Aux Communes
Champs Goudins
La Colombière
Aux Raviolles
Aux Saules
La Fontaine de Vosne
Au-dessus de la Rivière
Le Pré de la Folie
La Croix Blanche

GRANDS ORDINAIRES REGION

First-class wines, equivalent to modern *grand cru* appellations.

Second-class wines, equivalent to modern *premier cru* appellations.

Third-class wines, equivalent to modern *communale* appellations.

— Commune borders

COMMUNE / AOC	LIEUX-DITS	JULES LAVALLE'S CLASSIFICATION OF 1855	CLASSIFICATION BY THE AGRICULTURAL AND VITICULTURAL COMMITTEE OF THE COMMUNE OF BEAUNE, 1860	CAMILLE RODIER'S CLASSIFICATION, 1920	JASPER MORRIS'S CLASSIFICATION
Vosne-Romanée *grands crus* (27 ha)	La Grande Rue	1er cuvée	1er classe	1er cuvée	Grand cru
	Richebourg	Tête de cuvée	1er classe	Tête de cuvée	Grand cru exceptionnel
	Richebourg Les Véroilles	1er cuvée	1er classe	Tête de cuvée	Grand cru exceptionnel
	La Romanée	Tête de cuvée	1er classe	Tête de cuvée	Grand cru exceptionnel
	La Romanée-Conti	Tête de cuvée	1er classe	Tête de cuvée	Grand cru exceptionnel
	Romanée Saint-Vivant	1er cuvée	1er classe	Tête de cuvée	Grand cru
	La Tâche	Tête de cuvée	1er classe	Tête de cuvée	Grand cru exceptionnel
Vosne-Romanée *premiers crus* (48.19 ha in the commune of Vosne-Romanée)	Les Beaux Monts	1er cuvée	1er classe	Beaux Monts Bas: 1er cuvée / Beaux Monts Hauts: 2e cuvée	1er cru exceptionnel (Bas)
	Aux Brûlées	1er cuvée	1er classe: +/- 85% // 2e classe: +/- 15% (15% = lieu-dit Combe Brûlée)	1er: +/- 85% // 2e: +/- 15% (15% = lieu-dit Combe Brûlée)	1er cru exceptionnel
	Les Chaumes	2e cuvée	2e classe	2e cuvée	1er cru
	Clos des Réas	2e cuvée	2e classe	2e cuvée	1er cru
	La Croix Rameau	—	2e classe	—	1er cru
	Cros Parantoux	3e cuvée	2e classe	2e cuvée	1er cru exceptionnel
	Les Gaudichots	1er cuvée	2e classe	1er cuvée	1er cru exceptionnel
	Aux Malconsorts	1er cuvée	1er classe	Tête de cuvée	1er cru exceptionnel
	Dessus des Malconsorts	—	2e classe	2e cuvée	1er cru
	Les Petits Monts	3e cuvée	2e classe	1er cuvée	1er cru exceptionnel
	Aux Reignots	2e cuvée	2e classe	1er cuvée	1er cru
	Les Suchots	1er cuvée	1 classe / 1er classe: +/- 40% // 2e classe: +/- 60% (60% in 2e classe = low)	1er cuvée and 2e cuvée (2e cuvée = low)	1er cru exceptionnel
Vosne-Romanée *premiers crus* (11.42 ha in the commune of Flagey-Echezeaux)	Les Beaux Monts	1er cuvée (Bas)	Beaux Monts Bas: 1er classe / Beaux Monts Hauts: 2e classe	Beaux Monts Bas: 1er cuvée / Beaux Monts Hauts: 2e cuvée	1er cru exceptionnel (Bas) / 1er cru (Hauts)
	En Orveaux	1er cuvée	En Orveaux Bas: 1er classe / En Orveaux Hauts: 2e classe	1er cuvée	1er cru
	Les Rouges du Bas	1er cuvée	Les Rouges du Bas: 1er classe / Les Rouges des Dessus: 2e classe	1er cuvée	1er cru
Flagey-Echézeaux *grands crus* (45.40 ha)	Grands Echézeaux	Tête de cuvée	1er classe	Tête de cuvée	Grand cru
	Echézeaux (En Orveaux)	1er cuvée	1er classe	1er cuvée	Grand cru / 1er cru
	Echézeaux (Champs Traversins)	1er cuvée	1er classe	1er cuvée	Grand cru / 1er cru
	Echézeaux (Les Poulaillères)	1er cuvée	1er classe	1er cuvée	Grand cru
	Echézeaux (Rouge du Bas)	1er cuvée	1er classe	1er cuvée	Grand cru / 1er cru
	Echézeaux (Echézeaux du Dessus)	1er cuvée	1er classe	Tête de cuvée	Grand cru
	Echézeaux (Beaux Monts Bas)	1er cuvée	1er classe	1er cuvée	Grand cru / 1er cru
	Echézeaux (Loächausses)	1er cuvée	1er classe	Tête de cuvée	Grand cru / 1er cru
	Echézeaux (Cruots ou Vignes Blanches)	1er cuvée	1er classe	1er cuvée	Grand cru
	Echézeaux (Clos Saint-Denis)	2e cuvée	1er classe	1er cuvée	Grand cru
	Echézeaux (Les Treux)	2e cuvée	1er classe: +/- 50% // 2e classe: +/- 50%	1er cuvée	Grand cru / 1er cru
	Echézeaux (Quartiers de Nuits)	2e cuvée	1er classe	1er cuvée	Grand cru / 1er cru

The acceptance of Chablis as an AOC was debated at length, with criteria that developed over years, and it is a perfect example of the complexity involved in approving appellations and terroirs.

The invention of a terroir: the Kimmeridgian

As far as wine-lovers are concerned, if ever a French appellation seemed intimately associated with its geology, that appellation is Chablis, whose Kimmeridgian terroir of Jurassic marl limestone (about 150 million years old) is said to give its Chardonnays their unique personality. This assertion is routinely bandied about, but hides a reality that is considerably more complex. In fact, the area of the appellation is not even defined by a geological (that is, Kimmeridgian) criterion. Other justifications are used, and these are addressed by Olivier Jacquet and Éric Vincent (one of INAO's boundary engineers) in their article "Le Kimméridgien à Chablis: un argument géologique pour la construction sociale du terroir". (All quotes in this passage are from this essay.) Since the region was first established, no unanimity has been achieved in demarcating the borders of Chablis, despite geological studies in 1902–4 that linked it to Kimmeridgian rocks. Two positions had solidified, and their opposition was to continue throughout the 20th century: a narrow view of appellation area, advanced principally by historically established wine-growers, and a broader perspective advocated first by regional merchants and then by newcomers with no historic roots in the region. Each camp organized itself into a syndicate and a federation, and it was to be their more or less powerful links with decision-making bodies and the political powers-that-be, combined with the support of local producers, that played a role in redefining the borders of the AOC.

The first demarcation ratified in the Tonnerre and d'Auxerre courts in 1920 worked to geological standards and classified the slopes of only eight villages and their immediate surroundings (400 ha). This judgment was appealed by the Burgundy wine trade and revised in 1929: "Chablis was then extended to 20 villages, and the judgment no longer made any reference to Kimmeridgian geology. This was indeed a political demarcation made by syndicates."

Chablis was officially recognized as an AOC in 1938 with a new statute that acknowledged the 20 villages but re-stated the Kimmeridgian connection, which resulted in the declassification of the surrounding areas – and a further appeal. A commission of expert geologists and agronomists that had been commissioned to demarcate the extent of the Kimmeridgian terroirs had to re-evaluate these borders. Conflict then arose on even the definition of "Kimmeridgian", between the strict French interpretation ("the upper extent of the layer corresponding to the border between the *Exogyra virgula*, Kimmeridgian marls, and the limestone of Barrois from the layer of hard Portland limestone, forming the highest ridge") and international convention, which included a large area of the Barrois limestones. A crisis ensued among the experts, with objections raised against an artificial convention compared with the reality of the terrain, followed by a string of resignations. The final upshot was that the commission continued its work with no geologists. The outcome was an expansion by 500 ha that was approved in 1960 in the face of protests from advocates of the stringent, historical area.

A struggle involving syndicates, politics and geology

A new and hotly contested turning point came in 1971, when the Federation of Chablis Vineyards was created to fight for expansion of the borders and inclusion of the villages to the north, where the federation founders happened to have some vineyards. This was opposed by the Syndicate of Chablis Vineyards, which wished to narrow the limits. Pulling the strings of their government connections, the former managed to get a new commission appointed that "highly conveniently" eschewed geological criteria in favour of a purely agronomic demarcation. Its work (1976–8) resulted in the demarcation that is still in force: Kimmeridgian geology is a historical footnote that plays no role, and 5,200 ha are officially classified, included many areas of Portland bedrock. The Chablis AOC is a far cry from the position represented by the historic local viticultural community and is rather a reflection of a change in vision decided by networks of experts in Paris, based on new scientific and agronomic arguments. This example demonstrates how an appellation can be manifested as an economic, political and social instrument, and geological standards can be used as a tool whose relevance and definition will be mutable, depending on the interests of those who happen to be in power at any given time.

From origins to typicity

In addition, the market mechanisms highlighted by Dion came into play. The quality of wines depends on demand from the consumer and is difficult to impose via production. Despite their proliferation, AOCs didn't sell, and they accounted for no more than four per cent of purchases in France in 1946. For one thing, their wines did not stand out

> Appellations were born of crisis, but their institution was made possible by very specific political circumstances

enough from run-of-the-mill produce; and for another, the less discerning majority of consumers, who were used to the low standards of branded wines, were unskilled in tasting the difference and did not associate AOC with quality. So why would they change their consumption habits?

As Jacquet has shown in *Le goût des vins d'origine. Genèse, construction et triomphe des AOC au XXe siècle* (2024), INAO set up two initiatives to address these problems. The first was to improve wines through strict quality control and by training wine professionals in collaboration with the new technical institutions like ITV and INRAE, agricultural colleges, oenological faculties and laboratories and the like that were then appearing. INAO would then contrive to change standards in tasting, to develop a new vocabulary and get the message across that a wine that was characteristic of its appellation should have a particular organoleptic profile that attested to its quality in every sense of the word. This certification by tasting, which was highly controversial in the 1930s, became compulsory in 1974. A link had now been established between quality and typicity, which was a major turning point in the definition of terroir. What had hitherto been a pejorative term, used to dismiss unsophisticated wine with a poor, earthy taste, would henceforth be used to endorse a wine's origins, its fine aromas evaluated and attested by experts. The flavour of terroir became something positive and sought after. Journalists, sommeliers and cellarmasters alike took up the term, and it began to spread.

The sale of AOCs finally began to pick up in the mid-1970s as consumers learned to discern quality and typicity – and to insist on them. In a parallel development, buyers were also being introduced, by the media and during their annual holidays, to the various rustic back-stories wine regions had been putting out since the 1920s and 1930s, in an effort to sell their wines by pushing regional food or local scenery. This was wine marketing before wine marketing was invented.

The success of the AOCs

In less than a century, the AOC system has proved to be the most suitable way to guarantee the authenticity of a wine and to underwrite a certain taste – first in France and then further afield. In 1992, the EU created the PDO (protected designation of origin) classification, directly inspired by AOCs, which guaranteed that the ingredients of a product all came from a specified geographical area in which it had also been made.

Italy and Spain in particular also systematized their production of quality wine with (respectively) DOC/DOCG and DO/DOca designations, both inspired by the French system but with less detailed regulations. Having been recognized as the elite of French wines in the 1970s, AOCs also became the most produced by volume in the 2000s. In 1990, the designa-

From outsider to "Super Tuscan"

A revolution shook Italy's wine industry to the core in 1971, when Marchese Mario Incisa della Rocchetta presented his first bottle of Sassicaia 1968, which until then had been produced on a small scale in his family-run vineyard at Bolgheri. The marchese, a great wine-lover, used Cabernet Sauvignon vines planted in 1944 in which he had noted a similarity to the wines of Graves in Bordeaux. While wine and Tuscany go back a long way, their shared history had hitherto mainly featured Sangiovese in the hills of Chianti between Florence and Siena, rather than French cépages aged in barrels on the Maremma coast.

Tenuta San Guido was an immediate success even though it was sold as *vino da tavola* (VdT, table wine), untrammelled by the rules of DOC wines. In 1974, Niccolò Antinori brought out Tignanello, another left-field Sangiovese/Cabernet Sauvignon blend, another VdT (the Chianti DOC rules required Sangiovese to be blended with other local cépages, including white grapes) and another global smash hit.

Many such wines appeared in the wake of these two, and this new style found itself dubbed "Super Tuscan" at the turn of the 1980s. In 1992, the Italian government was forced to recognize the success of these VdTs, which were often sold at prices far higher than those commanded by bottles of the most prestigious appellations, and instituted the category of *indicazione geografica tipica* (IGT), a ranking between VdT and DOC/DOCG, which ratified international varieties and single cépages. Two years later, Bolgheri modified its rules to become the first Super Tuscan DOC. Initially a subregion, Bolgheri-Sassicaia was classified as a DOC in 1994 and then became its own stand-alone appellation in 2013, in an arc of acknowledgment that was closer in spirit to the New World than fusty old Europe.

THE WORD "WINE" AND ITS ROOTS IN VARIOUS INDO-EUROPEAN LANGUAGES

tion was expanded to include other produce such as cheeses, vegetables and meats, for which the regulations used for winemaking were not suitable. The definition of the function of terroir had to be reconsidered, and human factors reintegrated, in order to bring balance to the naturalist definition.

In 2006, INAO incorporated into the specifications for all AOCs an explanation of the wine's "link to its origins", a particular characteristic on which the wine's reputation was based, and experts in the human sciences would now be involved in determining this. By 2021, there were thus 386 PDO/AOC wines, ciders and spirits, 51 dairy PDOs and 54 agri-food PDOs for vegetables and fruits, as well as IGP, or *indication géographique protégée* wines. Despite this success, however, and the fact that the quality of wine has never been higher, some producers have decided to bid their appellations farewell and market their wine as Vin de France (VdF), waiving the right to lay claim to a specific place of origin, since that is not permitted for VdFs.

Challenging the AOCs

AOCs were created to dig winemaking out of a deep hole by promoting a wine's origins and quality, but for a growing number of winemakers they have become an straitjacket that has paradoxically ceased to guarantee the authenticity of the flavours of a terroir. From the outset, the notion of typicity posed a problem for many producers of fine wines, since they maintained it implied a specific taste and thus standardization. By normalizing typicity, accreditation tastings deny diversity and variability – and this is effectively what has been happening over the years. As production volumes increase, most wines are standardized and lose their special characteristics. As a result, more and more producers are turning their backs on the AOC system, having seen their wines refused accreditation for being atypical, even though they have complied with the rules and the wines are popular with the public.

Accreditation tasting, which had achieved very variable results from one AOC to the next, has not been compulsory since 2009 and is now carried out randomly on bottles already on the market. In a parallel development, the number of AOC wines increased, and from being the exception they became the rule. Their image of quality suffered as a result, and consumers were often disappointed. The system became a fog of names, with each following its own rules. The delineation of AOC wine terroirs has no uniform process; each one is different, and geological and human criteria do not necessarily have the same weighting in each. Other criteria, such as soil health or the industrialization of the vinification process, are not considered, so it can be entirely legal to create an AOC wine in the same way that you would produce an ultra-processed agri-food product, without even informing the consumer. Ultimately, it's a complete jungle.

This is compounded by a system that has become increasingly cumbersome: creating or modifying an AOC still takes years, indeed decades, while commercial and environmental endeavours have accelerated. The Judgment of Paris, a blind-tasting competition organized in 1976, had a bombshell effect: wines that did not lay claim to a terroir in the same way that the French contenders did proved equal in quality to icons that had based their status on their soil and their history. The solutions suggested doubled down on traditional positions: entrenching the AOCs in even more history, like the agronomist monks of Burgundy, at the risk of fossilizing them, and pushing for increased standardization of cépages and styles in order to be more competitive against the New World wines that customers liked so much. The French over-production crisis of the first decade of the 21st century was a real wake-up call.

> " The AOC system and its proponents will have to uphold strict but evolving standards as the only possibility for preserving terroir as a common good

Should the AOC system be abandoned?

Arguably the AOC system should not be abandoned, but its function must be reconsidered with a view to returning to the original idea of preserving a common heritage. The current classification is often the result of several centuries of vine cultivation, production methods and negotiations over demarcation. Each and every AOC has its own particular history that, despite all the desire for objective facts, has often been embodied in the interests of a select few – a manifestation of the political and economic balance of power rather than of the community as a whole. That community, as we now know, includes not only producers, consumers and institutions, but also every form of human, animal, vegetable and microbial life, with each being part of the dynamic complexity of the terroir and therefore of its typicity and quality.

By its very nature, terroir is in flux, because it depends on the interactions of humans with their environment. If the AOC system wishes to guarantee typicity, authenticity and integrity, it must not deny the variability and diversity inherent in terroir wines. If it does, it will end up with some kind of grape-based, fermented agri-food product instead of wine. The AOC system and its proponents will have to uphold strict but evolving standards as the only possibility for preserving terroir as a common good – because neither the taste of wine nor terroir itself is immutable.

Old Europe versus the New World – a distinction to be discarded

The advent of New World wines on the international market in the 1980s upset Europe's domination and ushered in a new trend for wines based on grape variety. This collision of two worlds – cépage wines from the newcomers and established terroir wines – goes some way toward explaining the evolution of wines over the subsequent 40 years. By 2023, however, these "emerging" countries were producing a growing number of terroir selections while, conversely, Old Europe was increasingly playing the brand and cépage card. Does this Europe/New World division still hold, given that almost every winemaker has the technical capacity to make good wines anywhere; that the exchange of goods and services is easier than ever; and that skills and markets are opening up and influencing one another? What was this split even based on? Is a new kind of wine quality emerging from modern viticultural landscapes?

The globalization of viticulture

Cast your eye across almost any vineyard vista in California, Argentina or Australia, and one pattern will strike you immediately: a chessboard grid, stretching as far as the eye can see, that is a far cry from the quirky little plots of the Rhône or Alsace. The vineyards of the so-called New World of winemaking – the Americas, Oceania (Australia and New Zealand), South Africa, and now even Asia, with China – seem to share the same monotonous geometry. Why should that be the case? Schirmer (in *Civilisations du vin*) once again has an answer.

The globalization of viticulture began in the 16th century, when Europeans packed a few vines onto their flimsy boats and set off to colonize the world. The Conquistadors planted vineyards in Mexico (1524) and Peru (1530), then in Chile and Argentina (1550). The French were doing the same on the eastern coast of North America (1560–1800) even as the Huguenots were taming the Franschhoek Valley in South Africa (1650). The 17th and 18th centuries saw the establishment of many French and Hispanic settlements in North America and Australia, in addition to the arrival of migrants from Italy, Germany and Switzerland.

Wave after wave of colonists would bend these vast wildernesses to their will using techniques and practices they brought with them from their homelands, to the detriment of the indigenous people, who were colonized and dispossessed (and often killed). The land was carved up and distributed into plots of equal size, forming a loose lattice rather like the grid pattern beloved of the US. These newcomers initially reproduced their national traditions, often at the encouragement of politicians wishing to create a land-owning middle class – landscapes that are still fairly recognizable as English or German can be seen in the Hunter and Eden Valleys in Australia. However, market developments and the influence of the US after the phylloxera crisis were to radically transform the look of such landscapes.

California revolutionizes Planet Wine

Besides being the bicentenary of American independence, 4 July 1976 now a legendary date in the California wine revolution. The bottles that triumphed at the Judgment of Paris, the famous blind taste-off between French and American wines – 1973 Chateau Montelena Chardonnay and 1975 Stag's Leap Wine Cellars Cabernet Sauvignon – have now even been selected as part of the Smithsonian's "101 Objects that Made America" collection.

America's obsession with marks, quality and commercial success goes back to the time of the pioneers. Following in the wake of Thomas Jefferson (1743–1826) and Agoston Haraszthy (1812–69), the latter being the man considered the "father of modern California winemaking" who had imported more than 500 varieties by 1862, came dozens of late 19th-century wine entrepreneurs, often of European origin, who wished to line their pockets in the wine trade.

Vineyards were laid down all around San Francisco, where the climate suits *Vitis* perfectly. The expansion of the railroads gave access to local, national and international markets: gold prospectors and oil-well drillers, Franciscan communities, passengers in dining cars and the urban elite were all possible customers. The first wineries to be founded in Sonoma and Napa were Charles Krug (1861), Beringer (1876) and Inglenook (1880).

Growers were soon turning to scientists to improve yields, but this took on a whole new dimension at the end of the Prohibition era (1920–33), when vineyards had to reinvent themselves from first principles. André Tchelist-cheff (1901–94), a Russian émigré who had trained at the Institut Pasteur, became the winemaker-in-chief of modern America, supported by researchers Maynard Amerine and Albert Winkler of UC Davis (founded 1905) and the visionary Robert Mondavi (1913–2008).

Everyone was trying to make the best wines possible, indirectly influenced by critic Frank Schoonmaker (1905–76), who had been teaching America about taste in wine since the 1930s. American wine, he said, should no longer borrow European names. ("Burgundy", "Margaux" or "Chablis" were commonly used for generic, blended wines.) Instead, labels should indicate the place of production, the vintage and the producer, but especially the cépage. The wineries would then be obeying the market in a land where it was the consumer who had the last say in matters of quality.

The final element in this boom in production was a legal consideration: there were no campaigns here to protect from industrialization, merchants or fraud. "Such an approach gained no traction in the countries known as the New World, beginning with the US. With no traditional countryside to speak of. . . they perceived wine as an industry," says Schirmer. Any hindrance was considered unfair competition, and manufacturing regulations were reduced to a minimum: the market spoke, and commercial brands took precedence. The US was getting ready to reform the landscape of the wine world.

"Ageographical" wines

The principle governing the organization of the majority of wineries in the Americas is that the process of wine production is industrial, rather than agricultural, and that grapes are simply a raw material. At one end, there is a host of anonymous "grape growers", often with a background in orchard farming, who grow grapes that are sold not by the hectolitre per hectare, but by the short ton, the price of which is determined by a rating system based on cépage,

supply and demand. At the other, there are winemakers who, thanks to spectacular scientific progress in oenology, are now able to produce large volumes of wine with a pre-determined taste, intended for specific markets, with total control of the costs. Regulation that is more flexible than in Europe allows them to add aromatics or water, or remove alcohol, in order to smooth out variations and ensure

> " Underwritten by stunning successes, the influence of the American formula went global in the 1980s

consistent results. The economic model is thus no longer based on viticulture but on "viniculture", or winemaking – on volume and technique rather than typicity.

This industrialization has allowed great corporations such as E&J Gallo, The Wine Group and Constellation Brands to spring up, equipped with research centres and commercial teams. These produce and sell tens of millions of cases every year. In so doing, they are bringing wine to the people: grape variety is what matters on the bottle, and packaging is weaponized. With a characteristic, easy-to-recognize taste, they bring reassurance even among the welter of brand names, with prices that are value, premium or icon.

Their success was immediate on a young market where purchases were principally made in supermarkets. If a cépage ceases to sell (the 2004 film *Sideways* introduced Pinot Noir to America but killed Merlot stone dead), the vines will be grafted so that the new and fashionable cépage can be harvested the following year. Vineyards are concentrated, rationalized and homogenized. Underwritten by these stunning successes, the influence of the American formula went global in the 1980s, with the vast majority of viticultural landscapes, especially in the the New World, transformed by this geographical, agri-food wine, inundated by a flood of vineyards devoid of any originality.

The New World has reassessed its terroirs…

There would seem to be a yawning gulf between the geographies permitted by laxer regulation, aiming at industrial wine, and those arising from robust demarcation by terroir – between the New World and old Europe – but the actual state of affairs is more complex, because these two geographies interpenetrate and overlap.

Let's look at the New World first. In addition to this industrial production, boutique, often family-run wineries are ubiquitous, producing top-quality wines on the European model of terroir – Oregon, a region highly influenced by Burgundy, is a good example, as is the Yarra Valley in

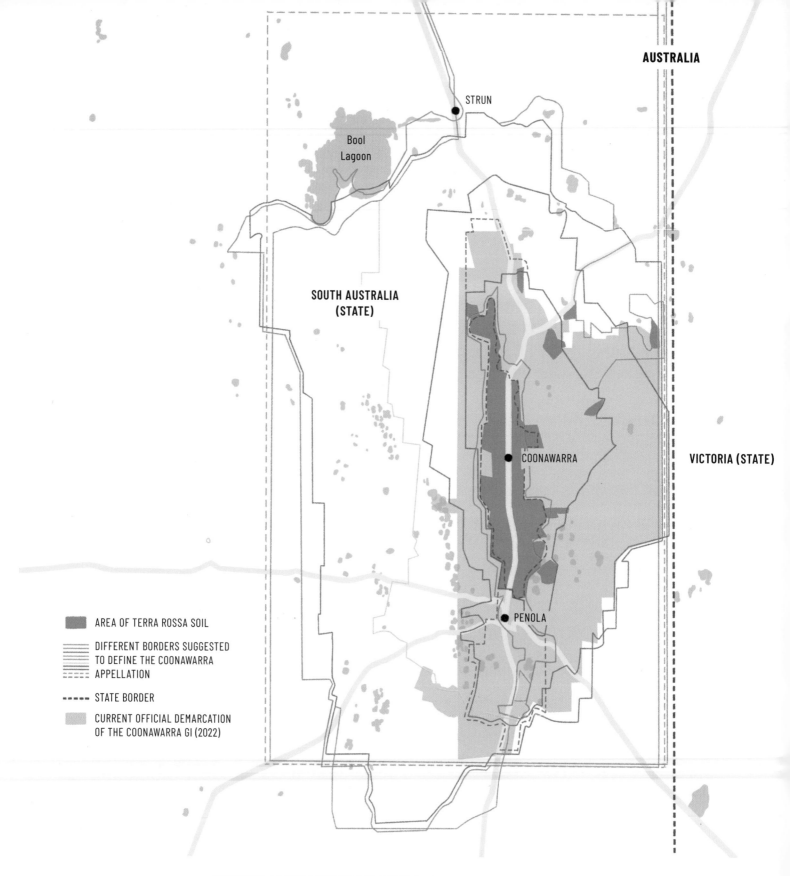

AUSTRALIA

STRUN

Bool
Lagoon

SOUTH AUSTRALIA
(STATE)

COONAWARRA

VICTORIA (STATE)

PENOLA

AREA OF TERRA ROSSA SOIL

DIFFERENT BORDERS SUGGESTED
TO DEFINE THE COONAWARRA
APPELLATION

STATE BORDER

CURRENT OFFICIAL DEMARCATION
OF THE COONAWARRA GI (2022)

THE VARIOUS ATTEMPTS TO DEMARCATE COONAWARRA IN SOUTH AUSTRALIA

This geographical indication (GI) has been defined as much by history and commercial
interests as it has by its legendary terra rossa soils.

To Kalon – a common good, or a private brand?

To Kalon is often considered the finest Cabernet Sauvignon from the Napa Valley. This Oakville vineyard now covers 274 ha and was founded in 1868 by Hamilton Crabb, who planted it with more than 300 cépages and turned it into an international beacon of quality. The vineyard changed hands several times after his death in 1891, and Robert Mondavi purchased 4.8 ha in 1966. Having gradually expanded his landholding and produced his first vintage of To Kalon Fumé Blanc Reserve, he trademarked "To Kalon" in 1987, followed by "To Kalon Vineyard" in 1994, thus resurrecting a brand created in 1906.

At about the same time, Andy Beckstoffer, a renowned Napa grape-grower, was acquiring 36 ha of the vineyard, where he replanted Cabernet. In 1999, he began selling grapes to winemakers, who marketed the wine under the name "Beckstoffer Oakville". In 2003, he persuaded Schrader Cellars, one of his high-profile customers, to use the name "Beckstoffer Original To Kalon Vineyard". Mondavi immediately sued for violation of copyright, and Beckstoffer responded that the vineyard was a place, not a brand. The matter was settled out of court the same year, with Beckstoffer retaining the right to allow his customers to use "To Kalon" if 95 per cent of the grapes were from the vineyard. "To Kalon" thus has two very different meanings. For Mondavi, it is a brand that he can use unfettered by the TTB (Tax and Trade Bureau) restrictions that govern wine production in the US; as his son Tim has pointed out, they could use it for a wine produced in Nairobi if they really wanted to. For Beckstoffer, it is an indication of geographical origin, a single vineyard that falls squarely under the strict regulations of the TTB.

The situation has now become even more complex because there are no longer two owners but six, including Constellation Brands, which has bought Mondavi and wishes to extend the original trademark; Beckstoffer; Detert; and the McDonald family, who have had the name "To Kalon Creek" protected and are trying to get To Kalon Vineyard inscribed in the National Register of Historic Places. At the time of writing, only Constellation Brands/Mondavi and Beckstoffer, and those WHO have bought grapes from that part of the To Kalon Beckstoffer plot, have the right to use the name. The legal wrangling over ownership of the terroir, as a private brand or a common good, shows no signs of abating.

Victoria, Australia. Europe, the world's premier market, also requires that countries wishing to export to its shores provide an indication of geographical origin and has got tough on blends: if a vintage, a cépage or a place of origin is listed, at least 75 per cent of the grapes have to comply. This has led to changes in many national regulations, in particular obliging the Australians to create geographical indications (GIs). Some countries had already anticipated this request and established geographical norms, such as Chile's *denominaciones de origen* (DO) in 1984, and the US's American Viticultural Areas (AVA) in 1980. Initially no more than a commercial tool, these designations are now being more closely defined at the request of winemakers who wish to produce quality terroir wines, as can be seen in the US: by 2024, there were more than 272 AVAs, compared with 26 in 1982.

While all these regulations deal only with provenance, some places, such as Oregon, are adopting stricter rules on blending. This has been complemented by a move toward recognizing old and original cépages, as large conglomerates buy up vineyards for their ultra-premium wines, with the vineyard indicated first and foremost.

... and Europe its cépages

In a parallel development, the old vineyards of continental Europe are being shaken awake under the twin influences of origin and brand. In the 1970s and 1980s, some French AOCs imposed "improvement cépages", banning local grape varieties that were considered to be of poorer quality and sold less well. The EU standardized the system in 2011, partially de-restricting the category of table wines with no stated geographical origin, in order to level the playing field. Indi-

1770
1560–1800
1530
1520
1530
1700
1550
1650
1788
1819

DISTRIBUTION OF *VITIS VINIFERA*
AT THE END OF THE 18TH CENTURY

MIGRATION OF *V. VINIFERA*
IN THE 16TH CENTURY
IN THE 17TH CENTURY
IN THE 18TH CENTURY
IN THE 19TH CENTURY

THE SPREAD OF *V. VINIFERA* AND THE GREAT WAVES OF COLONIZATION

Colonization was one of the principal vectors carrying *V. vinifera* and viticulture throughout the world between
the 16th and 19th century, for reasons that were religious, commercial and political.

cation of cépage and vintage, which had previously been prohibited for this category, were now permitted. (They remained optional for AOCs and IGPs.) Vinification rules were relaxed; the only requirement was an obligation to indicate national or European origin.

The best-selling wines in France in 2018 were branded lines from the Castel conglomerate, the French and European market leader, including more than 46 million bottles of Roche Mazet Cabernet Sauvignon, where the name of the cépage is twice as large as that of the place of origin (Pays d'Oc) on the label, and 26 million bottles of Ormes de Cambras produced on the same model, with purchasing contracts for grapes from the industrialized plains of Languedoc. The group also owns Baron de Lestac, France's best-selling Bordeaux AOC (8.5 million bottles) and produces, in a giant factory in Blanquefort, wine whose taste and profitability have been thought through down to the last little detail. Surely the Old Europe/New World "division" should be reconsidered?

"Wines for places"

The world of wine is in the throes of a sea change: Europe is striving to relax its regulations while seeking out greater typicity, in particular by promoting indigenous cépages, even as the New World is being "terroirized". Might there be some benefit in examining this global geography on a smaller scale, by nation or region? Schirmer has done just that, demonstrating that wine regions are subject to different and more subtle rationales, whose dynamics have become more and more intertwined since the 1980s.

- **Viticultural areas with a strong geographical element**: villages or *crus* where the fragmentation of the land is synonymous with its quality. Burgundy was the poster child here; viticultural landscapes were its beating heart, and viticulture reigned supreme. This still applies to Burgundy.
- **Commercially branded areas** such as Cognac or Champagne worked on the opposite principle, with price often determined by the reputation of the company rather than by the place of origin, which is considered a given. Everything was decided in town, not on the estate, and viniculture predominated over viticulture. This still applies but is more nuanced now, with the rise of small independent growers and bottlers.
- **Mixed areas**, such as Porto or Jerez, veered between regional denominations and commercial brands, and still do. Consumer confidence may rest on both, but here again, vinification is the deciding factor for quality.
- **Some areas feature both a strong generic element and an indication of cépage**. A large majority of these were in the New World. While they are still evolving, there is still a dominant suggestion that quality is all about the winemaking skills of a company or person who knows how to blend musts of differing origins, even though we are slowly but surely seeing more estates highlighting their terroir.
- **There are many areas that make up a disparate group that is difficult to define**. These too are in the process of (re)constructing themselves, as in Italy, with a mix of influences at the discretion of the producers.

Schirmer's fine distinctions as a way of reading viticultural landscapes make perfect sense in understanding the genealogy of historic wine regions and releasing us from the straitjacketed caricature of the Old Europe/New World split. When applied at an even more granular level, looking at groups of producers within a region, they are more compelling still. As noted, the evolution of Champagne – between its famous houses and independent growers, between branded wines and bottles from a single vintage, vineyard or cépage – is a sterling example of such, as was confirmed by its inscription as a UNESCO World Heritage Site in 2015. We need to think beyond the Europe/New World opposition, or we shall never understand the constantly shifting dynamics and land capes of the wine markets – dynamics whose acceleration has been spectacular in recent decades.

> " It is time to think beyond the Europe/New World opposition, or we shall never understand the constantly shifting dynamics and landscapes of the wine markets

Preserving viticultural landscapes

Vineyards may be among the first things that spring to mind when we think of the countryside, but we have only really taken an interest in the aesthetics of viticultural landscapes since the 1990s. Vines are "creative" plants, unleashing a wealth of ingenuity in people, sculpting nature and prompting the invention of agricultural methods; the end results are uniquely harmonious landscapes, some of which have even been inscribed as World Heritage Sites. These are living landscapes, however; just as the AOC system strives to safeguard tradition and terroir in an ever-changing environment, any attempt at preserving these remarkable ecosystems must take place within a context of constant technical and economic evolution. What are these landscapes? How can they be sustainably preserved without being turned into museums? What role should wine tourism play?

UNESCO World Heritage viticultural landscapes

In 1972, UNESCO adopted the Convention Concerning the Protection of the World Cultural and Natural Heritage after it had saved the temple of Abu Simbel from the waters rising behind Egypt's Aswan High Dam, which in 1964 threatened to engulf it. As Joël Rochard, an engineer at the Institut Français de la Vigne et du Vin, has pointed out in *Classement des sites viticoles "Patrimoine mondial Unesco". État des lieux et perspectives* (2016), this event helped the international community understand the necessity of protecting sites of "Outstanding Universal Value" in human history, for all the peoples of the world. The World Heritage List includes sites that may be cultural or intangible.

UNESCO has committed itself to protecting and promoting these sites and practices. The idea of "cultural landscape" was developed in 1992, allowing wine regions to lay claim to the highest degree of recognition for their heritage, and this also brought global visibility.

Sixteen viticultural cultural landscapes have been recognized since 1997. In France the first was the Juris-diction of Saint-Émilion (1999), followed by the Loire Valley (2000), the Champagne Hillsides, Houses and Cellars (2015) and the Climats of Burgundy (2015). Germany boasts the Upper Middle Rhine Valley (2002), while Portugal has the Alto Douro Wine Region (2001) and the Pico Island Vineyard Culture (2004). Switzerland has Lavaux (2007), Austria has the Wachau Cultural Landscape (2000) and Hungary the Tokaj Wine Region (2002), with the latter two countries sharing the Fertö/Neusiedlersee Cultural Landscape (2001). Last but not least, Italy has no fewer than five designated wine sites: the Costiera Amalfitana (1997), Cinque Terre (1997), the Val d'Orcia (2004), the Sacri Monte of Piedmont and Lombardy (2014) and Le Colline del Prosecco di Conegliano e Valdobbiadene (2019).

UNESCO is aware of the fragile nature of these locations and, since 2005, has designated them "evolving cultural and natural" heritage sites that still play an active role in the communities to which they are home. Their authenticity and continued inclusion on the list depend on the preservation of traditional assets and skills that have so far resisted modern socio-economic developments. There is every risk that they will fall prey to change, however, as is the case with many vineyards around the world. How can a balance between individual and collective interests be struck, creating heritage without fossilizing it? The question is only compounded as wine tourism increases in importance as a way of appreciating terroirs.

Wine tourism as a way of preserving viticultural landscapes

Developments in viticulture and the global economy have rapidly turned landscape and tradition on their heads. The restructuring of land by producers to facilitate use of machinery and increase productivity, the abandonment and uprooting of vineyards, infrastructure such as railways, connection to the electricity grid, bridges such as those over the Mosel river in Germany, and urbanization are just some of the threats viticultural landscapes have faced – and in some cases are still facing, since they are seen as a constraint on certain kinds of economic and technical progress.

Every heart is lifted by a "nice view", however, and emotion sells, so it is no surprise that people are taking another look at the landscape with a view to monetizing it in a competitive winemaking world in crisis. Vineyards are not only being turned into heritage sites to be protected and promoted by local and international associations, they are also at the heart of the wine-tourism initiatives that have become necessary avenues for many estates and regions as a means of supplementing their revenue. Not everyone has benefited to the same degree, however, as landscape geographer Soazig Darnay has explained in "Wine-Growing Landscapes: Rural Landscapes? Their Evolution Under the Influence of Tourism and their Heritagisation" (2018).

While wine tourism began back in the 1920s with the first wine routes, purchasing habits have brought about rapid change, and it was Robert Mondavi, in his Napa winery, who inspired its current incarnation as an integrated gastronomic, artistic, environmental and commercial experience. Not all approaches to wine tourism are the same, however. Breathing new life into a historic area in crisis, like Beaujolais, is a very different undertaking from trying to put a new wine region like the Okanagan Valley in Canada on the map. They do have one thing in common, however: a commercial ambition that will require investments of time and money to bring in the public and create an experience that benefits the estate and, indirectly, the region as a whole.

Paradoxically, the real or projected efforts to meet the expectations of a clientele that is increasingly international and discerning may result in profound changes to the viticultural landscape. Is it possible to square the circle of establishing successful tourist amenities while also preserving the authenticity of a heritage landscape? How can we avoid falling into the trap of creating vineyard amusement parks?

Viticultural landscapes are living common goods

The interests and avenues of opportunity available to independent, family-run wine businesses are not necessarily congruent with those of estates owned by financial institutions, merchants, cooperatives, sectors of the wine industry or national politicians. Rural flight from villages, lukewarm enthusiasm for protecting landscapes of scattered small wine-growers and a lack of cohesion within the sector have therefore conspired to prevent Rioja's recognition by UNESCO, despite the wine tourism initiatives undertaken by big-name estates and the money invested in a particular vision of the region, with terroir conceived as a marketing communications tool. Wine tourism undoubtedly creates employment both directly and indirectly, but the tourism is generally seasonal and the jobs low-skilled. There is a need for a common goal that includes every stakeholder – and this includes both local communities and ecological biotopes – in order to revitalize and preserve living winemaking traditions.

The unique aspect of wine tourism is its interest in vineyard culture within a specific natural environment. As with AOCs, it is a question of establishing and promoting unique terroirs and landscapes as guarantors of a particular taste, with a long-term vision of preserving the dynamic between winemaking customs and environments, without turning them into a museum or faking them to excess in the interest of short-term economic advantage. By their very nature, viticultural landscapes are also living common goods and should be treated and supported as such.

Lavaux – a victim of its own success

The terraces in Lavaux in the Canton of Vaud in Switzerland are one of the most extraordinary viticultural landscapes in the world. The Benedictine and Cistercian monks came to build their low walls in the 10th century, but these steep hillsides, falling away to Lake Geneva, had already been cultivated since ancient times. Lavaux is also a pioneer of wine tourism, with circular paths along the terrace embankments that allow tourists to explore a location that has been listed as a UNESCO World Heritage Site since 2007. That is not to say there has not been the occasional hiccup: the first visitors were surprised to find that these trails would also be used by vineyard tractors, for example. Despite the 30 per cent rise in tourist numbers, wine sales have dropped some 10 or 15 per cent, and heavy-handed protective heritage measures have had an impact on viticulture. As rural ethnologist Isac Chiva (1925–2012) pointed out in *Une politique pour le patrimoine culturel rural* (1994), "We have moved on from viewing heritage as a sum of beautiful, exceptional and irreplaceable testimonies from the past to understanding it as a collection of everyday artifacts representative of lifestyles that have disappeared or are on the way out," and this is precisely what is at stake with any incorporation of "living cultural landscapes" into the heritage industry. A better balance has now been struck on the back of cooperation between the various interest groups, but it is still obviously the case that it is the landscape – the holy trinity of vineyards, mountains and lakes – that is the real tourist attraction, rather than any winemaking activity or the built and cultural heritage.

Portovenere, Cinque Terre and the Islands
[Palmaria, Tino and Tinetto] (Italy, 1997)

Costiera Amalfitana
(Italy, 1997)

Jurisdiction of Saint-Émilion
(France, 1999)

Alto Douro Wine Region
(Portugal, 2001)

VINEYARDS AND VITICULTURAL LANDSCAPES INSCRIBED AS UNESCO WORLD HERITAGE SITES

The Loire Valley between Sully-sur-Loire and Chalonnes (France, 2000)

Wachau Cultural Landscape (Austria, 2000)

Fertö/Neusiedlersee Cultural Landscape (Austria/Hungary, 2001)

Tokaj Wine Region Historic Cultural Landscape (Hungary, 2002)

Upper Middle Rhine Valley (Germany, 2002)

Landscape of the Pico Island Vineyard Culture (Azores, Portugal, 2004)

Val d'Orcia (Italy, 2004)

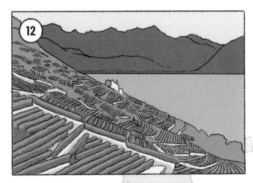

Lavaux, Vineyard Terraces (Switzerland, 2007)

Vineyard Landscape of Piedmont: Langhe-Roero and Monferrato (Italy, 2014)

Champagne Hillsides, Houses and Cellars (France, 2015)

The Climats, terroirs of Burgundy (France, 2015)

Le Colline del Prosecco di Conegliano e Valdobbiadene (Italy, 2019)

READING WINES

It is no exaggeration to say that wine is "alchemical"; its double birth, first in the cellar and then in the mind of the person who enjoys it and gives it meaning, is a transcendent transformation that still has the power to amaze, even though it has been going on for more than seven thousand years. While some of its mysteries have been solved by technological progress (the discovery of the world of the infinitely small, for example), the intricacy of wine is such that many still remain.

Wine is the most complex of all food and drink, but what is it that makes it so? It is all down to the nature of vines and their grapes – along with, once again, the tumult of microbial life in the vineyard and in the cellar. Man's longstanding companionship with *V. vinifera* has its counterpart in our alliance with *Saccharomyces cerevisiae*: reciprocal and intuitive domestication has taken place with these tiny creatures, with humans learning to make the best use of the magic of fermentation for their health and pleasure, even as yeasts have thrived in the new ecological niche represented by wine.

Winemaking was a small-scale, artisanal practice for centuries, but the scientific revolution has transformed oenology and tasting into a pragmatic science; it is now all about explanation, correction and prevention, and intuition has been supplanted by rational analysis in order to control the final results as much as possible. But at heart, is wine still an agricultural product that varies by vintage and terroir, or a manufactured marketing product? Should it be flawless – but sterile – or should it embody all the imperfections of living forces? Is it a danger to health or a fundamental element in social cohesion? Does our humanity as *Homo sapiens* not ultimately depend on our nature as *Homo imbibens*, with living wine reconnecting us with our nature, our liberty and our future?

MAKING WINE

What's in a grape?

Wine is made with grapes, and grapes alone, according to the official definition offered by the OIV, which regulates wine production in 50 countries, including France. But why should it be the berries of the vine, rather than any other fruit? One reason is their very particular composition, which makes it possible to arrive at a stable, fermented drink naturally, without and correction of the process. If we wish to understand vinification and the enormous diversity of wine styles and characteristics, we must examine the grape and its 1,500 compounds. Which are the most important? Why do the berries of the *Vitis* plant yield a fruit so ripe for fermentation? Are they affected by the challenges of viticulture?

Fruit wines and grape wines

Fermented drinks can be made naturally from almost any fruit, and although such alcoholic beverages are to be encountered wherever such produce is grown, they have become especially widespread in areas where vines are less common. Pineapple wine is made in Thailand, Nigeria and Hawaii, where the Maui Wine estate has made it a speciality; wines made from date palm sap are not unknown in Africa, and plum "jerkum" is a traditional drink in Worcestershire, UK; but it is the US that boasts the greatest diversity of commercially produced fruit "wines" anywhere in the world, and because the country is not a member of the OIV, it's all perfectly legal. Production is regulated by the TTB (which supervises alcohol and tobacco sales), and the wines may be made from any fruit, with special legislation reserved for berry wines and citrus wines (including "orange wines", which should not be conflated with the macerated grape-vine wines of the same name). The TTB only allows "wine" to come from grapes, and it doesn't have to be labeled grape wine. Fruit wine has to be labeled as such. Cherry, raspberry, blueberry and strawberry wine are routinely produced, not to mention wines made from rhubarb, watermelon, mango and peach.

None of these fruits can be "vinified" without some kind of additive, however, be it water, sugar, or the acids required to stabilize them and prevent microbial intervention.

Very few fruits have natural equilibrium, in fact; apart from grapes, there are only really apples and pears, and this characteristic is acknowledged in France with AOC recognition of certain ciders and perries (from Pays d'Auge, Cornouaille, Cotentin, Perche and Domfrontais). There are even increasing numbers of professionals who maintain that these "tree wines" (a term coined by French journalist Dominique Hutin) can perfectly express terroir and vintage. Grapes have prevailed, however, and this is all thanks to their particular chemical make-up; with some help from the ease of domestication of *Vitis*, no doubt.

A unique balance

The very existence of viticulture is proof positive that grapes have a natural tendency to produce a delicious fermented drink, and they are also the fruit best equipped to stabilize, both microbially and chemically, a resultant brew that would otherwise naturally tend to degrade and spoil. The quality and nature of their composite compounds are as crucially important as the quantities in which they occur. The spontaneous fermentation of sugars results in alcohol levels that are initially propitious for yeasts and bacteria but become toxic as the ethanol levels rise. Acidity controls microbial development within this environment: the greater the acidity and the lower the pH, and the higher the alcohol content, the less hospitable it is to such organisms. The controlling factors are a range of different acids that determine the pH of the wine and play a major role in its structure, aromas, stability and potential for ageing. The small size of the berries and the seed content may provide the must with high concentrations of polyphenols, antioxidants and antimicrobial agents. Lastly, grapes have enough water to allow fermentation processes.

All these elements are not homogeneously spread throughout the grape cluster, or indeed from one cépage to the next, however. The skin accounts for somewhere between 5-15 per cent of the weight of a ripe berry and principally contains phenolic and aromatic compounds, along with some organic acids. The pips, which comprise less than five per cent of the berry, are rich in oils and phenolic compounds. The pulp, comprising 75-85 per cent of the berry, is made up of water, sugars and organic acids, with the remainder of the grape's phenolic compounds and aromatics. The stems (the structure within clusters that makes up five per cent of the bunch and is sometimes used in winemaking) contains water, polyphenols and potassium. Every part of the bunch also contains mineral substances whose composition and levels will differ according to the cépage, terroir, type of viticulture, that year's weather and the date of harvest; all these parameters play a role in defining both the grape's potential for vinification and a wine's organoleptic profile.

The base compounds – water, cellulose, sugars…

Grape composition and quality are of crucial importance for good wine. Like many foods, a bunch of grapes is primarily made up of water that has been absorbed by the plant's roots. Water is also the main molecule present in wine. Next in line is cellulose, the main component of plant cells, which

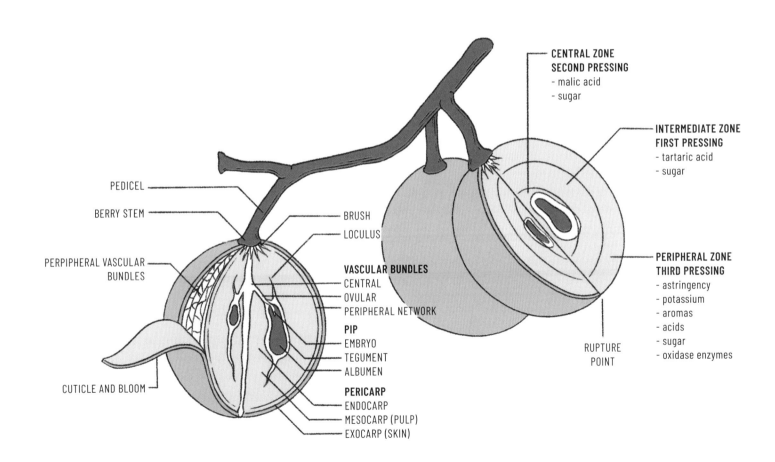

CROSS-SECTION AND STRUCTURE OF A GRAPE BERRY

205

is removed during racking and pressing. After that, there are carbohydrates; a grape has a sugar content of 15–25 per cent, which comes from photosynthesis – the hotter and sunnier the climate, and the later the season, the higher the sugar level. As the berry ripens, sucrose is hydrolysed into fructose and glucose, both fermentable sugars, with the former present in slightly higher quantities. The berry also contains very low levels of non-fermentable sugars such as arabinose and xylose, but these have no effect on the ultimate sweetness of the wine in the mouth. Wine grapes contain more sugars than table grapes – 20 per cent as opposed to 16 per cent, on average – although this concentration may even exceed 40 per cent in raisined or botrytized grapes destined for sweet wines. The zone immediately surrounding the pip is richest in sugars.

… organic acids…

Grapes are known to be one of the sweetest fruits, but they also contain acids, and many acidifying products can be extracted from them. Their acids are also varied in nature, with different flavours and potencies; the latter is determined by the potassium present in the skin, which influences the pH of the must. Tartaric and malic acids are responsible for 90 per cent of a grape's acidity and are created through the plant's photosynthesis. The former, which is largely specific to *Vitis* is found in higher levels in grape berries and owes its name to the tartar that is deposited in winemaking containers. It remains stable after veraison and does not degrade when heated, unlike malic acid, merely becoming diluted as the berry swells. It is a key acid in vinification. Malic acid is the acid found in green apples (from the Latin *malus*, "apple tree"), and levels drop as the berry ripens because it's metabolized and used as a carbon source. Citric acid is typically found in citrus fruits and is the third major acid in grapes.

There is also a host of other acids - like ascorbic, gluconic, coumaric, and more besides - that are present in much smaller quantities and contribute to the organoleptic complexity of wines. Some come from fungi; noble rot (*Botrytis cinerea*) produces gluconic, succinic and acetic acids. Because the concentration of acids increases from the skin to the pip, some wine regions, such as Champagne, have developed specific methods of pressing and vinifying grapes to achieve maximum acid content or otherwise.

… a world of phenolic compounds…

Phenolic compounds, or polyphenols, are a large family of molecules that are not specific to vines; they are used as natural defences throughout the plant kingdom and are found in various forms, providing plants with colours, odours and flavours, as is explained by Selosse in *Les Goûts et les couleurs du monde* (2019). These highly complex structures (there are more than 8,000 phenolic plant compounds) are yet to give up all their secrets; they are toxic by nature, and we consume very few of them, with notable exceptions to be found in tea, and to a lesser extent coffee, chocolate, beer and cider – and of course, red wine, to which they contribute colour, bitterness and astringency. Polyphenols play a fundamental role in the organoleptic qualities and preservation of grapes and, in fact, of all wines, and this is no doubt the reason that the wine industry has sought to enhance their presence by planting vines on terroirs drier than the damp soils originally favoured by *Vitis*; subjecting the plants to stress makes them produce protective tannins. This must only be to a moderate degree, obviously, otherwise the results would be problematic for the wine.

Polyphenols include an assortment of several phenols, ranging from simple molecules, such as gallic acid, to very large ones, such as lignin. They break down into two groups:
- The first of these comprises **non-flavonoid compounds**, including phenolic acids and volatile aromatic phenols, which affect the bouquet of the wine, and antioxidants such as resveratrol, a stilbene synthesized as a response to fungal attacks.
- The second includes **flavonoid compounds** that have polymerized, this being a reaction among small molecules that results in larger molecules. The best known are the anthocyanins, flavonols and tannins. The first two of these are responsible for the colour of grapes: red/blue/violet for the anthocyanins (from the Greek *anthos*, "flower", and *kuanos*, "deep blue") and yellow for the flavonols. Tannins come in various shapes and sizes.

The concentration and composition of polyphenols vary within a grape; the pips contain tannins, the pulp has phenolic acids, and the skin, which has the greatest concentration (obviously, because the skin is the berry's protective membrane) features anthocyanins, flavonols, tannins and phenolic acids. Pressing and maceration are therefore clearly important aspects of winemaking, since they optimize or not the extraction of these compounds.

… and other compounds, faint but essential

There are many other substances that are present in tiny quantities but that are nonetheless essential to the complexity of a wine and its links to its place of origin. Potassium is the most important mineral matter, influencing the pH of the must and the wine. It is present in a much higher molecular concentration than the polyphenols, and it is critical to winemaking. Grapes, especially the skin, also contain calcium, magnesium, iron and nitrogenous substances essential for fermentation, along with vitamins, including vitamin B.

The odorants responsible for a cépage's aromas are mostly to be found in the skin rather than the pulp. These are classified into families – for example, terpenes, pyrazines and thiols. They may be free, thus providing odour upon tasting, as with certain cépages such as Muscat, or odourless and tasteless as they are chemically bonded with sugars, fats or other compounds. These will then be the precursors of aromas that are released only during vinification, fermentation and ageing. These aromatic molecules evolve as the berry ripens; notes of over-ripeness, for example, may be due to lactones or furaneol-type compounds, while terpenes tend to disappear if the grapes are withered or botrytized.

Grapes also contain lipids. While some of these may present some problems for winemakers, such as the unsaturated fatty acids in the pips, others, such as the phytosterols, are essential to the dynamics of fermentation. One other "super-antioxidant" must be mentioned: glutathione, a substance of growing interest to wine scientists. There is up to 30mg/l present in grapes, and this amino acid (that is essentially made up of the cells of living creatures) protects wines during maturation. It is one of the secrets of the freshness of Muscadet *sur lie*, along with its saline taste.

Maturity today, maturity tomorrow

The date for harvesting is decided by the style of wine intended, in conjunction with meteorological and logistical conditions each year. The levels and balance of these compounds will essentially depend on the maturity of the grapes – or rather, on their maturities, since there are several to be considered separately, and their arrival dates are becoming less and less consistent; technological maturity – the maturity of sugars and acids, which depends on light, heat and precipitation – no longer necessarily coincides with phenolic or aromatic maturity. Phenolic compounds such as tannins may thus be astringent and unripe despite high levels of sweetness. Increased and repeated water stress, disease, frost and hail, in conjunction with elevated levels of CO_2 in the atmosphere, plus the UV light in certain wine regions, can modify the composition of the grape and force the plant to defend itself. Increases in alcohol levels are but one symptom of the complexity of reality for winemaking as climate extremes multiply.

More than with any other fruit, the taste of the grape and the flavours revealed by fermentation bear witness to the terroir in which the vine was grown; the current challenges in winemaking imperil these complex balancing acts and the way they are expressed. While oenologists are now enjoying more success than ever in using various processes to rebalance grapes and musts in the cellar, there is a part of the wine industry whose aesthetic and agricultural convictions are prompting it to look for solutions in the vineyard, so that there will be as little interference as possible in the winemaking process and it will continue to be possible to produce wines that express their place of origin and time.

The future is far from certain but will no doubt involve development of viticultural techniques capable of producing grapes that are as balanced as possible.

Products derived from grapes

Grapes produce a lot more than just wine and grape juice, and increasing numbers of products are extracted for a wide variety of markets. These include the marc (the residue left after vinification), which is still strictly regulated due to its residual content of alcohol and sugars. In Europe, this has to be distilled into neutral alcohol, except where an exemption has been obtained to produce eau de vie, compost or methane. Developments in industrial processes now promise new uses for skins, pips and stalks, however – from essential oils to biomaterials such as plant leathers, polyethylene to make corks, and glues made from condensed tannins. The skin and pulp provide winemaking additives such as Mega Purple®, a pigment developed in the US and usually sourced from Rubired, a red-fleshed cépage; the dye-making properties of anthocyanins have been known since antiquity.

Not many people know that the top product from the Finger Lakes, the largest wine region in New York State, is neither wine nor juice, nor even jam, but tartaric acid (cream of tartar), which is extracted from the pulp. This is a booming market worth hundreds of millions of dollars; the acid is much used in wine research and the agri-food industry as an acidifier, stabilizer and flavour enhancer, as well as in pharmaceuticals. The pharma and cosmetics industries are marketing more and more antioxidant products derived from polyphenols, including the famed resveratrol, from glutathione or from grape pip oil, which contains tocotrienol, a rare form of vitamin E. The industry segment based on grape pip extracts is thus set to rise in value to US$220 million by 2027, and the global market for polyphenols to a billion, while wine production will be in excess of US$430 billion, compared to 2020's total of US$326 billion.

207

From grapes to wine – a journey of microbial ecology

The transformation of grape must into wine has been shrouded in mystery since the earliest times. Fermentation long remained unexplained and was even considered by some an instance of transubstantiation, but it has been progressively studied and controlled since the 1860s. This does not mean that the process is now perfectly understood, however; we have moved on from a highly chemical and mechanical model based on the action of a few micro-organisms to an understanding of dynamic microbial communities interacting in extremely complex ways. Winemakers may supervise fermentation, but they are not directly responsible for it; to quote Selosse (*Jamais seul*, 2017), vinification is "microbial maturation", a mutual undertaking between winemakers and microbes, with the former nourishing the latter and creating conditions that allow them to develop, ferment sugar into alcohol and other compounds, metabolize acids, and produce a stable and tasty liquid. How does must turn into wine? Does "spontaneous" fermentation lend wine greater complexity? Can yeasts be a clue to terroir? Is there such a thing as microbial terroir?

Fermentation: sorcery, chemistry, microbiology

Although Fermentation is not exclusive to wine, it was through wine that the process came to be understood. This phenomenon, which stabilizes and preserves perishable ingredients, has long been associated with effervescence, as seen in wine, beer and sourdough. Over time, the idea was expanded to include other chemical transformations that do not release gas, such as the formation of lactic acid. What all these processes have in common is the production of certain elements from the decomposition of ingredients such as ethanol, acids and other compounds, with flavours and odours that are appetizing to a greater or lesser degree; when the substances produced smell bad and seem toxic, the process is called putrefaction rather than fermentation. Millennia of attempts to describe, and thus better control, the mechanisms at work in this phenomenon were doomed to failure, since the process takes place in the realm of the infinitely small; the first scientific explanations did not emerge until the 18th century and the invention of the microscope.

Fermentation was initially viewed as a purely chemical process. In 1789, Antoine Lavoisier (1743–94) was the first to demonstrate that the amounts of carbon, hydrogen and O_2 in the alcohol and gas produced were equal to those in the sugar consumed, from which he proposed his law of the conservation of mass: "nothing is lost, nothing is created; everything is transformed". In 1810, Joseph Gay-Lussac derived the chemical equation for the transformation of sugar into ethanol and CO_2, but it was not until 1837–8 that yeast was posited as anything more than a simple, indirect physical vector. Related research by Charles Cagniard de la Tour, Friedrich Kutzing and Theodor Schwann concluded that it was a living organism that reproduced through budding. F J F Meyen, a colleague of Schwann's, named it *Saccharomyces* (from ancient Greek *saccharo*, "sugar", and *myces*, "fungus"; *Saccharomyces* is abbreviated below as a capital S) and subdivided it into *S. cerevisiae* for beer, *S. pomorum* for cider and *S. vini* for wine. There was heated debate between the chemists, who denied any chemical aspect in yeast's action, and the naturalist school until the matter was finally settled by Louis Pasteur (1822–95) in 1857.

Pasteur's revolution

After being commissioned to conduct research by brewers who were encountering issues during production, and by Napoleon III, who was concerned about the problem that the contamination of wine might present for France's finances, Pasteur, who was from the Jura, published his results in *Études sur le vin* (1866). The work was a revolutionary contribution to the nascent sciences of microbiology and oenology and demonstrated that the presence of living germs was essential to all fermentation, scotching the hypothesis of spontaneous "generation". Pasteur showed that harvesting brought not only sugar but also fermenting agents into cellars with a still-famous experiment in which grapes were wrapped to prevent the intrusion of insects, which he presumed to be the disseminators of the yeasts: the swaddled grapes failed to ferment. He realized it was micro-organisms that were responsible for the spoiling of wine ("acetification", or turning to vinegar). These were viewed as harmful, and he invented the process that became known as pasteurization to cleanse the environment in which they were present.

In 1870, German botanist Max Reess (1845–1901) published a study that identified several species of yeast capable of fermenting sugar into alcohol (including *S. pastorianus*, which was named in honour of his French forerunner). Pasteur isolated two: *S. apiculatus* (now known as *Hanseniaspora uvarum*), which triggers alcoholic fermentation and *S. pastorianus* that completes it (widely used for beers). Further scientific progress in Pasteur's research into fermentation has shown us that a diversity of populations is at work in the process, giving rise to different metabolisms and results.

More than 350 strains of yeast on grapes

Yeasts are microscopic and single-celled: around 3–10μm in size. They differ from bacteria in that they have a cell nucleus in which their DNA is stored, and by their size: they are 10 times larger. They are ubiquitous in nature – on fruit, in tree bark and soils, and the wineries of wine estates, which are filled with fermentative and oxidative yeasts. They are able to multiply very rapidly via reproduction that may be sexual or asexual (the latter via budding). Approximately 100 million yeasts are present per kilogram on the skin of ripe grapes; the pulp contains none.

The taxonomy of oenological yeasts has come on in leaps and bounds with the development of molecular biology: we know of 149 genera and more than 1,500 species that are even now difficult to classify, because yeasts hybridize, adapt and mutate with ease. Those involved in vinification mainly come from the Saccharomycetaceae family, which includes thousands of species. More than 350 strains have been identified in the immediate environment of the vinification process; they may be on vines but also, and in particular, in grape musts and wineries; these are present in greater or lesser quantities depending on the ripeness of the berries, the vintage, the cépage, the cleanliness of the grapes, cultural prac-

tices and phytosanitary treatment. These yeast populations generally tend to be oxidative – that is, they transform little or no sugar into alcohol, and come mostly from the *Rhodotorula*, *Candida*, *Pichia* and *Aureobasidium pullulans* genera, with a sprinkling of *Kloeckera apiculata*, *Metschnikowia pulcherrima* and *Hansenula anomala* among others.

One important point to note is that *S. cerevisiae*, the principal agent of alcoholic fermentation, is rarely found in isolation on grape skins. There are nonetheless many wine producers who believe they have a yeast population that is unique to their vineyard and adapted to their grapes, giving their wine a unique flavour that is exclusive to their terroir. They are supporters of the notion of "spontaneous" or "indigenous" fermentation. The apparent absence of *S. cerevisiae* raises the question of "terroir yeast flora" and its relevance; what links are there between microbial micro-organisms from vines and those from the winemaking floor in fermenting wine?

> " Fermentation involves microbial diversity, the physical and chemical conditions in the environment and the chemical transformations that modify it

Fermentation is competition

Yeasts adapt according to their surroundings; the skin of the grapes in the vineyard is nothing like the pressed must or the finished wine. Those that survive are those best adapted to each particular environment. Fermentation thus always involves three factors: microbial diversity with metabolisms of its own, the physical and chemical properties of the environment, and the chemical transformations that modify this (the synthesis of new chemical compounds, for example). Vinification is therefore characterized by a steady decline in yeast diversity as a result of the intolerance of the majority of strains to the conditions of alcoholic fermentation – sensitivity to ethanol, anaerobic environments or SO_2, for example, or a lack of assimilable nitrogen. There are several different microbial phases that can be identified in a must that has fermented spontaneously.

• At the beginning of fermentation, the grape must is an acidic environment with a pH between 2.9 and 3.8 and high levels of fermentable sugars. It also contains nitrogen, lipids, vitamins and minerals, allowing for **extremely rapid yeast growth**. These include grape yeasts, species with little or no facility for fermentation and low tolerance of ethanol, whose numbers are greatly reduced by pressing and clarification: *Aureobasidium pullulans* (which comes from grapes) disappears entirely, while *Kloeckera apiculata*, *Metschnikowia*

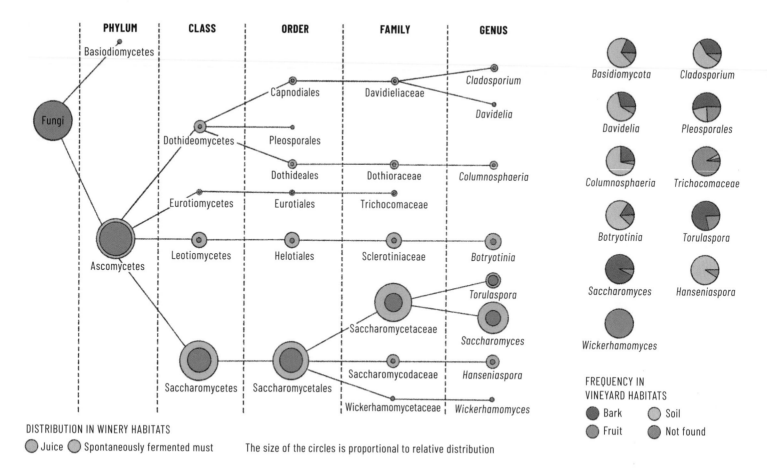

PHYLUM · CLASS · ORDER · FAMILY · GENUS

- Basiodiomycetes
- Fungi
- Capnodiales — Davidieliaceae — *Cladosporium*
- Davidieliaceae — *Davidelia*
- Dothideomycetes — Pleosporales
- Dothideales — Dothioraceae — *Columnosphaeria*
- Eurotiomycetes — Eurotiales — Trichocomaceae
- Ascomycetes
- Leotiomycetes — Helotiales — Sclerotiniaceae — *Botryotinia*
- Saccharomycetaceae — *Torulaspora*
- Saccharomycetaceae — *Saccharomyces*
- Saccharomycetes — Saccharomycetales — Saccharomycodaceae — *Hanseniaspora*
- Wickerhamomycetaceae — *Wickerhamomyces*

Pie charts (right): *Basidiomycota*, *Cladosporium*, *Davidelia*, *Pleosporales*, *Columnosphaeria*, *Trichocomaceae*, *Botryotinia*, *Torulaspora*, *Saccharomyces*, *Hanseniaspora*, *Wickerhamomyces*

DISTRIBUTION IN WINERY HABITATS
- Juice
- Spontaneously fermented must

The size of the circles is proportional to relative distribution

FREQUENCY IN VINEYARD HABITATS
- Bark
- Fruit
- Soil
- Not found

YEASTS AND HABITATS

This diagram shows juice and must yeasts in proportion to their presence in different habitats in a vineyard, as determined by a study undertaken by Peter Morrison-Whittle and Matthew Goddard in New Zealand (2018).

pulcherrima and *Hanseniaspora uvarum* (minority presences on the berry) flourish; the *Candida* or *Pichia* genera may also appear.

- After a few days, fermentation undergoes **a phase of growth for yeasts actively resistant to the absence of O$_2$**, thanks to the release of CO$_2$ and the ethanol that is gradually being produced. *S. cerevisiae* is obviously present, but *S. uvarum*, *Torulaspora delbrueckii* or *Schizosaccharomyces* may also crop up. Oxidative species will also appear, depending on the winemaking techniques, be they aeration of wines in the vat, pump-overs with air, stirring, SO$_2$ and so on.

- **Yeast multiplication slackens at the end of fermentation** as the sugars are exhausted and there is less of the assimilable nitrogen that yeast requires, or too high a concentration of ethanol. Non-*Saccharomyces* species that are highly resistant to ethanol (such as *Brettanomyces bruxellensis*)

may nonetheless continue to metabolize the wine. Others, such as *S. bayanus* (or *oviformis*, all considered part of the same *S. cereviseae* super group now), may bring about alcoholic fermentation (AF) in environments that are even richer in sugars, such as sweet wines.

It was long believed that different yeasts alternated during fermentation, but the situation is in fact far more complex. There is a consortium of numerous individual strains from which one or two dominant strains emerge, with the minority species surviving and at work for no more than a matter of days. These strains may also change from one year to the next, which explains the difficulty of mastering alcoholic fermentation and variations in wine. This is without even considering factors such as grape maturity, the year's climate, the integrity of the berry, hygiene levels in the cellar and a host more besides.

What about bacteria?

Yeasts are not the only micro-organisms involved in fermentation: bacteria are just as essential, but we had to wait until the technological progress of the 1960s, with its microscopes, microbiology and genetics, to realize it. Although Pasteur said, "Yeasts make wine, bacteria destroy it," referring to *Acetobacter* and other microbes that metabolize wine into vinegar, Robert Koch (1843–1910) and Émile Peynaud (1912–2004) highlighted the positive role they play. In 1939, Peynaud, a renowned oenologist, demonstrated the importance of malolactic fermentation (MLF) for the stability and quality of Bordeaux wines. The conversion of malic acid into lactic acid is the work of lactic bacteria, including *Oenococcus oeni*.

Although MLF does not produce alcohol, its effects are physical, chemical, biological and organoleptic. It involves natural deacidification in which the two acid functions of malic acid are metabolized into a single acid function (lactic) and CO_2. This drop in acidity will alter the intensity and subtlety of the wine's colour and produce secondary compounds such as diacetyl, with notes of fresh butter, and other aromatic molecules.

MLF had long caused unwanted secondary fermentations in the bottle and remained unexplained and unconstrained before gradually being brought under control in the 1960s. Winemakers can opt to let it happen or to provoke it for their whites and rosés, depending on the style required, or they can block it with SO_2 or by using filtration (less than 0.4μ). This is strongly recommended for red wines and is even obligatory in certain AOCs.

As with yeasts, only a few bacteria from the grapes survive in the must, and these include acetic and lactic bacteria. Both of these require O_2 to grow, unlike yeasts, but they have differing metabolisms; *Gluconobacter* dies away as soon as sugar levels drop and the presence of alcohol increases, while *Acetobacter* can grow by consuming ethanol and turning it into acetic acid. Lactic bacteria (*Lactobacillus, Leuconostoc, Pediococcus, Oenococcus*) are senstive to acid and yeast toxins and flourish mainly toward the end of alcoholic fermentation (AF), stabilizing the wine via MLF while also potentially synthesizing problematic aromatic compounds like mousy flavours.

Good and bad yeasts?

There are no good or bad yeasts or bacteria, per se; the role they play is merely more or less useful in vinification, as oenologist Christian Foulonneau has explained (*La Vinification*, 2019).

The deciding factor for quality has long been the capacity to produce alcohol, coupled with an ability to produce quality secondary aromas by synthesizing only a few higher alcohols while acting rapidly at both low and high temperatures, and this has led to the adoption and popularity of *S. cerevisiae* in lockstep with developments in oenological technology.

Recent microbiological research, such as that conducted by oenologist Jean-Luc Legras (in "De la diversité à la domestication chez *Saccharomyces cerevisiae*", 2018) has further shown that it is also capable of assimilating amino acids and vitamins from the must, along with sterols, the lipids it requires for growth. Additionally, it synthesizes deadly toxins and inhibitory metabolites such as SO_2 and acids from other micro-organisms. This is not to say that other yeasts are not of interest, however, although some have historically been considered harmful, producing little alcohol even as they consume sugar, and synthesizing volatile acids. Some may produce unpleasant smells, including solvent (ethyl acetate), rotten eggs (hydrogen sulphide), hot iron (aldehyde) and stables (ethyl, phenol). They can also produce foam and allow bacterial populations to increase, while some are not very sensitive to SO_2 and may even ferment fortified wines. (These include *Candida mycoderma, Saccharomyces ludwigii* and *Brettanomyces*.)

As our understanding of microbiology has developed in parallel with winemaking techniques and environmental change, however, some strains are being re-evaluated by researchers and winemakers alike. Some have attracted interest as fermentation has become more difficult and the market is looking for quality wines that are more complex, and these include *Saccharomyces* (*S. ellipsoideus* and *S. bayanus*, which complete fermentation) and the non-*Saccharomyces*, along with some that were long spurned (*Torulaspora delbrueckii, Candida stellata, Pichia fermentans*, and others). These are being reviewed, because they naturally lower alcohol levels and acidify (*Kluyveromyces thermotolerans, Lachancea thermotolerans*) or deacidify (*Issatchenkia orientalis, Schizosaccharomyces pombe*) the must, reduce acescence or ethanol levels (*Torulaspora delbrueckii, Candida zemplinina, Metschnikowia pulcherrima*), or indeed act as biocontrol agents, particularly in the vinification of wines with no added sulphites. How can they be controlled?

Controlling this microbial ageing

Before it became technologically possible to inoculate wine with a yeast of our choice, control of this microbial ecology was carried out indirectly, by manipulating the environmental parameters of fermentation. This is sometimes still the case. Those most commonly used include:

• **Temperature**. Most yeasts grow at temperatures between 15°C and 35°C (59°F and 95°F), with the exception of a few strains that are active in colder conditions, such as the *S. pastorianus* used in lager beers. Others will hibernate at such temperatures and reawaken only when heat levels rise – hence the resumption of spring fermentation in northern regions. Few can survive above 40°C (104°F).

• **Aeration**. "Fermentation is life without air," according to Pasteur, but O_2 is actually essential, permitting the growth of yeast populations that respire and transform sugars into new cells rather than ethanol, while boosting their capacity for fermentation and their ability to synthesize sterols, for example. Yeasts find it more difficult to flourish in anaerobiosis, so anaerobic strains tend to

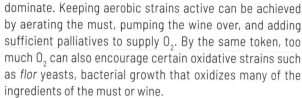

S. cerevisiae – *a long partnership*

Much like *V. vinifera*, there are certain yeasts with a long history with humanity. Foremost among these is the *Saccharomyces* genus, and in particular *S. cerevisiae*. Having been present on Earth for at least 80 million years, initially carving out its ecological niche by producing ethanol, CO_2 and heat inhibitors for many other micro-organisms, it became the first eukaryotic genome to be entirely decoded in 1996. As it cohabited with human populations, it was gradually domesticated for their local needs in Asia, West Africa, the Americas and Europe, being used to produce appetizing and stable fermented foods with a range of very different flavours. The work of microbiologist Jean-Luc Legras "De la diversité à la domestication chez *Saccharomyces cerevisiae*" (2018) has compared the results from genetic sequencing of more than 650 strains of *S. cerevisiae* with the history of our production of fermented foods to understand the yeast's evolution, highlighting the ecological niches created by humans that obliged micro-organisms to adapt and specialize. He suggests that, in the case of wine, this long companionship began in Mesopotamia, which was also one of the areas in which *Vitis* was domesticated, and then continued along human migration routes through the Danube Valley and the Mediterranean basin in a co-evolution of oenological yeasts, vineyards and the progress in winemaking that is still ongoing.

dominate. Keeping aerobic strains active can be achieved by aerating the must, pumping the wine over, and adding sufficient palliatives to supply O_2. By the same token, too much O_2 can also encourage certain oxidative strains such as *flor* yeasts, bacterial growth that oxidizes many of the ingredients of the must or wine.

• **SO_2 erroneously called "sulphur"**. Thanks to its antiseptic, antioxidant, antioxidasic and solvent properties, this is one of the most commonly used agents, although excess quantities can block the development of the must and wine and cause unpleasant smells of burned matches and rotten egg. As fermentation begins, however, it has the ability to clear out the incumbent microbial environment by selecting the most tolerant strains, including *S. cerevisiae*, which has co-evolved with its use. The lower the pH, the more efficient the free SO_2 will be. Other substances can be substituted, such as ascorbic acid (vitamin C, an antioxidant), sorbic acid, an antiseptic, and lysozymes that break down lactic bacteria. Tannins are also antioxidants and interact with proteins in micro-organisms to limit their growth.

• **Nutrient supply**. The presence of phosphates (yeasts and bacteria compete for these) and nitrogenous substances is controlled by adding ammonia – historically, workers would urinate while treading the grapes, according to Selosse – or vitamin B11 and thiamine, especially when fermenting botrytized grapes.

• **Inhibitors**. Fermentation produces selective substances – ethanol, obviously, but also saturated fatty acids, the action of which can be mitigated through the addition of yeast hulls. Pesticide (fungicide) residue on the grapes will also act as an inhibitor. The fungus *Botrytis cinerea* produces botryticine, an antifungal. Some "killer" yeasts also secrete a toxin capable of destroying competing strains.

Although winemakers may use such methods in an attempt to guide microbiota toward the kind of fermentation desired, the most direct means of control remains inoculation of yeast, which takes over the whole environment.

Choose your yeasts

Selecting the right fermenting agents has been a historic obsession. In the 19th century, Austrian and German bakers were turning to brewers for the yeast to leaven their *Kaisersemmel*, little imperial rolls that were not as sour as other breads of the time. The transition to low-temperature brewing using *S. pastorianus* had caused them problems here. Empirically, winemakers were using "yeast starters" they thought would provide high-quality fermentation to inoculate other containers. However, targeted inoculation was not possible until scientific progress developed techniques for isolating, selecting and disseminating the yeast populations desired.

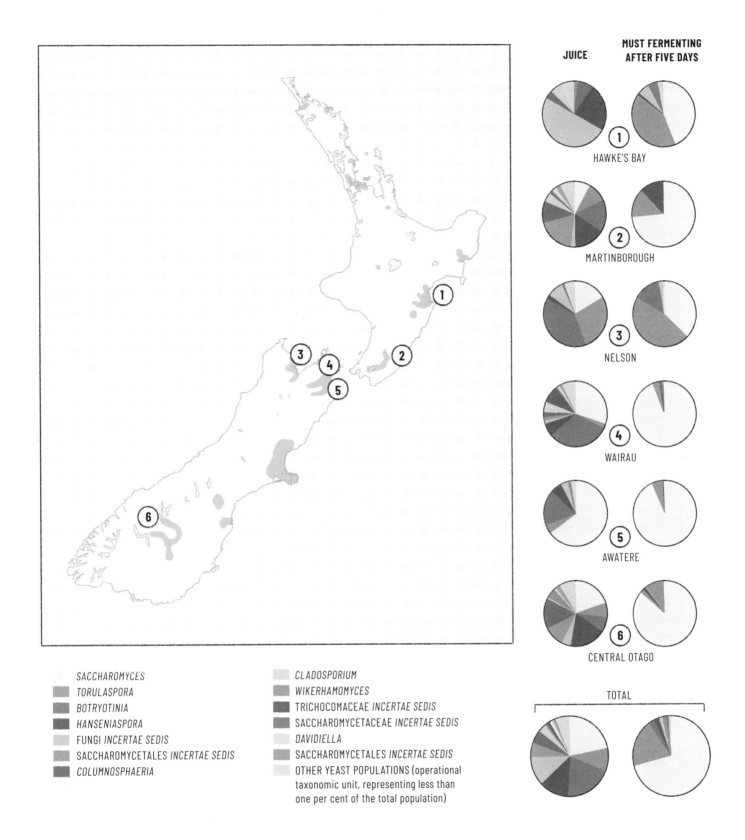

MUST FERMENTING
AFTER FIVE DAYS

1

HAWKE'S BAY

2

MARTINBOROUGH

3

NELSON

4

WAIRAU

5

AWATERE

6

CENTRAL OTAGO

TOTAL

SACCHAROMYCES

TORULASPORA

BOTRYOTINIA

HANSENIASPORA

FUNGI *INCERTAE SEDIS*

SACCHAROMYCETALES *INCERTAE SEDIS*

COLUMNOSPHAERIA

CLADOSPORIUM

WIKERHAMOMYCES

TRICHOCOMACEAE *INCERTAE SEDIS*

SACCHAROMYCETACEAE *INCERTAE SEDIS*

DAVIDIELLA

SACCHAROMYCETALES *INCERTAE SEDIS*

OTHER YEAST POPULATIONS (operational
taxonomic unit, representing less than
one per cent of the total population)

PRESENCE AND DISTRIBUTION OF FUNGAL SPECIES IN THE JUICE AND MUST
OF WINES FROM SIX WINE REGIONS IN NEW ZEALAND

In 2007, biologists Peter Morrison-Whittle and Matthew Goddard demonstrated that the microbial communities present
in juice and fermented products varied from one wine region to the next and that, while vineyard fungi were responsible
for 40 per cent of this diversity, external, uncultivated ecosystems were also an important source.

German botanist, Hermann Müller pioneered inoculation with a pure strain of *S. cerevisiae* in 1890, and the first selected yeasts were sold in liquid form in the 1920s. After World War Two, their use spread gradually through North America, Australia and New Zealand but did not really take off until the 1960s and the development and marketing of dried active yeasts (DAYs). These remain dormant until reheated and rehydrated, and can be stored more easily and for much longer than their liquid cousins.

While these first strains of *S. cerevisiae* had been isolated from their natural environment, technological progress since the 1990s has made it possible to hybridize strains for specific purposes in a laboratory. These selections were initially intended to guarantee reliable fermentation but are now used in ever more targeted ways – for synthesizing specific aromas, minimizing production of volatile phenols or SO_2, better use of sugar or assimilation of nitrogen, for example. Non-*Saccharomyces* strains have been included in these selections since 2005. By 2020, more than 350 strains of yeast had been marketed in France, and advances in genetics have accelerated research into the potential yeasts of tomorrow; while GMO yeasts are prohibited in Europe, one Canadian laboratory has developed strains that can trigger both alcoholic and malolactic (ML 01) fermentation, and another in the US is working on the Synthetic Yeast 2.0 project, using biology to construct the perfect winemaking yeast based on the genome of *S. cerevisiae*.

Indigenous fermentation, selected yeasts and the complexity of wine

While almost all fermentation was spontaneous until the 1970s, the opposite now holds true, with the majority of global producers making use of inoculation. The new viticultural countries are thought to be greater users than Europe, with its inherited winemaking traditions, but irrespective of where the producer might be located, a distinction is generally drawn between industrially produced wine and wine that is claimed to reflect its terroir. One of the ideas underpinning this distinction is that self-starting fermentation produces wines that are more complex and more "natural", with inoculation seen as a major intervention that would simplify and standardize the output. There are two aspects to this: the complexity of the wine is linked to the wide diversity of the yeasts, and the origin of the yeasts plays a part in determining the quality (in every sense of the word) of the wine.

According to the IFV, 30 years of research into the issue has still not managed to find a link between yeast diversity and wine complexity; the only consequence of increasing the number of different strains of *Saccharomyces* is to prolong fermentation. The IFV also maintains that spontaneous fermentation presents far more risks than benefits, including higher levels of volatile acidity and ethyl acetate arising from the rapid growth of *Kloeckera apiculata*; greater production of SO_2 and the presence of reduction aromas, acetaldehyde and a "mousy taste"; and a slow end to fermentation. The wide range of DAYs employed and the fact that, even when cleansed with SO_2, a must will never be totally sterile and will thus allow some indigenous yeasts to grow and complement the action of the inoculated yeasts are just two arguments to counter the idea that wine is standardized.

There is also another factor to be considered here, and that is the tasting grid used to evaluate the qualities and defects of a wine – tasting criteria that are now rightly being challenged by supporters of low-intervention wines such as natural wines. By the same token, Nicolas Joly – a champion of biodynamics and the owner of Coulée de Serrant, the top AOC in Savennières – is just one of many high-profile producers who claim that adding yeast is "absurd", because the indigenous yeasts transmit all the subtleties of the vintage and the terroir. Beyond the scientific question, there are two divergent ideological positions, with differing visions of wine quality and the criteria for its appreciation. And this is begging another question entirely: is there such a thing as microbial terroir?

The concept of "microbial terroir" is born...

Once we grasp the role played by yeasts in determining the organoleptic profile and quality of a wine, it is easy to see the full importance of their origins and their links to a particular terroir. As with soil and plants and their respective and sometimes shared microbial dimensions, however, this significant factor has long been overlooked; scientists have only really started to take an interest in the subject since around 2010 or so, and it has not been without controversy. A new debate has now arisen about the sources and habitats of yeasts:

- **The cellar**, long considered the predominant source of alcoholic fermentation, especially for *S. cerevisiae*, which is able to survive on equipment between two harvests.

- **The environment around the vine, including the grapes**. Unexpectedly, research has however shown not only that these are short-term habitats but also that the yeasts they accommodate are not those essential for alcoholic fermentation.

Progress in genetics and genomics has nonetheless brought new insights, such as the notion of "microbial terroir" and the importance of the environment. In 2013, Italian microbiologists Duccio Cavalieri and Irene Stefanini (in "Role of social wasps in *Saccharomyces cerevisiae* ecology and evolution", 2012) showed that certain wasps

Different types of fermentation

Fermentation is anaerobiosis – in environments starved of O_2 where respiration is not possible, certain yeasts and bacteria will produce their energy from carbohydrates, and fermented foods are a by-product of this microbial survival mode. The simplified formula for alcoholic fermentation is $C_6H_{12}O_6$ (glucose and fructose) $\rightarrow 2\, CO_2 + 2\, CH_3CH_2OH$, or ethanol – so called because the most visible result is the production of ethyl alcohol: on average, 16–17g of sugar will give 1% alcohol by volume. Enzymatic reactions synthesize other compounds, however:

· **CO_2** breaking down 1g of sugar produces 0.5g of CO_2, or 225,000 litres of CO_2 from a 5,000-litre vat of must for a wine of 12% alcohol by volume.

· **Heat** 180g of sugar releases around 138kJ – the temperature of an insulated, uncooled vat in the middle of fermentation can rise by more than 30°C (54°F).

· **By-products** on average, five per cent of the sugar produces by-products such as glycerol, higher alcohols, esters, aldehydes, sulphur compounds, organic acids, fatty acids and others besides, all of which contribute to every wine's unique organoleptic profile, structure and aromas – more than 400 secondary aromas in all.

Another transformation is sometimes wrongly associated with wine: lactic fermentation (wrongly since there is no lactose in grapes; malolactic is the direct decarboxylation of malic acid to lactic). Lactic fermentation is the conversion of lactose into lactic acid by lactic bacteria. This is an ancient technique for food preservation and is used to make yoghurts, cheeses, sausages, fish sauce, miso, sauerkraut, kimchi, kefir and kombucha, all of which have a recognizably sour taste. Inspired by spontaneously fermented beers such as lambic and gose, brewers have explored its potential by adding lactose to their mashes. It is also sometimes incorrectly called malolactic or acetic fermentation; the former is a transformation of acids by bacteria, while the latter refers to *Acetobacter's* metabolization of ethyl alcohol into acetic acid or vinegar, requiring neither O_2 nor carbohydrates. Either of these may occur during vinification.

and hornets (*Vespa crabro* and *polistes*) were reservoirs and vectors of the *S. cerevisiae* that is found on vines year after year. This discovery shows the close links between the fauna and microflora in vineyards and barrel stores. The same year, US microbiologists Nicholas Bokulich and David Mills posited the idea of biogeography, or microbial terroir, suggesting that yeast populations in Sonoma and Napa vineyards will differ depending on the year, the climate and the cépage, and hypothesizing that this diversity could influence the characteristics of the wines from these respective regions. These findings were backed up by another US study the following year that found micro-organisms could play a significant role in determining the organoleptic profile of a wine. Having researched 380 strains of *S. cerevisiae* present in the Kumeu River Estate to the west of Auckland (a region of New Zealand inhabited by humans for less than 700 years, where wine has been produced for less than a century), New Zealand microbiologist Matthew Goddard concluded in 2011 ("Geographic delineations of yeast communities and populations associated with vines and wines in New Zealand", 2011, and "From vineyard to winery: a source map of microbial diversity driving wine fermentation", 2018) that local spontaneous fermentation was dominated by strains of *S. cerevisiae* that came from the vineyard. These did not match any commercial strain that might have returned to nature, and were also almost unique to the region, having 0.4 per cent of correspondence with international yeasts, some of which would have come from new barrels that had been imported and used for ageing. Further work in 2017 made it possible not only to highlight the importance of vineyard *S. cerivisiae* in fermentation, but also to show that a proportion lived in uncultivated ecosystems such as bark, flowers and the surrounding native forest, and was brought into wineries by insects.

… and so is the controversy that surrounds it

The concept of microbial terroir and its corollary, the notion of terroir microbes, has attracted criticism from certain parts of the scientific community ever since it was first suggested. There are still questions of scale and scientific technique (metagenomic or genomic analysis) to be resolved, as Bordeaux oenologist Isabelle Masneuf-Pomarède and microbiologist Patrick Lucas have pointed out (in "Vendanges du savoir: La controverse des micro-organismes de terroir", 2021), and no stability of bio-geographical difference has been observed over time; indeed, quite the opposite. Studies of strains specific to wine that have been collected from all over the world (*S. cerevisiae*, *Torulaspora delbrueckii*, *Oenococcus oeni*) have shown that there are no geographical characteristics but that yeasts vary by product: microbial populations in wine differ from those in sake or cider. They are now increasingly widespread, thanks to speedy modern international transport – a fact that would seem to refute the idea of exclusive location.

Last but not least, there has never been a formal demonstration of the link between the action of such a strain, be it from the soil or from the vine, and the distinctive character of the wine produced; there is no such thing as a "*cru* yeast".

Some of this controversy has arisen because not every scientist employs the same definitions of microbial terroirs and terroir micro-organisms: according to the Anglo-Saxon school of thought, these would include every micro-organism, since they all have a direct influence on the sensory characteristics of a wine, while the European understanding is that micro-organisms in the vineyard affect the grape, and other strains that have adapted genetically to the type of wine influence the organoleptic profile. Despite this difference of opinion, there are nonetheless points of consensus between the two approaches:

- Yeast populations develop in wineries and on vines over the course of time, influenced by a complex network of factors which include individual yeast metabolisms and changes in the environment.
- Vineyards inoculate wineries, and vice versa.
- Yeasts spread very easily.
- Micro-organisms interact with one another.
- The exact chemical function of a strain within the organoleptic character of a wine is a shifting relationship that is still difficult to capture.
- There are acknowledged exceptions – very specific stress environments – that might indicate the existence of fermentation micro-organisms for types of wine or terroir wines such as *flor* wines, Icewines, and wines from certain islands.
- Any environmental change will have consequences for the biodiversity of oenological yeasts.
- New strains of yeast are constantly co-evolving – indeed, being co-created – through human domestication and environmental change.

Whether direct or indirect, there is an almost symbiotic synergy between winemakers and these oenological microbes. Although it still cannot be explained in every detail, we can only marvel at it and leave it the freedom to do its work unhampered – or not, and address the question of how new biotechnology can speed it up in unimagined ways.

Making wine as close to the terroir as possible

It is difficult to make out the necks of the amphorae buried beneath the head-pruned vines and the low drystone walls of the Sicus estate, but it is here, in the unspoiled landscape of the Massís de Bonastre between Barcelona and Tarragona, that Catalan wine-grower Eduard Pié Palomar is making wine among the vines. A champion of his region's local cépages, like Xarel·lo and Monastrell, and a proponent both of no-till and the preservation of the natural biodiversity of his vineyard and the surrounding fallow land, since 2012 he has been fermenting his Sicus Sons vintages in jars buried at the end of the vine rows. His aim is to fully express every aspect of the terroir, including the yeast, and he thinks vinifying with no additives within the plot where it grew is the best way to achieve this.

He is not alone, as biologist and wine journalist Jamie Goode (*Wine Science: The Application of Science in Winemaking*, 2005) has reported. Since 2013, Dom Maxwell, the New Zealand oenologist who runs the Greystone estate in the Waipara Valley, has also been making a Pinot Noir (named Vineyard Ferment) among his vines. In 2019, he began a research programme with Lincoln University to study its yeast populations. Other New Zealand winemakers have since followed suit, in particular Helen Morrison from Villa Maria, one of the largest estates in the country, who vinifies whole bunches of Sauvignon grapes among her vines in Marlborough. Less spectacularly, there are now many producers who work with laboratories to select the yeast for their wine from strains that have been collected from their land and cellar, isolated and identified; these can then be inoculated to control vinification without seeming to resort to external yeasts.

Vinification – art, craft and science

There is not just one wine – there are a thousand; as many as there are cépages, regions and cultures. Colours and flavours have evolved as winemaking and oenology have progressed to arrive at the diversity of styles we know today: red, white or rosé, effervescent or sweet, or even wines that may be *nouveau*, fortified, fermented under a biofilm of yeast, aromatized or even macerated. Originally seen as an art or a craft, vinification has become a science as technology has progressed, and the winemaker is now an "oenologist" (from the Greek *oinos*, "wine", and *logos*, "science" or "discourse"). Although diversity and quality have never been greater, a chorus of discontent is nonetheless making itself heard, denouncing the standardization of wines and the loss of any expression of terroir, either because wines are too "natural" or too "transformed". How did the styles of wine with which we are familiar come about? What production techniques are being used? And what physical processes and chemical modifications are winemakers using to make their wines?

The first vinifications

In days gone by, wine was consumed after the harvest; storing it without it turning into vinegar was tricky. This "new" wine was something like modern *federweisser*, a very sweet must with between one and three per cent alcohol that was drunk in viticultural areas when fermentation was in full swing after the harvest. *Vin primeur* (or *vin nouveau*) is another distant cousin that is officially regulated in France and marketed on the third Thursday of October (for wines sold as IGP) or November (for appellation wines such as the renowned Beaujolais Nouveau); these must state their year of production and are supposed to be drunk within 12 months or so.

From the work of Patrick McGovern, a molecular archaeologist specializing in fermented drinks (*Ancient Wine: The Search for the Origins of Viniculture*, 2003), André Tchernia and Jean-Pierre Brun (*Le Vin romain antique*, 1999), we know that the first wines were often minimally macerated light rosés, a mixture of grapes and plants, spices, honey, fruit and other ingredients that later also included gypsum, lead and seawater. There were two reasons for this: to extract compounds that might improve vinification and conservation, and to add aromas to make the wine more pleasant - hence the "marvellous preparation" mentioned in the 10th-century *Geoponica*, a compilation of the wisdom of previous centuries. It included the likes of aloe, incense, cardamom, saffron and myrrh, all plants with antiseptic, antifungal and antibacterial properties.

Despite the occasional problem entailed by certain adjuvants such as lead, which was used to reduce acidity, we can only admire the intuition of the ancients, which lacked any understanding of oenological microbiology. Flavoured wines were to endure into the Middle Ages as wines for pleasure, like hippocras, or medical use - Valencian physician Arnaldus de Villa Nova left us dozens of recipes, such as for cabbage or nettle wine – before eventually coming down to us in the form of vermouth, chinato and retsina. However, these texts also noted that such additions should be reserved only for wines of lower quality; the rarest and best wines, those most enjoyed, were those that had the fewest additives and were often aged under a veil of *flor*.

Flor wine – biological and physical oxidation

The oldest still wine in the world that is available for tasting, for those with deep pockets, is thought to be a *flor* wine from Arbois (Jura) made in 1774. The Greeks knew and enjoyed this style of wine, which involves an alcohol-rich must, sometimes 15 per cent or more, on which a layer of white yeast or *flor* develops, protecting the wine from O_2 and acetic bacteria, and encouraging unique aromas. This is an essential feature of Jura Vin Jaune and Fino and Manzanilla from Andalusia, as well as Szamorodni from Hungary and Vernaccia di Oristano from Sardinia; the wine is deliberately aged in contact with air and with no topping-up, allowing a biofilm, the *Mycoderma vini* or velum, to form. These are oxidative *S. cerevisiae* yeasts (beticus, cheresiensis, rouxii and montuliensis) that

What about SO₂?

Sulphur dioxide (SO₂) is a hotly discussed additive in vinification and should not be confused with sulphur (S) in winemaking processes. It has been used since ancient times, although it was first officially sanctioned for use in 1487, and its popularity spread with the use of SO₂ wicks to clean barrels, the first recorded use of which in Bordeaux is 1765. Its mechanisms have been understood since the end of the 19th century: it inhibits enzymatic and chemical oxidation of wine, it is an antiseptic to which bacteria are more sensitive than yeasts and it is also a solvent. Sulphur dioxide is used during harvesting, pressing and clarification, after fermentation, during maturation and before bottling. When added, a fraction of the chemical combines with the sugars and acetaldehyde, while the rest remains "free", and it is this active part (molecular SO₂) that is protective.

Its action is greatly improved by low pH levels where less SO₂ is usually required, and the ratio of free SO₂ to the total content is important in controlling uptake during vinification as the SO₂ combines with other compounds. It is a potentially toxic additive, with the World Health Organization recommending a daily intake of no more than 0.7mg/kg, which for an adult would be less than half a bottle containing 150mg/l. The amounts used are thus very carefully regulated; the maximum permitted in Europe is between 150mg/l and 400mg/l depending on the type of wine (sugars allow for more), with less allowed for organic and biodynamic wines. The latter are making increasing use of volcanic S rather than its form as potassium metabisulphite (which is obtained from the petrochemical industry), arguing that this makes for greater efficiency and an improved taste, neither of which has been scientifically proven. An increasing number of winemakers are also seeking to reduce and even halt the use of SO₂ for philosophical, aesthetic or marketing reasons; some are using other complementary additives that are more curative, such as sorbic acid, microbial biocontrol using selected yeasts, or nothing at all – in which case, hygiene is essential. An indication on the label that the wine "contains sulphites" is mandatory if the level is above 10mg/l, whether this was added or produced naturally by yeasts during fermentation.

have adapted to this extreme environment of high acidity, alcohol and SO₂, with little or no sugar, by floating in a layer on the surface and using O₂ to metabolize the wine's ethanol and residual sugars, thereby producing glycerol and protecting the wine from turning to vinegar. The yeasts transform the sugars into acetaldehyde, with its green-apple aroma, in drier wineries and into sotolon, which smells of curry and nuts, in damper conditions where the wine will lose viscosity and gain in acidity (volatility). The thickness of the layer varies with humidity and temperature, and the yeasts will die naturally if the environment becomes too nutrient-poor, the air too dry or the alcohol levels too high.

This style of ageing is what distinguishes biologically aged Sherries, Fino and Manzanilla, from those aged by physical oxidation; if necessary, Olorosos are usually fortified to 17 per cent immediately to prevent such a layer from forming, while Amontillado and Palo Cortado have a layer for a limited period and are then fortified. Physical oxidation involves direct contact between O₂ and the wine, oxidizing its compounds but also allowing tannins to polymerize, creating long-chain molecules that are perceived as softer. This is the gentle art of ageing a wine.

Maderization and cooked wine

The ancient world knew how to cook grape must and wine to preserve it, thus making it more appetizing and stable; the Greeks called the brew *glyxis* and the Romans *defrutum*, *caroenum* or *sapa*. The technique survived into the 19th century with Germany's *Feuerweine*, or "fire wines", that were often made with the best grapes by renowned specialists who preferred them to the uncooked wines that were often still too sour or bitter, or had been highly flavoured to hide their flaws. Provence's *vin cuit* and Italy's *vino cotto* are the spiritual heirs to this legacy, along with the *mosto cotto* ("cooked must") added to some Sicilian Marsalas. The term is also improperly retained for wines that are not cooked but fortified.

There is really only one wine that is made with deliberate heating, and that is Madeira. Originally a still wine from the eponymous volcanic archipelago in the Atlantic off the coast of Morocco, Madeira is produced using a technique that was developed after it was noted that wines shipped around the world in barrel and exposed to high temperatures, evaporation and oxidation on their journey became apparently indestructible and delicious. This process was then artificially reproduced on the island, first by fortifying the wines and then leaving them to age in uninsulated barrel stores for years or even decades so that they would be exposed to the vagaries of the subtropical climate. This method was called *canteiro* and is still used for the best

Madeiras. Progress in the 20th century made it possible to speed up this process with *estufagem*, in which wine is heated to 45-50°C (113-122°F) in a stainless-steel vat for a minimum of three months. *Armazéns de calor* is a related technique in which the wine is heated in a room adjacent to the *estufagem*. In all three cases, the components of the wine undergo a host of chemical transformations, including the Maillard reaction, enhanced with oak ageing and carefully managed contact with air. The compounds produced include acetaldehyde (green-apple notes), furfural (spices, almond, woody), lactones (coconut, nuts, musk), acetic acid and others, creating an extremely complex aromatic profile of caramel, dried and jammy fruits, olives, umami and more besides. The cépages, whose varietal notes fade away with age, give a hint to the style: Sercial is the driest, Malmsey the sweetest. Madeiras from the 17th century are still drinkable today.

Residual sugars

Until sugar became widely available in the mid-20th century, sweet wines were the most sought after and expensive. Things are very different today, however, with a less enthusiastic market and retail prices often lower than production costs, despite quality that has never been more impressive. Such wines are distinguished by both their sweetness and the manner of concentration. European wines may be dry (less than 4g/l, medium dry (4-12g/l), medium sweet (12-45g/l), and sweet (more than 45g/l), but in certain regions such as the Mosel in Germany or Alsace in France, these bands will vary, depending on the level of acidity, which mitigates the sensation of sweetness in the mouth – think of lemonade. Other AOCs may also have higher minimum levels, either for sweetness at harvest or in the finished wine. Even where the grapes are normally rich in sugars at harvest (240g/l will give c. 14% alcohol by volume), preserving and concentrating

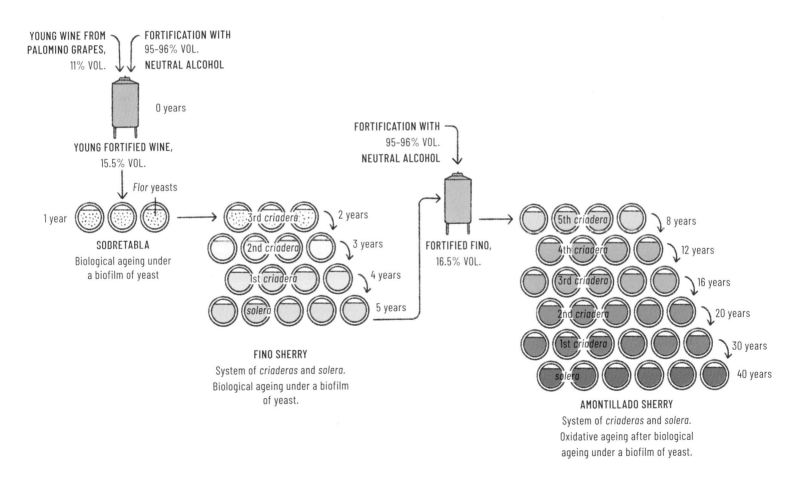

EXAMPLES OF SHERRY AGEING: FINO (BIOLOGICAL) AND AMONTILLADO (BIOLOGICAL AND OXIDATIVE) WITH FORTIFICATION

these any further is a challenge. As fermentation progresses, wines become drier, so making a wine with residual sugar means either stopping fermentation quickly, adding sugar in one form or another, or vinifying more concentrated grapes. This last option, which is the most complex, gives exceptional outcomes.

Overripeness can be achieved in different ways, depending on the climate, with each environment having its own organoleptic characteristics.

Raisin wines, made from shrivelled, *passerillé* grapes, or late-harvest wines are produced in regions where low risk of disease in the autumn coincides with cépages with thicker skins and higher levels of acidity that will retain some sharpness even as the sweetness increases. Such cépages include Riesling, Manseng and Chenin. These wines have vibrant notes of crisp, often citrus and tropical fruits, with little hint of oxidation.

In hot regions where acidity fades rapidly, wines made with dried grapes, or "straw wines", are produced: the grapes are harvested at normal maturity, halting the natural metabolization of grape compounds on the stem, and are left to dry in a cellar, as in Jura, Hermitage and Valpolicella for *appassimento* Amarone,or in the sun, as in Montilla-Moriles, Pantelleria and Samos, allowing water to evaporate. Such wines have notes of cooked fruits, often complemented with volatile acidity that is created during the drying process and vinification.

Botrytis cinerea produces "noble rot", a fungus that generates very high concentrations of sugar: Hungary's *eszencia* has a minimum of 450g of sugars per litre, with very low levels of alcohol. It is in fact the same fungus as grey rot, but in particular environments, where there are morning mists with wind and heat in the afternoon - as in Sauternes, Tokaj, Layon, Austria's Rust and along the Mosel - it can grow, dry out and ennoble itself. Enzymes attack the skins, drying out the berries by up to 50 per cent of their weight. Glycerol levels rise, and alcohols are formed through enzymatic reduction of sugars. Levels of malic, citric, acetic and succinic acids increase as tartaric acid drops. Muscat cépages lose their varietal rose aromas, while others gain in complexity. The fungus also synthesizes sotolon, giving notes of beeswax and nuts. Grapes affected with noble rot are harvested berry by berry for the finest selections such as *Trockenbeerenauslesen* and *aszú* Tokaji; these wines have a more umami, oxidative and viscous profile, and longer fermentation times than raisin wines.

Icewine, another wine with extreme concentrations of sugars, was known to the Romans; grapes that have been raisined, botrytized, or both are left on the stem until temperatures drop to −8°C/18°F (in Canada or China) or −7°C/19°F (in Germany and Austria). Successive freezing and thawing concentrates the sugars and develops new aromas, and the frozen water is not extracted at pressing, rendering the wines extremely crisp despite their sweetness. This technique can be reproduced artificially via cryoextraction in a cold room - the results will obviously be less complex, but the process is less expensive and less freighted with risk.

Lastly, entry-level sweet wines can be obtained via chaptalization, the addition of sugar, often beet or cane sugar. Prices are thus often as much an indication of origins and sweetness levels as they are of quality.

Fortification

Before SO_2 or filtration became the standard methods to kill off microbial activity and preserve sugars, fortification was the most popular stabilization technique from the moment the art of distillation was mastered. Valencian physician Arnaldus de Villa Nova is credited as the first to mention *mutage* in 1258, a technique involving the addition of alcohol to a must in order to halt alcoholic fermentation and fortify a wine, and it became popular in Roussillon to produce *muté* wine. The British took up the baton in the 17th century and spread the technology to Port and Madeira, to Spain for Sherry, to Italy for Marsala and even to Australia's Rutherglen, creating new styles that have since become classics. There are three methods for fortifying the musts of white, *gris* and red grapes:

- **Before fermentation has started**. These are known as *mistelles* or sweet liqueur wines - for example, France's *vin de liqueur* (VDL). They are often linked with wine regions. The alcohol used is specific and non-neutral, which contributes to the aromatic profile of the final wines. Pineau des Charentes uses Cognac, Floc de Gascogne uses Armagnac, and Macvin du Jura and Ratafia de Champagne both use eaux de vie from the region.
- **During fermentation**; between 5 and 25 per cent neutral alcohol, with an average titration between 77 and 96 per cent, is added to obtain a final product that is often between 15 and 22 degrees of alcohol depending on the appellation. These are called *vins doux naturels* (VDN) in France, or natural sweet wines, even though some alcohol is added to retain the sweetness. Some of the most famous are Banyuls and Muscat de Rivesaltes. Port is made the same way.
- **Once fermentation has finished**; the wine is fortified with neutral alcohol in proportions close to those for VDNs. The best known are Sherries and certain Marsalas.

Maturation also divides these wines into two groups; they are either protected from O_2 during ageing, which preserves varietal aromas and tannins, as in the case of

Rimages, and Ruby and Vintage Ports, which are deliberately exposed to air and variations in temperature that lead them to develop tertiary aromas, soften the texture and oxidize the colour, hence their names: Tawny Ports, *rancios* and *ambrés*. Fortification leaves such wines able to age for centuries.

Maceration and whole grape clusters

Contrary to popular belief, red wines as we know them became popular only quite recently in the wider context of the history of wine. Before techniques for preserving them were fully mastered, red wines were made by adding water to *marc* or pressed grape skins, and were closer to vinegar than to wine. They were the preserve of the lower classes. (Those further up the social scale drank white and rosés, cooked wines or flavoured wines.) Everything was to change in the 17th century, as techniques evolved and the market changed; clairet wine took on a deeper hue, and the "new French claret" became the preferred tipple of the aristocracy.

Maceration principally involves extracting elements including colour, phenolic compounds and aromatics from the skins of the berries during fermentation. Various factors may influence this extraction: temperature (heat promotes extraction); the presence of alcohol and water; the maturity of the grapes; whether the producer favours punching-down, pumping over or whatever; the fermentation vessel; the addition of enzymes; and many other factors.

Hot maceration is a technique that has been in use since the end of the 19th century: the grapes are heated to 70–75°C (158–167°F) to promote the rapid extraction of colour and aromas with few tannins, to polish up a harvest that may not have been the best. Thermovinification, hot pre-fermentation maceration (HPM) and "flash détente" (also known as flash release) are different refinements of this principle. Cold pre-fermentation maceration aims to extract as many water-soluble compounds – anthocyanins, for example – as possible before alcohol is produced.

Winemakers may carry out post-fermentation maceration, in particular to soften tannins, and may even choose to macerate entire harvests; this practice was the norm before mechanical destemming and has resurfaced with climate change and evolutions in taste. In the 1970s and 1980s, the stalks usually lacked maturity and so would bring green tannins to the wine.

There is a difference between maceration – where the entire cluster is included and crushed, thus macerating the stalk along with the juice – and carbonic maceration; the former is classic maceration, but the stalks add phenolic compounds and aromas, and absorb acids and colours. This has now become a strong stylistic choice for Pinot Noir and Syrah among others.

Skin-contact wines

Also known as orange or amber wines, skin-contact or macerated wines are made from white or *gris* grapes that have been vinified like red ones. In just a few years, they have become a category of wine in their own right and are now produced all over the globe, although the technique is anything but new – it is in fact one of the oldest in the world. It re-emerged in the 1990s thanks to Josko Gravner and Stanko Radikon who, on sites in Friuli (Italy) and Slovenia, have rediscovered the tradition of maceration once used to stabilize white wines and promote fermentation in hot climates. The skins also provide nutrients for the yeasts and help to extract antioxidant phenolic compounds. These historic wines, with their amber colour and powerful tannins, had come under fire from oenologists in the 1960s just as Italy's modern Pinot Grigio, a straightforward, crisp wine with a faint aromatic profile, was enjoying its first successes. Fortunately, they lived on in their birthplace, the Republic of Georgia, where the tradition had been preserved for millennia despite multiple invasions and the agricultural industrialization imposed by the Soviet administration. Grape skins are macerated in clay amphorae, known as *qvevri*, for a varying length of time – anything from a few days to several months, depending on the cépage, the region and the expression of tannins sought. The wine is then often aged for nine months, reminiscent of a human baby growing in the womb. Tasting such wines is an immersive aesthetic experience, transporting the senses back in time.

In carbonic maceration, the bunches of grapes have to remain perfectly intact to allow "fermentation" to occur within the berries with a minimum of intervention from the yeasts. This intracellular enzymatic metabolization was developed by oenologist Michel Flanzy in the 1930s; it transforms malic acid and sugar into up to two degrees of ethanol and metabolizes highly specific aromatic compounds – think of the aromas of bananas, candy, strawberry Haribo Tagada – and what are known as amylic aromas. The CO_2 produced will cause the berry to burst after a few days. The vat is generally also flooded with CO_2 to delay the start of fermentation of the juice that runs out naturally under the weight of the berry clusters, in cases of strictly carbonic maceration.

This juice is run off every day into a separate vat, and starts its alcoholic fermentation. This process is repeated until the producer decides to stop – at which point, most of the berries will still be intact. They are pressed and then blended with the free-run fermenting must.

Beaujolais is a classic example, whether obtained via strict carbonic maceration or semi-carbonically, in which case the juice squeezed out by weight is left in the vat. The alcoholic fermentation starts in the vat alongside the intracellular processes, and the alcoholic fermentation encourages the skins to break more easily. When there is enough extraction and enough amylic aromas, the juice is run off and the skins pressed. The result of both systems is fruity, rounded, soft wines.

Red wines and rosés, with rare exceptions, have to be macerated, but macerating white grapes is by no means a new phenomenon; macerated or skin-contact wine is as old as viticulture. Two methods are used nowadays: one produces amber and phenolic wines, while the other is shorter and more subtle, extracting only certain compounds and aromatic precursors.

Mastering effervescence was a collective undertaking

All wines contain CO_2, but those with levels above a perceptible threshold (0.8–1g/l, on average) that impart a tingling sensation on the tongue are considered sparkling. Effervescence is an ancient phenomenon, but the popularization of this style of wine was directly linked to the winemaker's ability to manage it. This required the invention of containers capable of withstanding pressure while preserving and controlling the gas generated by fermentation: Pliny the Elder (in *Natural History*, Book XIV) praised the *aigleucos* of the Vocontii. *Aigleucos* was a sweet, naturally sparkling wine and an ancestor of Clairette de Die. Barrels of it were immersed in Alpine streams until the winter solstice, and the Romans were known to pierce holes in amphorae to prevent them from exploding.

The technique of stopping fermentation before allowing it to restart, often in the spring, is the forerunner of an old method thought to be first officially documented with the mention of a flask of Languedoc Blanquette de Limoux from 1544. It was the English, however, who, with the industrialization of the glassmaking industry in England and cork-making in Portugal, became the driving force behind the secondary fermentation method. They produced more robust glass bottles with their new-fangled carbon furnaces, and they used corks to bottle barrels of still wine imported from Champagne, but they had known how to make sparkling wine by adding sugar since the 1660s. By the same token, it was merchants from Champagne (spurred on by demand from the English and Louis XV's permission, granted in 1728, to market bottled Champagne wines) that gradually formalized the *méthode champenoise*, what we now know as the traditional method: the fine art of harvesting, pressing, blending, secondary fermentation and *dosage*, the adding of sugar.

It would not be until the invention of *liqueur de tirage* (a solution of yeasts, wine and sugar added to the still base wine) in the mid-19th century, however, that Champagne could be produced via two controlled fermentations rather than one, and Chaptal's work on the relationship between sugar and ethanol in 1801 helped to promote the industrialization of this process. With the development of manual riddling and the wire frame and cap to protect the cork, bottles would also no longer explode quite so dramatically in the cellar. In 1800, the production total was 300,000 bottles, but by 1850 it had risen to 20 million.

Following the major success of these sparkling wines, the inventors of the eponymous Martinotti/Charmat method (patented in 1895 and 1907 respectively) upped the pace still further; secondary fermentation could now take place in a large pressurized vat at a controlled temperature, rather than in the individual bottle, drastically reducing production times and costs. The Soviets industrialized this technique still further with a method involving a series of pressurized vats and continual addition of *liqueur de tirage*, in constant contact with the lees. This technique is still in use to this day for very cheap wines. Lastly, carbonation (the injection of CO_2) has also become more common for entry-level sparkling wines.

Different types of bubble

Effervescent wines are legally classified according to EU legislation by their mode of production and their pressure; they may be semi-sparkling (2–4g/l or 1–2.5 bar) or (quality) sparkling (more than 4.5g/l or more than 3–6 bar), be they white, rosé, red or skin-macerated. Historically, the category of *perlant* or *moustillant* (slightly sparkling), with 1–2g/l of CO_2 or less than 1 bar of pressure, has also been used.

Because it involves the completion of first fermentation in the bottle, the "ancestral method" has less pressure (hence *pétillant naturel*, its modern name, often abbreviated to pét-nat). Such wines spend only a brief period on the lees, and the bouquet is dominated by varietal rather than fermentation aromas. Certain AOCs that produce a specific style, like Bugey Cerdon or ancestral-method Clairette de Die, require precise amounts of sugar and yeast to ensure the legally required final effervescence and sweetness; other, more natural wines, are less hands-on, and the results may vary from aggressive, leesy, fermentation bubbles, to a precise and gently fizzy pét-nat.

HARVESTING BY HAND

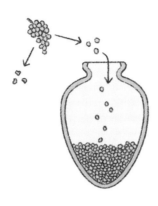

SORTING AND CRUSHING
The grapes may or may not be macerated with
the skins and stalks, depending on the region.

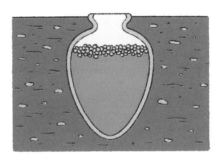

FERMENTATION

THE *QVEVRI* IS RACKED AND SEALED

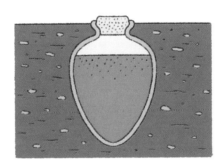

AGEING

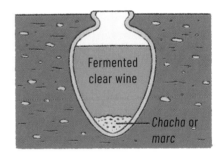

Fermented
clear wine

*Chacha or
marc*

**THE *QVEVRI* IS OPENED, AND THE
CLEAR WINE IS SIPHONED OFF**

BOTTLING

WHITE, ORANGE AND RED WINES, VINIFIED IN *QVEVRI*

Vinification in *qvevri* ("buried amphorae") is a technique that has been in use in the Republic of Georgia
for millennia, and it has been recognized as Intangible Cultural Heritage by UNESCO since 2013.
In Europe, it is rated as a protected geographical indication (PGI).

The traditional method is completely controlled, however. Originating in northern regions – with their favourable conditions of cold winters, wines with enhanced acidity and underground cellars – it then spread as barrel stores came to be equipped with air conditioning. First, a base wine is produced. This is often a white or a rosé that is a blend of different plots and cépages – indeed, even of different vintages – with high acidity and low levels of alcohol, and with or without malolactic fermentation and wood ageing. Reds are rare – though can include some Italian Lambrusco, Australian sparkling Shiraz and Portuguese sparkling Baga in Bairrada – because integrating the tannins, CO_2 and the lees can be tricky, and often goes hand in hand with the addition of sugar to soften the results. The combination of phenolic compounds with CO_2 is generally complex, hence the often very strict regulations on the way musts are pressed. Botrytis is avoided because of the organoleptic irregularities it causes, including bad acetaldehydes, oxidation and bitterness. The *liqueur de tirage* is then added for the second fermentation with a concentration of 1–2 million (often higher) cells per ml wine of "finishing" *Saccharomyces* (these have to re-ferment the wine, which is already at 9–11.5 degrees alcohol) required to break down 24g/l of sugar to obtain 10–12g/l of CO_2 (6 bar) and boost the alcohol content by 1.3–1.45 degrees.

This second fermentation, which is speedy, lasting only a few weeks, is followed by ageing on fine lees, which are in fact dead yeasts. Enzymatic autodegradation, known as autolysis, then synthesizes amino acids such as glutathione, polysaccharides and glycoproteins, and a Maillard reaction may also occur. The longer the wine is aged on lees in the cellar, the more this autolysis will alter the aroma and texture of the wine: a creamier texture with notes of butter and *rancio* and a more or less pronounced umami taste will result, depending on whether a breathable cork stopper or an impermeable capsule closure is used.

When ageing is over, the lees are removed by "disgorgement" – that is, freezing the neck of the bottle and removing a plug of sediment. This dry wine is then ready for *dosage* and a liqueur containing beet or cane sugar or rectified concentrated must is added at the producer's discretion.

Champagne, Crémant, Cava and Franciacorta are all made with traditional historic methods, which take between six months and several years. A far speedier option is the Martinotti/Charmat closed-vat method, which is completed in just a few weeks – the wines lack strong autolytic notes but have a more fermentative profile with notes of pear (isoamyl acetate and ethyl acetate) and the bubbles are larger at the same pressure. Production costs are far lower for decent quality: Prosecco is a typical example.

Whites and rosés of the 20th century

Technical and oenological progress in the 20th century made it possible for the white wines and rosés we know today to emerge, thanks to control of temperature, oxidation, malolactic fermentation and extraction of ingredients. Wines have become fresher, more aromatic, less strongly coloured and more lively. Bordeaux oenologists have made significant contributions to advances in varietal aromas and aroma precursors, establishing procedures for preserving these by addressing harvest quality and temperature, the duration of contact with skins, cold and reductive fermentation and the use of inert gases; they have certainly changed the way we experience Sauvignon Blanc, for example. While rosés made from crushed grapes are as old as winemaking itself, production of such wine is now strictly monitored.

In France, only Champagne allows red and white wines to be mixed to produce AOC rosé; it can also be obtained by short maceration. Otherwise, rosé is obtained either by direct pressing, by a process known as *saignée* in which a fermenting red wine, while still pale in colour, is "bled" of some juice, both to concentrate the remaining red wine and to turn the juice that has been removed into rosé. It is all too easy to extract too much, and there is a whole gamut of oenological techniques to mitigate this: for direct-pressed wines, charcoal or finings such as polyvinylpolypyrrolidone (PVPP) are added to lighten the colour. For the vast majority of the market, however, it is the colour of rosé that gives it its identity, rather than its taste or origins. With climate change producing ever more concentrated grapes, finding a balance for such wines is becoming increasingly tricky.

Winemaking craftsmanship and oenological science

Winemaking has undergone a dazzling evolution over the course of several decades, from an art and a craft to an oenological science, and it is now possible to produce almost any type of wine from almost any type of grape. But with a hands-off approach or complete control in the winery, with correction or promotion of terroir, to what extent do we detect the intervention of the winemaker and the origins of the vines when tasting a wine? There are still lively exchanges between those "add nothing, remove nothing" natural-wine supporters – who sanction only minimal physical intervention to preserve the expression of terroir – and those using all the legal ontological tools to produce a wine without technical fault and which is, according to them, a better presentation of the wine's origin. The debate continues, and the vast majority of modern producers lie somewhere between these two poles.

The alchemy of ageing

While fermentation is the most active – and most symbolic – phase of the transformation of must into wine, any number of physical and chemical reactions also occur during ageing, taking the liquid from its juvenile phase, as it were, to an expression of maturity that will depend on the producer's stylistic choices. By stirring, topping-up, racking, adding SO_2 and other techniques, winemakers make use of the lees and the phenomenon of redox (reduction-oxidation) to fashion their wines, and containers in many shapes and materials also shape the wine. These choices have no theoretical underpinning for the longest time; while Pasteur laid the scientific foundation in the second half of the 19th century, it was not until the 1980s that oenology really began to investigate the chemistry of ageing and the enhancement of wines. What transformations take place during ageing, and why are oak and wine such good friends?

Ageing wine is a complex business

Ageing wine has not always been synonymous with quality: in the past, the process was carried out in vessels or barrels that were not only too porous and poorly maintained but also expensive to use, so wine was mostly drunk rapidly. There were a few exceptions, such as the finest Roman wines like Falernian or Sorrentino; these were aged for decades, acquiring desirable notes of *flor*, *rancio* and maderization. There is a description by Tchernia and Brun in *Le Vin romain antique* (1999). Improvement of hygiene in wineries, the use of sulphur wicks and the development of tastes in England for aged wines, in the form of fortified wines, then clarets, all promoted organoleptic interest in ageing. Peynaud dates the first willful decision of ageing wine to the turn of the 18th century, but difficulties in the period after World War Two, the rising popularity of concrete and then stainless-steel vats, the often disproportionate difference in costs between barrel wines and vat wines, and complications in bottling all presented problems. Until around 1970, producers sought to prevent or eliminate the flavour of new barrels with finings or charcoal. The hunt for quality ageing and an interest in wood did not begin until the economic and scientific turning point of the 1980s.

The chemistry of redox: reductive ageing...

Ageing is playing with fire – or rather, with O_2. This element is both a scourge and a blessing for wine, which is a reservoir of hundreds of oxidizable molecules including ethanol, aromatic compounds, organic acids, tannins and pigments. Oxygen is essential for vinification but can also destroy the balance of the wine, with a multitude of extremely complex chemical reactions taking place, depending on the extent of the wine's exposure to the gas. These reactions are determined by the quality of the base grape and its redox potential (that is, the potential for reduction-oxidation), as well as by the environment in which they occur, and the skill of the winemaker. They may be very rapid or very slow, beneficial or undesirable, and will vary with the proportion of oxidizing elements in the wine, such as polyphenols and sulphites. Temperature and humidity influence potential absorption and the "angels' share" (evaporation); in a dry atmosphere, water evaporates more quickly than alcohol, thus concentrating the alcohol, while the opposite is true in a humid atmosphere, so the alcohol content should drop in a damp cellar. Some people entertain themselves by comparing ageing in their barrel store with containers submerged in the sea. Depending on the style of wine sought, producers may choose between reductive and oxidative ageing.

Extreme reductive vinification involves minimizing contact with O_2 as much as possible: this means pressing and vinification in a hermetically sealed stainless-steel or stoneware vat, the use of SO_2 and inert gases, and little racking. Ageing is often short, with minimal contact with air

> " Barrels have evolved from a simple tool for transporting produce into nothing less than an instrument for ageing wines

to preserve the primary varietal aromas, which are easily oxidized, especially certain sulphur compounds metabolized during fermentation. The most sought after are thiols: 3MH (with notes of grapefruit, passion-fruit, blackcurrant), 3MHA (exotic fruit, white flowers) and 4MMP (boxwood and blackcurrant leaves) impart an aromatic freshness that is now very much in fashion. Sauvignon Blanc is a cépage that is particularly well suited to this technique.

Red wines made with carbonic maceration are also vinified and aged to preserve their amylic aromas of strawberry and fruit drops and to be drunk young. When poorly controlled, however, such ageing may become too reductive, even when short, and other sulphur compounds that are considered defects in wine may form. These may be anything from hydrogen sulphide (cabbage, rotten egg – H_2S) to ethanethiol (stagnant water, the odour added to mains gas – C_2H_5SH), for which we have a very low detection threshold.

... and oxidative ageing

In 1873, Pasteur stated (in *Études sur le vin, ses maladies, causes qui les provoquent. Procédés nouveaux pour le conserver et pour le vieillir*), "It is oxygen that makes wine, and it is oxygen that alters the acerbic aspects of new wine and banishes its bad taste." Oxidative ageing seeks to impart controlled oxidation to wine without oxidizing it completely; Spanish *gran reservas* and Italian *riservas*, with their obligatory years of ageing in contact with air, are well-known examples of this. It is a difficult technique to master, however; alcoholic fermentation is the only point during vinification at which large quantities of O_2 can be introduced, to support the dynamics of yeast growth and, in the case of certain whites, to hyperoxygenate the must. Wines that are thus deprived of oxidizable compounds are paradoxically more stable thereafter in respect of oxidation. Any subsequent massive or uncontrolled intake of O_2 can degrade aromatic terpene and thiol molecules or produce *rancio* flavours; it may also oxidize the colour or increase the population of lactic and acetic bacteria or of other yeasts that can cause upsets - for example, lactic or acetic spoilage. Madeira, notably, is a fully oxidized wine, but this is an exception.

It takes controlled micro-oxygenation to construct red wines for ageing, by reducing astringency, softening tannins and stabilizing colour, and to influence the aromatics, unctuousness and stability of whites. Avoidance of reduction and oxidation has been estimated to require an average total O_2 of 20–50mg/l for white wine and 40–80mg/l for red, and the gas may be administered in doses or continuously, depending on the containers and techniques employed. Progress in oenology has created a wide variety of procedures to achieve this, such as the micro-oxygenation developed by Patrick Ducournau in 1991, which seeks to reproduce in a vat the oxygenation phenomena that occur in a barrel of Tannat, a tannic cépage from Southwest France: a microporous ceramic or a stainless steel element very slowly diffuses a continuous and precise dose of pure O_2. Macro-oxygenation makes use of the same principle to replace racking. Both techniques are extremely economical in terms of time and money by comparison with long ageing in wood.

Oak is made for wine

Historically, wood has replaced the terracotta used for amphorae; it is easier to transport, less fragile, and watertight. It is also more effective in promoting micro-oxygenation and diffuses into the wine plant compounds that are likely to improve its quality. Barrels are said by some to have been invented by the Celts and first made from locally sourced wood species such as fir, pine and beech; it was not until the 3rd century that oak (*Quercus*) began to rise in popularity because of its physical and chemical qualities. Acacia is still sometimes used for its aromatic properties: it can impart honey, lemon and floral notes. Chestnut, which had long been used for large containers for transporting goods, was eventually rejected as being too tannic.

Oak wood is a complex matrix comprising cellulose, hemicellulose (fibres made of sugar that link cellulose) and lignin, one of the polyphenols responsible for the rigidity of wood. It also has extractable compounds available in greater or lesser quantities according to the species of oak and the skills of the stave-makers and coopers. It has waterproofing qualities of its own, being rich in tyloses; these viscous cellular outgrowths block the sap vessels, allowing air but not liquid to pass through.

Quality is determined by species and origins but also by grain - that is, the average width of the tree's rings, which will vary with its speed of growth: the slower the growth, the closer together the rings, fed by sap vessels, and the finer the grain. The finer the grain, the more porous the wood will be, as the sap leaves room for air, and the fewer ellagitannins it will impart. Grain infuses and filters, guaranteeing high-quality micro-oxygenation and reducing the angels' share. It adds aroma and precipitates out the tannins that not only shape the organoleptic profile of the wine but also act as natural antiseptics, which was their original function. These tannins are also antioxidants that interact with the wine's proteins, stabilizing its colour and boosting its potential for ageing. Tannins form the framework of a wine, as Selosse explains in *Les Goûts et les couleurs du monde* (2019) - but not all oaks and tannins were created equal.

Wood *crus* – just like wine *crus*

There are terroirs for oaks just as there are terroirs for wines; these are based on a longstanding dynamic between a botanical species, a physical environment and human skills and requirements. Of the 250 varieties of oak growing in the temperate zones of the northern hemisphere, five have been favoured for vinification, one for corks (*Q. suber*) and four for cooperage.

- **North American white oak (*Q. alba*)** has a wealth of tyloses but few ellagitannins. It slows down O_2 transfer and can be sawn without losing its watertightness. The species is rich in lactones (with coconut aromas), eugenol (cloves) and scopoletin (balsamic notes). It has an average grain width (1–5mm/$\frac{1}{32}$–$\frac{13}{64}$in) and is very popular for spirits such as whisky. It tends to sweeten wines and impart dill aromas.

- **American northern red oak (*Q. rubra*)** was traditionally used in California for large containers but very rarely for barrels. It has a strong concentration of tannins and aromatic compounds of vanilla and resin that are lacking in the subtlety required for fine wines. It is very rarely used today.

- **English oak (*Q. robur* or *pedunculata*)** is found everywhere from the Iberian peninsula to the Urals, and throughout France. It is rich in ellagitannins and phenolic compounds but has low levels of coconut-flavoured whisky lactones, and it is the wood of choice for brandies such as Armagnac. It has an average-width grain (3–10mm/$\frac{1}{8}$–$\frac{3}{8}$in).

- **Sessile oak (*Q. sessiliflora* or *petraea*)** is the species recognized as best suited for ageing fine wines and is found from the northern shores of the Mediterranean to Scandinavia, as well as in Hungary and the Croatian region of Slavonia.

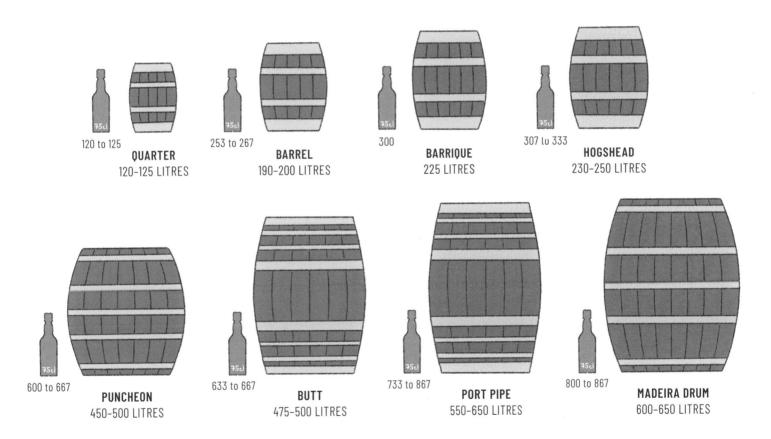

120 to 125
QUARTER
120–125 LITRES

253 to 267
BARREL
190–200 LITRES

300
BARRIQUE
225 LITRES

307 to 333
HOGSHEAD
230–250 LITRES

600 to 667
PUNCHEON
450–500 LITRES

633 to 667
BUTT
475–500 LITRES

733 to 867
PORT PIPE
550–650 LITRES

800 to 867
MADEIRA DRUM
600–650 LITRES

NUMBER OF BOTTLES IN EACH BARREL

THE VARYING SIZES OF THE MOST COMMON WHISKY BARRELS AND THEIR EQUIVALENTS IN 75-CL BOTTLES

The power of lees

The total lees form a fluffy carpet at the bottom of the barrel or vat at the end of fermentation. These are different from "gross" lees, which include press residues and impurities and are removed during racking after pressing. Fine lees are attracting more and more interest as a way of ageing wines. Working with fine lees is risky, however, and requires certain precautions to avoid introducing defects, particularly reduction.

Although they may potentially take up O_2 and risk the creation of reduction aromas, or even block the action of free SO_2, good fine lees bring benefits through autolysis, the enzymatic breakdown of dead yeast cells. They can release polysaccharides, nitrogen compounds (including amino acids), mannoproteins, esters, lipids and other compounds that render the wine's aromas more complex, bringing richness and length in the mouth while also stabilizing the wine and preserving its colour and freshness. This said, ageing on lees clearly restricts the aromatic perception of esters because the lees partially adsorb these. Glutathione – an antioxidant and detoxifying tripeptide that is found in both vines and humans – is of particular interest because it preserves thiols. Redox potential may be amplified by stirring, an active resuspension of the lees that accelerates decomposition and micro-oxygenates the wine. Ageing on lees is an essential aspect of the viticultural history of certain regions, whether in vats in Muscadet, in barrels in Burgundy or in bottles in Champagne. The technique was used for reds before malolactic fermentation became popular and is more usually applied to preserve colours and soften tannins without introducing further chemicals, even though there is also a greater risk of *Brettanomyces* development. Natural wines or those with fewer additives will necessarily make greater use of it.

In France it is particularly common in the Loire, central France, the Vosges and Normandy. It has low levels of ellagitannins but plenty of lactones and eugenol. It also boasts the finest grain (1–3mm/$\frac{1}{32}$–$\frac{1}{8}$in).

The price of a new 225-litre (60-US gallon) barrel can be anything from €500 to more than €1,500 before tax, depending on the species, the origins of the wood, and the cooper. Although Eastern Europe produces high-quality wood, France is still the yardstick, with Tronçais (Allier), Jupilles (Sarthe) and Bertranges (Burgundy) timber commanding the highest prices.

French forests are renowned equally for their terroir and their good management; aware that forests are a fragile resource and that short-term, local human interests have to be weighed against the long-term conservation of the trees and national interests, Jean-Baptiste Colbert established the first centralized Forest Code in 1669. One of its objectives was military: a competitive navy required rapid growth of dense, hard woods that were ill suited to cooperage. It fell to Bernard Lorentz (1775–1865), the first director of the forestry school in Nancy, to impose legislation managing the forest of Tronçais as a timber forest, yielding tall and slender cylindrical oaks with a fine grain. Just like vines, forests are a heritage to be conserved, and their influence on the climate, and vice versa, has been known since the 18th century. In modern France, publicly accessible forests, which are 25 per cent of the total, are managed by a national agency, while private holdings, 75 per cent of the total, are regulated by the National Centre for Forest Property (CNPF), which controls planting, pruning and sales.

From the heart of the oak tree to the alchemy of the barrel

Barrels have evolved from a simple tool for transporting produce into nothing less than a delicate instrument for ageing fine wines, although they are used for no more than two to five per cent of total global production; the volume is much higher for spirits. The heartwood, the central portion of trees between 70 and 250 years old, is cut into logs or billets, ideally during a waning moon to minimize the sap content of the wood. Twenty per cent of the lumber is squared off to make staves, long wooden slats several metres long, while the remaining eighty per cent is sold off for plywood, chips or other products at a lower price.

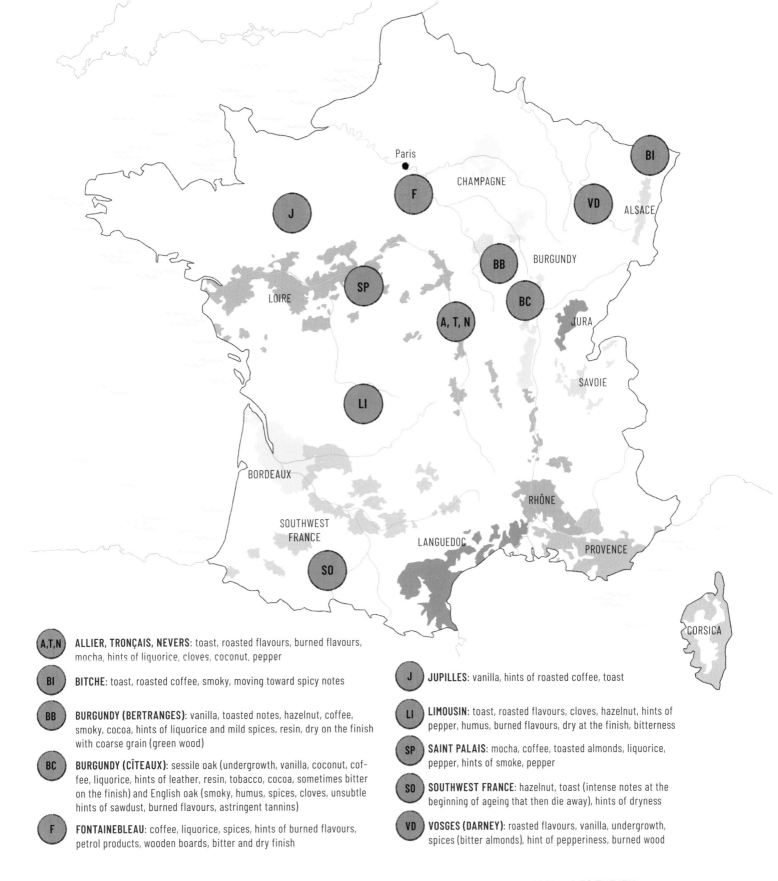

A,T,N **ALLIER, TRONÇAIS, NEVERS:** toast, roasted flavours, burned flavours, mocha, hints of liquorice, cloves, coconut, pepper

BI **BITCHE:** toast, roasted coffee, smoky, moving toward spicy notes

BB **BURGUNDY (BERTRANGES):** vanilla, toasted notes, hazelnut, coffee, smoky, cocoa, hints of liquorice and mild spices, resin, dry on the finish with coarse grain (green wood)

BC **BURGUNDY (CÎTEAUX):** sessile oak (undergrowth, vanilla, coconut, coffee, liquorice, hints of leather, resin, tobacco, cocoa, sometimes bitter on the finish) and English oak (smoky, humus, spices, cloves, unsubtle hints of sawdust, burned flavours, astringent tannins)

F **FONTAINEBLEAU:** coffee, liquorice, spices, hints of burned flavours, petrol products, wooden boards, bitter and dry finish

J **JUPILLES:** vanilla, hints of roasted coffee, toast

LI **LIMOUSIN:** toast, roasted flavours, cloves, hazelnut, hints of pepper, humus, burned flavours, dry at the finish, bitterness

SP **SAINT PALAIS:** mocha, coffee, toasted almonds, liquorice, pepper, hints of smoke, pepper

SO **SOUTHWEST FRANCE:** hazelnut, toast (intense notes at the beginning of ageing that then die away), hints of dryness

VD **VOSGES (DARNEY):** roasted flavours, vanilla, undergrowth, spices (bitter almonds), hint of pepperiness, burned wood

THE MAIN FRENCH OAK FORESTS USED IN COOPERAGE AND THEIR AROMATIC PROFILE, ACCORDING TO THE IFV

The IFV has analysed the aromatic profile of the oak trees grown in France, highlighting the importance of terroir and species in a barrel's organoleptic input to a wine.

The staves are left in the open air to age, usually for 18 to 36 months; rain, micro-organisms and wind decrease their humidity from 50 to 16 per cent, leaching out bitter tannins and oxidizing others as eugenol and vanillin begin to appear. After several years of drying and ageing, the staves are split into smaller sections that will form the barrel.

After a first, damp heating cycle (cintrage), these can be curved and formed into a circle, followed by a second, dry bake to between 120 and 200°C (248 to 390°F), which changes the chemical composition of the wood (bousinage). Caramelization and other reactions release aromatic molecules of toasted cyclotene, vanillin, eugenol, smoked syringol and sour guaiacol, while others fade away. Various molecules will appear, including almondy furfural and whisky lactones, depending on the species of oak. When buying barrels, winemakers will stipulate a particular level of toast and empyreumatic intensity (the family of aromas related to fire) depending on the style of wine desired: gentle heating has vanilla notes; medium heating imparts spicy and smoky aromas; and high heat roasts or even burns certain fragile compounds such as vanillin and whisky lactones.

> " The last few years have also witnessed a return to the earth, with clay wine jars of the sort in use as early as the Neolithic period

Producers can also choose a shape and size from the dozens available. Dimensions differ throughout Europe, and there are even regional variations across France, despite the adoption of a uniformly metric system in the 19th century – a last vestige of the historical diversity of barrels.

Containers of 225 litres (just short of 60 US gallons, the longest Bordeaux barrel) and 228 litres (just over 60 US gallons, the largest Burgundian option) are the most commonly used nowadays, although there is also the foudre, which holds more than 1,000 litres (264 US gallons). The largest barrel known is owned by the Byrrh estate and can hold a million litres (264,000 US gallons). The larger the container, the fewer its effects; the thickness of the staves is of crucial importance in the alchemy that takes place between the wine, the wood and the atmosphere. Something like 0.4mg/l of O_2 dissolves into a new barrel every year, 80 per cent of which enters through the bunghole.

Six months of ageing are required to obtain anything more than simple aromatization of the wine by the wood, and Bordeaux is generally aged for 18 months, and Burgundy, 10–18 months. Through the formation of acetaldehyde, O_2 is able to combine tannins and anthocyanins to stabilize the colour of the wine. The extractable elements – phenolic acids, volatile phenols, tannins and aldehydes – dissolve, and volatile acidity may increase; these exchanges will be more integrated for a wine that is fermented in barrels rather than just aged, as is more often the case for white wines.

Sustained use exhausts the wood; after a couple of years, it will be no more than a simple container that has actually become more airtight because its exterior pores have been clogged. It may also harbour bad flavours if it has been treated. Contrary to popular belief, old wood is never entirely neutral; some may even taint wine with "floorboard" tastes – alchemy can sometimes become contamination.

Oenological wood chips and tannins

There are alternative options, replacing barrels and avoiding the associated cost; woodchips greater than 2mm (1/16in) have been legally permitted for ageing in Europe since 2005, and roasted staves or boards have been allowed during vinification since 2009. Sawdust is still banned. Wood chips dissolve their extractable compounds more rapidly because of their greater contact surface area, but with variations in quality similar to barrels; as a result, they are left in the vat for less time to avoid causing astringency. Anything between 1 and 10g/l of wood chips is generally used, costing from €0.15 to €13 per hectolitre after tax; staves cost between €5.50 and €27 per hectolitre after tax, as opposed to from €83 to more than €127 per hectolitre after tax for a barrel, amortized over three years, according to the IFV's figures. The technique has attracted criticism from some quarters but can add complexity to entry-level wines – and is part of a tradition dating back centuries, as the work of Selosse has established. From the addition of spices and resins in ancient times, to later during antiquity with the addition of oak galls (caused by hymenoptera wasps, also used to make ink), to the modern use of industrially extracted liquid tannins, it can be seen that these practices have historically always been part of winemakers' toolkits in the quest to improve the quality of wine.

Alternatives to wood

Alternatives to wood can be used to track the history of materials, oenology and market tastes.
- **Concrete** has been in use since the end of the 19th century and may be vitrified or unlined, in which case it must be treated with tartaric acid to avoid deacidifying the wine. It has high thermal inertia, allows gas exchanges when unlined, is relatively easy to maintain, and can be formed into containers of many different shapes and in large volumes. Stainless steel briefly took over, but concrete is now making a comeback in the form of truncated conical vats, amphorae and ovoid tanks. Egg-shaped containers are very popular and are thought to cause convection currents that permanently stir the lees, encouraging autolysis.

- **Stainless steel** became popular in the 1970s, despite its cost. It is entirely inert, very easy to maintain and light in weight, with low thermal inertia and the required thermoregulatory properties. Its popularity rose in line with the spread of reductive winemaking techniques.
- **Fibreglass** and polyethylene tanks are light, relatively inert and inexpensive. They are used more for vinification than for ageing.
- **Granite**, which is similar to vitrified concrete, can still be found in long-isolated regions such as the Douro.
- **Glass**, which is hermetic, is traditionally used for ageing some fortified wines, especially in Roussillon.

In the wake of a movement resisting over-oaking, the start of the 21st century witnessed a return to the earth, with clay wine jars of the sort in widespread use as early as the Neolithic period. Vinification in amphorae was superseded with the invention of the barrel but nonetheless survived in locations scattered across Europe: with the *talhas* of Alentejo in Portugal, the imposing *tinajas* south of Madrid, the *qvevri* of Georgia, the *pithoi* of Greece and Italy's *dolia*. It was in Italy that a revival of the use of amphorae, and of skin-contact wines, came about in the first decade of the 21st century, after Friulian winemaker Josko Gravner returned from a trip to Georgia. However, there is not one amphora but thousands of amphorae, since this is a catch-all term for all kinds of different container. Materials may include clay, terracotta, porcelain and sandstone, among others, and the composition will determine the manufacturing method, firing and porosity: terracotta is very porous, while porcelain behaves like glass. If the jar is not coated on the interior, often with wax or resin, for their antiseptic properties, it may release minerals into the wine and oxidize it.

The shapes of the containers are similarly disparate. *Qvevri*, which hold anything from 200 to 8,000 litres (53 to 2,113 US gallons), are oblong to encourage sedimentation and natural clarification. They are also coated with lime and are often buried in the *marani*, the garden of the family home. They benefit from the thermal inertia of the ground, with minimal gas exchanges by comparison with jars that are not buried, which absorb vast amounts if they are porous. Faced with exponential demand from wine-growers all over the world, many potters have relocated part of their production and can be found from Oregon to South Africa, taking in France and Australia.

Ageing wine, a science and art (or craft) entirely forgotten and neglected 40 years ago, has now become one of the busiest areas of experimentation among winemakers. Proponents of natural ageing are looking at it, as are institutions in Bordeaux. Ageing plays a crucial role in a wine's quality and potential for laying down.

Ageing eaux de vie and "double ageing"

With casks used for bourbon, Marsala, Oloroso Sherry, Madeira barrels, Port pipes and Cabernet Sauvignon barriques, no fewer than six sorts of barrel of different origins are required to finish ageing the King Alexander III single-malt whisky produced by the Scottish distillery Dalmore, with the final product finished in Sherry butts. It is the only whisky in the world with so many cask finishes. Wood gives eau de vie its brown hue, and the art of ageing in wood is an integral part of Cognac, Armagnac, old rum and whisk(e)y. The used barrels employed for Scotch whiskies, since there were no forests to hand, and the new barrels preferred for many American whiskeys each bring different compounds to eau de vie depending on their provenance and potential previous contents: flavonols, oligonols and fatty acids from a bourbon barrel, quercetin and sugars from a Sherry barrel, anthocyanins from a barrel from Bordeaux and so on. Tannins and other aromatic extractable compounds diffuse through the alcohol, changing its colour and its taste, helped along by the action of micro-oxygenation. This influence is so pronounced that distilleries offer what are known as "cask finishes" – several months' finishing of these eaux de vie in specific woods, in addition to their traditional and regulated ageing, to add a further touch of originality to their product. All bourbon barrels experience a second life: bourbon must be aged in new wood, often *Q. alba*, so a lot of barrels are made, and none can be reused for bourbon. Barrels used for the great fortified wines of the Iberian peninsula or for Sauternes, Vin Jaune and others are similarly highly prized by the extremely competitive and creative spirits industry.

THE MAJOR STAGES IN VINIFICATION

When making wine, producers take a series of decisions to bring about the physical and biochemical transformation of grapes. Depending on their approach, they may choose to be more or less hands-on. The difference between white, red, rosé and skin-contact wine happens at the maceration stage.

Stages common to all wines

- **Harvesting**. This is carried out manually or by machine, depending on AOC regulations and the resources available.
- **Sorting and destemming**. Grapes are generally sorted. Destemming, which separates the berries from the stems, may be manual or mechanical. For carbonic maceration,, the cluster is left whole. The grapes may be crushed, bringing the juice into contact with the skins' colour and aromatic compounds; whites and some rosés are pressed directly to avoid coloration, while other wines are macerated to take on colour and phenolic structure.

Simplified vinification of reds, rosés and skin-contact wines

- **Vatting**. The juice and solid elements are placed in a vessel of concrete, wood, stainless steel, terracotta or other material.
- **Maceration, *pigeage*.** The length of the maceration depends on the extractable elements and the style of wine desired. It may be intensified by:
  - **Punching-down** – pushing the solid material down into the juice: as a result of the CO_2 from the alcoholic fermentation, a "cap" composed of agglomerated grape skins floats to the top of the vessel, leaving only a minority of its surface in contact with the must beneath. The cap is pushed down to mix them back.
  - **Pumping-over** – pumping juice up from the bottom of the tank and over the cap to moisten it. Emptying the entire tank to pour back over the crust is known as rack and return, or *delestage*.
- **Alcoholic fermentation**. Sulphur dioxide, selected yeasts, sugars, acids or other oenological additives can be added to the must. Fermentation may also be spontaneous, without added yeasts. Alcoholic and malolactic fermentation sometimes coincide (in French, *malo sous marc*), but winemakers prefer to avoid this.
- **Racking**. Once the desired level of extraction has been achieved, the "free-run" wine is drained off. The *marc* is removed to be pressed.

- **Pressing**. The solid elements are pressed to extract the press wine, which is richer in polyphenols.
- **Blending and racking**. The free-run and press wines can be blended or matured separately. If the wine is cloudy, it can be left to settle and clarify before racking.

Simplified vinification of white wines

- **Pressing and vatting**. The clusters are generally pressed whole. The choice of press is of crucial importance: extraction levels vary with the type of press, affecting the compounds extracted and their potential oxidation, among other factors.
- **Clarification and racking**. The must is often settled to allow coarse lees to deposit under the action of cold or enzymes. The clear juice is racked into the fermentation vessel. Fine lees are often retained to feed the yeasts and the must.
- **Alcoholic fermentation**.

Stages common to all wines

- **Malolactic fermentation, ageing and *bâtonnage*.** Malolactic fermentation may or may not be desirable (it is compulsory for reds in certain regions), and this natural deacidification process is either spontaneous or triggered by the addition of lactic bacteria. It can be blocked with SO_2, cold or filtration. During ageing, the lees may either be racked off or reintegrated to achieve a particular organoleptic profile. This is known as *bâtonnage*. It is most frequent for white wines.
- **Racking, adding sulphites, topping up**. The wine is racked off if it exhibits notes of reduction, which come from volatile sulphur compounds. It can also be sulphured to protect it. The wine is topped up to compensate for the portion that has evaporated.
- **Racking, blending, *mise en masse*.** The wine is racked before bottling and blended as required. The final batches are blended to homogenize them and allowed to settle before being prepared for bottling.
- **Fining**. The wine may be further clarified with organic or mineral finings, which trigger flocculation of aggregates. It may be chilled to precipitate out tartrate crystals. (These do not impair the taste but may make the final wine less visually appealing.)
- **Filtration, bottling**. The wine may be filtered for limpidity and eliminate micro-organisms that could trigger secondary fermentation. Filtration may be gentle or rigorous, although wines can also be bottled as "unfined and unfiltered"; some winemakers think this promotes complexity. Bottling is carried out mechanically; it is rare for this to be done by hand today.

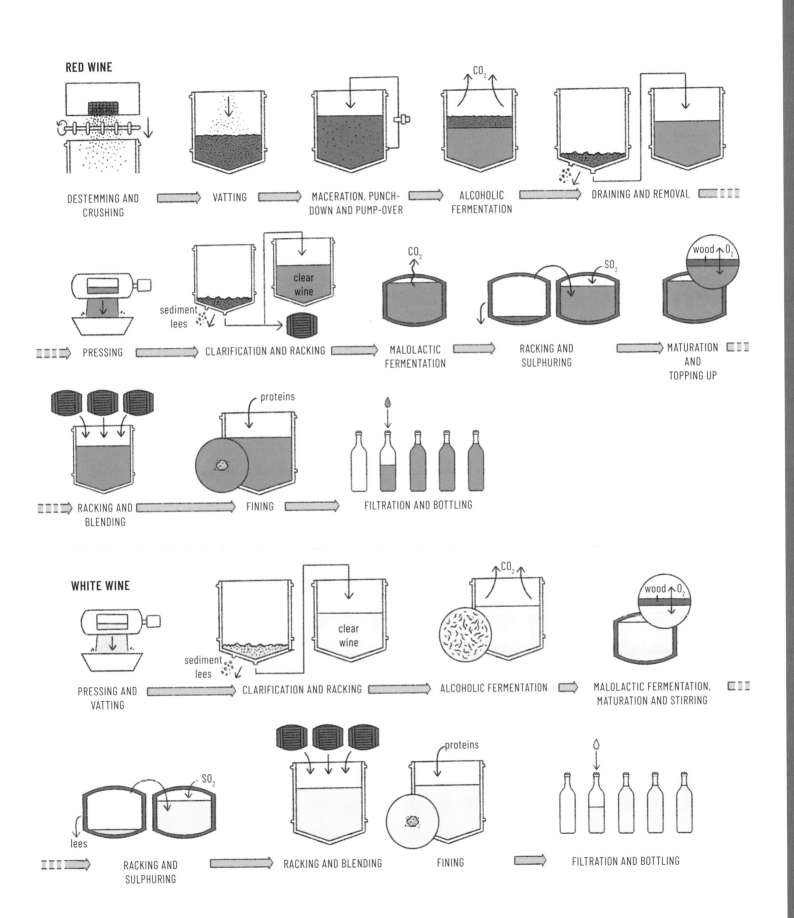

RED WINE

DESTEMMING AND CRUSHING → VATTING → MACERATION, PUNCH-DOWN AND PUMP-OVER → ALCOHOLIC FERMENTATION → DRAINING AND REMOVAL

CO_2

PRESSING → CLARIFICATION AND RACKING → MALOLACTIC FERMENTATION → RACKING AND SULPHURING → MATURATION AND TOPPING UP

sediment lees · clear wine · CO_2 · SO_2 · wood O_2

RACKING AND BLENDING → FINING → FILTRATION AND BOTTLING

proteins

WHITE WINE

PRESSING AND VATTING → CLARIFICATION AND RACKING → ALCOHOLIC FERMENTATION → MALOLACTIC FERMENTATION, MATURATION AND STIRRING

sediment lees · clear wine · CO_2 · wood O_2

RACKING AND SULPHURING → RACKING AND BLENDING → FINING → FILTRATION AND BOTTLING

lees · SO_2 · proteins

233

The oenologist's century

Tasting a standard Bordeaux or Burgundy from the turn of the 20th century would no doubt bring a host of surprises; we would not be expecting their low alcohol, occasionally sharp acidity, green tannins, *rancio* aromas, *coupage* blending or a pronounced whiff of sulphur… Only the best wines have come down to us, however, and it is difficult to get a proper sense of the metamorphosis undergone by wine in scarcely a century. We will have to move beyond romanticizing the past ("those were the days") if we wish to acknowledge and understand the role played by oenology in this transformation. Our understanding of wine – which itself was born of the progress made in numerous fields, microbiology in particular – has become a science in its own right, evolving from the empirical art of managing vinification into an applied discipline that seeks to cure and prevent disease as it shapes the health and organoleptic quality of a wine. While global quality has never been higher, the industry is regularly accused of distorting and standardizing wine to the point of negating its capacity to express terroir. Where do the roots of oenology lie, and what progress has it made? How should we understand the role it may play for the wines of the past, present and future?

From the empirical art of making wine to scientific oenology

The search for the best-quality wine has been going on for millennia, but compared with the number of treatises on growing wine, records of winemaking techniques are few and far between until the beginning of the 19th century. Peynaud set about cataloguing them. He suggested that wine was either deemed the product of seasonal agricultural labour and an individual effort, with vinification a secondary affair that was of little interest to chroniclers, or conversely, that it was an insider affair that had to be kept secret – or indeed both of these.

Until 1800, the art of making wine would remain mainly empirical and evolve very little. The advice offered by de Serres in his *Théâtre d'agriculture* (1600) merely compiles skills previously mastered by the ancient world, of harvesting healthy grapes when they are ripe, destemming where possible, paying attention to how long the wine is in the vat, topping up and so on. Such sage advice did not stop wine from spoiling, however, and treatises of this kind were more like compendia of recipes and additives than explorations of the root causes of problems. It was not until the 17th century that "oenology", a term first used by Louis Meyssonnier, physician to France's Louis XIII, in his *Oenologie ou Discours*

du vin et de ses excellentes propriétés of 1636, was able to come into its own as the science of winemaking, even as our understanding of wine itself was expanding. As an experimental field for other sciences, oenology became more clearly defined as progress was made first in physics, then chemistry, and then biology at the beginning of the 19th century, undergoing a paradigm shift with Pasteur's *Études sur le vin* (1866) and the emergence of microbiology and biochemistry.

The Bordeaux school – from curative to preventative

Pasteur made an exceptional number of revolutionary discoveries in just three years, but it would take decades for knowledge of these to spread and be applied. Until the 1950s, there were some managers of Bordeaux wineries, harbouring doubts about the sciences and clinging to the secrets of the cellar, who would not consider a wine with more than 1g/l of volatile acidity, H_2SO_4, to be spoiled – indeed quite the contrary. By comparison, the current legal limit in France is 0.88g/l for white wines and 0.98g/l for reds. Harsh, sour, oxidized and with low levels of alcohol, the wine of the era was a far cry from our current standards, and the changes to come would thus also involve a development of our palates; "Analytical restructuring of wines necessarily entails a rebalancing of tastes," as Peynaud said. The Station Agronomique de Bordeaux research institution (founded 1874) and its various later incarnations were to play a crucial part, not only in studying wine but also in employing and understanding it in the field, not to mention pioneering a new tasting approach.

While the research conducted by Alexandre Baudrimont (1806–80) and Ulysse Gayon (1845–1929), the institute's first directors, built on Pasteur's work, it is Jean Ribéreau-Gayon (1905–91), the latter's grandson, and Peynaud, his pupil, who can lay claim to having established the modern science of oenology. They progressed from cure to prevention by introducing basic science into wineries. Commissioned by winemaking companies to research ways of treating defects in wine, they managed to find explanations for many of the upsets and accidents that rendered wine unstable and unfit for sale, with their laboratory addressing everything from tartaric precipitation to copper, protein and oxidation turbidity, and more besides. They developed treatments for these, and Ribéreau-Gayon established the use of potassium ferrocyanide to counter iron turbidity, the most problematic fault of the time, along with acetic souring: its use had previously been banned in France for fear of harmful doses but ultimately led to the establishment of the Diplôme National d'Oenologue (DNO) qualification in 1955, theoretically underpinned by the *Traité d'oenologie* of 1947 that is still the standard reference work to this day.

Pascal Ribéreau-Gayon (1930–2011), Jean's son who took up the reins of the oenology faculty, summarized some of the progress made in his *Histoire de l'oenologie à Bordeaux* (2001); this includes microbiological control of fermentation including malolactic fermentation; a study of phenolic compounds and the transformations they undergo during vinification; the chemistry of the aromas of white wines, in conjunction with Professor Denis Dubourdieu's work on thiols; and the chemistry of *Botrytis cinerea* and wood, along with much else. These findings, which now seem so obvious, have been acquired in only since the 1960s and have transformed wine production.

Under the leadership of these pioneers, the oenologist's true calling was also to emerge. Among all the chemists, agronomists and pharmacists, oenologists had initially been few and far between, but from the 1960s onward, a period when few winemakers had any scientific training, the profession began to assert its authority with the vinification of wines that were riper, fresher and more supple. The results prompted producers to become oenologists themselves or to hire a consultant. As techniques developed, oenologists also became guarantors of compliance with the regulations currently in force.

The technological evolution of oenology

Oenology is involved at every juncture during vinification, with both must and wine: before fermentation even begins there is the need to protect the crop, extract the juice and clarify it. The harvested crop must be acidified, deacidified and enriched with sugar. Fermentation, stabilization (both microbial and tartaric, with finings or clarification), ageing and bottling all require oenology.

> 66 Until 1800, the art of making wine remained mainly empirical and evolved very little

The advent of new technologies has accelerated greatly with the integration of scientific advances in chemistry (which is where it all began), plant biology, biochemistry, soil sciences, analytical tasting and process management. The winemaker's chemical pharmacopeia of curative oenology has become prophylactic oenology that is based on a host of new technologies, including (and the decades when they became legal and widely used in Europe):

- **1960s** Horizontal presses, control of temperature during fermentation stages.
- **1970s** Dried active yeasts, pre-fermentation maceration extracting aroma precursors.
- **1980s** Mechanical destemming, flash pasteurization.
- **1990s** Flash détente (flash release), extraction enzymes and micro-oxygenation.
- **2000s** Use of inert nitrogen or CO_2, lactic fermentation, development of membrane-based techniques that make it possible to concentrate must and wine, removal of alcohol, sterile filtering, stabilizing acidity, removal of compounds such as ethylphenols and volatile acidity.
- **2010s** Wood chips, inactive yeasts in fermentation and new flotation techniques.

There have been more and more innovations: seven new processes, including exposing grapes to pulsed electric fields and treating crushed grapes with ultrasound to promote extraction of the compounds within, and two oenological compounds, fumaric acid to inhibit malolactic fermentation and Aspergillopepsine-type protease for protein turbidity, were approved by the European Commission at the turn of 2022.

Closely regulated practices

In most winemaking countries, use of these techniques is regulated by the OIV's International Code of Oenological Practices, which is regularly updated and available online. The OIV was founded in 1924 and now includes 50 countries, representing 87 per cent of global production, along with 18 organizations or territories with observer status,

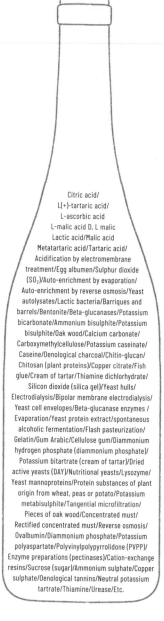

Citric acid/
L(+)-tartaric acid/
L-ascorbic acid
L-malic acid D, L malic
Lactic acid/Malic acid
Metatartaric acid/Tartaric acid/
Acidification by electromembrane
treatment/Egg albumen/Sulphur dioxide
(SO_2)/Auto-enrichment by evaporation/
Auto-enrichment by reverse osmosis/Yeast
autolysates/Lactic bacteria/Barriques and
barrels/Bentonite/Beta-glucanases/Potassium
bicarbonate/Ammonium bisulphite/Potassium
bisulphite/Oak wood/Calcium carbonate/
Carboxymethylcellulose/Potassium caseinate/
Caseine/Oenological charcoal/Chitin-glucan/
Chitosan (plant proteins)/Copper citrate/Fish
glue/Cream of tartar/Thiamine dichlorhydrate/
Silicon dioxide (silica gel)/Yeast hulls/
Electrodialysis/Bipolar membrane electrodialysis/
Yeast cell envelopes/Beta-glucanase enzymes /
Evaporation/Yeast protein extract/spontaneous
alcoholic fermentation/Flash pasteurization/
Gelatin/Gum Arabic/Cellulose gum/Diammonium
hydrogen phosphate (diammonium phosphate)/
Potassium bitartrate (cream of tartar)/Dried
active yeasts (DAY)/Nutritional yeasts/Lysozyme/
Yeast mannoproteins/Protein substances of plant
origin from wheat, peas or potato/Potassium
metabisulphite/Tangential microfiltration/
Pieces of oak wood/Concentrated must/
Rectified concentrated must/Reverse osmosis/
Ovalbumin/Diammonium phosphate/Potassium
polyaspartate/Polyvinylpolypyrrolidone (PVPP)/
Enzyme preparations (pectinases)/Cation-exchange
resins/Sucrose (sugar)/Ammonium sulphate/Copper
sulphate/Oenological tannins/Neutral potassium
tartrate/Thiamine/Urease/Etc.

CONVENTIONAL

150-200

total SO_2 permitted (mg/l)
white/rosé-red

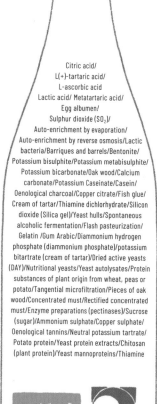

Citric acid/
L(+)-tartaric acid/
L-ascorbic acid
Lactic acid/ Metatartaric acid/
Egg albumen/
Sulphur dioxide (SO_2)/
Auto-enrichment by evaporation/
Auto-enrichment by reverse osmosis/Lactic
bacteria/Barriques and barrels/Bentonite/
Potassium bisulphite/Potassium metabisulphite/
Potassium bicarbonate/Oak wood/Calcium
carbonate/Potassium Caseinate/Casein/
Oenological charcoal/Copper citrate/Fish glue/
Cream of tartar/Thiamine dichlorhydrate/Silicon
dioxide (Silica gel)/Yeast hulls/Spontaneous
alcoholic fermentation/Flash pasteurization/
Gelatin /Gum Arabic/Diammonium hydrogen
phosphate (diammonium phosphate)/potassium
bitartrate (cream of tartar)/Dried active yeasts
(DAY)/Nutritional yeasts/Yeast autolysates/Protein
substances of plant origin from wheat, peas or
potato/Tangential microfiltration/Pieces of oak
wood/Concentrated must/Rectified concentrated
must/Enzyme preparations (pectinases)/Sucrose
(sugar)/Ammonium sulphate/Copper sulphate/
Oenological tannins/Neutral potassium tartrate/
Potato protein/Yeast protein extracts/Chitosan
(plant protein)/Yeast mannoproteins/Thiamine

ORGANIC

100-150

total SO_2 permitted (mg/l)
white/rosé-red

Tartaric acid (on derogation)/Egg albumen/
Sulphur dioxide (SO_2)/Nitrogen/Lactic bacteria
(on derogation)/Bentonite/Potassium bicarbonate
(on derogation)/Potassium bisulphite/potassium
bitartrate/Casein/Carbon dioxide/Yeast hulls/
Exogenous yeasts (on derogation)/Potassium
metabisulphite/Microfiltration/Tangential
microfiltration/Concentrated must/ Rectified
concentrated must /Pea or wheat proteins/Sugar

BIODYNAMIC

70-90

total SO_2 permitted (mg/l)
white/rosé-red

NATURAL WINE
Natural wine < 30mg/l

$SO_2 < 30$

NATURAL WINE

Traces*

Labelling by *cuvée*
(systematic control)

L'ASSOCIATION DES VINS NATURELS

Traces*

On at least 80 per cent
of production volume

VINS S.A.I.N.S
(NO ADDITIVES OR SULPHITES)

Traces*

On all production
every year

* only natural sulphites present

NATURAL

< 30

total SO_2 permitted (mg/l)
white/rosé-red

PRODUCTS AND PRACTICES AUTHORIZED IN FRANCE BY TYPE OF VITICULTURE

European legislation authorizes the use of a certain number of products and technological adjuvants;
since December 2023, some of these have to be indicated on labels. Legislation governing organic wines has stricter
regulations for what is permitted, and biodynamic certification has even more stringent restrictions.

The natural wine movement, which was initially reticent about any regulation, has now adopted Vin Méthode Nature,
a privater charter authorizing less than 30mg/l maximum total SO_2.

including the EU. Its primary function is to develop international standards for the entire production process in the form of non-binding resolutions that are used as reference points for national legislation; European regulations are therefore largely based on these norms. At the request of member states or the OIV's specialist commissions, products and techniques are examined by scientific delegates and experts nominated by members. There is a network of more than 500 experts currently affiliated to four commissions, namely viticulture, oenology, economics and law, and health and safety, and these will submit summary reports and recommendations. Some are voted on by the General Assembly to be adopted as resolutions. The OIV thus maintains a positive list of 106 products in use, and anything not listed is prohibited, unlike negative lists with a more "liberal" approach, whereby anything not mentioned is *de facto* authorized. Products, techniques and maximum doses are strictly regulated, and it takes several years for a new technique to be approved by the OIV and then ratified by European and national legislative bodies. In 2016, for example, the OIV voted to distinguish between additives (substances added and intentionally incorporated into the final product) and technological adjuvants (substances added and remaining present in the final product unintentionally but inevitably); no distinction had previously been drawn. This difference was ratified by the European Commission in 2019 to apply labelling rules to wine where there had previously been none.

A step toward obligatory labelling

Ever since 1889 and France's Griffe law, wine has been one of the most regulated food products from production to sale and consumption. Paradoxically, though, until very recently it was one of the rare exceptions that was not obliged to list its ingredients on the label. Labelling is a fundamental aspect of wine law to protect consumers, yet until 2023, only information related to the conformity and traceability of the wines had to be indicated on European labels. These are: category denomination; % alcohol by volume; provenance; volume; name and address of bottler; lot number; sulphites (if above 10mg/l); a health warning for pregnant women; and sugar content for sparkling wines – along with optional additional information including vintage, cépage, sugar content for non-sparkling wines, traditional details or information relating to production methods, geographical indication, company name and symbols relating to quality. There was no list of ingredients, however, either for wine or any other alcoholic drink.

This situation, which had been deliberately maintained by a number of professional wine organizations under the pretext that consumers would probably misunderstand it,

risking a drop in consumption, undoubtedly contributed to the criticism surrounding the composition of wine, the dangers it posed, and its "artificiality". Bowing to demands from consumer associations, and wishing to harmonize with the Codex Alimentarius, the European Commission announced the end of this exemption in 2017. The most recent Common Agricultural Policy (CAP 2023–27) requires nutritional information and ingredients to feature on the label or to be accessible via a QR code for all wine sold in Europe from December 2023.

Two visions of wine

Oenological technologies are in fact based on natural phenomena that they intensify and/or accelerate, ensuring higher quality and greater production efficiency because they are able to make corrections to occasionally defective raw materials. By the same token, however, could it then not be

> 66 Until December 2023, wine was one of the rare products that was not obliged to list its ingredients on the label in the EU

said that oenology is standardizing wine, even distorting it out of all recognition, in this use of increasingly space-age technologies? It is now technically possible to change the molecular composition of a wine, to extract its constituent elements and reassemble them as one wishes, to guarantee consistency and mitigate variations in the pursuit of agro-industrial interests. Scientists are now also able to take advantage of more and more external products, and oenological additives have become significant factors in the competition between large parts of the wine industry, including manufacturers. But with oenological science in constant evolution, with the aim of improving both the quality of wine and the productivity of its manufacturing process, at what point can these new procedures be acknowledged as legitimate? Here, the questions of the quality and the authenticity of the wine must be considered, and there are two opposing approaches.

- In one corner, there is the notion of wine that is "healthy, reliable and merchantable", according to the law passed in 1999 defining wine suitable for consumption in France. This replaced a commercial law of 1905 on "local, trusted and consistent techniques in the manufacture, storage and sale of drinks". Wine is defined by its manufacturing process and its final state.
- In the other, there is an approach linked to terroir and the skills of the wine-grower within a corpus of oenological practices regulated by a positive list that gives most weight to the final composition of the product, which need be no more than compatible with the wine's non-harmful nature and consumer demand.

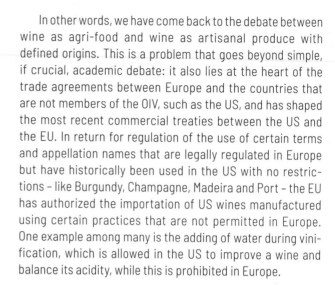

Émile Peynaud and the oenology of tomorrow

"The goal that modern oenology has set itself is to reach a point where wine no longer has to be treated, or at most has to undergo a simple process of clarification." Peynaud recounts in his *Vin et les jours* (1988) how an Italian winemaker once asked his advice on making better wines. He was already doing everything that was permitted at the time, such as adding sugar, tartrates, citric acid, bentonite, gelatine, ferrocyanide, charcoal, gum Arabic, ascorbic acid and tannins, using a centrifuge, inoculating yeast, clarifying with finings and flash pasteurization. Peynaud answered, "If you want to make good wine, forget all these brutal procedures and use no more than a little sulphurized wick and a little air when racking; some clarification for red wines with a few egg whites, filtration of white wines after the cold of winter, and that is enough. Great wines are delicate – the less we do to them, the better they are and the better off we are." Having advocated for harvesting only the best grapes when they were ripe – for more supple tannins, and for hygiene in wineries and barrels at the many estates where he was brought in as a consultant – he attracted accusations of "Peynaudization", but he revolutionized the quality of wines, many of which had been incapable of expressing their origins. He was one of the first "flying winemakers", dealing with more than a hundred estates in Bordeaux and around the world as his influence became international. He refused to standardize, however, seeing oenologists as those who would help by correcting and preventing faults but, above all, by uncovering the potential of a terroir. Peynaud was already issuing a battle cry for the oenology of tomorrow several decades ago. "The new doctrine for vinification is as follows: to make wines that preserve the taste of the original grapes, right into the glass, whatever the age of the wine... Fundamental quality is acquired in the vineyard."

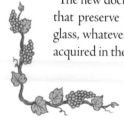

In other words, we have come back to the debate between wine as agri-food and wine as artisanal produce with defined origins. This is a problem that goes beyond simple, if crucial, academic debate: it also lies at the heart of the trade agreements between Europe and the countries that are not members of the OIV, such as the US, and has shaped the most recent commercial treaties between the US and the EU. In return for regulation of the use of certain terms and appellation names that are legally regulated in Europe but have historically been used in the US with no restrictions – like Burgundy, Champagne, Madeira and Port – the EU has authorized the importation of US wines manufactured using certain practices that are not permitted in Europe. One example among many is the adding of water during vinification, which is allowed in the US to improve a wine and balance its acidity, while this is prohibited in Europe.

Quality is a matter of convention

The question of quality is part and parcel of vinification and consumption. As Alessandro Stanziani, director of research at the Centre National de la Recherche Scientifique (CNRS) and a specialist in the history of both food and competition, has suggested, the quality of a wine "is less to do with the essential characteristics of products and more a matter of a complex interplay of economic agents whose interests sometimes overlap but are often incompatible, and... the quality associated with maintenance of tradition was invented at the turn of the century, at precisely the moment when agro-chemical progress was first challenging the traditional definitions of agricultural and natural products." (*La falsification du vin en France, 1880-1905: un cas de fraude agrialimentaire*, 2003).

This interplay of influences was in full swing at the dawn of the 20th century and remains so today in international trade deals, the question of labelling and pressure from various lobbies. Opposition between local or traditional interests and the internationalization of markets is nothing new, but the increasing interest in wine and the issues it embodies with its unique position in the agri-food industry lend it an unprecedented dimension. Is "authentic" wine one that exhibits a constant, average quality corresponding to predetermined standards, or as an agricultural product, should it not instead embody its geographical and natural origins and reflect its inevitable variations as they are brought out with human skill? The question is not an either/or, however; much like the definition of terroir, it is a sliding scale reflecting the interests of a large number of actors – but oenologists are certainly involved in the debate.

A defect – or a characteristic?

If there is one wine that is legendary, it has to be 1947 Château Cheval Blanc, a Saint-Émilion *grand cru* whose sweetness and pronounced balsamic notes are evidence of a rapid harvest in a sunny year, with fermentation that was not without its difficulties. Château Beaucastel 1990 is a similarly legendary wine; this remarkable Châteauneuf-du-Pape vintage is renowned for using 13 local cépages, for its terroir of pebbles and for its smoky notes. However, it also exhibits levels of 4-ethylphenol that are so high as to suggest strong involvement of *Brettanomyces* in its organoleptic profile. Indeed, its levels of Brett, not to mention acetic acid and phenols, would be unacceptable by current oenological standards – and yet these defects make up the personalities of these wines. Just as a medicine can become a poison, how and why can an element of a wine's character become a fault? How does organoleptic alteration come about in a wine? Is it always absolute, or is there cultural relativity among "defects"?

Defects in wine are almost inevitable

The question of defects in wine is not a simple matter. More than ever before, oenological laboratories are able to use chemical or spectrographic analysis, DNA sequencing or gas chromatography to identify the majority of the components of a wine; mass spectrometry can detect molecules and microbial populations even at trace level. However, as Jamie Goode points out in one of his books on the subject (*Flawless: Understanding Faults in Wine*, 2018), the problem of defects in wine goes far beyond the chemistry and microbiology of wine, touching instead on human perception and value judgments. So just what is a defect, exactly?

By its very nature, wine is a variable product of incredibly complex composition: with cépage, vintage, terroir, fermentation phenomena, ageing, laying down and human decision-making in the mix, the quality of wine is almost by definition unpredictable and unstable, unless the must is sterilized and vinified like an agro-industrial product. On a certain scale, it is this very variability that makes wine interesting, in fact – consider the oxidation-reduction phenomenon responsible for a wine's particularly sought-after tertiary aromas. However, certain molecules, when present at levels beyond a threshold set by authorities that may be scientific, political, professional or cultural, are considered a defect. They overpower the other compounds and distort the nuances of the unique expression of terroir, cépage and vintage. So what are these compounds, and under what conditions do they appear?

Chronology and classification of defects

A wine may have any number of potential defects, and these can occur at any stage in production, from vine to bottle. A distinction can be drawn between faults directly linked to winemaking practices, which are caused by potentially overlapping physical and biochemical processes, and faults arising from external contamination, such as smoke from a fire. One way of arranging these is by the order in which they appear during vinification, as attempted by oenologist Jean-Michel Monnier in his *Vin au fil des saisons. Un an dans le costume d'un oenologue* (2022). This a short summary, and the elements within it are expanded upon in research by Goode and Monnier, as well as on the Australian Wine Research Institute (AWRI) website, which is at the cutting edge of these questions, with solutions to correct and prevent these deficiencies.

Defects associated with harvesting

The first defects to appear are found on the vine: fungal disease, insects, climatic conditions during the year and treatments that have been used may all affect the quality of the grapes and thus be problematic, especially if the harvest and grape-sorting are not carried out with care. Besides the herbaceous odours associated with under-ripeness of grapes, the most critical tastes are linked to fungal disease: earthy, mouldy flavours in rainy years when grey mould (*Botrytis cinerea*) develops, and moulds with tastes ranging from cloves (eugenol) to musty. In particular, they can produce geosmin, a sesquiterpene with the scent of tilled earth and a very low detection threshold that was identified as a defect in wine in the early 2000s. Twenty per cent of the population are unable to smell it, however, and it is sometimes conflated with the taste of cork. Downy mildew and black rot can impart odours of iodine, fungus or even ivy.

> " The quality of wine is almost by definition unpredictable and unstable, unless the must is sterilized and vinified like an agro-industrial product

Insects commonly contaminate harvests: ladybirds crushed along with the grapes bolster concentrations of isopropyl-methoxy-pyrazine with notes of asparagus, while other insects are responsible for bitter mould.

Lastly, treatments applied to the vines – sulphur against botrytis, for example – can remain on the grapes, despite adhering to a very precise calendar for their use before harvesting, which will affect the wine, either organoleptically or by causing problems with fermentation.

Lastly, some defects arise from a wine or vine's environment, with the best known being the burned odour of smoke taint. During fires, volatile phenols become fixed in the the powdery coating, the bloom (or *pruine*) on the grape cuticle, and the sugars in the berries. If this occurs, the latter may release compounds such as guaiacol, 4-methyl-guaiacol and cresol during fermentation and ageing; these chemicals, which are also released by new wood but in lesser quantities, will overtake the wine with smoky, burned notes.

Another defect involves too great a concentration of cineole, which comes from the eucalyptus trees surrounding certain vineyards, especially in Australia and California; if the leaves are not carefully sorted and removed, they can find their way into the press, producing heady notes of camphor.

Defects associated with fermentation and ageing: acetic acid and ethyl acetate…

Oxygen and microbial action are to blame for the majority of defects appearing during vinification, often as a result of carelessness or poor hygiene in the winery. One of the most common defects is acetic acid, which forms in various ways and can appear in any wine as fermentation begins, in quantities that will vary depending on the yeast. It can appear during fermentation, when lactic bacteria produce it from sugars – this is lactic souring or afterward, when *Acetobacter* flora metabolizes ethanol (acetic souring) upon contact with air. Berries may also already be contaminated with bacteria, and in 2014, fruit flies were the cause of acetic rot in red grapes in parts of northern France. Acetic acid accounts for 95 per cent of volatile acidity, and depending on its concentration, it may lend depth to a wine or make it sour like vinegar and unsaleable. In Europe, there is a maximum threshold for the acid, expressed in equivalent grams per litre or in milliequivalents of sulphuric acid (H_2SO_4): 0.98g/l or 20mEq for reds, 0.88g/l or 18mEq for whites – a level that has been in force in France since 1921. Ethyl acetate is often associated with this acid; it is an ester of acetic acid and ethanol, and its aroma ranges from notes of glue and lacquer to full acescence. Other oxidation – such as of ethanol to form acetaldehyde, with notes of green apple, celery and nuts – is desirable in oxidative wines but less so in others. It binds with free SO_2, inhibiting its antioxidant and antimicrobial action.

… Brett and mouse…

If acidity and protection with SO_2 are low, with high levels of phenolic acids and alcohol and a poorly disinfected winery, undesirable micro-organisms such as *Brettanomyces* and *Pichia* may develop. These yeasts impair fruit aromas and metabolize volatile phenols that include 4-ethylphenol (4-EP; notes of leather, ink, stables) and 4-ethylguaiacol (4-EG; cloves), among others. They are very common and generally contaminate reds, more rarely affecting whites. A mousy flavour that can be tasted but not smelled was a historic defect that has recently reappeared in wines using fewer additives and SO_2, and it will depend on the pH of the taster's saliva, with wide variations from individual to individual. The finish of the wine may then be marked with aromas of anything from basmati rice to sausage, and even rodent urine. Lactic bacteria such as *Lactobacillus*, *Oenococcus oeni* and *Pediococcus* will sometimes occur in tandem with Brett to metabolize pyridines such as ATHP, ETHP and APY. While these molecules have been identified, the mechanisms through which they appear and disappear, and how the phenomenon might be treated, are still being studied. Lactic bacteria can also produce strong concentrations of biogenic amines that are undesirable and problematic for health, including histamine, which can provoke allergic symptoms, tyramine, and putrescine, which smells like a corpse. They are also responsible for bitter wine (known in France as *maladie de l'amer*), which is caused by the breakdown of glycerol; for "fat" wines (*maladie de la graisse*), caused by the production of glucan; and for *maladie de la tourne*, a breakdown of tartaric acid that causes precipitation upon contact with air. These affect both the structure and the aromas of a wine.

… reduction and oxidation

Reduction is often described as the opposite of oxidation, but the chemistry of both is more complex than that, and a wine can be reduced and oxidized at the same time.

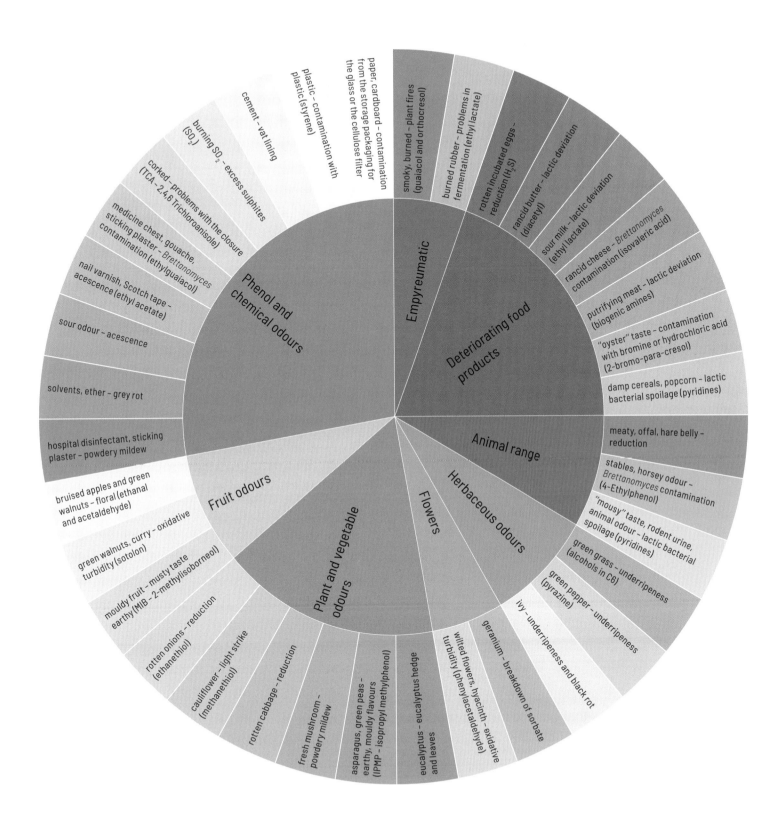

JEAN-MICHEL MONNIER'S WHEEL OF WINE FAULTS (2022)

Volatile acidity – when wine becomes unfit for sale

Initially an issue of interest only to professionals, volatile acidity has become a talking point for the wider public in the 21st century. It involves two different molecules: acetic acid, which turns wine into vinegar, and ethyl acetate with its acescent notes of lacqueur. When levels in Europe exceed the ceiling (20 mEq/l for red wines, with some exemptions if the wine is stronger than 13% alcohol by volume), the wine is declared unsaleable. This is precisely what happened to Bourgueil wine-maker Sébastien David, who was commanded by the Direction Générale de la Concurrence, de la Consommation et de la Répression des Fraudes (DGCCRF), France's regulatory body, to withdraw a batch of his 2016 vintage from the market and destroy it because its levels of volatile acidity were too high, according to the authority's analyses. The matter – and the winemaker's protests – attracted much media attention, but even though counter-analysis had indicated that the levels were not excessive, and despite the economic consequences for the estate, the judgment was upheld. This decision raises questions about the validity of such a threshold when the molecule does not present a health risk. Should it now be re-evaluated, given that low-intervention winemaking is on the rise, using riper grapes that are more likely to contain these compounds? There are some classic wines that even make a virtue of them to balance their power, such as Amarone della Valpolicella. This is a question worthy of debate.

Reduction, and its musty odours, is the result of volatile sulphurized compounds caused by residues of sulphurized products on grapes, by yeasts with low nitrogen levels, or by other complex phenomena. Some of these odours are desirable, like flinty notes from disulphane in Chardonnay, citrus-fruit notes from the thiols in Sauvignon, black-fruit aromas from dimethylsulphide in red wines; others are less so, including hydrogen sulphide (H_2S), mercaptan, methionol, methanethiol and ethanethiol, listed here in ascending order of unpleasantness. Diacetyl, which is produced by lactic bacteria from citric acid during malolactic fermentation, can also range from attractive hazelnut and cream, to repellent rancid butter, and it may react with cysteine (an amino acid) to give notes of popcorn much sought after for some white wines, but here too there is a permeable membrane between negative and positive, between chemistry and perception. Contamination may also arise from winemaking materials, like the epoxy used for vats, and filtration agents, or even from an excess of SO_2, which should be handled with care because of its toxicity.

Defects associated with laying down

The best-known defect in wine arising from laying down is the taste of cork taint, which affects roughly three per cent of wines worldwide, according to the Cork Quality Council, which is also responsible for cork promotion. The threshold of perception is extremely low – imagine a single drop of water in an Olympic swimming pool – and several kinds of contamination are possible, depending on the source and the offending molecule. Cork is the main culprit, but the wine may also be altered by wood used in the winery or the barrel, which can contaminate whole batches that have never even seen a cork. Three molecules have been identified:

- **TCA (2,4,6-Trichloroanisole)** notes of mouldy card-board, which is present in 70 per cent of cases, and in more than 9 cases out of 10 is the fault of the cork.
- **TeCA (2,3,4,6-Tetrachloroanisole)** odour of rotting wood.
- **TBA (2,4,6-Tribromoanisole)** phenolic notes.

These are synthesized by moulds acting on chlorophenols or tribromophenols derived from the chlorine, insecticides and other products used to treat wood. The wine is irreparably contaminated and only preventative solutions are currently of any use. These include risk-free closures such as capsules, carefully monitored corks, the use of untreated wood and so on; trials of absorbant plastic films are under way but are not currently widespread. This defect remains a major concern for the entire industry.

Apart from possible contamination associated with bottling – oxidation, for example – the final defects to mention are light strike and the effects of temperature. The former affects products in transparent bottles, including spirits, because certain light wavelengths metabolize the amino acids in sulphur compounds, imparting a taste of onions and turning the wine brown. The latter causes premature ageing of the wine and occurs if a bottle is stored at more than 20°C (68°F) for a certain period and there have been wide variations in temperature over time.

Defect, beauty – and *wabi-sabi*

Scientific research can now explain the vast majority of defects in wine, with specialist centres in Adelaide and Bordeaux, for example, determining the thresholds of perception and helping to set upper limits for wines to be marketed. The science of oenology incorporates these findings into professional training courses, and this has all made a major contribution to a global improvement in quality by limiting risk factors as much as possible for most producers.

Should every defect be viewed negatively, however? Goode actively addresses this question in the positive connotations of the title of his book *Flawless*. He suggests that "the presence of a flaw in a wine does not necessarily make a wine flawed", and cites the Japanese aesthetic of *wabi-sabi*, which appreciates the fleeting, transient beauty revealed by imperfect nuances. Within certain limits, defects can indeed make a wine more complex, interesting and appealing. Just as ambergris, which is repulsive in high concentrations, applies the finishing touch to a perfume, volatile acidity plays the same role for the 1947 Cheval Blanc or for Musar, to take another example cited by Goode. The relentless hunt for flaws risks throwing out the baby with the bathwater, especially with a product as complex and shifting as wine. A flaw is a flaw only in context.

Is it just a question of convention here as well?
Such a context will include both the product and the moment of tasting, not to mention the culture within which it has been produced. A defect in one style of wine is to be positively encouraged in another: an excess of diacetyl, with its buttery taste, is undesirable in a white Sancerre but sought after in a California Chardonnay, for example. Genetically, not everyone has the same sensory perception threshold. Indeed, there are some who lack any ability to smell or taste certain molecules (anosmia or ageusia, respectively) – so those who can't taste cork taint, a flaw that is objectively a defect, can enjoy a corked bottle.

Professionals are not always unanimous in detecting and identifying defects in a wine. While there may be a consensus on certain levels and compounds, lived experience is generally far more complex, and the upper boundaries are often not as clear-cut. The cognitive aspect of tasting is informed by context and experience and cannot be ignored; a palate may be desensitized to certain compounds, or there may be cultural considerations or adaptations, or even a lack of experience, so identification of flaws is anything but universal.

There are of course prohibitive defects that essentially transform the wine, such as turning it to vinegar or *maladie de la tourne*, and others that can be quantified, but standards and tastes evolve over time. Who is to decide when a characteristic becomes a defect? Is the quality of a wine no more than an absence of flaws? Does "healthy, reliable and merchantable" just mean sterilized? Is the essence of wine not being discarded in favour of some standardized, grape-based alcoholic drink? As with the quality of a wine being defined by its origins, here too it is a question of conventions that purport to be more or less objective, according to criteria that may be scientific or legislative and arise from particular interest groups and specific aesthetic pronouncements – as has been ably demonstrated by the evolution of wine tasting over the centuries.

The phenomenon of premature oxidation

At the turn of the millennium, people tasting fine Burgundy Chardonnays began to notice that certain bottles from the previous decade – the 1995 and 1996 in particular – were exhibiting hints of ageing that were unexpected after such a short period of time, including brown coloration, fruity, sometimes *rancio* tastes, and lowered acidity; wines with historic potential for laying down and ageing were proving almost still-born. In the space of just a few years, the phenomenon of premox (premature oxidation) was to crop up in a number of white and sparkling wines of all styles, geographical origins and cépages, in a completely random fashion. While some causes have now been identified, not every mechanism is perfectly understood. These may include changes in the climate or winemaking techniques, reduced use of SO_2, over-exposure of the wine to O_2, modifications made to wine presses, diminished extraction of phenolic compounds and the quality of corks or glass, or it may be that these tastes and notes favoured young wines that were more ready to drink. The underlying question is of the essential ageing of wine, of the balance between its oxidizable and oxidized compounds and the antioxidants that ultimately come from the grape and that vinification can only attempt to preserve. How are they formed within the berry? This is a further mystery that emphasizes the essential links between wine quality, terroir and winemaking practices.

TASTING WINE

Wine tasting tells a story of expertise and quality

Although scientific analysis has become an essential tool in guaranteeing the saleability of wines and in combating fraud (isotopic analysis can be used to identify a wine's place or year of origin), tasting remains an essential part of judging quality. It is impossible to enjoy a wine without using the senses, but to taste properly it must be possible to isolate a sensation, identify and describe it, and thus apply a grid of descriptors that have been corroborated with other tasters. While tasting for pleasure is an ancient practice, expert analysis has evolved over time and witnessed changes in techniques, fashions, markets and interests. Improvement in the quality of wine is undoubtedly a function of technical, ampelographic and scientific progress, but it is also driven by changes in approaches to tasting, since it is this that sets the bar, establishing objective standards and applying them to rate wines for marketable quality and typicity. How has tasting evolved over the past century? What are its aims and objectives? Who actually tastes wine – oenologists, merchants, sommeliers, enthusiasts, critics, collectors? Why do they do it, and what criteria are applied? And how has tasting come to reinforce a positive notion of terroir?

Tasting for pleasure and for experts

As Axel Marchal – an oenology researcher and course leader for the diploma in tasting skills, the Diplôme Universitaire d'Aptitude à la Dégustation (DUAD) – at Bordeaux University, explains: "Wine is born twice: once in the tran formation from grape into wine, and once again in the mind of the person who tastes it. Hitherto, oenology has taken a great interest in this first birth, the composition of wine, but we are now launching a pioneering project that will unite two fields. . . neurosciences, with the Neuro-Magendie Centre, and oenology, with the ISVV. The aim of this collaboration. . . is to better understand what goes on in a person's brain when they taste wine – in other words, to lift the veil on the mechanisms of wine's second birth." While a topic of only recent interest to researchers, tasting is as old as the drink itself, with the elites of the Near East enjoying and differentiating wines more than five thousand years ago. The Latin term was *degustatio* (from *degustare*, "to taste"), but "wine tasting" seems to have appeared only in 1519 and was little used until the end of the 18th century, moving away from the notion of simple consumption to signify ingestion with care to appreciate, verify and enjoy the characteristics of a product.

By its very nature, wine has encouraged an ever-more analytical approach over the centuries. The tastings for pleasure practised by enthusiasts since time immemorial – "I like this", "I don't like that", and the reasons why – proved to be inadequate for wines that had been demanding a more reasoned approach from the very outset, unlike other foods and drinks that have been tasted analytically only recently. Empirical frameworks for evaluating beer, coffee, tea and even chocolate and cheese really date no further back than the end of the 19th century. However, the analytical grid of wine tasting as a deliberate act of codified sensory evaluation to categorize sensations and express them with specialized vocabulary has its roots in ancient Greece.

The appreciation of wine in ancient Greece

"One smells of violets, the other of roses, and yet another of hyacinths. . ."; "a wine with neither sweetness nor fullness, restrained and dry, with remarkable power. . ." These tasting notes, which sound as if they could have flowed from the pen of American critic Robert Parker, are respectively the work of Hermippus, a poet of Old Comedy from the 5th century BCE, and Eparchides, a historian from the 2nd or 3rd century BCE.

It is to Thibaut Boulay, a winemaker in Sancerre who holds a PhD in Ancient History, that we owe our understanding of the points of resemblance and fundamental differences between our approach to wine tasting and the Classical world's (*Wine Appreciation in Ancient Greece*, 2015). During this period, wine was not only a commercial good, an object of pleasure and a token of social recognition, it was also an essential component of a person's diet and wellbeing. While the ancient Greeks appreciated wine three ways with a visual, olfactory and gustatory examination and served it in a precisely codified manner, with specific glassware and at specific temperatures, it was not until the Classical period that they refined their vocabulary to fall in line with the theories of the fathers of medicine, Empedocles and Hippocrates. The former defined the four elements of matter (earth, water, air and fire), while the latter described the elemental qualities deriving from these (hot or cold, dry or humid) and developed his theory of the humours and temperaments: blood linked with air, phlegm with water, yellow bile with fire, and black bile with earth. These laid the foundations for medicine until the Renaissance. The wine reserved for banquets would thus be enjoyed for its intrinsic qualities as defined by this approach and for its medicinal properties, although both physicians and philosophers were aware of the differences in perception between individuals and sought to clarify the semantics of the descriptors. Aristotle defined the eight basic tastes as a continuum that ran from bitter to sweet via salty, sour, pungent, astringent, rough and oily, and the

Graeco-Roman approach to organoleptic and expert wine tasting was synthesized in the writings of Galen, a physician of the 2nd century CE.

Wine tasting according to Galen

Galen contended that the diversity of wine meant that five-stage analysis was necessary: colour first, then taste, constitution, bouquet and relative strength, or "quality".

> " Wine is born twice: once in the transformation from grape into wine, and once again in the mind of the person who tastes it

- The sense of **sight** was used to determine colours of wine, of which there were five main shades, graded from cold to hot. Galen goes on to describe their nuances and intensity, as well as their purity, or absence or presence of sediment, their transparency and brilliance. Colour is of secondary importance in confirming the therapeutic quality of a wine, but it anticipates qualitative appreciation in the mouth.
- **Taste** is based on a synthesis of the theories of Empedocles, Hippocrates and Aristotle, refined with the notions of rhythm and tonality drawn from the musical theory formulated by Pythagoras. Wine is thus judged on the harmony of its flavours on a spectrum running from sweet (*glukus*) to bitter (*pikros*), taking in sharp (*drimus*), astringent (*austeros*), harsh (*struphnos*), acid (*oxus*) and salty (*halmuros*), to which Aristotle further adds unctuous (*liparos*).
- **Constitution** (*sustasis*), in which volume and texture combine with aromas and are judged according to mouthfeel: alcohol is full-bodied, acid is sharp, astringency warms the palate. This suggests that there is a somatosensory dimension here – in other words, sensations coming from different parts of the body (pressure, heat and so on) are used metaphorically According to Galen, "Depending on their constitution, wines can be divided into aqueous and fluid, or fairly full-bodied, with a median stage of no distinct quality between these two categories, of course, as well as those intermediate between the middle and the extremes" (*Commentary on the Hippocratic Epidemics*). Wine was considered light (*kouphos*), rough (*skleros*), dry (*xeros*), full-bodied (*pachus*) and so on.
- Lastly, relative strength, or **quality** (*dunamis*), which involves the structure, dry extracts, alcohol and so on, and indicate the wine's potential for ageing, along with the concentration of grapes at harvest. The strongest are the *oinodes* and the lightest are aqueous (*hudatodes*).

The vocabulary is limited as far as odour is concerned: wine may be pleasant (*edus*) or not (*luperon*), with an odour of quality (*euosmos*) or none (*aosmoi*). Galen maintains that odours derive from aromas and that these are difficult to

Degree of pleasure	Tastes (Greek)	Tastes (Latin)	Tastes (French)	Tastes (English)	Elements	Elemental qualities	Humours
Most pleasant	τὸ γλυκύ	dulcis	doux	sweet			
	τὸ λιπαρόν	pinguis	onctueux	oily, smooth	Air	hot and humid	blood
	τὸ δριμύ	acer	âcre, piquant	acrid, pungent, sharp			
	τὸ αὐστηρόν	austerus	astringent	astringent	Fire	hot and dry	yellow bile
	τὸ στρυφνόν	acerbus	âpre, acerbe	harsh			
	τὸ ὀξύ	acidus	acide	acid, sour	Earth	cold and dry	black bile
	τὸ ἁλμυρόν	salsus	salé	salty			
Least pleasant	τὸ πικρόν	amarus	amer	bitter	Water	cold and humid	phlegm

THE GREEK SPECTRUM OF TASTES ACCORDING TO THIBAULT BOULAY

pin down; there is occasional identification of secondary aromas from vinification and tertiary aromas from ageing, and sometimes even primary aromas from the cépage itself, but the bouquet does not play a fundamental role in general appreciation of wine. This lack of interest, which is shared by any number of scholars from the ancient world, was to have consequences. The semantics of smell were to be relegated to a minor role for centuries, which in part explains the lack of a specific vocabulary for odours in Western societies; we find ourselves obliged to reach for metaphors and analogies to express our olfactory perceptions.

In addition to his medical skills, Galen was a great lover of wine, and his writings, including *On the Nature and Powers of Simple Medications*, demonstrate the use of an immediately understandable and precise vocabulary along with spatial and anthropomorphic metaphors to acknowledge the enjoyable and therapeutic qualities of wine and determine its origins. Boulay glosses it thus: "Unlike wine that is weak and lacking in nutrition (*atrophos*), potent (*dunamikos*) wine is nourishing. Particularly rich in dry matter, it was qualified as thick or plump (*pachus*) or even as 'fleshy' (*sarkōdēs*), benefiting from a generous alcohol level and procuring a sensation of density, strength and warmth (the *aithops* wine of Homer is both dark in colour and glittering). Other anthropomorphic metaphors were frequently deployed: a wine that possessed the potential to become *dunamikos* was then qualified as 'robust' (*ischuros*). Warmer and more nourishing, the old rich wines could be diluted with more water" ("Tastes of Wine: Sensorial Wine Analysis in Ancient Greece", in *Taste and the Ancient Senses*, edited by Kelli C Rudolph, 2017).

Graeco-Roman wine tasting is little known but impressively modern; it was not until the mid-20th century that such a level of precision and richness of vocabulary was to return. In the meantime, this knowledge was gradually forgotten in the wake of barbarian invasions, obscurantism and less importance being attached to wine's therapeutic values, so that such precision was no longer required. Tasting notes became terse at best, and it was not until the 19th century that a renewed interest was shown in the semantics of organoleptic enquiry, as manifested in the works of C Redding, H Vizetelly, A Jullien et al. – with no gains in analytical precision, however.

Wine tasting – out of the hands of physicians, into the hands of merchants

Analytical criteria are ultimately driven by the purpose of wine tasting and the interests of those involved, as has been amply demonstrated by historian Olivier Jacquet, who has researched how the torch was passed on in sensory wine tasting from the end of the 19th century (*Le goût des vins d'origine*, 2024). During this period, wine would no longer be tasted by physicians, and although winemakers produced wine, they rarely bottled and sold it directly, so its evaluation was left to the merchants and brokers who blended it for sale under geographical or commercial brand names. Analytical tools and criteria were thus adapted to their approach, which involved the use of a *tastevin*, a flat-bottomed metal cup, as they rooted around in dark cellars, trying to check if the wine was clear, tipping their heads forward to taste it – it was mainly about mouthfeel. Turbidity arising from the presence of sediment would make it unsaleable, if it had turned or was likely to do so. What they were looking for in a wine was the greatest suitability for blending, so structure was the main criterion, because it held the key: whether the base wine was delicate, firm, acid, alcohol-rich or whatever else, the merchants would create blends based on the particular make-up of each batch to suit specific types and markets. A wine sold under the Gevrey brand would be more powerful than a Volnay, for example.

Bouquet was hardly ever described, tending mainly to be a value judgment (pleasant or not), and the vocabulary used was thus generally very limited. Even though such a thing had been known to the ancient world, there was a marked absence of what Jacquet has called "collective sensory canons" – terms from the world beyond wine that are used by analogy but understood by all, making it possible for anyone to find their bearings among smells and aromas. Jacquet mentions the hazelnuts of Meursault, the blackcurrants of Chambertin, the violets of Hermitage and the raspberries of Saumur, but these are rare and extremely limited examples compared to our contemporary descriptors. As a final note, he mentions another canon, that of terroir, but this had negative connotations of an earthy taste that should be avoided at all cost in fine wines.

Oenologists revolutionize tasting

This tasting by merchants continued into the first half of the 20th century. Despite the appearance of a new generation of tasters. such as gourmets, gastronomic clubs, journalists, critics and the sommeliers who had emerged from their cellars and made their way into restaurant dining rooms, analysis remained very telegraphic in style, and Jacquet cites an example of such commentary from the *La Revue du vin de France* of 1964 in reference to a 1949 Château Lafite-Rothschild: "finesse, distinction and elegance, the usual qualities of this *grand cru*, are not lacking. Still a trifle tannic. At its peak. Should remain so for several years."

It was to be the oenologists who had brought about a technological revolution in the quality of wine who ultimately initiated evolution in wine tasting in the 1920s; faults had to be identified so they could be corrected. They began to use collective sensory canons ("dry taste", "bitter mould", "rotten") to describe defects, but these were always essentially related to the mouth rather than the nose. Jean Ribéreau-Gayon and Peynaud accelerated this progress between the wars, more precisely describing certain organoleptic criteria such as alcohol, acidity and SO_2, but linking their chemistry merely to characteristics of touch, and evoking only "fat", "vinosity", "harshness" and so on. The rare odours and aromas that were mentioned were associated with defects.

The role of the AOC

A transformation of expert tasting in the 20th century came about with the introduction of new production and marketing standards and the creation of the *appellations d'origine contrôlée* (AOCs). Winemakers, who were gradually turning from wine wholesale to retail, were first in line, because they had to learn how to taste wine in order to guarantee its quality and typicity, but no one did more to revolutionize approaches to tasting than INAO, which oversaw

> " Graeco-Roman wine tasting is little known but impressively modern

regulation of the AOC system. The stakes were high: for the system to work, it had to prove that AOC wines possessed unique "essential qualities" that made them far better than branded wines; they had to stand out through their unique link to their origins. These organo-leptic characteristics, arising by their very nature from the terroir, were to be identified as the true guarantors of quality, typicity and authenticity, and it had to be possible to taste them, differentiate between them and discuss them.

AOCs accounted for less than six per cent of wine sales in France during the 1940s, however, and in 1943, in a move that rapidly attracted support from certain AOCs, Joseph Capus, president of the national committee that in 1947 was to become INAO, decided to introduce approval tastings to check compliance with the standards for each appellation. The practice was blocked by the Ministry of Justice, which refused to make it compulsory, but was voluntarily intro-duced first in Bordeaux, then Muscadet and Burgundy. The objective was obviously to promote the AOCs' image of quality and establish a link between the wines' characteristics and their place of origin, while also resolving the problem of how to demarcate the appellation areas. However, they soon ran into a major problem. The vocabulary was very dated and incapable of describing the wines precisely enough to tell them apart; expert tasters were unable to settle the turf war over the extent of the Chablis area because they were forced to admit they could not unambiguously distinguish between Chablis from Kimmeridgian soils and Chablis grown on Portland limestone. The old terminology of 1959 was unsuitable to tell if wines were typical of their terroir, and it was not until the next decade that a new approach to tasting would emerge that was capable of distinguishing the substantial quality of a wine's typicity.

Wine tasting by Jules Chauvet

Jules Chauvet was an exceptional taster, a talent he employed throughout his life in a quest to understand wine better. As a scientist, merchant, winemaker and gourmet with close links to the greatest chefs of this time, such as Fernand Point and Alain Chapel, he turned tasting into a vocation in which enjoyment informed expertise, and vice versa. His works were little read even, though they shed light on contemporary questions, and his tasting notes, which were so pioneering, still seem to be remarkably up to date, with a synthesis of analysis and enjoyment and a use of geosensorial tasting.

Saint-Julien, Médoc Grand Cru Classé, Château Beychevelle, 1946
(tasted in front of the hotel schools in May 1952)
Wine made mostly from Cabernet Sauvignon grapes grown on poor, gravelly, siliceous soils with a clayey subsoil. The 1946 vintage of Bordeaux reds tends to present with very decent average quality.

1. Colour: beautiful garnet coloration.

2. Strict olfactory impression:
- reminiscent of truffle (a scent arising from bottle-ageing)
- spicy and herbal notes from the green parts of the vine (aromas arising from vinification)
- resin (aromatic substance from the Cabernet Sauvignon plant)
- liquorice or catechu (tannic, introduced by the plant or during vinification)
- fine Oriental tobacco; ambergris derived from incense (scent of reduction, which appears only with bottle-ageing)
- violets (the grape already has this scent)
- seems to be a slight hint of rose (siliceous soil)
- lastly, a herbal aroma from the green parts of the vine, second harmonic (resulting from vinification).

3. Overall impression or olfactory form: expansive, even blossoming, although limited by the tannic element; this overall olfactory impression allows us to anticipate the taste of the wine.

4. Strict taste impression: the wine spreads nicely through the mouth but quickly collects itself, first impressing the tip of the tongue and then, almost simultaneously, the base of the tongue (with its bitterness). Its ultimate form is reminiscent of a crown or ring.

5. Aromatic taste:
- liquorice, catechu (tannic)
- resin
- violets.

The olfactory impression is along the same lines as the sensation of form: taking these together allows us to conclude that the wine's harmony is incomplete because of this discontinuity in the sensation of taste (the emptiness of the crown) and the dominant tannins that eclipse other elements. The wine is representative of its type and will benefit from a few more years of bottle age.

Jules Chauvet, "Quelques wines dégustés en public" in *Jules Chauvet ou le Talent du vin* (1997)

EARLY STAGE OF DEVELOPMENT

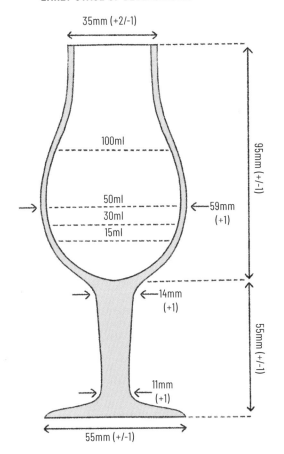

35mm (+2/-1)

100ml

50ml
30ml

15ml

59mm (+1)

95mm (+/-1)

14mm (+1)

55mm (+/-1)

11mm (+1)

55mm (+/-1)

FINAL VERSION

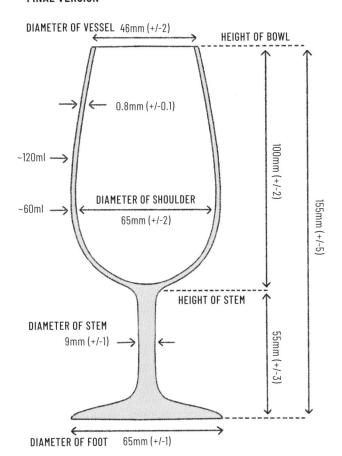

DIAMETER OF VESSEL 46mm (+/-2)

HEIGHT OF BOWL

0.8mm (+/-0.1)

~120ml

DIAMETER OF SHOULDER

~60ml

65mm (+/-2)

100mm (+/-2)

155mm (+/-5)

HEIGHT OF STEM

DIAMETER OF STEM

9mm (+/-1)

55mm (+/-3)

DIAMETER OF FOOT 65mm (+/-1)

THE INAO'S STANDARDIZED AFNOR GLASS

The work done by Jules Chauvet and André Vedel helped toward the creation of the first standardized tasting glass, the AFNOR, adopted by France's INAO as its standard glass in 1970.

The major influence exerted by Jules Chauvet

Although INAO had set up tasting commissions by 1954, these had no truly objective analytical methods until the end of the 1960s, when Chauvet's theoretical work was put into practice. This Beaujolais merchant and qualified chemist is best known as the father of the natural-wine movement, because of his sulphur-free vinification, but he was also instrumental in developing the way we taste wine today. Having written essays on the mechanisms of tasting, the physical chemistry of aromas and even glassmaking since the 1950s, Chauvet, who had an exceptional sense of smell, made use of his experience with perfume-makers in Grasse and a host of experiments with Beaujolais wines to develop scientific and sensory analytical procedures that concentrated on bouquet. Within just a few years, his work had "completely reshaped. . . the practice of wine tasting and

provided new tools capable of distinguishing between very similar appellations" (Jacquet, "Le Goût du terroir. . . histoire d'une prescription internationale au XXe siècle", in *Territoires du vin*, 2021) by referring to collective sensory canons like truffle, apricot, peppermint or kirsch, and improving the older descriptors for structure revised by the Bordeaux school; thanks to its members, the "negative" taste of terroir had become a positive quality, the typicity of each wine arising from its unique origins. This was compounded by a desire to move away from vague vocabulary that was sometimes freighted with unwanted connotations, like "masculine", "elegant", "naive" or ""thin", toward more analytical terms.

Despite lacking the scientific underpinning of other experts of the period, such as Peynaud, Chauvet's works were widely read and within 15 years had been complemented by studies conducted by other INAO engineers; the 1966

ENERGY					
1	Intensity	Absent	Weak	Perceptible	Strong	Powerful
2	Life	Dead	Tired	Alive	Vibrant	Exuberant
3	Luminosity	Cold				Warm

SALIVATION					
7	Quality	Defensive		Neutral		Welcoming
8	Intensity	Null	Weak	Moderate	Strong	Extreme
9	Location	Tip and middle of the tongue		Sides of the tongue		Back of the tongue

GEOMETRY					
12	Direction	↕ Vertical		↔ Horizontal		📶 Radiating
13	Shape	△ Sharp	— Broad		☐ Square	○ Round
14	Surface	✳ Chiselled		✴ Angular		☁ Rounded

TEXTURE					
18	Structure	Loose	Relaxed	Undulating	Tense	Tight
19	Grain	Large grain	Medium grain	Fine grain	Polished grain	No grain
20	Fabric	Burlap	Denim	Velvet	Satin	Silk

CONSISTENCY					
23	Thickness	Thin				Thick
24	Weight	Airy	Light	Medium	Heavy	Weighty
25	Fluidity	Watery	Juicy	Velvety	Creamy	Viscous

FINAL ASSESSMENT					
29	Terroir wine	Yes				No
30	Message clarity	Inaudible	Garbled	Audible	Clear	Crystal clear
31	Purity	Tarnished	Fair	Cleaned	Refined	Pure
32	Length	Short	Moderate	Long	Persistent	Infinite
33	Complexity	Vacuous	Simple	Layered	Complex	Sophisticated
34	Balance	Unbalanced	Unharmonious	Balanced	Harmonious	Symphonic

AN EXTRACT FROM THE GEOSENSORIAL TASTING GRID

This geosensorial tasting grid was developed from work carried out by Alsace winemaker Jean-Michel Deiss and Jacky Rigaux from Burgundy, based on gourmet tasting. It was further refined by Julien Camus and his team and is now taught as part of the Approaching Terroir Through Geosensorial Tasting higher diploma at the University of Strasbourg and in Wine Scholar Guild training courses.

oenological colloquium of the institution of which he was a member was dedicated to tasting, and in 1970 he co-created the INAO glass with Vedel, who went on to publish his *Essai sur la dégustation des vins* in 1972. Approval tasting was made compulsory for AOC wines in 1974, and in 1980 Peynaud himself and Jacques Blouin published *Le Goût du vin*. The wine-tasting module for the diploma in nology at Bordeaux University was replaced by sensory analysis in 1982. This analytical method has spread beyond professional circles, with winemakers, sommeliers, chefs, teachers, critics and journalists making use of it, popularizing this approach to wine tasting and its collective sensory aromatic canons, and moving away from the mouth-based tasting that had previously prevailed.

The worldwide spread of Anglo-Saxon tasting

Anglo-Saxon wine-growing areas have not been sitting on their hands; in the 1950s, oenologist Maynard Amerine at UC Davis developed a tasting grid scoring from 1 to 100, analysing appearance (10), colour (10), bouquet (15), volatile acidity (10), taste (15), total acidity (8), sweetness (6), astringency (10) and overall quality (16). Much like the French approach, he wished to rank California terroirs to create value for consumers and owners, and his work was to inspire the sensory analytical model developed soon after by the Institute of Masters of Wine (founded in 1953), the Wine & Spirit Education Trust (WSET, 1969) and the Court of Master Sommeliers (1977), the standard Anglo-Saxon institutions awarding wine qualifications.

These bodies were to train a remarkable number of authoritative figures who emerged in the 1970s and 1980s and who went on to manage their alma maters. Master of Wine Michael Broadbent (1960) published ground-breaking works that included *Wine Tasting* (1968), considered the first book on tasting written in English for the general public – the key writers of the 1930s such as Alexis Lichine and Frank Schoonmaker had no interest in critical tasting – Steven Spurrier, the founder of the Académie du Vin and the organizer of the Judgment of Paris tasting, was similarly a supporter of this method.

As the network spreads and the number of academies multiplies, Anglo-Saxon specifications (tasting by analytical reduction, quantitative appreciation and making notes and comparisons), enhanced by INAO's work in France, are slowly becoming a global yardstick. A classic example is the WSET's Systematic Approach to Tasting Wine (SATW®), the entry ticket to the Institute of Masters of Wine; in 2021, it was being taught in 800 centres around the world, with more than 108,000 students in training, and it has served in part as inspiration for the far more in-depth university diploma in wine-tasting skills offered in France.

New forms of tasting

In becoming the touchstone for expert tasting, sensory analysis has undeniably enabled a standardization of approaches to wine tasting in a very short period of time and has been a part of the globalization and popularization of a particular notion of the quality of wine. As wine production has become more uniform, however, this quest for objectivity has also contributed to a standardization of typicity, and the increasing numbers of wines refused for approval tasting is proof positive of this. Might there be more than a coincidence of interests between the

> ❝ Sensory analysis is no stranger to the current crisis in the appellation system

qualities specific to one type of production, the methods used to appreciate it, and the way these are taught? History would seem to bear this out.

Sensory analysis is no stranger to the current crisis in the appellation system. Peynaud had already warned that it was anything but a goal in itself, but rather a necessary step toward an approach to wine tasting that was more holistic. Sensory analysis was undoubtedly a science, but it was also an art, a way of understanding the full complexity of wine, and much more than mere rote learning of categories applicable to standardized wines. Its limitations would certainly explain the emergence of new approaches intended to suit certain wines better, in particular those that had been refused, hence the development of geosensorial tasting by French wine critic Jacky Rigaux and Jean-Michel Deiss; to balance out the preponderance of aromas and colour, he returned to mouthfeel to appreciate what he calls *vins de lieu*, local wines, in a sense that goes even further than that intended by the brokers of the 19th century.

The idea was taken up and refined by a team under the aegis of Julien Camus and is now taught at the University of Strasbourg and the Wine Scholar Guild. With its language of energy, geometry, texture, consistency and salivation, it harks back to the Greeks' approach to tasting in a remarkable fashion. Without falling into overly exotic, figurative descriptions, an expansion of the vocabulary of wine is entirely possible to capture its ever-increasing diversity of new terroirs, cépages and styles. This is precisely the paradox of tasting: it defines itself as an objective method even as it uses subjective means, with the object, the wine, and the subject, the taster, mutually constructing one another in a process that is nothing less than a double birth.

Wine tasting – from the senses to the brain

Every wine, whether run-of-the-mill or iconic, is far more complex than merely the sum of the parts that can be identified through sensory analysis. While, as we have seen, it is efficient to break it down into simple elements (the data collected by the eye, then the nose, and then the mouth), such an approach will fail to tell the whole story because it analyses without synthesizing; a perception never exists in isolation but is part of a dynamic multisensory bundle captured by our senses and mediated by our brains. Taste is a holistic experience, a faculty that neuroscience is only beginning to unravel. Indeed, tasting a wine is an invitation to understand our perceptual relationship with the world. How do our senses work during a wine tasting? What role does the brain play? Is all tasting necessarily subjective? How are advances in cognitive science pointing toward another approach to tasting that is more global?

Wine is fireworks for the brain

Of all the foods we can taste, wine, with its chemical complexity, is among those that stimulate the senses the most – sight, smell and taste, obviously, but also touch in the mouth and even hearing: opening the bottle, pouring the wine into the glass, words and sounds in context. All tasting is thus multisensorial, and this experience, long neglected in favour of study of the physical and chemical composition of the wine, is now the research subject of choice for neuroscience.

Gabriel Lepousez, a neurobiologist at the Pasteur Institute and a great lover of wine, is a global expert on the matter, which he has explored in numerous publications for a general readership and in tasting workshops teaching a "neuro-oenological" approach (a term he has borrowed from American neurobiologist Gordon M Shepherd's standard work *Neuroenology: How the Brain Creates the Taste of Wine*, 2016). He maintains that wine provides a sensory and cognitive experience that should be addressed by the tools we use to adapt to the world that surrounds us – that is, not only our sensory brain, which is genetically wired for one response or another, but also our subjectivity, which can be thought of as the interaction between our genes, our experience and our culture. The brain receives, selects and ranks information transmitted by our senses, and this will vary depending on our perception threshold and past experience, the context of the tasting, our physiological and nutritional state, and even our emotions. All of these are used to construct a mental image of the wine that facilitates a decision: "I shall describe the wine in such and such a manner; I like it or I don't; I shall buy it or I shan't." Tasting a wine, which is a dynamic object in itself, is indeed a holistic, aesthetic and cognitive experience whose physiological mechanisms must be deconstructed if we wish to understand them better.

The supremacy of sight

Sensory analysis teaches us to taste a wine in three steps: looking, smelling and tasting. This order is culturally codified and therefore entirely artificial (you could taste a wine wearing a blindfold before smelling it and taking the blindfold off, for example) but may be explained by the hierarchy of our senses. Sight is the human species' primary sense, to which 15–17 per cent of the cerebral cortex is devoted, as opposed to one per cent for the sense of smell. The brain tastes first with the eyes, not least because sight is often the first step in tasting. The same white wine, tasted with its natural hue or artificially coloured red, will be described with vocabulary typical for whites in the first instance and for reds in the second, as shown in an experiment on the taste of colours carried out at the Bordeaux Oenology Institute in 2000. The preliminary encounter with colour projects information into the brain that influences our anticipation of the rest of the experience. The way to avoid this is to taste wearing dark glasses or a blindfold, as with geosensorial tasting.

The natural complexity of smelling

There are two ways that olfactory stimuli are detected: orthonasally and retronasally. Both pathways converge toward the olfactory epithelium, where the smell molecules are detected before being encoded by the olfactory bulb. Olfactory information is then transmitted to the piriform cortex, the hub of olfactory perception and memory, which helps us to recognize and distinguish odours. It is then sent on to the orbitofrontal cortex, the multimodal integration centre that collates it with other sensory data – colour, taste and so on – and ascribes an enjoyment value. In a parallel development, the information is also transmitted to the amygdala, the brain's emotive centre, which automatically generates an emotional response. This simultaneously delivers a twin cognitive and affective relationship with odour that both enables taste and explains the feelings underpinning the simple fact of liking something or not. This perception will differ depending on the pathway along which it originates.

- When the information is obtained through the nose, volatile compounds reach the olfactory mucosa at ambient temperature via airflow from the nostrils; this is **the orthonasal pathway**. As the nostrils open pretty much alternately, one will often perceive more of the very volatile molecules while the other will be increasingly receptive to more enduring background notes.
- When the information is obtained through the back of the buccal cavity – the mouth – this is known as **the retronasal pathway**. The wine is enclosed in a smaller space and warmed by the temperature of the mouth, triggering the production of other compounds in contact with the saliva with which it mixes, and the results are classified as aromas rather than odours. This may involve changes for some of these, while other new ones may appear, such as the metallic taste of red wine when matched with some fish (the iron associated with tannins induces an oxidation of fatty acids that is perceived only in the mouth and not on the nose) or a mousy flavour, which is an exclusively retronasal sensation. Experiments have also shown that retronasal aromas – spices and fruits, for example – are remembered better than simple odours smelled only via the nose and not perceived in the mouth, such as flowery smells.

Olfactory perception is the result of a complementary synergy between the orthonasal and retronasal pathways. These each supply different information, with the former being immediate to the nose and outward-facing, while the latter is gradual in the mouth and already enhanced by tastes and touch sensations; this would go some way toward explaining their currently predominant role in tasting.

The mouth tastes…

The mouth is the most multisensory locus of tasting; it is where volatile aromas arise along the retronasal pathway, flavours are analysed, and tactile, thermal and irritant stimuli are detected, so it is no surprise that it was of central importance for the Graeco-Romans, the merchants of the 19th century and the modern geosensorial approach alike.

As Lepousez explains, we have three kinds of taste bud: small, circular fungiform papillae on the surface of the tongue, foliate papillae on the sides, and large circumvallate papillae at the base. All feature gustatory cells able to perceive tastes via receptors, each of which specializes in detecting certain ions and molecules. When a particular compound is encountered, the receptor is activated, the gustatory cell on which it is located is stimulated, and an electric nervous impulse is sent to the gustatory cortex in the brain. Five tastes and their receptors have been identified so far.

> " Tasting a wine is a holistic, aesthetic and cognitive experience with fascinating physiological mechanisms

- First is **acidity**, for which we have a single receptor that remained undiscovered until 2019. This receptor detects the hydrogen ions (H^+, measured by pH) liberated from wine by organic acids like tartaric, malic, citric, lactic or succinic. These ions are released differently by different acids, and each gives us a stronger or weaker sense of acidity. Perception of acidity can be further altered by the presence of other compounds, so the CO_2 in sparkling wines also activates this receptor and enhances the sensation of acidity.
- We also have only one receptor for **sweetness**, which is stimulated by a wide variety of molecules: sugars per se (carbohydrates like fructose, sucrose, glucose and lactose) and sweetening compounds that come from ageing in new wood.
- We have only a single receptor for sensing **salt**, and this detects two mineral ions, the sodium (Na^+) in table salt and potassium (K^+). These two ions are in fact poorly represented in wine, and we often speak mistakenly of the "salty" flavour of wine. (The same is true of "sapidity", which refers to tastes in general rather than just saltiness.) This taste, which is essentially experienced first on the mouth before rapidly dissipating, is often conflated with umami.
- **Umami**, which was discovered by Japanese researcher Kikunae Ikeda in 1908, is unfortunately yet to be part of the vocabulary of wine tasting. An umami taste is triggered by a receptor that detects specific amino acids, principally glutamate, made up of proteins that are freed by biological or thermal change, like cooking, fermentation or long ageing.

Umami, which means "savoury" is an enveloping taste, at once sweet and salty, that is extremely persistent on the finish. It is associated with thick salivation, distinguishing it from the perception of salt (short and aggressive), which provokes aqueous salivation. Other molecules activate the umami receptor, in particular the nucleotides released by autolysis, as in long-aged Champagnes, and succinic acid.

- Lastly, for **bitter** tastes, there is not just one but 25 receptors. Unlike for other tastes, the detection threshold is very low, and the receptors will be stimulated by a very small quantity of more than 1,000 different compounds, including polyphenols, terpenes and metal ions. We are hypersensitive to bitterness and have an innate aversion to it, a vestigial evolutionary necessity for survival: many bitter molecules actually indicate potential toxicity. A taste for bitter things will vary between cultures and individual training: Italy has embraced it, while France still has little time for this flavour in its taste education or gastronomy.

> Our saliva is essential for wine tasting – and in our everyday life

It is still common to teach those learning how to taste that flavours have an exclusive position on the tongue - the infamous taste map - but is this actually the case? The answer is no. The limitations of the theory of four tastes, which was based on a map of tastes developed in Germany at the beginning of the 20th century and poorly translated in the US in the 1940s, were demonstrated with the discovery of umami, and it has proved to be entirely erroneous despite its popularity. Each taste bud perceives all tastes, which are more numerous than the four or five commonly cited. Research carried out since the turn of the 21st century suggests that we may have receptors to detect fatty acids, calcium and possibly even magnesium, along with water-soluble and non-volatile compounds that should be added to the list of tastes and therefore to the criteria for tasting. We have to rethink a new "geography" for the mouth.

... the mouth also feels

In addition to smelling and tasting, the mouth is highly tactile. It is innervated by the endings of the trigeminal nerve, which allow it to detect hot and cold, either from the temperature of wine or from certain molecules such as menthol, which gives the illusion of a cool sensation, or ethanol, which "warms" the palate. Other receptors detect spiciness and irritation – CO_2, for example, activates the same receptor as mustard or horseradish. We also now know that 20–25 per cent of all our touch receptors are located in the muscles and mucosae of the oral cavity, and there is a greater concentration in the mouth than on the hands.

Describing the feel of a wine in the mouth is thus highly relevant, as the Greeks knew; these receptors detect its consistency and texture and are extremely sensitive to the pressure, vibrations and resistance of the liquid tasted. Current sensory analysis underestimates this information and fails to draw finer distinctions because we are still learning how to isolate tastes; we over-simplify and refer only to creaminess, effervescence or astringency, which is often conflated with bitterness. Astringency is not a taste, however, but a tactile sensation arising from the interaction of tannins with the proteins in saliva; these polymerize on contact, forming aggregates of different sizes and changing the fluid feel of the saliva into a more or less rough sensation. We then indirectly sense the grain size of the tannin as the texture of a surface. As with a fabric or stone, whose granularity we feel by moving our hands against it, this is a dynamic experience. "We would be unable to read the tannins in a wine without saliva," Lepousez pointed out.

Saliva – invisible but essential

We have little awareness of the essential role played by our saliva, the "invisible" accompaniment to wine tasting and a part of our everyday lives. The primary functions of this viscoelastic gel are to lubricate the mouth and protect the teeth and mucous membranes. It also allows us to speak, preserves the mouth from the attacks of acids, regulates oral pH and prepares food for digestion; it contains anti-bacterial, antifungal and antiviral compounds, along with opiorphin, a natural analgesic released during salivation that raises the perception threshold of pain. Through all these qualities that derive from our biological evolution and the need to survive, saliva indirectly allows us to taste wine extremely precisely, rendering certain molecules soluble so we can perceive them even as it changes the wine itself.

Saliva is made up of 99 per cent water with a few electrolytes (calcium, phosphate, bicarbonate and potassium) but also, and in particular, more than 3,000 proteins, the proportions and roles of which will vary according to the salivary gland that has produced it. Mucin plays a key role in the perception of astringency, for example. The parotid gland located at the base of the oral cavity secretes a highly aqueous saliva toward the rear and sides of the mouth that is rich in water and low in proteins, while the submandibular glands and the sublingual glands beneath the tongue produce a thicker saliva with a higher protein content.

As soon as we put something in our mouths, and even by simply thinking of certain foods, we begin to salivate. Salivation is dynamic and reactive, and it differs according to the quality and quantity of the elements present. These do not all reveal themselves simultaneously but are perceived

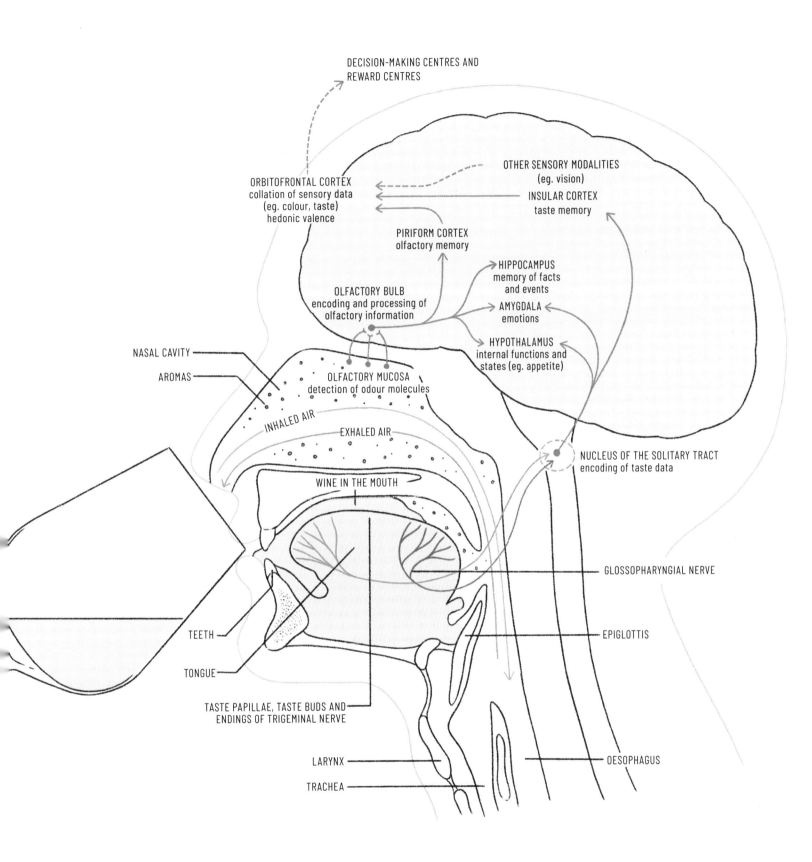

DECISION-MAKING CENTRES AND
REWARD CENTRES

ORBITOFRONTAL CORTEX
collation of sensory data
(eg. colour, taste)
hedonic valence

OTHER SENSORY MODALITIES
(eg. vision)

INSULAR CORTEX
taste memory

PIRIFORM CORTEX
olfactory memory

OLFACTORY BULB
encoding and processing of
olfactory information

HIPPOCAMPUS
memory of facts
and events

AMYGDALA
emotions

HYPOTHALAMUS
internal functions and
states (eg. appetite)

NASAL CAVITY

AROMAS

OLFACTORY MUCOSA
detection of odour molecules

INHALED AIR

EXHALED AIR

WINE IN THE MOUTH

NUCLEUS OF THE SOLITARY TRACT
encoding of taste data

GLOSSOPHARYNGIAL NERVE

TEETH

TONGUE

EPIGLOTTIS

TASTE PAPILLAE, TASTE BUDS AND
ENDINGS OF TRIGEMINAL NERVE

LARYNX

OESOPHAGUS

TRACHEA

THE BRAIN – THE CO-CREATOR OF THE ODOUR AND TASTE OF WINE

gradually in the mouth: acidity is experienced aggressively, with more fluid salivation to the sides of the mouth; umami on the finish produces thicker saliva; and sweet and bitter tastes induce only very low levels of salivation. These tastes are not juxtaposed but make up a dynamic and living sequence, a continuum. The way we salivate is a precise transcription of the composition of a wine, so why do we pay so little attention to our salivary reactions when they reveal so much?

We all smell differently

Every wine taster shares these physiological mechanisms, and yet we all taste differently; with any glass of wine, there will be as many descriptions as there are individual drinkers. But what causes this inconsistency? The reasons may be genetic or physiological, cultural or hedonic. For a start, we all have different perception thresholds due to our genetic differences, especially in our ability to smell, which of all our senses has the greatest genetic variations. Humans have 400 different olfactory receptors that are highly sensitive and capable of distinguishing the contours of several billion odours.

While our sense of smell is extremely effective in differentiating between two odours, it is much less effective in identifying the molecules that make them up. This initial capacity is actually counterbalanced by extraordinary inconsistency. Research has shown that at least 30 per cent of receptors function differently from one individual to the next in the population of the Western world, and the perception threshold for a smell molecule may vary by a factor of 1,000 to 10,000 between two people, which makes it difficult to share our olfactory perceptions. To draw an analogy with colour vision, we are all "colour blind" to some odours; if a group of tasters is offered the odour of β-ionone to smell, for example (a molecule that evokes the smell of violets and is in fact part of the flower's chemical composition), statistically, 30–50 per cent will be unable to detect it.

We all taste differently

Taste also varies genetically, but to a lesser degree; we have only one receptor to detect acidity, umami, saltiness and sweetness respectively, rather than 400, and the variability factor is no greater than 10. The field of descriptors for tastes is undoubtedly more circumscribed than for odours, but there is also far less genetic variation, which allows for greater standardization of perceptions; if a wine is sweet, it will be so for the vast majority of tasters. Only bitterness, with 25 receptors, varies widely; for any given compound, like phenylthiocarbamide (PTC), for example, detection thresholds that vary by a factor of 1,000 can be identified thanks to the existence of supertasters (individuals who are genetically better disposed to detect this bitter molecule). Such people are more sensitive and tend to avoid PTC, along with other similar compounds found to a certain extent in cabbages (brassicas) and other ingredients such as coffee, tobacco and ethanol. Tolerance of bitterness varies within a population but also across individuals and by age: children are more sensitive than adults, which is due in part to changes in the composition of saliva. Physiology influences genetic dispositions, as hunger and satiety clearly show. Chauvet would always taste wine around 11am, just before lunch, when his sense of smell and his palate were more stimulated by hunger.

The buffering effect of prolonged exposure

One other variable to consider is previous exposure. While past olfactory experience may help with recognition of odours, it can, by the same token, reduce sensitivity if the event is too recent and was too prolonged, because the human sensory system adapts and temporarily desensitizes. Wine tasting in cellars can be like this – the damp odour, which is initially very pronounced, will disappear after a few minutes – and the same is true of a series of wines with very similar organoleptic characteristics; the nuances of the next wine become less perceptible because of the one we have just tasted and to which we have "adapted". There is less genetic variability involved in tasting for the other senses – sight, in particular. That said, there will of course be cultural variations, and not everyone will find the same things pleasant. A colour or a sound may have positive or negative effects, and we are all educated to eat food that is sweeter or more savoury, with differing tolerances for bitterness. We also give different names to ingredients and perceptions depending on our origins – isobutyl-methoxypyrazine (IBMP), for example, a pyrazine present in Cabernet Franc, evokes green pepper in Europe but ginseng root or asparagus in southern China, and this is of course compounded by the question of the limits of language and the impossibility of recognizing something of which one has no knowledge. Descriptive points of reference clearly correlate with specific cultures and lived experience. One example is *xing*, a slightly metallic, spicy taste detected by Chinese tasters and identified in certain Pinot Noirs and Syrahs. As a descriptor, it would mean nothing to the majority of Western palates.

Tasting is an incredibly complex synthetic reconstruction

Wine is a multidimensional object that stimulates all our senses, whose capacity to detect the sensations it delivers will be influenced by both internal and external factors. When wine is tasted, a phenomenal amount of information arrives in the brain in a very short period of time – indeed, almost simultaneously – from each of our senses and their synergetic interactions. Depending on how well this information slots together, the brain constructs a mental image of the wine; if an odour and a taste correspond, their perception is reinforced, but if two pieces of information are contradictory, the brain will reconcile them based on the other information it has received and its probability. It is thus a "predictive machine", anticipating taste according to colour, since sight is our primary and dominant sense. Given two identically sweet solutions, we will find the one flavoured with vanilla sweeter, however, so the brain is not just a passive filter; it anticipates, imagines and works to reconstruct the taste of a wine in conjunction with the correlation of information and past experience.

By trying too hard to anticipate, though, it can sometimes lead us into error, and an awareness of this reality is what separates professional tasters from amateurs. Regular practice also conditions cerebral responses that are faster, more consistent and more analytical in professionals than in amateurs, whose brains tend to activate their emotional centres more. It is this distinction in the mind - separating analysis and emotion - that allows us to evaluate wines without liking them, and vice versa. This ability can be rapidly taught, however; in just a few days, a novice can learn how to detect compounds just as well as a sommelier. What many years of practice brings to sommeliers - and perfumemakers, too - is an enhanced ability to distinguish, identify, memorize, imagine and verbalize the components of the wine (or perfume).

With all this genetic variation, cerebral conditioning and cultural subjectivity, it must be understood that tasting can never be universal or objective, even when it complies with the most codified sensory analysis. Instead of decrying this state of affairs, we should become more aware of the mechanisms at work during tasting and, more broadly, in our perceptions and our relationship with the world. This is in order both to mitigate our cognitive biases and to imagine other ways of tasting that place greater emphasis on the synergy of the senses, on the continuum of experience and on other perceptions of which we are not yet aware, either because our culture has not yet instilled them in us or science is yet to discover them. We should also marvel at the fantastic potential for progress that we enjoy if we make the effort to educate our senses, especially our senses of taste and smell. Wine tasting is indeed an object lesson in humility, but what a window it can offer us both on ourselves and on our world!

Interoception – our sixth sense?

The anecdote about Chauvet tasting at 11am is of far greater significance that it might seem; when we are hungry, our sense of smell is far more attentive and precise than when we are full. The body produces hormones signalling to the brain that it should boost the sensitivity of the senses used to seek food, in particular by lowering our perception threshold for certain odours. Wine is made to be examined, sniffed and tasted – but also to be drunk. As Lepousez has pointed out, the human digestive system might be considered a "sixth sense" here, even though its sensory activity is far more unconscious. He cites as an example the notion of "drinkability", a concept that is being increasingly used to judge the quality of a wine. It refers to the digestibility of a wine as experienced in the pharynx and stomach when it is consumed. This ability to sense how messages from our body interact with our cognition and emotions makes use of a sixth sense – interoception. The idea was first put forward and studied in the 1870s by physiologist Claude Bernard (1813–78) and is now attracting more and more research interest. Tasting a wine is both exteroception (the reception of information from the outside world) and the perception of information coming from within our bodies. This unconscious information (we are not aware of what is happening in our stomachs) is more protracted and longer-lasting but less conclusive than our external perceptions; it nonetheless influences all our brain activity by modulating our internal and emotional states. If a wine is perfect according to traditional organoleptic analysis but is lacking in digestibility, how should it be judged? This, too, is an invitation to rethink our approaches and criteria for tasting.

Seeing wine

In *Le Goût du vin*, Peynaud describes how we taste wine "with our eyes" in much the same way as we eat food. Pliny the Elder maintained that fine wine was *albus* (pale and white), *fulvus* (a yellowed, tawny amber), *sanguineus* (blood red) or *niger* (dark and black), and although tasters have always been consciously – and unconsciously – aware of a wine's colour, the visual aspect of a liquid also encompasses its transparency, its viscosity and even its effervescence. Sight is an extremely immediate sense that grasps an object as a whole, and while the first impression of a wine conveyed by sight may contain a wealth of information, it can also encourage illusory expectations. We shall take a look at the molecules that are involved in visual analysis, examining their origins, their interaction with the human sensory system and any cognitive biases they may induce, before doing the same with the senses of smell and taste. So, what is it about wine that we see, and how do we see it? Can we literally drink colours?

The origins of colour in wines

Whether resplendent with flecks of yellow and green, whether magenta or sparkling, whether a turbid shade of brick red or deep purple, the visual appearance of a wine is defined by its physical aspect, the nuances of its colour and its intensity. The colour of a wine, along with its chemistry, has become increasingly important during the 20th century, and research is ongoing because the processes are so complex. The colour of reds and rosés comes almost exclusively from polyphenols, and more specifically from anthocyanins, themselves a type of flavonoid that tints water and alcohol, both colourless liquids. Reds, with all their hues, from purple and violet to blue, are natural shades widely represented in the plant kingdom, and they appear both during and after veraison, as Goode has pointed out (*Wine Science*, 2021). Light encourages their synthesis, but heat reduces their concentration, so a cool but bright climate will paradoxically produce darker wines than one that is hot and sunny.

There are five types of anthocyanin present in *V. vinifera*, and these appear in greater or lesser quantities depending on the cépage and terroir, although malvin predominates in varieties with black berries; the anthocyanins bond with one or two sugars (glucosides) and other compounds, like flavonols or metal ions, that modify their colour. This interaction with glucosides, known as acylation, enhances their stability and solubility in water but will vary between cépages, which explains the pale colour of certain wines; it is less intense in Pinot Noir because the grape's anthocyanins are less numerous and stable in the must. This may also be the case with Nebbiolo, which produces reds of low colour intensity.

Tannins are other polyphenols with colour, although this is much less pronounced and the colours are ochre/yellow/brown; various phenomena, such as contact with O_2, aggregation with other polyphenols and the like, can increase their concentration.

The anthocyanins found in grape skins are water-soluble: during maceration, the colour is extracted before the tannins, which require a certain level of ethanol, hence the use of pre-fermentation maceration to produce supple wines with strong colours. When extraction is completed, stabilizing the colour requires the formation of polymers – that is, the bonding of anthocyanins with other polyphenols. The colour intensity will fade rapidly without this polymerization.

Much less is known about the origins of the colour of white wines, although it is known that it is the absence of genes for biosynthesizing anthocyanins that makes a cépage "white". As with black grapes, their skins contain flavonoids and flavonols but in far lower quantities, and they are a very pale yellow. The skins also contain traces of carotenoids, but the golden yellow colour of a white wine comes more from the oxidation of aldehyde compounds from the grape and wood over time. In the case of wines made with *Botrytis cinerea*, it is laccase, an enzyme coming from the fungus, that oxidizes the grape polyphenols upon contamination with noble rot, producing an amber must.

Nuance and colour intensity

According to the OIV, the colour of a wine is determined by its hue (the colour itself), its luminosity and its "chromatism", or its intensity of colour. This will depend on a number of parameters arising from the grape's cépage, terroir and vintage; its vinification, including extraction, ageing, the amount of O_2 absorbed at every stage in the life of the wine; and the way it has been stored. Hot (70°C/158°F) pre-fermentation maceration extracts anthocyanins very quickly, but traditional long maceration reduces the colour intensity even as it makes it more stable over time. Low pH produces red tones, while high pH elicits shades of deep purple. Sulphur dioxide is sometimes used at the start of the harvest for "sulphitic maceration"; this facilitates the release of polyphenols, but wine may discolour during post-fermentation maceration.

Ageing in new wood oxidizes wine but also helps stabilize, indeed even enhance, the colour, with the tannins in the wood polymerizing the anthocyanins. This is the difference between a Rioja *gran reserva* aged for two years in a used American barrel and a Ribera del Duero aged for the same period of time in a new barrel; the Tempranillo will be pale brick red in the first instance, and opaque, deep violet in the latter. As the wine ages, its colour intensity drops as its hue evolves: purplish red turns to garnet, brick red, then brown, while yellowish-green turns orange, amber, and then brown. All this information about colour and intensity contains valuable clues, but these are always qualified.

The physical characteristics of wine: "legs"

Every wine is a liquid with unique physical properties. The discreet emulsion that it makes with air upon pouring is an indicator of alcohol in varying quantities, and this determines its consistency; it is more viscous than water and more "wetting", as can be seen from its "legs". This phenomenon, now known as the Marangoni effect, was first addressed by physicist James Thomson in 1855 but is still not perfectly explained by wine educators. When a glass of wine is swirled, a film of liquid appears on the walls of the glass, forming drops that slide back in a more or less regular fashion. Since alcohol is more volatile than water, it is quicker to evaporate from the surface, leaving a more aqueous liquid with greater surface tension – that is, a stronger attractive force between the water molecules. Capillary action causes the liquid to rise up the glass, and water then acts as a wave, pushing the unevaporated alcohol down and forming the legs. The thicker and slower these are, the more alcohol the wine contains, although not necessarily the more glycerol or sugar, as is sometimes taught (even though these molecules affect the viscosity of wine). External factors also influence their appearance; temperature will of course affect evaporation, and a very clean glass will hold the legs for less time. The legs may also be coloured or not, depending on the colour intensity of the wine.

Transparency, clarity, effervescence

The transparency and clarity of a wine are a function of its age and the precision of its vinification. Its appearance, which may be more or less crystal-clear, murky or milky, depends on the penetration of light rays in inverse proportion to the presence of particles. If clarity is not affected by visible sediment, like tartrate crystals (sometimes called "wine diamonds") or deposits of polyphenols, microscopic particles of yeasts and bacteria, especially when wines are neither filtered nor fined, reflect light in all directions. This

> " According to the OIV, the colour of a wine is determined by its hue, its luminosity and its chromatism

affects the turbidity, which is measured in NTUs (nephelometric turbidity units) and is similarly independent of colour.

The presence of micro-bubbles is not the exclusive preserve of sparkling wines. Certain still wines, such as Muscadet *sur lie* and Albariño from Rías Baixas in Galicia can be very slightly sparkling, with 1,200–1,400mg/l of CO_2 deliberately retained to enhance crispness in the mouth; CO_2 can be sensed above 850mg/l. The quality of the bubbles in sparkling wines is a source of information about the manner of vinification, providing clues to the base wine, protein content, second-fermentation technique, duration of ageing *sur lattes* with the bottles stacked on their side, and type of cork. Fast second fermentation at a high temperature or the addition of gas results in larger bubbles, and the bead of bubbles at the surface will dissipate more quickly. As Gérard Liger-Belair, professor in the Effervescence, Champagne and Applications combined research unit at the University of Reims-Champagne-Ardenne, has shown, the physics of bubbles is as much to do with a wine's production as with how it is served; during the three phases of their life (genesis/nucleation, rising, and bursting at the surface), the appearance of the bubbles depends equally on the quantity of gas dissolved, the shape of the glass and the presence of nucleation sites.

The less CO_2 there is, the finer the bubbles will be, but the taller the glass, the larger they will be when they reach the surface. For there to be bubbles at all, however, there has to be a nucleation site – an active surface where CO_2 is trapped, most often a hollow cellulose fibre left over from glass-polishing, a mote of dust or a fault in the glass wall. When too much gas accumulates, a bubble is formed, the

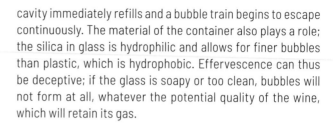

Rosé

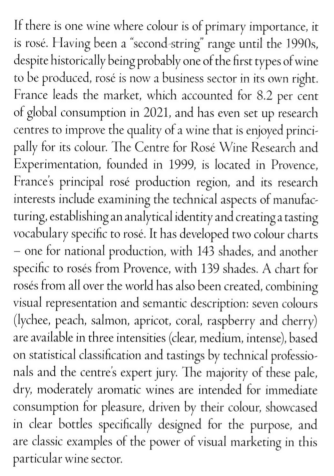

If there is one wine where colour is of primary importance, it is rosé. Having been a "second-string" range until the 1990s, despite historically being probably one of the first types of wine to be produced, rosé is now a business sector in its own right. France leads the market, which accounted for 8.2 per cent of global consumption in 2021, and has even set up research centres to improve the quality of a wine that is enjoyed principally for its colour. The Centre for Rosé Wine Research and Experimentation, founded in 1999, is located in Provence, France's principal rosé production region, and its research interests include examining the technical aspects of manufacturing, establishing an analytical identity and creating a tasting vocabulary specific to rosé. It has developed two colour charts – one for national production, with 143 shades, and another specific to rosés from Provence, with 139 shades. A chart for rosés from all over the world has also been created, combining visual representation and semantic description: seven colours (lychee, peach, salmon, apricot, coral, raspberry and cherry) are available in three intensities (clear, medium, intense), based on statistical classification and tastings by technical professionals and the centre's expert jury. The majority of these pale, dry, moderately aromatic wines are intended for immediate consumption for pleasure, driven by their colour, showcased in clear bottles specifically designed for the purpose, and are classic examples of the power of visual marketing in this particular wine sector.

cavity immediately refills and a bubble train begins to escape continuously. The material of the container also plays a role; the silica in glass is hydrophilic and allows for finer bubbles than plastic, which is hydrophobic. Effervescence can thus be deceptive; if the glass is soapy or too clean, bubbles will not form at all, whatever the potential quality of the wine, which will retain its gas.

Do we all see the same colours?

As with the senses, we are all different as far as our genetics and experiences are concerned. Colours do not actually exist, as such; they are no more than electromagnetic waves of light absorbed or reflected by objects, from which the cone photoreceptors in our retinas and our brains construct colour. These photoreceptors absorb light via three visual pigments that react to different wavelengths: short waves tend toward blue, medium toward green and long toward red. This difference in sensitivity encompasses all the wavelengths of visible light; infrared and ultraviolet are below and above this. The colour perceived therefore depends on the type of cone reached by the photons – there are three different ones for trichromatic vision – and their intensity and number. We can distinguish thousands of shades, although the visible spectrum varies with each individual and their age.

This genetic variation is compounded by variable precision of vocabulary. The common terms generally used to describe the colour of wine are often ambiguous, indeed even incorrect: we speak of white, *gris* and black grapes, when in fact they are more yellow, pink and blue; and the same is true of wines. Anthropology goes some way to explaining the reasons for such discrepancies between the way colours are perceived and named; in Western civilizations in particular, white, red and black are the three fundamental colours, with the strongest symbolic connotations, and so these were the categories in which wine, itself a symbolic object, was soon classified. Other colours qualifying this – like green, yellow, blue, brown, violet, pink and orange – appeared gradually over the centuries, with their own associations, and these were joined by cultural variants. Colours are accorded different meanings by different cultures, each of which educates its members to categorize and distinguish the shades of use to it, thus "seeing" or overlooking certain hues.

To resolve this genetic and cultural variability and reconcile our visual descriptors for wine tasting, might it not be useful to use one of the many colour charts that offer precise physical definitions of colours? On the Pantone colour chart, for example, 13-0752 TCX corresponds to lemon yellow, while 123 C is the colour of cycling's yellow jersey. This type of scientific approach is already used, in fact, and the OIV has set precise calculation parameters for the various

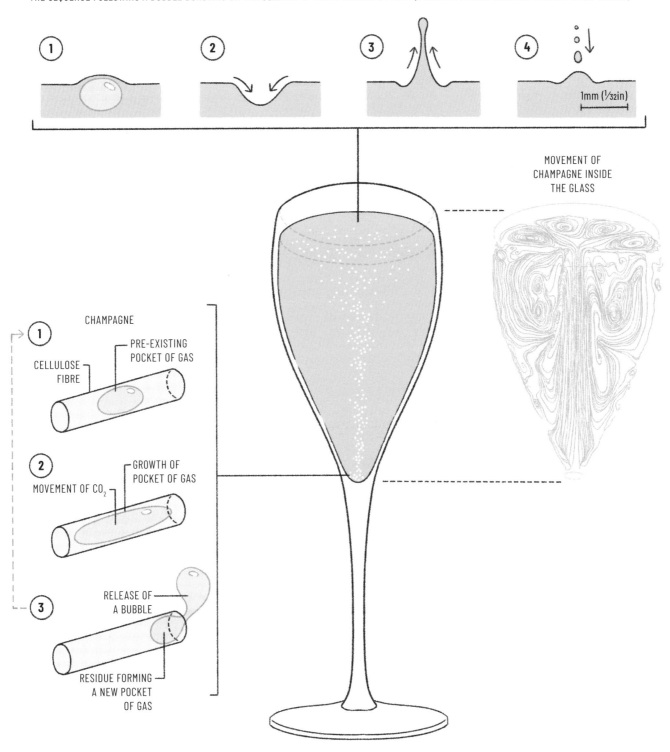

THE SEQUENCE FOLLOWING A BUBBLE BURSTING ON THE SURFACE OF CHAMPAGNE IN A FLUTE (BASED ON PHOTOS TAKEN BY GÉRARD LIGER-BELAIR)

1

2

3

4

1mm (1/32in)

MOVEMENT OF
CHAMPAGNE INSIDE
THE GLASS

1 CHAMPAGNE

CELLULOSE
FIBRE

PRE-EXISTING
POCKET OF GAS

2 MOVEMENT OF CO_2

GROWTH OF
POCKET OF GAS

3 RELEASE OF
A BUBBLE

RESIDUE FORMING
A NEW POCKET
OF GAS

NUCLEATION, RISING AND BURSTING OF BUBBLES IN A CHAMPAGNE FLUTE, AS DESCRIBED BY GÉRARD LIGER-BELAIR

The life cycle of a bubble in a liquid saturated with CO_2 breaks down into three phases: genesis in a rough hollow (nucleation), rising (in which it takes on aromatic compounds) and bursting, where the liquid encounters air at the surface. Bubbles also create invisible convection movements as they rise.

Wine and carafes

One of the reasons given for decanting a wine into a carafe is being able to admire its appearance, and a clear glass container does indeed make it possible to appreciate the nuances of the wine's colour, along with its brilliance and lustre. A decanted wine is also supposed to be of better quality, although this is obviously not always the case. The primary goal of using a carafe is to alter the bouquet and taste of the wine, either by aeration, by pouring directly into the carafe to oxygenate young wines, or by decanting old wines off their sediment.

Decanting is a more complex science than you might think, however, and involves two physical and chemical mechanisms, namely evaporation and oxidation. The first of these not only allows certain more volatile aromatic sulphur compounds to dissipate rapidly, removing notes of egg or cabbage, but also permits alcohol and other more fragile aromatic compounds to evaporate; the greater the surface exposed to air, the greater the evaporation and rise in temperature. Oxidation releases compounds over several hours, and modifies our perception of the structure of a wine – its tannins, alcohol and acidity – although reactions will be different for each bottle, even of the same wine.

So what does it bring us? Spanish wine merchant Vila Viniteca has carried out a tasting under strict conditions and published online its findings for four wines served five different ways (vilaviniteca.es/en/blog/to-decant-or-not-to-decant). The experiment established that aromatic intensity does not increase with decanting, that wines become more astringent and bitter when decanted, that acidity and sweetness are not affected, that decanting reduces the sensation of the weight of a wine but not its volume, and that decanted wines and those left in the bottle developed a similarly wide range of aromas.

components of the colours in wines. Certain AOC wines, such as Côtes du Rhône and Côtes du Rhône-Villages, have their own criteria set out in their specifications and have to exhibit a particular level of colour intensity (respectively, IC ≥ 4.5 and ≥ 7). In both of these cases, however, few people are able to make use of such formulae, no matter how precise they might be, and this is the whole problem in communication and choice of language.

Sight: predictor and precedent

Analysis of a wine's colour plays a major role in its general appreciation, but is it possible that too much attention is paid to this criterion? Indeed, could it even be deceptive? Tasting a young Barolo is a classic example: the wine is pale, almost rosé, implying lightness, faint aromas and a reasonable price; instead, it is highly aromatic, with a broad range of varietal notes, tannic, fairly high in alcohol and relatively expensive. Sight is our primary sense, overriding the others, especially taste and smell, and it is trained from the youngest age, while the others are generally neglected in Western societies. As Lepousez has pointed out, the fact that we generally take a look at wine before tasting only accentuates this primacy. Making use of our remembrance of things past, our brains anticipate what we are potentially about to smell and taste based on all the visual indices; if the wine is thick and amber-coloured, it is probably going to be oxidative and sweet, and descriptors for sweet wine will spring to mind.

Such was the experiment carried out by Gil Morrot, Frédéric Brochet and Denis Dubourdieu at the Bordeaux Oenology Institute in 2000 mentioned earlier, where colouring a white wine fooled tasters into using the vocabulary of red fruits. Intensity also plays a role; the more intense the hue, the more powerful we believe the aromas to be. Vision is so dominant that it can also inhibit the olfactory and taste centres of the brain. The easiest way to rebalance these perceptions is to close your eyes; because vision takes precedence when there is contradictory information, taking it out of the equation helps to mitigate our cognitive biases. The predictive and precedent nature of sight is also unconsciously incorporated beyond just the colour of a wine: the type of glass, the label, the shape of the bottle and the price, if visible, are just some of the factors that will influence our tasting. What is the solution if we want to be as objective as possible? Ignore the bottle, and taste with the mouth first, then with the nose, in a black glass, before pouring the wine into a transparent glass; both science and experience are beckoning us to rethink the way we taste.

Smelling wine

"Those people [looking for strong wines] shouldn't drink Beaujolais. Strong wines are everywhere, they're ten a penny, really, but a wine with a nice bouquet is difficult to find. If only people would learn to use their noses, learn how to smell again…" Chauvet revolutionized olfactory analysis and knew that wine was the result of extremely complex interactions (that were poorly understood and taught in his time) between volatile and non-volatile compounds and our senses. The former – odours and aromas – are essential for identifying and appreciating the quality of wine. The thousands of chemical molecules that interact to provide a bouquet that varies with time and between bottles include alcohols, esters, acids, aldehydes, ketones, lactones, terpenes, volatile phenols and so on. But how are aromas created in wine? Why does smelling seem so subjective? How does the historic neglect of the sense of smell in Western civilizations influence the way we analyse things with our noses?

Odour, aroma and the olfactory buffer

Humans have two ways of perceiving the volatile molecules that make up the scent of wine: directly, via the nose (the orthonasal pathway) and indirectly, via the mouth (the retro nasal pathway). We call the scents detected in the former case odours, and in the latter, aromas. All aromas are odours, but not vice versa; saliva, with its specific pH and enzyme content, and the temperature of the oral cavity can produce or alter aromas that are indetectable to the nose, such as a mousy taste. The two are entirely complementary, but for ease of reading this section, the term "aroma" should be understood as subsuming the concept of odour.

Between 700 and 1,000 aromatic volatile compounds have been recorded in wine: primary aromas arising from the grapes, secondary aromas from vinification and tertiary aromas from ageing. A large majority of these lie beneath our perception threshold, which of course does not prevent them from exerting a positive, neutral or negative influence on the complexity of the wine's aromas. Studies carried out by the likes of Vicente Ferreira, head of research at the Laboratory of Aroma Analysis and Oenology at the University of Zaragoza have shown that all wines share a basic aromatic structure that includes ethanol and about 30 aromatic compounds, most of which are by-products of fermentation, including ethanol, higher alcohols, acetic acid, β-damascenone and the like. When combined, these compounds release the characteristic aroma of wine, the "vinous" scent, forming an olfactory buffer that tends to eclipse the other aromatic compounds present, in particular those linked with notes of fruit. Depending on its ability to break through this buffer, a compound can be classified as:

- **A high-impact compound** – where the aroma is clearly recognizable.
- **A major contributor** – that, whether identifiable or not, its absence would fundamentally change the aroma.
- **A net contributor** – one whose absence would change the intensity but not the aromatic quality.
- **A subtle aromatic compound** – whose absence might not be noticed.
- **An activator or depressant/aromatic mask** – which intensifies or diminishes the perception of other compounds.

High-impact compounds from the grape or from vinification are perceptible unaltered in the finished wine – for example, linalool, a highly complex aroma encompassing everything from aniseed to orange flowers, found in the flesh of Muscat grapes. While these may be present in almost every V. vinifera, the particular cépage can be identified by their concentration.

Varietal or primary aromas

Aromas are most usually classified according to their origins and their synthetic path, which often produce molecules with the same chemical structure. Varietal or primary aromas stem from the grape and its environment and are characteristic of a cépage or a family of cépages; they will vary according to variety, maturity, cleanliness, vintage and terroir. These aromatic molecules are principally located in the skin, and more rarely in the flesh, of the grape. They may produce a smell in the fruit, as is the case with the aroma of Muscat, which is present in both the grape and the wine, but are often found in the form of non-volatile aroma precursors, a form in which the smell molecule is bonded with a non-volatile chemical compound that will then be released by fermentation to reveal the final aroma. *Vitis vinifera*'s primary aromas include the following.

> Vinification causes wine to lose fruitiness and gain "microbial complexity"

- **Methoxypyrazines** are molecules with herbal notes that are also present in the *Capsicum* genus of peppers. They are mostly associated with Cabernet Franc and Cabernet Sauvignon, Sauvignon Blanc and other cépages from the broader area of Southwest France. They can also be secreted by ladybirds, whose presence in the vines and thus the wines of Burgundy in 2004 left an aromatic stamp on the vintage.
- **Monoterpenes** are also to be found in every variety but are particularly pronounced in the Muscat family and in Gewürztraminer, Torrontés and Viognier. These volatile terpenes are extremely aromatic in the berry, smelling of rose, lemongrass, sweet citrus fruits and lychees, and change little during vinification but become less intense with ageing. *Botrytis cinerea* also mitigates them, which may explain why Muscat is not a cépage often used for nobly rotten sweet wines. These compounds include linalool, geraniol (geranium, verbena), citronellol (lemongrass) and cis rose oxide (the lychee and rose notes in Gewürztraminer). Cépages with high terpene levels are particularly suitable for making skin-contact wines.
- **Norisoprenoids** produced by the breakdown of carotenoids are more concentrated in the flesh of red grapes ripened in a sunny climate. Of particular note are α- and β-ionones, smelling of violets and raspberries, β-damascenone (blackcurrants, although this is also a net contributor) and trimethyl dihydronaphthalene (TDN), an indicator of a hot year that gives Rieslings a petroleum odour.
- **Rotundone** is a sesquiterpene identified as recently as 2005 and one of the molecules responsible for the peppery notes in Syrah, Pineau d'Aunis, Grüner Veltliner and Mourvèdre. It has a very low perception threshold, but studies have shown that 20 per cent of the population are unable to smell it.
- **Varietal thiols**, also known as mercaptans, are compounds of sulphur that have no smell in the berry but are nonetheless present in the form of aroma precursors chemically bonded with sugars or amino acids (cysteine); the bond is broken during vinification, at which point they become volatile. Chewing the skin of a Sauvignon grape for a few seconds can trigger the release of thiols, probably through the action of enzymes present in saliva. Many factors can influence the concentration of thiols: the nature of the clone, growing conditions, yield, climate, human intervention (treatment with copper can destroy such compounds), ripeness (thiols gradually change as the berry matures) and choices in vinification – for example, mechanical harvesting, maceration, addition of yeast and hydrogen sulphide levels. Some thiols determine the profile of some cépages: 4MMP, with its notes of blackcurrant, boxwood and grapefruit, is typical of Sauvignon Blanc, Cabernet Sauvignon and Manseng, among others; A-3MH and 3MH, with hints of passion-fruit, lychee and rhubarb, are more widespread, being present in lots of varieties, including those just mentioned plus Semillon, Grenache, Merlot and Melon – they are especially common in young wines and rosés. They can become pungent if concentrations are too high, however.

Other primary aromas include furaneol, lactone and foxy aromas.

Vinification or secondary aromas

Vinification causes wine to lose fruitiness and gain "microbial complexity" (per Selosse) and "fermentation acts to reveal aromas", as Peynaud has pointed out. The almost alchemical nature of the process is revealed at this point; in addition to alcohol, vast numbers of volatile and non-volatile compounds are produced that all contribute to the aroma of a wine.

According to oenologist Guillaume Antalick, the greater part of the pool of primary aromas are odourless in the grape and released only during fermentation. Peynaud and Blouin, in *Le Goût du vin*, add that "secondary aromatic compounds are created only during this process and may result from all kinds of fermentative conditions". These compounds may be produced in an artificial environment without the addition of grape must: C_6 compounds such as hexanol can help impart notes of fresh fruit or floral notes, for example, but at very low levels in such a case; these would be higher in the presence of must because it contains precursor aldehydes. These tend to be pre-fermentation aromas. By contrast, if a *Saccharomyces* yeast is brought into contact with sugars, water and nutrients such as lipids, ammonium, amino acids and vitamins, it will be capable of producing higher alcohols, esters and volatile fatty acids, for example, and these are what make up "vinous" aromas. The composition of the grape must (which will vary with the terroir, the cépage and the viticultural techniques applied) may, however, affect the make-up of some of these secondary aromas (esters in particular) by influencing metabolization by the yeast.

In addition to ethanol, upward of 20 secondary alcohols (measured by comparison to the quantities of ethanol) or higher alcohols (those with more than two carbon atoms) are formed by yeasts. Some are floral, such as 2-phenyle-thanol, (which has a sweet scent like rose petals), while others are heavy and unctuous. Yeasts and bacteria also metabolize a host of fermentative acids that will influence the bouquet either directly or indirectly. These may include fatty acids, which can be soapy or rancid, such as butyric acid, or even the highly volatile acetic acid, which imparts a shot of energy to wine when present in small quantities but can turn it to vinegar and make it legally unsaleable if levels climb too high. Alcohols and acids, the two main products of fermentation, combine to form esters, a third category of volatile fermentative compounds that play a considerable role in the bouquet of a wine. Their highly complex perfumes can be anything from light and floral to rich and acescent (acetates, for example, which are formed from acetic acid). The most important of these include:

- **Ethyl acetate**, which is found in all fermented drinks, with notes ranging from floral to ethereal and even with a hint of vinegar. According to Peynaud, "It contributes to olfactory complexity at concentrations of 50–60mg/l, then tends toward harshness at around 80–100mg/l before being identified as an unpleasant factor from 120-150mg/l, depending on the wine".
- **Isoamyl acetate**, a fruity ester produced by yeasts as fermentation begins, is found in young white wines and in German wheat beers. Its notes of banana and chewing gum are easily identified but fade rapidly with age as they react with the water in the wine and are hydrolysed. Synthesis of the chemical is enhanced by cold fermentation and the use of carbonic maceration, of which it is a strong aromatic indicator, even to cartoon proportions in the case of industrially produced Beaujolais Nouveau, which has long used 71B, a yeast that metabolizes it.
- **Ethyl hexanoate and ethyl octanoate** are fruity esters with the scent of fresh pears or green apples.

In addition to these acids, alcohols and esters is another product of fermentation:

- **Diacetyl** is formed by lactic bacteria breaking down malic acid at the tail end of malolactic fermentation. Its intensity depends on fermentation conditions; in weak concentrations, it features aromas of hazelnut, butter and brioche, but this can turn to rancid butter in higher concentrations.

Finally, fermentation also produces ketones, aldehydes and acetals, including:

- **Lactones** (cyclic esters of various origins). While these may be found in some overripe grapes during fermentation and

ageing, the vast majority come from the barrel; these are whisky lactones.

- **Sulphur compounds** metabolized by sulphurized amino acids from the berries or from added SO_2. These have a very low perception threshold but are highly odorous, ranging from smoky to a stale, fermented scent. Good aeration or a piece of copper can reduce their intensity. Some are of interest, such as dimethyl sulphide (DMS), a very common compound found in cooked meats, cheese, and citrus fruits that is not yet entirely understood and produces notes of corn and molasses in white wines and blackcurrants and raspberries in reds. With ageing, there are also hints of white and black truffle. When too heavily concentrated, it can be reminiscent of cooked cabbage and seafood. It is

The Nose School and Le Nez du Vin

Taking inspiration from the way perfume-making was taught, Jean Lenoir, Burgundian by birth, created Le Nez du Vin® in 1981 to help people recognize the aromatic compounds found in wine. It is a true compendium; the 54 odours it contains have been identified in the majority of bouquets and users can practise identifying, memorizing and recognizing them. Lenoir followed this up first with Le Nez du Café in 1997, then Le Nez du Whisky, and he also offers products exploring oak aromas and explaining wine faults. In 2016, he joined Lepousez in founding L'École du Nez, which offers a unique training course in neuro-oenology; the aim is to make use of cutting-edge scientific findings in sensory perception to explain why "taste is in the head", as American neurobiologist Gordon M Shepherd has put it. By understanding how the brain decodes, comprehends and memorizes olfactory information to generate positive or negative emotions, how it is constantly seeking to simplify the dynamic, multimodal and multisensory experience provided by wine, we can begin to get a handle on the cognitive biases inherent in the way we taste. Achieving a better understanding of ourselves is the only way we will be able to appreciate wine and develop a precise, shared language that best describes this vibrant complexity.

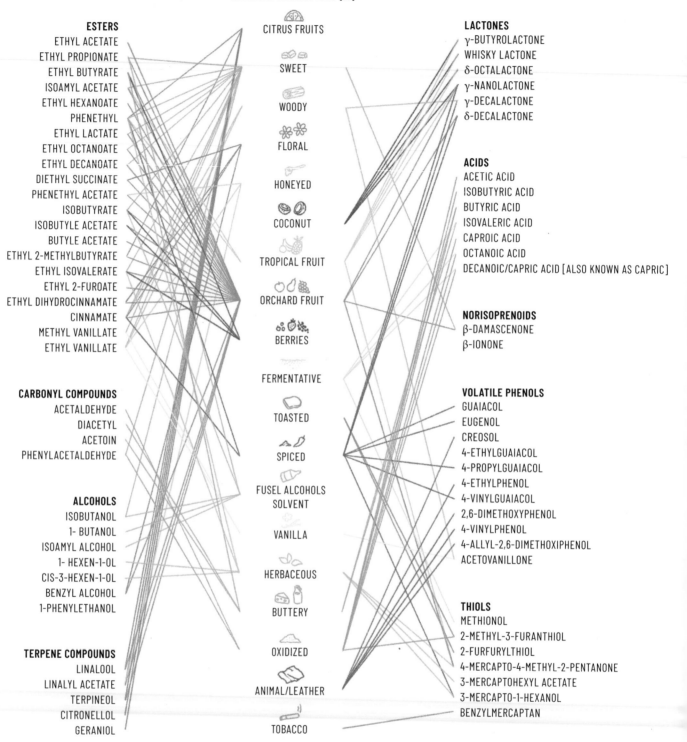

AROMATIC DESCRIPTORS (19)

ESTERS
ETHYL ACETATE
ETHYL PROPIONATE
ETHYL BUTYRATE
ISOAMYL ACETATE
ETHYL HEXANOATE
PHENETHYL
ETHYL LACTATE
ETHYL OCTANOATE
ETHYL DECANOATE
DIETHYL SUCCINATE
PHENETHYL ACETATE
ISOBUTYRATE
ISOBUTYLE ACETATE
BUTYLE ACETATE
ETHYL 2-METHYLBUTYRATE
ETHYL ISOVALERATE
ETHYL 2-FUROATE
ETHYL DIHYDROCINNAMATE
CINNAMATE
METHYL VANILLATE
ETHYL VANILLATE

CARBONYL COMPOUNDS
ACETALDEHYDE
DIACETYL
ACETOIN
PHENYLACETALDEHYDE

ALCOHOLS
ISOBUTANOL
1- BUTANOL
ISOAMYL ALCOHOL
1- HEXEN-1-OL
CIS-3-HEXEN-1-OL
BENZYL ALCOHOL
1-PHENYLETHANOL

TERPENE COMPOUNDS
LINALOOL
LINALYL ACETATE
TERPINEOL
CITRONELLOL
GERANIOL

CITRUS FRUITS
SWEET
WOODY
FLORAL
HONEYED
COCONUT
TROPICAL FRUIT
ORCHARD FRUIT
BERRIES
FERMENTATIVE
TOASTED
SPICED
FUSEL ALCOHOLS
SOLVENT
VANILLA
HERBACEOUS
BUTTERY
OXIDIZED
ANIMAL/LEATHER
TOBACCO

LACTONES
γ-BUTYROLACTONE
WHISKY LACTONE
δ-OCTALACTONE
γ-NANOLACTONE
γ-DECALACTONE
δ-DECALACTONE

ACIDS
ACETIC ACID
ISOBUTYRIC ACID
BUTYRIC ACID
ISOVALERIC ACID
CAPROIC ACID
OCTANOIC ACID
DECANOIC/CAPRIC ACID [ALSO KNOWN AS CAPRIC]

NORISOPRENOIDS
β-DAMASCENONE
β-IONONE

VOLATILE PHENOLS
GUAIACOL
EUGENOL
CREOSOL
4-ETHYLGUAIACOL
4-PROPYLGUAIACOL
4-ETHYLPHENOL
4-VINYLGUAIACOL
2,6-DIMETHOXYPHENOL
4-VINYLPHENOL
4-ALLYL-2,6-DIMETHOXIPHENOL
ACETOVANILLONE

THIOLS
METHIONOL
2-METHYL-3-FURANTHIOL
2-FURFURYLTHIOL
4-MERCAPTO-4-METHYL-2-PENTANONE
3-MERCAPTOHEXYL ACETATE
3-MERCAPTO-1-HEXANOL
BENZYLMERCAPTAN

CREATING A CHEMICAL AROMA FINGERPRINT FOR PORTUGUESE BAIRRADA CÉPAGES

Teams from the universities of Zaragoza and Aveiro have identified a "chemical aroma fingerprint" for six cépages
(three whites, Arinto, Bical and Sauvignon; and three reds, Touriga Nacional, Castelão and Baga).

found in Manseng, Grenache and Syrah grapes and also plays an important role as the bouquet of Champagne develops.

Fermentative aromas are essentially shaped by yeasts, bacteria and fermentation conditions, as is ably demonstrated by wines made with traditional methods: ageing with bottles stacked on their sides and the use of CO_2 imparts a particular bouquet of fresh cream, brioche and white truffle.

The alchemy of the barrel

Fashion, technological progress and barrel quality all play a part in balancing the aromatic influence of wood on wine, which may vary from extremely subtle to almost a caricature. Several dozen different molecules will infuse into wine when a barrel is new, but once the container is old, it will no longer be neutral and can even impart a taste of old floorboards. The nature of these compounds and the ease with which they are extracted into the wine varies by species and origins of the wood, and how it has been dried or heated and so on. The most important volatile compounds include:

- **Whisky lactones** from the lipids in the wood. These molecules have a very low detection threshold and impart sweet notes of coconut, with American *Quercus alba* containing higher levels than Europe's *Q. petraea* and *Q. robur*. They are destroyed if heated too severely.
- **Phenolic aldehydes** such as syringaldehyde, with hints of maplewood and vanillin. Levels of the latter increase when lignin is broken down under the effects of heat, and American wood also contains higher quantities of it. If wine is fermented in barrel, it will be less concentrated because it is metabolized into vanillyl alcohol, which is odourless. Levels will also decrease in the bottle.
- **Phenols**, which increase during heating. These include eugenol (smelling of cloves, with levels rising if the wood is dried or toasted), guaiacol (smoky; this is formed as wood breaks down during toasting) and its derivatives (carnations, pepper, soot), cresol (pharmaceutical, even peaty notes), phenols and their derivatives, ethylphenols, for red wine (ink, stables). *Brettanomyces*-type yeasts can also produce some of these molecules.
- **Compounds produced by heating**, especially furfural, an aldehyde produced by the breakdown of carbohydrates in wood, with notes of toasted almonds. Furfurylthiol, a sulphurized derivative of furfural that comes indirectly from wood, has a coffee aroma.

In addition to creating these aromas, wood may also, depending on its age, facilitate slow oxygenation of the compounds in wine. This will of course alter its organic profile and may increase the extraction of certain compounds.

Aromas from ageing (tertiary aromas)

These aromas first develop during ageing, then in the bottle. Most aromatic esters hydrolyse and reduce in vats and barrels, with few new instances being esterified. There are two kinds of bouquet, depending on the type of maturation.

- An **oxidative bouquet**, rich in **aldehydes**, smells of quince, nuts, *rancio*. Prolonged exposure to O_2 renders this extremely stable once the wine is bottled, but with an intense aromatic signature. This phase of oxidation gives rise to two molecules from the lactone family in particular: sotolon – with hints of curry, nuts and fenugreek, a typical feature of Jura Vin Jaune – and solerone, which is characteristic of wines from Jerez: dried figs, roast chestnuts.

> As Émile Peynaud has pointed out, "fermentation acts to reveal aromas"

- A **reductive bouquet**, rich in **sulphur compounds** and smelling of matches, garlic, fermented cabbage and sulphurous water, appears if there is insufficient O_2.

The in-bottle ageing phase is still poorly understood as far as the mechanisms of aromatic transformation are concerned. We know from the work of Jean Ribéreau-Gayon and Peynaud (1976) that only tiny amounts of O_2 enter through the cork and that oxygenation is carried out by the O_2 dissolved in the wine and in the neck of the bottle – but it is not the primary agent of in-bottle ageing.

An aroma is never alone – a real strength

With so many processes having a hand in its production, including chemical biosynthesis in the grape berry, maturation, double fermentation, oxidative and reductive maturation the introduction of wood, and even cooking and aromatization, in the cases of Madeira and vermouth, it is no coincidence that wine is one of the foodstuffs containing the most aromatic compounds. This also makes it an ideal subject for study, and it is indeed the most researched food of all.

Note the role of interactions between volatile and non-volatile compounds, especially in red wines, and probably in macerated whites too. "The lighter the tannic structure of a wine, the more opulent its aromatic component will be," as Peynaud points out. In 2010, the María-Pilar Saenz-Navajas team in Zaragoza showed how the non-volatile component was almost more important than the aromatic component in the aromatic expression of reds.

In addition, ethanol is a substance that preserves and concentrates, hence its use in perfumes; as a solvent, it plays a role in both extracting and diffusing odours. As

Lepousez reminds us, the field of perfume-making has been extremely useful in helping us understand the olfactory analysis of wines; we never smell a single, fixed volatile molecule on its own – instead, we perceive the evolution of a matrix of molecules over time, and perfumiers separate this out into "notes".

- **Top notes**, the smallest, are highly volatile and evaporate in a few seconds or minutes.
- **Middle notes**, evaporate more slowly, in around a minute.
- **Base notes**, the heaviest fragrances, evaporate over several hours.

This dynamic explains the analysis of wine by its "first nose" (immediate exposure, at rest), second nose (with aeration, increasing the surface area exposed and thus volatilizing other molecules), in the mouth (increase of surface area and temperature, dissolution in the water present in saliva, enzymatic metabolization revealing other molecules), and third nose, in an emptied glass (when the ethanol has evaporated and other molecules continue to appear).

Depending on the temperature at which the wine is served, the shape of the glass and its position in respect of the nose and mouth, the olfactory bulb will also receive odours differently – so not only do molecules change over time, we actively influence their diffusion during the tasting procedure. This is compounded by the fact that these molecules interact with each other – the buffering effect, for example. Because they can combine, they may multiply the effects of another or mask it entirely, or a new odour may appear; the bouquet of a wine is thus never the same.

Wine odours travel…

The hundreds of volatile compounds present in a glass of wine and their combination are perceived by the receptors of a unique organ, the olfactory epithelium at the top of the nasal cavity located between the eyes. This is a mucous membrane, a few square centimetres in size, made up of millions of olfactory sensory neurons. Each of these has several specialized cilia, protected within a film of mucus, that are in more or less direct contact with the air in the nasal cavity. These olfactory cilia feature receptors that are able to accept several nearby olfactory molecules that fit like keys into locks. The receptors are not exclusive, however, so odorant molecules can activate, or "open", several different receptors, enabling a complex combinatory interplay between the 400 olfactory receptors and thousands of volatile compounds. In theory, this encoding would allow us to detect more than 1,000 billion different odours, some with very low thresholds of perception in the order of 0.0007 to 100 parts per million, but this powerful combinatory code has one inconvenient drawback: a mixture of several compounds is perceived as a single odour – the olfactory system does not allow us to access the different elements that make up the mixture – only the overall impression.

… across our brains

Once a receptor has been stimulated, the olfactory neurons on which it is located relay this activation toward a precise zone of the olfactory bulb, the first cerebral relay of olfactory processing.

Several receptors are activated for each odour, and these activate various specific zones of the bulb, creating a unique olfactory map of its characteristics. Every time we smell a different wine, individual specific maps are created from the hundreds of volatile compounds that it contains, and these maps are then sent to the olfactory cortex, the seat of our olfactory memory. Sensory analysis thus consists of recognizing this complex bouquet of aromas, which presupposes that we have previously encountered and memorized these aromas. The analytical task of the olfactory cortex will therefore include comparing the olfactory map produced by the wine with the olfactory maps stored in memory, and the task of deconstructing the bouquet of aromas will involve successfully isolating from this map an element similar to one that has been memorized.

Olfactory information does not stop uniquely in the olfactory cortex, however. It follows multiple pathways within the brain, travelling to the amygdala, for processing in a more emotional way; the hypothalamus, a centre that controls our physical behaviours and internal states, such as appetite; the hippocampus, a key centre for episodic and semantic memory that plays an essential role in establishing a link between the taste of a wine and its associated words and memories; and the orbitofrontal cortex, an important centre for multisensory analysis, among others. Throughout this journey through the brain, olfactory information, whether perceived consciously or unconsciously, helps us to identify and recognize aromas but is also subject to transformation by its context: when we see its colour, whether we are hungry or have just eaten, whether we feel emotions of pleasure or disgust and so on.

Variability and subjectivity – the shortcomings of smelling

As remarkable as it may be, our sense of smell's ability to discriminate is freighted with a number of shortcomings. For a start, the brain perceives these odours only as a whole, non-analytically – in other words, we are neurophysiologically incapable of breaking down the individual molecules that make up an odour. This is probably because, in our daily lives, we are only ever exposed to complex aromatics, never basic smells: while a banana releases nigh on 200 different smell molecules, we experience the odour of the banana as a whole and are unable to read the 200 elements of which it is composed. Without the use of chemical analysis like gas chromatography, mass spectrometry and electro-olfactography, we would never know precisely what we are smelling and which receptors were being stimulated.

In addition, studies have shown that the more complex an odour is, the less able we are to recognize its compounds. Intensity may also be deceptive; we tend to think that the more intense an aroma is, the more complex the aroma must be, but this is not necessarily the case. If a particular odour is strong and pervasive – a damp cellar, for example – we may even unconsciously adapt to it to the point of no longer smelling it, and we will perceive other, less striking smells instead. This is known as adaptation and desensitization. Our hypersensitive sense of smell is therefore also imprecise.

This is compounded by genetic variability; studies have shown that at least 30 per cent of receptors are functionally different from one person to the next, with distinct and individual thresholds of detection. This has a powerful effect on particular perception thresholds; the same molecule may sometimes have a detection threshold that differs by a factor of 1,000 to 10,000 between individuals, as opposed to a 5- or 10-fold difference for most tastes, with the exception of bitterness.

This is further complicated by the fact that we do not necessarily give a compound the same name, depending on its concentration and our perception threshold: what may be white truffle for one person is rotten egg for another, even though both of these are dimethyl sulphide. While we all share the same olfactory zoning map of stimuli in the olfactory bulb, the way our memories code these is also entirely individual, using emotions, memories, other sensations and so on. Essentially, it is impossible for two individuals to have the same sensations or the same ability to distinguish and interpret, even for the same wine tasted at the same moment under the same conditions, and this is without even considering all the variables of olfactory analysis itself: context, order of presentation and physical and psychological state, among others.

Devaluing the sense of smell – poor vocabulary and analogy

"I'm getting violets!" But a taster who describes a bouquet thus is not really suggesting there is a smell of Violaceae flowers in the glass, or that the wine has been infused with their petals; it merely means that an element has been identified on the global scent map of wine that by analogy is reminiscent of the olfactory map of violets. The vocabulary for single odours

is in fact highly limited in Western societies. We resort to comparison and metaphor for odours and aromas from our lived experience and of objects we have encountered, using recollections stored away in the sensory memory. When we talk about something, it is always in the sense of "This reminds me of the smell of such and such a thing" – the bouquet of this wine is reminiscent of violets.

> "I'm getting violets!" But a taster who describes a bouquet thus is not really suggesting there is a smell of Violaceae flowers or that the wine has been infused with their petals

As linguist Martine Coutier points out in her *Dictionnaire de la langue du vin* (2007), "In the absence of specific descriptors, expression of these complex sensations, which are all no more than nuances, must refer back not only to sensory analogy but also to the imagination."

Why should there be such a lack of direct descriptors? Anthropology may provide some clues. In the first instance, being a primate implies the superiority of sight and vision for perceiving stimuli at a distance; the fact that we walk upright means that humans are distanced from the ground and its olfactory sources – with the caveat that a reduction in functional olfactory receptor genes had already begun in the great apes, and this reduction seems to coincide in human evolution with the emergence of trichromatic vision. Evolution has thus conditioned the senses that we were to educate first, and in Western societies, since the time of the ancient world, vision and hearing have been at the front of the queue.

Until the end of the 20th century, the sense of smell was considered an inferior sense of an almost animal nature and was valued and intellectualized far less than sight, unlike in other societies. In addition, the standards of hygiene that had developed over centuries to facilitate social life in increasingly large urban centres resulted in "silent judgment" that spread throughout the world of odour, with a social discourse that stigmatized smells, whether they were bad or not. The story of this massive dynamic of deodorization in Western society from the end of the 18th century is told by historian Alain Corbin in *The Foul and the Fragrant* (English ed: 1996).

This also has repercussions for scientific research: the sense of smell was long neglected, and it was not until the discoveries made by Richard Axel and Linda Buck about recognition of odours in 1991 (which earned them the Nobel Prize in Medicine in 2004) that a sudden and large-scale expansion of work on olfaction was to be seen. For a long time, in fact, aromas had been of interest to no one, and this was certainly a factor in the history of wine tasting. Chauvet, who in the 1960s was suggesting odours and aromas as a specific way of

The particularities of the human sense of smell

Although our sense of smell is relatively underdeveloped compared to many other animals – like dogs, mice, butterflies or elephants – Lepousez suggests that the olfactory system nonetheless retains several peculiarities: the way in which odours are perceived (both orthonasally and retronasally simultaneously); the multidimensional classification of odours (we have around 400 olfactory receptors, compared with three for colours); wide genetic variety; and the synthetic and global perception of smell (it is impossible to separate the elements that make up an odour). In addition, there is multiple, parallel processing of this information (analytical vs emotional, conscious vs unconscious) and a highly associative odour recognition memory (odours are named according to the olfactory source) that rarely operates on an abstract level. There is no abstract word to describe odours to compare with the word "blue" to describe a colour, for example.

This wealth of resources is a delight for the brain, which takes a fascinated interest in analysing, memorizing and categorizing the world of smells that goes far beyond the simple detection of odours for the survival of the species.

That said, the unique nature of our genetics, our experiences, our olfactory education and our culture makes it unlikely that any two people smell things in the same way – and this is, in part, the source of the problem of the language and communication of aromas.

distinguishing fine wines, now looks like a visionary; not only did he establish their credibility as subjects for study, he also broadened the fields of comparative evocation and analogy.

How can we talk about aromas now?

Taking inspiration from 19th-century colour wheels, Ann Noble, a chemist at UC Davis, created the Wine Aroma Wheel® in 1980 in an attempt to organize the comparative odours used in wine tasting, classifying them by their apparent similarity. This approach encourages an almost infinite number of analogies, culminating in the most grotesque excesses that ultimately chip away at the credibility of tasting: they generate remarks that are both incomprehensible to the average amateur and hollow clichés to professionals. In striving for absolute precision, some even refer to specific molecules by their chemical names, but this too has raised a communication barrier, as with colour, with such scientific language proving difficult to share.

So, how can we talk about aromas, a fundamentally subjective experience, without falling prey to oversimplification or solipsism? The solution is to develop a codified vocabulary and categories within a system of commonly accessible reference points that the taster can use in accordance with their own taste sensitivity. The subjectivity of experience, however, renders neither the linguistic fact, nor the referent itself, subjective. This has been demonstrated by the work of Richard Pfister, a Swiss oenologist working in perfume creation who has specialized in this field, summarizing his findings in Les Parfums du vin (2013). Because the only objective constant is the source of olfactory analogy, we must relearn how to classify these families as we were once able to do with the Aroma Wheel, for example. This was one of Pfister's achievements, with the oenology department of the Changins school of engineering (the École d'Ingénieurs de Changins, or EIC Changins), in 2004, using the Oenoflair classification concept. "Odours are not classified by their olfactory similarities, as each individual reacts differently," he states. "Here, it is odorous 'objects' that are classified together, rather than their odours: redcurrants and blackberries are in the berry family because they are both berries, not because they smell alike. Narcissi are classified in the garden flower family, irrespective of the fact that their odour can have hints that are more animal than floral in nature." This has enabled Pfister to identify 10 dominant odours and 19 families.

In this system, if a red wine smells of strawberries, it would be more logical also to evoke pineapple than raspberries, since the odour of strawberries is chemically closer to the former than the latter; our brains and our upbringing in wine would spontaneously balk at this, however – a dry red wine can't smell like a sweet, yellow tropical fruit! And pineapple does not in fact feature in the same family as strawberry on the Aroma Wheel. Given the desire to develop tasting methods that are better adapted to the growing diversity of wines produced, the emergence of new complexities, the advances made by science in understanding olfactory perception and the wine world's increasingly cosmopolitan openness to other cultures and thus to other vocabularies and frames of reference, the smell of wine promises to be an extremely exciting field of research and analysis in the future.

Tasting wine

The mouth, where we both taste and feel wine, is the most synaesthetic part of the wine-tasting experience. It is stimulated by chemical and physical sensations, sending to the brain thousands of messages that were once used for survival but are now employed for pleasure. During a wine tasting, we become fully aware that wine is a "total sensory object", whose appreciation depends as much on its physical and chemical composition as – once again – on the structure of our brains and the sensory information they receive. Our mouths may be packed full of biochemical receptors, but they are also steeped in our unconscious experience and are embedded in a specific culture. Much like our sense of smell, our sense of taste has long been neglected in Western societies and is still disregarded, with a poverty of vocabulary to express its incredible complexity. What are flavours and taste sensations? How do we perceive them? And is it possible to truly describe the taste of wine?

Taste – flavours and dynamic sensations

Wine provokes chemical sensations that are gustatory (taste), tactile (astringency, smoothness, tingling and so on), thermal and algesic (causing pain or irritation). The last three are also categorized as somatosensory or somaesthetic, from the Greek *soma*, "body", and *aisthesis*, "sensation": they relate to sensations essential for our survival and are perceived by the whole body. In the mouth, there are also what are known as "trigeminal" sensations, as the tactile, thermal and pain sensations in the oral cavity are transmitted by the trigeminal nerve. The mouth, which is the location of some 20 per cent of the body's tactile receptors, has become uniquely sensitized in order to prevent all kinds of food poisoning. The oral cavity is thus a dynamic centre of several million taste cells grouped together on 2,000 to 10,000 taste receptors, making up several hundred taste buds that are mainly concentrated on the upper surface of the tongue, with a few scattered outposts located in the pharynx and the soft palate.

We now know that each taste bud is not exclusively specialized for one taste, but there are nonetheless differences in sensitivity between the various parts of the mouth, not least because taste buds are more concentrated at the front and back of the tongue. For this reason, you should take in a sufficient amount (10ml, or slightly less than a tablespoon) to perceive the taste of a wine correctly, so that the saliva does not dilute it too much, and it should be chewed, like any food, for 10–15 seconds. This will ensure the vast majority of the taste buds are coated, allowing the taster to move on from reflexive impressions to analysis; you can inhale at the same time to boost retronasal perception of aromas. Once the wine has been spat out, the length of time that its taste and aromas persist in the mouth can be evaluated and quantified in seconds, or *caudalies* in French; the quality of a wine is judged on the duration of these lingering sensations.

The taste of a wine is highly dynamic: sweetness, acidity and salinity are immediately apparent on the attack, while umami and bitterness tend be on the finish, as is the tactile sensation of astringency that tends to emerge at the end. This last depends on the interaction between tannins and the proteins in saliva, which only comes about if the wine is chewed. This makes it clear that the taste and structure of a wine – this skeletal framework made up of basic elements such as acids, alcohol, sugars, tannins and CO_2 – must be understood within the dynamics of their components – their qualities, their persistence and their interactions.

Sweetness

The sweetness of a wine, the first sensation to be perceived in the mouth, essentially refers to the unfermented residual sugars in the wine rather than to any aroma of ripe fruit. Unless they have been introduced as chaptalization, they come from the grape itself or are released by new wood as triterpenoid-style natural sweeteners. These are sweet molecules identified in 2020 by Axel Marchal and his Bordeaux team, not to be conflated with aromatic compounds such as vanillin or lactones that are not in themselves sweet.

Grapes mainly accumulate glucose and fructose, hexoses that have equal molar mass in the must but are unmatched in the wine; glucose, the sugar of choice for yeasts, is fermented more quickly, leaving fructose, which tastes twice as sweet and is perceived more rapidly in the mouth. Our point of reference, sucrose, or table sugar, has a sweetening power midway between fructose and glucose and is generally used for chaptalization or *dosage*; more will thus be required to obtain the same sensation as that delivered by fructose. Wine also contains traces of non-fermentable sugars, including arabinose and xylose. As a rule, we do not notice a sweet taste if glucose is less than 2g/l, but other molecules may stimulate our receptors and act in synergy to give us the impression of sweetness.

- **Ethanol**, which has a sweet taste in low concentrations before it begins to bite, also enhances the perception of sugars when these are present. It plays an essential role in balancing a wine in the mouth, which explains the difficulty of finding an alcohol-free wine that is not a little off-kilter.
- **Glycerol** is a polyol and a by-product of fermentation, present in greater amounts with noble rot. It exerts little effect at low concentrations in the vast majority of wines, but feels viscous and sweet above 8g/l. In sweet wines, however, the sugar concentration will mask any sweetening effect of glycerol.

Diethylene glycol, a synthetic polyol, was involved in a major fraud in Austria in 1985, when unscrupulous producers added it to round out wines, an illegal practice that led to comprehensive reform of wine quality control in the country. Incorporation of amino acids such as peptides may also have a sweetening effect: research has shown that autolysis releases a peptide that sweetens both white and red wines left on their lees. The perception of sweetness may also be either enhanced or masked by other elements: acid and bitter tastes and salinity and cold will diminish it. Some aromas, like vanilla, ripe fruit, maltol and furaneol, are sometimes called "sweet". Even though these volatile molecules are incapable of activating the sweet taste receptor in the mouth, they reinforce the sense of sweetness in the brain because they hint at and predict something sugary.

Acidity – the backbone of wine

Acidity is the second taste to emerge in the mouth and is the backbone of a wine, which in any case is one of the most acid-rich beverages, containing something like a hundred different examples from the grape or from fermentation, each with a different capacity to release H^+ ions. It is these last that stimulate our unique acidity receptors. Acids have different strengths, and acidity may be fixed or volatile, and the compounds may be mineral or organic. Some of the latter

are bonded with bases, such as potassium, to produce salts and play no role in the perception of acidity.

All these elements add up to produce the total acidity of a wine, which is measured in grams per litre (g/l): this is expressed in sulphuric acid equivalents in France (which is odd, since H_2SO_4 is rarely or never found in wine) and in tartaric acid equivalents in the rest of the world. The upshot is often confusion because these two indices have different values: a wine with 4g/l of acidity in France will have 6g/l in the US (the conversion factor is 1.5). The other way of measuring acidity refers not to weight but strength – the well-known pH value, which is a logarithmic representation of H^+ ion activity. While the correlation between acidity and pH is actually indirect and complex, the basic principle is that the higher the pH value is, the lower the acidity, and vice versa, bearing in mind that a pH that is too high will compromise microbial stability and the wine's potential for ageing. On average, the acidity of a wine will lie somewhere between 2.5 and 8g/l (H_2SO_4), with a pH between 3 and 4, which corresponds to a variation of 1 to 0.1mg/l of H^+ ions, or a factor of 10, which is not inconsiderable.

The acids in wine

The main acids present in wine are fixed organic acids that come from grapes. They seem to have a taste of their own – besides acidity – even though there is no scientific consensus on this point.

- **Tartaric acid** is the acid most commonly present in wine and most associated with grapes because of its concentration. It is the strongest acid present, increasing the concentration of H^+ ions to the greatest extent, and may be precipitated by potassium or calcium, or metabolized into acetic acid by lactic bacteria. It has a hard and slightly astringent taste and plays a prominent role in salivation. It is the acid most used for artificial acidification.
- **Malic acid** is far more widespread, particularly in fruit and especially apples, from which it takes its name. It functions as an indication of the maturity of grapes because levels drop after veraison, and it may impart a rather harsh character to wines from years with cold summers. It is converted during malolactic fermentation, which naturally deacidifies the wine. Some styles of wine, like Muscadet, Sancerre and Vinho Verde, avoid it more or less systematically to preserve freshness, but with the progression of climate change, which reduces it naturally, some winemakers have been re-examining the role it plays in a wine's feeling of freshness. It has an intense taste, with sharp, green undertones.
- **Citric acid** is present in all grapes but is most concentrated in those with noble rot. It is the main acid in lemons and citrus fruits. Levels in wine vary considerably, with reds

containing little or none. During fermentation, it is often broken down into acetic acid by lactic bacteria. It is also used to acidify white wines and has a fresh and sharp taste.

Other grape acids found as trace elements in wine include ascorbic acid, which tastes crisp, gluconic acid and coumaric acid, which is an ethylphenol precursor. Others may appear during fermentation.

- **Lactic acid** is produced from sugar and malic acid by lactic bacteria. It is a lighter acid with a fresh and pleasant taste. It is found in yoghurts and lacto-fermented vegetables.
- **Succinic acid** is also synthesized in small quantities. It features a slightly bitter and umami taste that is characteristic of all fermented drinks and is found in larger quantities in sake.
- **Acetic acid** is a volatile acid that tastes and smells sour and vinegary – and indeed is the acid in vinegar.

When an organic acid is tasted, the acidity is never perceived in isolation. There is also a tactile aspect that is more or less astringent, because acids are able to act on the proteins in saliva and affect the contraction of mucous membranes. As a result, the mouth produces aqueous saliva, rich in water, when the pH of the mouth drops below a threshold that poses a danger to our teeth or mucosae; we will therefore only ever experience a diluted mixture of wine and saliva. However, the composition and quantity of saliva produced will vary widely from one individual to the next: between 0.1 and 1.5ml/min with a pH that can alter the base reading by anything from +0.2 to +0.9. According to Peynaud, "These wide variations in oral pH, which are far greater than those of the acidity analysed in wines, would go some way toward explaining the differences in perception of, and preference for, acidity between individuals and circumstances. Too little attention is paid to this simple but essential mechanism of 'tasting acidity'". The sensation of acidity is mitigated by sweetness but boosts astringency and bitterness; it plays a role in the sensation of freshness, tension and minerality.

Bitterness

Bitterness is not a taste commonly found in wine. It develops more gradually and slowly in the mouth than sweet or acid tastes but dominates on the finish. It is a highly complex taste that has only just begun to be studied. We have 25 receptors that are stimulated by more than 1,000 compounds that can be detected at far lower concentrations than any other taste molecule. This is a physiological protection mechanism, because many natural toxins are bitter, which is why the taste is often perceived as unpleasant or provoking reactions of disgust. One explanation for this innate rejection of the taste is that the taste cells that detect bitterness are hardwired to induce in our brains, and in the brains of most mammals,

an avoidance response. Appreciating bitterness is therefore a culturally acquired behaviour that is developed gradually.

Depending on the compound encountered, there can be an enormous variation in genetic and cultural sensitivity between individuals, with the perception threshold potentially fluctuating by a factor of 1,000 from one person to the next. The bitter taste in wine arises mainly from phenolic compounds

> " One of the great challenges in taste analysis of wines is to re-educate the palate not to conflate "salty", "savoury" and "umami"

and tannins, which can sometimes cause it to be conflated with astringency. Some mineral ions, such as magnesium, have a bitterness that is amplified by alcohol and acidity and can be attenuated with salt, umami and sugars.

Salinity – not only salt, but also…

One of the great challenges in wine taste analysis is to re-educate the palate not to conflate "salty", "savoury" and "umami". Saying that a wine is salty is often an imprecise use of language: wines contain very little – if indeed any at all – sodium chloride (NaCl), the table salt that is our point of reference. This saltiness, which is transmitted by a dedicated taste receptor, is the way we detect sodium and potassium ions, which are found in seawater, for example.

Among the 2–4g of mineral substances that wine contains on average, however, there are other mineral and organic compounds that also seem to have a salty taste – although at such concentrations, these compounds are not perceived as such. Instead, they tend to act by indirectly modifying the taste of the wine by enhancing sweetness and balancing bitterness and astringency. We are aware at some level that wine is not salty like seawater, and we betray this, says Lepousez, by using words such as "savour" and "salinity" instead of "saltiness". We taste something different, but we have only a poor grasp of concepts to describe it, resulting in imprecision in the way we tell these apart. There are in fact several types of salinity in wines.

… umami…

The sensation of salinity mainly comes from umami, for which we have a primary taste receptor that detects certain amino acids, nucleotides and succinic acid. As previously mentioned, umami was discovered at the beginning of the 20th century by Japanese researcher Kikunae Ikeda and has been considered a taste since the 1990s. Umami has been highly popular since the very origins of culinary tradition: Roman *garum*, a fish-based fermented sauce, was a boiled-down version; soy

Liger-Belair and the science of effervescence

Bubbles provide what may be the most synaesthetic wine experience of all, stimulating the senses of sight and hearing – the pop of the cork, the fizz of the bubbles – along with smell, taste and touch – the tingling of the nostrils and on the tongue in the presence of CO_2. Carbon dioxide, their essential ingredient, is much more than a somatosensory agent in wine, tickling the mucous membranes and heightening the sensation of acidity and astringency. Gérard Liger-Belair, a specialist in the physical chemistry of effervescence at the University of Reims-Champagne-Ardenne, has been studying bubbles for more than 15 years. His findings, published in *Un monde de bulles* (2020), show that the generation, rise and bursting of bubbles owe nothing to chance. Forming on tiny imperfections or motes of dust in the glass, they grow larger and capture aromas as they rise to the surface, releasing CO_2 and aromatic compounds. Their rise is not continuous and will depend on the wine itself – its viscosity, the quantities of gas dissolved, sugar content and so on – the temperature at which it is served, the shape of the glass and the duration of the tasting session. These are thus all parameters that shape our perception of an effervescent wine. Understanding these physical mechanisms and the neurophysiological processes at work when we experience them increases the pleasure of tasting a flute of Champagne tenfold – the first sip, a truly enjoyable sensation if ever there was one, takes on a whole new taste.

sauce is an ancient Asian condiment; and we can assume that French gourmand Jean Anthelme Brillat-Savarin was an enthusiast from his descriptions, in 1825, of the "osmazome" (pure essence of meat) in the stocks and sauces of his *Physiology of Taste* (English ed: 1949). The taste of umami is found in some vegetables, like tomatoes, asparagus and shiitake mushrooms, in green tea, in meat, fish and crustaceans, and in fermented and matured products such as cheese, ham, miso and nýớc mắm, and more besides. It is also found in human breast milk. While the perception of umami can be stimulated by several molecules in our food, the most common trigger in wine seems to be glutamate.

So, what creates umami in wine? Studies are only just beginning, and we can offer no more than food for thought, as it were.

The autolysis of yeasts during lees-ageing releases amino acids and small umami peptides. The longer the ageing, as with Champagne and *flor* wines, the more umami the wine is likely to have. Low nitrogen levels in the must, resulting from low-fertility, low-water-retention terroirs, induce metabolic stress that may cause yeasts to produce more succinic acid, with an umami taste, during fermentation. It should be remembered that umami is a particular taste with a synergetic dynamic, and the simultaneous presence of two umami compounds will impart a sensation that is logarithmically greater than their sum, as can be tasted, for example, when glutamate-rich Champagne is matched with nucleotide-rich caviar: the results are intensely umami. In wine tasting, umami resembles saltiness but differs from it through its length in the mouth and its persistence – the saline impression at the finish – with an enveloping character and enhanced salivation.

... and calcium

The same is true of the calcium in wine, the scientific study of which is in its infancy. Calcium (Ca) and the mineral ions Ca^{2+} and Mg^{2+} (magnesium) would give rise to a harder salinity that is desiccating and slightly bitter. In addition to the taste receptor for saltiness, which detects sodium (Na) and potassium (K) ions, it is thought we have a sixth taste sense with a specific receptor dedicated to the perception of Ca^{2+} and Mg^{2+} ions and certain compounds that the Japanese call *kokumi*, "rich taste", a taste familiar to us from heavily mineralized water.

The calcium in wine comes from the grapes, but it has to be present in quantities greater than that contained by our saliva, which is about 40mg/l, for us to perceive it. It also has to be lower than 80mg/l to avoid precipitation in contact with tartaric acid, which will cause stability problems. Because our perception of calcium takes place within a rather limited spectrum, it tends to be magnesium that is responsible for expressing salinity.

There are thus two types of salinity: one is organic, umami, created by yeasts and perceptible on the finish, generating a soft film of saliva that is of great interest for food and wine pairings; the other is mineral coming from the soil, expressing saltiness from sodium or potassium, a very direct taste perceived in the mouth, and calcium/magnesium, which tends to be bitter and slightly desiccating in the mid-mouth. These new criteria and terms cannot be ignored by modern sensory analysis.

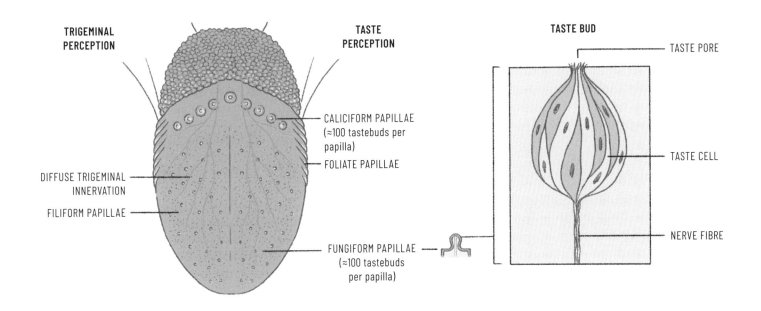

SENSATION	MOLECULE TRIGGERING THE SENSATION	NUMBER OF RECEPTORS	DETECTION THRESHOLD (µM)
ACID	PROTON (H^+) organic acids, CO_2	1	1,000
SALINITY	NA^+ , K^+	1	10,000
SWEETNESS	GLUCIDES sweeteners	1	10,000
UMAMI	GLUTAMATE peptides, succinic acid	1 (+1?)	10,000
BITTERNESS	POLYPHENOLS alkaloids, terpenes etc.	25	10
FAT	FATTY ACIDS	2–4	10,000
CALCIUM	$CA^{?+}$, $MG^{?+}$ kokumi	1	10,000
"SWEET"	OLIGOSACCHARIDES derived from starch	1?	10,000
"WARM"	PEPPER	1 (+1?)	0.1
"COLD"	MENTHOL	1 (+1?)	10
SPICY/ IRRITATING	MUSTARD/ PEPPER ethanol, CO_2, acid	1–3	1

THE TASTES OF WINE AND THE AGENTS, RECEPTORS AND DETECTION THRESHOLDS THAT CREATE THEM, AS DESCRIBED BY GABRIEL LEPOUSEZ

Astringency and tannins

"Wine is a Gothic cathedral of tannins confected by man, made with a finesse and elegance that evolves over time." Selosse's *Les Goûts et les couleurs du monde* (2019) explores the tannins or polyphenols, ubiquitous in nature and our everyday lives, that are found in the colour, odour and taste of wine. As they react with our saliva, they turn the ritual of tasting into a fundamentally dynamic experience, revealing to us the development of wine over time in the mouth.

The corollary of this is that saliva and changes in its properties allow us indirectly to analyse the tannins in wine. Tannins combine with the proteins in saliva, triggering the formation of aggregates that are precipitated out. This phenomenon reduces the lubricant properties of the saliva and triggers a sensation of friction and roughness between the tongue and the sides of the mouth.

Tannins are a complex subject that is generally poorly understood by wine tasters; these compounds perform a protective role for plants and are toxic in certain concentrations but nonetheless provide the foundations for the architecture of wine. Astringency, from the Latin *astringere*, "to squeeze", is a somesthetic sensation essential in red wines, although less so in whites and rosés; it is also found in skin-contact wines. It imparts a sensation of dryness and absence of lubrication in the mouth and is principally caused by polyphenols, the great diversity of which shapes the sensation of astringency. Polyphenols are chemical groups of greater or lesser complexity, with a basically phenol function.

Learning to distinguish the different types of tannin

There are two large families of tannins.
- **Flavonoids**, or condensed tannins, come principally from the skin and pips. This is a broad category and includes anthocyanins, procyanidines and flavonols such as catechins and epicatechins. Some of these small phenolic compounds are also able to impart a bitter taste. The quality and concentration of these tannins are determined by cépage, viticulture and vinification.
- **Non-flavonoids**, or phenolic acids, are water-soluble and metabolized in plant bark. These include the ellagitannins in oak and gallotannins in oak gall that are introduced to the wine during ageing in contact with the wood.

When tasting wine, we tend to group all these compounds together under the heading "tannin". While this approach is understandable, it comes at the price of a proper comprehension of their origins and the different sensations in the mouth that they provide.
- **Tannins from grapes** (flavonoids) polymerize more readily with saliva proteins. Tannins from pips are greener and sharper; those from skins are silkier. Anthocyanins have no flavour.
- **Tannins from wood** (non-flavonoids) are more diffuse and pronounced on the finish, with an aspect of bitterness. They vary depending on the species of the wood and how it has been treated at the cooperage, and give off less of a desiccating astringency.

Tannins can bring out a wide range of nuances in the mouth, varying in intensity; there are specific astringencies, such as the sensation of particles of powder or chalk, astringencies that are reminiscent of textile or fabric surface textures – silky, velvety or rough – and desiccating and aggressive astringencies.

While we still take the power of tannins as an indication of their quantity in a wine, tasting is really still the only way to evaluate their quality, since this will vary with the composition of the saliva and the presence of acids: tannins react more strongly with the proteins in saliva when the pH is low. Conversely, astringency is modified by the presence of sugar or proteins, and by higher pH levels. Finally, the sensation of astringency is cumulative and grows during tasting.

As with bitterness, the appreciation of astringency as a sensation is acculturated; we learn to transcend our initial rejection of this disagreeable sensation, warning of possible danger, to transform it into an aspect of a wine that is particularly enjoyed, if it is of good quality. Enjoying it ultimately tells us something about ourselves as well.

Richness and consistency

The counterpoint to astringency might be richness and unctuousness, which give a feeling of consistency and thickness to a wine, like a solid food. Research carried out in 2005 identified a receptor present in the taste buds of both humans and rodents that is activated by fatty acids. While fat is thus technically a new potential taste, it is of less use in tasting wine, because wine contains very few fatty acids, and if we perceive them at all, it will tend to be more in the form of aromatic volatile compounds. While autolysis of the lees also releases a few fatty acids, current use of milk, be it skimmed or full-fat, as an analogy to understand the consistency of wine is still a misuse of language. When we speak of the "unctuousness" of a wine, we are referring more to the tactile perception of alcohols, both ethanol and glycerol, polysaccharides, glycoproteins (mannoproteins) and of proteins in our saliva that are released under the effects of certain components of the wine. It is therefore the combination of umami compounds from the wine and polyphenols that trigger the production of unctuous, textured saliva that is thought to create this impression of a wine's consistency. But this sensation is only a by-product of its interaction with our mouths rather than a characteristic per se.

The touch of wine

We have all experienced the dynamic construction of wine, which is what we mean by its "feel" or "touch". Our mouths contain dedicated filiform papillae, five receptors sensitive to mechanical deformation, called mechanoreceptors, and five muscular receptors that complement the somatosensory information provided by the receptors of the trigeminal nerve, which detect temperature and pain. Located on the lips, tongue and pharynx in the oral cavity, they detect changes in pressure, vibrations and deformation of the mucous membranes, such as contraction. It is these receptors that allow us to sense the texture and consistency of a wine extremely precisely; the mouth is the part of our body best able to sense textures and tell them apart. It is an active sense, however – the wine has to be poured, and we have to chew it. The tongue has to move or we will perceive almost nothing, just as a hand simply placed on a surface will perceive very little; it must move across it. Salivation plays an active role by polymerizing tannins and diluting acidity, for example, so we sense a great deal through the prism of our saliva and its changes in texture, but here too our vocabulary is limited. To remedy this, scientists have developed educational tools to expand the terms at our disposal and define them, thereby improving the precision of sensory analysis.

In 2000, Australian researcher Richard Gawel created a "mouthfeel wheel", divided into 13 categories that use 53 terms to describe the mouthfeel of red wines, the majority of which are orientated around astringency; the rest relate to acidity and different tastes. In describing textures, Gawel makes particular analogical use of different materials, like talcum, satin, plaster, chamois leather, silk, velvet, suede, fur, emery board, corduroy, glass paper and burlap, which he supplements with dynamic descriptors – different types of dryness, hardness, underripeness and so on.

In 2008, Gary Pickering from Canada's Brock University suggested another wheel, intended this time for white wines, with notable differences: it was less focused on astringency and included parameters for intensity and sequence – attack, finish, evolution and so on. The descriptors are arranged around the wheel in their supposed order of mouthfeel. This time patisserie, in the form of meringue, whipped cream, mousse or marshmallow, is used as an analogy for volume, with no aromatic references.

These two wheels represent undeniable progress in categorizing the mouthfeel of wine. While their differences

may lead to confusion, applying them in practice can only help to educate us and expand our vocabulary and our language when describing taste and mouthfeel, which was so neglected in wine tasting in the 20th century.

How should we talk about taste?

Coutier's *Dictionnaire de la langue du vin* points out that "perceptions of taste are the most complex to identify, and thus to name, because of the close contact that the perceiver has with the object perceived, which excludes the type of comparison possible for visual and olfactory perceptions. In addition, French is particularly deficient in specific vocabulary for taste. . . And this is why the vocabulary of taste is largely metasemic; the taster has to rely on a metaphorical process, making use of shared language in particular to draw on analogies with recurrent themes." She goes on to list the following themes.

- **Intersensory metaphors** and metaphors relating to the properties of materials – these are consistent, crunchy, hard and so on.
- **Anthropomorphism**, which she considers the oldest and most productive association: the "body" of a wine, of course, but there are also allusions to its construction ("skeleton"), its "legs", its figure ("slender"), its nerves ("tension"), its strength ("athletic"), its gender ("masculine") and, among 19th-century tasters, even extending to erotic connotations like "thighs" and "bodice".
- **Spatial metaphors** designate shape, volume and contours, which Peynaud called "stereotasting", depending on the proportions of its constituents, angular, rounded or vertical.
- **Temporal metaphors** relate to the persistence of the taste and potential for ageing: "short-term", "accomplished" or "over".
- **Building metaphors** include terms such as "architecture", "construction" and "frame".
- **Textile-related metaphors**.

Coutie also notes that new terms have emerged to supplement this vocabulary: "crunchy" in 1989, "pumped" in 1999. So there is now a vast analogical vocabulary available to describe these tactile sensations in our mouths, mitigating semantic poverty and evoking taste sensations. While this figurative vocabulary allows us to express what literal language would struggle to describe, one problem still remains: the necessity of establishing a common frame of reference to decode these metaphors, given that the link between chemical compounds and the sensations perceived is still poorly understood. It is this that new multisensory approaches, which are also all new languages of wine, hope to address.

The language of wine

Tasting a wine loosens tongues. For some, a tasting is not really a tasting until it has been shared and discussed. The tongue used for tasting is also used for talking, and this presents a problem – the specialized language of wine is not standardized, even among experts, however abstract and opaque non-professionals might consider it. Much wine language attracts criticism for having moral connotations. The meaning of a term will vary from specialist to specialist over time, depending on the style of wine. Use of extremely wide-ranging semantic fields seems a necessary evil, complicating things still further and raising questions about the relevance of such commentaries, including those from critics, and the possibility of describing wine. How can we speak about such a subjective experience? Don't our syntax and vocabulary distort our perception? Can we do without words? What language can be used not only to evaluate but, more fundamentally, to understand wine?

Knowing how to drink wine means knowing how to talk about it

Of the many and varied aesthetic experiences, including fine dining, tasting wine seems to be the only one that almost as a matter of course elicits commentary about both the enjoyment – "it's good" or "I don't like it" - and the explanation of the object itself and the taster's experience. For most people, there is a disconnect between tasting a wine alone and in silence and sharing the experience with others. The ultimate purpose of critics who blind-taste in isolation to guarantee maximum objectivity is to communicate their experience of the wine. So, whether we are tasting for ourselves, as wine-lovers, for pleasure, or for others, knowing how to drink wine also means knowing how to talk about it. This is far from a clear and simple process, however, and it often involves learning by imitation, perhaps of other tasting notes, or assimilation of sensory profiles or normative grids, lists of points of reference and words used to describe this or that wine, descriptors fashioned by experts who strive to agree on the perception to which they might refer. This specialized grammar, which aims to be codified and objective, goes some way toward structuring, expressing and sharing the multimodal and multisensory experience that is wine, but there are limits to its precision and objectivity. As oenologist Max Léglise (1924–96) pointed out, those tasting wine do not describe it by saying that "it contains high levels of isoamyl acetate, alpha ionone,

glycyrrhizin and benzaldehyde-cyanohydrin, for example, but, much more simply, state that it smells of candy crisp, violets, liquorice and cherries." There is in fact not a single specialized language but many, determined by the wine taster's training and linguistic baggage, along with the circumstances in which they are describing the wine.

There is not one language of wine, but thousands

Peynaud and Blouin's *Le Goût du vin* identifies six types of tasting note, five professional and one amateur, for the same wine, with vocabularies that run from the most specific to the most general. They typically come from:

- **Technicians and agronomists**, with a global perspective and the most specific vocabulary;
- **Cellarmasters**, whose interest in wine production prompts use of the physical and chemical vocabulary of vinification;
- **Wine brokers**, using more generalized vocabulary than an oenologist;
- **Sommeliers**, who taste to match food with wines, with vocabulary suited to the restaurant trade but also generalized;
- **Reviewers**, with some interest in organoleptics but inclined more toward criticism and advertising, allowing themselves literary analogies that are constrained to different degrees, depending on the readership;
- **Wine-lovers/-drinkers**, with an enjoyment-based approach, making use of vague, generalized and holistic vocabulary.

These lexicons are increasingly overlapping because

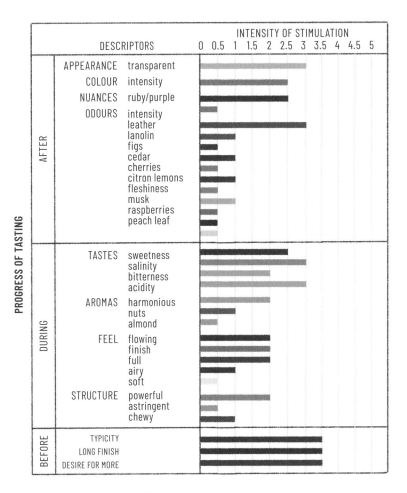

	DESCRIPTORS		INTENSITY OF STIMULATION 0 0.5 1 1.5 2 2.5 3 3.5 4 4.5 5

The appearance of Chateau Musar when served agreeably cool is as dark as one would wish, coloured with warm hints of ruby in the foreground and a touch of fuchsia that together define the parameters of this young wine. A multitude of textures are easily discerned on the nose, including tanned leather, lanolin, figs, cedar, cherries, citron lemons, fleshiness, musk, raspberries, and peach leaves.

Its subtlety asserts itself in the mouth, exposing a smooth and soft body with a silhouette accentuated by supple flavours that endow the wine with a delicate but tenacious chewiness. Everything is in balance, its power is relentless in translating the wine's wish to be tasted again and again; it has no desire to leave, and nor do we. So we take another sip to better savour the high-altitude countryside with its pure air where the vines flourished. This is a wine that flows into us with precision and persistence. Delicate dishes should be chosen to serve with it and bring out its best; some spiced squab like those served up by Alain Senderens, or noisettes of lamb nestling in a delicate chickpea purée scattered with a few shavings of black truffle. A wine of light and tranquillity.

Jacques Puisais

Description of a wine and analysis of sensory intensity by Jacques Puisais

THE FINGERPRINT OF A WINE, BY JACQUES PUISAIS AND DIDIER MICHEL: CHROMATIC ID CARD AND CORK FOR CHATEAU MUSAR 1995
Didier Michel painted cork barks (c. 60cm/23½in high) to visually represent the wine in 3D. Compounds are allocated a colour swatch and the intensity of each is reflected in its size on the painted surface according to Jacques Puisais' tasting notes and analysis.

279

of the growing popularity of wine in the 20th century and beyond, and as the vocabulary expands, our approach to tasting is changing. This conceals a fundamental problem with language and its relationship with perception: it is a tool for understanding but also an agent of change, of both the world and the way it is perceived. We taste through the filter of the words we possess, so if we have a wider vocabulary, does that mean that the wine has become more complex or that we are better at tasting? How much does our language inform our tasting?

Language models our relationship with the world – the Sapir-Whorf hypothesis

The question of whether language determines not only our perceptions but also our cognition is a hoary philosophical chestnut; is the world perceived differently depending on the language used? Colour, a continuum of wavelengths that each language divides up using specific vocabulary, is a case in point: essentially, no two languages make use of the same concepts or deploy them in the same societal context. A study of the Himba tribe from Namibia conducted by British psychologist Jules Davidoff has shown that, because they have no concept corresponding to "blue", they are unable to distinguish it from green, for which by contrast they have a wide variety of words. This view partly corroborates a controversial thesis in sensory anthropology, the linguistic relativism put forward in the Sapir-Whorf hypothesis (named after the American anthropologists who developed it at the beginning of the 20th century) to counter the universalist hypothesis that holds the perceptual categories influenced by our physiology to be universal.

According to Benjamin L Whorf, "We dissect nature along the lines laid down by [our] native languages." Words unconsciously construct reality even as they allow us to know it and share this knowledge. From this perspective, the subjectivity of the sensory experience of wine is compounded by the cultural determinism of language, making the objective communication of the experience of tasting a wine nigh on impossible. Taking this to its logical conclusion, the reality of a wine would always elude us, because language is an insurmountable filter. However, the very experience of tasting a wine limits the strong version of this hypothesis, as developed by anthropologist Joël Candau ("Vin, arômes, couleurs et descripteurs sensoriels. Quel partage de la dégustation?", 2005), in analysing the "natural language of odours".

A natural lack of words to describe odours

Visual recognition is extremely acute in humans, as demonstrated by our memory for faces, but however adept we may be at detecting odours and aromas, and accurate in distin-

guishing them, we lack skill in describing them. Thanks to the complex processing of olfactory stimuli by the brain, "odour and language don't go well together", says Candau. Physiology is therefore one reason why the olfactory lexicon is inherently imprecise and erratic: one word can describe several molecules, and several words can describe a single stimulus. It also explains why we find it difficult enough to name an aroma, let alone construct a mental image of one: try to imagine the odour and label of your favourite wine, the latter is far easier to picture mentally. Where learning colours is codified, and this can indeed structure the experience, capturing an odour in a single word proves almost impossible. Due to the way the brain works, the language of aromas is holistic and far more emotional, and tends to be prototypical – an odour resembles other members of its family – rather than analytical – an odour has this or that characteristic. Even Peynaud has acknowledged that tasters, professional and amateur alike, will therefore "struggle against the impotence of words".

This is compounded by the fact that not all the aromas we perceive are expressed verbally; there are too many for us to name each one, and we lack the necessary vocabulary to span the aromatic continuum. This would contradict the Sapir-Whorf hypothesis for odours and aromas at least, but it also opens up avenues toward a common language based on other points of reference without being purely subjective; few people tasting wine choose to say nothing, despite the difficulty of the olfactory experience, as Candau notes. In fact, they square the circle by inventing a language at the very moment of tasting: "When words encounter difficulty in establishing a reference point, everything plays out as if the process of language production was looking for a solution by generating terms in a more or less controlled manner. . . The sense of smell is multisensory by its very nature, and no less so on a lexical level." Descriptions will thus, by necessity, be allegorical, not to mention impressionist, indeed even synaesthetic, using figurative terms to create imagery and neologisms embedded within a metaphorical network: in the 1990s, wine was suddenly "exuberant", "mineral" or even "Parkerized". In her *Dictionnaire de la langue du vin*, Coutier dates the appearance of these terms in wine literature to 1991.

Because this figurative characterization is a deliberate choice, however, such analogies will indeed collate sensory representations from different semantic fields that nonetheless share fundamental traits. In other words, while the aromatic lexicon of wine tasting might have figurative characteristics, this is not so much a poetic preference as a real, strong correspondence between the properties of the wine and the things to which they are compared; one condition of many being that they have common points of reference, even if this ultimately breaks the bounds of the meaning of words.

A multisensory approach to the mouthfeel of wine

Though long neglected, the sensation of a wine's mouthfeel has again become an increasingly common feature of tasting notes since the 2010s. Dominique Valentin and Jordi Ballester are researchers in sensory sciences at the Centre for Taste and Feeding Behaviour in Dijon, and in 2016 they conducted a study intended to establish the usefulness of the tactile vocabulary available, since its relevance was not clearly evident: we don't have the same type of receptors on the tips of our fingers as we do in our mouths, so sensations will differ. How, then, can we use the same vocabulary? That said, we use a wide variety of metaphorical vocabulary to compensate for our lack of descriptive terminology for physical and chemical sensations, using terms relating to anatomy (full-bodied. . .), textiles (velvety. . .), a physical nature (hard. . .) or geometry (round, rectilinear. . .).

This type of language is necessary – it would be too difficult to express the sensations literally – but poses endless problems with interpretation and common points of reference: what do we actually mean by tannins that are "green", "unctuous" or "chalky"? Such designations are, in the first instance, intellectual shortcuts with no scientific value. Tannins are in fact brown and contain neither lipids nor calcium carbonate!

The more metaphors tasters use, the more difficult it becomes to interpret what they are describing. Even Gawel's mouthfeel wheel of sensations, which is an attempt to clarify such language, is not always crystal clear; leaving aside the problem of translating from English to another language, its categories lack coherence. This is what prompted the Dijon team to suggest a "multisensory approach aimed at using synaesthesia to describe sensations in the mouth with the aid of materials we can touch".

To achieve this, the researchers first convened a panel trained in wine tasting to carry out a semantic analysis of the vocabulary used to describe wine sensations perceived in the mouth, which allowed them to identify nine semantic fields. The panel then linked the tactile aspects identified by this analysis to materials that can be touched, either as a surface, like fabrics, bubble wrap or sandpaper, or held in the hand, like flour, rice, cotton or feathers. Finally, the panellists used the materials selected to characterize a series of wines.

There is nothing particularly original in using synaesthesia to describe a wine, but this experiment and its findings are undoubtedly unique in that they suggest it may be possible to develop a standardized lexicon of texture and perhaps even to create a portable tool, a chart of different materials to describe wine. This idea is just beginning to gain in popularity, but it confirms the relevance of multisensory

Natural wine and punk rock – synaesthesia according to Punkovino

Synaesthesia is a non-patholgical neurological phenomenon, rather than a condition, in which two or more senses are associated: "A black, E white, I red, U green, O blue", as Arthur Rimbaud wrote in "Vowels" (1883). With advances in cognitive neurobiology, wine tasting is now regarded as a kind of synaesthesia. Associating sensations or memories arising from several senses is part and parcel of memorizing, identifying and talking about wine. The television series *Punkovino* made by Yoann Le Gruiec and Tina Meyer for Arte, a European public service channel dedicated to culture, has demonstrated this in a stimulating and provocative way, presenting portraits of 10 winemakers from Anjou to Majorca, taking in everywhere from Germany to Georgia, in random productions culminating in a sequence dubbed "vinaesthesia". A local musician or a band "interprets" one of the wines that has been presented and that may have been produced in a vineyard thousands of miles away, without ever meeting the winemaker. They then improvize a piece as they taste the wine, symbolizing the vital and creative force that this movement champions. It would be great for this spontaneous vinaesthesia to be examined in detail, exploring the rhythms and tonalities chosen and how they match with the energy and changing power of the wine in the mouth. In any case, this field is wide open for exploration.

tasting for mouthfeel, at least, by inviting us to explore communication of the experience using methods other than spoken language, on condition, of course, that all the points of reference – the signifiers and signified, as it were – are common to all members of the group using them.

Tasting wine is an experience of the self

Whether the language is tactile, figurative or analytical, or synaesthesia, tasting wine requires us to develop forms of communication that evoke in others as precisely as possible what a wine is making us feel. When we are tasting a wine in a group or are compiling tasting notes, we are trying to share our perceptions with others who may not experience it in the same way, either due to physiological, genetic or cultural differences, or because the person simply cannot taste the wine. It is a kind of empathy; sensations have to be elicited in our audience that are as similar as possible to the way we feel on tasting the wine, using words and occasionally other "languages" such as graphics, sound and so on. A good note is therefore one that allows the person who reads or hears it to form a picture of the wine tasted, and so it will be made up of more than just a list of standardized descriptors; it has to capture both the wine and the taster's multimodal and dynamic experience of the wine. As Peynaud and Blouin wrote in *Le Goût du vin*, "We are moving from a very concrete world – of alcohol, acidity, tannins – that is largely universal, to a world that is increasingly abstract and, above all, increasingly personal. . . When used well [because they are well known], the vocabulary of wine helps us to know [and know ourselves], to understand [and understand ourselves] and to appreciate [and appreciate ourselves]."

In addition to its unique complexity in the sensory universe, wine also has incomparable figurative and symbolic power, which explains the central place it occupies in the social expression of taste: knowing how to taste and talk about wine translates into a skill that is both reflexive and performative, expressed in a shift from expert and analytical discourse toward forms of tasting and sharing that are more sensitive, more structured and more experiential. It is legitimate to invoke aesthetics and synaesthetics. This is made equally clear in the immersive tours of the Cité du Vin cultural centres in Bordeaux and Dijon, where images, sound and so on are put to good use, as in these new forms of tasting.

Judging and understanding the taste of fine wine

Developments in cognitive science and linguistics, and their growing interest in wine) have vastly expanded our understanding of the way we perceive and talk about it. There is still much left to discover, but this progress has validated more aesthetic and synesthetic approaches that encourage us to create and develop other forms of tasting. Lepousez proposes a number of different approaches drawing on critical rationality, emotions and associative imagination, all of which mutually enrich one another and enable us to express, as universally and as sincerely as we can, the way we taste and therefore appreciate wine.

• **Analytical, Cartesian tasting** works by taking things apart and focusing on details, judging quantitatively rather than qualitatively, and analyses fine wine by the absences of defects when compared against a standard sensory profile. It is a good starting point for learning to connect the senses with the major components of wine, but it has its limits. It

does not take salinity into account, has little to say about the finer nuances of bitterness, and passes over the different aspects of mouthfeel and the experiential changes that occur in wine over time.

• Analytical tasting needs to be enriched by a more **global tasting** approach that focuses on the concept of balance between tastes and odours, the harmony of the different sensory strata, energy, structure, minerality and freshness. By the same token, however, addressing a global concept like minerality prompts us to wonder what sensory modality (or modalities) we might be introducing to this overall experience. If a wine is "mineral", is it because of its flinty aroma, its saline aspects or its sharp acidity?

• Another kind of tasting, with **symbolic and metaphorical associations** (such as "feel"), will enhance the experience still further by making us think in terms of shape, tension and energy, suggesting new options for matching food and wines, as well as new ways of considering the relationship between wine and its terroir – human, organic, mineral and so on, the signature of the soil.

• **Emotions** must also be reintegrated into tasting, because they can help us make links between different perceptions, as long as we can tell the difference between emotion and enjoyment – "I like it/I don't like it". Teams at the ISVV at Bordeaux University led by Sophie Tempère, who holds a PhD in cognitive sciences and sensory neuroscience, are currently working on these questions, examining the role of emotions and olfactory mental imagery in tasting. Lastly, we should also remember that it is emotions that generally trigger reactions such as salivation, excitement, an attentive state or indeed apathy, and that these are essential to interoception, the unconscious internal state that allows us to appreciate the digestibility of a wine.

In this way, we will be able not only to assess but also to understand a wine and to understand ourselves. Wine, the object of all tasting, demands this. The question of "what is a good wine?" now goes far beyond a simple affirmation of standardized and normative categories as the problem of approval tasting has amply demonstrated. Wine tasting allows us to make judgment calls in taste and to cultivate a thoughtful relationship with our senses, taming them but also freeing them by making use of symbolism, imagination and emotion. Belgian writer Jean-Claude Pirotte in "Au vin la parole" (the foreword in Coutier's *Le Dictionnaire de la langue du vin*) could not have summed it up more aptly: "Wine also imposes many obligations upon us, including one duty that is absolute: to resist the reduction of the world to banality. . . The effort to translate the cadences of the vocabulary of wine is an act of resistance and a vital contribution to the primacy and liberty of the mind."

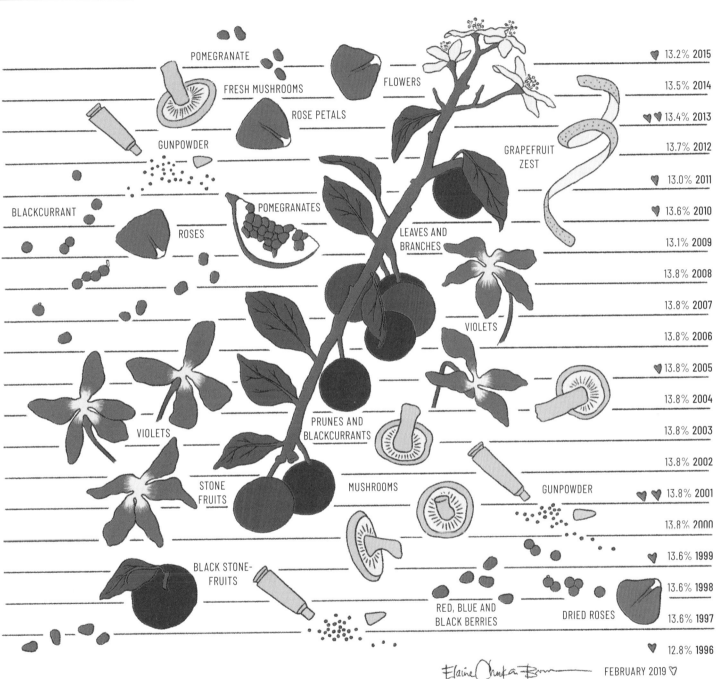

POMEGRANATE

FRESH MUSHROOMS

FLOWERS

ROSE PETALS

GUNPOWDER

GRAPEFRUIT
ZEST

BLACKCURRANT

POMEGRANATES

ROSES

LEAVES AND
BRANCHES

VIOLETS

VIOLETS

PRUNES AND
BLACKCURRANTS

STONE
FRUITS

MUSHROOMS

GUNPOWDER

BLACK STONE-
FRUITS

RED, BLUE AND
BLACK BERRIES

DRIED ROSES

13.2% 2015
13.5% 2014
13.4% 2013
13.7% 2012
13.0% 2011
13.6% 2010
13.1% 2009
13.8% 2008
13.8% 2007
13.8% 2006
13.8% 2005
13.8% 2004
13.8% 2003
13.8% 2002
13.8% 2001
13.8% 2000
13.6% 1999
13.6% 1998
13.6% 1997
12.8% 1996

FEBRUARY 2019

A GRAPHICAL INTERPRETATION OF CATHY CORISON'S KRONOS CABERNET SAUVIGNON,
AS DEPICTED BY ELAINE CHUKAN BROWN

Elaine Chukan Brown, a philosopher, lecturer and wine journalist hailing from Alaska, is one of the wine professionals
rethinking tasting codes by opening up new avenues in graphic design. Their unique composition evokes 20 years
of Cathy Corison's Kronos, a renowned Cabernet Sauvignon from California's Napa Valley.

Tasting minerality – myth or reality?

Minerality has been a central concept in the world of wine since the 1990s, with labels indicating the name of the bedrock, and promotional blurbs and critical notes expounding on the mineral characteristics of wines; sommeliers have even been known to lick rocks and winemakers to infuse stones directly into their wine… The word "minerality" has gone from obscurity to media ubiquity and has prompted some unlikely practices. Long poorly defined and thus controversial, the idea it refers to has been the focus of studies since around 2010 that, given its global popularity, have striven to define its semantic, sensory and chemical parameters. What do we mean by minerality, and why is this term so confusing? What might a mineral wine taste like? Are there other ways to think about this concept? How does it shed light on the way we see ourselves and the way we view wine and its links to terroir?

A very recent (and highly confusing) concept

"Uderan wine worked wonders in loosening the tongues they usually held [as if speaking on a weekday were a sin]; it was a white wine, a little dry, that had acquired the mineral taste of the plateaus." In 1943's *The Impudent Ones* (not published in English until 2021), Marguerite Duras is said to be the first writer in French to use the concept of minerality to describe a wine, a term previously entirely unknown in tasting notes. However, it wasn't until 40 years later that it would became a fixture in the language of wine, making its official and resounding debut in wine literature in 1991 (Coutier, *Dictionnaire de la langue du vin*). Although "mineral" has been properly defined since the 16th century ("any inorganic material located within the Earth or on its surface"), minerality is a neologism still unrecorded in general dictionaries and contemporary thesauruses. What do tasters mean by this concept?

The answer is confusing and contradictory for amateurs and professionals alike, and there are many ways of understanding minerality, even among experts. Various studies, including by sensory analysis researchers Wendy Parr and Jordi Ballester and their teams, have addressed its meaning and implications (*Minerality in Wines: Towards the Reality behind the Myths*, 2018). The concept can be understood in ways that relate to geology (bedrock) or organic chemistry (the trace elements absorbed by the plants), or in the sensory sense (a taste or flavour). It is multimodal, encompassing olfaction, taste and mouthfeel, and features in a wide range of semantic fields, including rocks and minerals like flint, silex, chalk and graphite, organic compounds like kerosene, petroleum and ink, the sea (iodine, algae, seashells) and fire-related terms like smoky or toasted. In the mouth, it is associated with acidity (tension, freshness), bitterness, saltiness and salinity. Perceptions also vary depending on the cépage, style (white more than red) and region, and responses tend to conflate elements classically associated with organic chemistry (carbon compounds) and mineral chemistry. One constant has emerged, however: a strong link with the notion of terroir - it has been suggested that we do indeed taste directly in the wine the minerality of the soil in which the vine was grown.

Soil minerality, wine minerality – a syllogism?

We know that a wine terroir is made up of rocks containing minerals that the vine needs in order to grow. It would therefore seem logical that the wine should be rich in these and that we should be able to taste them. British geologist Alex Maltman is one of many scientists who have regularly taken this syllogism apart. For a start, there is some confusion about the very meaning of mineral; the minerals in the bedrock are solid crystals that have to be eroded into chemical elements and rendered soluble and assimilable by roots, so the vine does not absorb the rock itself but its dissolved form, as ions of potassium or calcium and so on. This erosion is such a long process that the majority of trace elements that the vine requires are in fact sourced from the mineralization of humus; in other words, from organic matter - and, in some cases, synthetic fertilizers. In addition, vines are not passive; they absorb only what they need, in micro-quantities. Plant cells push sodium chloride (our cooking salt) beyond the cell wall; the salt in the ground is not the salinity in wine. This is the major difference with mineral waters, which contain a far greater diversity of soluble mineral ions, collected unfiltered along the way at levels that make them perceptible, like the sodium bicarbonate filtered by vines.

Lastly, rocks, with rare exceptions, have no taste or aroma (just try licking a pebble), only texture. There can thus be no direct link between the *Exogyra* – marine mollusc fossils with no taste of their own – in the Kimmeridgian soils of Chablis and the iodized mineral taste of the region's wines, but this does not mean that geology has no influence on the characteristics of a wine; merely that such an influence takes other routes – drainage, albedo, microbiota and so on. There is no literal or causal link, however.

Deceptive geological metaphors

We are also misled by the frequent use of geological metaphors to express sensations in wine tasting; these odours are organic rather than of mineral origin, but confusion still reigns. The odour of turned earth may come from geosmin, a terpene produced by bacteria in the soil. Petrichor notes, typical of the odour of soil after rain, come from a suspension of lipids broken down from plants and, once again, from geosmin. The metallic odour of copper coins in contact with skin comes from the oxidative reaction of certain lipids catalysed by metal ions, triggering the production of ketone and aldehyde-style volatile compounds. The most treacherous metaphor is undoubtedly that of flint, which you can smell when two pieces of silex are struck together. This does not come literally from the flint present in terroirs – flint is in any case rare in viticultural soils and has no taste per se – but from sulphur compounds released by friction, as demonstrated by the work of Swiss researchers Christian Starkenmann, Pascale Deneulin et al. ("Identification of Hydrogen Disulfanes and Hydrogen Trisulfanes in H_2S Bottle, in Flint, and in Dry Mineral White Wine", 2017). In this case, hydrogen disulphide emerges from the oxidation of mercaptan (H_2S, a sulphur compound metabolized during fermentation, with notes of rotten egg). These smoky notes of burned matches are often associated with minerality by test panels of tasters. As early as 2003, Takatoshi Tominaga, Guy Guimberteau and Denis Dubourdieu (all at Bordeaux University) had identified another sulphur compound, the volatile thiol benzenemethanethiol (BMT), as the source of a strong smoky (empyreumatic) odour, in concentrations in wines that in this instance, as in the other, were perceptible at very low thresholds.

What do we perceive as mineral?

Many research studies carried out since 2012 have tried to shed some light on the correlation between the chemical composition of wine and its perceived minerality. What are we noticing that causes us to identify minerality as a reference point? There is no simple answer but instead a host of possibilities that specialists consider worthy of far greater in-depth study. First of all, it can't be the minerals themselves. Wine contains between 1 and 2g/l of these, principally potassium and traces of calcium, magnesium and sodium, often at levels below direct perception thresholds, and some of these minerals also originate from the winemaking process, because of fertilizers, cellar products and so on. Acidity – notably tartaric, malic and

> What are we noticing that causes us to identify minerality as a reference point? There is no simple answer but a host of possibilities worthy of far greater in-depth study

succinic acid – is a taste frequently and globally associated with tactile analogies, conjuring up notions of tension and spiky crystals, but it does not seem essential to the perception of a wine as mineral. Sulphur dioxide and reduction seem to be of central importance: reduced wines and wines with high levels of SO_2, whether free or in total, are more often described as mineral, as are those containing sulphur compounds, like BMT or hydrogen disulphide, with smoky notes. Added to this are compounds that cause salinity, either of an organic nature (umami) or mineral (sodium, calcium). Wines with discreet, closed aromas tend to be described as mineral, while fruity, sweet wines that have been aged in wood are not. Lastly, retronasal and orthonasal perceptions seem to predominate over mouthfeel.

Current conclusions tend to suggest that there is not one "minerality" but many, of great chemical complexity and with no universal definition, and our understanding of these will vary with the tasting group and the cépage. With so many questions left open, it would probably therefore be wiser to refrain from using a notion so lacking in consensus, although it cannot be ignored that this ubiquitous concept has a communicative force among wine tasters, which would certainly explain its popularity.

Minerality and mineralization, according to David Lefebvre

Oenologist and Alsace winemaker David Lefebvre also sees a correlation between soil, agronomic and oenological practices and the mineral constitution and taste of a wine, giving it its own inimitable identity. He has developed a theory of his own, as explained in two articles in the magazine *Le Rouge et le Blanc* (issues 100 and 112).

Lefebvre suggests the use of a "minerality index" based on the minerals in a wine, defined as stable compounds that

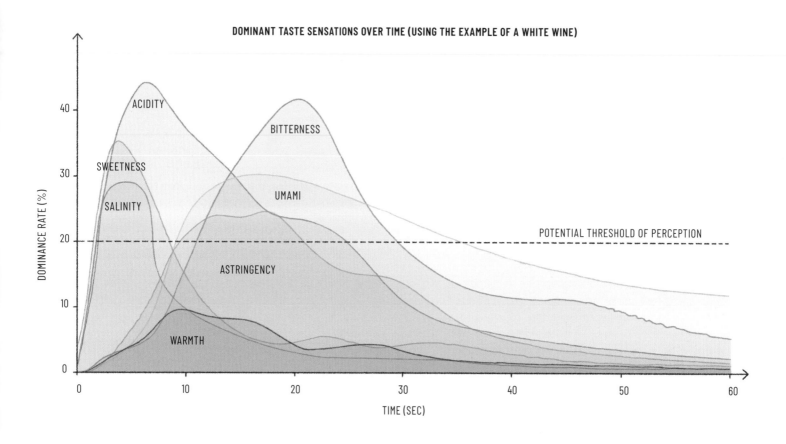

DOMINANT TASTE SENSATIONS OVER TIME (USING THE EXAMPLE OF A WHITE WINE)

PERCEPTIONS OF TASTE AND MINERALITY OVER TIME

**Different taste sensations may be involved in what wine tasters can interpret as minerality –
especially salinity and umami, which have their own dynamic in the mouth.**

do not change over time, like water, CO_2, salts and so on –
a minerality that can be tasted but has no aroma. This is a
property of organic compounds. This index, relating to the
mineralization of the wine in question, is linked to the ash
of the wine (what remains after the wine has been burned)
less the potassium, and it should not be confused with
the dry extract (what remains after evaporation, such as
sugars and tannins).

The mineralization process of wine begins at fermentation: in the strictly agronomic sense, this is the decomposition of organic matter into a more stable, mineralized
state: fermented must becomes wine. Lefebvre draws a
distinction between mineralization that is biological (by
micro-organisms), chemical (by oxidation, for example) and
physical (during pressing). The richer the base grape is in
minerals, the more these will be released from their organic
matrix by decomposition during fermentation and minera-

lization, creating salinities. He considers Champagne and
Vin Jaune to be classic examples of this.

Mineralization causes the loss of varietal aromas, but the
unique identity of the wine is revealed in its tactile dimension
and persistence over time. Such mineralized wines are in fact
rare, with most winemakers trying to produce organic wines
that are rich in alcohols, sugars and aromatic compounds.
These are wines in which the process of mineralization
has been deliberately halted and that pay little attention to
the mineral composition of the grape and how it has been
obtained (from biodiversity, living soil, mycorrhization and so
on). Lefebvre maintains that it is impossible to identify the
correlation between minerality and a specific terroir, because
the parameters are too complex; there are too many biological, chemical and physical mechanisms involved, and we
are physiologically too limited too perceive it anyway. But it
is nonetheless possible to think of wine from the perspective

of mineralization through different processes of oxidation if we define it as the result of many complex breakdowns arising from the mineral content of the soil and the capacity of the plant to absorb and restore this. Some wines would therefore be far more mineralizable and thus mineralized than others, with a potential for laying down and a unique identity that is the hallmark of their terroir. This is an exciting approach that deserves to be explored.

Good use of minerality

Since the mid-1990s, minerality has established itself as an important concept in tasting, both among amateurs and a certain number of winemakers, journalists and somme-liers. To spread so widely and enjoy such success, it clearly has a purpose and meets a need. Quite remarkably, Swiss researchers determined that the first peak in the term's popularity in French wine writing occurred in 1994, just as use of the word terroir began to decline, and have suggested that "minerality" has slowly been replacing "terroir", which had become hackneyed through its use for other agricul-tural products. It is also no coincidence that this sudden popularity coincides with an evolution in taste for wine among both amateurs and professionals – one might note the rise and fall of the influence of critic Robert Parker; the emergence of organic, biodynamic and natural wine-growing; and so on   and a transition from an analytical approach to wine tasting toward more holistic methods such as geosensorial tasting. In much the same way as the terms "drinkability" and "digestibility" are bandied about in tasting notes today, minerality was the symptom of a growing awareness of new perceptions that could not have seen the light of day without an evolution in wine, including greater links to the soil and less intervention in wineries, as well as in our aesthetics – yet further confirmation that wine transcends the nature/culture divide.

Sensitive crystallization

What if we could actually see the mineral quality of a wine? This is said to be possible through "sensitive crystallization", a method involving the interpretation of crystals as an image of a product's composition. It was developed by Ehrenfried Pfeiffer (1899–1961), a pupil of Rudolf Steiner, the founder of biodynamics. It is mainly used by adherents of the movement, who claim it can describe a wine, its oenological characteristics, the stresses undergone by the vine and indeed the nature of its terroir. The principle involves adding a solution of copper chlo-ride to a sample of the wine diluted with pure water, then placing this solution in a temperature-controlled room. The reaction of the two compounds gives rise to a dendritic pattern of crystals, and the arrangement and size of these can then be interpreted.

What should we make of this method, which has found use in renowned estates and institutions? While the physical mechanics of crystallization are well known and understood, there are problems with exactly how to measure and interpret the results. Whether we agree or not about the beauty and harmony of the structures arising, quite why they came about is more controversial still. For its practitioners (Christian Marcel and Margarethe Chapelle, both experts in sensitive crystalli-zation), this experimental interpretation doubles as an anthro-posophical spiritual exercise – in itself a contentious discipline if ever there was one. Marcel has suggested that its many scep-tics can at least agree that sensitive crystallization undeniably reveals something that we are currently unable to understand.

SERVING WINE

Wine containers

"Who cares about the bottle, as long as there's drunkenness," wrote Alfred de Musset in an era that saw the glass bottle sweep the field as the essential container for transporting, marketing, serving and storing wine. The advent of this object, so mundane and unremarkable to us today (more than 30 billion bottles of wine are consumed every year, let alone the bottles containing other liquids), was essential to the rise in quality of wine, its identification with terroir and its social symbolism. Here, as so often elsewhere, it was demand that stimulated supply, driving human ingenuity to invent new containers for better drinking. Where did the bottle come from, and why did it become so popular? How did it evolve from a simple utensil to an integral part of wine's identity? And why, despite our contemporary environmental crises, are we unable to do without it?

Containing, transporting and storing wine – from skin…

Any examination of the glass bottle must include a study of the relationship between wine production and consumption from the perspective of geographical history, and Jean-Robert Pitte, a geographer specializing in landscape and gastronomy, does just that in his *La Bouteille de vin. Histoire d'une révolution* (2013). The spread of viticulture relied equally on the domestication of *Vitis* and the invention of containers that made it possible to vinify, store and transport wine while protecting it from air and acetification, and thus on the technical abilities of different civilizations to adapt the skilled processing of materials to market requirements. Animal skins, particularly goatskins, are the first known containers for liquid, from the Palaeolithic era. These were available, easily sealed, lightweight and re-usable, and though practical for the perils of transporting wine, they were of less use for vinification and storage; they could change the organoleptic profile of wine over time, and their seams were liable to fail

under gas pressure during fermentation. Some modern-day Chilean producers are trying to revive their use, including Carolina Alvarado and Arturo Herrera, who vinify their Cuero de Vaca wine in a container made of cow leather.

… to earthenware and wood

Before the 3rd century, terracotta, both inert and malleable, was the main material used to make the various *qvevri*, *pithos* and *dolia* required for making wine, the amphorae for selling it and even the jugs for serving it. Their shapes and sizes would vary from region to region, probably due to the success of a particular pioneer model that ended up symbolizing the area of origin and thereby guaranteeing the provenance of the wine. The amphora most used by traders, according to archaeological evidence, had an average capacity of 20-30 litres (5-8 US gallons) and was intended for commercial use or service at large banquets; it was too large for individual consumption, suggesting that wine was most often enjoyed in company.

Stopping and sealing amphorae with cork closures, a practice already known to the Romans, showed how storage would improve wine, and the ability to save wine for later reciprocally changed vinification techniques. Lighter, simpler and more delicate wines were drunk rapidly to satisfy day-to-day consumption, while wines made with finer grapes from the most acclaimed vineyards were vinified for ageing and enjoyed by wealthy wine lovers who would save these amphorae for decades, just like contemporary collectors. The growing popularity of hermetically sealed jars changed both the way wine was enjoyed and the wine itself. Despite their advantages, these containers nonetheless had drawbacks: once opened, the wine had to be drunk immediately so it would not spoil, and the containers were fragile, heavy and difficult to stack, which complicated their transport and storage. This was not the case for the barrel, which was to emerge at the dawn of the Christian era.

Whether called a "barrel" or a "cask" (these two generic terms are pretty much interchangeable and give no particular indication of volume, unlike a barrique, which is of a specific size), these containers grew in popularity from the 1st century BCE. Pitte suggests a link with the carpentry skills of the Rhaetians, in particular the wooden containers this Central Alpine tribe used for milk and cheese. While archaeological evidence is scarce (unlike terracotta, wood rots), we know that the technique spread very quickly, first to Gaul and then throughout Europe. Barrels were only a quarter of the weight of amphorae in proportion to the weight of the liquid (45–50 kg for 220 litres of wine, or 100–110 lb for 58 US gallons; as opposed to 20 kg for 20 litres, or 44 lb for a little over 5 US gallons, with terracotta). They used cheap and available materials and were easy to move by rolling. They were stackable, recyclable, easy to empty and clean, and much more efficient for transport, but they still suffered from the same drawback as amphorae when it came to final consumption. once the barrel had been "tapped", or opened, the wine had to be drunk quickly before it spoiled. Preservation techniques were still poorly understood and the containers available unsuitable. Gradual neglect of old skills, including the use of sulphur and cork, during late antiquity and the Middle Ages, periods of political upheaval and invasion, marked a hiatus in improvement of wine quality, and it was not until the revolutionary arrival of the bottle and the re-emergence of markets for wealthy, enlightened wine-lovers that great progress was to be made in the wine industry.

Wine and glass
The invention of glass obviously predates the invention of the bottle. The Egyptians were already cutting naturally vitrified silica, such as obsidian or rock crystal, into small vases, cups and carafes, and the hardness and transparency of these fascinating objects prompted artisans to master the technique of reproducing them. Glassware from the 3rd millennium BCE has certainly been discovered in Mesopotamia; lye, which was widely used at the time, would have been mixed with sand that contained silica, saltpetre or ash, along with mineral oxides to add colour. The invention of the closed kiln, with temperatures higher than open-air ovens, enabled vitrification of this new base material, which also had a lower melting point (1,300°C or 2,372°F, as opposed to 1,700°C/3,092°F). Glassware was prized by the elite, and its use spread and evolved as techniques improved: moulds appeared in the 2nd millennium BCE and canes for blowing glass in the 1st century BCE, which made it possible to use less glass and to vary the shapes and fine details of the finished objects. Then there was the use of manganese dioxide to make glass colourless and glass shards to promote melting.

> " Glassware was already associated with gastronomy as it neither changed the taste of food and wine nor retained their smell, and its transparency allowed the contents to be admired

Although glass became more common during the time of the Roman Empire, it was not until the 16th century that technological progress was to enable mass production of bottles. By this time, glassware was already associated with gastronomy because it neither changed the taste of food and wine nor retained their smell, and its transparency allowed the contents to be admired and appreciated. Carafes, flasks and cups were initially the preserve of high dignitaries, in particular those hailing from Murano, a Venetian island that had excelled in glassmaking since the 13th century. Glass remained an extremely fragile material, however, and fiaschi and bottles, whether spherical or flattened, still came equipped with a jacket of straw, wicker or leather. Despite these limitations, their usefulness and practicality for service made them popular with every social class during the 16th century. The word "bottle", which had previously referred to any container, from wineskin to tun, would then take on the almost exclusive meaning of a glass container for all kinds of liquid, especially wine.

The English revolutionize bottles…
While wine was still generally consumed and served from stoneware containers, ceramic or pewter jugs, and more rarely carafes or bottles in 17th-century England, this was to change as glass started to be produced in coal-fired kilns.

WINE BOTTLE SHAPES IN EUROPE AT THE BEGINNING OF THE 21st CENTURY

Pitte's *La Bouteille de vin. Histoire d'une révolution* (2013) traces the history and cultural geography of the glass bottle, three styles of which – Bordeaux, Champagne, Burgundy – are now found all round the world.

PORTUGAL, SPAIN, NORTH AFRICA, FRANCE (SOUTHEAST), CORSICA, GREECE:
Both types of bottle (Burgundy and Bordeaux) are to be found.

ITALY:
Both types of bottle (Burgundy and Bordeaux) are to be found, but most are Bordeaux style.

FRANCE (AS FAR NORTH AS BURGUNDY-AUVERGNE):
Both types of bottle (Burgundy and Bordeaux) are to be found, but most are Burgundy style.

FRANCE (ROUSSILLON):
Both types of bottle (Burgundy and Bordeaux) are to be found.

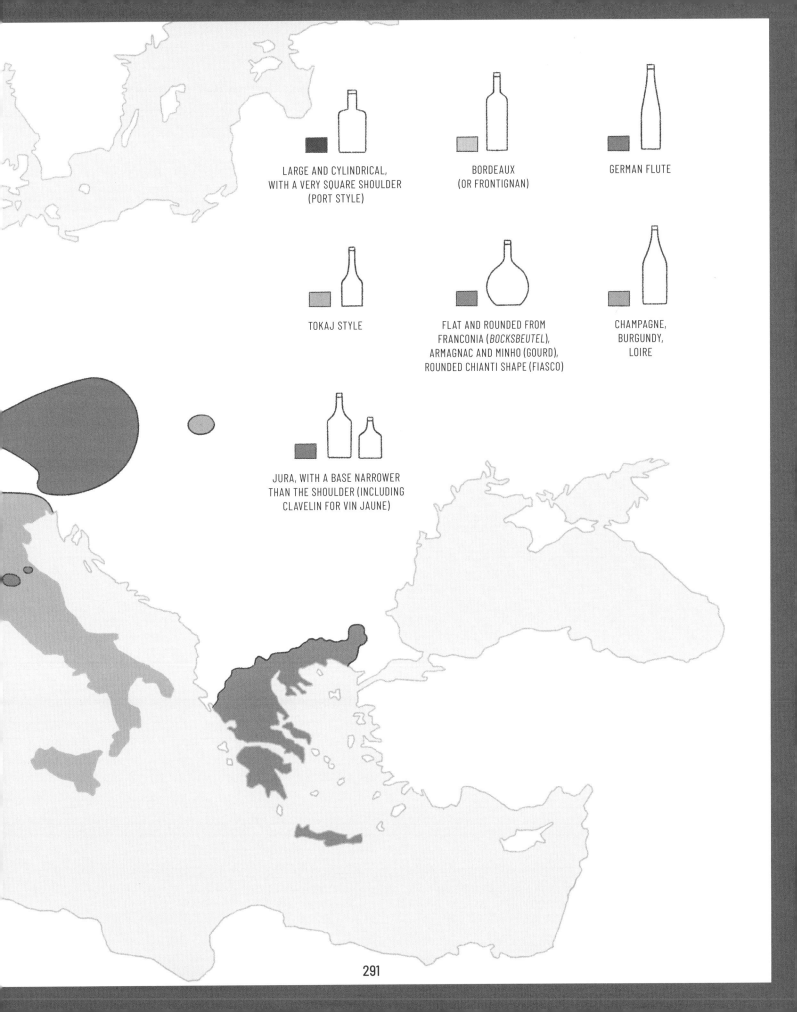

LARGE AND CYLINDRICAL,
WITH A VERY SQUARE SHOULDER
(PORT STYLE)

BORDEAUX
(OR FRONTIGNAN)

GERMAN FLUTE

TOKAJ STYLE

FLAT AND ROUNDED FROM
FRANCONIA (*BOCKSBEUTEL*),
ARMAGNAC AND MINHO (GOURD),
ROUNDED CHIANTI SHAPE (FIASCO)

CHAMPAGNE,
BURGUNDY,
LOIRE

JURA, WITH A BASE NARROWER
THAN THE SHOULDER (INCLUDING
CLAVELIN FOR VIN JAUNE)

There was also a growing need for bottles on the national market for wines imported in quantity, like Port, Marsala and Bordeaux, but wholesale deforestation of the country began to threaten the wood required by the navy and for construction. Robert Mansell (1573-1656), a savvy adviser to James I, persuaded the king to sign an edict prohibiting wood-burning kilns and to award him a monopoly on the production of glass in coal-fired kilns, which he set up among the high-yielding coal-fields of Newcastle. This new technique developed by Mansell made it possible to melt glass at higher temperatures, making it more robust. Kenelm Digby (1603-65) refined the process soon after, producing thick-walled black bottles from a mould, and therefore of a regular size, with a reinforced base and a punt that aided stability.

> The English bottle gradually revolutionized not only the serving and transportation of wine but also its vinification and connection with terroir

The new generation of bottle met with immediate acclaim – it was robust enough to transport wine over long distances, and could be stacked and resealed. The neck was even strong enough to accept the cork closures that had been less favoured after the fall of the Roman Empire but were rediscovered in Portugal.

... "invent" the traditional method...

The English bottle gradually revolutionized not only the serving and transportation of wine but also its vinification and connection with terroir. It spread throughout Europe as bottle production was established in new locations and producers took back control of marketing their wine. Until the 17th century, wines were essentially sold in barrels by brokers and merchants, with tapping and bottling (for service) being carried out on the premises of the final consumer. With the advent of this new type of container, English merchants could begin to bottle wine for sale, thereby at the end of the 17th century "inventing" what became known as the traditional method and providing Champagne with its bubbles. To mitigate the sharp acidity of Champagne wines, which at the time were still rather than sparkling, they added cane sugar, which had become more readily available. In the autumn, this mixture was bottled in the thicker, new-fangled glass bottles, and they were stopped with cork, rather than straw. Not only did these not break, but the wine was far more reliably full of bubbles by the time spring came; the uncontrolled fizz they knew all too well had suddenly become the effervescence they were looking for. It was an immediate success and soon found its way across the Channel.

Producers in Champagne quickly decided to take control of the process and followed suit in bottling their produce to "Champagnify" their wine. It nonetheless took decades and (as Pitte states) "a host of developments from small-scale production to industrial output", before the technique was properly established, including local construction of coal-fired glassworks, quality control of materials to minimize breakages, royal assent to sell bottles in France in 1728 (it had previously been prohibited, to limit fraud from selling short weight) and standardization of weight and volume of bottles. By around 1770, Champagne glassmakers were producing more than 2.5 million bottles, and Champagne's entire output no longer travelled via England but was sourced directly from a region that had been reinvented by the European success of its bubbles.

... and dub it the "new French claret"

Wines from Champagne were not the only ones to benefit from being bottled in these new English containers. Bordeaux wines were also to rise in quality during the 17th and 18th centuries, and here too there were several factors at work. There had been developments in the field of oenology, for one thing, with the Dutch rediscovering the antiseptic and antioxidant properties of the sulphur with which they asked Bordeaux merchants to treat their barrels. This made it possible to extend maceration and ageing times, and the wines became stronger and more colourful. Racking, topping up and fining further refined the tannins of Bordeaux cépages and made it easier to lay them down. These "new French clarets", which the English raved about, were also bottled in thick-walled, hermetically sealed bottles that were laid down in cellars. Merchants soon noticed how much the wines improved after several years of storage, and the world of wine rediscovered benefits of ageing that had been forgotten since the Romans. Bordeaux converted to this new style, closely followed by wine producers all over France, lending new momentum to the glassmaking industry.

A "cultural geography of the bottle" – the Bordeaux bottle...

Glassmakers initially used containers in shapes inspired by Belgian and Dutch alembics and onion-shaped bottles, but a response to customers' demand for bottles that would stack more easily also expanded their market share. Containers rapidly became more cylindrical, with longer necks and squarer shoulders. This new design would prove extremely useful for addressing the presence of sediment, an unanticipated inconvenience to which the wines of Bordeaux - not to mention the Ports, Sherries, Madeiras and other aged wines drunk in the British Isles - were all too prone. A right-angled shoulder allowed the dregs to be retained during pouring, and the Anglo-Dutch shape soon became the bottle of choice for any wine requiring decanting.

Acceptance of the design was accelerated as glassmakers settled in wine production regions, taking up residence on the Quai des Chartrons in Bordeaux in 1723; their influence on bottle style was such that the shape had become known as the "Bordeaux bottle" by 1837. Wine was still mostly shipped in barrels, and it was not until the turn of the 20th century that estate-bottling was gradually adopted, a development that was also enabled by technical progress in glassmaking.

Glass-blowing was back-breaking, dangerous work that required a large workforce and was progressively automated after 1887. In 1880, it had taken 13 hours of gruelling work to produce 100 bottles, but by 1938 it could be done in 3 hours. By 2015, production was up to 6–8,000 bottles an hour. Simultaneously, the glass industry was also rationalizing; France had 3,000 companies in the 18th century, but by 1928 it was only 30; and by 2022, only 2. Production rose from 100 million bottles in 1860 to 370 million in 1928, and 600 million by 1960. The success of Bordeaux wine was due in part to its packaging, and this also played a part in the success of the Bordeaux bottle, which is now the best-selling shape in the world.

… the Champagne bottle, the Burgundy bottle and others

The two other most common shapes are the Champagne bottle and the Burgundy bottle. The shape of the former has scarcely changed since the end of the 19th century, since there has been no need for technical improvement, but it has given rise to derivatives, and these include the latter. Neither wine has historically needed to be decanted, and Pitte even maintains that decanting is in fact a cultural practice linked to a notion of purity typical of the Puritan mentality of Protestant countries. In Burgundy and Champagne, which are mostly Catholic, sediment was not considered a mortal sin, and bottles there have mostly retained a broader profile with soft shoulders. Burgundian Pinots also do not have the same tannic substance as Bordeaux cépages. Estate-bottling came to Burgundy much later and only really took off with the creation of the AOCs, which were based on direct links between a wine and its original terroir, and thus encouraged estate-bottling. The shape of the bottle has therefore evolved very little to the present day.

In the absence of commercial pressure for estate bottling, the bottle spread relatively slowly to other French and European wine regions, whose markets were mainly local; when the need to bottle wine arose, some decided to use their own model, while others, with no particular heritage to fall back on, simply chose one of the big three shapes according to the

values they ascribed to it – the style of wine, the aesthetic value and so on. The most notable regional shapes included:

- **Rhine flute**, found in Austria, Alsace, Château-Grillet and Muscadet is almost exclusively used for white wines;
- *Fiasco*, from central Italy is one of the oldest bottle shapes and a strong sign that the Italian wine industry modernized only recently;
- *Bocksbeutel*, a flattened bottle from Franconia whose origins are said to be ancient; the name can be translated as "goat scrotum" and is reminiscent of the containers made of hide or glass that would hang from travellers' belts;
- **Long-necked bottle**, used for sweet wines from Tokaj in Hungary and Constantia in South Africa;
- **Provence flute**, known as an *anfora* in Italy, a possible inheritor of a Venetian aesthetic;
- *Clavelin*, a container unique to the Vin Jaune of the Jura, whose particular shoulder shape, which is of no practical use, since the wine throws no sediment, and 62-cl volume would have been chosen arbitrarily by some local glassmaker in the 19th century, takes inspiration from old English bottles.

Use of these regional bottle shapes was long a matter of choice but is now regulated by EU directives. But where does bottle design stand now? Its cultural importance is unmistakable, and production has largely freed itself from technical constraints, but it is striking to note how little the wine bottle has evolved over the past 150 years or so, either in shape or materials. Growing global demand, ever scarcer resources and the ecological cost suggest that there is a need for innovation here; despite some new packaging designs developed since the 1960s, the traditional glass bottle still leads the field – but why?

Symbolic weight versus urgent need for innovation

Wine in glass bottles accounts for 75 per cent of global sales, some 30 billion units, and despite some fluctuations in consumption – a drop in traditional countries, a rise in new consumers – the symbolism of the bottle is still an essential part of the act of purchasing, as marketing studies have shown. A glass bottle is associated with ideas of quality, and because the majority of French AOCs have historically been packaged this way, their image of tradition, prestige and guaranteed origins has become bound up with it. By association, the glass bottle has become a symbol of quality, even to the point where it must be increasingly visible: a number of estates market their high-end vintages in heavier and darker bottles, as if the weight and colour were guarantors of the quality of the wine. The glass bottle is highly charged with symbolism and has been promoted as an essential marketing device by traditional producers keen to attract the classic wine market, but paradoxically, the major innovation of a few centuries ago has become a drag factor for the change that is now required. Current wine consumption no longer justifies its use as much as it once did: 80 per cent of wines are drunk within 24 hours of purchase rather than being laid down, and the bottle is thrown away as soon as it is emptied and is not recycled enough.

Ultimately, 68 per cent, on average, of the wine industry's CO_2 emissions are due to packaging in glass bottles, and the energy required to manufacture and transport them, and to recycle them when possible, makes them less environmentally friendly containers for wine for immediate consumption, which often takes place at a significant distance from their home vineyard. It has even become one of the market's paradoxes: for most producers and consumers, the "naturalness" of a wine and its "local" heritage do not appear to conflict with sending heavy bottles, whose contents do not need to be protected for years of cellar storage, to the other side of the world. There has been increasing public discussion of this issue since around 2010 or so, with critics as renowned as Jancis Robinson MW joining the fray; she now even publishes bottle weights alongside her tasting notes.

What solutions are there today or tomorrow?

Alternative solutions have been developed to contain wines not intended for laying down, including Tetra Pak, bioplastic containers and bag-in-boxes, recycled plastic bottles, aluminium cans and kegs. Technological innovation in materials has provided solutions to the problems of weight, energy consumption and recycling, and the impact of these can be quantified according to various metrics, such as life-cycle analysis (LCA). Other solutions considered include transporting wine in bulk and bottling it at the sales market, transporting it using wind power, or a revival of refundable deposits for bottles. So, what is stopping us? Local and international legislation – which mandates specific glass bottle shapes for a number of AOCs, for example – sometimes hampers initiatives and the preferences of materials manufacturers, such as glassmakers with a particular kind of stopper, have been accommodated to preserve such conglomerates' financial interests, but ultimately, the biggest hindrance is the consumer.

Wine and its bottles have become a symbol of belonging and recognition, and when the moment of consumption poses a social, financial or qualitative "risk", drinkers tend to plump for a glass bottle as a tried and trusted vessel. It is only on less risky occasions that a novel container might more easily be chosen – for individual use or drinking on the go, for example. Only new consumers, especially the young, who are less prone to preconceptions and more aware of societal issues, are accepting such developments, but the glass bottle must change, and the major regions are showing the way. Champagne has ordered a reduction in the weight of its bottles from 900g (32oz) to 835g (29oz), saving thousands of tons of glass and fossil fuel. Some major brands have been promoting changes in their packaging by doing away with boxes, but it is time to go even further in altering mentalities – like supporting consignment and reuse of empty bottles. This will involve producers, tastemakers and legislators joining forces to persuade consumers to surrender the convenience they have enjoyed since the postwar period, and once again it is our consumer habits that have to change.

Volume and capacity

Whether quart, magnum or Jéroboam, the volumes and names of the various bottle sizes have retained a fanciful dimension despite the standardization imposed over the course of time by regional and then national legislators. Knowing the capacity of a bottle has been a fraught and complex matter ever since the beginnings of the wine trade and the imposition of taxes on alcoholic drinks. The difference between the advertised and actual quantities was always an opportunity for fraud in an era when containers like glass bottles were still being blown by hand and could vary wildly in size. The metric system was not adopted in France until 1837, before which time regional measures such as Beaujolais's 46-cl (15.7-fl-oz) *pot* (a thick-bottomed glass bottle) were permitted. The standard capacity of 75cl (a little over 25 fl oz) was initially adopted in Bordeaux in the first half of the 18th century, under the influence of the British, either because of the old measure of a "reputed quart" (0.7577 litre) or because a Bordeaux barrel contains 225 litres (50 imperial/60 US gallons), corresponding to 300 bottles at 0.75 litre, which would explain the contemporary packaging of wine in half-cases of six bottles (the equivalent of a gallon) or cases of 12 (2 gallons). In 1866, 75cl became the legal standard in France, although volumes have multiplied since then, with the largest bottles emerging in Champagne at the end of the 19th century. It is still a mystery why Biblical names were chosen.

Looking for closure – how can wine be sealed?

Cork or plastic, screwcap or glass? Choosing a stopper is one of the most difficult decisions for a producer, almost as important as selecting a date for harvesting or bottling, because the means of closure has a direct impact on how a wine ages. Options have multiplied with the rise in consumption and increasing globalization of production since the 1970s, from entry-level to super-premium wines. The cork stopper, the use of which has gone hand-in-hand with the success of the glass bottle and the rise in the quality of wines since the 17th century, no longer enjoys a monopoly. Despite its mechanical qualities, it can sometimes cause irreversible harm to wine either by giving it the taste of cork taint or by indirectly accelerating its oxidation. Why have corks historically been the closure of choice? What alternatives have been developed? What does the cork stopper symbolize, and why is it still around today?

The cork stopper has been invented, forgotten…

According to Pitte in *La Bouteille de vin. Histoire d'une révolution*, cork stoppers date not from the 17th century but from the ancient world. They are sourced from cultivated cork oak (*Quercus suber* L.), a species of oak found on the acidic terroirs of the Mediterranean Basin, from Sardinia to Roussillon, taking in northwest Africa, Spain and in particular Portugal, which now has 730,000 ha of cork plantations given over to *Q. suber*, representing 33 per cent of global production. *Q. suber* is mostly cultivated in Alentejo, a region in southern Portugal where the landscape has been redrawn by an industry that is essential to the country's economy: it has an annual turnover in excess of a billion euros, equating to 60 per cent of global market share by value.

The Greeks and Romans were already making use of the mechanical qualities of the bark of this tree, which was found throughout their empires. Archaeological excavations, including underwater exploration, have revealed amphorae still sealed with corks and containing remnants of wine. Cements made from wax, lime, pozzolans, terracotta and even pitch would help to seal the jars, which could preserve liquids for years, providing evidence of the elite's taste for aged wine. However, the fall of the Roman Empire, the rise of the barrel to replace the amphora and the all-too-infrequent use of sealable containers caused the cork stopper to drop from use and be forgotten for centuries.

… and rediscovered

Until the English invented their thick-walled glass bottle with its long, reinforced neck in the 17th century, wine was stored in barrels, jugs or carafes that were sealed as well as possible with a range of materials of varying watertightness, such as twists of dried grasses. These were known in French as *bousches*, from the Latin *boscus*, which became the modern word *bouchon*, meaning cork. There were also wooden pegs wrapped in greased hemp or linen (the ancestor of the barrel bung) and oakum or leather stoppers. In Italy, it was not uncommon to pour oil directly onto the surface of the wine to protect it, and attempts were made to pump this out before it was served. Only glass stoppers sealed at the neck with emery paste would make the container completely airtight, but these had to be broken in order to consume the liquid, so could not be reused. A combination of technical progress and the English trading presence in Portugal and Spain revived interest in corks; the cork floats used for fishing nets in Jerez, Málaga and Porto struck English merchants as perfect for sealing bottles with sufficiently robust necks, and the use of cork spread in less than a century throughout all the wine regions that had adopted thicker bottles. These new stoppers were instrumental in creating new styles of wine, such as Champagne, and revived interest in laying down wine in bottles. The corkscrew, a by-product of this development, became widespread from 1730.

Corks have many benefits…

Thanks to its phellogen cells, the cork oak has the enviable property of being able to produce an even outer bark that regenerates when removed – and unlike other species, the tree does not die when its bark is stripped. A tree 20m (66ft) high can be harvested up to 16 times, producing around 4,000 corks in total if it is properly managed over the 200 years of its lifespan. The first stripping is carried out when the tree reaches 25 or 30 years of age, yielding "male" or "virgin" cork that is used as insulation or cladding, because it is too hard and irregular for use with bottles. This starts a nine-year cycle (a period established in law in Portugal in 1937) that includes the *secundeira*, the first regrown cork, which is still irregular, and then *amadia*, or black cork, which is finally suitable for use in quality stoppers, 43 years after the tree was first planted.

> Modern producers can choose a closure to suit a wine, its structure and its ageing potential

Cork cells resemble the compartments of a beehive, and there are around 800 million of these minute hexagonal or pentagonal prisms in a single stopper. They are all filled with an air-like gas that accounts for 60 per cent of their volume, and it is here that the secret of the lightness and elasticity of the material is to be found. These alveolar cells are made up of lignin for its structure, polysaccharides for texture, tannins for colour, ceroids for waterproofing, and especially suberin, which gives cork its resilience.

Cork possesses some remarkable intrinsic properties: it floats on water; it is totally impermeable to most liquids and (up to a point) gases; it resists humidity; it can be compressed to half its thickness without losing either shape or plasticity; it absorbs heat, vibrations and sound but not dust; it withstands frictional wear; and it burns slowly, emitting neither flame nor toxic gases.

… and a few drawbacks

Cork oak is a miraculous material, providing a natural barrier against fires, and is an essential resource for Portugal, whose leaders are well aware of its status. The tree is protected by a 1209 law that prohibits illegal felling and has even become the country's symbol. Portugal's cork industry has been without competition for centuries, and the country seeks to preserve cork as an ecological and financial benefit.

However, despite cork's undeniable qualities, since the 17th century critics have painted a more nuanced picture: in his *Vinetum Britannicum* (1676), English agronomist John Worlidge mentions variability in watertightness – a somewhat unfair accusation, since this problem is largely due to the irregularity in bottle necks – but also highlights the taste it can sometimes leave in wine. The first of these problems can be solved by reinforcing and lengthening the neck, allowing the cylindrical cork to be pressed in and seated more effectively. The second, caused by the inconsistent quality of the bark, nevertheless did not prevent cork stoppers from becoming established, thanks to more meticulous preparation of the bark, which was gradually codified. Glass bottles were routinely sealed with corks for more than 300 years, and it was not until the 1960s that any alternative closures were to emerge.

The rise and rise of the screwcap

The screwcap was invented in France in 1959 for the spirits industry and owes its success to a particular combination of circumstances, including developments in the wine-bottling process pioneered by Le Bouchage Mécanique, a Burgundian company, and the boom in the Australian wine industry in the 1990s. It did not immediately take off in France, however, where aluminium was considered rather cheap and cheerful, or in Europe, and it was initially only Swiss producers who took an interest, because the system's watertightness protected the discreet aromas of Chasselas, one of the country's iconic cépages. The product marketed under the Stelvin brand name was left treading water until it was adopted by a group of high-end producers from South Australia, including Penfolds, Yalumba and Hardys. It should be noted, though, that synthetic corks became the closure of choice for some wineries before screwcaps took over. The cause was dismay at the losses incurred through cork-tainted wines: Southcorp, for example, had a packaging division that produced synthetic stoppers, and supermarkets in the UK were instrumental in encouraging a change to synthetic corks. The year 2000 was the turning point: the winemakers of Australia's Clare Valley collectively moved to screwcaps, and large Australian companies joined forces to import from France the minimum order of 250,000 bottles adapted for screwcaps. (Australia still did not have the technology to manufacture them.) They bottled and marketed their wines in record time.

This snowball effect and the interest it attracted hit the mark. In 2004, 10 per cent of Australia's national output was bottled with screwcaps, rising to 88 per cent in 2013 and exceeding 90 per cent by 2019. Only New Zealand, which had established the New Zealand Screwcap Wine Seal Initiative in 2001, maintained a higher rate (99 per cent). With two such major exporting countries adopting the screwcap and markets such as the UK cheerfully accepting the system (the screwcap has had equal consumer recognition with corks in the UK since 2014), a shift in attitude was clearly taking place.

This has not escaped the attention of both cork manufacturers and certain new entrepreneurs, and there has been an unprecedented surge in innovations aimed at finding solutions to the organoleptic problem factors (TCA, or "cork taint") that cause wine to be tainted, without sacrificing the system's intrinsic qualities.

An embarrassment of choice

Modern producers can choose a closure to suit a wine, its structure and its ageing potential. All closures claim organoleptic "safety" in that they do not impart a taste, especially the haloanisoles of TCA, to wine, so choices are based on the O_2 transmission rate (OTR) through the closure system. The aim is to prevent or control the introduction of O_2, which influences the development of the wine and its economic and environmental cost. There are currently five major types of closure available, using different materials, but in the absence of solid, independent data, their distribution is hard to gauge. Figures relating to contamination rates and trends are contradictory and appear to depend on the manufacturers' specialities.

• **Natural cork** still seems to dominate the sector despite having lost a third of its market share between 2000 and 2009. Its position has even been strengthened with the development of faster, lower-cost techniques to detect haloanisoles using mass spectrometry and the NDtech screening technology supplied by Amorim, the leading corkmaker. These technologies are now at the cutting edge of cork-taint detection.

Cork production is nonetheless still very much in the hands of artisans. Once stripped, the bark is processed in accordance with the International Code of Cork Stopper Manufacturing Practice that is in force in Europe. The slabs of material are air-dried for a minimum of six months, allowing rain, wind and sun to oxidize and leach out tannins as the cork structure tightens, and then boiled to sterilize them and increase their elasticity. They are then sorted, dried and cut into transverse strips, ready to be made into plugs of the size selected for the final corks. These are washed, disinfected and sorted according to the number of lenticels (surface pores), which in some cases may be sealed – "colmated", or filled with cork powder. As a finishing touch, they are stamped with the name of the estate or cork manufacturer and treated with paraffin wax and/or silicone to facilitate insertion and removal.

The average diameter of a cork is 24mm (1in) to fit into a neck 18mm (¾in) across. The length varies with the type of wine, and the more important ageing is, the longer the cork will be. Measured in increments of 2.256mm (twelfths of an inch), the length can be anything from 15 (34mm/1¹¹⁄₃₂in) to 24 (54mm/2⅛in) in fine wines for laying down, at a cost of more than €1 each.

Is it the closure or the neck?

While the vast majority of wines purchased around the world are consumed in under 18 months, with some studies even suggesting a waiting time of less than 24 hours, the question of which closure might be best for wines to be laid down remains unresolved. This is a matter of some importance, because the chosen closure becomes a symbolic mark of quality and therefore a criterion for sales, with a knock-on effect for the marketing of wines for immediate consumption. Market conditions are such that studies have proved contradictory in assessing the respective qualities of natural cork, Diam-style synthetic closures, screwcaps and glass stoppers. Producers routinely bottle the same vintage with different closures, hoping to confirm one or other of the choices for their wines with a critical comparison of the bottles a few years later. When he was managing director of Château Margaux, Paul Pontallier (1956–2016) joined the Laroche estate in Chablis, Château d'Agassac in Bordeaux and even Tyrrell's in Australia (a great champion of the screwcap) in publishing results indicating that screwcaps and corks were relatively close in terms of appreciation, although they also noted variations from bottle to bottle in every case for both reds and whites. These were certainly less extreme for screwcaps, but the question was not definitively settled.

There is one little-mentioned point that requires further study, however: the regularity of the neck, and therefore its adhesion to the closure. This may be one of the major causes both of variation from bottle to bottle and of the oxidation that occurs in some wines, and it is one of the avenues of enquiry pursued by a team under the aegis of Thomas Karbowiak, a professor of chemistry at AgroSup Dijon, in *Le Vieillissement du vin: une question d'obturation?* (2019). It may be the bottle, rather than the cork, that ultimately holds one of the answers.

Natural cork is recyclable, with a low ecological footprint. It also helps to preserve cork forests, but it is still not perfect; figures suggest that three per cent of bottles will still be affected by cork taint. It is a living material, and variations from bottle to bottle cannot be prevented. When laid down for very long periods, cork can also deteriorate and yet has retained a virtual monopoly on the high-end wine market, with between 84 and 90 per cent of the wines selected for the *Wine Spectator*'s top 100 annual rankings featuring natural cork stoppers during the period 2016–21.

- **Stoppers made from agglomerated cork granules** also come from cork trees but are made from scraps of different sizes rather than being a solid piece of bark. Some may be colmated (made from average-quality bark whose lenticels have been plugged with glue and cork powder), while others are multipiece, with two or more discs glued together; these are often made of agglomerated material, as is the case with many sparkling-wine corks. There are also agglomerated corks, which are similar to cork mats, where the particles are welded together by glue and pressure; these are intended for wine for immediate consumption. Or there are micro-agglomerated stoppers, of which Diam is the best-known example. These are also known as technical-cork stoppers and are made of boiled raw cork that is then crumbled and treated under pressure with supercritical CO_2 (an intermediate state between liquid and gas), making it possible to extract more than 150 compounds, including the polychlorophenols and polychloroanisoles responsible for cork taint. The stopper is then reconstituted with synthetic or natural glue based on castor oil and beeswax and moulded into the desired shape. Different O_2 transmission rates are possible, depending on the wine. These closures may be recyclable, with their price varying from a few cents to more than 40 cents each. One constraint on their use is the relatively unpredictable behaviour of glue over time.

- **Aluminium** is the main constituent material of screwcaps, which consist of a metal cap whose upper section is coated on the inside. This kind of closure was developed as a solution to the problem of cork taint and provides a hermetic seal that reduces gas exchange. It therefore offers better protection for varietal and fermentation aromas and allows less SO_2 to be added, because bottling is also routinely carried out under inert gas. Screwcaps assure consistent quality, need no corkscrew and represent good value. They cost 6–20 cents each. But they also have their weak points: there is an ecological price to pay, and their almost complete impermeability can give rise to reduction aromas. There are two types of seal in general use, the Étain-Saran (tighter seal) and Saranex (more permeable). Whether they have the same potential for market development as was the case in Australia and New Zealand is up for debate, but the majority of such closures are intended for wines for immediate

> **Much like the label and the bottle itself, how a wine is sealed has also become a major aspect of wine marketing**

consumption. Crown caps (beer bottle tops) are also being increasingly used, especially for pét-nats.

- **Plastic** lies somewhere between aluminium and cork in terms of its physical properties. Technological innovations to find alternatives to synthetic polymers use either recycled plastic that is suitable for food use, or plant extracts such as sugar cane, as used in Nomacorc Smart Green corks. These stoppers do not crumble, are cheap (between 5–40 cents each) and easy to customize, but suffer from three main defects: they are not suitable for ageing, because the polymers harden and molecules are able to pass through, so they are not often recommended for wines to lay down; they may impart a taste to the wine; and they come at a high ecological price. One brand has nonetheless established itself: ArdeaSeal closures have been used for several years by renowned winemakers from Burgundy and Italy. These feature a rigid outer layer with a central element that passes through the middle of the stopper and allows a regulated amount of O_2 to enter; a coating ensures good adhesion to the neck and facilitates opening, although they are not easy to reseal. These closures have a smaller carbon footprint than screwcaps or other synthetic stoppers, and the designers have emphasized their potential for ageing.

- **Glass** is centuries old and has been used by the brands Vinoseal and Vinolok since 2003. Here, a glass cap is enclosed by a plastic collar to guarantee a hermetic seal, making it possible to control the OTR. This type of closure is completely inert, discreet and smartly designed; some are recyclable, and all can be removed without a corkscrew, so their properties are very similar to those of the screwcaps with which they share the market for wines for immediate consumption. They are considered slightly more upmarket because of their production costs (50 cents apiece) and technical requirements: like screwcaps, they require bespoke bottling plants.

The cork – another powerful symbol

In 2019, Diam calculated that some 18 billion bottles of wine had been fitted with a closure: nine billion with a cork, another five billion with a screwcap, two billion with Diam products and another two billion with plastic. While these figures differ slightly from Amorim's, corks still come out on top. The expansion of the American and Asian markets, which prefer corks, and the boom in effervescent wines would rather confirm this tendency. Where does this preference come from? It is no doubt something to do with the emphasis that has recently been placed on ecological costs (cork has scored well here for several years), but the symbolic power of the material cannot be overlooked. In a study carried out in 2017 – and financed by the cork industry, it must be said – British psychologist

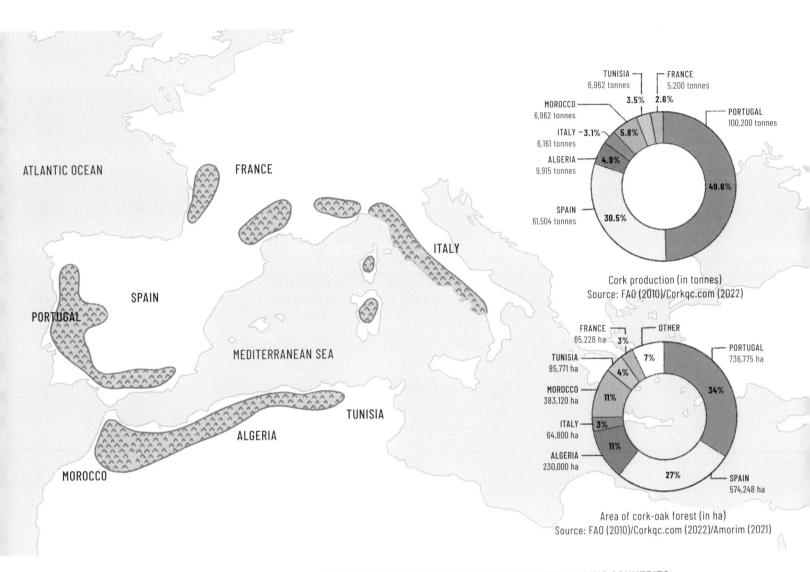

TUNISIA
6,962 tonnes

FRANCE
5,200 tonnes

MOROCCO
6,962 tonnes

ITALY —3.1%
6,161 tonnes

PORTUGAL
100,200 tonnes

3.5% 2.6%

5.8%

ALGERIA
9,915 tonnes

4.9%

49.6%

SPAIN
61,504 tonnes

30.5%

Cork production (in tonnes)
Source: FAO (2010)/Corkqc.com (2022)

FRANCE
65,228 ha

OTHER

3%

7%

TUNISIA
85,771 ha

4%

PORTUGAL
736,775 ha

MOROCCO
383,120 ha

11%

34%

ITALY
64,800 ha

3%

ALGERIA
230,000 ha

11%

27%

SPAIN
574,248 ha

Area of cork-oak forest (in ha)
Source: FAO (2010)/Corkqc.com (2022)/Amorim (2021)

THE MAIN CORK-OAK FORESTS AROUND THE MEDITERRANEAN AND MARKET SHARE OF CORK-MAKING COUNTRIES

There are more than 2.1 million ha of cork-oak forest in the Mediterranean region; Portugal alone boasts around 736,000 ha, representing 50 per cent of global cork production, with the other major producers being Spain, Morocco, Algeria, Tunisia, France and Italy. All tonnes are metric tonnes (1 tonne = 1.1 imperial [US] tons).

Charles Spence and his team showed that the sight and sound, the "pop" of a bottle sealed with a cork compared with a screwcap, influenced consumer appreciation of the wine: on average, 15 per cent thought the wine to be of superior quality with a cork, with 20 per cent suggesting that it was more suitable for celebrating a special occasion, even though it was actually the same wine in both glasses. This confirms the importance of context in tasting, the involvement of all our senses and, above all, the effects of our cognitive biases – in this case, the association of corks with quality.

The closure system is clearly essential to the quality of a wine, but much like the label and the bottle itself, how a wine is sealed has also become a major aspect of wine marketing – sometimes more important than the contents of the bottle. Barbe Nicole Ponsardin-Clicquot, the eponymous 19th-century widow Veuve Clicquot, who branded her corks and checked them all herself, knew very well the importance of the closure. Those seeking to taste objectively must acknowledge the influence of the subconscious.

Label mythology

We are all label drinkers; for the vast majority of consumers, the second criterion after price when choosing a bottle of wine is the label. This small slip of paper certainly plays a role at the moment of purchase, but it is also an integral part of the pleasure of tasting a wine, and the right label can encourage loyalty in drinkers. It is not just of interest to producers and buyers, however – the label is of far greater importance than one might imagine for historians as well, who have long treated it as a secondary archive. It is an extremely effective marketing tool in places such as France, where the wine industry is not permitted to use other media to promote sales, while also serving as a silent witness of the sector's current norms and codes. Every label is a treasure trove of highly informative clues to the status of wine within a given culture – its economic, legal, social and cultural environment. How did these labels originate, and how did they become so symbolic? How can semiotics help us to decipher their codes and meanings, when both the creativity and standardization of labels has never been so great?

A label is born

Authenticating and naming wines is a practice as old as time. The Egyptians of the New Kingdom (1500-1000 BCE) were already engraving a considerable amount of information on their wine jars, indicating the quality and type of the wine, the originating vineyard and its geographical location, the name of the producer and even the regnal year of the pharaoh who happened to be on the throne when the inscription was made. The wines were consumed by an elite but also presented as funerary gifts, with such jars being found in the tombs of the greatest rulers, indicating the Egyptians' appreciation for quality wines. The seals and stamps on Assyrian jars, Roman amphorae and modern barrels (the branded B of the Bandol appellation, for example) are ever more distant descendants of these Egyptian "labels". Only containers used for production and transportation were marked in even a rudimentary way, often as palimpsests, and it was not until the first bottles were produced for wines to be consumed or laid down that metal collars or basic stamped glass appeared.

Wine labels as we know them today emerged with the invention of lithographic printing in Germany at the end of the 18th century. At a time when the cork and glass industries had been busy spreading the use of bottles for selling and storing wine, a way had to be found to identify their contents. Dating from the turn of the 19th century, the first labels were plain rectangles of paper, often handwritten, that bore a minimal amount of information: the region, perhaps a merchant or a year, surrounded by a simple border. Germany's industrialization of lithographic printing soon made these more colourful, more stylized and, most importantly, cheaper and easier to produce: during the 19th century, these labels spread first through Germany, then on to Champagne and Bordeaux, and the prestige of these regions would accelerate the adoption of printed labels in every wine region and for all kinds of production, including spirits. The motifs and typefaces were selected from catalogues and, although initially generic and all-purpose, became increasingly differentiated to meet the evolving requirements of various participants in the wine market, with normative specifications to satisfy the legislators and rhetorical flights of fancy from the producers.

From normative specifications to evocative rhetoric

The mass use of labels during this period came about as a result of production crises and industrialization: wine, which had been subject to large-scale fraud in the wake of the phylloxera disaster, became the flagship product at the heart of a new public health regulatory regime for foodstuffs. The primary role of the label had been confirmed; even the Egyptians had grasped the necessity of demonstrating authenticity. As legislation on appellations and origins was introduced, labels became legally standardized to make them easier to understand. In France, this codification was further extended over the course of the 20th century. As the

PEOPLE

SIMPLE CONTEMPORARY

BRIGHT

PRESTIGE

STATELY CLASSIC

CLASSIC TEXT

SIMPLE BOLD

SURREALIST

BOLD TEXT

DISTINCTIVE

BOUTIQUE

ARTISAN/VINTAGE

MODERN GRAPHIC

ELEGANT

FOURTEEN MARKET RESEARCH CATEGORIES FOR CLASSIFYING WINE LABELS

According to Wine Intelligence, a UK market research agency, the wine labels sold on the Australian market in 2021 could be categorized into 14 broad types, a greater number than in 2017.
Research also found that certain designs were more successful in specific consumer markets.

Direction Generale de la Concurrence, de la Consumption and de la Répression des Fraudes (DGCCRF), the body responsible for the legal monitoring of labelling in France, puts it, the aim was to "provide purchasers with both criteria of choice and reliable information, promoting fair competition with a view to protecting consumer health and ensuring the traceability of products".

Under European legislation, eight separate pieces of information must now be listed for all wines in France, plus a ninth, the *dosage*, for sparkling wines and a tenth, the denomination, for AOCs and IGPs. The position, colour and size of these details are regulated, as are certain words and

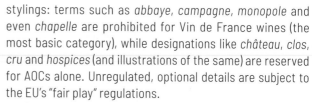

Iconic labels and iconoclasts

Some estates understood the power of labels long before marketing was even a thing. While French wines tend to privilege classic design, we are indebted to Baron Philippe de Rothschild who, in 1924, dared both to start bottling at the estate (a revolutionary move) and to ask artist Jean Carlu (1900–97) to design the label for his Château Mouton Rothschild. The idea provoked an outcry and did not really find acceptance until 1945, but it eventually became an iconic visual signature anticipated with each vintage. The design fascinatingly tracks the development of both art and wine market trends. French artists, including Jean Cocteau and Georges Braque, were followed by an increasingly international and avant-garde scene: Salvador Dalí, Marc Chagall, Wassily Kandinsky, Pablo Picasso, Andy Warhol, Keith Haring and Francis Bacon. Asian artists have been highlighted recently. Anything is permitted, but certain topics are perennial, like vines, the pleasures of drinking and the estate's signature ram. Mouton has proved an inspiration both directly – as for the labels of Leeuwin Estate in Western Australia, whose Art Series began in 1981, and Taittinger Champagne, whose Collection launched in 1983 – and indirectly. Elsewhere, the iconoclastic labels supplied by artists from the satirical magazine *Charlie Hebdo*, such as Charb, Cabu and Wolinski, helped to break down the hide-bound traditions of wine in the 1980s and 1990s, just when natural wines were first putting in an appearance in France. Labels and drinking styles are constantly being reinvented, hand-in-hand.

stylings: terms such as *abbaye*, *campagne*, *monopole* and even *chapelle* are prohibited for Vin de France wines (the most basic category), while designations like *château*, *clos*, *cru* and *hospices* (and illustrations of the same) are reserved for AOCs alone. Unregulated, optional details are subject to the EU's "fair play" regulations.

Christophe Lucand, a historian working on labelling in Burgundy, has suggested that the label has therefore become more than "a simple piece of extra information about regulations; it represents a vector of individual and collective strategic orientation. Labels are also used to shore up a story – or a fiction – with an aspect of propaganda about it that is used to persuade customers of the authentic character of the product, convincing them of the credibility of the producer and raising the product to the rank of a luxury product intended for specific markets and keeping it there. . . Labels have thus become a marketing ploy as they have the potential to encourage or clinch a purchase."

Seen but not read – label marketing

Through the use of explicit and implicit messaging, labels began to use design to offer a narrative, real or imagined, to identify with a wider audience or indeed to stand out from the crowd. As a mundane object consisting of text and images, a label is "seen without begin read", perceived by the eye without being analysed by the mind, as communications research scientists Yves Jeanneret and Emmanuël Souchier point out ("L'étiquette des vins: analyse d'un objet ordinaire", *Communication & Langages*, 1999). Its messaging is based on the interrelation of lexical, typographical and iconographic choices. The science that allows us to describe these signifiers and to study the mechanisms through which this system creates sense is known as semiotics. Marketing researcher Franck Celhay ("Sous le design des étiquettes de vins, la variété des 'storytellings de marque'", *The Conversation*, 2017) has conducted a semiotic analysis of wine labels, highlighting four main categories of signifier systems that are all freighted with meaning for consumers to some extent or other.

• **Shape, layout and composition**, indicating the positioning of the brand and place of origin: a centred layout suggests a palette of "classic", "traditional" values; an asymmetrical label suggests a "modern" and "innovative" approach. Horizontal lines imply stability and credibility. Centring the brand name underlines its importance, and the position and size of each detail are an indication of their relative importance.

• **Typography**: fonts have associations – gothic type suggests centuries of tradition, serif capital letters such as *capitalis monumentalis*, Roman square capitals, carry connotations of grandeur and classicism. Fine shapes imply subtlety,

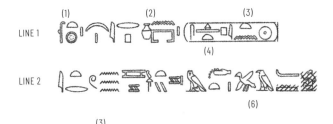

LINE 1 (1) (2) (3)
(4)
LINE 2 (6)
(3)

ILLUSTRATION OF A JAR LABEL (RECORDED AS COA III, LABEL NO. 111) FOUND AT TELL AL-AMARNA, THE CAPITAL CITY OF THE PHARAOH AKHENATEN (1371/1365 BCE–1338/1337 BCE)

TRANSLATION OF LINE 1:
Year 1, month 1, wine from the estate of Sehetep-Aton

TRANSLATION OF LINE 2:
The Eastern river, for which Pahou is responsible

The information recorded can be broken down as follows:
DOCUMENT: COA III, label no. 111
PROVENANCE: Amarna
DATE (1): year 1, month 1
QUALITY (2): jrp (wine)
STATUS (3): royal estate
"NAME" (4): Shtp Jtn
GEOGRAPHICAL PROVENANCE (5): Jtrw jmnty
WINEMAKER (6): Pahou

This label is typical of the pharaonic era and identifies the estate of Shtp Jtn (He-who-satisfies-Aton). Wine-jar labels provide a great deal of information about wine production of the time.

ORNAMENTAL MEDALLION LABEL, AROUND 1820

MULTIUSE LABEL, AROUND 1820

Appearing at the end of the 18th century, the oldest labels were simple rectangles with woodcut or leather engraving, handwritten with a minimum of details. These were transformed when lithography emerged in the 1820s and gradually spread throughout Europe.

JEAN CARLU'S LABEL FOR THE 1924 VINTAGE OF CHÂTEAU MOUTON ROTHSCHILD (PAUILLAC, BORDEAUX)

In 1924, for the first time, that Baron Philippe de Rothschild bottled Mouton Rothschild's entire production at the estate. To mark the occasion, he commissioned Jean Carlu, a young poster designer, to create the label. While estate-bottling was imitated, the label's innovative marketing did not find favour, and it was not until 1945 (and Philippe Jullian's "V for Victory" label) that the use of works by avant-garde artists was to become a signature (and much-copied) style of Mouton.

BARTOLO MASCARELLO'S LABEL FOR HIS 1990 AND 1999 BAROLO

Bartolo Mascarello is remembered as a legendary winemaker, a redoubtable champion of Piedmont tradition and an opponent both of the use of new barrels and the "Parkerization" of Barolos. Nicknamed the 'Last of the Mohicans', he designed labels that he used as tools in the political struggle, underlining his opposition to the internationalization of taste and the dangers of populism. The "NO BARRIQUE, NO BERLUSCONI" label was censored for a while in Italy but has now become a collector's item.

LABELS THAT MADE HISTORY

and handwritten scripts are linked with meticulous crafts-manship. The size and hierarchical arrangement of the words indicate their relative importance.

- **Colours**: as a rule, white paper signifies quality; slight yellowing implies tradition. The colours used for the typeface and illustrations are also obviously significant.
- **Illustrations**: these can make reference to more or less literal images, conveying recognized values that are easy to identify - like a vine or a chateau, but also works of art - or may be symbolic and so pre-select their "reader" who has the key to the code. Some wines no longer even want or need to use literal means to show they are wines; the absence of iconography becomes itself their image. Researchers call this "sublimation", with wine per se becoming a cultural object.

So, how can we pick our way through the minefield of all these signs and millions of labels, whose design no longer leaves anything to chance?

"Jupiterian ego-centrics" and "consumption-orientated Bacchanals"

Semiotician François Bobrie distinguishes between two main categories of labels. Having studied those that made the annual top 100 of the American *Wine Spectator* magazine between 2009 and 2013, he identifies two categories telling two types of narrative.

- **"Jupiterian ego-centrics"** talk about the wine itself, its history, its *savoir-faire*, its prestige, its origins and so on. Celhay delves deeper into this category, analysing 166 labels from Australia's Barossa Valley and identifying four thematic sub-categories that differ through the emphasis they place on the producer or place of production. He suggests they tell stories that distinguish between **wine as a work of art**, whose qualities stem from the artist-winemaker; **farm wine**, a rustic product crafted by the farmer-winemaker; **château wine**, a cultural product born of historic expertise and a prestigious estate; and **wine as a gift of nature**, whose qualities are due to the exceptional nature of its physical terroir.
- **"Consumption-orientated Bacchanals"** no longer talk about the wine itself but address the taster and what benefits they might gain from its consumption. Using the same study data, Celhay further identified four sub-categories that differ through the emphasis they place on pleasure and mutual enjoyment. He found narratives about **relaxation wine**, enjoyed alone and for pleasure in moments of downtime and when taking it easy - individual, restrained pleasure; **liberation wine**, allowing you to escape and free the imagination - untrammelled individual pleasure; **seduction wine**, shared with a loved one, with themes ranging from romance to eroticism - restrained, shared pleasure, and

celebration wine, representing partying, drunkenness and madness - unbridled, shared pleasure.

These different interpretations reveal a whole new side of wine. Drinkers are obviously not completely taken in by these stories, but the label certainly contributes to the overall pleasure of tasting. What is particularly interesting is to note the wine producers' bias revealed by this powerful communications tool.

Popularization and naturalization

Labels are akin to banners - something to rally around, allowing tasters not just to identify the wine but to find an identity for themselves, whether consciously or unconsciously. A punchy label can make it easier to reach the consumers targeted. Is the bottle intended as a luxury product to be collected, a wine for everyday drinking or a counter-cultural symbol? What audience is it addressing, and how can it attract interest as competition grows fiercer? The answer, to put it quite simply, is by creating a narrative that speaks to the consumer. The dominance of supermarket sales and the rise of online sales and social media promotions only underline the importance of visuals over information. The use of graphic art, which historically has been associated with great European wines (Château Mouton Rothschild's inspired labels were brilliant pioneers of wine marketing), is spreading and becoming more popular under the influence of the "new" wine-producing countries.

A 2011 exhibition at the San Francisco Museum of Modern Art (*How Wine Became Modern: Design + Wine 1976 to Now*) provided further evidence that a modern label may no longer have anything at all to do with the actual wine. In ostensibly presenting itself as a lifestyle, using powerful aesthetic codes such as music, film and fashion, it attracts the interest of new consumers who are often young, and as the wine becomes fashionable, it draws in more experienced segments of the market as a knock-on effect. The wine is bought and drunk less on its own merits and more for the symbolism it conveys via its label and its story, whether real or fictional.

Another strategy is emerging in parallel with this process of popularization - the idea of getting back to nature and returning to the essentials. The natural-wine movement has a notable tendency to combine these two approaches in labels that are often hyper-symbolized, identity-based and sometimes highly provocative, associating "naturalness" with counter-culture values. More than ever, drinking wine requires an understanding of different aesthetic judgments - of the wine itself, the label and the values it represents, all of which come into play when the wine is consumed. The wine and the label feed off one another, mutually reinforcing one another in a symbiotic relationship intended to satisfy the consumer's wants and needs.

Drinking wine

Is wine a tipple or a toxin? Should we drink fancy or inexpensive wine? Indulge in binge drinking or have a little snifter? Is it the doorway to the divine, or a speculative investment? Much like the techniques of viticulture and winemaking, the styles and colours of wines and the ways in which they are served and drunk have evolved over the centuries, writing a history of consumption in which the beacon of wine sheds a light on the history of the civilizations that drank it. Why and how do we drink? What is the key to reading this history of drinking, which is also the history of our becoming human? Is *Homo sapiens* not also, fundamentally, *Homo imbibens*?

Wine is a social good

How and why do we drink wine? The human sciences – history, geography and anthropology – have only been taking an interest in the history of food and drink since the 1930s, and even more recently in wine. Until then, the subject had primarily been approached through anecdotes, and it was not until the work of Dion, followed by research into sociology and food history, that systematic studies began to emerge. The act of drinking wine ceased to be examined from an exclusively economic perspective and was instead acknowledged as an expression of culture with its own rhythms and trends that did not necessarily track the grand narratives of history, politics or religion. Wine occupied a very particular place within this field: "[A] singular difference in attitude becomes immediately apparent in respect of solid and liquid foods. The former represents the body's obligations, the latter its luxuries. One is used to nourish, the other to honour. . . unlike 'today's special', wine is a personal good, a social good" (Claude Lévi-Strauss, *The Elemental Structures of Kinship*, 1949).

The whys and wherefores of drinking thus reflect a necessity that is physical but also determined by civilization – the practices that in equal measure influence and embody changes in the context in which drinkers drink, be that political, technical, cultural or agronomic. This role has become clearly apparent since the 1970s, and there is no shortage of international research laboratories and reference works – those instituted by the UNESCO chair for the Culture and Traditions of Wine, in particular – shedding light on the central position occupied by wine as a social constructor of humanity. This question has been addressed in many studies – in *Le Goût de l'ivresse. Une histoire de la boisson en France* (2017), for example, historian Matthieu Lecoutre outlines a way of reading the interactions at play in this co-production between mankind and society.

A wine drinker under the influence

Wine proliferated because sections of humanity chose to drink it. As Dion sums up, "Man. . . loves wine like a friend he has chosen: out of preference, not out of duty." While the antiseptic, energy-giving and intoxicating properties of wine go some way toward explaining its almost essential usefulness before modern developments in healthcare, nutrition and medicine, it should nonetheless be noted that plenty of other alcoholic drinks also possessed the same properties and were generally accessible. The specific consumption of wine therefore went beyond purely pragmatic necessity. This idea has been developed by Lecoutre: choosing to drink a particular product is an act of affirmation and differentiation, an act of sharing, of discovery and of taste. Drinkers hierarchize and codify beverages by deciding whether and how to drink them, and in drinking, they acknowledge both their purported effects and their symbolic significance. In fact, wine drinkers are consuming far more than fermented grape juice, since wine – a "hyper-culturalized" drink that in certain eras has even been used in cult worship – occupies a singular place in human history. As sociologists are quick to point out, the patterns of wine consumption can also be explained by the political, economic and social environment; drinkers of wine stand at the crossroads of their individual tastes and the possibilities offered by the area and the community to which they belong. Lecoutre identifies three sources of influence:

- **Intergenerational transmission** by parents or the older generation;
- **Intragenerational transmission** by peers – siblings, friends, colleagues;
- **Extended transmission** by a new social group to which the drinker wishes to belong.

Drinkers are influenced but not strictly motivated by these and retain a certain freedom of choice for what seems symbolically good. This choice is affected by drinkers' tastes, financial means and a desire either to maintain traditional links or integrate into new social, political, religious or political models adjudged superior. Drink is an essential social driving force: "Drinking thus makes it possible to integrate oneself by creating links with one's group of origin or other groups, but also to exclude particular drinks and drinkers [or non-drinkers] and certain ways of drinking from authorized normality" (Matthieu Lecoutre, *Le Goût de l'ivresse*). Drinking and offering a drink can be seen as one of the most universal forms of social bonding, an assertion of social power and an affirmation of identity. How did these cultural circumstances arise around the Mediterranean and in Western Europe over the centuries? The various successive stages have mainly been studied in a number of specialist works and will help us to better understand the status of wine and intoxication in our contemporary society.

> **It was in Greece, with the cult of Dionysus, that wine was to emerge as a vector of humanization and civilization**

The wine of the ancient world – a drink for the gods and the elite

The various peoples of antiquity thought wine so miraculous that it could only be of divine origin. The gods loved wine so much that it was used as an offering, and the ruling classes were quick to take it up to get closer to the heavenly spheres, whereas the masses contented themselves with other fermented beverages such as beer. In Egypt, for example, wine played an important role in rituals where the alternative state of "noble" inebriation brought one closer to the gods; the Egyptian divinities Hathor, Sekhmet and Osiris were even described as "masters of wine". The work of Egyptologist Pierre Tallet has shown that particular interest was taken in wine beyond the religious aspect revealed by pharaonic tombs, however. During the New Kingdom (1550–1070 BCE), an "art of drinking" was established that ritualized sexual desire within the morality of enjoyment; consuming wine was part of the art of seduction and pleasure. It was stored in meticulously "labelled" amphorae and consumed in the company of women at elite banquets, where it was served with great precision, no doubt mixed with water and other adjuvants.

In Mesopotamia, however, wine (the "beer of the mountains") was associated with Gilgamesh, the legendary second-millennium king who discovered a vine that offered him immortality. Wine graced the tables of high dignitaries, affirming their power and magnanimity. Intoxication was actively pursued in such situations, although plebeian drunkenness, often the result of indulgence in beer, was generally condemned. As *V. vinifera* spread to the western Mediterranean, wine came to exert an even greater influence on civilization.

Dionysus in the city – from living in the wild, to a life of culture

It was in Greece, with the cult of Dionysus, that wine was to emerge as a vector of humanization and civilization. Despite numerous works dedicated to the determinative role played by myths and gods, including those by Walter Otto, Jean-Pierre Vernant, Maria Daraki and Jean-Robert Pitte, the significance of the Dionysiac movement is still poorly understood by the general public – and with it, the role played by wine in the codification of "the city" through the establishment of rites such as the Dionysiac Mysteries. "By introducing vines and wine into the Greek world, Dionysus translated humanity from *bios agrios* to *bios héménos*, living in the wild to a life of culture" (Thibaut Boulay, "Dionysos, les cultes bachiques and les travaux viticoles", 2015). With Dionysus, wine was not merely a means of accessing the gods or forging an alliance with them; it became the physical incarnation of the god himself, sharing all his ambiguities and powers. Dionysus, known as Bacchus in Roman mythology, was an ambivalent god, the son of Zeus and a mortal woman, Semele, who became pregnant and then died of her overpowering desire to see her lover in all his splendour. To save the child, Zeus sewed him into his thigh, symbolizing for some the vatting required for fermentation. As a child, Dionysus was dismembered by the Titans, an image interpreted as the pruning of vines. Zeus then brought him back to life, evoking the rebirth of nature and, for exegetes, the resurrection of Osiris and Christ.

Dionysus was a central and ambiguous god, embodying the vital dynamic that mankind has to face and whose apparent paradoxes we must learn to overcome: nature and culture, wild thinking and civilized reason, the chthonic world below and the universe of plants above, man and woman, life and death.

God of vines and all vital liquids – sap, milk, wine, semen – the worship of Dionysus was intended to codify the destructive effects of excessive drunkenness for society and the individual, enabling us to transcend the constraints of the human condition. In a great leap forward for civilization, theatre and tragedy were invented for Dionysus (including Euripides' *Bacchae*, written in 405 BCE, the archetype of the genre), along with the Bacchanal (one of the rites of the Dionysiac Mysteries, the forerunner of carnival with its cross-dressing, excessive drinking and abandonment of

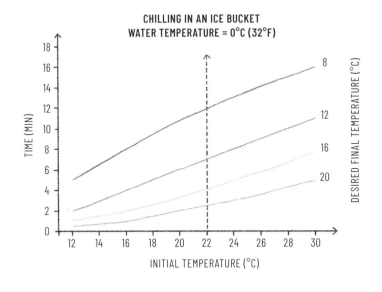

CHILLING IN AN ICE BUCKET
WATER TEMPERATURE = 0°C (32°F)

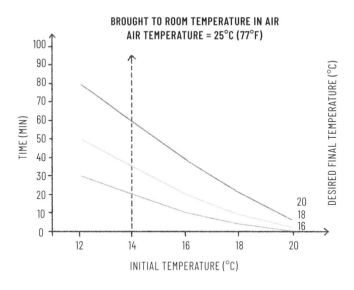

BROUGHT TO ROOM TEMPERATURE IN AIR
AIR TEMPERATURE = 25°C (77°F)

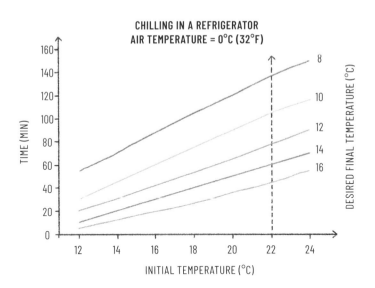

CHILLING IN A REFRIGERATOR
AIR TEMPERATURE = 0°C (32°F)

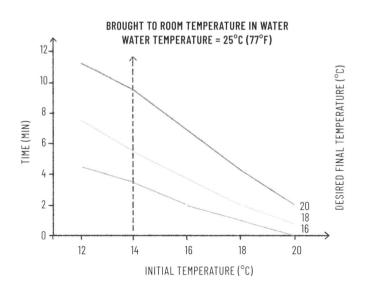

BROUGHT TO ROOM TEMPERATURE IN WATER
WATER TEMPERATURE = 25°C (77°F)

TEMPERATURE CONTROL FOR SERVING WINE

Preparation time will depend on the initial temperature of the wine and the type of chilling desired, irrespective of bottle size (half-bottle, bottle, magnum and so on). Immersion in water helps wine to come to temperature rapidly, whether chilled in an ice bucket or at room temperature. Oenologists Émile Peynaud and Jacques Blouin highlight the importance of serving temperature and the time required to achieve it in their book *Le Goût du vin. Le grand livre de la degustation*.

THE AUCTION MARKET AND PRICE PERFORMANCE OF PREMIUM WINES LISTED FOR RESALE ON THE LIV-EX INDEX

The market for premium wines (from Burgundy, Bordeaux, Champagne, the Rhône, Italy and California, for example) has seen record sales since 2021, with Liv-ex figures and indices suggesting growth in purchases by both volume and value. New life has also been breathed into the auction market, highlighting the role played by Asian and American buyers in this price boom. Certain wines have now become investment products just like any other and are traded by specialist investment funds.

LIV-EX PRICE INDICES SINCE THE END OF 2019

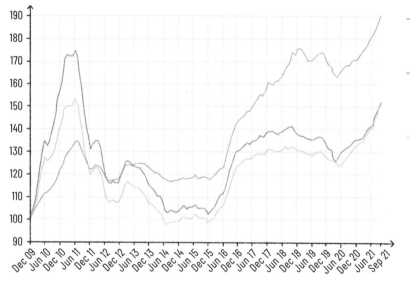

— LIV-EX FINE WINE 1000 INDEX:
Index of monthly movement in the resale price of the 1,000 most-traded wines from across the regions

— LIV-EX FINE WINE 50 INDEX:
Index of daily movement in the resale price of Bordeaux First Growths, the wines considered the most sought-after, over the 10 most recent vintages

— LIV-EX FINE WINE 100 INDEX:
Index of daily movement in the resale price of the 100 most-traded wines on the secondary market (resale)

LIV-EX REGIONAL PRICE INDICES DURING THE FIRST NINE MONTHS OF 2021

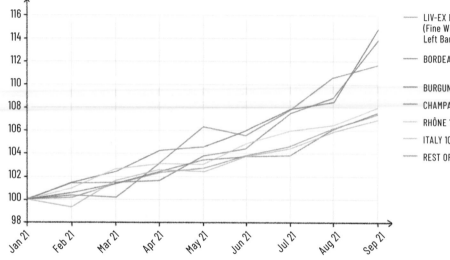

— LIV-EX BORDEAUX 500
(Fine Wine 50, Second Wine 50, Right Bank 50, Left Bank 200, Sauternes 50)

— BORDEAUX LEGENDS 50; MOST-TRADED

— BURGUNDY 150; MOST-TRADED
— CHAMPAGNE 50; MOST-TRADED
— RHÔNE 100; MOST-TRADED
— ITALY 100; MOST-TRADED
— REST OF THE WORLD 60; MOST-TRADED

GLOBAL AUCTION SALES REVENUE FOR Q1–Q3 (JANUARY TO SEPTEMBER) SINCE 2016

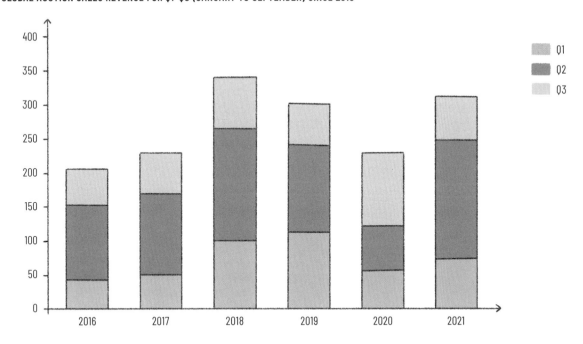

GLOBAL AUCTION SALES REVENUE FOR JANUARY TO SEPTEMBER 2021 BY COUNTRY AND CONTINENT

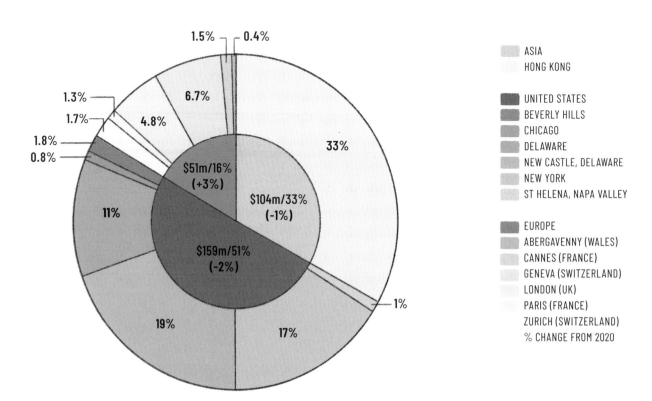

Is Homo sapiens *actually* Homo imbibens?

British journalist Andrew Jefford wrote a famous article for issue 60 of the *World of Fine Wine* magazine ("*Homo Imbibens*: The Work of Patrick McGovern", 2018) in which he examined the work of this American anthropologist and global expert in biomolecular archaeology and brought to a wider public McGovern's conclusion that man is in fact *Homo imbibens*. As McGovern recounts in *Ancient Wine: The Search for the Origins of Viniculture* (2007), humanity has been driven by biological, social and religious imperatives to consume alcohol, which we are able to assimilate thanks to a genetic evolution we share with our primate ancestors: alcohol dehydrogenase and aldehyde dehydrogenase enzymes. This relationship with alcohol is even one of the keys to understanding the development of our species and our civilizations: "What came first, bread or beer?", McGovern enquires. "You need food to exist; but if you want to have a good time, if you want to drink something safer than water, if you want to have something reliable with which to take medicine and so live longer, if you want a social lubricant, if you want to stimulate your sexual desire and thus have more children, alcoholic drinks are going to help. You are left with mind-altering effects that are shrouded in mystery to a greater or lesser extent in that there seem to be supernatural forces at work both in the process of fermentation and in your brain. You are able to relate this to some meaning within the universe, and this is why alcoholic drink is generally involved at the heart of all religions... Ultimately, humanity will always come back to it – we like to drink alcohol. I would also mention that what we seem to be adapted for is moderate consumption, and this probably goes back to the Palaeolithic era. Alcohol is so easily available now that people abuse it, but that doesn't mean we should ignore its positive effects."

inhibition), and even the banquet – as "institutionalized transgressions with the power to cement human association"', to quote Greek historian Maria Daraki.

The symposium, or the civilizing art of drinking

The banquet essentially embodies the exemplary normalization of wine consumption and, by analogy, represents a code of conduct in a democratic city. The meal itself (*deipnon*) is followed by the symposium (from the Greek *sumpinein*, "to drink together"), where the guests take refreshment and discuss matters. Because unadulterated wine was reserved for Dionysus, who alone was capable of withstanding its effects, it would be provided diluted with water and mixed with spices. It was served using dedicated vessels that would warm the heart of any contemporary sommelier, including a *péliké* vase to transport it, a *hydria* to hold the water, a *krater* for mixing, a *kylix* for drinking and a *psykter* for cooling. The symposiarch, the master of ceremonies, who would normally remain sober), would decide the proportion of the mixes and the number of cups assigned to each guest – a ritual still enacted in Georgia and overseen by a *tamada*, the MC of the *supra*, Georgia's traditional banquet.

The symposium is a perfect symbol of Greek society. It is certainly not a drinking binge, being more concerned with accessing the Dionysiac world through controlled inebriation while cultivating the self through debate, games of skill, music and poetry. By dint of its religious nature, such a banquet is also pedagogical and philosophical, as Plato recounts in his famous text, *Symposium* (380 BCE): during a symposium in which he is the only person not to get drunk, Socrates explains the maieutic method (a philosophy that draws out analytical minds) and the search for beauty and truth through love and virtue.

Two millennia later, German philosopher Friedrich Nietzsche was to explore the topic of Dionysism from his first work (*The Birth of Tragedy*, 1872) through to his last (*Dionysian Dithyrambs*, 1888). Nietzsche was a strict teetotaller and even considered alcohol one of the greatest corruptors of human nature, but he still saw in Dionysus the only potentially civilizing figure capable of forcing us to accept humanity's deep roots and transcend its deadly illusions. His writings are a critique of Platonism and Christianity, which he viewed as misleading apprehensions of "true" Dionysism that distorted it for fear of its power. They identify a fundamental link between the Dionysiac myth and the Christian religion's role in Western civilization.

A Dionysiac Christ

In *Le Désir du vin* (2004), Pitte develops multiple analogies between Dionysus and Christ: both transformed water into wine, both died and were resurrected like a vine in winter, and both were celebrated on 6 January. (Epiphany is thought to have been fixed on this date because it was the day of the Dionysiac feast celebrating the rebirth of the vine.) Christian scripture has, in fact, undeniably assimilated its pagan, essentially Graeco-Roman heritage in making the vine and its fruit the symbol of the one God; it accords wine a central place both literally and symbolically. The Gospels take up the basic theme of the temperance required to forge a religious bond (by contrast to Islam, which forbids any consumption of alcohol) in the Eucharist, a ritual taught to the disciples of Jesus during. . . a banquet. And don't believers access the divine by drinking the wine that has become the blood of Christ through transubstantiation?

The zenith of Dionysism also coincides with the origins of Christianity, which may explain the dazzling success of the Christian religion in the ancient Mediterranean world. Vines reached the southern end of the Italian peninsula from Greece around the 5th century BCE and were rapidly adopted first by the Etruscans and then the Romans. Here, too, wine began as a luxury beverage reserved for the elite but spread to the people as the empire expanded, with its consumption, in place of beer, even becoming a symbol of Romanization. At the same time, the quest to "drink well" continued among those with knowledge and experience of the hierarchy of wines and guaranteed origins, during banquets that, while tradition was being upheld, were gradually changing in appearance and function. As they slowly lost their philosophical dimension, banquets, which had been conceived as a time of "drinking together" (but not to excess – this is Seneca's collective "sober drunkenness" rather than selfish inebriation) still met religious, social and hedonistic needs.

The greater the growth of Christianity, however – it became the official religion of the empire in 392 CE – the more the sacred aspect of the banquet tended to crumble. From that moment on, divine Communion was to be taken only during Mass. Through the course of the centuries to follow, it was also the Church that remained the underwriter of winemaking skill and modes of consumption, despite the disruption caused by the invasion by Germanic tribes and the fall of the Roman Empire. As the sole bastion of stability in these times of political chaos, the Church preserved both the art of winemaking among the laity and the norms of the Eucharist rite and divine offerings among the clergy. For the rest of the population, wine became a palliative for everyday ills, with intoxication losing any liturgical associations to become a constitutive – and accepted – element of society.

Wine and pharmacopoeia

While the elites of the Middle Ages may have also consumed wine for religious, political and economic reasons, every class of society made use of it primarily for nutritional and medical purposes. Drawing directly on Hippocrates and Galen's doctrine of the humours, the contemporary understanding of diet essentially saw disease as an imbalance that a well-chosen wine could rectify. Depending on the harmony of an individual's four humours (blood, phlegm, yellow bile and black bile) linked to the four elements of the universe (earth, fire, air and water), which themselves are associated with the four qualities (hot, cold, humid, dry), a physician might administer one of the four recognized types of wine: white, black, red or clairet. Their therapeutic and blood-thinning properties were based on tasting criteria similar to those used in antiquity, and a sound knowledge of these was required to prevent the medicine becoming a poison. Daily consumption did no harm anyway, as well as providing calories and sterilizing water. Wine was thus the most essential foodstuff in this pharmacopoeia, which remained the case in France until the 18th century and the dawn of modern medicine. For Fagon, Louis XIV's physician, the humours of Burgundy wine provided far better remedies than those from Champagne for treating royal afflictions, igniting a controversy about the ostensible virtues of this or that wine that lasted almost a century (1650–1730).

> **The Greek banquet is a perfect example of the normalization of wine consumption**

Toward the end of the 17th century, however, certain quarters of the medical profession began to question the therapeutic properties of wine, and doubts were raised about the purported beneficial effects of the mild intoxication advocated by Hippocrates and Galen, who believed that getting drunk once or twice a month was claimed to be good for the digestion; this was now the disease, not the treatment. This point of view took some time to establish itself, since wine was considered a "national religion", as historian Didier Nourrisson explains in *Crus et Cuites. Histoire du buveur* (2013). Its political place within the nation's economy had nothing at all to do with it, of course.

Cult wine, tonic wine, socializing wine...

Awarding the 1853 Academy of Sciences prize to Magnus Huss for his book *De l'alcoolisme chronique*, which examined aquavit consumption in Sweden, physician Joseph Reinach declared that "France has plenty of drunkards, but there are fortunately no alcoholics", when the Swedish writer coined

A WIDE CHOICE OF WINE GLASSES: HYPER-SPECIALIZED OR UNIVERSAL?

There has been a wild proliferation of glass shapes since the 1990s, thanks to technological innovation and diversification in wine styles. Riedel, a family-run Austrian firm founded in 1756, is the market leader and has been striving for the greatest harmony between glass, cépage and style since 1958, with its Sommeliers range including 31 different shapes as of 2022. At the other end of the spectrum, there has been a movement to explore the versatility of a single glass to suit every style of wine, like that created by Jancis Robinson MW and Richard Brendon in The Wine Glass in 2018.

WIDTH
90mm (3½in)

VOLUME
500ml (16.9fl oz)

YEAR CREATED
2018

HEIGHT
224mm (8¹³/₁₆in)

Jancis Robinson
×
RICHARD BRENDON

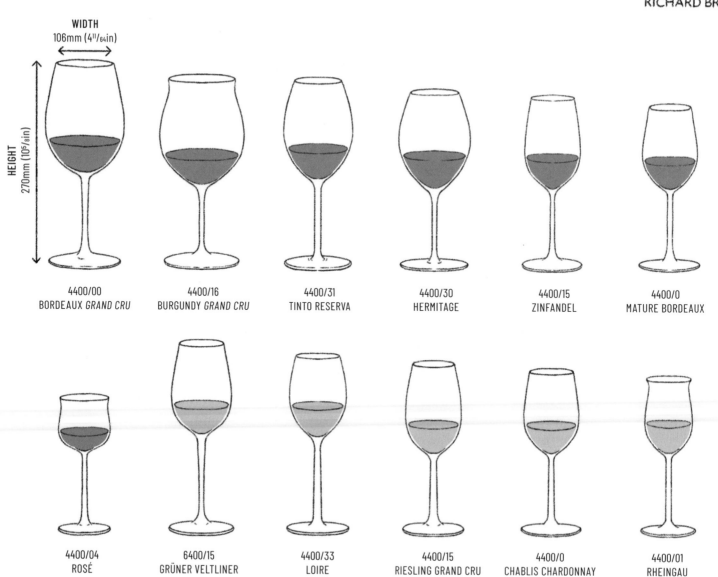

WIDTH
106mm (4¹¹/₆₄in)

HEIGHT
270mm (10⅝in)

| 4400/00 | 4400/16 | 4400/31 | 4400/30 | 4400/15 | 4400/0 |
| BORDEAUX *GRAND CRU* | BURGUNDY *GRAND CRU* | TINTO RESERVA | HERMITAGE | ZINFANDEL | MATURE BORDEAUX |

| 4400/04 | 6400/15 | 4400/33 | 4400/15 | 4400/0 | 4400/01 |
| ROSÉ | GRÜNER VELTLINER | LOIRE | RIESLING GRAND CRU | CHABLIS CHARDONNAY | RHEINGAU |

RIEDEL
THE WINE GLASS COMPANY

4400/07
MONTRACHET

4400/55
SAUTERNES

4400/05
ALSACE

4400/28
VINTAGE CHAMPAGNE

4400/08
CHAMPAGNE

4400/58
CHAMPAGNE WINE

4400/88
SPARKLING WINE

4400/20
WATER

4400/18
SHERRY

4400/18
TEQUILA

4400/60
VINTAGE PORT

4400/70
COGNAC XO

4400/71
COGNAC VSOP

4400/80
SINGLE-MALT WHISKY

4400/17
MARTINI

4200/03
GRAPPA

4200/04
ORCHARD FRUIT

4200/06
STONE FRUIT

8400/15
BLACK GLASS FOR
BLIND TASTING

313

the term. There was nothing paradoxical about such a statement at the time: wine was a health product and was viewed as a remedy against the dangers of alcohol. It had fortified farmers, workers and the middle classes through the Industrial Revolution and its "virtues" transcended class and gender. And France was certainly getting through it: by 1880, there were more than half a million *mastroquets* (village drinking establishments – that is, one for every 82 inhabitants), with average annual consumption of 162 litres (43 US gallons) per head, including children, all cheerfully taxed by the state. Louis Pasteur considered wine to be the hygienic drink *par excellence*, and even the temperance leagues that formed toward the end of the 19th century drew an emphatic distinction between fermented drinks and the strong spirits to be resisted. The French state, supported by the Academy of Medicine, backed this approach because it represented both an economic issue and a source of national pride; schoolchildren were taught to tell the difference between "good" wine and "bad" alcohol, and red wine was served in school canteens until 1956. It should be noted that, back then, more than 23,000 municipalities still had no running water, and only cider, beer or wine was routinely available to quench thirst. Wine was at the heart of France's "30 glorious years" in the wake of the world wars as the country became a consumer society deluged in advertising. As philosopher and semiologist Roland Barthes described it, "Wine is socialized because it is based not only on a morality but also on a scenario. It adorns all the most trivial ceremonials of French daily life, from a quick snack (a rough-and-ready red with some Camembert), to a feast, from chatting at the bistro to speeches at a banquet" (*Mythologies*, 1957). Perspectives were to shift in the 1950s, however.

> **Such circumstances expose the fundamental ambiguity of wine, which is both a vector of the dangers of ethanol and a driver of socializing ritual**

... wine as the enemy, wine as a choice, wine as world heritage

Since 1943, the French Resistance medical committee had been describing alcoholism, including dependence on wine, as a "social disease" entailing healthcare and economic problems that were finally quantified in 1952. The annual cost was estimated at between 150 and 200 billion francs. Nourrisson comments that, "this national scourge was becoming a burden on the economy". The anti-alcohol lobby became more vocal, and from the wine code instituted by Pierre Mendès France and the French government in 1954 to the present day, there has been a host of laws and campaigns designed to reduce consumption, set against a thorny background of conflicting socio-economic interests. A raft of legislation to combat drink-driving (still the leading cause of alcohol-related deaths) was put in place in France as early as 1959, and the words "drink in moderation" have been mandatory on packaging since 1989, followed by regulation of advertising under the Évin law of 1991. Campaigns recommending maximum daily consumption have been produced for all parts of the wine-drinking public, with dependence no longer seen as just over-consumption of alcohol but a syndrome caused by multiple psycho-social, behavioural and neurobiological factors. Medical research has achieved a far better understanding of the addictive and harmful effects of excessive consumption at a neurological and physiological level and has dispelled a number of the untruths relating to its purported benefits – that it stimulates physical activity or is invigorating, for example. Studies of the potential benefits of very moderate wine consumption (phenolic compounds and ethanol are said to have beneficial effects for cardiovascular problems in particular) have returned contradictory results, with potential confirmation *in vitro* but a mixed picture *in vivo*.

Legal prohibition and pressure from society have proved effective in any case, with annual per capita consumption in France sinking from 135 litres (35 US gallons) in 1950 to 46 litres (12 US gallons) by 2022. Abstinence has been encouraged by medical authorities but has had a largely negative image that has persisted to this day, although this seems to be changing with the recent emergence of the concept of "de-consumption", which means drinking a lot less but drinking far higher quality. As Lecoutre points out, drinking is part and parcel of the rituals and traditions of wine-based civilizations. Not drinking means rejecting the norms of the group, unless those norms change – a development that seems to be taking place.

This brings us back to the fundamental ambiguity of wine, which is both a vector of the dangers of ethanol and a driver of socializing ritual, giving rise to the discourses that continue to set wine apart – less as a "hygienic beverage" these days but as a unique and civilizing alcoholic drink that tells a story. It has even been indirectly ratified by UNESCO: French dining, at the heart of which is the service of wines and foods, was recognized as an example of UNESCO Intangible Cultural Heritage in 2010.

An accelerated revolution in codes

The wine drinker and the codes surrounding the consumption of wine have changed considerably over the centuries, alternating between what Nourrisson called "coarse" and "refined" drinking, drunkenness and prohibition, in search of a socially acceptable compromise and a model for moderate consumption. Why have things evolved so over the course of time? Wine and drinking in general have diversified: the social functions of alcohol – wine's role in religion and debate, wine as a tonic, for health, to combat disease – have been transformed; the places where it is consumed, be they palaces, churches, cabaret clubs or the home, have changed; and external and internal norms for controlling drinking – legislation, education and enjoyment – have fluctuated. Having initially changed slowly over long timescales, all these norms have undergone an increasingly rapid evolution since the early 20th century, proving that wine has lost none of its power to shape culture. Two aspects are particularly revealing: one is marketing, the way the retailer addresses the consumer; the other is the role of the sommelier, the way the moment of consumption is aestheticized, especially by pairing food and wine.

Wine drinkers have become wine enthusiasts – a marketing revolution

Joëlle Brouard, a professor of marketing and a member of the UNESCO Culture and Traditions of Wines board, has identified four key periods in wine consumption:

- **1920–1940 and "folklorization".** This period of standardization and re-evaluation of wine was dominated by tradition and the AOC model. Food tourism took off and was championed by specialist publications. A regional mythology was established, with the creation of dishes and food-and-wine pairings.
- **1950–1985 and "democratization".** At this time, AOCs expanded both geographically and socially, with rising demand, followed by production. There was an emphasis on terroir, with collective, branded appellations winning out over owners or estates. Local consumption of table wine spread to other regions, thanks to large-scale distribution. This was also the era of wine fairs and mass publicity.
- **1985–2012 and "Parkerization".** This is when US critic Robert Parker was active, an era characterized by a search for simplified typicity with easily understood tasting notes. The audience for wine expanded, attracting more women, and consumers began to take an interest, with more wine clubs being founded, wine tourism expanding and drinkers entering the world of wine as a cultural product, against a backdrop of structural decline in consumption, and overproduction.
- **2013 onward, and "fan-clubization".** Social media has become an exponential echo chamber in the search for the unique and the "natural". The personality of the winemaker – whose ethics are highlighted by new forms of re-selling such as wine merchants, wine bars, "bistronomies" and specialist

Wine and misogyny

The place of women in the world of wine is a decidedly complex issue but fortunately one that is now increasingly coming under discussion. Throughout the history of every civilization, women have been excluded from the winemaking professions and their consumption of wine seen as shameful, with women drinking wine ostracized on the basis of superstition, taboos, traditional prejudice and stereotypes that have proliferated over a long period. It was a world that until very recently remained highly gendered. Although women were essential to the sector's economy, in particular through their work in vineyards and at harvest, they were relegated to junior roles in the majority of cases. This gender imbalance has gradually been changing, as has the role of women in society as a whole, thanks to a range of different feminist movements. The introduction of women to the world of winemaking was led by pioneers in the 19th century but has accelerated since around the 1980s, and women are now represented at every level within the industry, as winemakers, oenologists, cellar managers, importers, critics, sommeliers, wine merchants and teachers, among other roles. They have also become lovers and consumers of wine.

Although women have acquired a certain legitimacy and recognition, and brought a different dynamic and perspective to the world of wine, it should not be forgotten that social structures and representations evolve only over a long timescale, and any current progress is still highly fragile.

For a better understanding of the finer points of these highly critical issues, refer to the work of Laure Ménétrier or publications by the food historian Ségolène Lefèvre, especially *Les Femmes et l'amour du vin* (2009); *Le Vin. Quand les femmes s'en mêlent* (2019) by researchers Carmela Maltone and Maylis Santa-Cruz; *Les Femmes et la Vigne. Une histoire économique et sociale* (2016) by economist Jean-Louis Escudier and, lastly, on a lighter note but an equally serious issue, *In Vino Femina* (2022) by Alessandra Fottorino and Céline Pernot-Burlet.

online sites – has become a key component. This is wine as a "narrative" that has to enter the drinker's world, rather than vice versa. In a fiercely competitive drinks market, consumption of wine is no longer necessary but a choice, to quench thirst and to socialize. From this point onwards, it is the experience that counts more than the product itself, curiosity wins out over loyalty, and any allegiance is emotional, with a strong tendency toward de-consumption.

> " In scarcely a hundred years, the acts of eating and drinking have changed in meaning almost entirely

Commodification, speculation and fakes

We should add a fifth key period in consumption that has emerged since the **1990s: "speculation"**. This took off in the wine trade around the turn of the millennium with the installation of the market for young Bordeaux wines, and it has since spread as global demand has increased for wines that are available in limited quantities, especially in Burgundy. A narrow tranche of wine production has become first collectors' items and then financial investments: celebrity winemakers, rare vintages, social-status symbols and specific labels are listed as if on a stock market, and their market value has skyrocketed since the mid-1990s in a trend that has established certain wines as undisputed luxury goods. A boom in the buying power of new wine-lovers, in Asia and the US in particular, has caused the price of certain wines to rise dramatically, as is clear from the indices published by Liv-ex. Vineyard land prices have soared, and problems with distribution have emerged. Much like the commodification of works of art, speculation in certain wines is also a symptom of a society in which monetization and short-term profit taking is the norm.

As a result, a shadow market has also exploded with a proliferation of fakes, giving rise to some extraordinary stories, such as that recounted in Benjamin Wallace's *Billionaire's Vinegar* about counterfeiter Hardy Rodenstock, or the documentary *Sour Grapes* dealing with Rudy Kurniawan, who was nicknamed "Doctor Conti" for his unbridled enthusiasm for wines from Domaine de la Romanée-Conti.

In scarcely a hundred years, the acts of eating and drinking have changed in meaning almost entirely, with a reinvention of the codes and imaginations that are associated with them. New consumer expectations are shaking up the industry and its historic tenets. Wine is no longer essential for the individual in society: professionals need to give it new meaning and to provide wine drinkers with an experience that will help them rediscover its unique nature beyond mere financial gain or social recognition of the consumer. This is one of the roles of the sommelier and the work of pairing food with wine.

Why do we drink wine?

I am borrowing the simple and provocative title of a small treatise published in 2019 by Belgian mathematics professor Fabrizio Bucella, a beer specialist who also holds a PhD in physics. He pursues an enquiry into the deep connections between wine and the human condition with all his characteristic wit and erudition. Calling upon philosophers, anthropologists, physicians, sociologists and other specialists, he concludes that it is impossible to answer this question satisfactorily without raising many others, and so opts for the following tautology as a solution: "Ultimately, if we drink. . . it is for the sake of drinking. . . In these times of a return to a certain kind of Puritanism, where some would like to condemn all forms of excess, all deviance, every pleasure, it pleases me to imagine that drinking could become an act of resistance."

When we drink wine, we have special intimate access – intimate because it is ingested – to a natural and infinite reality beyond ourselves. We make it a reflection of our own nature and so can endow it with new meaning. In a society that has been commodified and rationalized to an absurd degree, re-enchanting the world through controlled, cultured and Dionysiac consumption of the product of the vineyard may also be an invitation to reappropriate for ourselves the experience of tasting and the power of our palates – and so to taste the world around us in a different way, a world of which wine is just one possible incarnation, although one of the most powerful. This is where viticulture and a respectful sampling of the living world come together. By rediscovering the pleasure of tasting living wine (rather than industrial, processed wine), drinkers may perhaps understand and transcend the mechanisms by which taste is made and escape the diktats of the market by constructing their own definition of what is good or bad.

The art of serving wine – pairing with food and the role of the sommelier

In 2010, UNESCO inscribed "the gastronomic meal of the French" on its list of Intangible Cultural Heritage in recognition of the cultural aspects of this style of eating and drinking together. Among the defining criteria is an art that was also "made in France", the "pairing of food with wine". This should come as no surprise, since these pairings reveal the specific links between wine and gastronomy, two of the country's greatest specialities. Much more importantly, however, they embody the notions of taste and terroir – in other words, a vision of the world that is specific to a certain culture. Behind what might seem to be simply enjoyment for aesthetes lurk political issues that have shaped the collective imagination of an idiosyncratic "art of living", hence its power as a peaceful force in international relations – the "gastro- diplomacy" that Laurent Fabius, France's then Minister of Foreign Affairs, brought back into play in 2014. How did these pairings of food and wine come about? Who sets the rules for "good" matches? How has sommellerie made a speciality of recommending them? What do contemporary gastronomic pairings say about how we view the world?

The prerequisites for gastronomic pairing

While we have been drinking wine with meals in every vine-growing civilization since the skills of vinification were first mastered, the art of matching particular *cuvées* with specific dishes is a practice that has been codified only very recently in the broad scope of human history. Guillaume Tirel (also known as Taillevent) wrote his *Viandier* (a collection of recipes) in the 13th century, followed a century later by *Le Ménagier de Paris* (1393), which described specific wines, including whites, clairets and those to be diluted with water, along with elaborate dishes that were testament both to the richness of the medieval kitchen and the supremacy of the medical theory of the four humours in choosing and serving wine.

It was the modern era, however, in particular the period between the 17th and 19th centuries, that was to see the practice become the norm in France. This was on the back of an evolution in table manners, technical progress and political upheaval: the much-contested endorsement of the fork at the side of the plate, the arrival of glasses on the table, the staging of a meal, the gradual hierarchization of the serving of courses, a diversification of wine production and the appearance of the restaurant and the gourmets who dined there were just some of the conditions that paved the way for the emergence of wine tasting and pairing. This genealogy and the gastronomic family tree it produced have been detailed in *Les Accords mets-vins. Un art français* (2017), an interdisciplinary compendium edited by Pitte, who also wrote an enlightening introduction.

À la française or à la russe

Meals served to France's elite at the end of the 18th century made use of what was known as "French service", which did not really allow for precise pairing of food and wine. All the dishes were served simultaneously, like a buffet, with no particular coordination between them. Appetizers, starters, soups, fish, roasted and sauced meats, vegetables, palate cleansers and desserts were all put on the table together, leaving guests free to snack on whatever took their fancy. Glasses were not included in table settings, and the choice of wines was long limited to clairets or whites, with sweet, red and sparkling wines putting in only rarer appearances; these were drunk for their own sake and with no connection to the food. The common herd made do with *piquette* (water mixed with grape pomace), broth and bread.

Things changed rapidly after the French Revolution, however. For a start, technological progress in winemaking,

DEVELOPMENTS IN THE LEADING THEORIES ON PAIRING FOOD AND WINE SINCE 1800

Josep Roca and Ferran Centelles have developed a chronology of theories on pairing food and wines since the turn of the 20th century. The overview here also includes foundational works from the 19th century and new, contemporary approaches, such as the use of artificial intelligence.

SUBJECTIVITY

REGIONALITY
Proximity and wine routes

OBJECTIVITY
Great literary works

Luigi Veronelli
Il vino giusto

THE SCIENCE OF TASTE
JM Kamen
Food research

TRIAL AND ERROR
Raymond Dumay
The Wine Guide

GREAT LITERARY

Philippe Bourguignon
Accord parfait

Pierre Casamayo
École des Alliance

THE FOUNDATIONS
Grimod de La Reynière
Manuel des amphitryons

PHYSIOLOGY OF TASTE
JA Brillat-Savarin
The Physiology of Taste

CATEGORIZATION INTO COMPLEMENTARY AND OPPOSITIONAL PAIRINGS
Alain Senderens

CHEF COLLABORATING WITH WINEMAKERS
Alain Chapel

DICTIONARY
Plon editors
General Dictionary of Old and New French Cooking

POPULARIZATION OF WINE TASTING AMONG THE MIDDLE CLASSES
Raymond Brunet
Le Mariage des vins et des mets

NOUVELLE CUISINE STAR LISTENING TO WINE
Alain Senderens

THE OENOLOGIST TRAINS THE CHEFS
Jacques Puisais
Le vin met sur à table

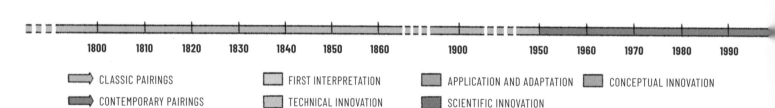

1800   1810   1820   1830   1840   1850   1860   1900   1950   1960   1970   1980   1990

➡ CLASSIC PAIRINGS   FIRST INTERPRETATION   APPLICATION AND ADAPTATION   CONCEPTUAL INNOVATION

➡ CONTEMPORARY PAIRINGS   TECHNICAL INNOVATION   SCIENTIFIC INNOVATION

FIRST USE OF ARTIFICIAL INTELLiGENCE
Peter Coucquyt, Bernard Lahousse, Johan Langenbick
The Art & Science of Foodpairing: 10,000 Flavour Matches that Will Transform the Way you Eat

NEW STUDY ON THE HISTORY OF THE CONSUMPTION OF DRINKS, INCLUDING WINE
L Melo, C Delahunty, D Cox
A new approach using consumers' "drinking histories" to explain current wine acceptance

OVERVIEW OF BINARY INTERACTIONS
RSJ Keast, PAS Breslin
An overview of binary taste/taste interactions

THEORY OF INTENSITY AND COMPLEXITY
Ferran Centelles

UNESCO Chair: Culture and Traditions of Wine
Wine and Gastronomy: Converging Views

WINE & CULINARY INTERNATIONAL FORUM
Bodegas Torres

100% MATCH, ALL PAIRINGS ARE EXPLAINED IN WRITING ON THE LUCAS CARTON MENU
Alain Senderens

NEUROLOGICAL PLASTICITY
"pairing the wine with the diner, not the meal"
Tim Hanni MW
Why You Like the Wines You Like

...ORKS

GREAT METHODOLOGICAL WORKS

...ppe Faure-Brac
...veurs complices

Evan Goldstein MS
Perfect Pairings

A Dornenburg, K Page
What to Drink with What You Eat

Robert H Harrington
Food & Wine Pairings

Enrico Bernardo
Savoir marier le vin

Alain Franck
La Méthode Franck basée

METHODOLOGIES
FM Marzi, P Mercadini, R Rosella, G Vaccarini, *Tecnica dell'abbinamento CIBO-VINO*

NEUROBIOLOGY AND GENETICS REVEAL INDIVIDUAL VARIATIONS IN PERCEPTION OF BITTERNESS (PROP) AND TACTILE SENSATIONS (TTS) WITH FOOD PREFERENCES
R Bajec, J Pickering

elBulliFoundation/
Ferran Centelles
Sapiens del Vino

THEORY OF RELATIVITY AND EMOTIONAL INTELLIGENCE OF EACH INDIVIDUAL AT THE HEART OF A PAIRING
Josep Roca

WINE FIRST
Enrico Bernardo
Il Vino restaurant

Ferran Centelles
¿Qué vino con este pato?

...XTH SENSE, INTEGRAL
...RMONIES AT EL CELLER
DE CAN ROCA
Josep Roca

MOLECULAR SOMMELLERIE
François Chartier

GEOGRAPHICAL AND ANTHROPOLOGICAL STUDIES
led by J-R Pitte
Les accords mets-vin. Un art français

Fiona Beckett
matchingfoodandwine.com

VERSATILITY
Jeannie Cho Lee MW
The Asian Palate

2000 2001 2002 2003 2004 2005 2006 2007 2008 2009 2010 2011 2012 2013 2014 2015 2016 2017 2018 2019 2020 2021

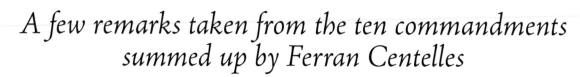

A few remarks taken from the ten commandments summed up by Ferran Centelles

At the end of his book *¿Qué vino con este pato?* (2016), Ferran Centelles draws a number of conclusions and sums up his main argument in a series of points to help us think about the culinary pairings of the future. His insights include the following.

· Plenty of myths and pseudo-science about pairings remain to be debunked.

· The most precise pairings will be those devised together by a sommelier and a chef who has a recipe that can always be tweaked to suit the wine.

· Victory is particularly sweet when the food and wine create synergies (1 + 1 = 3).

· There are no such things as so-called "enemies of wine", and there is an infinite number of imaginative combinations.

· Complementary pairings are the easiest to make and the most reliable.

· Contrasting pairings are riskier but tend to be more memorable.

· A pairing can be both complementary and contrasting at the same time.

· The use of versatile wines and other beverages can be an appropriate way to bring harmony to long and complex tasting menus (such as sake with *kaiseki*).

· One question yet to be answered is whether olfactory sensations are more or less important than taste sensations in a pairing.

· Cultural factors and personal experience are almost as important as genetics in understanding taste preferences.

· No one has the absolute authority to insist on what is a good or bad pairing; relativity rules.

· Emotion plays a fundamental role in how we experience pairings, and it is almost impossible to remove it from the equation in order to taste objectively.

· Showing empathy toward your guests will help you give the best advice. You have to know how to "get a sense of" the people to whom you are suggesting pairings.

· Every sommelier should employ their critical faculties and ask the question implicit in the title of Tim Hanni's book *Why You Like the Wines You Like*: Why *do* you like the wines you like?

from the vineyard to the winery to the bottle, had considerably improved the quality, ageing potential and diversity of the wines available. Cellars were being laid down, and wine-lovers were beginning to take an interest in how wines were served. Grimod de La Reynière, the critic considered the father of modern Western gastronomy, used his *Manuel des amphitryons* (1808) to impart the first advice on what had yet even to be properly identified as sommellerie. He recommends serving wine in bottles, placing these on the table and chilling them as required, and drinking unadulterated wine rather than having drinks diluted by some invisible lackey. He also suggests choosing the style of wine to suit the hosts.

Even for this gourmet, however, pairing wine still came down to whites or reds for the starters and main courses and sweet wines for desserts. Only the evolution of the dining process during the nineteenth century would allow this approach to be refined, and the first step was the invention of the modern restaurant. A descendant of the tavern and the coaching inn, the name restaurant came from an establishment offering *bouillon restaurant* ("restorative broth") set up in Paris by a Monsieur Boulanger in 1765, in which patrons could sup on hearty meat soups and whose Latin motto promised, "O come to me, all ye whose stomachs cry out in misery, and I shall restore ye". There was a rash of court cooks forced into unemployment by the French Revolution, and with the loss of the patronage of the aristocracy, along with their brigades of servants and heaving larders, service had to adapt: either alone or in small groups, customers would choose dishes

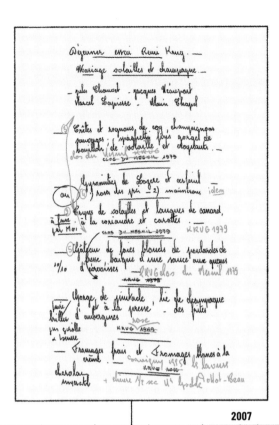

1900

1987

2007

07/08/2007

Le dessert "albarizas" et le Xérès VORS Matusalem Cream
Oloroso Dulce de González Byass, un des rares accords
spécifiques proposés par Ferran Centelles à elBulli.

elBulli

gin fizz frozen caliente
aceitunas verdes sféricas-I
galleta de mango
pepitas de oro
oliva crujiente
merengue/profiteroles de remolacha y yogur
nori-quinoa
catanias saladas
bombones de mandarina, cacahuete y curri
pistacho con su miel y roquefort
bizcocho de pistachos con mousse de leche ácida
bizcocho de sésamo y miso
fondant de frambuesas y vinagre de frambuesa
flores de horchata
yogur de ostras con px en tempura
judión son panceta Joselito
cajú con yogur
anchoa con jamón y ruba de yogur
cáscara de gorgonzola, nueces, apio y manzana
ñoquis de polenta con café y yuba al azafrán
nueces tiernas
"pie de muiños"
fideua de shimensi
caracoles "a la llauna"
ventresca de caballa teriyaki
anguila-chirimoya
jugo de liebre
miel de ciprés con shots de melocotón y mazapán de almendra tierna
"trufitas"
albarizas
Morphings....

THE EVOLUTION OF WINE AND FOOD PAIRINGS OVER A CENTURY

Pairing food and wine was almost unheard of at the
Mayors' Banquet in Paris in 1900, but the idea has attracted
extraordinary levels of interest since around the 1960s, from
research into pairing wine with food by chefs such as Alain
Chapel (above right, with Krug Champagnes) to avant-garde
gastronomic exploration by Ferran Adrià or Ferran Centelles
at El Bulli, for example (pictured above): "Albarizas" (a dessert)
and González Byass VORS Matusalem Cream Oloroso Dulce
Sherry, one of the few specific pairings suggested by Ferran
Centelles at El Bulli.

from a given menu and – to cut losses – consume individual portions brought to them by a small number of serving staff. The same approach went for wines, sweet cordials and *digestifs*, which were served by the bottle and the glass, as can be seen from the oldest menu surviving from Véry's restaurant at the Palais-Royal in Paris, which dates from 1790; there is a selection mainly of Burgundy, Champagne and Bordeaux for the first courses, although the choice becomes more exotic as matters progress: Málaga, Constance, Calabria and Scetuvalle – for Setúbal in Portugal, spelling still being in its phonetic infancy. A little later, necessity became the mother of invention for a style of service to the upper classes dreamed up by the Russian Ambassador. Having been injured in a fire, he asked his butler to serve dishes pre-sliced and presented individually to the guests he continued to receive. This was the origin of "Russian service", which was to supplant its French counterpart during the second half of the 19th century. The table was also set with a wider range of glassware as the cellars continued to swell with wines from every region. For Pitte, such developments were the mainspring of "a new form of sensitivity to taste that sought to identify harmonious pairings of food and wine".

The teachings of the *Physiology of Taste*
Two months before his death, lawyer and gourmet Brillat-Savarin published *Physiologie du goût, ou Méditations de gastronomie transcendante* (1825), a magisterial treatise, although not without humour, that took an aesthetic, intellectual and educated approach to fine dining and drinking in an attempt to establish gastronomy as a science. The foreword, which comprised 20 aphorisms, anticipated the work as a whole in suggesting gastronomy as the convergence of many complex disciplines, including biology, economics, agriculture, medicine and chemistry. Some of these maxims are anthropological: "Tell me what you eat and I will tell you who you are"; "Animals feed, humans eat, but only a man of intellect knows how to dine". Others are political: "The destiny of nations depends on the way they feed themselves"; or metaphysical: "The discovery of a new dish does more for the happiness of the human race than the discovery of a star." Others again set out rules for pairing food and wine.

> X. Those who gorge themselves or get drunk know neither how to drink nor how to eat.
>
> XI. The order in which to eat foods is from the most substantial to the lightest.
>
> XII. The order for drinks is from the blandest to the smokiest and most fragrant.
>
> XIII. Any claim that wine should not be changed is a heresy; the tongue becomes overburdened, and after the third glass, even the best wine will evoke only a dull sensation.

Specific pairings are suggested throughout this spectacularly successful opus, which was to influence the arts of cooking, serving and tasting food for decades to come and awaken a new generation of wealthy gourmets to the subtleties of taste. Following on from Brillat-Savarin and La Reynière, the entry for "wine" in the *Dictionnaire général de la cuisine française ancienne et moderne* (1853) suggested the first modern standardization of pairings. For a typical meal, still served *à la française*, the unknown author suggests in particular:

> "Before and after soups: vermouth. Dry Madeira. Loka. Sicilian white wine. Dry Pacaret. Agrigente. Rota-Rancio...
>
> "With roasts (red wines): Clos-Vougeot. Romanée-Conty [*sic*]. Chambertin. Pomard [*sic*]. Clos Saint-Georges. Nuits. Volnay. Vosne. Côte-Rôtie. Red Hermitage. Jurançon. Roussillon. Old port...
>
> "For palate cleansers [*sic*]: Morachet [*sic*]. Hermitage blanc. Saint-Péray. Condrieux [*sic*]. Blanquette de Limoux. Arbois wine. Pink Champagne. Coulée de Serrant. Val-de-Pennas. Italian wines."

The vast range of suggested pairings is remarkable, and the matches are guided by a pleasure-based pragmatism to be appreciated by men and women "of taste". They are based on the need for social distinction – drinking is a great divider – and the availability and quality of wines rather than any precise organoleptic rules, even though certain trends are discernible. It should also not be forgotten that, at the time, 80 years before the creation of the AOC system, the styles of even famous wines were still in the hands of merchants rather than producers and were anything but perfectly consistent. From this time on, however, matching food and wine started to become a feature of official and prestigious banquets, such as the banquet for the mayors of France given by President Émile Loubet in 1900, where specific wines were selected although not paired dish by dish, along with restaurant dining rooms, where the first sommeliers were to emerge. Wine followed cooking's lead until the 1920s or 1930s, however, which brought changes in standards and the development of a culture among the new rural elites, including wine-growers.

The establishment of regional cuisine
Food and wine pairings in the Middle Ages had initially followed medicinal prescripts before the modern era turned them into an ostentatious indicator of education and wealth based on vague physiological and organoleptic rules. At the turn of the 20th century, however, they became a truly political issue, symbolizing the final expression of a particular aspect of gastronomy that is peculiar to France, that of regional cuisine. The work of historian Julia Csergo has shed considerable light on the subject: in antiquity, as in the

Middle Ages, specialities from local and regional terroirs were already known and accepted as such, but it was the political centralism that took hold in France from the 16th century onward that encouraged their integration into a certain vision of France as a nation apart, with a wealth of natural resources that should be recognized and united.

The French Revolution only accelerated this understanding of regional gastronomic output. Since highly pronounced regional cultural differences were threatening to derail the entire revolutionary undertaking by encouraging secession, there was a need to construct a collective sense of belonging to a "single and indivisible" Republican nation. Gastronomy was thus to play a key role: unlike other elements that made up regional identity, in particular language, which were suppressed, regional food, agriculture and industry were itemized, acknowledged and even turned into local features by the state officials sent out into the provinces. On the first "gastronomic" map of France published by Charles-Louis Cadet de Gassicourt in 1809, historical monuments and areas of outstanding natural beauty were replaced by foods that symbolized the French regions. This may seem like a cliché these days, but at the time it occupied a key position in the nation's collective imagination and played a vital role in promoting the international tourism that was in its infancy. "Food production was fully integrated into the construction of the Republic. . . The Belle Époque saw the emergence of the exploration of regional popular cultures by folklore specialists, which continued into the interwar period. The political will to build a nation remained undiminished, but there was now a sense of a rural world that was being lost and that a new age of urban and industrial modernity was dawning. . . From this point on, terroir became the way to unite a land that was shared, and popular culture became a crucible of what was to be accepted as national tradition" (Julia Csergo, *L'invention française des "gastronomies régionales"*, 2022). An "eternal" mythology of gastronomy and wines was thus invented.

The Club des Cent, the Michelin Guide, folklore and mythology – Burgundy and gastro-tourism

Many of the food and wine pairings we imagine as having been around forever are in fact political creations of the 1920s and 1930s underpinned by overt economic perspectives. The driving forces were the advent of mass tourism and the protection of French national interests. High-end cuisine and wines had previously been viewed and retailed as prestige products reserved for an elite – an approach symbolized by Auguste Escoffier (1846-1935), the most famous and imitated chef of his time, who created luxury international gastronomy, served by brigades of staff in the great houses of Paris, London, New York and Monte Carlo and revered by a sophisticated cosmopolitan clientèle. While such cuisine used mostly French food and drink, it was seen in some politically influential circles as symptomatic of the dangers of modernism embodied by two competing powers, Germany and the US (countries that, unlike France, could not lay claim to any particularly impressive gastronomic heritage).

Among these groups, the Club des Cent – founded in 1912 by a coterie of male decision-makers from the worlds of politics, industry and the media – was determined to promote the gastronomic riches they had discovered as they crisscrossed France in their cars. This patriotic and principled crusade in defence of provincial culinary tradition (and motor tourism, which was in its infancy) also promised an auspicious financial windfall for France as a whole. The scheme was most perfectly realized in Burgundy, with the renowned RN7 (the motorway connecting Paris and Italy) and the *Route des vins*, or wine road. The idea was rapidly reproduced elsewhere, as sociologist Gilles Laferté and Olivier Jacquet explain (*La Route des vins et l'émergence d'un tourisme viticole en Bourgogne dans l'entre-deux-guerres*, 2013).

In the absence of any outstanding natural beauty or impressive monuments capable of diverting holiday-makers from their inexorable descent on the Mediterranean, and with the image of wine-growing landscapes being no more than one of "productive ugliness", the great and the good of Burgundy adopted a novel approach and elected to mythologize their living heritage as folklore. This was to be, in the words of Laferté and Jacquet, a "folklore of tourist information centres, less concerned with respectful reproduction of the past and more about attracting sightseers". The mayor of Dijon was the main driving force behind a sustained local and international advertising campaign, with conferences on Burgundy wines attended by hundreds and the founding of the Foire Gastronomique culinary association (1921), which ran a competition for rural specialities that had been adapted and stylized to suit the demands of Parisian palates and even renamed for the occasion to flag up their regional allegiances: Burgundy snails, Bresse chicken, Dijon sauce, allusions to history and the dukes of Burgundy. "The whole enterprise," they add, "was conceived as the creation *ex nihilo* of a regional cuisine that drew on local produce but was arranged to suit bourgeois and urban notions of hygiene and taste – and adapted to the sociology of the era's car-borne tourists." And it worked a treat, with Curnonsky, the "prince of gastronomy" and a contemporary critic of immense influence, hailing it a complete success.

Wine was not forgotten in all this and similarly became a guarantor of quality and tradition; it was even an essential factor in the birth of the AOC system. Unlike in Champagne or

THE GROWTH OF GOURMET MAPS:
BURGUNDY (1809–1929)

In scarcely a century, regional food has grown from being a neglected aspect of cooking to an issue of national importance to be showcased as a first priority, as highlighted by the differences between Charles Louis Cadet de Gassicourt's gastronomic map (1809, one of the first recorded), below, and Alain Bourguignon's (1929), opposite. With the advent of paid vacations for workers, local specialities and recently created pairings of food and wine became a major draw for tourists.

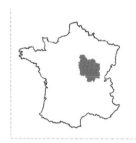

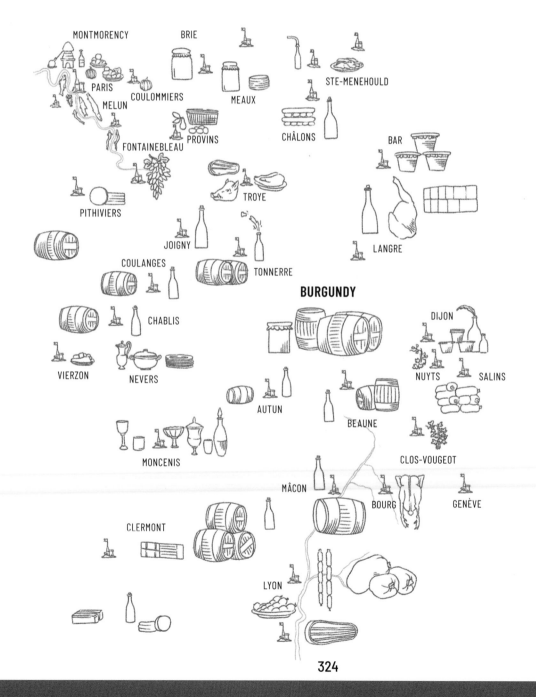

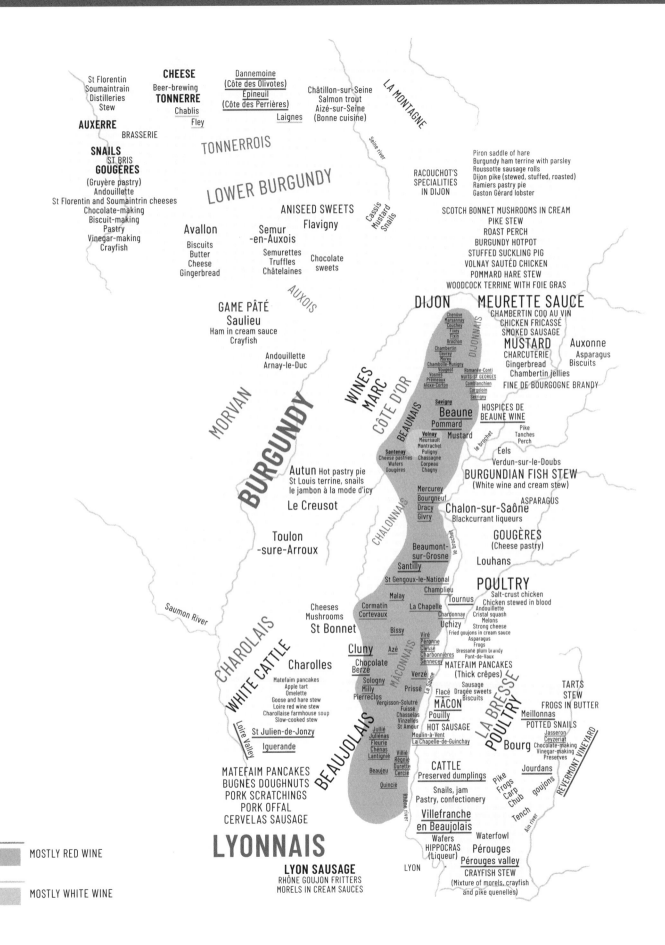

St Florentin
Soumaintrain
Distilleries
Stew

CHEESE
Beer-brewing
TONNERRE
Chablis
Fley

Dannemoine
(Côte des Olivotes)
Epineuil
(Côte des Perrières)
Laignes

Châtillon-sur-Seine
Salmon trout
Aizé-sur-Seine
(Bonne cuisine)

LA MONTAGNE

AUXERRE
BRASSERIE

TONNERROIS

Seine river

SNAILS
ST BRIS
GOUGÈRES
(Gruyère pastry)
Andouillette
St Florentin and Soumaintrin cheeses
Chocolate-making
Biscuit-making
Pastry
Vinegar-making
Crayfish

LOWER BURGUNDY

Cassis
Mustard
Snails

RACOUCHOT'S
SPECIALITIES
IN DIJON

Piron saddle of hare
Burgundy ham terrine with parsley
Roussotte sausage rolls
Dijon pike (stewed, stuffed, roasted)
Ramiers pastry pie
Gaston Gérard lobster

ANISEED SWEETS

Flavigny

Avallon
Biscuits
Butter
Cheese
Gingerbread

Semur
-en-Auxois
Semurettes
Truffles
Châtelaines

Chocolate
sweets

SCOTCH BONNET MUSHROOMS IN CREAM
PIKE STEW
ROAST PERCH
BURGUNDY HOTPOT
STUFFED SUCKLING PIG
VOLNAY SAUTÉD CHICKEN
POMMARD HARE STEW
WOODCOCK TERRINE WITH FOIE GRAS

AUXOIS

GAME PÂTÉ
Saulieu
Ham in cream sauce
Crayfish

DIJON

MEURETTE SAUCE
CHAMBERTIN COQ AU VIN
CHICKEN FRICASSÉ
SMOKED SAUSAGE
MUSTARD
CHARCUTERIE
Gingerbread
Chambertin jellies
FINE DE BOURGOGNE BRANDY

Auxonne
Asparagus
Biscuits

Chenôve
Marsannay
Couchey
Fixey
Fixin
Brochon
Chambertin
Gevrey
Morey
Chambolle-Musigny
Vougeot
Vosnes
Prémeaux
Aloxe-Corton

Romanée-Conti
NUITS-ST GEORGES
Comblanchien
Corgoloin
Serrigny

DIJONNAIS

Andouillette
Arnay-le-Duc

MORVAN

BURGUNDY

WINES
MARC
CÔTE D'OR

BEAUNAIS

Savigny
Beaune
Pommard

HOSPICES DE
BEAUNE WINE

le brochet

Pike
Tanches
Perch

Volnay
Meursault
Montrachet
Puligny
Chassagne
Corpeau
Chagny

Mustard

Autun Hot pastry pie
St Louis terrine, snails
le jambon à la mode d'icy

Santenay
Cheese pastries
Wafers
Gougères

Eels
Verdun-sur-le-Doubs

BURGUNDIAN FISH STEW
(White wine and cream stew)

Le Creusot

Mercurey
Bourgneuf
Dracy
Givry

Chalon-sur-Saône
Blackcurrant liqueurs

ASPARAGUS

CHALONNAIS

Toulon
-sure-Arroux

GOUGÈRES
(Cheese pastry)

Beaumont-
sur-Grosne

Santilly

le brochet

Louhans

St Gengoux-le-National

Champlieu

POULTRY
Salt-crust chicken
Chicken stewed in blood
Andouillette
Cristal squash
Melons
Strong cheese
Fried goujons in cream sauce
Asparagus
Frogs
Bressane plum brandy
Pont-de-Vaux

Saumon River

Malay

Cormatin
Cortevaux

La Chapelle

Tournus

Cheeses
Mushrooms
St Bonnet

Chardonnay
Bissy
Uchizy

CHAROLAIS

WHITE CATTLE

Charolles

Cluny

Azé

Viré
Péronne
Clessé
Charbonnières
Sennecer

MATEFAIM PANCAKES
(Thick crêpes)

MÂCONNAIS

La Saône

Chocolate
Berzé

Sologny
Milly
Pierreclos

Verzé

Prissé

Flacé

Sausage
Dragée sweets
Biscuits

TARTS
STEW
FROGS IN BUTTER

Meillonnas
POTTED SNAILS

Matefaim pancakes
Apple tart
Omelette
Goose and hare stew
Loire red wine stew
Charollaise farmhouse soup
Slow-cooked stew

Vergisson-Solutré
Fuissé
Chasselas
Vinzelles
St Amour

MÂCON
Pouilly
HOT SAUSAGE

LA BRESSE
POULTRY

Jasseron
Ceyzeriat
Chocolate-making
Vinegar-making
Preserves

REVERMONT VINEYARD

St Julien-de-Jonzy

Iguerande

Loire Valley

Jullié
Juliénas
Fleurie
Chénas
Lantignié

Moulin-à-Vent
La Chapelle-de-Guinchay

Bourg

BEAUJOLAIS

Villié
Régnié
Durette
Cercié

Beaujeu

Quincié

CATTLE
Preserved dumplings

Snails, jam
Pastry, confectionery

Jourdans

Pike
Frogs
Carp
Chub

goujons

MATEFAIM PANCAKES
BUGNES DOUGHNUTS
PORK SCRATCHINGS
PORK OFFAL
CERVELAS SAUSAGE

Rhône river

**Villefranche
en Beaujolais**

Wafers
HIPPOCRAS
(Liqueur)

Waterfowl

Pérouges

Pérouges valley

Tench

Ain river

LYONNAIS

LYON SAUSAGE
RHÔNE GOUJON FRITTERS
MORELS IN CREAM SAUCES

LYON

CRAYFISH STEW
(Mixture of morels, crayfish
and pike quenelles)

MOSTLY RED WINE

MOSTLY WHITE WINE

Bordeaux, the great estate owners of Burgundy decided to portray themselves as wine-growing sons of the soil rather than aristocratic merchants. They also invented their own folklore, first with the Paulée de Meursault (1923), a reinvention of the traditional meal at the end of the harvest, and then the Brotherhood of the Knights of the Tastevin (1934), a Bacchanalian cadre of wine devotees who saw themselves as heirs to the traditions of medieval fraternities and courted French and international tastemakers with fanciful traditionalist marketing. In both cases, dishes from the Foire Gastronomique were served, initially with whatever random wines guests may have brought with them, and then, over the course of time, with specific wines that would gradually cement pairings now viewed as classic.

Lastly, there was the *Route des vins* wine road, which took in every *grand cru* from Dijon to Santenay. Created in 1937, a year after the first of its kind was set up in Germany, it reinforced the idea that wine, gastronomy and the marrying of the two were the very embodiment of Burgundy.

Proof of the undeniable success of these pioneering initiatives in wine tourism came when the *Michelin Guide* (itself founded in 1900) dubbed Burgundy and the axis of the RN7 an centre of world gastronomy, awarding it a remarkable number of stars, compared to the rest of the country, from the 1930s onward.

This mythologization of the centuries-old traditions to be found in every region of France became an exceptional springboard for generations of chefs and sommeliers. In appropriating such a heritage, which over time had lost some of its earlier political trappings, they sought to rethink in their own way the links between produce and terroir and the pairing of food and wine – with some achieving this in a remarkable fashion, such as the three-star chefs and oenophiles Alain Chapel (1937–90) and Alain Senderens (1939–2017).

And sommeliers take charge of serving wine

One figure in particular was to emerge as this specific understanding of gastronomy established itself and became more widespread in restaurants. Historically restricted to serving wine but now presiding over water, sake, beer, tea and all kinds of beverage, the sommelier was also a mirror of the evolution of the social role of drinking, the manufacturing of taste and of the unmistakable transformation of the viticultural system. In some ways taking up the mantle of those serving at the Greek symposium, sommeliers now normalized, socialized and aestheticized the acts of drinking and eating to a greater degree than ever before. Sommeliers of both sexes (more and more women have been entering the profession) have become mediators and authorities for taste

in a sector where the economic and ecological stakes have multiplied tenfold.

Sommellerie as we know it today only really emerged with the switch to restaurant dining in the 19th century. Prior to this, it had fulfilled several functions that had become increasingly specialized over the course of time: French monasteries and courts of the high Middle Ages would have had a cellarmaster responsible for looking after the wine from vineyard to bottling, a bottler, and a wine steward to decant and serve, with the latter gradually taking on major responsibilities for the crown, like stewardship of the household, but also of royal vineyards and revenues. In a parallel development, the role of the *sommier* (from the Latin *sagmarium*, "driver of a beast of burden") was by extension to become the *sommelier* responsible for transporting the court's trunks and luggage during its numerous peripatetic travels through the country, then specifically the person in charge of setting the table and preparing service of meals. Sommeliers also took care of everything from the royal coat of arms (*sommelier d'armes*) to the bakery (*sommelier de panneterie*) until the role was specialized as the steward (*sommelier d'échansonnerie*) responsible for the ewers in which water and wine were served to royal diners before the French Revolution and the emergence of restaurants. The profession then entered its modern phase, although it is still a far cry from the role that we know today.

In the cellar, in the dining room and centre stage

Until the first half of the 20th century, sommeliers were principally involved in the practical management of wine, taking charge of its purchase and storage: almost all wines were sold in barrels rather than bottles. There was no qualification available at the time to certify a profession for which the wine merchant André Jullien wrote a practical guide in 1822 (*Manuel du sommelier, ou Instruction practique sur la manière de soigner les vins*). Sommeliers were mainly concerned with the logistics of transporting, storing and then bottling at the point of sale a drink that could all too easily spoil. Serving wine was a secondary consideration, and it was only with the emergence of restaurants and the needs of their customers that a more or less precise division of labour was established between sommeliers of the dining room and the cellar. History records the name of Caradot, sometime sommelier of the renowned Café Riche, who helped to burnish the reputation of the establishment by choosing wines and controlling the temperatures at which they were stored and served.

The phylloxera crisis and the proliferation of fraud were to reinforce the importance of sommeliers working in the cellar over those in the dining room. In search of recognition, the profession created a structure for itself, founding the Union of Paris Sommeliers in 1907 and carving out an essential role as front-of-house staff during the boom in tourism. It was more marginally involved in the creation of the AOC system. Pairing suggestions were still few and far between, generally following either the recommendations of the previous century or the new regional pairings promoted by the folklore movement, and sommeliers were thus involved in spreading culinary canons as common cultural backgrounds.

Despite these initial successes, however, the profession almost disappeared in the 1960s: the restaurant industry was in crisis, industrial bottling had mitigated the need for a cellar sommelier and the maître d' had hijacked the role in the dining room. It was to be a close-run thing, but sommellerie did survive, thanks initially to competitions, as historian Sénia Fedoul explains in *L'oenologue et le sommelier, ambassadeur de la qualité des vins. Le "discours oenologiquel froid" and le "discours oenologique chaud"* (2018). In 1961, food journalist Henry Clos-Jouve and editor-in-chief of *La Revue du vin de France* Odette Kahn, noticing the disappearance of the sommelier from the restaurant floor – for them, a symbol of the French way of life – organized the first competition for the best sommelier in France in three categories (best restaurateur/sommelier, best maître d'/sommelier, best sommelier). The success of the competition reinvigorated the profession and encouraged it to reorganize itself more effectively. New professional associations were created, including the Association des Sommeliers Lyonnais et Rhône-Alpes (ASLERA) in 1964, followed (in 1969) by the Association des Sommeliers de Paris (ASP), the Union de la Sommellerie Française (UDSF) and the Association de la Sommellerie Internationale (ASI) in partnership with Italy, Belgium and Portugal. The first competition to recognize the best sommelier in the world was organized the same year, marking the ongoing liberation and internationalization of the profession, which gained a new authority that was legitimized by newly instituted qualifications (in France, the CAP vocational certificate in 1980, the Brevet Professionnel, another vocational diploma, in 1984, and the Mention Complémentaire, a Level 4 certificate for a specialist field of study). As Stéphane Olivesi, a philosopher specializing in information sciences explains (*Le sommelier. Un médiateur, artisan du goût*, 2015), "The profession of sommelier as we know it today – freed from the practical management of wine in the cellar and focused on advising the customer – only came to prominence much later, from the 1960s onwards. . . and is largely the result of proactive intervention by people in the wine world, rehabilitating and radically transforming an ancient profession in order to associate and involve it with the cultural and commercial renewal of wine."

A "world as unknown and abstract as food and wine pairings" (F Adrià)

Since the 1960s, gastronomy and sommellerie – much like society in general – have undergone a series of revolutions that have brought to light the mechanisms involved in the manufacture of taste and ideas of quality. The relationships between food (what style of cuisine?) and drink (what method of production?) embody the ethics and aesthetics of chef and sommelier, who have been increasingly freed from the constraints of social codes and practical imperatives. By analogy, they also reveal a notion of good taste, or the "right" taste, that can be anything from hypernormalized to a completely free and deconstructed flow, a kind of world where a multitude of cultures and gastronomies intersect and everyone can choose whatever they want. In *¿Qué vino con este pato?* Ferran Centelles, the sommelier of a restaurant that has transformed contemporary gastronomy with molecular cuisine (El Bulli), has provided the most comprehensive analysis of the evolution in pairing drinks with food since the 1960s. Interestingly, Ferran Adrià, his renowned chef, has said that he undoubtedly created extremely complicated menus for food and wine pairings, but Centelles has become a specialist. Although more and more is being written on the subject, he has identified the key elements, players and methodologies of this evolution as summarized below.

Classic pairings were common until the end of the 1960s, based on:

- **Subjectivity** – personal taste had historically been the driver of classic pairings, and subjectivity still dictated many contemporary matches.
- **Regionality** – pairings based on the products' availability and geographical proximity had been in existence since ancient times.
- **Objectivity** – the first great written works, often anonymous, tried to articulate objective rules for pairings.
- **Trial and error** – Raymond Dumay's *Le Guide du vin* (1967) encouraged experimentation with pairings even if it meant making mistakes.

Contemporary pairings began to emerge from the 1970s onwards, involving:

- **The adaptation of objectivity** – chefs and sommeliers like Luigi Veronelli, Alain Senderens and Josep Roca applied and modified these rules, giving rise to a new set of standards; Jacques Puisais might also be included here.
- **The science of taste** – research in the agri-food industry helped provide a better understanding of the chemical, physiological and emotional interactions between wine and food.
- **Great literary works** – leading sommeliers published their books of advice: the likes of Philippe Faure-Brac, Philippe

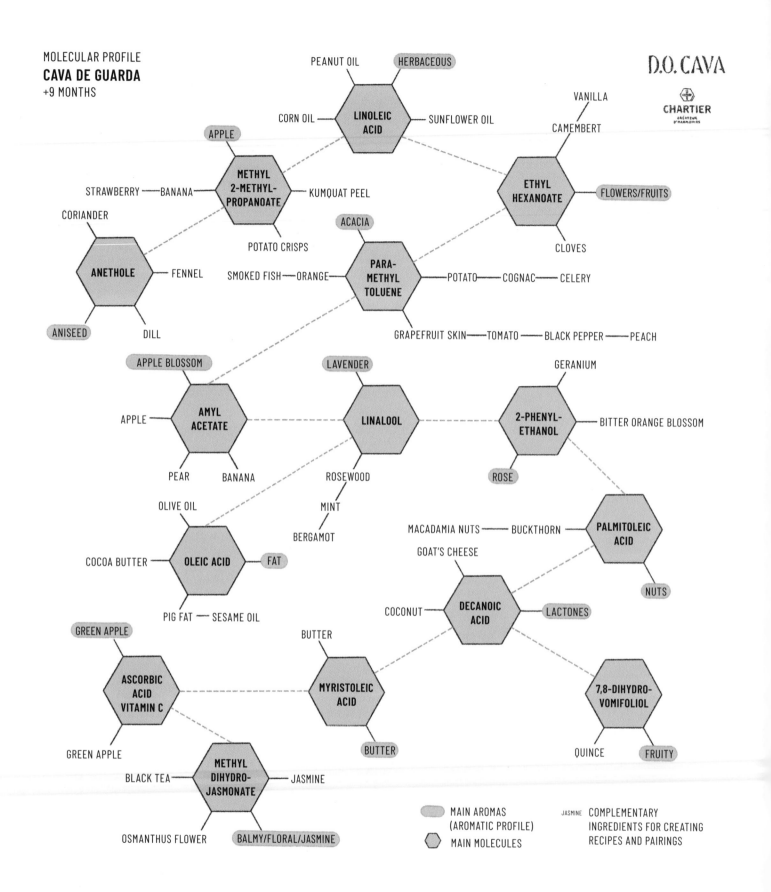

D.O. CAVA

CHARTIER
CRÉATEUR D'HARMONIES

LINOLEIC ACID
PEANUT OIL
HERBACEOUS
CORN OIL
SUNFLOWER OIL

ETHYL HEXANOATE
VANILLA
CAMEMBERT
FLOWERS/FRUITS
CLOVES

METHYL 2-METHYL-PROPANOATE
APPLE
STRAWBERRY — BANANA
KUMQUAT PEEL
POTATO CRISPS

ANETHOLE
CORIANDER
FENNEL
ANISEED
DILL

PARA-METHYL TOLUENE
ACACIA
SMOKED FISH — ORANGE
POTATO — COGNAC — CELERY
GRAPEFRUIT SKIN — TOMATO — BLACK PEPPER — PEACH

AMYL ACETATE
APPLE BLOSSOM
APPLE
PEAR
BANANA

LINALOOL
LAVENDER
ROSEWOOD
MINT
BERGAMOT

2-PHENYL-ETHANOL
GERANIUM
BITTER ORANGE BLOSSOM
ROSE

OLEIC ACID
OLIVE OIL
COCOA BUTTER
FAT
PIG FAT — SESAME OIL

PALMITOLEIC ACID
MACADAMIA NUTS — BUCKTHORN
NUTS

DECANOIC ACID
GOAT'S CHEESE
COCONUT
LACTONES

ASCORBIC ACID VITAMIN C
GREEN APPLE
GREEN APPLE

MYRISTOLEIC ACID
BUTTER
BUTTER

7,8-DIHYDRO-VOMIFOLIOL
QUINCE
FRUITY

METHYL DIHYDRO-JASMONATE
BLACK TEA — JASMINE
OSMANTHUS FLOWER
BALMY/FLORAL/JASMINE

MAIN AROMAS (AROMATIC PROFILE)
MAIN MOLECULES

JASMINE COMPLEMENTARY INGREDIENTS FOR CREATING RECIPES AND PAIRINGS

FRANÇOIS CHARTIER'S SCIENCE OF "MOLECULAR HARMONY" APPLIED TO CAVA DE GUARDA

Bourguignon and Evan Goldstein; Olivier Poussier, Karen Page and Andrew Dornenburg might also be included.

- **Senderens and Puisais** – after training with oenologist Puisais, who also founded France's Institute of Taste, Senderens, the Michelin-starred chef at Lucas Carton, was the first to base the food on the wines, with a menu that was created specifically for them and the pairings explained in writing; he formalized the idea of complementary and contrasting pairings.
- **Veronelli** – the Italian critic outlined the role played by the intensity of tastes, an idea put into practice by sommelier Giuseppe Vaccarini, who also set out the notion of oppositional pairings.
- **Roca** – the sommelier at El Celler de Can Roca developed "complete" matching, including the "sixth sense" of emotion and memory in creating a pairing; he proposed a theory of relativity that puts the emotional intelligence of the guest at the heart of the experience.
- **Jeannie Cho Lee MW** – the Korean-American critic published *Asian Palate* in 2009, taking an interest in pairing wines with Asian cooking and comparing American, Asian and European tastes.
- **François Chartier** – after working with El Bulli and reading the work of culinary chemist Hervé This, the Canadian sommelier developed a theory of molecular harmony in his 2009 book *Papilles et molecules.*
- **Enrico Bernardo** – the Italian sommelier opened Il Vino, the first restaurant where the wine was systematically selected before the dish and influenced the way in which the latter was prepared.
- **Tim Hanni MW** – working with scientists on neuroplasticity, he asserted that "wine should be matched to the diner, not the dinner"; the taster's "vinotype" must be identified.
- **Ferran Centelles** – in 2012, he developed a theory at El Bulli that saw the taste intensity and complexity of a dish as the limiting factors for any pairing; his research was published in his monumental series Sapiens del Vino (2018-24).
- **Human sciences** – this list should also include the research carried out by food historians, geographers and anthropologists who have provided ways of reading and understanding these changes: the UNESCO Culture and Traditions of Wines chair, Pitte et al.
- **Artificial intelligence** – algorithms and AI are at the forefront of exploring new frontiers in pairings, both for smartphone applications and more ambitious projects, such as the collaboration between Chartier and Sony and the work at foodpairings.com on "flavour intelligence".

Manufacturing taste, or how we should live in the world

In a somewhat abrupt break with tradition within a context of acculturation, gastronomic globalization, scientific research and economic wealth, virtually anything is now possible in the aesthetics of pairing food and wines. But is it really better to astonish just for the sake of astonishing, with consideration for neither the product nor the diner, nor even necessarily for the taste itself, just the experience alone? Or, instead, to return to heritage sources, to fundamental ingredients, to organoleptic pleasure? Construction or deconstruction? Local or global? Matching or contrasting? Wine first, food first, or patron first? Rely on the neurology of taste, or turn to synaesthesia? The Krug Champagne house works with musicians to create "harmonious experiences" combining music with its *cuvées* and foods.

If there is no absolute truth here, it is because we are dealing with the way taste is manufactured, a norm that is being continually redefined at the intersection of aesthetics, ecology, economics, politics and social mores, all of which reflect the cultures in which it is constructed. In a culinary universe where the European – and, in particular, the French – model has long prevailed, the cards are being reshuffled, from the structure of service (*kaiseki*, Japanese service influenced by Shintoist and Buddhist thought featuring multiple courses, has been copied all over the world) to techniques, ingredients and a host of alternative drinks like sake, beer, cider, tea or water instead of wine. The table – a place first of consumption, then of tasting, and now of experiencing – has changed, as have the expectations of those who sit at it. Some people now think that the mission of restaurants is more to entertain than to feed, in an experience, broadcast to the entire world via social media, that has become more exhilarating even than the tastes of the food and wine.

For others, however, its role – now more than ever – is to nourish both body and mind and to reconnect us to all that surrounds us by transforming the act of eating and drinking into an absolute aesthetic experience. This quest, this eternal apprenticeship in Puisais's "right taste" of things (or at least "as right as possible"), embodies our way of wanting to be in the world – a powerful political act if ever there was one, because it transcends our individuality to summon up our universality and liberty. Gastro-politics or intangible cultural heritage – however superficial it might seem, the gentle art of eating and drinking well nestles at the heart of our humanity and the way we wish to live in our world.

CONCLUSION

So, what shall we drink tomorrow?

In June 2022, more than 35 international experts from 17 different countries gathered at the Act for Change symposium organized by Bordeaux's Cité du Vin cultural centre to debate the future of wine. A month earlier, the international Green Wine Future conference – featuring virtual contributions from over 160 speakers including scientists, producers, journalists, politicians and economists – had addressed a host of issues relating to the future of the wine industry, from regenerative viticulture to the role of wine tourism, taking in greenhouse-gas emissions, the preservation of the genetic heritage of old vines, producers' social responsibilities, the dangers of greenwashing, government policy and alternatives to the circular economy.

The general conclusion was the same in both cases: given the environmental problems it faces, urgent action is required to ensure the survival of the world of vineyards and wine. The question remains of how this might be achieved, however – and why should we even bother, when wine seems to have lost its meaning for the majority of consumers, or at the very least has got bogged down in a mire of contradictions. It is a cultural heritage product and a major sector of France's economy, as well as the embodiment of France's prestige abroad, and yet it is under constant fire from the anti-alcohol lobby. Wines are being targeted by irrationally exuberant financial speculation just as increasing numbers of producers are going bust, even in wine areas as prestigious as Bordeaux. Among producers and wine tasters, trust in the AOC system, which was supposed to guarantee the highest levels of quality, is at an all-time low. Wine is increasingly being passed over for everyday consumption even as

sophisticated enthusiasts are collecting it like works of art. Once an essential foodstuff, it is now a superfluous luxury product; the drink of the people has become a beverage for the chosen few. While it was long considered a pure product plucked straight from the vine, there is now a rising wave of criticism about the lack of transparency and health consequences of the way it is produced. It is naturalness incarnate and yet has never been so hyper-cultivated; as an embodiment of the entrenched nature of terroirs and a talisman of their preservation, it has never been so globalized and transported to the four corners of the Earth.

Wine, as we have seen, holds up a mirror to our civilization: its crises are our crises, its status and the way it is defined are our social choices, its taste and appearance are made in the image of our aesthetic and moral requirements – and its paradoxes are a reflection of our own contradictions.

Inventing a new mythology of wine

"Actually, like all resilient totems, wine supports a varied mythology which does not trouble about contradictions." While there is no longer any real evidence of wine being a "totemic drink" for the "French nation" as described by Roland Barthes in *Mythologies* (1957), in the first instance this is because it has been deprived of its mythology as a "binding collective act" rather than its mythological power per se: drinking wine is no longer a societal necessity. Belgian professor of physics and beer specialist Fabrizio Bucella addresses this question, concluding that wine is no longer a given; it has been denormalized. No longer either a food or a social necessity, it has become a leisure product. No longer passively accepted, it is now actively chosen; there is a wine for everyone, a totem that has been created and is no longer imposed. Drinkers have changed with the evolution of society: "as the status of wine changes, the status of those who drink wine changes with it." Wine is thus being drunk less for what it is than for what it represents, and we drink it less than we talk about it or post about it on social media. Wine has become an archetype; its function has never ceased to evolve but is now probably under more pressure than ever as a result of the societal and health-related norms that constrain it and view it only as a risk to public health, rather than something with the power to civilize.

Its existence is also threatened by the industrial commodification of production; the taste is of little interest as long as it has alcohol and symbolic value. "What is wine for?" is a reasonable question when the majority of bottles available on the market contain a product standardized to suit globalized demand, incapable of providing the full experience of what it can embody. It is a question immediately rendered moot, however, when we taste a wine that has been produced with the very different intention of respecting and revealing the living complexity of the terroir where it first saw the light of day. These are the wines that invite us to imagine a new mythology and a new way of being in the world – a far cry from the greenwashing and dubious narratives of marketing.

Rediscovering the taste of living wine is an eminently joyful and political act of resistance

This mythology to be invented is, I believe, already in the process of being crafted, narrated and created, with many clues to its nature appearing throughout the pages of this book. Its most evident incarnation is undoubtedly in the form of "natural wines", which, since the 1980s, have brought about an entirely beneficial revolution in taste. It was not so much a love of ecology but rather a quest for untainted Bacchic elation, a fellowship in mind and body – the joy of "drinking together" – that prompted the pioneers of this movement to strive to produce wines without recourse to chemistry, in order to rediscover the taste it had "back in the day". It was the search for a wine that slips down easily, rather than packing a punch, that has led these pioneers to wonder about yeasts, the life of the soil, and the deadly impact of intensive chemical viticulture. It must have been the spirit of the age, a zeitgeist, that brought together a scientist-cum-merchant like Chauvet, a winemaker and born communicator like Lapierre, a sommelier-philosopher like Néauport, a bistro manager and journalist like François Morel and a chef and aesthete like Chapel. This synergy of perspectives has breathed life into this new mythology of "living wine", a wine ideal for rediscovery that in fact had to be invented from first principles.

Make no mistake, the wine "back in the day" was never, and will never be, either the wine of that time or of this. This living wine appeared in the 1980s, in a world very different from back in the day, because our relationship with this world has fundamentally changed. We will never know what wine might have been or what it meant to the ancient Greeks, for whom "nature" did not exist as an entity distinct from themselves. Back then, agriculture was an ethical and religious practice, and polyculture was the rule; monoculture did not make an appearance until after antiquity. Winemaking farmers had a living relationship with the animal, vegetable and mineral kingdoms, toward which they maintained an attitude of humility, respect and devotion.

As anthropologists – and Philippe Descola, in particular – have been reminding us since the 1970s, the notion of nature as a classification system organizing things external to mankind is the exception rather than the rule in human history. This division between nature and culture is in itself a construct, nothing more than a particular way of seeing things that emerged in the city of Athens in the 4th century BCE, although it has accompanied the development of modern science and economics, first in the West and then the entire known world, into the 20th century. In no way does it imply an intangible barrier between the natural and human world, but it is a "Great Divide" that has been constantly disputed, displaced and designed anew, in particular by a number of "natural winemakers" – an expression that, when understood in this way, is no longer an oxymoron. Like it or not, the natural-wine movement is thus one that is eminently joyful, based as it is on a desire to reforge a social bond by drinking wine that is alive and unadulterated, and eminently political, in that it has awoken within some of its advocates a desire for some new kind of relationship with others – "others" in this case being not only humans but also all living things, which are to enjoy the same rights and status.

The same holds true, in a less "extreme" – and more "civilized" – instance (like Dionysus, appeased by the establishment of the Symposium) for terroir wines: the desire to drink wines with guaranteed provenance has bred alternative approaches to viticulture that alone can express all the nuances of the microbial life of soils, of grapes and of humans. Organic agriculture, followed by biodynamics, then permaculture and now regenerative agriculture, have progressively redefined a relationship with vines that are no longer simply "plant material" or a means of production, but a living ecosystem with which we need to coexist. The fact that many of these wines, nonetheless celebrated by wine tasters, stem from the AOC system is proof positive that they are pushing toward a new definition of the rules for organizing territory and demanding the inclusion of all living communities, visible and invisible, according to new criteria that transcend terroir that may be physical, geological, climatic or administrative. To quote Pitte, these same wines also offer a new form of sociability; unlike industrially produced wines, they are – thanks to their qualities, their nuances and their complexity – original creations that transcend cultural differences and forge new links in taste and aesthetics. It is not by chance that these wines form part of the arsenal of "gastro-diplomacy" and their terroirs and their practices have been inscribed by UNESCO as intangible cultural heritage.

Future wine, future drinkers and future freedom

So, what wine shall we invent for the future? Tomorrow's wine, which now more than ever will be chosen rather than imposed, will depend more than ever on tomorrow's drinkers – as has always been the case, after all. Through the course of human history, every vineyard has experienced highs and lows, change and decay, resilience and profound transformation of what it produces and the way it produces it. Wine is mired in crisis in some countries with a proud wine history, even as it is singularly in the ascendant in others. The Western white male, the classic drinker of wine, often revered and rarely criticized, is making way for an exceptional diversity of drinkers of every age, religion, gender and outlook who – each in their own way – give a legitimate meaning to the bottle they consume. So, wine still has meaning, but it's the meaning that each individual wishes to give to their own existence.

The wines of the future will be as many and as various as the thousand vines and thousand palates that bring them into the world. This living freedom for the wine of the future should not, if possible, be construed as an ineluctable historical inevitability, however – indeed, anything but; there must be a sincere belief in this mythology and a wish to live it out. Jonathan Nossiter, the cosmopolitan director of the renowned *Mondovino* documentary, could not have put it better: "The fight to defend the individuality of wine, the fight for the survival of individual taste in the face of the levelling effects of impersonal power (especially when that power is wielded by a handful of individuals) is thus a fight. . . that involves us all. . . I am entirely convinced of the religious aspect of wine. It is an act of faith. . . whether you are a believer or not. As with any leap of faith, however, there will be many things that are 'less likely', let's say, that you are going to accept. From the very beginning to the very end, you have to have confidence, you have to tell yourself that the winemaker is not a fraud" (*Le Goût et le pouvoir*, 2007).

Given the distressing and stultifying environmental and political crises that are raging, living wine offers joyful ways to resist a system that wishes to see us dispirited, delimited and deprived of meaning – educating our taste, respecting the living world, creating a dialogue between cultures and fields of knowledge, sharing a bottle in a new diplomacy of nature, inventing new languages and new economics, marvelling at the beauty and the diversity of the world, in a life full of freedom and creative vigour. How we eat and drink has the power to change how we live. By educating our palate, the needed revolution will be possible – transforming both taste and tasting, in a win-win relationship with our world.

APPENDICES

Index

2,3,4,6-tetratrichloroanisole (TeCA) 242
2,4,6-tribromoanisole (TBA) 242
2,4,6-trichloroanisole (TCA) 241, 242, 297
2-methylisoborneol (MIB) 241
4-ethylguaiacol 240, 241, 266
4-ethylphenol 240, 241, 266
4-methyl-guaiacol 240
45th parallel 1136

A

Aarrouf, Jawad 108
abscisic acid 110
acacia 226
acetaldehyde 214, 218, 219, 224, 230, 240, 241, 266
acetic acid 6, 211, 215, 219, 220, 240, 242, 263, 265, 266, 272, 273
acetic fermentation 215
Acetobacter 211, 215, 240
acidity 47, 62, 113, 114, 115, 120, 205, 206, 253, 271, 272–3, 275, 286
Adama 125
additives 236, 237
Adelaide 54, 243
adjuvants 236, 237
Adrià, Ferran 321, 327
ageing 218–19, 224, 228, 230, 231, 267, 292; oxidative 217, 218, 219, 221, 225, 226; premature 242; reductive 220, 225–6
Agnel, Henri 26
agroecology 90, 101
agroforestry 86, 91, 99
AgroSup 297
Ahr 115
Ajaccio 128, 130
Alba 22
Albariño, Alvarinho 122, 177, 259
albedo 138, 143, 285
alcohol dehydrogenase 19, 310
alcoholic fermentation (AF) 210, 211–15, 220, 226, 232
alcoholism 314
alcohol levels 52, 64, 114, 115, 120, 121, 122, 205, 220, 237
aldehydes 211, 215, 230, 258, 263, 264, 265, 267, 285, 310
Aleatico 29
Alentejo 231, 295
Alicante Bouschet 35
Aligoté 29
Allaby, Robin 20
Allier 229
Alsace 152, 166, 192; cellars 166; climate 112, 151; geology 128, 129, 134, 138, 142, 185; glasses 293, 313; grafting 58; heroic viticulture 116; insects 121; oak forests 229; organic/biodynamic viticulture 95; soil 158, 161; terroir 146; volcanic wines 132; wine sweetness 219
Altamira 148
Altieri, Miguel 101
Alto Douro 168, 198, 200
aluminium 178, 134, 142, 144, 163, 296, 298
aluminium cans 294
aluminium closures 296, 298
Alvarado, Carolina 288
amadia 296

amadou 61
Amarone 220, 242
amber wine *see* orange wine
American Viticultural Area (AVA) 112, 195
Amerine, Maynard A 108, 110, 193, 251
Amerine-Winkler index 108, 110
Aminea 22
amino acids 81, 211, 224, 228, 242, 264, 272, 273, 274
ammonia 212
amoebae 86
Amontillado 218, 219
Amorim 297, 298
ampelographic collections 33
ampelography 19, 22–3, 24–5, 26–30, 31, 46
ampelometry 24, 26
ampelonyms 24
amphibolite 136, 137, 138
amphorae 183, 216, 221, 222, 223, 226, 231, 288, 295, 300
amylic aromas 221, 222, 226, 241
anaerobiosis 212, 215
andesite 132
Andlau 138
angel's share 225, 226
Anjou 128, 132, 137, 146, 164
Antalick, Guillaume 264
anthocyanins 26, 44, 47, 64, 105, 206, 207, 221, 230, 231, 258, 259, 276
anthracnose 68
anthropization 103, 158, 160, 163
Anthropocene 118
anthropomorphism 277
anthroposoils 149
Antinori, Niccolò 189
antioxidants 205, 206, 207, 212, 221, 226, 243
AOC *see* appellation d'origine contrôlée
AOP *see* appellation d'origine protégée
Aosta Valley 39, 116, 161
Ao Yun 113
apex 40, 42, 64
apomixis, vegetative 21
apoplexy 68
appellation d'origine contrôlée (AOC) 33, 35, 88, 114, 122, 146, 148, 155, 158, 182, 183, 184–5, 188–91, 195, 198, 204, 211, 219, 222, 232, 247, 260, 293, 294, 315, 323, 327, 332
appellation d'origine protégée (AOP) 161
Aramon 55
Aramon Noir 35
Arbois 22, 174, 185, 217, 322
arbustive system 86
ArdeaSeal 298
Areni 20
Argentina 51, 112, 113, 119, 121, 148, 159, 161, 166, 192
Ariège 166
Arinarnoa 122
Aristotle 49, 70, 245
Armagnac 35, 173, 185, 220, 227, 231, 291
Armazéns de calor 219
Armenia 20, 29
Arnaldus de Villa Nova 217, 220

aromas 88, 114, 207, 220, 253, 263–4, 267–70; amylic 221, 222; aroma wheel 270; primary 226, 246, 263–4; secondary 211, 215, 246, 264–7; tertiary 221, 239, 246, 263, 267
aromatic precursors 47, 207, 222, 235, 264
Artaban 36, 100
Artificialization 158
Asprinio di Aversa 100
artificial intelligence (AI) 329
Association de la Sommellerie Internationale (ASI) 327
Association des Francs de Pied 52
Association des Sommeliers de Paris (ASP) 327
Association des Sommeliers Lyonnais et Rhône-Alpes (ASLERA) 327
Association des Vins Naturels (AVN) 97
Assyrtiko 44
aszú 220
Atkinson, John 145
Aube 185
Aubun 37
Aureobasidium pullulans 209
Australia 166, 192, 194, 196; climate 104, 117, 118, 121, 148; effervescent wines 224; eucalyptus 240; fortified wines 220; geology 130; GIs 195; labels 301, 304; measures 294; natural wines 100; organic/biodynamic viticulture 95
Australia's Wine Future 104, 121
Australian Wine Research Institute (AWRI) 88, 239
Austria 36, 116, 135, 138, 166, 178, 198, 220, 272, 293
autolysis 224, 228, 230, 254, 272, 274, 276
Auvergne 116, 128, 132, 154, 166, 177
Auxerre 153, 154
Auxerrois 22, 28
Avignon University 108
AWRI *see* Australian Wine Research Institute
Axel, Richard 269
AxR1 55
Azay-le-Rideau 147
Azerbaijan 20, 29
Azores 116, 132, 200

B

Bacchanals 304, 310
Bacchus *see* Dionysus, Bacchus
Bachet 28
Bacillus pumilis 86
Baco, François 35
Baco 22A 35
Bacon, Francis 302
bacteria: plants 44, 47, 72, 85–6; soil 78–81, 84, 143, 285; soil formation 133, 139; 205, 211; wine production 212, 215, 217, 218, 226, 232, 240, 241, 242, 259, 265, 267, 272, 273
Baga 224
bag-in-boxes 294
Baïf, Jean-Antoine de 22
Arnaldus de Villa Nova 217, 220

Baillod-Baglioni system 62
Bairrada 224
Baixo Corgo 168
Bajec, R 319
Ballester, Jordi 281, 284
Bandol 128, 300
Banyuls 116, 128, 160, 185, 220
Barbaresco 125
Barolo 115, 125, 262, 303
Baron de Lestac 197
Baroque 122
Barossa Bailey 51, 54, 304
barrels 226–30, 259, 267, 289, 292, 295
barriques 227
Barthes, Roland 314, 331
Bartoli, Marco de 174
basalt 132, 136, 139, 143, 164
basic terroir units (BTUs) 146, 147, 148
basket pruning 44, 171
bâtonnage *see* stirring
Baudrimont, Alexandre 235
Baumert, Nicolas 155
Bazille, Gaston 50
BBCH-scale 62
Beaujolais 97, 115, 173, 222, 249, 263; geology 125, 128, 130, 132, 139; measures 294; natural wines 100; organic/biodynamic viticulture 95
Beaujolais Nouveau 217, 265
Beaune 162, 182, 183
Beaunois 22
Beckett, Fiona 319
Beckstoffer, Andy 195
beer 18, 19, 153, 156, 206, 208, 209, 212, 215, 245, 265, 298, 310, 311, 314, 326, 329
Belgium 36, 120, 153, 327
Bellussi brothers 83
bench-grafting 57, 66
Benedictines 177, 183, 199
Bensin, Basil 101
benzenemethanethiol (BMT) 285
Bercy 179, 184
Bergerac 172
Bérillon, Lilian 67
Beringer 193
Berlandieri Rességuier S2 56
Bernard, Claude 257
Bernard, Olivier 113
Bernardo, Enrico 319, 329
Bertranges 228, 229
Besançon 165
Bezin, Basil 101
Bierzo 177
Bigando, Eva 168
biocontrols 54, 86, 87, 91, 211, 218
biodiversity 26, 76, 78, 87, 89, 99
biodynamic agriculture 73, 93, 96, 97, 101, 138, 214, 236, 287, 332
Biodynamic Agriculture Movement (MABD) 73
bio-indicators 89
biotite 130, 137
bioturbation 98, 140
Birebent, Marc 57, 61
Bisson, Jean 28, 29, 30
bitterness 245, 246, 254, 255, 256, 271, 273, 274, 275, 286
Black Corinth 45
black dead arm 86

Black Muscat 29
black rot 69, 86, 240, 241
Black Zinfandel 23
Blanquette de Limoux 222, 322
Blanquefort 197
Blatt 72, 73
blending 182, 183, 184, 193, 195, 232, 247
Blouin, Jacques 251, 264, 278, 282, 307
bluestone 132
BMT *see* benzenemethanethiol
Bobrie, François 304
bocksbeutel 293
Bodega Colomé à Salta 121
Bodegas Güell 166
Bodegas López de Heredia 166
Bodegas Torres 319
Bodega Ysios 168
Bofill, Ricardo 166
Bokulich, Nicolas 215
Bolgheri 189
Bolivia 100
Bombino Bianco 27
Bonarda 161
Bonnes-Mares 185
Bordeaux 89, 153, 166, 178, 184, 185, 224, 234–5, 238, 243, 244, 249, 251, 252, 282, 285, 316, 322, 331; approval tastings 247; barrels 230, 231; bottles 290–1, 292–3, 294; cépage diversity 122; Chartrons district 182; Cité du Vin 179, 182; climate 112, 113, 151; closures 297; enclosed vineyards 165; Fête de la Fleur 45; geology 125, 128, 135; glasses 312; labels 300; malolactic fermentation 211; Merlot 61; mildew 80; oak forests 229; organic/biodynamic viticulture 95; price index 308; soil 142, 143, 145, 162; sulphur dioxide 218; sulphur usage 51; terroir 146, 148; transport 154, 172, 173, 175; UNESCO site 179; UV light 108
Botrytis cinerea (noble rot) 46, 86, 111, 160, 206, 212, 220, 224, 235, 240, 258, 264, 272
bottles 222, 242, 288, 289–93; neck 224, 267, 292, 293, 295, 296, 297
Bouchange Mécanique, Le 296
Bouffard, Michelle 122
Boulanger, Monsieur 320
Boulanger-Fassier, Sylvaine 93
Boulay, Thibaut 245, 246, 306
bouquet 247, 249; oxidative 267; reductive 267
Bouquet, Alain 36, 37, 55
bourbon 231
Bourguignon, Alain 325, 326
Bourguignon, Claude and Lydia 78, 144
Bourguignon, Philippe 318, 329
Boursiquot, Jean-Michel 24, 26, 27, 29–30
Bouschet de Bernard, Louis and Henri 35
bousinage *see* toasting
Bowen, Norman 130
Bowers, John 26
Branas, Jean 50, 64
Brancellao 177

335

Brancott 101
Braque, Georges 302
Brazil 118
Breslin, PAS 319
Breton 22
Brettanomyces 211, 228, 239, 240, 241, 267
Brettanomyces bruxellensis 210
Brillat-Savarin, Jean Anthelme 274, 318, 322
Broadbent, Michael 251
bromine 241
Bronner 37
Brouard, Joëlle 315
Brotherhood of the Knights of the Tastevin 326
Brown, Elaine Chukan 283
Brun, Jean-Pierre 217, 225
Brunet, Raymond 318
BTUs *see* basic terroir units
Bucella, Fabrizio 316, 331-2
Buck, Linda 269
buds 42, 43, 58, 62, 63
Bugey 95, 165
Bugey Cerdon 222
Bull, Ephraim Wales 34
Burgundy 29, 79, 154, 193, 197, 238, 264, 308, 316, 322; ageing 228, 230; AOC system 183, 185; approval tastings 247; bottles 290-1, 293; cellars 166; climate 151; *climats* 124, 183, 184, 186, 194, 198, 201; closures 298; drystone walls 159-60; enclosed vineyards 159, 165; geology 124, 125, 128, 134, 135; glasses 312; grafting 55; hail nets 161; harvesting 104, 120; hillsides 115; insects 121; labels 302; medicinal effects 311; oak forests 228, 229; organic/ biodynamic viticulture 95; soil 145, 158, 162; sulphur usage 51; terroir 146, 148; transportation 154, 174, 175; truffles 84; UNESCO site 201; uneven fruit set 47; wine tourism 323-6
Busch, Clemens 138
butyric acid 265, 266
butts 227
Byrrh 166, 230

C

Cabernet Franc 24, 27, 29, 146, 159, 256, 264
Cabernet Sauvignon 24, 26, 29, 37, 61, 88, 110, 122, 189, 195, 197, 231, 248, 264, 283
Cabernet Severny 18
cabottes 159, 165
Cadet de Gassicourt, Charles Louis 323, 324, 326
Cahors 128, 172, 177
Cagniard de la Tour, Charles 208
Caíño Tinto 177
Calabria 322
calcium 78, 138, 142, 206, 254, 272, 274, 275, 284, 285
calcium carbonate 127, 132, 134, 139, 148, 281
Calera 135
California 192-3, 195, 196, 243, 308; climate 108, 109, 110, 112, 115, 116, 117; eucalyptus 240; geology 130, 132, 134, 135; grafting 57; oak 227; soil 142; sunblock 105; Terret 122; terroir 148, 251; Zinfandel 23, 26
Calvo, Paco 94, 96
cambium 16, 40, 42, 61
Camino de Santiago 177
Camino Francés 177
Campy, Michel 125

Camus, Julien 250, 251
Canada 113, 132, 138, 220
canals 172, 175
Canary Islands 51, 116, 130, 132
Candau, Joël 280
Candida mycoderma 211
Candida stellata 211
Candida zemplina 211
canteiro 163, 218
Cape Doctor 112
Capone, Dimitri 88
Capus, Joseph 185, 247
Caradot 326
carafes 262, 289
Caramany 138
carbonation 222
carbon dioxide (CO2) 118, 212, 235; aromas 267; closures 298; effervescence 222, 224, 259, 261, 274; emissions 294; fermentation 208, 210, 211, 221; minerality 286; plants and 44, 77, 85, 113, 114, 121, 207; regenerative agriculture 98, 100; soil formation 139; taste 253, 254, 271
carbonic acid 139
carbonic maceration 221, 222, 226, 265
Carbonneau, Alain 50, 61, 104, 106, 110, 117, 147, 169
Carignan 29, 42
Carlu, Jean 302, 303
Carmenet group 28, 29
Carpentras 64
Carson, Rachel 92
Carton, Lucas 319, 329
Casamayor, Pierre 177, 318
cask finishes 231
casks *see* barrels
Cassis 185, 325
Casteel, Mimi 100
Castel 197
Castets 122
cation exchange capacity (CEC) 78, 140, 163
Caucasus 19, 20, 29
Caucinum 115
Cava 224, 328
Cavalieri, Duccio 214
Cayuga White 35
Cederberg 137
Celhay, Franck 302, 304
cellars 166, 167, 214, 225, 256
cellulose 206, 226, 241, 259, 261
cement 241, 295
Centelles, Ferran 318, 319, 320, 321, 327, 329
Central Asia 176
Central Coast 117
Central Otago 137
Central Valley 110
Centre for Research, Environmental Sustainability and Advancement of Mountain Viticulture (CERVIM) 116
Centre National de la Recherche Scientifique (CNRS) 238
cépages 13, 22-30, 34, 146, 147
cerebral cortex 252, 253
Cévennes 165
Chabin, Jean-Pierre 151
Chablis 118, 128, 151, 185, 188, 193, 247, 285, 297, 312
Chagall, Marc 302
chalk 134, 140, 276, 281, 284
Chambertin 158, 247, 322
Chambourcin 35

Champagne 152, 153, 154, 178, 182, 185, 238, 308, 322; ageing 228, 274; aroma 267; bottles 222, 291, 292, 293, 294; cellars 166; climate 151; corks 295; distillation 173; enclosed vineyards 165; geology 128, 129, 134, 135; glasses 313; grafting 55; hillsides 115, 198, 201; labels 300; medicinal effects 311; *méthode champenoise* 206, 222, 224, 292; oak forests 229; organic/biodynamic viticulture 95; rosé 224; soil 140, 161, 162; taste 254, 274, 286; terroir 148; UNESCO site 197, 200, 201; UV light 108; *V. sezannensis* 16
Chancellor 35
Changins 270
Chapel, Alain 248, 318, 321, 326
Chapelle, Margarethe 287
Chaptal, Jean-Antoine 33, 222
chaptalization 220, 222, 271, 272
charcoal 224, 225, 238
Chardonnay 26, 28, 47, 49, 65, 115, 118, 122, 145, 185, 242, 243, 312
Charente 27, 58, 64, 174, 175, 220
Charlie Hebdo 302
Charnay 100
Chartier, François 88, 319, 328, 329
Chartogne, Alexandre 52
Chasselas 29, 55, 159, 296
Château Beaucastel 239
Château Beychevelle 248
Château Cheval Blanc 166, 239, 243
Château Cos d'Estournel 166
Château d'Yquem 160
Château d'Agassac 297
Château de Fosse-Sèche 99, 101
Château de Parnay 159
Château Fortia 185
Château-Grillet 293
Château Haut-Brion 178, 179, 180, 181, 182
Château La Coste 166
Château La Dominique 166
Château La Mission Haut-Brion 178, 179, 180
Château Lafite-Rothschild 166, 247
Château Les Carmes Haut-Brion 166, 178
Château Margaux 166, 297
Chateau Montelena 192
Château Mouton Rothschild 302, 303, 304
Château Musar 243, 279
Château Pape-Clément 178
Châteauneuf-du-Pape 104, 113, 115, 122, 134, 135, 139, 144, 185, 239
châteaux 164, 165, 166, 182, 302, 304
Chaume de Marsannay 162
Chauvet, Jules 97, 248-51, 256, 263, 269
Chenin 22, 25, 29, 52, 147, 159, 220
Chenôve 162
Cher 154
chestnut 165, 226
Chevalier-Montrachet 160
Chevallier, Maurice 155
Chianti 125, 189
Chidaine, François 52
Chile 51, 116, 117, 119, 130, 132, 166, 192, 195, 288
China 19, 49, 113, 117, 118, 176, 220, 256
Chinato 217
Chinon 154
Chinook 112
chip-bud grafting 58, 59
Chiva, Isac 199
chlorine 218, 221
chlorophyll 44, 72
chloroplasts 44, 72, 85

chlorosis 55, 68, 146
Christ, Christianity 152, 306, 310, 311
Chusclan 173
cider 153, 204, 206, 208, 216, 314, 329
cilia 268
Cima Corgo 168
cineole 88, 240
Cinque Terre 116, 198, 200
cintrage 230
cis rose oxide 264
Cistercians 183, 199
Cîteaux 183, 229
citric acid 19, 206, 220, 238, 242, 272-3
citronellol 264, 266
Clairet 173, 221, 317
Clairette 29
Clairette de Die 185, 222
clarification 209, 232, 238
clarity 259
claret 225; new French clarent 179, 221, 292
Clare Valley 296
Class, Nicolas 73
clavelin 293
clay-humus complex 76, 78-9, 81, 139, 140, 142
clays 78, 132, 133-4, 135, 136, 138, 139, 140, 141, 142, 143, 144-5, 146, 160, 163
clay wine jars 221, 231, 288
cleft-grafting 49, 58, 59, 61
climate change 54, 67, 101, 104, 109, 119, 120-1, 122, 169
climate classifications 117-18, 148
Clinton 35
clonal selection 64-5, 179
clones 21, 24, 29-30, 31, 32, 33, 64, 65
clos 302
Clos de Bèze 184
Clos de la Roche 185
Clos d'Entre-les-Murs 159
Clos-Jouve, Henry 327
Clos des Lambrays 185
Clos Lanson 178
Clos Saint-Georges 322
Clos-Vougeot 322
Club des Cent 323
Cluny 176, 183
Cocteau, Jean 302
Codex alimentarius 237
Code of Œnological Practices 235
Cognac 27, 50, 55, 134, 154, 173-4, 182, 185, 197, 220, 231, 313
Colbert, Jean-Baptiste 238
Collioure 116
Colombard 27
colour 258-9, 260, 262
Columbia Valley 132, 139, 142
Columella 49, 58
Comblanchien 138
Commandaria 21
companion planting 88
complantation 21, 67, 88
complexolysis 142
Concord 34
concrete 225, 230
Condrieu 173, 322
Conques 177
Constance 322
Constantia 293
Constellation Brands 193, 195
consumption-oriented 304
Contra Costa 115, 135
cooked wine 218, 221
cool night index (CNI) 108, 110
Coonawarra 194

copper 86, 89, 100, 235, 265, 285
copper chloride 287
Corbin, Alain 269
cordon de Royat pruning 169
cordon pruning 60, 171
Corinthian 22, 29, 45
Corison, Cathy 283
cork 40, 227, 240, 242, 289, 292, 295, 296, 297, 298, 299
corks 207, 222, 224, 227, 242, 259, 267, 289, 292, 295, 297, 298-9
corkscrews 295
cork taint 241, 242, 243, 296 297
Cornas 128
Cornell University 33, 35, 108
Corner, Edred 72
Cornouaille 204
Corsica 95, 128, 129, 137, 229, 290
cost of production 148, 152
Côte Brune 137
Côte chalonnaise 128
Côte de Beaune 184
Côte de Brouilly 132
Côte de Nuits 145, 184
Côte des Bar 128, 153
Côte des Blancs 115, 128, 148
Coteaux du Layon 115, 132, 220
Côte d'Or 115, 124, 128, 134, 135, 145, 146, 158, 161, 165
Cotentin 204
Côte-Rôtie 116, 118, 128, 137, 138, 173, 174, 322
Côtes-de-Provence 128
Côtes-de-Roussillon 128
Côtes du Forez 138
Côtes-du-Rhône 173, 262
Cots 28
Coucquyt, Peter 319
Couderc 35
Coulée de Serrant 214, 322
coulure 45
Courtiller, Auguste 33
Court of Master Sommeliers 251
Coutier, Martine 269, 277, 280, 284
Cox, D 319
Crabb, Hamilton 195
Crémant 224
cresol 240, 241, 266, 267
Criolla 161
Cristal, Père 159
Crljenak Kaštelanski 23
Crozes-Hermitage 128
crus 124, 185, 302
cryoextraction 220
Csergo, Julia 322, 323
Cuero de Vaca 288
Cukierman, Jérémy 122
cultivars 23, 24, 30, 56, 66, 110
culture of wine consumption 305-16
curettage 58
Curnonsky 323
cuttings 66, 74
CVNE 166
cyanobacteria 44, 85
Cyprus 21, 51, 87, 138, 152, 172
cysteine 242, 264

D

Daktulosphaira vitifoliae 50
Dal, François 58
Dali, Salvador 302
Dalmore 231
Daniel, Lucien 51-2
Dantan, Hervé 178
Dão 130
Daraki, Maria 306, 310
Darnay, Soazig 199
Darney 229
Darricau, Léa and Yves 86
Darwin, Charles 72

Dattier de Beyrouth 29
Daumas Gassac 123
David, Sébastien 242
Davidoff, Jules 280
DAYs see dried active yeasts
decanting 262, 293
de-consumption 314, 316
defects 239–43
defrutum 218
degree days 108
Deiss, Jean-Michel 250
Delahunty, C 319
Delaware 34
Delay, Étienne 155
delestage 232
Democritus 22
Deneulin, Pascale 285
denominación de origen (DO) 177, 189
denominaciones de origen (DO) 195
denominazione di origine controllata (DOC) 114, 189
Descola, Philippe 93, 94, 96, 332
Detert family 195
DGCCRF see Direction Générale de la Concurrence, de la Consommation et de la Repression des Fraudes
diacetyl 211, 241, 242, 243, 265, 266
Diam 297, 298
diatomite 133, 134, 135
Didier-Michel 279
diethylene glycol 272
Digby, Kenelm 292
Dijon 153, 183, 184, 281
Dillon, Clarence 179, 181
dimethyl sulphide (DMS) 242, 265, 269
Dion, Roger 149, 150–5, 158, 176, 177, 305
Dionysus, Bacchus 20, 70, 115, 306, 310–11
diorite 132
Diplôme National d'Oenologue (DNO) 235
Diplôme Universitaire d'Aptitude à la Dégustation (DUAD) 244
Direction Générale de la Concurrence, de la Consommation et de la Repression des Fraudes (DGCCRF) 242, 302
diseases and disease resistance 30, 35–6, 37, 68–9, 86, 108
distillation 173
disulphane 242
DNA sequencing 23, 26, 27, 30, 36, 239
DNO see Diplôme National d'Oenologue
DO see denominación de origen; denominaciones de origen
DOC see denominazione di origine controllata
Dokuchaev, Vasily 139
dolia 231, 288
dolomites 134
Domfrontais 204
Dominus 166, 168
Dordogne 154, 172
dormancy 41, 42, 43, 62, 66, 105, 108
Dornenburg, Andrew 319, 329
Douro 116, 137, 161, 166, 168, 172, 198, 231
Douro Superior 168
drainage (land) 111, 115, 132, 135, 143–4, 160–1, 162, 164, 274, 285
draining (wine) 232, 233
dried active yeasts (DAYs) 214, 235
drinkability 257, 287
drought resistance 122
drunkenness 288, 304, 306, 311, 315

Dry Creek 134
dryness index 108
drystone walls 159–60
DUAD see Diplôme Universitaire d'Aptitude à la Dégustation
Dubois, Jehan 162
Dubourdieu, Denis 235, 262, 285
Ducerf, Gérard 89
Ducournau, Patrick 226
Dujac 135
Dumay, Raymond 318, 327
Duras, Marguerite 284
Dussard, Thierry 113
dyes 207

E
early anthropogenic hypothesis (EAH) 118
eau-de-vie 207, 220, 231
eco-geogroups 28, 29
ectomycorrhizae 77, 84
Eden Valley 192
Effective Microorganisms (EM) 86
effervescent wine 222–4, 237, 259–60, 261, 274, 292; perlant 222; pétillant naturel 222, 298
egg white 237, 238
Egypt, ancient 21, 166, 198, 289, 300, 303, 306
Eiffel, Gustave 166
El Celler de Can Roca 329
El Niño/La Niña 116
elBulli 319, 321, 327, 329
elevation 113–15
ellagitannins 226, 227, 228, 276
EM see Effective Microorganisms
Empedocles 245
empyreumatic 230, 241, 285
endocarp 47
endomycorrhizae 77, 81
endosymbiosis 44, 79
England 36, 120, 121, 134, 153, 174, 204, 222, 289–90, 292, 295, 296
English grafting 58, 59, 61
Enjalbert, Henri 123, 173
ENTAV-INRA 26, 65, 67
Entraygues-le-Fel 177
Entre-deux-Mers 128
Eparchides 245
epicarp 47
epoxy 242
Erasmus 91
Eratosthenes 150
erosion 161, 162
esca 58, 60, 61, 67, 72, 86
Escoffier, Auguste 323
Escudier, Jean-Louis 106, 117, 315
Estaing 177
esters 263, 264, 265, 266, 267
estufagem 163, 219
eszencia 220
ethanal 241
ethanethiol 241, 242
ethnobotanical 70, 92, 101
ethyl acetate 211, 214, 224, 240, 241, 242, 265, 266
ethyl hexanoate 265, 266
ethyl lactate 241, 266
ethyl octanoate 265, 266
ethylphenols 235, 239, 240, 241, 267
Etna 114, 132, 139
eucalyptus trees 88, 240, 241
eugenol 227, 228, 230, 240, 266, 267
Euripides 306
European Union 44, 148, 189, 195, 237, 238, 293, 302
eutypiosis 86
Euvitis 18
evaporation 218, 220, 225, 226, 232, 259, 262

evapotranspiration 42, 101, 110, 111, 112, 121, 144
Évin loi 314
Exogyra virgula 188
Eyrie Vineyards 98

F
F2 grafting 58, 59
Fabius, Laurent 317
Fabre, Jean-Henri 72
Fagon 311
Falernum 115, 126, 225
Falerno 22
fanleaf virus see grape vine fanleaf virus
fatty acids 207, 212, 215, 231, 253, 254, 265, 276
Faugères 101, 137
faults see defects
Faure-Brac, Philippe 319, 329
Faustianum 115
federweisser 217
Fedoul, Sénia 327
feldspar 127, 130, 132, 133, 138, 139
Fercal 55
fermentation 208–14; alcoholic 210, 211–15, 220, 226, 232; lactic 215, 235; malolactic 211, 214, 215, 224, 232, 235, 242, 265, 272
Ferreira, Vicente 263
fertigation 148
fertilizers 162–3; green 89, 143; mineral 78, 81, 92, 93, 143, 284
Fertő/Neusiedlersee 198, 200
Feuerweine 218
fiasco 293
fibreglass 231
Fiefs Vendéens 146
Figeac 177
field-grafting 57, 58, 59, 66
filtration 211, 232, 238, 242
Finca Altos Los Hormigas 159
Finger Lakes 108, 116, 118, 134, 207
fining, finings 224, 225, 232, 235, 238, 292
Fino 217, 218, 219
Fitch, Asa 50
Flagey-Echézeaux 186, 187
Flanzy, Michel 221
flash détente, flash release 221, 235
flavescence dorée 27, 66, 86, 121
flavonoids 81, 105, 206, 258, 276
flavonols 206, 231, 258, 276
Fleurie 130
flint 284, 285
Floc de Gascogne 220
floral aromas 226, 241, 253, 256, 264, 265, 269, 270
Floréal 36, 122
Florin, Jean-Michel 73, 75
Florio family 174
flor wine 216, 217, 274
flowers see inflorescences
flying winemakers 238
Foehn 111, 114
Foëx, Gustave 25, 33
Folle Blanche 27, 29, 50
Folles 28
folletage (sunstroke) 67
Fontainebleau 229
food and wine pairing 317–22, 325, 327–9
Foradori, Elisabetta 36
Forez 138, 176
Forrestel, Beth 110
Forst 132
fortified wine, fortification 174, 218, 219, 220–1
Foster, Norman 166
Fottorino, Alessandra 315
Foulonneau, Christian 211

France 26, 152–4, 197, 234, 235, 236, 314; AOC system 183–5, 191, 247; bottles 290, 292–4; cépages 27–8, 30; climate 112, 117, 151; cork 299; gastronomy 317, 326; geology 127–9; grafting 51, 55, 64–6; heroic viticulture 116; hillsides 115; ice wines 220; labels 302, 303; oak forests 227, 228, 229; organic/biodynamic viticulture 95; regional cuisine 322–3; rosé 260; soil 79, 142; sweet wine 220; terroir 148, 188; transportation 175, 177; UNESCO sites 198, 200–1; urban viticulture 178–82; wine tourism 323–6
France, Benoît 128
FranceAgriMer 24, 26, 66
Franciacorta 224
Franck, Alain 319
Franconia 134, 293
Frank, Albert 81
Frankenthal 27
Frankfurt 56
fraud 25, 26, 52, 184, 185, 244, 294, 300, 316
Freedom 56
French hybrids 25, 35
French Wine and Vine Institute (IFV) 64, 65, 198, 214, 229, 230
Friuli 221
frost 42, 89, 101, 105, 108, 112, 114, 115, 121, 133, 149, 172, 173, 207
fructose 206, 215, 253, 272
fruit wine 204
Fukuoka, Masanobu 98, 100
fumaric acid 235
fungicides 58, 85, 86, 92, 212
furanic acid 235
furfural 219, 229, 267
Furmint 29

G
gabbro 132
Gadachrili Gora 19, 20
Gadoury, David 108
Gaglioppo 36
Gaïa 94
Gaillac 128, 172, 174
Galen 245–6, 311
Galet, Pierre 24, 25–6, 29, 31, 47, 52, 62, 105, 113, 115, 162
Galicia 80, 116, 130, 137, 177, 259
Gallo, E & J 193
gallotannins 276
Gamay 28, 42, 46, 154
Ganzin, Victor 55
Garcia, Jean-Pierre 158, 162, 182, 183
Garonne 154, 160, 172, 175, 179, 182
gas chromatography 239, 269
Gaudi, Antoni 166
Gawel, Richard 277, 281
Gay-Lussac, Joseph Louis 208
Gayon, Ulysse 235
Gehry, Frank 166
Geisenheim 35, 121
Gemischter Satz 178
genetically modified organisms (GMOs) 35–6, 214
genetic diversity, lack of 33, 56, 66
genome 16, 26, 31, 34, 36, 71, 212
genotype 26, 30, 31, 36, 54
geographical indication (GI) 148, 194, 195
Geoponica 217
Georgia 19, 20, 29, 100, 113, 117, 221, 223, 231, 310
geosensorial tasting 248, 250, 251, 252, 287
geosmin 240, 285
geotropism 74

Geoviticulture Multicriteria Climatic Classification System 110
geraniol 264, 266
Germany 254, 265, 323; bottles 291, 293; cellars 166; cépages, hybrids 27, 35, 36, 37; climate 118, 151, 153; Feuerweine 218; geology 132, 137, 138; glasses 291; heroic viticulture 116; hillsides 115; ice wines 220; labels 300; natural wines 97; phylloxera 51; sweet wines 219; UNESCO sites 201; volcanic wines 132; wine tourism 198, 326; yeast 212
gesta 73, 75
Gevrey-Chambertin 184, 247
Gewurztraminer 24, 264
GFV see Grapevine Flowering and Veraison index
Gilgamesh, Epic of 20, 306
Girard, Michel-Claude 148
glass 222, 231, 288, 289, 292, 293, 298
glasses 249, 251, 311–14
glucan 240
Gluconobacter 211
glucose 206, 215, 253, 272
glutamate 274, 275
glutathione 207, 224, 228
glycerol 215, 218, 220, 240, 259, 272, 276
GMOs see genetically modified organisms
gneiss 136, 138, 164
goblet pruning 86, 171
Goddard, Matthew 210, 213, 215
Godello 177
Goethe, Johann Wolfgang von 72, 73, 74, 75
Goldstein, Evan 319, 329
González Byass 166, 321
Goode, Jamie 121, 216, 239, 243, 258
Gorges 132
Gouais 27, 28
grafting 35, 40, 41, 49–50, 51–2, 54, 56, 57–61, 64, 66–7, 71; bench-grafting 57, 66; chip-bud 58, 59; cleft-grafting 49, 58, 59, 61; English 58, 59, 61; F2 58, 59; field-grafting 57, 58, 59, 66; mortise-grafting 58; omega-grafting 57, 58, 61; over-grafting 57, 58; regrafting 57; semi-mechanical 58; shield-bud 49, 58; T-bud 58, 59; whip-grafting 49, 57
Grahm, Randall 36
grands ensembles de références (GER) 140, 142
granite 130, 139, 140, 142, 164, 231
grapes: apyrene (seedless) 27, 29, 45, 47; berries 46–7, 62, 63, 205; clusters/bunches 48, 216, 221, 232; genetic diversity, lack of 33, 56, 66; maturity 29, 46, 62, 63, 108, 207; red 21, 35, 36, 47; seeds (pips) 23, 27, 30, 31, 34, 36, 37, 45, 47–8, 205, 207, 276; skins 205, 206–7, 209, 258; stems 205, 207, 221, 232; sun-dried (passerillé) 21, 172, 206, 220; table vs wine 27, 29; white 36, 47
grape varieties see cépages
grape vines see vines
grape vine fanleaf virus 18, 36, 61, 64, 81, 89, 159
Grapevine Flowering and Veraison index (GFV) 110
Grapevine Sugar Ripeness index (GSR) 110
grass 88–9, 101
Grasset, Charles de 55

Graves 128, 141, 179, 189
Gravesac 55
Gravner, Josko 221, 231
Greco di Tufo 132
Greece 27, 44, 51, 152, 172, 231, 290
Greece, ancient 21, 49, 218, 245–6, 254, 295, 306, 310, 311
greenwashing 101
Grenache 24, 29, 35, 37, 45, 46, 54, 91, 122, 144, 172, 264, 266
grey rot 220, 241
Greystone 216
greywackes 134
Grgich, Mike 23
Griffe law 52, 237
Grillon, Guillaume 183
Grimod de La Reynière 318, 320
Gringet 65
Grüner Veltliner 264, 312
GSR see Grapevine Sugar Ripeness index
guaiacol 240, 241, 266, 267
Guibert, Aimé 123
Guimberteau, Guy 285
Gulf Stream 115
Guyot, Jules 169
Guyot pruning 60, 169, 171
Guyot Poussard pruning 58, 169
gypsum 134, 217

H
Hadid, Zaha 166
hail 112, 114, 121, 161, 207
Hajji Firuz Tepe 20
Hallé, Francis 70, 71, 72, 85
Hanni, Tim 319, 329
Hanseatic League 174
Hanseniaspora uvarum 209
Haraszthy, Agoston 192
Harding, Julia 23, 24
Hardy, Auguste-François 33
Hardys 296
Haring, Keith 302
Haro 178, 179
Harrington, Robert H 319
harvesting 104, 119–20, 121, 207, 232, 239–40
Haudricourt, André-Georges 9, 97, 98
hautain system 86
Hawaii 118, 130, 204
head-pruning 86, 152, 169
healthy, reliable and merchantable 237, 243
Hében 27
Heitz Cellar 88
hens and chicks 45, 47
Heptaliko 27
Herbemont 33, 35
herbicides 88, 92
hermaphrodite hypothesis 21, 31
Hermippus 245
Hermitage 113, 128, 173, 174, 184, 220, 247, 312, 322
Herodotus 150
heroic viticulture 116, 162
Herrera, Arturo 288
Herzog & de Meuron 166
Hesiod 21
HI see Huglin heliothermic index
High Environmental Value (HEV) 93
Hill of Grace 54
hillsides 115
hippocras 217
Hippocrates 245, 311
histamine 240
hogsheads 227
Holmgren, David 98
holobiont 85, 96
homeostasis 89
Homer 246

Homo imbibens 19, 305, 310
Hope Well 100
hospices 302
hot pre-fermentation maceration (HPM) 221, 259
HPD see hybrides producteurs directs
Huarpes 117, 161
Huglin heliothermic index (HI) 108, 110
Humahuaca 113
Humboldt Current 115
humidity 225
humours, theory of the 245, 246, 311, 317
humus 76, 78, 89, 140, 145, 163, 284
Hungary 29, 116, 132, 198, 217, 227, 293
Hunter Valley 105, 192
Huss, Magnus 314
hybrides producteurs directs (HPD) 25, 35
hybrids, hybridization 18, 24–5, 29, 32, 34–6, 51, 55, 100, 113, 119, 122, 163, 214
hydrochloric acid 241
hydrogen disulphide (H2S2) 285
hydrogen peroxide 58
hydrogen sulphide (H2S) 211, 226, 241, 242, 264, 285
hygrometry 108

I
Ibn al-'Awwâm 49
Icewine 220
IFV see French Wine and Vine Institute
igneous rocks 125, 130–1, 138, 144
IGP/IGT see indication géographique protégée, indicazione geografica
Ikeda, Kikunae 253, 273
illite 144
INAO see Institut National de l'Origine et de la Qualité
Incisa della Rocchetta, Mario 189
India 118, 176
indication géographique protégée, indicazione geografica tipica (IGP/IGT) 114, 148, 161, 189, 191, 195, 217, 302
Indonesia 113, 118
industrialization 33, 61, 64, 92, 155, 197, 222
inflorescences (flowers) 16, 21, 26, 31, 42, 44–6, 48, 62, 63, 74
infrared light 108
Ingham, Benjamin 174
Inglenook 193
inoculation 214
Institute for Sustainable Plant Protection (IPSP) 39
Institute of Masters of Wine 251
Institute of Vine and Wine Sciences (ISVV) 58, 61, 244, 282
Institut National de l'Origine et de la Qualité (INAO) 23, 125, 146, 158, 161, 162, 185, 189, 190, 247, 249, 251
Institut national de la recherche agronomique (INRA) 35, 36, 37, 91
Institut national de recherche pour l'agriculture, l'alimentation et l'environnement (INRAE) 79, 122, 146, 147, 189
International Organization of Vine and Wine (OIV) 24, 25, 26, 35, 116, 149, 204, 235, 237, 259, 260
interoception 257, 282
IPSP see Institute for Sustainable Plant Protection
Irache 177
Iran 20, 29, 176

iron 54, 55, 78, 130, 132, 134, 138, 139, 165, 207, 235, 253
Irouléguy 177
Isabella 35, 119
isoamyl acetate 224, 265, 278
isobutyl-methoxypyrazine (IBMP) 256
isopropyl-methoxy-pyrazine 240
isopropyl methylphenol (IPMP) 241
Isovaleric acid 241
ISVV see Institute of Vine and Wine Sciences
Italy 21, 23, 166, 173, 192, 197, 308, 311, 322; ageing 226; bitterness 254; bottles 290, 293; cépages 26, 27, 36, 38–9, 221; climate and geography 113, 114, 116; closures 295, 298; cork 299; DOC/GIs 189; dolia, amphorae 231; effervescent wine 226; fraud 184; geology 125, 132, 134; grafting 58, 64; heroic viticulture 116; labels 303; pruning 169; soil 79; sommeliers 327; UNESCO sites 198, 200, 201; vino cotto 218; vite maritata all'albero 82–3, 86; vitiforestry 100; volcanic wines 132
Itata Valley 130

J
Jacquet, Olivier 183, 185, 189, 246, 247, 249, 323
Jacquez 33, 35
jalles 160
James I, King 292
Japan 98, 118, 155, 176, 243, 253, 274, 329
jars see clay wine jars
Jayer, Henri 47
Jeanneret, Yves 302
Jefferson, Thomas 179, 192
Jefford, Andrew 310
Jensen, Josh 135
Jerez 154, 166, 174, 197
Jilin Changbai Mountains Wine Company 18
Joly, Nicolas 214
Jones, Gregory 104, 109, 110, 124, 129
joualle system 82, 86, 88, 162
Judgment of Paris 110, 191, 192, 251
Juliénas 132
Jullian, Philippe 303
Jullien, André 97, 184, 246, 326
Jupilles 228, 229
Jupiterian egocentrics 304
Jura 30, 95, 121, 125, 127, 129, 135, 151, 174, 217, 220, 229, 267, 291, 293
Jura bow pruning 171
Jurançon 112, 134, 322

K
Kaefferkopf 185
Kahn, Odette 327
kaiseki 329
Kamen, JK 318
Kandinsky, Wassily 302
kaolinite 105, 144, 145
Karbowiak, Thomas 297
karez 117, 160
Kaštela 23
Keast, RSJ 319
Kenya 113
ketones 263, 265, 285
kieselguhr 134
Kimmeridgien 153, 188, 247, 285
Kloeckera apiculata 209, 214
Kluyveromyces thermotolerans 211

Koch, Robert 211
kokumi 274
koulouras 44, 171
Kronos 283
Krug 321, 329
Krug, Charles 193, 321, 329
Kuhlman, Eugene 35
Kuhnholz-Lordat, Georges 182
Kumeu River Estate 215
Kurniawan, Rudi 316
Kutzing, Friedrich 208

L
Labbé, Thomas 183
labels 193, 237, 300–4
Laboratoire d'Analyse Microbiological des Sols (LAMS) 145
La Cavale 166
Lachancea thermotolerans 211
Lachaud, Stéphanie 162
Lacombe, Thierry 21, 30
laccase 258
lactic acid 208, 211, 215, 273
lactic fermentation 215, 235
Lactobacillus 211, 240
lactones 219, 227, 228, 229, 263, 264, 265, 266, 267, 271, 328
ladybirds 240, 264
Laferté, Gilles 323
Lahousse, Bernard 319
Laliman, Léopold 51
Lambrusco 224
LAMS see Laboratoire d'Analyse Microbiological des Sols
Langenbick, Johan 319
Langhe-Roero 200
Languedoc 35, 95, 97, 122, 128, 148, 165, 172, 173, 178, 197, 222, 229
Lánia 87
Lanzarote 132
lapilli 132
La Rioja 112
La Rochelle 154, 173, 178
Larrère, Catherine and Raphaël 94
latitude 113
Latour, Bruno 93, 94
Lavalle, Jules 184, 187
Lavaux 116, 161, 198, 199, 200
Lavoisier, Antoine 208
layering 32
LCA see life-cycle analysis
lead 217
leaves 24, 25, 26, 42–4, 62
Lecoutre, Matthieu 305, 306, 314
Lee, Jeannie Cho 319, 329
Leeuwen, Kees van 122, 142
Leeuwin Estate 302
Lefebvre, David 285–7
Lefèvre, Ségolène 315
Léglise, Max 278
Legras, Jean-Luc 211, 212
legs 259
Le Hong, Pierre 125
Léon Barral 101
Léon Millot 35
Lenoir, Jean 265
Le Pallet 137
Lepousez, Gabriel 252, 253, 254, 257, 262, 265, 267, 270, 273, 275, 282
Le Roy de Boiseaumarié, Baron 185
Le Roy Ladurie, Emmanuel 119, 120
Letessier, Isabelle 125
Lett, David and Jason 98
Leuconostoc 211
levadas 160, 163
Levadoux, Louis 23, 28, 29, 30

Lévi-Strauss, Claude 305
Lichine, Alexis 251
Lichtenstein, Jules 50
life-cycle analysis (LCA) 294
Liger-Belair, Gérard 259, 261, 274
light strike 242
lignin 78, 101, 206, 226, 267, 296
Liguria 39
Liliorila 122
limestone 55, 123, 127, 133, 134, 142, 143, 145, 164, 188
Limousin 229
Limousin, Éric 177
linalool 263, 264, 266, 328
Linné, Carl von (Linnaeus) 22, 73
Lipari 132
lipids 207, 209
liqueur de tirage 222, 224
Liv-ex 308, 316
Lledoner Pelut 24
loam 141, 143
local, trusted and consistent 162, 182, 184–5, 237
Loire Valley 152, 153; bottles 291; climate 151; geology 128, 132, 134, 138, 164; glasses 312; grafting 67; hillsides 115; oak forests 228, 229; organic/biodynamic viticulture 95; soil 162; terroir 146, 147, 148; transportation 154, 173, 175, 176; UNESCO site 176, 198, 200; UV light 108
Lombardy 39, 198
Lorentz, Bernard 228
Lot 154, 177
Loubet, Émile 322
Loureiro 177
Louis XIV, King 179
Louis XV, King 222
Lovelock, James 94
Lucand, Christophe 302
Lucas, Patrick 216
lyre pruning 169, 171
lysozymes 212

M
MABD see Biodynamic Agriculture Movement
McDonald family 195
maceration 47, 206, 221–2, 232, 258, 259, 292; carbonic 221, 222, 226, 265; pre-fermentation 221, 235, 259; semi-carbonic 222; sulphitic 259
McGovern, Patrick 19, 217, 310
Mâconnais 128, 173
macro-oxygenation 226
Macvin du Jura 220
Madeira 132, 160, 163, 174, 218–19, 220, 226, 231, 267, 292, 322
Madeira drums 227
Magdeleine Noire des Charentes 27
Magliocco 36
magma 130, 131, 132, 136, 138
magnesium 78, 130, 132, 134, 138, 142, 143, 163, 207, 254, 274, 285
Maillard reaction 219, 224
maladie de l'amer 240
maladie de la graisse 240
maladie de la tourne 240, 243
Málaga 154, 295, 322
Malard, Alain 90, 145
Malbec 22, 26, 27, 61
malic acid 19, 46, 206, 211, 220, 265, 272, 273, 285
malolactic fermentation (MLF) 211, 214, 215, 224, 232, 235, 242, 265, 272
Malmsey 219
Maltman, Alex 130, 138, 284
Maltone, Carmela 315

Malvasia 152, 172
malvin 258
Mansell, Robert 292
Mansien group 28, 29
Manseng 29, 122, 220, 264, 266
Manzanilla 217, 218
Marangoni effect 259
Maratheftiko 21
marble 138
marc 207, 221, 232
Marchal, Axel 244, 271
Marcel, Christian 287
Marcillac 177
Maréchal Foch 35
Margaret River 47
Margaux 160, 166, 185, 193, 297
Marqués de Riscal 166
Marsala 174, 218, 220, 231, 289
Marsan, Benoît 132
Marselan 122
Martha's Vineyard 88
Martin, Jean-Claude 164
Martinotti-Charmat method 222, 224
Marzi, FM 319
Mascarello, Bartolo 303
Masnaghetti, Alessandro 125
Masneuf-Pomarède, Isabelle 216
massal selection 64, 65–6
Master of Wine 251
Master Sommelier 251
Maui Wine 204
Maxwell, Dom 216
Mazzorbo 178
medicinal effects 311, 314
Mediterranean climate and region 117, 151, 152
Médoc 128, 143, 154, 160, 165, 166, 248
Mega Purple 207
Melo, L 319
Melon 28, 29, 264
Mencia 177
Mendès, Pierre 314
Mendoza 112, 117, 121, 148, 159
Meneghetti, Stefano 36
Ménétrier, Laure 315
Mercadini, P 319
mercaptans 242, 264, 266, 285
Meredith, Carole 23, 26
Merlot 26, 27, 37, 45, 61, 193, 264
mesocarp 47
Mesopotamia 20, 212, 289, 306
Messiles 27, 28
metamorphic rocks 128, 130, 136–8, 144
methanethiol 226, 241, 242
methoxypyrazines 264
methyl anthranilate 35
Metschnikowia fruticola 86
Metschnikowia pulcherrima 209, 211
Metz 172
Meursault 247
Meuse 154
Mexico 117, 192
Meyen, FJF 208
Meyer, Tina 281
Meyssonnier, Louis 234
mica 127, 136, 137, 138, 139
mica-schiste 136
Michelin Guide 326
microbial terroir 208, 214–16
microbiota 77, 84, 85, 132, 142, 143, 146, 212, 285
micro-oxygenation 226, 231, 235
Middle East 117

migmatite 136, 138
Milanković, Milutin 118
mildew, downy 36, 37, 68, 80, 86, 108, 121, 152, 165, 240
mildew, powdery 36, 37, 51, 68, 86, 108, 121, 152, 165, 241
milk 276
Millardet, Alexis 35, 55
millerandage 45
Mills, David 215
Milton-Freewater 135
Minard, Charles 175
mineralization 76, 77, 78, 145, 163, 284, 286–7
minerality (wine) 78, 127, 138, 142, 273, 280, 282, 284–7
minerals 76–8, 127, 130, 133, 136, 139–40, 142–3, 146, 162, 163, 232, 274, 284–5
Minho 164
Minnesota 35
MIR see mycorrhiza-induced-resistance
MLF see malolactic fermentation
Moissac 177
molecular biology 26
Mollison, Bill 8, 13, 98
Monastrell 216
Monbazillac 185
Mondavi, Robert 166, 193, 195, 199
Monferrato 200
Monnier, Jean-Michel 239, 241
monoterpenes 264
Montepulciano 29
Montilla-Moriles 220
montmorillonite 138, 144
Morelot, Denis Blaise 184
Morizot, Baptiste 94
Morlat, René 147, 148
Morris, Jasper 187
Morrison, Helen 216
Morrison-Whittle, Peter 210, 213
Morrot, Brochet and Dubourdieu 262
mortise-grafting 58
Mosel Valley 51, 115, 116, 137, 138, 139, 140, 151, 154, 161, 172, 198, 219, 220
Mother Vine 18
mother vines 66
Mourvèdre 29, 54, 61, 264
moustillant 222
mousy flavour 211, 214, 240, 241, 253, 263
mouthfeel 245, 247, 251, 277, 281, 285
mucin 254
Müller, Egon 52
Müller, Hermann 212
Murano 289
murgers 159–60
Murray Darling 117
Muscadelle 27
Muscadet 22, 112, 132, 137, 138, 166, 169, 173, 176, 207, 228, 247, 259, 272, 293
Muscadinia rotundifolia 17, 18, 36, 37
Muscaris 36
Muscat 29, 172, 207, 220, 263, 264
Muscat de Rivesaltes 220
Muscat of Alexandria 48
muscovite 137
Musset, Alfred de 288
mutage 174, 220
mycorrhizae, mycorrhizal fungi 41, 72, 77, 78, 81, 84, 93, 98, 138, 142–3
mycorrhiza-induced-resistance (MIR) 81

N
Nantes 173
Napa Valley 23, 55, 88, 110, 115, 132, 139, 166, 168, 193, 195, 199, 215, 283
Napoleon III, Emperor 208

natural agriculture 98
natural wine 96–7, 214, 224, 228, 236, 249, 281, 302, 304, 332
Nature 2050 101
Near East 18, 19, 20, 117, 244
Néauport, Jacques 97
Nebbiolo 258
Negrul, Aleksandr 29, 30
Nelson, Horatio 174
Nemadex Alain Bouquet 5
nematodes 18, 56, 81, 89
nephelometric turbidity units (NTUs) 259
NeuroMagendie Centre 244
Nevers 229
New South Wales 118
New York (state) 108, 116, 118
New Zealand 101, 105, 112, 117, 134, 137, 192, 196, 210, 213, 214, 215, 296
Nietzsche, Friedrich 310
Nigeria 204
Niles, Meredith 101
nitrogen 47, 51, 52, 77, 78, 79, 81, 84, 89, 101, 142–3, 207, 209, 210, 212, 214, 228, 235, 242, 274
no-tilling 98, 100
Noah 35
Noble, Ann 270
noble rot see Botrytis cinerea
Noiriens 27, 28, 29, 30
Nomacorc Smart Green 298
Nomentura 22
non-flavonoids 276
norisoprenoids 264, 266
northern limit of commercial viticulture 113, 151, 152, 153
Norway 113
Nossiter, Jonathan 333
nouaison (fruit set) 45, 46, 62, 105, 120
Nourrisson, Didier 311, 314
Nouvel, Jean 166
NTUs see nephelometric turbidity units
nurseries 25, 33, 57, 61, 64–7, 84

O
oak 226–30, 267, 276
Oakville 166, 195
Observatoire National du Déploiement des Cépages Résistants (OSCAR) 37
Odart, Alexandre-Pierre 22
ODG see Organisme de Défense et de Gestion
Oenococcus œeni 211, 216, 240
Oenoflair 270
oenogeology 124–5
oenology 234–6
OIV see International Organization of Vine and Wine
Okanagan 138, 199
Olderman, Roelof 72
olfactory buffer 263
olfactory bulb 253, 268, 269
olfactory cortex 268
Olivesi, Stéphanes 327
Ollat, Nathalie 54
Oloroso 218, 231, 268
omega-grafting 57, 58, 61
Ontario 113, 116, 118
orange wine 221, 222, 223
Oregon 98, 112, 113, 117, 148, 193, 195
organic agriculture 66, 86, 91, 93, 95, 97, 98, 100, 218, 236, 287, 332
Organisme de Défense et de Gestion (ODG) 158
Orléans 153, 154, 176
Ormes de Cambras 197
OSCAR see Observatoire national du déploiement des cépages

osmazome 274
Otago 137
Othello 35
OTR see oxygen transmission rate
Otto, Walter 306
over-grafting 57, 58
Overnoy, Pierre 97
oxidation 217–18, 220, 224, 226, 232, 240, 242, 243, 253, 258, 262, 267, 285, 286, 287, 295, 297
oxidation-reduction see reduction-oxidation
oxidative ageing 217, 218, 219, 221, 225, 226
oxidative bouquet 267
oxygen transmission rate (OTR) 297

P
Page, Karen 319, 329
Palaeolithic hypothesis 19
Palladius 49
Palo Cortado 218
Pantelleria 116, 220
Pao Tscheou Kon 49
Paquet, Loïc 52
Parain, Charles 166, 167
Paraje Altamira 148
Paris 153, 162, 173, 178
Parker, Amber 110
Parker, Robert 280, 287, 315
Parr, Wendy 284
Parra, Pedro 125, 142, 148
parthenogenesis 50
Pasteur, Louis 79, 208–9, 211, 212, 226, 234, 314
pasteurization 97, 209, 235, 238
Patrimonio 128
Pauillac 160
Paulée de Meursault 326
Pays d'Auge 204
Pays d'Oc 197
Pays Nantais 164, 173
PDO see protected designation of origin
Pediococcus 211, 240
pedogenesis 84, 139, 140
Penfolds 296
Perche 204
pergola training 100, 163, 169, 171
permaculture 8, 90, 96, 98, 332
Pernot-Burlet, Céline 315
perries 204
Persians 160, 176
Perth 117
Peru 192
pests 89, 91
pesticides 78, 92, 93, 212
Petaluma Gap 112
pétillant naturel 222, 298
Petit Bouschet 35
Petit Manseng 29, 122
petrichor 285
Petrus 166
Peynaud, Émile 211, 225, 234, 235, 238, 247, 251, 258, 264, 265, 267, 273, 277, 278, 280, 282, 307
Pfeiffer, Ehrenfried 287
Pfister, Richard 270
PGI see protected geographical indication
pH (soil) 35, 54, 55, 140, 142, 146, 162–3
pH (wine) 64, 205, 206, 209, 212, 218, 253, 259, 272, 273, 276
phellogen 40–1, 296
phenylacetaldehyde 241
Philip the Bold, Duke of Burgundy 154
phloem 40, 49, 61
phosphates 81, 212, 254
phosphorus 77, 78, 79, 81, 142, 163

photoreceptors 260
photosynthesis 6, 16, 42, 44, 55, 74, 77, 81, 85, 101, 105, 110, 112, 121, 138, 206
phylloxera 21, 24, 25, 35, 41, 44, 49, 50–1, 53, 54, 55, 61, 119, 158, 184, 300
phytoremediation 89
phytosociology 86
phytosterols 207
Picasso, Pablo 302
Pichia fermentans 211, 240
Pickering, Gary 277
Pickering, J 319
Pico Island 198, 200
Piedmont 39, 113, 132, 198, 200
Pié Palomar, Eduard 216
pigeage 232
Pierce's disease 86
pilgrims 177
pine 165
Pineau, Christelle 96
Pineau d'Aunis 264
Pineau des Charentes 220
Pinot 21, 22, 24, 28, 29, 42, 46, 47, 293
Pinot Grigio 221
Pinot Noir 29, 30, 33, 47, 56, 65, 88, 115, 135, 145, 193, 216, 221, 256, 258
Piquette 317
Pirotte, Jean-Claude 282
pithoi 231
Pitte, Jean-Robert 150, 152, 174, 176, 288, 289, 292, 293, 295, 306, 311, 317, 319, 322, 329, 332
PIWI International (pilzwiderstandsfähig) 35
Planchon, Jules-Émile 50
plant leather 207
plastic 298
Plato 73, 310
Plavac Mali 23
Pliny the Elder 22, 49, 115, 132, 173, 222, 258
ploughing 98, 160
plutonic rocks 130
PMT see precision mechanical trimming
Pogue, Kevin 126, 133, 136, 142
Point, Fernand 248
Poitou 173
pollination 45
polyculture 82, 88, 91, 92, 98, 162, 174, 332
polyethylene 207, 231
polymerization 258, 259, 276, 277
polyphenols 44, 105, 108, 121, 143, 205, 206, 207, 225, 226, 232, 254, 258, 259, 276
polyvinylpolypyrrolidone (PVPP) 224
Pomerol 128
Pommard 322
Ponferrada 177
Ponge, Francis 71
Pontac, Jean de 179, 182
Ponsardin-Clicquot, Barbe Nicole 299
Pontailler, Paul 297
Popelouchum 36
porphyry 132
Port 130, 168, 173, 220–1, 289, 291, 292, 313, 322
Portland stone 124, 188, 247
Porto 153, 154, 168, 172, 174, 178, 197, 295
Portovenere 200
Port pipes 227, 231
ports 154, 173, 178

Portugal 168; bottles 290; climate 137; cork 222, 292, 295, 299, 296; fortification 220; geology 164; heroic viticulture 130; mildew 116; pruning 169; sommeliers 327; talhas 231; UNESCO sites 198, 200, 201
Portzamparc, Christian de 166
potash 81
potassium 47, 51, 77, 78, 130, 132, 138, 142, 143, 163, 205, 206, 253, 254, 272, 273, 274, 284, 285, 286
potassium ferrocyanide 235
potassium metabisulphite 218
Pouilly-Fuissé 134
Pouilly-Fumé 134
Poulsard 42
Poussier, Olivier 329
pozzolans 44, 132, 295
Prado de Irache 177
precision mechanical trimming (PMT) 169
premature oxidation (premox) 243
pressing 206, 209, 224, 232
price of wine 308–9, 316
Primitivo 23, 26
Priorat 116, 137
Prohibition 156–7, 193
Proles 29, 30
propagation *see* vegetative propagation
Prosecco 224
Prosecco de Conegliano et Valdobbiadene 198, 200
protected geographical indication (PGI) 223
protected designation of origin (PDO) 191, 302
proteins 212, 226, 235, 254, 259, 271, 273, 276
Provence 64, 95, 128, 166, 229, 260, 293
provignage 6, 32, 158
pruning 42, 58, 60, 86, 113, 118, 169, 170–1; basket 44, 171; cordon 60, 171, 169; Geneva double curtain 169, 171; goblet 86, 171; Guyot 58, 60, 169, 171; head-pruning 86, 152, 169; Jura bow 171; lyre 169, 171; stake 169, 171
Puisais, Jacques 10, 279, 318, 327, 329
Pulliat, Victor 25, 29, 51
puddingstone 134
pumice 132
pumping-over 232
puncheons 227
punching-down 232
Pünderich 138
Punkovino 281
putrefaction 208
PVPP *see* polyvinylpolypyrrolidone
pyridines 241
pyrazines 207, 240, 241, 256
Pythagoras 245

Q
qanat 160
quartz 127, 130, 132, 133, 138, 139, 144
quarters 227
Quebec 113
Quebrada 113
Quenol, Hervé 112, 122
quercetin 81, 231
Quercus alba 227, 267
Quercus robur/pedunculata 227, 267
Quercus rubra 227
Quercus sessiliflora/petraea 227, 267
Quercus suber 295, 296
Quigley, Brenna 125
qvevri 221, 223, 231, 288

R
Rabelais, François 22
racking 206, 225, 226, 228, 232, 238, 292
Radikon, Stanko 221
railways 178–9
rancio 174, 221, 224, 225, 226, 234, 243, 267
Ratafia de Champagne 220
Rauscedo 58
Ravaz, Louis 24, 26
Rayon d'Or 35
reduction 214, 220, 225, 226, 228, 231, 232, 241, 242, 248, 251, 267, 285, 298
reduction-oxidation (redox) 225, 228, 239
reductive bouquet 267
Reess, Max 209
Référentiel pédologique 140
regenerative viticulture 98, 332
Regenerative Viticulture Foundation 96
Regent 36, 37
regional cuisine 322–3
regrafting 57
Reims 153, 178
Reinach, Joseph 314
remontage 232
Rencontre des Cépages Modestes 33
replantation 67
reproduction, sexual 30, 31, 32
reproduction, vegetative 30, 31–2
ResDur 36, 37
Restinclières 88, 91
Retsina 217
Réunion 118
Rheingau 137, 151, 312
Rhine Valley 154, 172, 174, 198, 200
rhizosphere 77, 84, 161
Rhône Valley 95, 116, 125, 128, 130, 144, 146, 154, 161, 172, 173, 174, 229, 308, 327
rhyolite 132
Rías Baixas 177, 259
Ribeira do Ulla 177
Ribeira Sacra 177
Ribera del Duero 134, 177, 259
Ribéreau-Gayon, Jean 235, 247, 267
Ribéreau-Gayon, Pascal 235
Riedel 311, 312–13
Riesling 29, 45, 65, 138, 220, 264, 312
Rigaux, Jacky 250, 251
Riley, Charles 50
Rimagesor 207
Rimbaud, Arthur 281
Rioja 134, 165, 166, 168, 177, 178, 199, 259
Riparia Gloire 56
ripening classification 29
ripping 160
Riverina 117
Riverland 117
RN7 323, 326
Robinson, Jancis 23, 24, 294, 312, 314
Roca, Josep 318, 319, 327, 329
Rochard, Joël 198
Rochefort 174
Roche Mazet 197
Rodale, Robert 98
Rodenstock, Hardy 316
Romanée-Conti 135, 183, 187, 316, 322

Rome, ancient 21, 152, 174, 225, 311; cellars 166; cépages 22, 30; cooked wine 218; cork 295; effervescent wine 222; garum 273; glass 289; grafting 49; hillsides 115; ice wine 220; soil 126; tasting 245–6; vitiforestry 88
Rondo 35, 36
root rot 68, 86
roots 40–1, 74, 79, 140–2
rootstocks 18, 24, 25–6, 30, 33, 35, 41, 45, 49, 50, 52, 54, 55–6, 57, 66, 67, 89, 121, 140, 142, 146, 147
Rosella, R 319
rosé wine 224, 260, 312
Rothschild, Philippe de, Baron 302, 303
rotundone 264
Roupnel, Gaston 158
Roussillon 95, 97, 128, 137, 138, 165, 220, 232, 322
Rouvellac, Éric 173
Royer, Claude 165, 167
Rozier, François 33
Rubired 207
Ruddiman, William 118
Rudolph, Kelli C 246
Rupestris St George 56
Rust 220
Rutherglen 220

S
Sables-de-l'Océan 152
Saccharomyces 208, 211, 212, 224, 264
Saccharomyces apiculatus 209
Saccharomyces bayanus (*oviformis*) 210, 211
Saccharomyces cerevisiae 203, 208, 209, 210, 211, 212, 214, 216, 218
Saccharomyces ellipsoideus 211
Saccharomyces ludwigii 211
Saccharomyces pastorianus 209, 211, 212
Saccharomyces pomorum 208
Saccharomyces vini 208
Sachs, Philipp Jakob 22
Sahut, Félix 50
saignée 224
Saint-Aubin Murgers de Dents de Chien 160
Saint-Émilion 128, 198, 200, 239
Saint-Estèphe 160
Saint-Julien 160, 248
Saintonge 173
Saint Palais 229
Saint-Péray 322
Saint-Suliac 27
Saint-Vivant de Vergy 183, 187
sake 155, 216, 273, 320, 326, 329
Salamanca 172
Salette, Jean 146
salicylic acid 108
salination and salt (soil) 41, 121, 126, 134, 160, 285
saliva 240, 250, 253, 254–6, 263, 264, 268, 271, 272, 273, 274, 276, 277
Salta 121
saltiness, salinity (wine) 245, 246, 253, 271, 273, 274, 275, 285, 286
salt trade 154, 173, 174
Salvaniens 28, 29
Samos 220
San Carlos 121
Sancerre 67, 134, 152, 155, 243, 272
Sancerrois 128, 151
Sideways 134, 193
sand 115, 134, 141, 143, 164, 289
sandstone 134, 138, 140, 142, 144, 164, 231
Sangiovese 26, 189

San Juan 112
Sanlúcar de Barrameda 179
Santa Barbara 36, 109, 115, 134
Santa-Cruz, Maylis 315
Santiago de Compostela 177
Santorini 44, 111, 132
Saône 154
sapidity 253
Sapir-Whorf hypothesis 280
Sassicaia 189
SATW® *see* Systematic Approach to Tasting Wine
Saumur 33, 99, 101, 128, 146, 159, 164, 166, 247
Sauternes 160, 162, 220, 231, 313
Sauvignac 122
Sauvignier Gris 122
Sauvignon 46, 216, 242, 264, 266
Sauvignon Blanc 24, 47, 67, 101, 224, 226, 264
Savagnin 21, 24, 28, 29, 30
Savennières 132, 214
Savoie 82, 95, 165, 229
Schirmer, Raphaël 123, 165, 166, 168, 172, 174, 178, 179, 180, 181, 182, 192, 193, 197
schist 134, 136, 137–8, 140, 142, 143, 160, 164, 177
Schizosaccharomyces 211
Schizosaccharomyces pombe 211
Schneider, Christophe 37
Schoonmaker, Frank 193, 251
Schrader Cellars 195
Schwann, Theodor 208
Scott Henry pruning 169, 171
screwcaps 295, 298
sediment 224, 231, 233, 245, 247, 259, 262, 292, 293
sedimentary rocks 125, 128, 129, 130, 133–5
seeds 23, 27, 30, 31, 34, 36, 37, 45, 47–8, 74
Seguin, Gérard 141, 143, 145
Seibel, Albert 35
Seine 154
Selosse, Marc-André 76, 79, 85, 93, 206, 208, 212, 226, 230, 264, 276
Semillon 264
semi-mechanical grafting 58
semiotics 300, 302
Senderens, Alain 318, 319, 326, 327, 329
Seneca 311
sensitive crystallization 287
sensory analysis 251, 252, 254, 268, 277, 284
Sercial 219
Sérine 28, 29, 36
Serines group 29
serpentinite 138
Serres, Olivier de 22, 152, 154, 234
Sétubal 322
Seyval 35
Sézanne 152, 154
shales 134
shatter 45
Shepherd, Gordon M 252, 265
Sherry 217, 218, 219, 220, 231, 292, 313, 321
shield-bud grafting 49, 58
Shulaveri-Shomutepe culture 20
Shulaveris Gora 19, 20
Siberia 113
SICAVAC 67
Sicily 114, 126, 132, 174, 322
Sicus 216
Sideways *see above*
Sigales 125
Signet, Victor 50
silex 133, 134, 164, 284, 285
silica 78, 132, 134, 260, 289

Silk Road 174
Simonit & Sirch 58
Sitges 166
slate 136, 137, 138
Slovenia 221
smectites 144, 145
smell 245, 252–3, 256, 262, 263, 265, 268–70, 280
smoke taint 240
Soave 132
Socrates 310
sodium 121, 127, 130, 132, 253, 273, 274, 285
sodium arsenite 58, 61
sodium chloride 273
soil 41, 76–9, 84, 121, 125–6, 127, 139–42, 145, 146, 160, 161, 162, 180
Solaris 18, 36
solerone 267
somesthetic sensations 271, 276
Somló 132
sommeliers 189, 247, 251, 257, 278, 284, 311, 312, 315, 316, 317, 320, 326–7
Sonoma 115, 139, 193, 215
Sony 329
sortotypes 29
sotolon 218, 220, 241, 267
Souchier, Emmanuël 302
Sousão 177
South Africa 112, 116, 117, 121, 130, 137, 192, 293, 296
South Australia 51, 117, 194, 296
Southcorp 296
Southwest France 27, 29, 128, 166, 177, 226, 229, 264
Souvigner Gris 36, 100
Spain 166, 177, 216; ageing 226; bottles 290; cépages 27; cork 295, 299; DO/DOca system 189; flor wine 217; fortification 220; geology 137; grafting 64; heroic viticulture 116; pruning 169; tinajas 231
sparkling wine *see* effervescent wine
speculation 316
Speechly, William 34
Spence, Charles 298
Spurrier, Steven 251
spurs 42, 169
Sta. Rita Hills 134
Stag's Leap Wine Cellars 110, 132, 192
stainless steel 179, 219, 225, 230–1, 232
stake pruning 169, 171
stakes 86, 138, 165, 169
Stanziani, Alessandro 238
starchitects 166
Starck, Philippe 166
Starkenmann, Christian 285
Stefanini, Irene 214
Steiner, Rudolf 73, 74, 75, 287
Stellenbosch 116
Stelvin 296
stereotasting 277
sterols 211, 212
stone walls *see* drystone walls
stoniness 144
Strasbourg 250, 251
Strathbogie Ranges 130
straw wine 220
stirring (*bâtonnage*) 210, 225, 228, 230, 232
Styria 116
suberin 296
succinic acid 19, 220, 254, 273, 274, 285
sucrose 206, 272
sulphites 211, 218, 225, 232, 237, 241

sulphur 51, 78, 86, 97, 100, 142, 225, 232, 238, 240, 289, 292
sulphur dioxide (SO₂) 97, 209, 210, 211, 212, 214, 218, 225, 236, 240, 242, 243, 247, 259, 265, 285, 298
sulphuric acid (H₂SO₄) 234, 240, 272
Sultana 29, 45
sunburn, sunstroke 67, 68, 105, 121
sunshine 104–5, 113, 115, 116, 143
supertasters 256
Super Tuscan 189
sustainable viticulture 93
Sweden 113
sweet liqueur wine 220
sweetness 219, 222, 251, 255, 256, 271–2, 275, 286
sweet wine 21, 115, 160, 172, 210, 219–20
Switzerland 36, 116, 148, 161, 192, 198, 199, 201, 296
symbiosis 41, 44, 72, 77, 79, 81, 84, 85, 88, 93
symposium (banquet) 310, 326
synaesthesia 281, 282, 329
synthetic corks 296
Syrah 26, 29, 30, 36, 51, 54, 91, 115, 118, 221, 256, 264, 266
syringic acid 21
Systematic Approach to Tasting Wine (SATW®) 251
Szabo, John 132
Szamorodni 217

T
Tahiti 118
Taillevent 317
Taittinger 302
talhas 231
Tallet, Pierre 306
Tandonnet, Jean-Pascal 54
tannins 6, 46, 47, 64, 105, 114, 206, 207, 212, 221, 225, 226, 230, 231, 254, 258, 259, 276, 281, 292
Tannat 45, 122, 226
tartaric acid 19, 46, 52, 206, 207, 220, 230, 240, 272, 274, 285
tartrate crystals 259
taste buds 253, 254, 271, 276
tastevin 184, 246
tasting 184, 189, 191, 214, 244–57, 271–7
tasting terminology 278–82
Tavel 173, 185
T-bud grafting 58, 59
Tchelistcheff, André 193
Tchernia, André 217, 225
TDN see trimethyl dihydronaphthalene
Teinturier 28, 35, 47
temperature for growing grapes 101, 104, 105–8, 113, 115–16, 117–18
temperature for serving wine 307
Tempère, Sophie 282
Tempranillo 177, 259
Tenuta San Guido 189
tephras 132
Teroldego 36
terpenes 6, 88, 207, 226, 254, 263, 264, 266, 275, 285
terra rossa 194
terracing 161–2, 168
Terret 122
terroir 123, 146–9, 155, 182, 189, 207, 237, 287, 332; AOCs 185, 247; food and wine pairing 317; geology 127, 188; gradient and terracing 161–2; microbial 208, 214–16; roots 41; soil 78, 158–60, 162; water 160–1; yeasts 209
terroir-slogan 149
Tetra Pak 294

Texier, Éric and Martin 100
Thailand 113, 118, 204
Theophrastus 22, 49, 58
thermovinification 221
thiols 47, 207, 226, 228, 242, 264, 266
This, Patrice 24, 29–30
Thomery 159
Thomson, James 259
Thuir 166
Thünen, J H von 179
thyllosis 67
Tignanello 189
tinajas 231
Tirel, Guillaume 317
To Kalon 195
toasting (bousinage) 228, 267
tocotrienol 207
Tokaj 132, 166, 198, 200, 220, 291, 293
Tomasi, Diego 88
Tominaga, Takatoshi 285
Tonietto, Jorge 110
topping up 225, 232, 292
Torga, Miguel 168
Torregrossa, Laurent 104
Torrontés 264
Torulaspora delbrueckii 210, 211, 216
totipotency 71
Touraine 128, 146, 147, 165
Touriga Nacional 122, 266
Tours 165
training systems 42
trait de Jupiter 58
Traminer 24
transparency 259
transportation 172–5, 177, 289, 292, 294
Trebbiano 29, 48
trees 82–3, 86–8, 91, 99, 164–5
Treixadura 177
trellising 86, 165, 169, 170
Trepat 29
Tressots 28
Tribidrag 23, 23
Trichoderma fungi 86
Trier 154, 172
trigeminal sensations 271, 277
trimethyl dihydronaphthalene (TDN) 264
Trockenbeerenauslesen 220
Tronçais 228, 229
Truc, Georges 125, 126, 142, 144
truffles 84
Truyère 177
tufa 132, 133, 134
tuff 44, 132
tuffeau 132, 164
Tupin-et-Semons 138
Tupungato 121
turbidity 235, 241, 247, 259
Turkey 176
Turpan 117, 160, 176
Tuscany 86, 125, 189
TVMDI 108, 110
Tyrrell's 297

U
Uco 121
UDSF see Union de la Sommellerie Française
ultraviolet (UV) light 108, 207
umami 219, 220, 224, 253–4, 271, 273–4, 275, 276, 285, 286
UMT see units of macro-terroir
UNESCO Culture and Traditions of Wine 305, 319, 329
UNESCO Intangible Cultural Heritage 223, 315, 317, 333
UNESCO World Heritage sites 160, 168, 176, 178, 179, 184, 197, 198–201
Union de la Sommellerie Française (UDSF) 327

Union of Paris Sommeliers 327
United States 166, 192–3, 195, 196, 238, 272, 323; climate 110, 112, 116, 118, 148; fruit wine 204; geology 130, 132, 135; grape byproducts 207; hybridization 34, 35; native vines 18, 51, 55; oak 227; Prohibition 156–7, 193; regenerative viticulture 98; rootstocks 56; tasting 251; wine tourism 199; Zinfandel 23
units of macro-terroir (UMT) 148
University of California, Davis 33, 56, 108, 110, 193, 251, 270
Urban, Laurent 108
urban viticulture 178
urine 212
Urpflanze 73, 75
Uruguay 116, 118

V
Vaccarini, Giuseppe 319, 329
Valais 116
Val de Loire 162, 176
Val-de-Pennas 322
Val d'Orcia 198, 200
Valentin, Dominique 281
Valpolicella 220
Valtellina 161
Van Duzer Corridor 112
Van Volkenburgh, Elizabeth 37, 96
vanillin 230, 267, 271
Vannier, Françoise 125
Vassal-Montpellier Grape Vine Biological Resources Centre 30, 33
Vaudour, Emmanuelle 149
VDNs see vins doux naturels
VdT see vino da tavola
Vedel, André 249, 251
vegetative cycle 52, 54, 62–3, 75, 105, 108, 114, 121, 142, 143
vegetative propagation 30, 31–2, 37, 74
Velasco-Graciet, Hélène 179, 180, 181
Venice 172, 178
veraison 44, 46, 62, 63, 105, 108, 110, 120, 122, 143, 145, 206, 258, 272
Verband Deutscher Prädikats- und Qualitätsweingüter (VDP) 97
Verdelho 29
Vermentino 29
Vermorel, Victor 24, 31
vermouth 174, 217, 267
Vernaccia di Oristano 217
Vernant, Jean-Pierre 306
Veronelli, Luigi 318, 327, 329
Vertus 152, 154
Verzenay 115
Veuve Clicquot 299
Viala, Pierre 24, 31, 55
Victoria 117
Vidoc 36, 122
Vienna 178
Vienne 172, 173
Viento Blanco 112
Vignenvie 100
Vila Nova de Gaia 168, 178
Vila Viniteca 262
Villa Maria 216
Villard 35
Vincent, Éric 188
vin cuit 218
Vin de France 302
vin de goutte 232
vinegar 19, 154, 209, 211, 215, 218, 221, 240, 242, 243, 265, 273

vines: life cycle and morphology 41, 43, 62–3; diseases and disease resistance 30, 35–6, 37, 68–9, 86, 108; trained up trees 82–3, 86–8, 100
vineyards: creation of 158–9; enclosed 159, 165; geology of 130, 132, 134–5, 137; gradient 161–2; location of 106–8, 113–16, 121, 152–4; structures and buildings 164–8; urban 178–82
vin jaune 30, 217, 231, 267, 286, 291, 293
Vin Méthode Nature 97
vin nouveau 217
vino da tavola (VdT) 189
Vinolok 298
Vinoseal 298
vin primeur 217
Vinaesthesia 281
vinhos do roda 163
Vinho Verde 164, 272
vino cotto 218
vino da tavola (VdT) 189
vino de pago 177
vins doux naturels (VDNs) 220
Vins SAINS (Sans Aucun Intrant NiSulfite) 97
vintage 104, 112, 193, 195, 209, 224, 239
Viognier 264
Virgil 31, 115, 126
VitAdapt 122
vitamin B 207
vitamin E 207
vite maritata all'abero 82, 86
viti-agro-forestry, vitiforestry 86, 100–1
viticulture 15, 92–5, 98; heroic 116, 162; industrialized 33, 61, 64, 92, 155, 197, 222; *raisonné*/thoughtful 93; regenerative 98; sustainable 93; urban 178–82
vitipastoralism 91, 101
Vitis amurensis 17, 18
Vitis berlandieri 50, 55, 56
Vitis cordifolia 56
Vitis labrusca 17, 18, 22, 34, 35, 49
Vitis longii 56
Vitis lupina 22
Vitis riparia 17, 49, 50, 55, 56
Vitis rupestris 17, 42, 55, 56
Vitis sezannensis 16
Vitis vinifera subsp. *sativa* 15, 16, 17, 18, 19, 20, 21, 22, 24, 26, 56, 196
Vitis vinifera subsp. *sylvestris* 18, 19, 21, 48
Vitruvius 126
Vocontii 222
volatile acidity 184, 185, 211, 214, 218, 220, 230, 234, 235, 240, 242, 243, 251
volcanic rocks 130, 132
volcanic wine 132
Volnay 162, 247, 322
Voltis 36
Vosne-Romanée 183, 186, 187, 322
Vouillamoz, José 21, 23, 24, 26

W
wabi sabi 243
Wachau 138, 161, 198, 200
Wagner 57
Waipara Valley 216
Walker, Andrew 56
Wallace, Benjamin 316
Warhol, Andy 302
Washington (state) 51, 112, 132, 135
water 40, 41, 44, 51, 54, 78, 110–11, 115–16, 143–4, 145, 146, 160, 221, 225, 238

water stress 81, 100, 111, 112, 115, 121, 122, 207
Wegener, Alfred 126
Western Australia 302
whip-grafting 49, 57
whisky 231, 266, 313
whisky lactones 227, 230, 265, 267
White Palestine 48
white rot 61, 68
white wine 224, 232
Whorf, Benjamin L 280
Willaertia magna C2c Maky 86
Willamette Valley 98, 117, 139
Wilmotte, Jean-Michel 166
Wilson, James 124, 141
wind 112, 114
wine: as artisan product 238, 301; as industrial product 193, 238; as standardized 33, 191, 238, 332; word origins 190
Wine Australia 121
Wine Group, The 193
Wine Intelligence 301
Wine Scholar Guild 250, 251
Wine Spectator 304
Wine & Spirit Education Trust (WSET) 251
wine terroir units (WTUs) 147–8
wine tourism 91, 163, 168, 177, 178, 179, 198–9, 315, 323–6
Winiarski, Warren 110
Winkler, Albert J 108, 110, 148, 193
Wittendal, Frank 145
Wohlleben, Peter 81
women and winemaking 315
wood chips 230, 235
Woodhouse, John 174
World Health Organization (WHO) 218
World Reference Base for Soil Resources (WRB) 140
Worlidge, John 296
WSET see Wine & Spirit Education Trust
WTUs see wine terroir units

X
Xarel.lo 216
xing 256
Xinjiang 113, 117, 160, 176
xylem 40, 49

Y
Yalumba 296
Yang Dong 19
Yarra Valley 193
yeasts 86, 97, 208–10, 211–16, 265
Yunnan 113

Z
Zaragoza 263, 267
Zierfandler 23
Zinfandel 23, 26, 312
Zonda 112
Zuccardi, Sebastián 148

Bibliography

Sources available in English

Books

Altieri, Miguel A, *Agroecology: The Science of Sustainable Agriculture*, CRC Press, 2019.

Barthes, Roland, *Mythologies*, Jonathan Cape, 1972.

Bohling, Joseph, *The Sober Revolution: Appellation Wine and the Transformation of France*, Cornell University Press, 2018.

Brillat-Savarin, Jean Anthelme, *The Physiology of Taste, or Meditations on Transcendental Gastronomy*, Everyman's Library Classics, 2009.

Broadbent, Michael, *Wine Tasting*, Académie du Vin Library, 2019.

Calvo, Paco, *Planta Sapiens: Unmasking Plant Intelligence*, The Bridge Street Press, 2022.

Carson, Rachel, *Silent Spring*, Penguin Modern Classics, 2022.

Chartier, François, *Taste Buds and Molecules: The Aromatic Path of Wine and Foods*, John Wiley & Sons, 2012.

Chauvet, Jules, *Le Vin en question*, Éditions de l'Épure, 2018 (bilingual edition).
—, *L'Esthétique du vin*, Éditions de l'Épure, 2020 (bilingual edition).

Colman, Tyler, *Wine Politics: How Governments, Environmentalists, Mobsters, and Critics Influence the Wines We Drink*, University of California Press, 2010.

Columella, *On Agriculture*, Loeb Classical Library, 1989.

Corbin, Alain, *The Foul and the Fragrant: Odor and the French Social Imagination*, Harvard University Press, 1986.

Coucquyt, Peter; Lahousse, Bernard and Langenbick, Johan, *The Art & Science of Foodpairing: 10,000 Flavour Matches that Will Transform the Way You Eat*, Mitchell Beazley, 2020.

Davodeau, Étienne, *The Initiates: A Comic Artist and a Wine Artisan Exchange Jobs*, NBM, 2013.

Deleuze, Gilles, and Guattari, Felix, *A Thousand Plateaus: Capitalism and Schizophrenia*, Bloomsbury Revelations, 1987.

Descola, Philippe, *Beyond Nature and Culture*, University of Chicago Press, 2013.
—, *The Composition of Worlds, Interviews with Pierre Charbonnier*, Wiley, 2023.

Dufour, Jean-Jacques, *The American Vine-Dresser's Guide*, La Valsainte, 2003.

Duras, Marguerite, *The Impudent Ones*, The New Press, 2021.

Dussard, Thierry and Bernard, Olivier, *The Magic of the 45th Parallel*, Feret, 2014.

Euripedes, *Bacchae*, Cambridge University Press, 2024.

Fanet, Jacques, *Great Wine Terroirs*, University of California Press, 2004.

Feiring, Alice, *The Battle for Wine and Love: Or How I Saved the World from Parkerization*, Houghton Mifflin Harcourt Publishing Company, 2008.
—, *Naked Wine: Letting Grapes Do What Comes Naturally*, Da Capo Press, 2011.
—, *The Dirty Guide to Wine: Following Flavor from Ground to Glass*, Countryman Press, 2017.

Florin, Jean-Michel, *Biodynamic Wine-Growing: Understanding the Vine and Its Rhythms*, Floris Books, 2021.

Galet, Pierre, *Grape Varieties and Rootstock Varieties*, Oenoplurimedia, 1998

Gawel, Richard, *Wine Tasting Wheel*, 2003.

Gobat, Jean-Michel; Aragno, Michel and Matthey, Willy, *The Living Soil: Fundamentals of Soil Science and Soil Biology*, Science Publishers, 2004.

Goethe, Johann Wolfgang von, *The Metamorphosis of Plants*, The MIT Press, 2009.

Goldstein, Evan, *Perfect Pairings: A Master Sommelier's Practical Advice for Partnering Wine with Food*, University of California Press, 2006.

Goode, Jamie, and Harrop, Sam, *Authentic Wine: Toward Natural and Sustainable Winemaking*, University of California Press, 2007.

Goode, Jamie, *I Taste Red: The Science of Tasting Wine*, University of California Press, 2016.
—, *Flawless: Understanding Faults in Wines*, University of California Press, 2018.
—, *Wine Science: The Application of Science in Winemaking*, Mitchell Beazley, 2005 and 2021.
—, *Regenerative Viticulture*, Jamie Goode, 2022.

Frankel, Charles, *Land and Wine: The French Terroir*, University of Chicago Press, 2014.

Fukuoka, Masanobu, *The One-Straw Revolution*, New York Review Books Classics, 2009.

Hallé, Francis, *In Praise of Plants*, Hachette, 2002.

Hanny, Tim, *Why You Like the Wines You Like: Changing the Way the World Thinks about Wine*, New Wine Fundamentals, 2013.

Harding, Julia; Robinson, Jancis and Vouillamoz, José, *Wine Grapes: A Complete Guide to 1,368 Vine Varieties, Including Their Origins and Flavours*, Allen Lane, 2012.

Harrington, Robert J, *Food and Wine Pairing: A Sensory Experience*, John Wiley & Sons, 2007.

Holmgren, David, *Permaculture: Principles and Pathways Beyond Sustainability*, Permanent Publications, 2011.

Jackson, Nick, *Beyond Flavour: The Indispensable Handbook to Blind Wine Tasting*, Nick Jackson, 2020.

Jefford, Andrew, *The New France*, Mitchell Beazley, 2002.
—, *Drinking with the Valkyries: Writings on Wine*, Académie du Vin Library, 2022.

Johnson, Hugh, *The Story of Wine*, Mitchell Beazley, 1989.
—, *The Story of Wine: From Noah to Now*, Académie du Vin, 2020.

Johnson, Hugh and Robinson, Jancis, *World Atlas of Wine* (8th Edition), Mitchell Beazley, 2019.

Joly, Nicolas, *What Is Biodynamic Wine? The Quality, the Taste, the Terroir*, Clearview Books, 2007.

Keeling, Dan, and Andrew, Mark, *Wine from Another Galaxy: Noble Rot*, Quadrille Publishing Ltd, 2020.

Larousse Wine, Hamlyn, 2017.

Le Roy Ladurie, Emmanuel, *Times of Feast, Times of Famine: A History of Climate Since the Year 1000*, Farrar Strauss & Giroux, 1988.

Latour, Bruno, *Politics of Nature: How to Bring the Sciences into Democracy*, Harvard University Press, 2004.
—, *Facing Gaia: Eight Lectures on the New Climatic Regime*, Polity, 2017.
—, *We Have Never Been Modern*, Harvard University Press, 1993.

Le Breton, David, *Sensing the World: An Anthropology of the Senses*, Routledge, 2017.

Legeron, Isabelle, *Natural Wine: An Introduction to Organic and Biodynamic Wines Made Naturally*, CICO Books, 2020.

Liger-Belair, Gérard, *Uncorked: The Science of Champagne*, Princeton University Press, 2013.

Lévi-Strauss, Claude, *The Elementary Structures of Kinship*, Beacon Press, 1971.

Lovelock, James E, *Gaia: A New Look at Life on Earth*, Oxford University Press, 2016.

Maltman, Alex, *Vineyards, Rocks, and Soils: The Wine Lover's Guide to Geology*, Oxford University Press, 2018.

Margulis, Lynn, *Symbiotic Planet: A New Look at Evolution*, Basic Books, 1998.

Masnaghetti, Alessandro, *Barolo MGA. L'Enciclopedia delle grandi vigne del Barolo. The Barolo Great Vineyards Encyclopedia*, Enogea, 2015 (bilingual edition).

Masson, Pierre, *A Biodynamic Manual: Practical Instructions for Farmers and Gardeners*, Floris Books, 2014.

Mollison, Bill and Mya Slay, Reny, *The Permaculture Way: Practical Steps to Create a Self-Sustaining World*, Permanent Publications, 2004.

Mollison, Bill and Holmgren, David, *Permaculture One*, Intl Tree Corps Inst, 1978.

Morel, François and Galet, Pierre, *A Practical Ampelography*, Cornell University Press, 1979.

Morizot, Baptiste, *Ways of Being Alive*, Polity, 2022.
—, *Rekindling Life: A Common Front*, Polity, 2022.

McGee, Harold, *Nose Dive: A Field Guide to the World's Smells*, Penguin Press, 2020.

McGovern, Patrick E; Fleming, Stuart J and Katz, Solomon H (dir.), *The Origins and Ancient History of Wine: Food and Nutrition in History and Anthropology*, Routledge, 2015.

McGovern, Patrick E, *Ancient Wine: The Search for the Origins of Viniculture*, Princeton University Press, 2003.
—, *Uncorking the Past: The Quest for Wine, Beer and Other Alcoholic Beverages*, University of California Press, 2011.

Nietzsche, Friedrich, *Complete Poems of Nietzsche*, Grapevine India, 2023.
—, *The Complete Works of Nietzsche*, TGC Press, 2024.

Page, Karen and Dornenburg, Andrew, *What to Drink with What You Eat*, Bulfinch, 2006.

Palladius, *Opus Agriculturae ("The Work of Farming")*, Prospect Books, 2013.

Parker, Thomas, *Tasting French Terroir: The History of an Idea*, University of California Press, 2015.

Parra, Pedro, *Terroir Footprints. A Fascinating Trip to the Great World or Terroir (Burgundy, Barolo, Sonoma, Montalcino, Itata, Gredos, Oregon, Sicily and More)*, Alit Wines, 2021.

Paullin, Charles O and Wright, John K (ed.), *Atlas of the Historical Geography of the United States*, Carnegie Institution of Washington and the American Geographical Society of New York, 1932.

Peynaud, Emile and Spencer, Alan FG, *Knowing and Making Wine*, Houghton Mifflin Harcourt, 1984.

Peynaud, Emile, *The Taste of Wine: The Art and Science of Wine Appreciation*, Little, Brown, 1987.

Phillips, Rod, *9000 Years of Wine: A World History*, Whitecap Books Ltd, 2017.
—, *Wine: A Social and Cultural History of the Drink that Changed Our Lives*, Infinite Ideas Ltd, 2020.

Pitte, Jean-Robert, *French Gastronomy: The History and Geography of a Passion*, Columbia University Press, 2002.

Plato, *The Symposium*, Penguin Classics, 2003.

Pliny the Elder, *Natural History*, Penguin Classics, 1991.

Pomerol, Charles, *The Wines and Winelands of France: Geological Journeys*, Robertson McCarta, 1999.

Poussier, Olivier and Lenôtre, *Desserts and Wines*, Mitchell Beazley, 2004.

Rabelais, François, *Gargantua and Pantagruel*, Penguin Classics, 2006.

Regan-Lefebvre, Jennifer, *Imperial Wine: How the British Empire Made Wine's New World*, University of California Press, 2022.

Ribéreau-Gayon, Pascal; Glories, Yves; Maujean, Alain and Dubourdieu, Denis, *Handbook of Enology, Vol. 1: The Microbiology of Wine and Vinifications*, Wiley, 2021.
—, *Handbook of Enology, Vol. 2: The Chemistry of Wine— Stabilization and Treatments*, Wiley, 2021.

Rigaux, Jacky, *Terroir and the Winegrower*, Terre en Vues, 2006.
—, *Geosensorial Tasting: The Art and Manner of Tasting Wines of Origin*, Terre en Vues, 2015.
—, *A Tribute to the Great Wines of Burgundy: Henri Jayer, Winemaker from Vosne-Romanée*, Terres en Vues, 2019.

Robinson, Jancis and Harding, Julia, *The Oxford Companion to Wine* (5th Edition), Oxford University Press, 2023.

Roca Fontané, Joan, Josep and Jordi, *El Celler de Can Roca, The Book*, Librooks Barcelona, 2022.

Scott, James C, *Against the Grain: A Deep History of the Earliest States*, Yale University Press, 2017.

Segnit, Niki, *The Flavour Thesaurus*, Bloomsbury Publishing, 2010.

Shepherd, Gordon M, *Neuroenology: How the Brain Creates the Taste of Wine*, Columbia University Press, 2016.

Simmat, Benoist and Casanave, Daniel, *Wine: A Graphic History*, SelfMadeHero, 2020.

Simonit, Marco, *Simonit & Sirch's Spurred Cordon Methodology*, Edizioni L'Informatore Agrario, 2022.
—, *Simonit & Sirch's Guyot Methodology*, Edizioni L'Informatore Agrario, 2019.

Smith, Barry C (ed.), *Questions of Taste: The Philosophy of Wine*, Signal Books, 2007.

Smith, Clark, *Postmodern Winemaking: Rethinking the Modern Science of an Ancient Craft*, University of California Press, 2013.

Sommers, Brian J, *The Geography of Wine: How Landscapes, Cultures, Terroir and the Weather Make a Good Drop*, Plume, 2008.

Steiner, Rudolf, *Agriculture Course: The Birth of the Biodynamic Method*, Rudolf Steiner Press, 2004.

Szabo, John, *Volcanic Wines: Salt, Grit and Power*, Jacqui Small, 2016.

Tattersall, Ian and DeSalle, Robert, *A Natural History of Wine*, Yale University Press, 2015.

Unwin, Tim, *Wine and the Vine: An Historical Geography of Viticulture and the Wine Trade*, Routledge, 1991.

Virgil, *The Georgics*, Penguin Classics, 2010.

Wallace, Benjamin, *The Billionaire's Vinegar. The Mystery of the World's Most Expensive Bottle of Wine*, Crown, 2009.

Wilson, James E, *Terroir: The Role of Geology, Climate, and Culture in the Making of French Wines*, University of California Press, 1999.

Wohlleben, Peter, *The Hidden Life of Trees*, William Collins, 2017.

Woolf, Simon J, *Amber Revolution: How the World Learned to Love Orange Wine*, Interlink Books, 2018.

Selected articles and papers

Allaby, Robin G, "Two domestications for grapes: Glacial cycles and wild adaptations shaped grape domestication and the rise of wine", science.org, *Science*, Vol. 379, Issue 6635, 3 March 2023.

Altieri, MA and Nicholls CI, "The simplification of traditional vineyard based agroforests in northwestern Portugal: Some ecological implications", *Agroforestry Systems*, vol. 56, 2002.

Atkinson, John, "Terroir and the Côte de Nuits", *Journal of Wine Research*, vol. 22, 2011.

Bokulich, Nicholas; Mills, David; et al, "Microbial biogeography of wine grapes is conditioned by cultivar, vintage, and climate", *Proceedings of the National Academy of Sciences*, vol. 111, no. 1, November 2013.

Boulay, Thibaut, "Wine appreciation in ancient Greece", in John Wilkins and Robin Nadeau (ed.), *A Companion to Food in the Ancient World*, Wiley Blackwell, 2015.
—, "Tastes of wine: Sensorial wine analysis in ancient Greece", in Kelli C Rudolph (ed.), *Taste and the Ancient Senses*, Routledge, 2017.

Boursiquot, Jean-Michel; et al, "Parentage of Merlot and related winegrape cultivars of southwestern France: Discovery of the missing link", *Australian Journal of Grape and Wine Research*, 15(2), June 2009.

Dong, Yang; et al, "Dual domestications and origin of traits in grapevine evolution", science.org/doi/10.1126/science.add8655

Ferreira, Vicente, "The chemical foundations of wine aroma: A role game aiming at wine quality, personality and varietal expression", *Proceedings: 13th Australian Wine Industry Technical Conference*, January 2007.

Fischetti, Mark and Franchi, Francesco, "Wine's true origins", *Scientific American*, Vol. 329, No. 3, October 2023, p. 38.

Gilberta, Jack A; Van der Leliec, Daniel and Zarraonaindia, Iratxe, "Microbial terroir for wine grapes", *Proceedings of the National Academy of Sciences*, no. 111, December 2013.

Grassi, Frabrizzio; et al, "Phylogeographical structure and conservation genetics of wild grapevine", *Conservation Genetics*, 2006.

Hellman, Edward W, "Grapevine structure and function", *Oregon Viticulture*, 2003.

Jones, Gregory; et al, "Spatial analysis of climate in wine grape growing regions in the western United States", *American Journal of Enology and Viticulture*, 61(3), January 2010.

Karbowiak, Thomas; et al, "Wine aging: A bottleneck story", *Nature*, 2019.

Lacombe, Thierry; et al, "Palaeogenomic insights into the origins of French grapevine diversity", *Nature Plants*, 2019.

Monroe, James S, and Wicander, Reed, "The rock cycle", *Historical Geology: Evolution of Earth and Life Through Time*, Brooks Cole, 2014.

Morrison-Whittle, Peter, and Goddard, Matthew, "From vineyard to winery: A source map of microbial diversity driving wine fermentation", *Environmental Microbiology*, 20(1), 2018.

Parr, Wendy; Maltman, Alex J; Easton, Sally and Balester, Jordi, "Minerality in wines: Towards the reality behind the myths", *Beverages*, 4(4), 77, 2018.

Petronilho, Sílvia; et al, "Revealing the usefulness of aroma networks to explain wine aroma properties: A case study of Portuguese wines", *Molecules*, vol. 25, January 2020.

Raimondi, Stefano; Tumino, Giorgio; Ruffa, Paola; Boccacci, Paolo; Gambino, Giorgio and Schneider, Anna, "DNA-based genealogy reconstruction of Nebbiolo, Barbera and other ancient grapevine cultivars from Northwestern Italy", *Scientific Reports*, vol. 10, 2020.

Ruddiman, WF; He, Feng; Vavrus, SJ and Kutzbach, John, "The early anthropogenic hypothesis: A review", *Quaternary Science Reviews*, July 2020.

Shapin, Steve, "The tastes of wine: Towards a cultural history", *Rivista di Estetica*, 51: Wineworld – New Essays on Wine, Taste, Philosophy and Aesthetics, 2012.

Snyder, Scott and Hellman, Edward W, "Grapevine structure and function", *Oregon Viticulture*, 2003.

Spence, Charles and Wang, Qian (Janice), "Assessing the impact of closure type on wine ratings and mood", *Beverages*, 3(4), 52, 2017.

Starkenman, Christian; et al, "Role of social wasps in *Saccharomyces cerevisiae* ecology and evolution", *Proceedings of the National Academy of Sciences*, no. 109, August 2012.

Tandonnet, Jean-Pascal; et al, "Genetic architecture of aerial and root traits in field-grown grafted grapevines is largely independent", *Theoretical and Applied Genetics*, vol. 131, 2018.

Tandonnet, Jean-Pascal; et al, "Sciongenotype controls biomass allocation and root development in grafted grapevine", *Australian Journal of Grape and Wine Research*, May 2010.

Tomasi, Diego, "Influence of blackberry plants on the aroma profile of *Vitis vinifera* L. cv. Pinot Noir", *South African Journal of Enology and Viticulture*, 2017.

Tonietto, Jorge and Carbonneau, Alain, "A multicriteria climatic classification system for grape-growing regions worldwide", *Agricultural and Forest Meteorology*, vol. 124, 1-2, July 2004.

Valcárcel-Muñoz, Manuel J; Guerrero-Chanivet, María; Rodríguez-Dodero, María del Carmen; García-Moreno, María de Valme and Guillén-Sánchez, Dominico A, "Analytical and chemometric characterization of Fino and Amontillado Sherries during aging in *criaderas y solera* system, *Molecules*, January 2022.

Van Leeuwen, Cornelis; Roby, Jean-Philippe and Ollat, Nathalie, "Viticulture in a changing climate: Solutions exist", *IVES Technical Reviews, Vine & Wine*, October 2019.

Van Leeuwen, Cornelis; Roby, Jean-Philippe and de Rességuier, Laure, "Soil-related factors: A review", *OENO One*, 52(2), June 2018.

Wan, Yizhen; et al, "A phylogenetic analysis of the grape genus (Vitis L.) reveals broad reticulation and concurrent diversification during neogene and quaternary climate change", *BMC Evolutionary Biology*, 2013.

Wittendal, Frank, "Great Burgundy wines: A principal components analysis of "La Côte" vineyards", 2004.

Online

Amorim, *Sustainability report 2021*: amorimcork.com/xms/files/2_EN_-_Relatorio_Sustentabilidade.pdf

Australian Wine Research Institute (AWRI): awri.com.au

Brendon, Richard and Robinson, Jancis, *The Wine Glass*: richardbrendon.com/products/the-wine-glass

Capone, Dimitra, "Managing the eucalyptus character in Shiraz", awri.com.au/wp-content/uploads/2014/06/dimi-capone.pdf

Charest, Remy, "The science behind decanting wine", *Seven Fifty Daily*, September 2018.

Gaat-lab pm: mowse.blogspot.com/2018/05/the-mt-etna-viticultural-environment.html

Goode, Jamie: wineanorak.com/2023/03/02/big-news-new-genetic-evidence-shows-that-the-grapevine-was-domesticated-in-two-locations-and-3000-years-earlier-than-previously-thought

Guildsomm: guildsomm.com

IWSR: theiwsr.com

Jones, Gregory: climateofwine.com

Littler, Mark: marklittler.com/how-many-bottles-in-a-whisky-cask

McLeod, Murdick M and Williams, Roger, "Grape phylloxera", *Ohio State University Extension Fact Sheet:* teara.govt.nz/mi/diagram/18318/phylloxera-aphid-life-cycle

National Alcohol Beverage Control Association, *Control State Directory and Info,* 2022.

Oxford Geology Group: ogg.rocks/rocks

Robinson, Jancis: jancisrobinson.com

Spinner, Lauren: winesgeorgia.com/wp-content/uploads/2021/07/Winemaking-Process-Georgian-Qvevri-White.png

Stevens, Doug: perrybrissette.medium.com/in-a-warming-world-winemakers-search-for-cooler-ground-b9714627adcd

Riedel, *The Wine Glass Guide:* fliphtml5.com/eqghh/lvqc

UC Davis: ucdavis.edu

University of California, "Wine grapevine structure, cluster and berry size and shape", *Agricultural and Natural Resources, Wine Grape Varieties California:* ucanr.edu/sites/intvit/files/24344.pdf

Vine to Wine Circle: vinetowinecircle.com/en/history/the-american-plagues

Wine Folly: media.winefolly.com/parts-of-a-grapevine-training-methods.jpg#large

Wine Intelligence, "Which wine label is a wine?", Wine Intelligence Australia Wine Label Categories, 2020.

The Wine Scholar Guild: winescholarguild.org

Films

Mondovino, Jonathan Nossiter, 2003.

Sideways, Alexander Payne, 2004.

Sour Grapes, Jerry Rothwell, 2016.

Magazines

Decanter

Noble Rot

Wine & Spirits

Wine Spectator

The World of Fine Wine

Sources available in French and other languages

Books

Anon, *Dictionnaire général de la cuisine française ancienne et moderne* ("General Dictionary of Ancient and Modern French Cuisine"), Plon, 1853.

Argod-Dutard, Françoise; Charvet, Pascal and Lavaud, Sandrine, *Voyage aux pays du vin. Histoire, anthologic, dictionnaire* ("Voyage to the Land of Wine: History, Anthology, Dictionary"), Robert Laffont, 2007.

Association Française pour l'Étude du Sol (AFES), *Référentiel pédologique* ("Pedological Reference"), Quae, 2008.

Barbe, Noël and Bert, Jean-François, *Penser le concret. André Leroi-Gourhan, André-Georges Haudricourt, Charles Parain* ("Think Concretely: André Leroi-Gourhan, André-Georges Haudricourt, Charles Parain"), Créaphis, 2011.

Battle, Karimi; Chemidlin-Prévost Bouré, Nicolas; Dequiedt, Samuel; Terrat, Sébastien and Ranjard, Lionel, *Atlas français des bactéries du sol* ("French Atlas of Soil Bacteria"), Biotope/MNHN, 2018.

Beaumard, Éric, *Les Vins de ma vie* ("The Wines of My Life"), La Martinière, 2021.

Belcourt, Olivier and Salze, David, *Modules Roches métamorphiques* ("Metamorphic Rocks Modules"), Mine Alès, 2016.

Bérillon, Lilian and Gasparotto, Laure, *Le jour où il n'y aura plus de vin* ("The Day When There Is No More Wine"), Grasset, 2018.

Bernardo, Enrico, *Savoir goûter le vin* ("How to Taste Wine"), Plon, 2005.

—, *Savoir marier le vin* ("How to Match Wine"), Plon, 2011.

Bertin, Hélène and Chevalier, César, *Jacques Néauport, le dilettante* ("Jacques Néauport, the Dilettante"), Le Rouge & le Blanc, 2022.

Bisson, Jean, *Vignes et raisins en France. Diversité et utilisation* ("Vines and Grapes in France: Diversity and Use"), Féret, 2001.

—, *Classification des vignes françaises* ("Classification of French Wines"), Féret, 2009.

Bouché, Marcel B, *Des vers de terre et des hommes. Découvrir nos écosystèmes fonctionnant à l'énergie solaire* ("Earthworms and Men: Discover How Our Ecosystems Run on Solar Energy"), Actes Sud, 2014.

Bouffard, Michelle; Cukierman, Jérémy and Quénol, Hervé, *Quel vin pour demain? Le vin face aux défis climatiques* ("What Wine for Tomorrow? Wine Facing Climate Challenges"), Dunod, 2021.

Boulay, Thibaut, *Les Terroirs sancerrois. Un héritage géologique, culturel et immatériel* ("Sancerre Terroirs: A Geological, Cultural and Intangible Heritage"), Loubatières, 2020.

Bouneau, Christophe and Figeac, Michel, *Le Verre et le vin de la cave à la table du XVIIe siècle à nos jours* ("Glass and Wine from the Cellar to the Table from the 17th Century to Today"), Maison des Sciences de l'Homme d'Aquitaine, 2007.

Bourguignon, Alain, *Carte gastronomique de la France* ("Gastronomic Map of France"), E Girard, 1929.

Bourguignon, Claude and Lydia, *Manifeste pour une agriculture durable* ("Manifesto for a Lasting Agriculture"), Actes Sud, 2017.

—, *Le Sol, la terre et les champs. Pour retrouver une agriculture saine* ("The Soil, the Earth and the Fields: Rediscovering Healthy Agriculture"), Sang Terre, 2022.

Bourguignon, Philippe, *L'Accord parfait des vins et des mets* ("The Perfect Pairing of Wine and Food"), Éditions du Chêne, 2001.

—, *L'Accord parfait* ("The Perfect Pairing"), Hachette E/P/A, 2012.

Bourguignon, Philippe and Serroy, Jean, *Sommelier. À mots choisis* ("Sommelier: In Chosen Words"), Glénat Livres, 2018.

Brouard, Emmanuel, *La Loire et ses vins. Deux mille ans d'histoire(s) et de commerce* ("The Loire and Its Wines: Two Thousand Years of History and Commerce"), Flammarion, 2021.

Bucella, Fabrizzio, *Pourquoi boit-on du vin? Une enquête insolite et palpitante du Pr. Fabrizio Bucella* ("Why Do We Drink Wine? An Unusual and Thrilling Inquiry by Professor Fabrizio Bucella"), Dunod, 2021.

Burgat, Florence, *Qu'est-ce qu'une plante? Essai sur la vie végétale* ("What Is a Plant? Essay on Vegetal Life"), Seuil, 2020.

Cadet de Gassicourt, Charles Louis, *Cours gastronomique, ou Les Dîners de Manant-ville. Ouvrage anecdotique, philosophique et littéraire* ("Gastronomic Course, or the Dinners of Manantville: An Anecdotal, Philosophical and Literary Work"), 1809.

Campy, Michel, *Terroirs viticoles du Jura. Géologie et paysage* ("Viticultural Terroirs of the Jura: Geology and Landscape"), Mêta Jura, 2017.

Capatti, Alberto (dir.), *Luigi Veronelli. Camminare la terra* ("Luigi Veronelli: Walk the Earth"), Giunti Editore, 2015.

Carbonneau, Alain and Escudier, Jean-Louis, *De l'oenologie à la viticulture* ("From Oenology to Viticulture"), Quae, 2017.

Carbonneau, Alain; Torregrosa, Laurent; et al, *Traité de la vigne. Physiologie, terroir, culture* ("Treatise on the Vine: Physiology, Terroir, Culture"), Dunod, 2020.

Casamayor, Pierre, *L'École des alliances. Les Vins et les mets* ("The School of Alliances: Wines and Food"), Hachette Pratique, 2000.

Casamayor, Pierre and Limousin, Éric, *Les Vignobles des chemins de Compostelle* ("The Vineyards of the Roads to Compostella"), Hachette Pratique, 2003.

Catalogue de l'Ecole des Vignes de la Pépinière du Luxembourg ("Catalogue of the Luxembourg Nursery School of Vines"), 1848.

Centelles, Ferran, *¿Qué vino con este pato?* ("Which Wine with This Duck?"), Planeta Gastro, 2016.

Charnay, Pierre, *La Dégustation et ses disciples. La fiche de dégustation* ("Tasting and Its Disciples: The Tasting Sheet"), Buguet-Comptour, 1967.

Chauvet, Jules, *Études scientifiques et autres communications* ("Scientific Studies and Other Communications"), BBD Éditions, 2021.

Chauvet, Jules and Néauport, Jacques (ed.), *Jules Chauvet ou le talent du vin. Communications scientifiques* ("Jules Chauvet or the Talent of Wine: Scientific Communications"), Jean-Paul Rocher Éditeur, 1997.

Class, Nicolas, *Goethe et la méthode de la science* ("Goethe and the Scientific Method"), Astérion, 2005.

Cornot, Danielle; Pouzenc, Michaël and Strehaiano, Pierre (dir.), *Les Arts et les Métiers de la vigne et du vin. Révolution des savoirs et des savoir-faire* ("The Arts and Crafts of the Vine and Wine. A Revolution in Knowledge and Know-How"), Presses Universitaires du Midi, 2016.

Coutier, Martine, *Le Dictionnaire de la langue du vin* ("Dictionary of the Language of Wine"), CNRS, 2007.

Crespy, André, *Manuel pratique de taille de la vigne* ("Practical Manual of Vine-Pruning"), Oenoplurimedia, 2006.

Daniel, Lucien, *La Question phylloxérique, le greffage et la crise viticole* ("The Phylloxera Question, Grafting and the Viticultural Crisis"), BnF, 1908.

Daraki, Maria, *Dionysos et la déesse Terre* ("Dionysus and the Earth Goddess"), Flammarion, 1994.

Darricau, Léa and Yves, *La Vigne et ses plantes compagnes. Histoire et avenir d'un compagnonnage végétal ("The Vine and Its Companion Plants: The History and Future of Companion Planting")*, Éditions du Rouergue, 2019.

Descola, Philippe (dir.), *Les Natures en question. Colloque de rentrée du Collège de France ("The Natures in Question: Back-to-School Conference at the Collège de France")*, Odile Jacob, 2018.

Deyrieux, André, *À la rencontre des cépages modestes et oubliés. L'autre goût des vins ("Meeting Modest and Forgotten Grape Varieties: The Other Taste of Wines")*, Dunod, 2018.

Dion, Roger, *Le Val de Loire. Étude de géographie régionale ("The Loire Valley: Study of Regional Geography")*, Arrault et Cie, 1934.
—, *Le Paysage et la Vigne. Essais de géographie historique ("The Landscape and the Vine: Essays on Historical Geography")*, Bibliothèque historique Payot, 1990.
—, *Histoire de la vigne et du vin en France; des origines au XIXe siècle ("History of Wine and the Vine in France from the Beginning to the 19th Century")*, CNRS, 2010.

Doré, Claire and Varoquaux, Fabrice (coord.), *Histoire et amélioration de cinquante plantes cultivées ("History and Improvement of 50 Cultivated Plants")*, Quae GIE, 2006.

Dubrion, Roger-Paul, *Les Routes du vin en France au cours des siècles ("Wine Routes in France Over the Centuries")*, Campagne & Compagnie, 2011.

Ducerf, Gérard, *L'Encyclopédie des plantes bio-indicatrices, alimentaires et médicinales. Guide de diagnostic des sols ("Encyclopedia of Bio-indicator, Food and Medicinal Plants. Diagnostic Guide to Soils")*, Éditions Promonature, 2014.

Dumay, Raymond, *Le Guide du vin ("The Wine Guide")*, Le Livre de Poche, 1985.

École de Beaujeu, *Une agriculture du vivant. L'héritage de l'École de Beaujeu ("An Agriculture of the Living: The Heritage of the School of Beaujeu")*, Éditions du Fraysse & CEREA, 2006.

Enjalbert, Henri, *Un vignoble de qualité en Languedoc. Mas de Daumas Gassac ("A Quality Vineyard in Languedoc: Mas de Daumas Gassac")*, Imprimerie Chalaguier, 1985.
—, *Histoire de la vigne et du vin. L'avènement de la qualité ("History of Wine and the Vine: The Advent of Quality")*, Bordas, 1975.

Escudier, Jean-Louis, *Les Femmes et la Vigne. Une histoire économique et sociale (1850–2010) ("Women and the Vine: An Economic and Social History, 1850–2010")*, Presses Universitaires du Midi, 2016.

Faure-Brac, Philippe, *Saveurs complices ("Accompanying Flavours")*, E/P/A, 2002.
—, *Accords vins et mets ("Matching Wine and Food")*, E/P/A, 2020.

Fernandez, Jean-Luc, *La Critique vinicole en France. Pouvoir de prescription et construction de la confiance ("Wine Criticism in France: Power of Prescription and Building Trust")*, L'Harmattan, 2004.

Figeac-Monthus, Marguerite and Lachaud-Martin, Stéphanie (dir.), *Ville & Vin. En France et en Europe du XVe siècle à nos jours ("Town and Wine: France and Europe from the 15th Century to Today")*, La Geste, 2021.

Florin, Jean-Michel, *Viticulture biodynamic. Nouvelles voies pour régénérer la culture de la vigne ("Organic Viticulture: New Ways to Regenerate Wine-Growing")*, Mouvement de l'Agriculture Biodynamique, Section d'Agriculture au Goetheanum, 2018.

Fottorino, Alessandra and Pernot-Burlet, Céline, *In Vino Femina. Les tribulations d'une femme dans le monde du vin ("A Woman in Wine: The Tribulations of a Woman in the World of Wine")*, Hachette Pratique, 2022.

Foulonneau, Christian, *La Vinification ("Vinification")*, Dunod, 2019.

France, Benoît, *Le Grand Atlas des vignobles de France ("Grand Atlas of the Vineyards of France")*, Solar, 2008.

Franck, Alain, *La Méthode Franck. Pour réussir à coup sûr vos accords plats-vins ("The Franck Method: Making a Success of Your Food and Wine Matches")*, Le Muscadier, 2012.

Fumey, Gilles and Etchevarria, Olivier, *Atlas mondial des cuisines et gastronomies ("World Atlas of Cuisines and Gastronomies")*, Autrement, 2009.

Galet, Pierre, *Précis d'ampélographie pratique ("Summary of Practical Ampelography")*, Pierre Galet, 2000.
—, *Précis de pathologie viticole ("Summary of Viticultural Pathology")*, Pierre Galet, 1999.
—, *Précis de viticulture ("Summary of Viticulture")*, Pierre Galet, 2000.
—, *Dictionnaire encyclopédique des cépages et de leurs synonymes ("Encyclopedic Dictionary of Grape Varieties and Their Synonyms")*, Libre & Solidaire, 2015.

Garrier, Gilbert, *Histoire sociale et culturelle du vin ("Social and Cultural History of Wine")*, Larousse, 1998.

Godart, Fleur and Saint-Lô, Justine, *Pur jus. Cultivons l'avenir dans les vignes ("Pure Juice: Let's Cultivate the Future in the Vineyards")*, MARAbulles, 2016.
—, *Pur jus vinification ("Pure Juice Winemaking")*, MARAbulles, 2019.

Hallé, Francis, *Architectures de plantes ("Architecture of Plants")*, JPC, 2004.

Haudricourt, André-Georges and Hédin, Louis, *L'Homme et les plantes cultivées ("Man and Cultivated Plants")*, NRF Gallimard, 1943.

Henry, Albert, *La Bataille des vins. Édition, avec introduction, notes, glossaire et tables, Bulletin de la Classe des lettres et des sciences morales et politiques ("The Battle of Wines")*, Vol. 2, No. 1, 1991.

Hervier, Denis, *Lettres de goût. L'abécédaire de Jacques Puisais ("The ABC of Jacques Puisais")*, Féret, 2009.

Hinnewinkel, Jean-Claude (dir.), *La Gouvernance des terroirs du vin ("The Governance of Wine Terroirs")*, Féret, 2010.
—, *Les Terroirs viticoles. Origines et devenirs ("Wine Terroirs: Origins and Futures")*, Féret, 2004.

ICOMOS, *Étude thématique: Les Paysage culturels viticoles dans le cadre de la Convention du Patrimoine mondial de l'Unesco ("Cultural Landscapes in the Framework of the UNESCO World Heritage Convention")*, July 2005.

INRAE, *Atlas français des bactéries du sol ("French Atlas of Soil Bacteria")*, INRAE, 2018.

Jacquemont, Guy and Guicheteau, Gérard, *Le Grand Livre des vins de Loire ("The Big Book of Loire Wines")*, Le Chêne, 1998.

Jacquet, Olivier, *Le goût des vins d'origine. Genèse, construction et triomphe des AOC au XXe siècle ("The Taste of Original Wines: Genesis, Construction and Triumph of AOCs in the 20th Century")*, Presses Universitaires de Dijon, 2024.

Jullien, André, *Topographie de tous les vignobles connus ("Topography of All Known Vineyards")*, L Colas et Mme Huzard, 1816.
—, *Manuel du sommelier, ou Instruction pratique sur la manière de soigner les vins ("Sommelier Manual, or Practical Instruction on the Way of Caring for Wines")*, L Colas et Mme Huzard, 1822.

Lachaud, Stéphanie, *Le Sauternais moderne. Histoire de la vigne, du vin et des vignerons des années 1650 à la fin du XVIIIe siècle ("The Modern Sauternais: History of the Vine, the Wine and the Vignerons from the 1650s to the end of the 18th Century")*, Fédération Historique du Sud-Ouest, 2012.

Lachiver, Marcel, *Vins, vignes et vignerons. Histoire du vignoble français ("Wines, Vines and Winegrowers. History of the French Vineyard")*, Fayard, 1997.

Lagorce, Stéphane, *Le Grand Précis des vins au naturel. Du biologique au sans sulfites ajoutés ("Summary of Natural Wines: From Organic to No Added Sulphites")*, Homo Habilis, 2021.

Larrère, Catherine & Raphaël, *Du bon usage de la nature, pour une philosophie de l'environnement ("The Good Use of Nature, for a Philosophy of the Environment")*, Flammarion, 2009.
—, *Penser et agir avec la nature. Une enquête philosophique ("Think and Act with Nature: A Philosophical Enquiry")*, La Découverte, 2018.

Lecoutre, Matthieu, *Le Goût de l'ivresse. Une histoire de la boisson en France ("The Taste of Drunkenness: A History of Drinking in France")*, Belin, 2017.
—, *Atlas historique du vin en France. De l'Antiquité à nos jours ("Historical Atlas of French Wine: From Antiquity to Today")*, Autrement, 2019.

Lefèvre, Ségolène, *Les Femmes et l'Amour du vin ("Women and the Love of Wine")*, Féret, 2009.

Léglise, Max, *Les méthodes biologiques appliquées à la vinification et à l'oenologie, Vol. 1: Vinifications et fermentations ("Organic Methods Applied to Vinification and Oenology, Vol. 1: Vinifications and Fermentations")*, Le Courrier du Livre, 2003.
—, *Les Méthodes biologiques appliquées à la vinification et à l'oenologie, Vol. 2: Conservation, traitements, embouteillage, champagnisation artisanale ("Organic Methods Applied to Vinification and Oenology, Vol.2: Conservation, Treatments, Bottling, Artisan Champanisation")* Le Courrier du Livre, 2002.

Lemasson, Jean-Pierre and Csergo, Julie, *Voyages en gastronomies. L'invention des capitales et des régions gourmandes ("Gastronomic Travels: The Invention of Capitals and Gourmand Regions")*, Autrement, 2008.

Lenoire, B A, *Traité de la culture de la vigne et de sa vinification ("Treatise on Vine Cultivation and Winemaking")*, Wentworth Press, 2018.

Levadoux, Louis, *La Vigne et sa culture ("The Vine and Its Culture")*, Presses Universitaires de France, "Que sais-je?" collection, 1966.

Liger-Belair, Gérard and Rochard, Joël, *Les Vins effervescents. Du terroir à la bulle ("Sparkling Wines: From Terroir to Bubble")*, Dunod, 2008.

Malard, Alain, *Vignes, vins et permaculture. Prendre soin de la Terre, prendre soin des humains, partager équitablement les ressources ("Vines, Wines and Permaculture: Taking Care of the Earth, Taking Care of Humans, Sharing Resources Equitably")*, France Agricole, 2021.

Maltone, Carmela and Santa-Cruz, Maylis (dir.), *Le Vin. Quand les femmes s'en mêlent ("Wine: When Women Get Involved")*, Presses Universitaires de Bordeaux, 2019.

Michot, Alexandra, *L'Esprit Chapel ("The Chapel Spirit")*, Éditions de l'Épure, 2022.

Minard, Charles, *Carte figurative et approximative des tonnages des vins et spiritueux qui ont circulé en 1857 sur les voies d'eau et de fer de l'Empire français ("Figurative and Approximate Map of the Tonnages of Wines and Spirits that Circulated in 1857 on the Water and Rail Routes of the French Empire")*, 1860.

Monnier, Jean-Michel, *Le Vin au fil des saisons. Une année dans le costume d'un oenologue ("Wine Through the Seasons: A Year in the Costume of an Oenologue")*, Ellipses, 2022.

Morain, Éric, *Plaidoyer pour le vin naturel ("Plea for Natural Wine")*, Nouriturfu, 2019.
—, *Le Vin au naturel. La viticulture au plus près du terroir ("Natural Wine: The Viticulture Closest to the Earth")*, Sang de la Terre, 2020.

Morlat, René, *Traité de viticulture de terroir. Comprendre et cultiver la vigne pour produire un vin de terroir ("Treatise on Terroir Viticulture: Understanding and Cultivating Vines to Produce a Terroir Wine")*, Lavoisier, 2012.

Navarre, Colette and Belly, Patrice, *L'Oenologie ("Oenology")*, Tec & Doc Lavoisier, 2017.

Néauport, Jacques, *Réflexions d'un amateur de vins ("Reflections of a Wine-Lover")*, Jean-Paul Rocher, 1994.
—, *Les Tribulations d'un amateur de vins ("The Tribulations of a Wine-Lover")*, La Presqu'île, 1999.

—, *Petit traité de dégustation* ("A Little Treatise on Tasting"), L'Or des Fous Éditeur, 2010.

Nossiter, Jonathan, *Le Goût et le pouvoir* ("The Taste and the Power"), Grasset, 2007.

Nourrisson, Didier, *Crus et cuites. Histoire du buveur* ("Raw and Cooked: A History of the Drinker"), Perrin, 2013.
—, *Une histoire du vin* ("A History of Wine"), Perrin, 2017.

Odart, Alexandre-Pierre, *Ampélographie ou Traité des cépages les plus estimés dans tous les vignobles de quelque renom* ("Ampelography or a Treatise on the Most Esteemed Grape Varieties in All Renowned Vineyards"), 1845.

Panaitescu, Corina and Fosalau, Liliana (dir.), *Vigne, vin et ordres monastiques en Europe. Une longue histoire* ("Wine, the Vine and Monastic Orders in Europe: A Long History"), UNESCO Chair of Culture and Traditions of Wine, 2013.

Pasteur, Louis, *Études sur le vin: ses maladies, causes qui les provoquent, procédés nouveaux pour le conserver et pour le vieillir* ("Studies on Wine: Its Sicknesses, Their Causes, New Procedures for Keeping and Ageing It"), 1866.

Pérard, Jocelyne and Jacquet, Olivier (dir.), *Vin et gastronomie: regards croisés* ("Wine and Gastronomy: Combined Perspectives"), Éditions Universitaires de Dijon, 2019.

Peynaud, Émile, *Le Vin et les jours* ("Wine and Days"), Dunod, 2012.

Pfister, Richard, *Les Parfums du vin. Sentir et comprendre le vin* ("The Perfumes of Wine: Feeling and Understanding Wine"), Delachaux et Niestlé, 2013.

Pineau, Christelle, *La Corne de vache et le Microscope. Le vin "nature", entre sciences, croyances et radicalités* ("The Cow's Horn and the Microscope: 'Natural' Wine, Between Science, Beliefs and Radicalities"), La Découverte, 2019.

Pitte, Jean-Robert, *Le Vin et le Divin* ("Wine and the Divine"), Fayard, 2004.
—, *Le Désir du vin. À la conquête du monde* ("The Desire for Wine: Conquering the World"), Fayard, 2009.
– **(dir.)**, *Le Bon Vin. Entre terroir, savoir-faire et savoir-boire. Actualités de la pensée de Roger Dion* ("Good Wine: Between Terroir, Knowledge and How to Drink. Thoughts of Roger Dion"), CNRS, 2010.
—, *La Bouteille de vin. Histoire d'une révolution* ("The Wine Bottle: History of a Revolution"), Tallandier, 2021.
– **(dir.)**, *Les Accords mets-vins. Un art français* ("Pairing Food and Wine: A French Art"), CNRS, 2017.

Ponge, Francis, *Le Parti pris des choses* ("The Nature of Things"), NRF Gallimard, 1942.

Pouget, Roger, *Histoire de la lutte contre le phylloxera de la vigne en France* ("History of the Struggle Against Phylloxera and the Vine in France"), INRA, 1990.

Puisais, Jacques, *Le vin se met à table. 200 recettes autour de 14 familles de vins* ("Wine Comes to the Table: 200 Recipes around 14 Families of Wine"), Albin Michel, 2004.
—, *La France du vin* ("The France of Wine"), Éditions du Patrimoine Centre des Monuments Nationaux, 1996.
—, *Le Goût juste des vins et des plats* ("The Right Taste of Wines and Dishes"), Flammarion, 2013.

Puisais, Jacques and Didier, Michel, *Empreintes de vin* ("Wine Prints"), Délicéo, 2009.

Pulliat, Victor, *Mille variétés de vignes. Description et synonymies* ("A Thousand Varieties of Vine: Descriptions and Synonyms"), Hachette Livre et BnF, 2016.

Rambourg, Patrick, *Histoire de la cuisine et de la gastronomie françaises* ("History of French Cooking and Gastronomy"), Perrin, "Tempus" collection, 2010.

Reynier, Alain, *Manuel de viticulture. Guide technique du viticulteur* ("Manual of Viticulture: Technical Guide to Viticulture"), Tec & Doc Lavoisier, 2016.

Ribéreau-Gayon, Jean and Genevois, Louis, *Le Vin* ("Wine"), Hermann & Cie, 1947.

Ribéreau-Gayon, Pascal, *L'Histoire de l'œnologie à Bordeaux. De Louis Pasteur à nos jours* ("The History of Oenology in Bordeaux: From Louis Pasteur to Today"), Dunod, 2011.

Roca Fontané, Josep, *A l'avantguarda del vi* ("At the Vanguard of Wine"), Vibop, 2018.

Roupnel, Gaston, *La Bourgogne. Types et coutumes* ("Burgundy: Types and Practices"), Horizons de France, 1936.

Rowley, Anthony, *Les Français à table. Atlas historique de la gastronomie française* ("The French at Table: Historical Atlas of French Gastronomy"), Hachette, 1997.

Royer, Claude, *Les Vignerons. Usages et mentalités des pays de vignobles* ("Wine-Growers: Practices and Attitudes in the Wine Country"), Berger-Levrault, 1980.

Rozier, François (1734-93), *Traité de viticulture* ("Viticultural Treaty") (unpublished).

Schirmer, Raphaël, *Vignes et vins. Paysages et civilisations millénaires* ("Vines and Wines: Landscapes and Ancient Civilizations"), Glénat, 2018.
—, *Civilisations du vin. Comment les vignobles ont façonné le monde et les hommes* ("Wine Civilizations: How Vineyards Shaped the World and Mankind"), Prisma, 2019.
– **(dir.)**, *Bordeaux et ses vignobles. Un modèle de civilisation* ("Bordeaux and Its Vineyards: A Model of Civilization"), Éditions Sud-Ouest, 2020.

Seguin, Gérard, *Les Sols des vignobles du Haut-Médoc. Influence sur l'alimentation en eau de la vigne et sur la maturation du raisin* ("The Soils of the Haut-Médoc Vineyards: Influence on the Water Supply of the Vine and on the Ripening of the Grape"), Faculté des Sciences de l'Université de Bordeaux, 1970.
—, *Influence des facteurs naturels sur les caractères des vins* ("Influence of Natural Factors on the Character of Wine"), Dunod, 1971.

Selosse, Marc-André, *Jamais seul. Ces microbes qui construisent les plantes, les animaux et les civilisations* ("Never Alone: The Microbes that Build Plants, Animals and Civilizations"), Actes Sud, "Babel" collection, 2017.
—, *Les Goûts et les Couleurs du monde. Une histoire naturelle des tannins, de l'écologie à la santé* ("The Tastes and Colours of the World: A Natural History of Tannins, from Ecology to Health"), Actes Sud, 2019.
—, *L'Origine du monde. Une histoire naturelle du sol à l'intention de ceux qui le piétinent* ("The Origin of the World: A Natural History of Soil for Those Who Trample It"), Actes Sud, 2021.

Senderens, Alain, *Le Vin et la Table d'Alain Senderens. Le mariage idéal des mets et des vins en 80 recettes. Vins sélectionnés par Bettane et Desseauve* ("The Wine and the Table of Alain Senderens: The Ideal Marriage of Food and Wine in 80 Recipes—Wines Selected by Bettane and Desseauve"), Flammarion, 1999.

Séralini, Gilles-Éric and Douzelet, Jérôme, *Le Goût des pesticides* ("The Taste of Pesticides"), Actes Sud, 2021.

Serres, Olivier de, *Théâtre d'agriculture et mesnage des champs* ("The Theatre of Agriculture and Field Husbandry"), Actes Sud, 2001.

Sirven, Bruno, *Le Génie de l'arbre. Visages, paysages, usages* ("The Genius of the Tree: Faces, Landscapes, Uses"), Actes Sud, 2016.

Tallet, Pierre, *L'Égypte pharaonique. Histoire, société, culture:* ("Pharaonic Egypt: History, Society, Culture"), Armand Colin, 2019.

Tchernia, André and Brun, Jean-Pierre, *Le Vin romain antique* ("Ancient Roman Wine"), Glénat Livres, 1999.

Truc, Georges, *Châteauneuf-du-Pape. Histoire géologique & naissance des terroirs* ("Châteauneuf-du-Pape: Geological History and the Birth of Terroirs"), Syndicat des Vignerons de Châteauneuf, 2022.

Vaudour, Emmanuelle, *Les Terroirs viticoles. Définitions, caractérisation et protection* ("Viticultural Terroirs: Definitions, Characterization and Protection"), Dunod, 2003.

Velasco-Graciet, Hélène and Schirmer, Raphaël, *Atlas mondial des vins* ("World Atlas of Wines"), Autrement, 2010.

Veronelli, Luigi, *Il Vino giusto* ("The Right Wine"), Rizzoli, 1971.

Viala, Pierre and Vermorel, Victor (dir.), *Ampélographie. Traité général de viticulture* ("Ampelography: General Treatise of Viticulture"), 1901.

Wolikow, Serge and Jacquet, Olivier (dir.), *Bourgogne(s) viticole(s). Enjeux et perspectives historiques d'un territoire* ("Burgundy Vineyards: Historical Issues and Perspectives of a Territory"), Éditions Universitaires de Dijon, 2018.

Yengué, Jean-Louis and Stengel, Kilien (dir.), *Le Terroir viticole. Espace et figures de qualité* ("Viticultural Terroir: Space and Quality Values"), Presses Universitaires François Rabelais, 2020.

Selected articles and papers

Albertini, Louis, "La greffe végétale des origines à nos jours" ("The Vegetal Graft from Its Origins to Today"), paper presented to l'Académie des Sciences, Inscriptions et Belles-Lettres de Toulouse at the meeting of 13 November 2014.

Antalick, Guillaume, "Les esters du vin font leur révolution au vignoble et en bouteille" ("Wine Esters Are Causing a Revolution in the Vineyard and in the Bottle"), *Revue des œnologues*, No. 158, January 2016.

Baggiolini, M, "Les stades-repères de la vigne" ("The Benchmark Stages of the Vine"), *Revue suisse de viticulture, arboriculture et horticulture*, No. 28, 1993.

Bessis, Raphaël and Hallé, Francis, "L'homme colonaire et le devenir végétal de la société contemporaine. Un dialogue entre la botanique et l'anthropologie des réseaux" ("Colonial Man and the Plant Future of Contemporary Society: A Dialogue Between Botany and Anthropology"), *Alliage*, No. 64, "Du végétal", March 2009.

Bisson Jean, "Essai de classement des cépages français en écogéogroupes phénotypiques" ("Attempt to Classify French Grape Varieties into Phenotypic Ecogeogroups"), *Journal international des sciences de la vigne et du vin*, 33, No. 3, 1999.

Bigando, Eva, "La synecdoque paysagère, une notion pour comprendre les représentations des paysages viticoles bourguignon et bordelais" ("Landscape Synecdoche, a Notion for Understanding the Representations of Burgundian and Bordeaux Wine Landscapes"), Revue géographique des Pyrénées et du Sud-Ouest. Sud-Ouest Européen, 2006.

Bobrie, François, "La narration des qualités œnologiques et sensorielles des vins embouteillés par leur étiquetage: Une analyse sémiotique des étiquettes des vins du Top 100 du *Wine Spectator* de 2008 à 2017" ("The Narration of Oenological and Sensory Qualities of Bottled Wines by their Labels: A Semiotic Analysis of Wine Labels of the *Wine Spectator*'s Top 100 from 2008 to 2017"), CNRS MSHS, 2018.

Bouin, Philippe, "Une journée... Marc Birebent" ("A Day... Marc Birebent"), *Le Rouge & le blanc*, No. 119, winter 2015-2016.

Bouin, Philippe and Tabor, Yaïr, "Une soirée avec... Gabriel Lepousez. Voyage sous le crâne d'un dégustateur" ("An Evening With... Gabriel Lepousex: A Voyage Under the Skull of a Taster"), *Le Rouge & le blanc*, No. 139, winter 2020-2021.

Boulanger-Fassier, Sylvaine, "La viticulture durable. Une démarche en faveur de la pérennisation des territoires viticoles français?" ("Sustainable Viticulture: An Approach to Sustainability in French Vineyards?"), *Géocarrefour. Revue de géographie de Lyon*, Vol. 83, No. 3, 2008.

Boulay, Thibaut, "Dionysos, les cultes bachiques et les travaux viticoles" ("Dionysos, Bacchic Cults and Viticultural Work"), *Rencontres du Clos-Vougeot 2015. Vin et civilisation. Les étapes de l'humanisation*, 2016.

—, "Le γλεῦκος dans tous ses états. Le moût, le 'vin doux', le vin nouveau et la maîtrise du processus fermentaire dans le monde égéen de l'époque classique à l'époque byzantine" ("The Must in All Its States: The Must, the 'Sweet Wine', the New Wine and the Mastery of the Fermentation Process in the Aegean World from the Classical Period to the Byzantine Era"), text of a speech of 7 December 2020 before l'Association des Études Grecques.

Boursiquot, Jean-Michel and This, Patrice, "Essai de définition du 'cépage'" ("Trying to Define 'Cépage'"), *Progrès agricole et viticole*, 116, No. 117, 1999.

Boutaud, Jean-Jacques, "Le vin et l'éveil des sens. L'expérience du goût en partage" ("Wine and the Awakening of the Senses: The Shared Taste Experience"), *Hermès, La Revue*, No. 74, 2016.

Candau, Joël, "Vin, arômes, couleurs et descripteurs sensoriels. Quel partage de la dégustation?" ("Wine, Aromas, Colours and Sensory Descriptors: How Is Tasting Shared?"), *MEI*, No. 23, "Le corps, le vin et l'image", 2005.

Carbonneau, Alain, "Diversité des architectures de vigne dans le monde: contraintes environnementales et facteurs historiques" ("Diversity of Wine Architectures Around the World: Environmental Constraints and Historical Factors"), *Food & History*, Vol. 11, No. 2, 2013.

Chabin, Jean-Pierre, "L'excellence aux limites... ou le paradoxe des vignobles septentrionaux français d'après l'exemple côte-d'orien" ("Excellence at the Limits... Or the Paradox of Northern French Vineyards Based on the Example of the Côte d'Or"), *Revue géographique de l'Est*, Vol. 44, 1–2, 2004.

Chiva, Isac (dir.), Une politique pour le patrimoine culturel rural ("A Policy for Rural Cultural Heritage"), presented to Jacques Toubon, Ministre de la Culture et de la Francophonie, 1994.

Darnay, Soazig, "Paysages viticoles: paysages ruraux? Leur évolution sous l'influence du tourisme et de leur patrimonialisation" ("Wine-Growing Landscapes: Rural Landscapes? Their Evolution Under the Influence of Tourism and their Heritagization"), *Projets de paysage*, 17, 2017.

Delay, Étienne and Chevallier, Marius, "Roger Dion, toujours vivant!" ("Roger Dion, Still Alive!"), *Cybergeo. Revue européenne de géographie*, 2015.

Desbuissons, Frédérique, "L'étiquette éloquente. Le vin dans les éphémères de la Bibliothèque nationale de France" ("The Eloquent Label: Wine in the Ephemera of the Bibliothèque Nationale de France"), *Revue de la BnF*, No. 53, 2016.

Destrac-Irvine, Agnès; Gowdy, Mark; Suter, Bruno; Goupil, Willy; Thibon, Cécile; Ollat, Nathalie; Darriet, Philippe; Parker, Amber and Van Leeuwen, Cornelis, "La diversité des cépages est une puissante ressource d'adaptation au changement climatique" ("Diversity of Cépages Is a Powerful Weapon in Adapting to Climate Change"), *Revue française d'oenologie*, No. 297, Janaury–February 2020.

Fassier-Boulanger, Sylvaine, "Les mutations de la filière viticole en France. Des vignerons de plus en plus engagés dans des pratiques durables: l'exemple alsacien" ("Changes in the Wine Industry in France: Wine-Growers Increasingly Committed to Sustainable Practices—The Alsace Example"), *Revue géographique de l'Est*, Vol. 54, 1–2, 2014.

Fedoul, Sénia, "L'oenologue et le sommelier, ambassadeur de la qualité des vins: le 'discours oenologique froid' et le 'discours oenologique chaud'" ("The Oenologist and the Sommelier, Ambassador of Wine Quality: The 'Cold Oenological Discourse' and the 'Hot Oenological Discourse'"), *Territoires du vin. Patrimoine et valorisation des territoires de la vigne et du vin*, 8, 2018.

Gallet, Pierre, and Agnel, Henri, "Première étude d'ampélographie pratique et d'ampélométrie sur les porte-greffes" ("First Study of Practical Ampelography and Ampelometry on Rootstocks"), *Annales de l'école d'agriculture de Montpellier*, 1946.

Garcia, Jean-Pierre, "Le goût du lieu: la mise en place du discours sur la nature des sols comme référence au goût des vins en Bourgogne" ("The Taste of Place: The Establishment of the Discussion on the Nature of Soils with Reference to the Taste of the Wines of Burgundy"), *Cahiers d'histoire de la vigne et du vin*, No. 11, 2011.

Garcia, Jean-Pierre; Chevrier, Sébastien; Dufraisse, Alexa; Foucher, Marion and Steinmann, Ronan, "Le vignoble gallo-romain de Gevrey-Chambertin. Au-dessus de Bergis, Côte-d'Or (Ier-IIe siècle): modes de plantation et de conduite de vignes antiques en Bourgogne" ("The Gallo-Roman Vineyard of Gevrey-Chambertin – Above Bergey, Côte d'Or (1st to 2nd Century): Methods of Planting and Managing Ancient Vines in Burgundy"), *Revue archéologique de l'Est*, No. 59–2, 2010.

Garcia, Jean-Pierre; Labbé, Thomas and Quiquerez, Amélie, "La préservation et la pérennisation des sols viticoles en Bourgogne du Moyen Âge à nos jours" ("The Preservation and Sustainability of Viticultural Soils in Burgundy from the Middle Ages to Today"), *Rencontres du Clos Vougeot 2017*.

Garcia, Jean-Pierre; et al, "La construction des climats viticoles en Bourgogne. La relation du vin au lieu au Moyen Âge" ("The Construction of Viticultural Climats in Burgundy: The Relation of Wine to Place in the Middle Ages"), *Économie de la vigne et du vin*, 12: "Vignes et vins au Moyen Âge. Pratiques sociales, économie et culture matérielle", 2014.

Garcia, Jean-Pierre; et al, "Non, les moines n'ont pas goûté la terre pour délimiter les terroirs viticoles de Bourgogne" ("No, the Monks Did not Taste the Earth in Order to Delimit the Viticultural Terroirs of Burgundy"), *Crescentis, Revue internationale d'histoire de la vigne et du vin*, No. 3, June 2020.

Garcia, Jean-Pierre and Jacquet, Olivier, "Le terroir du vin: trajectoire historique d'un objet multiforme en Bourgogne" ("Wine Terroir: Historical Trajectory of a Multiform Object in Burgundy"), in Jean-Louis Yengué and Kilien Stengel (dir.), *Le Terroir viticole. Espace et figures de qualité*, Presses Universitaires François Rabelais, 2020.

Gatteron, Jean-Marc, "David Lefebvre et la minéralité" ("David Lefebvre and Minerality"), *Le Rouge et le Blanc*, No. 100 and No. 112, spring 2014.

Hallé, Francis, "Des données récentes sur les arbres" ("Recent Data on Trees"), Académie des Sciences et Lettres de Montpellier, *Bulletin mensuel de l'Académie des Sciences et Lettres de Montpellier*, Vol. 48, 2017.

Haudricourt, André-Georges, "Domestication des animaux, culture des plantes et traitement d'autrui" ("Domestication of Animals, Culture of Plants and Treatment of Others"), *L'Homme*, Vol. 2, No. 1, 1962.

Interloire, CTV, FranceAgriMer, Région Centre, *Cartographie et caractérisation des terroirs viticoles de l'AOP touraine Azay-le-Rideau et des terroirs arboricoles fruitiers* ("Mapping and Characterization of the Wine-Growing Terroirs of the AOP Touraine Azay-le-Rideau and the Fruit-Producing Arboreal Terroirs"), 2013.

Jacquet, Olivier, "Le goût de l'origine. Développement des AOC et nouvelles normes de dégustation des vins (1947–1974)," ("The Taste of Origin: Development of AOCs and New Norms of Tasting Wine, 1947–1974"), *Crescentis. Revue internationale d'histoire de la vigne et du vin*, 2018.

Kuhnholtz-Lordat, Georges, *La Genèse des Appellations d'Origine des vins* ("The Genesis of Wine Appellations of Origin"), Oenoplurimedia, 1963.

Lacombe, Thierry; Boursiquot, Jean-Michel and Marchal, Cécile, "Analyse de la diversité et du fonctionnement du génome de la vigne" ("Analysis of the Diversity and Functioning of the Vine Genome"), *Vigne et vin. Les Dossiers d'Agropolis International*, No. 21, November 2015.

Lacombe, Thierry, "Contribution à l'étude de l'histoire évolutive de la vigne cultivée (*Vitis vinifera* L.) par l'analyse de la diversité génétique neutre et de gènes d'intérêt" ("Contribution to the Study of the Evolutionary History of Cultivated Vines [*Vitis vinifera* L.] through the Analysis of Neutral Genetic Diversity and Genes of Interest"), thesis presented at Montpellier SupAgro Centre International d'Études Supérieures en Sciences Agronomiques, 2012.

Lacoste, Jean, "La métamorphose des plantes" ("The Metamorphosis of Plants"), *Littérature*, No. 86, May 1992.

Lasnier, Jacques and Vincent, Charles, "Le phylloxera de la vigne" ("Phylloxera of the Vine"), *Grapevines – Viticulture*, November 2019.

Legras, Jean-Luc, "De la diversité à la domestication chez *Saccharomyces cerevisiae*" ("From Diversity to Domestication in *Saccharomyces cerevisiae*"), Université de Montpellier, 2018.

Lopez Calleja, Sonia, "Cépages hybrides, futurs croisés de la vigne?" ("Hybrid Cépages, Future Vine Crosses?"), *Le Rouge et le Blanc*, No. 144, 2022.

Lucand, Christophe, "Le vin, le lieu, la marque par les étiquettes du vin en Bourgogne" ("The Wine, the Place, the Brand by Wine Labels in Burgundy"), *Crescentis. Revue internationale d'histoire de la vigne et du vin*, No. 2, 2019.

Luginbühl, Yves, "Paysages viticoles" ("Viticultural Landscapes"), ICOMOS, 2005.

Marchal, Axel, "La relation entre le vin et le bois. Une histoire de goût" ("The Relation Between Wine and Wood: A History of Taste"), 17e Matinée des Oenologues de Bordeaux: "Le vin, ça envoie du bois", March 2019.

Martin, Jean-Claude, "La création de paysages viticoles. Une histoire de matériaux" ("The Creation of Viticultural Landscapes: A History of Materials"), *Revue géographique des Pyrénées et du Sud-Ouest*, Sud-Ouest Européen, 2006.

Morizot, Baptiste, "Nouvelles alliances avec la terre. Une cohabitation diplomatique avec le vivant" ("Forging New Alliances with the Land: Toward a Diplomatic Cohabitation with Living Beings"), *Tracés. Revue de sciences humaines*, 2017.

Morlat, René; Barbeau, Gérard and Asselin, Christian, "Facteurs naturels et humains des terroirs viticoles français: méthode d'étude et valorisation" ("Natural and Human Factors in French Viticultural Terroirs: Method of Study and Valorization"), *Études et recherches sur les systèmes agraires et le développement*, INRA Éditions, 2001.

Morlat, René; Salette, Jean and Asselin, Christian, "Le lien du terroir au produit. Analyse du système terroir-vigne-vin: possibilité d'application à d'autres produits" ("The Link Between Terroir and Product: Analysis of the Terroir–Vine–Wine System – Possibility of Application to Other Products"), *Sciences des aliments*, 18, 1998.

Nicolas, Alexandre, "Le meilleur de la biodynamie en 187 vins enthousiasmants" ("The Best of Biodynamism in 187 Exciting Wines"), *La Revue du vin de France*, No. 647, January 2021.

Olivesi, Stéphane, "Le sommelier: un médiateur, artisan du goût" ("The Sommelier: A Mediator, Artisan of Taste"), *Politiques de communication*, No. 5, 2015.

Ollat, Nathalie, "Changement climatique: le matériel végétal peut-il permettre de répondre aux risques accrus de sécheresse?" ("Climate Change: Can Plant Material Help Us Respond to Increased Risks of Drought?"), Colloque EUROVITI, January 2014.

Parain, Charles, "La maison vigneronne en France" ("The Wine Estate Buildings of France"), *Arts et traditions populaires*, No. 4, October-December 1955.

Raimondi, Stefano; Tumino, Giorgio; Ruffa, Paola; Boccacci, Paolo; Gambino, Giorgio; Schneider, Anna; Rochard, Joël; Clément, Jean-Rémy and Srhiyeri, Abdelhaq, "Évolution des dates de vendanges en liaison avec les changements climatiques" ("Evolution of Harvest Dates in Connection with Climate Change"), "Réchauffement climatique, quels impacts probables sur les vignobles?" conference, March 2007.

Rochard, Joël, "Classement des sites viticoles 'Patrimoine mondial Unesco'. État des lieux et perspectives" ("Ranking of 'UNESCO World Heritage' Wine Sites: Current Situation and Outlook"), Revue des oenologues, No. 167, 2018, p.52–59.

Rouvellac, Éric, "Le terroir. Essai d'une réflexion géographique à travers la viticulture" ("Terroir: An Attempt at a Geographical Reflection Through Viticulture"), Université de Limoges, 2013.

—, "Vins, vignobles et viticultures atlantiques. Quelles trajectoires contemporaines?" ("Atlantic Wines, Vineyards and Viticulture: What Contemporary Trajectories?"), Norois, Vol. 2, No. 255, 2020.

Roy, Michèle and Mainguy, Julie, "Cycle de biologique du phylloxera de la vigne (adapté de William 1938)" ("Biological Cycle of Vine Phylloxera, Adapted from William 1938"), Ravageurs galligènes de la vigne au Québec, Laboratoire de Diagnostic en Phytoprotection MAPAQ, s.d.

Schirmer, Raphaël, "Le regard des géographes français sur la vigne et le vin (fin du XIXe–XXe siècle)" ("The View of French Geographers on Wine and the Vine – End of the 19th Century to the 20th Century"), Annales de géographie, No. 614-615: "La nouvelle planète des vins", July–October 2000.

—, "Le géographe et l'expertise dans le domaine des vins" ("The Geographer and Expertise in the Field of Wine"), UNESCO Chair of Culture and Traditions of Wine, international conference, "De Jules Guyot à Robert Parker: 150 ans de construction des territoires du vin", November 2008.

Spilmont, Anne-Sophie, "Production des plants et qualité du matériel végétal" ("Production of Plants and Quality of Plant Material"), IFV, "Recherche et transfert, quelles synergies?" conference, Beaune, January 2020.

Stanziani, Alessandro, "La falsification du vin en France, 1880–1905: un cas de fraude agro-alimentaire" ("The Falsification of Wine in France, 1880–1905: A Case of Agro-Food Fraud"), Revue d'histoire moderne & contemporaine, No. 50-2, 2003.

Tallet, Pierre, "Le vin en Égypte à l'époque pharaonique" ("Wine in Egypt in the Pharaonic Age"), thesis presented to l'Université Paris 4, 1998.

Valentin, Dominique; Brache, Solène; Peyron, Dominique and Ballester, Jordi, "Vers une approche polysensorielle de la description du toucher des vins" ("Toward a Polysensory Approach to the Description of the Feel of Wines"), Revue des oenologues, No. 155, April 2015.

Van Leeuwen, Cornelis; Roby, Jean-Philippe and de Rességuier, Laure, "Le terroir. Définir, mesurer, gérer" ("Terroir: Defining, Measuring, Managing"), FAO AGRIS, 2016.

Vincent, Éric and Jacquet, Olivier, "Le Kimméridgien à Chablis. Un argument géologique pour la construction sociale d'un terroir" ("The Kimmeridgian at Chablis: A Geological Argument for the Social Construction of a Terroir"), IXe Congrès International des Terroirs Vitivinicoles, 2012.

V'Innopôle Sud-Ouest France, "Plan de déploiement des cépages résistants en Occitanie" ("Deployment Plan for Resistant Cépages in Occitanie"), Bulletin d'information de l'IFV Sud-Ouest, 2017.

Vouillamoz, José, "Domestication de la vigne à la lumière du test ADN" ("Domestication of the Vine in Light of DNA Testing"), Académie Internationale du Vin, September 2015.

Yobrégat, Olivier, "La conservation de diversité génétique de la vigne en France. Enjeux, réalisations et travaux en cours" ("The Conservation of Genetic Diversity of the Vine in France: Challenges, Achievements and Work in Progress"), La Revue des oenologues, No. 158, January 2016.

Online

Adama: adama-terroirs.fr

Belluau, M, "223: Baie: Forme": plantgrape.plantnet-project.org/media/content/OIV_223_FR.pdf

Bérillon, Lilian, and Birebent, Marc, "La Vigne au 21ème siècle. Retour vers le futur" ("The Vine in the 21st Century: Return to the Future"), Account for the conference-debate at Château Simian, February 2015.

Bertrand, Alain, "Du vin de Noé à celui que nous buvons. Évolution d'une technique" ("From Noah's Wine to the One We Drink: Evolution of a Technique"), video UT2J Canal-U, April 2013.

Boursiquot, Jean-Michel, "L'odyssée des cépages, beaucoup d'appelés... et peu d'élus" ("The Odyssey of Cépages, Many are Called... and Few Chosen"), video Agora des Savoirs, 2019.

Brouard, Joëlle, "Nouvelles générations et consommation du vin. Évolution ou révolution?" ("New Generations and Wine Consumption: Evolution or Revolution"?), "Les Vendanges du Savoir" conference at La Cité du Vin, March 2021.

Canet, Alain and Bourdarias, Marceau, "Agroforesterie. Clé de voûte de la production" ("Agroforestry: Key to Production"), video produced during the Festival des Rencontres de l'Agroécologie du Bassin Méditerranéen, organized by Arbre et Paysage 66, at Elne, May 2021.

Celhay, Franck, "Sous le design des étiquettes de vins, la variété des 'storytellings de marque'" ("Under the Design of Wine Labels, the Variety of 'Brand Storytelling'"), The Conversation, June 2017.

UNESCO Chair of Culture and Traditions of Wine: chaireunesco-vinetculture.u-bourgogne.fr

Château de Parnay: chateaudeparnay.fr/histoire/le-clos-dentre-les-murs

Csergo, Julia and Collas, Benoît, "L'invention française des 'gastronomies régionales'" ("The French Invention of 'Regional Gastronomies'"), Retronews, BnF press site, January 2022.

ENTAV-INRA: selections.entav-inra.fr/en

Fédération Nationale d'Agriculture Biologique: produire-bio.fr/filiere-viticulture-bio

FranceAgriMer: franceagrimer.fr

GIESCO: giesco.org

Gille, Martin: http://monocepage.com/flagey-echezeaux-vosne-romanee-et-vougeot

Hautevelle, Yann: youtube.com/watch?v=MgYRbwsJnpM

IFV (Institut Français de la Vigne et du Vin): vignevin.com
—: vignevin.com/publications/fiches-pratiques/elevage-des-vins-en-barriques

IFV Occitanie: vignevin-occitanie.com

INRAE (Institut National de Recherche pour l'Agriculture, l'Alimentation et l'Environnement): inrae.fr
—: svqv.colmar.hub.inrae.fr/production-scientifique/faits-marquants/un-porte-greffe-transgenique-de-vigne-developpe-pour-lutter-contre-le-gflv

Jacquet, Olivier: preo.ubourgogne.fr/territoiresduvin/docannexe/image/2269/img-4.jpg

Julliard, Sébastien, "La plupart des porte-greffes actuels sont des créations centenaires" ("Most Current Rootstocks are Century-Old Creations"), Conservatoire du Vignoble Charentais: mon-viti.com/articles/viticulture/nous-sentons-un-regain-dinteret-pour-les-porte-greffe

La Cité du Vin de Bordeaux, "Les Vendanges du savoir" ("The Harvest of Knowledge"): youtube.com/c/Laciteduvin/playlists

Louapre, David, "D'où viennent les bulles du champagne?" ("Where do Champagne Bubbles Come From"?), Science Étonnante, 2013: scienceetonnante.com/2013/12/23/dou-viennent-les-bulles-du-champagne

Masneuf-Pomarede, Isabelle, and Lucas, Patrick, "La controverse des micro-organismes de terroir" ("The Controversy over Local Microorganisms"), "Les Vendanges du savoir" conference at La Cité du Vin, November 2021.

Morel, Alain: meteo05.sepcs.fr

Motta, Annalisa: quadoalmelo.it/il-vino-e-gli-etruschi-ii-la-vite-maritata-tremila-e-piu-anni-di-viticoltura-ed-arte

Observatoire des Cépages Résistants: observatoire-cepages-resistants.fr

Oenologues de France: oenologuesdefrance.fr

Organisation Internationale de la Vigne et du Vin (OIV): oiv.int/fr

Pépinières Hebinger, "Nos types de greffes. Oméga, anglaise et F2" ("Our Grafts: Omega, English and F2"): pepiniereshebinger.fr/FR/Nos-Types-De-Greffes

Pierre Le Hong: youtube.com/user/chateaujaja/featured

Plantgrape: plantgrape.plantnet-project.org/fr

Selosse, Marc-André, "Fonctionnement biologique des sols" ("Biological Functioning of Soils"), Ver de Terre Production, 2019.

Sigales: http://sigales.fr

Sosnowski, Mundy M: plan-deperissement-vigne.fr

Taillandier, Patricia, "La vinification. Du processus naturel aux nouvelles technologies" ("Vinification: From the Natural Process to New Technologies"), "Vins, vignes et vignerons: Passages, messages et métissages" conference, organized by In Vino Varietas du Centre d'Études et de Recherche Travail, Organisation, Pouvoir (CERTOP) et le Département de Géographie de l'Université de Toulouse II–Le Mirail, April 2013.

UNESCO: whc.unesco.org/fr/list/?search=vignoble&order=country

Ver de Terre Production: Thématique viticulture: youtube.com/playlist?list=PLQNBggapGeH9ytTOlwUFKzTutovUB9kHl

Vitisphère: vitisphere.com

Yobrégat, Olivier: technioloire.com/sites/default/files/diversite_selction_materiel_vegetal.pdf

Magazines

La Revue des oenologues

La Revue du vin de France

Le Rouge et le Blanc

Vigneron

ILLUSTRATION SOURCES AND CREDITS

P.8 Mollison, Bill, and Mya Slay, Reny (2013); p.17 Wan, Yizhen, et al. (2013); p.20 Boursiquot, Jean-Michel (2019) and Grassi, Frabrizzio, et al. (2006); Dong, Yang, et al. (2023); p.24 Galet, Pierre, and Agnel, Henri (1946); p.21 OIV (2001); p.28 Bisson, Jean (1999); p.32 Garcia, Jean-Pierre, Chevrier, Sébastien, Dufraisse, Alexa, Foucher, Marion, and Steinmann, Ronan (2010); p.37 V'Innopôle Sud-Ouest France (2017) and Lopez Calleja, Sonia (2022); pp.38–9 Raimondi, Stefano, Tumino, Giorgio, Ruffa, Paola, Boccacci, Paolo, Gambino, Giorgio, and Schneider, Anna (2020); p.41 Snyder, Scott (2003); p.42 Simonit, Marco, and Giudici, Massimo (2016), Sandre, Anne; p.46 Belluau, M; p.48 the University of California; p.53 McLeod, Murdick M, and Williams, Roger, Roy, Michèle, Mainguy, Julie, and Wynne, Patricia J (2015); p.56 Julliard, Sébastien; p.59 Worldwide Vineyards and Pépinières Hebinger; p.60 Simonit, Marco, and Giudici, Massimo (2016); p.61 Sosnowski, Mundy M, Crespy, A (2006); p.63 Galet, Pierre (2000), Baillot M, and Baggiolini, M (1993); p.65 Yobrégat, Olivier; pp.68–69 Larousse mensuel illustré (1907–1920); p.71 © Hallé, Francis (2017); p72 Goethe, Johann Wolfgang von; p.80 Vine to Wine Circle; p.82–83 Motta, Annalisa; p.87 from the Implementing Sustainable Agricultural Practices panel published by the Agro LIFE project: rbaps.eu/2017/04/28/rbaps-at-agro-life-cyprus; p.90 Malard, Alain (2021), and Fédération National d'Agriculture Biologique; p.95 Nicolas, Alexandre (2021); p.99 © Arnaud, Sarah, and Irys Graphisme pour le Château de Fosse-Sèche; pp. 106–109 Carbonneau, Alain, and Escudier, Jean-Louis (2017); p. 109 Stevens, Doug; p. 111 Morel, Alain; p.114 gaat-lab pm; p.119 Le Roy Ladurie, Emmanuel (2020) and Wilson James E. (1999); p.123 Enjalbert, Henri (1985); p.125 Monroe, James S, and Wicander, Reed (2010); p.128 France, Benoît (2008); p.129 © Fanet, Jacques (2008); p.131 Oxford Geology Group, and viagallica.com/auvergne/img/coupe_eruption_volcan_strombolien.gif; p.135 Maltman, Alex (2018), and Hautevelle, Yann; p.137 Belcourt, Olivier, and Salze, David (2016); p.141 Seguin, Gérard (1971); p.145 Malard, Alain (2021); p.147 Interloire, CTV, FranceAgriMer, Central Region (2013); p.151 Dion, Roger (2010), and Chabin, Jean-Pierre (2004); pp.156–7 Paullin, Charles O (1932), and National Alcohol Beverage (2022); p.159 le Château de Parnay; p.167 Parain, Charles (1955); p.170–1 Wine Folly; p.175 Minard, Charles (1860); pp.180–1 Velasco-Graciet, Hélène, and Schirmer, Raphaël (2010); p.186 Statistical map of vineyards producing the great wines of Burgundy (1861) and Monocépage/Martin, Gilles; p.190 Wikipedia Common PiMaster3 (2013); p.187 Gille, Martin; p.194 Velasco-Graciet, Hélène, and Schirmer, Raphaël (2010), Wine Australia, Coonawarra Geographical Indication (2022); p.196 Unwin, Tim (1991); pp.200–1 UNESCO; p.205 Ruiz Villarreal, Mariana (2008); p.210 Whittle-Morrison, Peter, and Goddard, Matthew (2018); p.212 Whittle-Morrison, Peter, and Goddard, Matthew (2018); p.219 Valcárcel-Muñoz, Manuel J, Guerrero-Chanivet, María, Rodríguez-Dodero, María del Carmen, García-Moreno, María de Valme, and Guillén-Sánchez, Dominico A (2022); p.223 Spinner, Lauren; p.227 Littler, Mark; p.229 Wine Folly, French Wine and Vine Institute (IFV); p.232 BIVB; p.236 Mendoza, Cédric and Association des vins S.A.I.N.S (2022); p.241 © Monnier, Jean-Michel (2022); p.246 Boulay, Thibaut (2017); p.249 Jacquet, Olivier; p.249 Chauvet, Jules; p.250 Wine Scholar Guild, File DGS V7.8 under CC SA (2021); p.255 Shepherd, Gordon M (2016) and Lepousez Gabriel (2022); p.261 Liger-Belair, Gérard (2009), Louapre, David (2013); p.266 Petronilho, Sílvia, et al. (2020); p.275 Bouin, Philippe, Tabor, Yaïr, and Lepousez, Gabriel (2020–2021); p.279 Puisais, Jacques, and Didier, Michel (2009); p.283 © Chukan-Brown, Elaine, Corison Kronos Vineyard Twentieth Anniversary (February 2019); p.286 Sokolowsky, et al. (2015); pp.290–1 Pitte, Jean-Robert (2013), p.299 Amorim (2021); p.301 Wine Intelligence; p.303 Tallet, Pierre (1998), Desbuissons, Frédérique (2016), Carlu, Jean, for Château Mouton-Rothschild, Bartolo, Mascarello, for Cantina Bartolo Mascarello; p.307 Peynaud, Émile, and Blouin, Jacques (2013); pp.308–9 Ashton, Chloe, "The fine-wine market: Back in business", *The World of Fine Wine* (2021), Liv-Ex, liv-ex.com; pp.312–3 Brendon, Richard, and Robinson, Jancis, and Riedel; pp.318–9 Centelles, Ferran (2016); p.321 Chapel, Alain (2022), elBulli, elBulliFoundation (2007); pp.324–5 Cadet de Gassicourt (1809), Bourguignon, Alain (1929); p.328 Chartier, François, Molecular Profile Cava de Guarda (2020)

Pascaline Lepeltier

After writing a master's thesis in philosophy on Henri Bergson, Pascaline chose to devote herself to wine. Hailing from Angers in the Loire Valley, she had learned the importance of respect for the living world from local visionary winemakers, while her training in gastronomy and pairing food and wine under chef Jacques Thorel was the gateway to her discovery of the great tradition of iconic, classic wines. These twin strands of her schooling led her first to Belgium and then to the US, where she created wine lists for Michelin-starred restaurants dedicated to "better drinking based on holistic sustainability". A host of international awards and recognitions soon followed, including Master Sommelier, Best French Sommelier and Un des Meilleurs Ouvriers de France 2018, and in 2019 she was voted Personality of the Year by *La Revue du vin de France*. Since 2022, she has been beverage director at Chambers, a farm-to-table restaurant in the Tribeca district of New York boasting a wine list of more than 3,000 mostly organic, biodynamic and natural selections. She teaches, regularly giving papers at conferences in Europe and North America, and writes the monthly "Vu d'ailleurs" column for *La Revue du vin de France*. In 2016, she put her name to the first vintage of Chëpìka ("roots" in the language of the Delaware Nation), a wine-growing project established in the Finger Lakes (NY) in collaboration with winemaker Nathan Kendall. She earned fourth place at the ASI Best Sommelier of the World competition in Paris in February 2023. *One Thousand Vines* is her first solo literary project.

Acknowledgments

There is the idea – the desire, even – and then there is making it happen. This book would never have seen the light of day without the initial boost (followed by unwavering support over three years) from Laurence Lehoux, the dedicated managing editor at Hachette Livre who brought this project to fruition. It would have had neither the style nor the appearance I was hoping for without the sterling work of my editor Franck Friès, whose extremely valuable contribution was to turn the whirlwind of my thoughts into clear and limpid text. Quality was essential for the illustrations, and the results have exceeded all my expectations thanks to Loan Nguyen Thanh Lan, whose smooth and precise lines breathed life into the beauty of this incredible universe of wine on paper. My thanks are also due to Charles Ameline for having orchestrated the design of the work.

Some say that translation is necessarily an act of betrayal, but I must recognize and applaud the fantastic work done by Malcolm Garrard, Jane Moseley and Jackie Strachan, who not only preserved the details and tone of the book but also made the text even better. Thanks also to Pauline Bache and Margaret Rand, the editors of the English-language edition, who helped to clarify and correct with such precision. Thanks are due to Alison Starling and the team at Octopus/Mitchell Beazley for believing in *One Thousand Vines*; it is an honour to be on the roster of such a respected publishing house. A final thank you goes to my agent Jonah Strauss, who made my dream of bringing this book out in English come true.

I was fortunate enough to be able to rely on help, advice and comments from the specialists whose remarkable work inspired this book. Despite their busy schedules, they took the time to read and correct the errors and inaccuracies in the text, and if any remain, the fault is mine alone. I am sincerely grateful to Olivier Yobrégat, Christelle Pineau, Hervé Quénol, Georges Truc, Olivier Jacquet, Jean-Michel Monnier, Gabriel Lepousez, Christophe Laudamiel, Jean-Robert Pitte, Guillaume Antalick, Jamie Goode, Kevin Pogue, Robert Pincus, Michael Cruse and Samuel Lyons. I would particularly like to thank Thibaut Boulay, who has given me the benefit of his critical vision as a winemaker, historian and Hellenist since the very first inklings of this book; long live Dionysus! Ferran Centelles and the El Bulli Foundation joined Olivier Krug and the House of Krug in generously opening their archives for the chapter on pairing food and wine, for which many thanks! And thank you to the Pire family for commissioning Sarah Arnaud's drawing of their magnificent estate at Fosse-Sèche to illustrate the chapter on cohabiting with vines. Thank you to Julien Camus and the Wine Scholar Guild for sharing their work on wine tasting, including the geosensorial tasting grid. Thanks also to Elaine Chukan Brown for her highly symbolic illustration of tasting Cathy Corison's Kronos Cabernet Sauvignon. Lastly, it was an honour to have such fertile and inspiring minds writing the forewords; a heartfelt thank you to Marc-André Selosse and François Régis-Gaudry for the French edition, and Raj Parr, Ava Mees List and René Redzepi for the English edition

Having an author in the house is not exactly easy for your loved ones . . . Obviously, my wife has been my secret weapon, day in, day out. Thank you to my mother and my best friend for their eagle eyes and their editing advice; they have undoubtedly made the text clearer. Thank you for your constant encouragements throughout the drafting process. I hope this book will make Alice Feiring, my "American mom", proud; she had been pushing me to pick up a pen since our first meeting! I still have some way to go before I write as powerfully as you! I would also, of course, like to thank all my loved ones for having put up with the hours I spent buried in books and sat in front of a screen instead of with them. Thank you to the team at Chambers NYC (more particularly, Jared David, Jonathan Karis, David Lillie, Chelsei OJoe, Andrew Lin and Ellis Srubas-Giammanco) for giving me the time I needed to write; it is a pleasure to work with you at the restaurant every evening and to share a vision of gastronomy that is passionate, generous and humble. Thanks to the Union of French Sommeliers and Team France, keepers and spreaders of the flame of sommellerie. This book is intended to make it shine more brightly still! Last but not least, thank you to my mentors, who got my foot on the ladder and who believed in me more than 20 years ago now, instilling in me their love of philosophy and of wine: Éric Beaumard, Thierry Hamon, Denis Moreau, Christophe Reignaud, Patrick Rigourd and Mr and Mrs Thorel.

Finally, this book would not exist without all the winemakers who have opened their wineries, their bottles and their vineyards to me since my first faltering steps as a sommelier; thanks to them and the way they live their daily lives with their vines and their wines, I have learned to read and taste the world differently. I am particular indebted to Mark and Martial Angeli, Catherine and Pierre Breton, François Chidaine, Bruno Ciofi, Didier Chaffardon, Sébastien Dervieux, Manue and Benoît Courault, Coralie and Damien Delecheneau, Elisabetta Foradori, Thierry Germain, Olivier Humbrecht, Virginie and Nicolas Joly, Nathan Kendall, Tessa Laroche, Richard Leroy, Raj Parr, Abe Schoener, Matt Taylor and Éric Texier for their takes on the vineyards and the wines of the future.

All illustrations and colouring by Loan Nguyen Thanh Lan

Loan Nguyen Thanh Lan is a freelance illustrator specializing in scientific illustrations. As a jack-of-all-trades, she has broadened her palette by exploring many different styles and techniques, allowing her to work with a wide range of stakeholders (such as agencies, editors and science professionals). The time she spent at the École Estienne (ESAIG) only fanned the flames of her burgeoning enthusiasm for science, and her work now aims to spread and promote knowledge.

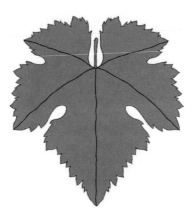

First published in Great Britain in 2024 by Mitchell Beazley, an imprint of Octopus Publishing Group Ltd
Carmelite House, 50 Victoria Embankment
London EC4Y 0DZ
www.octopusbooks.co.uk

An Hachette UK Company
www.hachette.co.uk

First published in France in 2022 by Hachette Livre

Distributed in the US by Hachette Book Group
1290 Avenue of the Americas
4th and 5th Floors, New York, NY 10104

Distributed in Canada by Canadian Manda Group
664 Annette Street, Toronto, Ontario, Canada M6S 2C8

ISBN 978-1-78472-923-3

A CIP catalogue record for this book is available from the British Library.

Printed and bound in Malaysia.

1 3 5 7 9 10 8 6 4 2

Director: Catherine Saunier-Talec
Editorial manager: Stéphane Rosa
Project manager: Laurence Lehoux
Editorial supervision: Franck Friès
Art director: Charles Ameline
Graphic designer: Marie Gastaut

English-language edition
Publisher: Alison Starling
Design director: Jonathan Christie
Senior Developmental Editor: Pauline Bache
Translator: Malcolm Garrard at JMS Books
Copyeditor: Margaret Rand
Editors: David Tombesi-Walton and Hilary Lumsden
Designer: Jeremy Tilston at the Oak Studio
Senior Production Manager: Katherine Hockley